MONTGOM[...]
ROCKVILLE[...]
ROCKVILLE, MARYLAND

W9-CHI-557

# Career Guide to AMERICA'S Top Industries

## Essential Data on Job Opportunities in 42 Industries

*Fifth Edition*

**Published by JIST Works, this book's industry descriptions are a complete reprint of the entire contents of the *Career Guide to Industries* (Bulletin 2541) as produced by the good people at the U.S. Department of Labor.**

*Part of America's Top Jobs® Series*

JIST Works

# Career Guide to America's Top Industries, *Fifth Edition*

*Essential Data on Job Opportunities in 42 Industries*

© 2002 by JIST Publishing, Inc.

Published by JIST Works, an imprint of JIST Publishing, Inc.
8902 Otis Avenue
Indianapolis, IN 46216-1033
Phone: 1-800-648-JIST     Fax: 1-800-JIST-FAX
E-mail: info@jist.com     Web site: www.jist.com

**Other books in the America's Top Jobs® series:**

*America's Top 300 Jobs*

*America's Fastest Growing Jobs*

*America's Top Jobs for People Without a Four-Year Degree*

*America's Top Jobs for College Graduates*

*America's Top Computer and Technical Jobs*

*America's Top Medical, Education & Human Services Jobs*

*America's Top White-Collar Jobs*

*America's Top Military Careers*

For other career-related materials, turn to the back of this book or visit www.jist.com. Quantity discounts are available for JIST books. Please call 1-800-648-JIST for more information and a free catalog.

Printed in the United States of America

04 03 02     9 8 7 6 5 4 3 2 1

The industry information contained in JIST's *Career Guide to America's Top Industries* presents a general, composite description of firms and jobs and cannot be expected to reflect work situations in specific establishments or localities. The *Career Guide*, therefore, is not intended and should not be used as a guide for determining wages, hours, the right of a particular union to represent workers, appropriate bargaining units, or formal job evaluation systems. Nor should earnings data in the *Career Guide* be used to compute future loss of earnings in adjudication proceedings involving work injuries or accidental deaths.

**Credits.** This book is a complete reprint of the original *Career Guide to Industries*, published by the good people at the Bureau of Labor Statistics, U.S. Department of Labor. Here is the text, from the original, providing credits to the many people who worked on this:

The *Career Guide to Industries* was produced in the Bureau's Office of Occupational Statistics and Employment Projections. General guidance and direction was provided by Mike Pilot, Chief of the Division of Occupational Outlook. Chester C. Levine and Jon Sargent, Managers, Occupational Outlook Studies, were responsible for planning and day-to-day direction.

Supervisors overseeing the research and preparation of material were Theresa Cosca, Douglas Braddock, Kristina Shelley, and Carolyn M. Veneri. Analysts who contributed material were Andrew Alpert, Jill Auyer, Hall Dillon, Tamara Dillon, Arlene K. Dohm, Henry Kasper, R. Sean Kirby, T. Alan Lacey, Kevin M. McCarron, Roger Moncraz, Andrew J. Nelson, Azure Reaser, Terry Schau, Lynn Shniper, Tiffany T. Stringer, Patricia Tate, and Ian Wyatt. The cover design and other artwork (for the original book) were contributed by Keith Tapscott. Word processing support was provided by Beverly A. Williams.

ISBN 1-56370-886-8

# About This Book

## Helpful Career Planning Information on 42 Major Industries Employing 75% of the Workforce

Most people, when planning their careers, think mainly about the job they want and the education or training needed to get it. Unfortunately, they often overlook the enormous importance of the industry where they work. This book is designed to help.

The *Career Guide to America's Top Industries* provides information on employment trends and opportunities in industries. It is a companion to another book, also published by the U.S. Department of Labor, titled the *Occupational Outlook Handbook (OOH)*. These books fulfill a Labor Department mission to provide useful information for career planning and job seeking.

While the *OOH* provides information on jobs, the *Career Guide to America's Top Industries* gives details on the industries where people hold these jobs. JIST suggests you use both of these important references in your career planning.

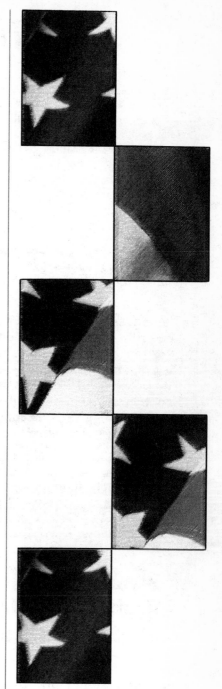

## The *Career Guide to America's Top Industries* Is Easy to Use!

This book was developed to assist you in making good career decisions. The information is presented in a readable and useful format. Use the table of contents to identify industries that interest you, and then find out more about them by turning to the page where each industry is described. You can also get a good overview on major employment trends by reading the short section titled "Major Trends in Industries and Employment."

# Table of Contents

## Industries Described in This Book

# Information Provided in the
# *Career Guide to America's Top Industries*

What kinds of workers are employed by a particular industry, and what jobs are you qualified for right now? What jobs require special education or training? And, what advancement opportunities do these jobs offer in the long run? The *Career Guide to America's Top Industries* addresses these questions and more for 42 diverse industries which, when combined, accounted for nearly 3 out of 4 wage and salary jobs in 2000.

As a companion to the *Occupational Outlook Handbook (OOH)*, the *Career Guide to America's Top Industries* discusses careers from an industry perspective. Why? Because many career-minded people think in terms of industries rather than occupations. Your personal circumstances or choice of lifestyle may compel you to remain in your area, limiting prospective jobs to those offered by the distinctive mix of industries in your state or community. Or, you may be attracted to a particular industry for other reasons—the potential for high earnings in the securities and commodities industry, the appeal of using advanced technology in aerospace manufacturing, the opportunity to work with children offered by the educational services industry, or the stability of jobs in the federal government, to name a few. By focusing on industries, the *Career Guide* provides information that the *OOH* does not. It shows the relationships between different occupations and how they cooperate within industries to produce goods and bring them to the market or provide services to businesses and the public. Furthermore, some occupations are unique to a particular industry and are not discussed in the *OOH*. And, some industries offer specific paths of career advancement that are not addressed in the *OOH*.

For each industry, the *Career Guide to America's Top Industries* includes a section with information on each of the following topics, although the information presented within each section varies slightly from industry to industry.

## Industry Title

This is the name the industry is most commonly called.

## SIC Number

To the right of the industry titles you will see numbers in parentheses. These numbers are called SIC codes. They are from a reference titled the *Standard Industrial Classification Manual*, a publication of the Federal Office of Management and Budget that defines and names industries and establishes a structure for relating industries to one another. Readers interested in obtaining more detailed definitions of the industries in the *Career Guide to America's Top Industries* should consult the *SIC Manual*, which is available in the reference section of many libraries. The *SIC Manual* may also be consulted on the Internet at http://www.osha.gov/oshstats/sicser.html.

## Significant Points

One or more key information items are presented at the beginning of each industry description.

## Nature of the Industry

* Description of the goods produced or the services provided

* Description of individual segments of the industry

* Description of production processes

* Changes in technology or business practices taking place

## Working Conditions

* Description of the physical environment in which workers perform their duties

* Hours of work, including frequency of night or weekend work, or split shifts

* Physical activities essential to successful job performance

* Proportion of part-time workers

* Rate of job-related injury and illness

* Extent and frequency of travel

## Employment

* Number of wage and salary jobs in the industry

* Number of self-employed persons in the industry, where significant

* Data on the age of workers, where significant

* Number of establishments and concentration of industry employment by state

* Distribution of establishments and employment in the industry by employment-size class

* Data on other unusual characteristics of industry workers, where significant

## Occupations in the Industry

* Description of the various jobs in the industry and how each fits into the process of producing goods or delivering services to consumers

* Current and projected wage and salary jobs by occupation

## Training and Advancement

★ Qualifications required or preferred for key occupations

★ Types of formal education and other training that employers in the industry generally require or prefer

★ Discussion of how experience, on-the-job training, formal employer training, and continuing education enable workers to advance in this industry

★ Paths of career advancement for key types of workers

★ Opportunities for self-employment

## Earnings

★ Average weekly earnings in the industry

★ Earnings of key occupations in the industry

★ Employee benefits that are often offered in the industry but which are uncommon in other industries

★ Principle unions representing workers in the industry

★ The proportion of workers who belong to unions or who are covered by union contracts

## Outlook

★ Rate at which jobs in the industry are projected to grow or decline

★ The projected rate of job growth compared to that of the economy as a whole

★ Factors expected to influence employment growth in the industry, such as new technology, changing business practices, and demographics

★ Occupations expected to grow or decline

★ Ease or difficulty of acquiring a job in the industry

## Sources of Additional Information

This section includes organizations providing additional information via the Internet or by mail on the industry and its job opportunities. It also lists jobs described in the *Occupational Outlook Handbook* that are typically found in the industry.

A great many trade associations, professional societies, unions, industrial organizations, and government agencies provide career information that is valuable to counselors and job seekers. For your convenience, some of these organizations and their Internet addresses are listed at the end of each industry statement. Although these references were carefully compiled, the Bureau of Labor Statistics has neither authority nor facilities for investigating the organizations or the information or publications that are sent in response to a request and cannot guarantee the accuracy of such information. The listing of an organization, therefore, does not constitute in any way an endorsement or recommendation by the Bureau either of the organization and its activities or of the information it supplies. Each organization has sole responsibility for whatever information it issues.

## Information Tables

Unless otherwise indicated, the Bureau of Labor Statistics is the source of data presented in the various tables.

# Major Trends in Industries and Employment

You have many factors to consider in targeting one industry over another when making job and career choices. Some industries pay more than others, are growing more rapidly, have more openings, fit your interests better, or have other advantages.

This section will give you a quick overview of the major employment trends in various occupations and industries in the U.S. economy.

The U.S. economy is made up of industries with diverse characteristics. For each industry covered in the *Career Guide*, detailed information is provided about specific characteristics: The nature of the industry, working conditions, employment, occupational composition, training and advancement requirements, earnings, and job outlook. This chapter provides an overview of these characteristics for the economy as a whole.

## Nature of the Industry

Industries are defined by the goods and services they provide. Because workers in the United States produce such a wide variety of products and services, the types of industries in the U.S. economy range widely, from aerospace manufacturing to motion picture production. Although many of these industries are related, each industry has a unique combination of occupations, production techniques, inputs and outputs, and business characteristics. Understanding the nature of the industry is important, because it is this unique combination that determines working conditions, educational requirements, and the job outlook for each of the industries discussed in the *Career Guide*.

Industries consist of many different places of work, called *establishments*, which range from large factories and office complexes employing thousands of workers to small businesses employing only a few workers. Not to be confused with companies, which are legal entities, establishments are physical locations in which people work, such as the branch office of a bank. Thus, a company may have more than one establishment. Establishments that produce similar goods or services are grouped together into *industries*. Industries that produce related types of goods or services are, in turn, grouped together into *major industry divisions*. These are further grouped into the *goods-producing sector* (agriculture, forestry, and fishing; mining; construction; and manufacturing) or the *service-producing sector* (transportation, communications, and public utilities; wholesale trade; retail trade; finance, insurance, and real estate; services; and government).

Each industry is made up of a number of subdivisions, which are determined largely by differences in production processes. An easily recognized example of these distinctions is in the food processing industry, which is made up of subdivisions that produce meat products, preserved fruits and vegetables, bakery items, beverages, and dairy products, among others. Each of these subdivisions requires workers with varying skills and employs unique production techniques. Another example of these distinctions is found in public utilities, which employs workers in establishments that provide electricity, sanitary services, water, and natural gas.

There were more than 7 million business establishments in the United States in 1999. The average size of these establishments varies widely across industries. Among industry divisions, manufacturing included many industries having among the highest employment per establishment in 1999. For example, the aerospace and steel manufacturing industries each averaged 200 or more employees per establishment.

Most establishments in the wholesale trade, retail trade, finance, and services industries are small, averaging fewer than 20 employees per establishment. Exceptions are the scheduled air transportation industry with 166.8 employees and colleges, universities, and professional schools with 433.4. In addition, wide differences within industries can exist. Hospitals, for example, employ an average of 717.5 workers, while doctors' offices employ an average of 8.7. Similarly, although there is an average of 13 employees per establishment for all of retail trade, department stores employ an average of 164.3 people.

Establishments in the United States are predominantly small; 54.2 percent of all establishments employed fewer than 5 workers in 1999. The medium-sized to large establishments employ a greater proportion of all workers. For example, establishments that employed 50 or more workers accounted for only 5.4 percent of all establishments, yet employed 59 percent of all workers. The large establishments—those with more than 500 workers—accounted for only 0.3 percent of all establishments, but employed 20.3 percent of all workers. Table 1 presents the percent distribution of employment according to establishment size.

Establishment size can play a role in the characteristics of each job. Large establishments generally offer workers greater occupational mobility and advancement potential, whereas small establishments may provide their employees with broader experience by requiring them to assume a wider range of responsibilities. Also, small establishments are distributed throughout the Nation; every locality has a few small businesses. Large establishments, in contrast, employ more workers and are less common, but they play a much more prominent role in the economies of the areas in which they are located.

**Table 1. Percent distribution of establishments and employment in all industries by establishment size, 1999**

| Establishment size (number of workers) | Establishments | Employment |
|---|---|---|
| Total ................................. | 100.0 | 100.0 |
| 1 to 4 ................................ | 54.2 | 5.9 |
| 5 to 9 ................................ | 19.4 | 8.1 |
| 10 to 19 ............................ | 12.5 | 10.7 |
| 20 to 49 ............................ | 8.5 | 16.3 |
| 50 to 99 ............................ | 2.9 | 12.8 |
| 100 to 249 ......................... | 1.7 | 16.4 |
| 250 to 499 ......................... | 0.4 | 9.6 |
| 500 to 999 ......................... | 0.2 | 7.2 |
| 1,000 or more ................. | 0.1 | 13.2 |

SOURCE: Department of Commerce, County Business Patterns, 1999

## Working Conditions

Just as the goods and services produced in each industry are different, working conditions vary significantly among industries. In some industries, the work setting is quiet, temperature-controlled, and virtually hazard free. Other industries are characterized by noisy, uncomfortable, and sometimes dangerous work environments. Some industries require long workweeks and shiftwork; in many industries, standard 40-hour workweeks are common. Still other industries can be seasonal, requiring long hours during busy periods and abbreviated schedules during slower months. These varying conditions usually are determined by production processes, establishment size, and the physical location of work.

One of the most telling indicators of working conditions is an industry's injury and illness rate. Overexertion, being struck by an object, and falls on the same level, are among the most common incidents causing work-related injury or illness. In 1999, approximately 5.7 million nonfatal injuries and illnesses were reported throughout private industry. Among major industry divisions, manufacturing had the highest rate of injury and illness—9.2 cases for every 100 full time workers—while finance, insurance, and real estate had the lowest rate—1.8 cases. About 5,900 work-related fatalities were reported in 2000; transportation incidents, contact with objects and equipment, assaults and violent acts, and falls were the most common events resulting in fatal injuries. Table 2 presents industries with the highest and lowest rates of nonfatal injury and illness.

Table 2. Nonfatal injury and illness rates of selected industries, 2000

| Industry | Cases per 100 full-time employees |
| --- | --- |
| **All industries** | 6.3 |
| **High rates** | |
| Transportation equipment manufacturing | 13.7 |
| Transportation by air | 13.3 |
| Lumber and wood products manufacturing | 13.0 |
| Primary metal industries | 12.9 |
| Food and kindred products manufacturing | 12.7 |
| Fabricated metal products manufacturing | 12.6 |
| **Low rates** | |
| Insurance carriers | 1.9 |
| Engineering and management services | 1.7 |
| Depository institutions | 1.5 |
| Legal services | 1.0 |
| Insurance agents, brokers, and service | 0.9 |
| Security and commodity brokers | 0.6 |

Work schedules are another important reflection of working conditions, and the operational requirements of each industry lead to large differences in hours worked and in part-time versus full-time status. In retail trade, 28.9 percent of employees worked part time in 2000 compared with only 4.4 percent in manufacturing. Table 3 presents industries having relatively high and low percentages of part-time workers.

The low proportion of part-time workers in some manufacturing industries often reflects the continuous nature of the production processes that makes it difficult to adapt the volume of production to short-term fluctuations in product demand. Once begun, it is costly to halt these processes; machinery must be tended and materials must be moved continuously. For example, the chemical manufacturing industry produces many different chemical products through controlled chemical reactions. These processes require chemical operators to monitor and adjust the flow of materials into and out of the line of production. Because production may continue 24 hours a day, 7 days a week, under the watchful eyes of chemical operators who work in shifts, full-time workers are more likely to be employed. Retail trade and service industries, on the other hand, have seasonal cycles marked by various events, such as school openings or important holidays, that affect the hours worked.

During busy times of the year, longer hours are common, whereas slack periods lead to cutbacks in work hours and shorter work-weeks. Jobs in these industries are generally appealing to students and others who desire flexible, part-time schedules.

Table 3. Part-time workers as a percent of total employment, selected industries, 2000

| Industry | Percent part-time |
| --- | --- |
| **All industries** | 15.3 |
| **Many part-time workers** | |
| Eating and drinking places | 37.8 |
| Department, clothing, and accessory stores | 31.3 |
| Grocery stores | 30.4 |
| Amusement and recreation services | 29.3 |
| Childcare services | 28.2 |
| Motion picture production and distribution | 23.0 |
| Educational services | 21.9 |
| Social services | 20.9 |
| **Few part-time workers** | |
| Public utilities | 3.2 |
| Chemical manufacturing, except drugs | 3.0 |
| Drug manufacturing | 2.6 |
| Electronic equipment manufacturing | 2.4 |
| Mining and quarrying | 1.9 |
| Aerospace manufacturing | 1.8 |
| Steel manufacturing | 1.5 |
| Motor vehicle and equipment manufacturing | 1.5 |

## Employment

The total number of jobs in the United States in 2000 was 145.6 million. This included 11.5 million self-employed workers, 169,000 unpaid workers in family businesses, and more than 133.9 million wage and salary workers—including primary and secondary job holders. The total number of jobs is projected to increase to 167.8 million by 2010, and wage and salary jobs are projected to account for more than 155.9 million of them.

As shown in table 4, although wage and salary jobs are the vast majority of all jobs, they are not evenly divided among the various industries. The services major industry division is the largest source of employment, with more than 50 million workers, followed by the wholesale and retail trade and manufacturing major industry divisions. Among the industries covered in the *Career Guide*, wage and salary employment ranged from only 216,000 in cable and other pay television services to 11.8 million in educational services. Three industries—educational services, health services, and eating and drinking places—together accounted for almost 31 million jobs, or nearly a quarter of the Nation's employment.

Although workers of all ages are employed in each industry, certain industries tend to possess workers of distinct age groups. For the reasons mentioned above, retail trade employs a relatively high proportion of younger workers to fill part-time and temporary positions. The manufacturing sector, on the other hand, has a relatively high median age because many jobs in the sector require a number of years to learn and perfect skills that do not easily transfer to other firms. Also, manufacturing employment has been declining, providing fewer opportunities for younger workers to get jobs. As a result, almost one-third of the workers in retail trade were 24 years of age or younger in 2000, compared with only 10 percent of workers in manufacturing. Table 5 contrasts the age distribution of workers in all industries with the distributions in five very different industries.

3

**Table 4. Wage and salary employment in selected industries, 2000 and projected change, 2000-2010**

(Employment in thousands)

| Industry | 2000 Employment | Percent distribution | 2010 Employment | Percent distribution | 2000-10 Percent change | Employment change |
|---|---|---|---|---|---|---|
| All industries ................................................ | 133,896 | 100.0 | 155,872 | 100.0 | 16.4 | 21,977 |
| **Goods-producing industries** ........................... | 27,984 | 20.9 | 29,728 | 19.1 | 6.2 | 1,745 |
| **Agriculture, mining, and construction** ................... | 9,514 | 7.1 | 10,682 | 0.0 | 12.3 | 1,167 |
| Agricultural production .......................................... | 1,120 | 0.8 | 1,092 | 0.7 | -2.5 | -28 |
| Agricultural services ............................................. | 1,099 | 0.8 | 1,524 | 1.0 | 38.6 | 425 |
| Construction........................................................... | 6,698 | 5.0 | 7,522 | 4.8 | 12.3 | 825 |
| Mining and quarrying............................................. | 231 | 0.2 | 199 | 0.1 | -14.0 | -32 |
| Oil and gas extraction .......................................... | 311 | 0.2 | 289 | 0.2 | -7.3 | -23 |
| **Manufacturing**........................................................ | 18,469 | 13.8 | 19,047 | 12.2 | 3.1 | 577 |
| Aerospace manufacturing ..................................... | 551 | 0.4 | 655 | 0.4 | 18.9 | 104 |
| Apparel and other textile products ....................... | 633 | 0.5 | 530 | 0.3 | -16.3 | -103 |
| Chemical manufacturing, except drugs ................. | 723 | 0.5 | 691 | 0.4 | -4.5 | -32 |
| Drug manufacturing .............................................. | 315 | 0.2 | 390 | 0.3 | 23.8 | 75 |
| Electronic equipment manufacturing ..................... | 1,554 | 1.2 | 1,657 | 1.1 | 6.6 | 103 |
| Food processing ................................................... | 1,684 | 1.3 | 1,634 | 1.0 | -3.0 | -50 |
| Motor vehicle and equipment manufacturing .......... | 1,013 | 0.8 | 1,100 | 0.7 | 8.6 | 87 |
| Printing and publishing ......................................... | 1,547 | 1.2 | 1,545 | 1.0 | -0.2 | -3 |
| Steel manufacturing .............................................. | 225 | 0.2 | 176 | 0.1 | -21.6 | -49 |
| Textile mill products .............................................. | 529 | 0.4 | 500 | 0.3 | -5.4 | -29 |
| **Service-producing industries**............................... | 105,912 | 79.1 | 126,144 | 80.9 | 19.1 | 20,232 |
| **Transportation, communications, and public utilities**............................... | 7,019 | 5.2 | 8,274 | 5.3 | 17.9 | 1,255 |
| Air transportation .................................................. | 1,281 | 1.0 | 1,600 | 1.0 | 24.9 | 319 |
| Cable and other pay television services ................. | 216 | 0.2 | 325 | 0.2 | 50.6 | 109 |
| Public utilities....................................................... | 851 | 0.6 | 893 | 0.6 | 4.9 | 42 |
| Radio and television broadcasting ........................ | 255 | 0.2 | 280 | 0.2 | 9.7 | 25 |
| Telecommunications ............................................. | 1,168 | 0.9 | 1,311 | 0.8 | 12.2 | 143 |
| Trucking and warehousing .................................... | 1,856 | 1.4 | 2,262 | 1.5 | 21.9 | 407 |
| **Wholesale and retail trade** ................................ | 30,331 | 22.7 | 34,200 | 21.9 | 12.8 | 3,869 |
| Department, clothing, and accessory stores ........... | 4,030 | 3.0 | 4,198 | 2.7 | 4.2 | 168 |
| Eating and drinking places ................................... | 8,114 | 6.1 | 9,600 | 6.2 | 18.3 | 1,486 |
| Grocery stores ..................................................... | 3,107 | 2.3 | 3,281 | 2.1 | 5.6 | 174 |
| Motor vehicle dealers ........................................... | 1,221 | 0.9 | 1,366 | 0.9 | 11.9 | 145 |
| Wholesale trade ................................................... | 7,024 | 5.2 | 7,800 | 5.0 | 11.1 | 776 |
| **Finance, insurance, and real estate** ...................... | 7,560 | 5.6 | 8,247 | 5.3 | 9.1 | 687 |
| Banking ............................................................... | 2,029 | 1.5 | 1,999 | 1.3 | -1.5 | -31 |
| Insurance ............................................................ | 2,346 | 1.8 | 2,497 | 1.6 | 6.4 | 151 |
| Securities and commodities ................................. | 748 | 0.6 | 900 | 0.6 | 20.3 | 152 |
| **Services** ................................................................ | 50,764 | 37.9 | 64,483 | 41.4 | 27.0 | 13,719 |
| Advertising .......................................................... | 302 | 0.2 | 400 | 0.3 | 32.5 | 98 |
| Amusement and recreation services ..................... | 1,728 | 1.3 | 2,325 | 1.5 | 34.5 | 597 |
| Childcare services ............................................... | 712 | 0.5 | 1,010 | 0.6 | 41.9 | 298 |
| Computer and data processing services ............... | 2,095 | 1.6 | 3,900 | 2.5 | 86.2 | 1,805 |
| Educational services ............................................ | 11,797 | 8.8 | 13,400 | 8.6 | 13.6 | 1,603 |
| Health services .................................................... | 11,065 | 8.3 | 13,882 | 8.9 | 25.5 | 2,817 |
| Hotels and other lodging places ........................... | 1,912 | 1.4 | 2,167 | 1.4 | 13.3 | 255 |
| Management and public relations services ............ | 1,090 | 0.8 | 1,550 | 1.0 | 42.2 | 460 |
| Motion picture production and distribution .............. | 287 | 0.2 | 369 | 0.2 | 28.7 | 82 |
| Personnel supply services ................................... | 3,887 | 2.9 | 5,800 | 3.7 | 49.2 | 1,913 |
| Social services, except childcare ......................... | 2,191 | 1.6 | 3,118 | 2.0 | 42.3 | 927 |
| **Government** ........................................................... | 10,238 | 7.6 | 10,940 | 7.0 | 6.9 | 702 |
| Federal Government.............................................. | 1,917 | 1.4 | 1,772 | 1.1 | -7.6 | -145 |
| State and local government ................................... | 7,461 | 5.6 | 8,318 | 5.3 | 11.5 | 856 |

**Table 5. Percent distribution of wage and salary workers by age group, selected industries, 2000**

| Industry | Age group | | | |
| --- | --- | --- | --- | --- |
| | 16 to 24 | 25 to 44 | 45 to 64 | 65 to 90 |
| All industries | 15 | 50 | 32 | 3 |
| Textile mill products manufacturing | 9 | 47 | 41 | 3 |
| Public utilities | 5 | 51 | 42 | 1 |
| Eating and drinking places | 45 | 39 | 15 | 2 |
| Computer and data processing services | 11 | 67 | 22 | 1 |
| Educational services | 11 | 43 | 43 | 3 |

Employment in some industries is concentrated in one region of the country. Such industries often are located near a source of raw or semifinished materials upon which the industry relies. For example, oil and gas extraction jobs are concentrated in Texas, Louisiana, and Oklahoma; many textile mill products manufacturing jobs are found in North Carolina, South Carolina, and Georgia; and a significant proportion of motor vehicle and equipment manufacturing jobs are located in Michigan and Ohio. On the other hand, some industries—such as grocery stores and educational services—have jobs distributed throughout the Nation, reflecting the general population density.

## Occupations in the Industry

The occupations found in each industry depend on the types of services provided or goods produced, as mentioned above. For example, because construction companies require skilled trades workers to build and renovate buildings, these companies employ large numbers of carpenters, electricians, plumbers, painters, and sheet metal workers. Other occupations common to construction include construction equipment operators and mechanics, installers, and repairers. Retail trade, on the other hand, displays and sells manufactured goods to consumers, and so hires numerous sales clerks and other workers, including more than 5 out of 6 cashiers. Table 6 shows the major industry divisions and the occupational groups that predominate in each.

The Nation's occupational distribution clearly is influenced by its industrial structure, yet there are many occupations, such as general manager or secretary, that are found in all industries. In fact, some of the largest occupations in the U.S. economy are dispersed across many industries. Because nearly every industry relies on administrative support, for example, this occupational group is the largest in the Nation. (See table 7.) Other large occupational groups include service occupations, professional workers, and production workers.

**Table 7. Total employment and projected change by broad occupational group, 2000-10**

(Employment in thousands)

| Occupational group | Employment, 2000 | Percent change, 2000-10 |
| --- | --- | --- |
| Total, all occupations | 145,571 | 15.2 |
| Management, business, and financial occupations | 15,519 | 13.6 |
| Professional and related occupations | 26,758 | 26.0 |
| Service occupations | 26,075 | 19.5 |
| Sales and related occupations | 15,513 | 11.9 |
| Office and administrative support occupations | 23,882 | 9.1 |
| Farming, fishing, and forestry occupations | 1,406 | 5.3 |
| Construction and extraction occupations | 7,451 | 13.3 |
| Installation, maintenance, and repair occupations | 5,820 | 11.4 |
| Production occupations | 13,060 | 5.8 |
| Transportation and material moving occupations | 10,088 | 15.2 |

## Training and Advancement

Workers prepare for employment in many ways, but the most fundamental form of job training in the United States is a high school education. Fully 87.5 percent of the Nation's workforce possessed a high school diploma or its equivalent in 2000. However, many occupations require more training than previously, so workers are responding by pursuing additional training. In 2000, 28.8 percent of the Nation's workforce had some college or an associate's degree, while an additional 27.5 percent continued in their studies and attained a bachelor's or higher degree. In addition to these types of formal education, other sources of qualifying training include formal company-provided training, informal on-the-job training, correspondence courses, the Armed Forces, and friends, relatives, and other non-work-related training.

The unique combination of training required to succeed in each industry is determined largely by the industry's occupational composition. For example, machine operators in manufacturing generally need little formal education after high school, but sometimes complete considerable on-the-job training. Training requirements by major industry division are shown in table 8.

Persons with no more than a high school diploma accounted for about 63.8 percent of all workers in agriculture, forestry,

**Table 6. Industry divisions and their largest occupational group, 2000**

| Industry division | Largest occupational group | Percent of industry wage and salary jobs |
| --- | --- | --- |
| Agriculture, forestry, and fishing | Farming, forestry, and fishing occupations | 45.4 |
| Mining | Construction and extraction occupations | 33.6 |
| Construction | Construction and extraction occupations | 67.6 |
| Manufacturing | Production occupations | 51.7 |
| Tranportation, communication, and utilities | Transportation and material moving occupations | 36.0 |
| Wholesale and retail trade | Sales and related occupations | 32.4 |
| Finance, insurance, and real estate | Office and administrative support occupations | 45.3 |
| Services | Professional and related occupations | 36.9 |
| Government, except State and local education and hospitals | Office and administrative support occupations | 26.8 |

**Table 8. Percent distribution of workers by highest grade completed or degree received, by industry division, 2000**

| Industry division | Bachelor's or higher degree | Some college or associate's degree | High school or equivalent | Less than 12 years or no diploma |
|---|---|---|---|---|
| All industries | 28 | 29 | 31 | 13 |
| Agriculture, forestry, and fishing | 14 | 22 | 34 | 30 |
| Mining | 17 | 26 | 45 | 12 |
| Construction | 10 | 25 | 44 | 21 |
| Manufacturing | 21 | 26 | 39 | 15 |
| Tranportation, communication, and other public utilities | 21 | 35 | 37 | 8 |
| Wholesale trade | 25 | 31 | 34 | 11 |
| Retail trade | 13 | 30 | 36 | 21 |
| Finance, insurance, and real estate | 39 | 33 | 25 | 4 |
| Business and repair services | 29 | 29 | 29 | 12 |
| Personal services | 13 | 28 | 38 | 22 |
| Entertainment and recreation services | 25 | 30 | 28 | 17 |
| Professional and related services | 48 | 27 | 20 | 5 |
| Government | 36 | 36 | 25 | 3 |

and fishing; 64.7 percent in construction; 53.4 percent in manufacturing; and 44.8 percent in wholesale trade and 57.4 in retail trade. On the other hand, those who had acquired at least some training at the college level accounted for 72.4 percent of all workers in government; 71.4 percent in finance, insurance, and real estate; and 75.1 percent in professional and related services.

Education and training also are important factors in the variety of advancement paths found in different industries. Each industry has some unique advancement paths, but workers who complete additional on-the-job training or education generally help their chances of being promoted. In much of the manufacturing sector, for example, production workers who receive training in management and computer skills increase their likelihood of being promoted to supervisory positions. Other factors that impact advancement and that may figure prominently in the industries covered in the *Career Guide* include the size of the establishments, institutionalized career tracks, and the mix of occupations. As a result, persons who seek jobs in particular industries should be aware of how these advancement paths and other factors may later shape their careers.

## Earnings

Like other characteristics, earnings differ from industry to industry, the result of a highly complicated process that reflects a number of factors. For example, earnings may vary due to the nature of occupations in the industry, average hours worked, geographical location, industry profits, union penetration of the workforce, workers' average age, and educational requirements. In general, wages are highest in metropolitan areas to compensate for the higher cost of living. And, as would be expected, industries that employ relatively few unskilled minimum-wage or part time workers tend to have higher earnings.

A good illustration of these differences is shown by the earnings of all wage and salary workers in petroleum refining, which averaged $1,099 a week in 2000, and those in eating and drinking places, where the weekly average was $177. These differences are so large because petroleum refining establishments employ more highly skilled, full-time workers, while eating and drinking places employ many lower skilled, part-time workers. In addition, many workers in eating and drinking places are able to supplement their low wages with money they receive as tips, which is not included in the industry wages data. Table 9 highlights the industries with the highest and lowest average weekly earnings.

Employee benefits, once a minor addition to wages and salaries, continue to grow in diversity and cost. In addition to traditional benefits—including paid vacations, life and health insurance, and pensions—many employers now offer various benefits to accommodate the needs of a changing labor force. Such benefits include childcare, employee assistance programs that provide counseling for personal problems, and wellness programs that encourage exercise, stress management, and self-improvement. Benefits vary among occupational groups, full- and part-time workers, public and private sector workers, regions, unionized and nonunionized workers, and small and large establishments. Data indicate that full-time workers and those in medium-sized and large establishments—those with 100 or more workers—receive better benefits than do part-time workers and those in smaller establishments.

**Table 9. Average weekly earnings of production or nonsupervisory workers on private nonfarm payrolls in selected industries, 2000.**

| Industry | Earnings |
|---|---|
| All industries | $474 |
| **Industries with high earnings** | |
| Petroleum refining | 1,099 |
| Pipelines, except natural gas | 956 |
| Aircraft and parts | 901 |
| Computer and data processing services | 897 |
| Electric, gas, and sanitary services | 895 |
| Coal mining | 871 |
| Blast furnances and basic steel products | 870 |
| Security and commodity brokers | 841 |
| Engineering and architectural services | 821 |
| Motion picture production and services | 811 |
| **Industries with low earnings** | |
| Agricultural services | 379 |
| Nursing and personal care facilities | 349 |
| Apparel and other textile products manufacturing | 338 |
| Drug stores and proprietary stores | 323 |
| Hotels and motels | 298 |
| Food stores | 281 |
| Department stores | 278 |
| Amusement and recreation services | 262 |
| Child daycare services | 258 |
| Eating and drinking places | 177 |

Union penetration of the workforce varies widely by industry, and it also may play a role in earnings and benefits. In 2000, about 15 percent of workers throughout the Nation were union members or covered by union contracts. As table 10 demonstrates, union affiliation of workers varies widely by industry. Approximately a third of the workers in government and transportation, communications, and public utilities are union members or are covered by union contracts, compared with fewer than 4 percent in business and repair services; agriculture, forestry, and fishing; and finance, insurance, and real estate.

**Table 10. Union members and other workers covered by union contracts as a percent of total employment in major industry divisions, 2000**

| Industry | Percent union members or covered by union contract |
|---|---|
| All industries | 14.9 |
| Government | 35.7 |
| Tranportation, communication, and public utilities | 31.9 |
| Construction | 20.4 |
| Manufacturing | 15.7 |
| Mining | 11.6 |
| Entertainment and recreation services | 10.5 |
| Personal services | 9.8 |
| Wholesale trade | 5.6 |
| Retail trade | 5.2 |
| Professional and related services | 5.2 |
| Business and repair services | 3.8 |
| Agriculture, forestry, and fishing | 3.3 |
| Finance, insurance, and real estate | 2.8 |

## Outlook

Total employment in the United States is projected to increase by about 15 percent over the 2000-10 period. Employment growth, however, is only one source of job openings; the total number of openings in any industry also depends on the industry's current employment level and its need to replace workers who leave their jobs. Throughout the economy, in fact, replacement needs will create more job openings than will employment growth. Employment size is a major determinant of job openings—larger industries generally provide more openings. The occupational composition of an industry is another factor. Industries with high concentrations of professional, technical, and other jobs that require more formal education—occupations in which workers tend to leave their jobs less frequently—generally have fewer openings resulting from replacement needs. On the other hand, more replacement openings generally occur in industries with high concentrations of service, laborer, and other jobs that require little formal education and have lower wages because workers in these jobs are more likely to leave their occupations.

Employment growth is determined largely by changes in the demand for the goods and services produced by an industry, worker productivity, and foreign competition. Each industry is affected by a different set of variables that determines the number and composition of jobs that will be available. Even within an industry, employment may grow at different rates in different occupations. For example, changes in technology, production methods, and business practices in an industry might eliminate some jobs, while creating others. Some industries may be growing rapidly overall, yet opportunities for workers in occupations that are adversely affected by technological change could be stagnant or even declining. Similarly, employment of some occupations may be declining in the economy as a whole, yet may be increasing in a rapidly growing industry.

As shown above in table 4, employment growth rates over the next decade will vary widely among industries. Employment in goods-producing industries is expected to increase as growth in agricultural services, construction, and manufacturing is partially offset by declining employment in agricultural production and mining and quarrying. Rapid growth in agricultural services will be driven by its landscaping and veterinary services components. Growth in construction employment will stem from new factory construction as existing facilities are modernized; from new school construction, reflecting growth in the school-age population; and from infrastructure improvements, such as road and bridge construction. Employment in agricultural production and mining and quarrying is expected to decline due to laborsaving technology. Reliance on foreign sources of energy also is expected to play a role in employment declines in mining and in oil and gas extraction.

Manufacturing employment will increase slightly, as strong demand continues for high technology electrical goods and pharmaceuticals despite improvements in production technology and rising imports.. Apparel manufacturing is projected to lose about 103,000 jobs over the 2000-10 period—more than any other manufacturing industry—due primarily to increasing imports. But other manufacturing industries with strong domestic markets and export potential are expected to experience increases in employment. The drug manufacturing and aerospace manufacturing industries are two examples. Sales of drugs are expected to increase with growth in the population, particularly among the elderly, and the introduction of new drugs to the market. An increase in air traffic, coupled with the need to replace aging aircraft will generate strong sales for commercial aircraft. Both drug and aerospace manufacturing also have large export markets.

Growth in overall employment will result primarily from growth in service-producing industries over the 2000-10 period, almost all of which are expected to have increasing employment. Rising employment in these industries will be driven by services industries—the largest and fastest growing major industry group—which are projected to provide almost 2 out of 3 new jobs across the Nation. Health, education, and personnel supply services will account for 6.3 million of these new jobs. In addition, employment in the Nation's fastest growing industry—computer and data processing services—is expected to nearly double, adding another 1.8 million jobs. Job growth in the services sector will result from overall population growth, the rise in the elderly and school-age populations, and the trend toward contracting out for computer, personnel, and other business services.

Wholesale and retail trade is expected to add 3.9 million jobs over the coming decade. More than 776,000 of these jobs will arise in wholesale trade, reflecting growth both in trade and in the overall economy. Retail trade is expected to add 3.1 million jobs over the 2000-10 period, the result of increases in both population and personal income. Although most retail stores are expected to add employees, nonstore retailers will experience the fastest growth rate—35 percent—as electronic commerce and mail-order sales account for an increasing portion of retail sales. Eating and drinking places will have the largest number of new jobs, nearly 1.5 million.

Employment in transportation, communications, and public utilities is projected to increase by nearly 1.26 million new jobs. The trucking and warehousing industry will have the biggest increase—407,000 jobs. Trucking industry growth will be fueled by growth in the volume of goods that need to be shipped as the economy expands. Air transportation is expected to generate nearly 319,000 jobs. Air transportation will expand as consumer and business demand increases, reflecting a growing population and increased business activity. Demand for new telecommunications services, such as Internet and wireless communications, will lead to an expansion of the telecommunications infrastructure. Employment growth is projected to add 143,000 jobs. While radio and television broadcasting will show average growth due to consolidations in the industry, employment of cable and other pay-television companies will increase by 51 percent as they upgrade their systems to deliver a wider array of communication and programming services.

Overall employment growth in finance, insurance, and real estate is expected to be around 9 percent, with close to 687,000 jobs added by 2010. Securities and commodities brokers, exchanges, and services will be the fastest growing industry in this group, add-ing more than 152,000 jobs. A growing interest in investing and the popularity of 401(k) and other pension plans are fueling increases in this industry. In contrast, employment in the largest industry in this group, banking, will decrease by 1.5 percent, or -31,000 jobs, as technological advances and the increasing use of electronic banking reduce the need for large administrative support staffs. Nondepository institutions—including personal and business credit institutions, as well as mortgage banks—are expected to grow as fast as the average, adding 111,800 jobs. Insurance carriers will grow more slowly than average, increasing by only 42,600 jobs.

All 702,000 new government jobs are expected to arise in State and local government, reflecting growth in the population and its demand for public services. In contrast, the Federal Government is expected to lose more than 145,000 jobs over the 2000-10 period, as efforts continue to cut costs by contracting out services and giving States more responsibility for administering federally funded programs.

In sum, recent changes in the economy are having far-reaching and complex effects on employment in each of the industries covered in the *Career Guide*. Jobseekers should be aware of these changes, keeping alert for developments that can affect job opportunities in industries and the variety of occupations that are found in each industry. For more detailed information on specific occupations, consult the 2002-2003 edition of the *Occupational Outlook Handbook*, which provides information on more than 275 occupations.

# The Industry Descriptions

This is the book's major part, which describes 42 major industries. Look in the table of contents for a complete list of the industries, arranged into these seven clusters:

* ★ Agriculture, Mining, and Construction
* ★ Manufacturing
* ★ Transportation, Communications, and Public Utilities
* ★ Wholesale and Retail Trade
* ★ Finance and Insurance
* ★ Services
* ★ Government

## Agriculture, Mining, and Construction

# Agricultural Production

## SIGNIFICANT POINTS

- Small family farms constitute 91 percent of all farms and own about two-thirds of all farmland, but large family and commercial farms account over half of the total value of agricultural production.

- Self-employed workers—mostly farmers—account for more than half of the industry's workforce.

- Employment in agricultural production is projected to decline, especially among self-employed farmers and ranchers.

## Nature of the Industry

Agricultural production—consisting of farming and ranching, including aquaculture—has long been a mainstay of the Nation's economy, successfully feeding and clothing the domestic population as well as exporting agricultural goods around the world. Once a labor intensive industry, providing jobs for at least 12 percent of the workforce as late as 1950, both agricultural employment and the number of farms have dropped significantly in recent decades because of mechanization and other technological improvements and wide fluctuations in farm incomes due to unstable agricultural commodity prices. Although approximately one-third the number of farms exists today as compared with 50 years ago, output has more than doubled, exports of agricultural goods continue to contribute positively to the foreign trade balance, and agricultural production remains one of the Nation's top industries in terms of total employment.

Thanks to generally temperate climates, rich soil, and a variety of growing conditions, the agricultural sector produces an abundance and wide selection of products. The industry is roughly divided into two major segments: livestock production, including animal specialties; and crop production. *Livestock production* includes establishments that raise livestock, such as beef cattle, sheep, and hogs; dairy farms; poultry and egg farms; and animal specialty farms, such as apiaries (bee farms) and aquaculture (fish farms). *Crop production* includes the growing of cash grains, such as wheat, corn, and barley; field crops, such as cotton and tobacco; vegetables and melons; fruits and nuts; and horticultural specialties, such as flowers and ornamental plants.

About 2.1 million farms make up the agricultural production industry. According to the U.S. Department of Agriculture, an establishment must sell at least $1,000 worth of produce per year to qualify as a farm. Almost 1.9 million, or 91 percent, are small family farms with less than $250,000 in annual sales, but they own about two-thirds of the Nation's farmland. Operation of these farms is the primary occupation of about one-third of their owners; two-thirds are operated as a secondary source of income, primarily as homes for the rural lifestyle they afford, or as limited retirement enterprises. Large family farms numbered about 150,000 and commercially operated farms barely 40,000, but together they were responsible for just over half of the total output of the agricultural production industry.

Production of some types of crops and livestock tends to be concentrated in particular regions of the country, on the basis of growing conditions and topography. For example, the warm climates of Florida, California, and Arizona are well suited for citrus fruit production. The Southern States are the major growers of tobacco, cotton, rice, and peanuts, while the Northeast, from Maine to New Jersey, produces blueberries, maple syrup, and apples. Cranberry bogs are found mainly in Wisconsin, Massachusetts, and New Jersey. Hogs, grains, potatoes, and range-fed cattle are major products in the Plains States, where cattle feedlots also are numerous. In the Southwest and West, ranchers raise beef cattle. In Washington State, apples are an important crop. In California, most vegetables and fruits are prominent, as well as grapes for wine. Poultry and dairy farms tend to be found in most areas of the country.

The nature of the work in the agricultural production industry varies, depending on the type of product. Consumption of, and demand for, cash grains tend to be strong and steady, and these grains account for a substantial part of agricultural output. They are generally grown in large-scale operations in several areas in the Nation, but particularly in the Midwest and Plains States. During the planting, growing, and harvesting seasons, workers are busy for long hours, plowing, disking, harrowing, seeding, fertilizing, and harvesting. Fieldwork on large farms consisting of hundreds, sometimes thousands, of acres often is done using massive, climate-controlled tractors and other modern agricultural equipment. In some cases, teams of operators with tractors, combines, or other agricultural equipment travel from one farm to another during harvest time in a practice known as "custom harvesting."

Small-scale establishments are more common in the Northeast, while larger establishments are located elsewhere in the country, particularly the Southwest and West. However, these small farms in States with limited growing seasons cannot provide produce for markets during the late fall, winter, and early spring. Therefore, fresh vegetables grown on large farms in warm States, such as California, Florida, and Arizona are shipped throughout the country in the cooler months. Vegetables generally are still harvested manually by groups of migrant farmworkers, although new machines have been developed to replace manual labor for some fruit crops. Vegetable growers on large farms of approximately 100 acres or more usually practice "monoculture," large-scale cultivation of one crop on each division of land.

Dairy farms provide the Nation with milk, from which cheese, butter, ice cream, and a variety of other products are made. Dairy farming requires outdoor, as well as indoor, work. Farmers, farm managers, and farmworkers must feed cows, heifers, and calves; clean their stalls; and take them outside to pastures for exercise and grazing. Workers also may plant, harvest, and store several crops to feed the cattle through the cold of winter or the drought of summer.

Though the nature of the work on large livestock ranches in the West and Southwest still entails the kind of activities—such as branding and herding—often seen in cowboy movies, the use of modern equipment and technology has changed the way the work is done. Branding and vaccinating of herds, for example, are largely mechanized; and the use of trucks, portable communications gear, and geopositioning equipment now is common and saves valuable time for ranchers. The work on such establishments still tends to be seasonal and to take place largely outdoors. Common activities include raising feed crops, rotating cattle from one pasture to another, and keeping fences in good repair.

Most poultry and egg farms are large operations resembling production lines. Although free-range farms allow fowl some time outside during the day for exercise and sunlight, most poultry production involves mainly indoor work, with workers repeatedly performing a limited number of specific tasks. Because of increased mechanization, poultry growers can raise chickens by the hundreds—sometimes the thousands—under one roof. Eggs still are collected manually in some small-scale hatcheries, but, in larger hatcheries, eggs tumble down onto conveyor belts. Machines then wash, sort, and pack the eggs into individual cartons. Workers place the cartons into boxes and stack the boxes onto pallets for shipment.

Aquaculture farmers raise fish and shellfish in salt, brackish, or fresh water—depending on the requirements of the particular species. Farms usually use ponds, floating net pens, raceways, or recirculating systems, but some fish farms are actually in the sea, relatively close to shore. Workers on aquaculture farms stock, feed, protect, and otherwise manage aquatic life to be sold for consumption or used for recreational fishing. Horticulture farms raise ornamental plants, bulbs, shrubbery, sod, and flowers. Although much of the work takes place outdoors, in climates with cold seasons, substantial production also takes place in greenhouses or hothouses.

Although most agricultural establishments sell their products to food processing and textile companies and food retailers, some cater directly to the public. For example, some fruit and vegetable growers use the marketing strategy of "pick-your-own" produce, or set up roadside stands. Nurseries and greenhouses, which grow everything from seedlings to sod, also provide products directly to individual consumers as well as to retail establishments and other industries.

## Working Conditions

Agricultural production attracts people who enjoy working with animals, living an independent lifestyle, or working outdoors on the land. For many, the wide-open physical expanse, the variability of day-to-day work, and the rural setting provide benefits that offset the sometimes hard labor, the danger that unseasonable or extreme weather may stunt or ruin crops, and the risk that unfavorable commodity prices may reduce income.

Although the working conditions vary by occupation and setting, there are some characteristics common to most agricultural jobs. Hours generally are uneven and oftentimes long; work cannot be delayed when crops must be planted and harvested, or when animals must be sheltered and fed. Weekend work is common, and farmers, agricultural managers, crew leaders, farm-equipment operators, and agricultural workers may work a 6- or 7-day week during planting and harvesting seasons. Graders and sorters may work evenings or weekends because of the perishable nature of the products. Almost 1 out of 4 employees in this industry work variable schedules, compared with fewer than 1 in 10 workers in all industries combined. Because much of the work is seasonal in nature, many farmworkers must cope with the difficulty in obtaining year-round, full-time employment. Migrant farmworkers, who move from location to location as crops ripen, live an unsettled lifestyle, which can be stressful.

Much farm and ranch work takes place outdoors in all kinds of weather and is physical in nature. Harvesting vegetables, in particular, requires manual labor and workers do much bending, stooping, and lifting. Some field workers may lack adequate sanitation facilities, and their drinking water may be limited. The year-round nature of much livestock production work means that ranch workers must be out in the heat of summer, as well as the cold of winter. Those who work directly with animals risk being bitten or kicked.

Farmers, farm managers, and agricultural workers in crop production risk exposure to pesticides and other potentially hazardous chemicals that are sprayed on crops or plants. Those who work on mechanized farms must take precautions when working with tools and heavy equipment to avoid injury. Farmwork has long had one of the highest incidences of illnesses and injuries of any industry. In 1999, crop production had 7.0 injuries and illnesses per 100 full-time workers, compared with an average of 6.3 throughout private industry.

## Employment

In 2000, agricultural production employed a total of about 2 million workers, making it one of the largest industries in the Nation. This industry is unusual in that self-employed workers account more than 40 percent of its workforce. Among workers in all agricultural production occupations, over 1.1 million were wage and salary workers, 885,000 were self-employed, and 34,000 were unpaid family.

Among the industry's wage and salary workers, the single most common occupation was that of farmworkers, who made up nearly 54 percent of the overall workforce. The majority of self-employed workers were farmers and ranchers, but they accounted for only about 3.3 percent of wage and salary employment in this industry. Agricultural production is one of the few remaining areas of the economy in which unpaid family workers remain a significant part of the workforce. Most unpaid family workers on farms assist with the farmwork, but a small number do bookkeeping and accounting or act as farmers.

Employment is fairly evenly distributed between livestock production and crop production, with livestock-producing establishments employing about 50 percent of all workers and crop-producing establishments employing the other 50 percent. Establishments specializing in ornamental nursery products employed the largest number of workers in 2000, followed by vegetable- and melon-producing farms and fruit orchards. Crop farms, dairy farms, and vineyards also employed significant numbers of workers. Most individual agricultural-production establishments, however, employ fewer than 10 workers (chart).

Workers in agricultural production tend to be older than workers in other industries. In 2000, 50 percent of the workers livestock production were age 45 or older, compared with 35 percent for all workers in all industries.

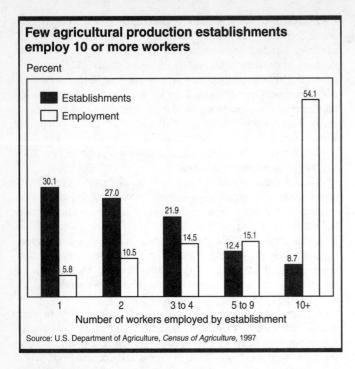

**Few agricultural production establishments employ 10 or more workers**

Percent

Legend: ■ Establishments □ Employment

- 1 worker: Establishments 30.1, Employment 5.8
- 2 workers: Establishments 27.0, Employment 10.5
- 3 to 4 workers: Establishments 21.9, Employment 14.5
- 5 to 9 workers: Establishments 12.4, Employment 15.1
- 10+ workers: Establishments 8.7, Employment 54.1

Number of workers employed by establishment

Source: U.S. Department of Agriculture, *Census of Agriculture*, 1997

## Occupations in the Industry

It takes several kinds of occupational specialties—from book-keepers, accountants, and auditors to mechanics and repairers—to keep the industry functioning (table 1). However, despite upgrades in technology, new forms of machinery, and the complex financial records that must be kept, three occupations still compose the overwhelming majority of workers in agricultural production: Farmers, agricultural managers, and agricultural workers.

*Farmers and ranchers* are the self-employed owner-operators of establishments that produce agricultural output. Their work encompasses numerous tasks. They keep records of their animals' health, crop rotation, operating expenses, major purchases, bills paid and income due, as well as pay bills and file taxes. Computer literacy has become as necessary for farmers as it has for many other occupations.

Farmers and ranchers must have additional skills to keep a farm or ranch operating day in and day out. A basic understanding and working knowledge of mechanics, carpentry, plumbing, and electricity all are helpful, if not essential, for running an agricultural establishment. The ability to maintain and repair equipment and facilities is important to keep costs down and the farm or ranch running smoothly.

Farmers who work large commercial farms for cash crops make decisions as much as a year in advance about which crop to grow. Therefore, a farmer must be aware of prices in national and international markets to use for guidance, while tracking the costs associated with each particular crop. When dealing in hundreds or thousands of acres of one crop, even small errors in judgment are magnified, so the impact can be substantial. Thus, large-scale farmers strive to keep costs to a minimum in every phase of the operation. Furthermore, risk management of portfolios—the practice of juggling stocks, buying and selling futures, and engaging in other paper deals like bond trading—is now becoming more important for farmers of large commercial farms.

*Farm, ranch, and other agricultural managers* operate the farm or ranch on a daily basis for the owners. Agricultural managers perform many of the functions of farmers and ranchers themselves, with the added tasks of managing the schedules and work of the employees. They assign, monitor, and assess individuals' work day in and day out. They may keep in order all the paperwork needed to satisfy legal requirements, including payroll records and State and Federal tax records.

Besides managing farms and ranches, agricultural managers also oversee nurseries, greenhouses, timber tracts, cotton gins, and packing houses, among other agricultural establishments.

Large commercial farms may have a manager for different operations within the establishment. On smaller farms, managers oversee all operations. They purchase the inputs used in the farm's production: Machinery, seed, fertilizers, herbicides and pesticides, fuel, and labor. They must be aware of any laws that govern the use of such inputs in the farm's locality. Additionally, they may hire and oversee other farm employees as they plow, disk, harrow, plant, fertilize, harvest, and care for livestock. Agricultural managers must be knowledgeable about crop rotation, soil testing, and various types of capital improvements necessary to maximize crop yields.

Agricultural workers perform the whole spectrum of daily chores involved in crop or livestock production. *Graders and sorters* ensure the quality of the agricultural commodities that reach the market. They grade, sort, or classify unprocessed food and other agricultural products by size, weight, color, or condition. *Farmworkers and laborers, crops, nurseries, and greenhouse* manually plant, maintain, and harvest food crops; apply pesticides, herbicides, and fertilizer to crops; and cultivate plants used to beautify landscapes. They prepare nursery acreage or greenhouse beds for planting; water, weed, and spray trees, shrubs, and plants; cut, roll, and stack sod; stake trees; tie, wrap, and pack flowers, plants, shrubs, and trees to fill orders; and dig up or move field-grown and containerized shrubs and trees. Additional duties include planting seedlings, transplanting saplings, and watering and trimming plants.

*Farmworkers, farm and ranch animals* care for farm, ranch, or aquaculture animals that may include cattle, sheep, swine, goats, horses and other equine, poultry, finfish, shellfish, and bees. They also tend to animals raised for animal products, such as meat, fur, skins, feathers, eggs, milk, and honey. Duties may include feeding, watering, herding, grazing, castrating, branding, debeaking, weighing, catching, and loading animals. They also may maintain records on animals, examine animals to detect diseases and injuries, and assist in birth deliveries and administer medications, vaccinations, or insecticides, as appropriate. Daily duties include cleaning and maintaining animal housing areas. These farmworkers also repair farm buildings and fences. For farmworkers on dairy farms, the work may include operating milking machines and other dairy-processing equipment and hauling livestock products to market.

Some agricultural workers share duties as farm-equipment operators, and handle the tractors and equipment used for plowing, sowing, and harvesting using machinery such as fertilizer spreaders, haybines, raking equipment, balers, combines, and threshers.

## Training and Advancement

The agricultural production industry is characterized by a large number of workers with low levels of educational attainment. More than 30 percent of this industry's workforce does not have a high school diploma, compared with only 12.5 percent of all workers in other industries. The proportion of workers without a high school diploma is particularly high in the crop-production sector, where there are more labor-intensive establishments employing migrant farmworkers.

**Table 1. Employment of wage and salary workers in agricultural production by occupation, 2000 and projected change, 2000-2010**
(Employment in thousands)

| Occupation | Employment, 2000 Number | Employment, 2000 Percent | Percent change, 2000-2010 |
|---|---|---|---|
| All occupations | 1,120 | 100.0 | -2.5 |
| **Management, business, and financial occupations** | 198 | 17.6 | 4.1 |
| Farm, ranch, and other agricultural managers | 154 | 13.7 | 5.2 |
| Farmers and ranchers | 36 | 3.3 | 0.4 |
| **Service occupations** | 19 | 1.7 | -1.7 |
| Building and grounds cleaning and maintenance occupations | 14 | 1.3 | -0.5 |
| **Office and administrative support occupations** | 46 | 4.1 | -10.1 |
| Bookkeeping, accounting, and auditing clerks | 18 | 1.6 | -11.1 |
| Secretaries and administrative assistants | 9 | 0.8 | -11.8 |
| **Farming, fishing, and forestry occupations** | 771 | 68.8 | -3.8 |
| First-line supervisors/managers/contractors of farming, fishing, and forestry workers | 35 | 3.1 | 1.2 |
| Farmworkers | 610 | 54.5 | -5.0 |
| Graders and sorters, agricultural products | 8 | 0.7 | -8.3 |
| All other farming, fishing, and forestry workers | 116 | 10.4 | 1.1 |
| **Installation, maintenance, and repair occupations** | 21 | 1.9 | -1.5 |
| Heavy vehicle and mobile equipment service technicians and mechanics | 8 | 0.7 | -1.6 |
| Other installation, maintenance, and repair occupations | 10 | 0.9 | -2.0 |
| **Production occupations** | 13 | 1.2 | -1.8 |
| **Transportation and material moving occupations** | 37 | 3.3 | -1.8 |
| Truck drivers, heavy and tractor-trailer | 13 | 1.1 | 1.3 |
| Truck drivers, light or delivery services | 9 | 0.8 | 0.1 |
| Material moving occupations | 12 | 1.1 | -4.5 |

NOTE: May not add to totals due to omission of occupations with small employment.

Training and education requirements for general farmworkers are few. Some experience in farm or ranch work is beneficial, but most tasks require manual labor and are learned fairly quickly on the job. Advancement for farmworkers is somewhat limited. Motivated and experienced farmworkers may become crew leaders or farm-labor contractors. Because firsthand knowledge of farm produce is good preparation for grading, sorting, and inspecting, some farmworkers may become agricultural inspectors. Farmworkers who wish to become independent farmers or ranchers first must buy or rent a plot of land.

Becoming a farmer generally does not require formal training or credentials. However, knowledge and expertise about agricultural production are essential to success for prospective farmers. The traditional method for acquiring such knowledge is through growing up on a farm. This background is becoming less and less common as the percentage of the U.S. population raised on farms continues to dwindle. But even with a farming background, a person considering farming would benefit from the formal schooling offered by land-grant universities in each State. Programs usually incorporate hands-on training into the curricula to complement the academic subjects. Typical coursework covers the agricultural sciences (crop, dairy, and animal) and business subjects such as accounting and marketing.

Experience and some formal education are necessary for agricultural managers. A bachelor's degree in business with a concentration in agriculture provides a good background. Work experience in the various aspects of farm or ranch operations enhances knowledge and develops decision-making skills, which further qualifies prospective agricultural managers. The experience of having performed tasks on other farming establishments as a farmworker may save managers valuable time in forming daily or monthly workplans and in avoiding pitfalls that could result in financial burdens for the farm.

Whether it is gained through experience or formal education, both farmers and agricultural managers need enough technical knowledge of crops, growing conditions, and plant diseases to make sound scientific and business decisions. A rudimentary knowledge of veterinary science, as well as animal husbandry, is important for dairy and livestock farmers, ranchers, and agricultural managers.

It also is crucial for farmers, ranchers, and agricultural managers to stay abreast of the latest developments in agricultural production. They may do this by reviewing agricultural journals that publish information about new cost-cutting procedures, new forms of marketing, or improved production using new techniques. County cooperative extension agencies serve as a link between university and government research programs and farmers and farm managers, providing the latest information on numerous agriculture-related subjects. County cooperative extension agents may demonstrate new animal breeding techniques, or more environmentally safe methods of fertilizing, for example. Other organizations provide information—through journals, newsletters, and the Internet—on agricultural research and the results of implementing innovative methods and ideas.

Some private organizations are helping to make farmland affordable for new farmers through a variety of institutional innovations. The Land Link program, run by the Center for Rural Affairs, matches old farmers up with young ones. In the matching process, farmers approaching retirement arrange to pass along their land to young farmers wishing to keep the land under cultivation. This program has now been expanded to at least 18 States, and is now coordinated by the National Farm Transition Network.

### Earnings
In 2000, median earnings for workers in agricultural production were $335 a week, substantially lower than the median of $580 a week for all workers in private industry. In fact, only the highest 10 percent of workers in agricultural production earned more than $630 a week. Lower than average earnings are due in part to the low level of skill required for many of the jobs in the industry and the seasonal nature of the work.

Farm income can vary substantially, depending on a number of factors, including: The type of crop or livestock being raised, price fluctuations for various agricultural products, and weather conditions that affect yield. For a growing number of farmers and ranchers, particularly those working noncommercial farms, crop or livestock production is not their major occupation or source of income.

## Outlook

Increasing productivity in the highly efficient U.S. agricultural production industry is expected to meet domestic consumption needs and export requirements with fewer farms and less farm labor than in the past. Market pressures should continue to drive the consolidation trend toward fewer and larger farms through the 2000-10 period, resulting in a 7.8 -percent decline of overall employment in agricultural production. The decline will be fastest, at 14 percent, among self-employed and unpaid family workers, most of whom are farmers. Employment of wage and salary workers will decline 2.5 percent.

In recent decades, new technology in the form of larger and more efficient farm machinery and computerization of farm equipment and financial systems have resulted in higher yields and increased productivity. Further technological improvements will continue to boost output between 2000 and 2010.

Federal Government subsidy payments traditionally have shielded many agricultural producers from the ups and downs of the market. Currently, Federal policy is to open up the industry to competitive forces. In the United States, the 1996 Federal Agriculture Improvement and Reform Act (also known as the 1996 Farm Act) was enacted to phase out price supports for agricultural produce such as wheat, corn, grain sorghum, barley, oats, rice, and upland cotton. If price supports disappear entirely, farm establishments that grow such crops may experience wide fluctuations in incomes as they deal with the adverse affects of climate and price changes. The 1996 Farm Act also calls for replacing the Federal price support system for milk with new loan programs beginning in the year 2000, allowing the milk prices received by dairy farmers to be determined by market forces. Under these conditions, the larger and more financially sound farms will be best able to cope with international and domestic competitive forces. Owners of farms that do not have sufficient funds to withstand the changes in the marketplace and still cover all operating costs may eventually be forced to consolidate with larger operations or leave agricultural production altogether. However, full implementation of the 1996 Farm Act may take several years, and some aspects of the legislation may eventually be revised.

Employment on many farms will most likely continue to be characterized by low wages and lack of benefits. This, combined with continuously rising agricultural productivity, should translate into a further reduction in the workforce. Employment of farmers and ranchers is projected to decrease. Employment of agricultural managers, farmworkers, and graders and sorters is projected to rise, but more slowly than the average for all occupations. Prospects should be best for agricultural workers working in nurseries and greenhouses.

Employment declines resulting from growing productivity and consolidations might be counterbalanced somewhat by other changes taking place in the agricultural production industry. Employment in aquaculture, for example, has been growing steadily over the past 10 years in response to growth in the demand for food fish. Because of low prices for some agricultural commodities, more farmers—including some in the Midwest—are switching to aquaculture production. New developments in marketing milk and other agricultural produce through farmer-owned and -operated cooperatives hold promise for many dairy and other farms. Furthermore, demand for organic farm produce is growing. Consumers are becoming more conscious about the pesticides and fertilizers used in conventional agriculture, allowing farms of small acreage—which only 12 years ago appeared to have almost no future as working farms—to

remain economically viable. Also, Federal, State, and local governments programs may increasingly provide assistance targeted at small farms. For example, some programs allow farmers to sell the development rights to their property to non-profit organizations pledged to preserving green space. This immediately lowers the market value of the land—and the property taxes levied on it—making farming more affordable.

## Sources of Additional Information

For general information about farming and agricultural occupations, contact:

➢ Small Farm Program, U.S. Department of Agriculture, Cooperative State, Research, Education, and Extension Service, Stop 2220, Washington, DC 20250-2220. Internet: **http://www.reeusda.gov/agsys/smallfarm**

For general information about academic programs and aquaculture, contact:

➢ The Alternative Farming Systems Information Center (AFSIC), 10301 Baltimore Ave., Room 132, Beltsville, MD 20705-2351. Internet: **http://www.nal.usda.gov/afsic**

For information about Community Supported Agriculture and internships in organic farming, contact:

➢ The Biodynamic Farming and Gardening Association, Inc., Building 1002B, Thoreau Center, The Presdio, P.O. Box 29135, San Francisco, CA 94129-0135. Internet: **http://www.biodynamics.com**
➢ Appropriate Technology Transfer for Rural Areas, P.O. Box 3657, Fayetteville, AR, 72702. Internet: **http://www.attra.org**

For information on a career as a farm manager, contact:

➢ American Society of Farm Managers and Rural Appraisers, 950 South Cherry St., #508, Denver, CO 80222. Internet: **http://www. asfmra.org**

For information on Land Link Programs, contact:

➢ The National Farm Transition Network, ISU Extension Outreach Center, 2020 DMACC Boulevard, Ankeny, IA 50021. Internet: **http://www.extension.iastate.edu/ pages/bfc/national/netwpart.html**

For information about State agencies involved in the purchases of development rights of farmland, contact:

➢ American Farmland Trust, 1200 18th St., NW, Washington, DC 20036. Internet: **http://www.farmland.org**

For information about working in a nursery or as a farmworker, contact:

➢ National FFA Organization, The National FFA Center, Attention to Career Information Requests, P.O. Box 68690, Indianapolis, IN 46268-0960. Internet: **http://www.ffa.org**
➢ The New England Small Farm Institute, 275 Jackson St., Belchertown, MA 01007. Internet: **http://www.smallfarm.org**

Information on the following occupations may be found in the 2002-03 *Occupational Outlook Handbook*:

- Farmers, ranchers, and agricultural managers
- Agricultural workers
- Grounds-maintenance workers
- Bookkeeping, accounting, and auditing clerks

# Agricultural Services

## SIGNIFICANT POINTS

- About 41percent of all agricultural service workers are employed in California, Florida, and Texas.

- Entry-level jobs that can be learned on the job in less than a week—including those of animal caretakers, farmworkers, and grounds maintenance workers—constitute a substantial portion of employment.

## Nature of the Industry

The agricultural services industry is composed of several diverse segments that provide services to an equally diverse clientele. Groups using services from the industry range from agricultural producers seeking stronger financial returns to their farmland through skilled farm management, to individual urban dwellers needing veterinary care for their pets, and urban and suburban property owners wishing to boost "curb appeal" of their establishments through professional landscaping. Many of the jobs in this industry require agricultural knowledge or skills, but only about 28 percent of wage and salary employment is directly related to the production of crops or the raising of livestock.

*Landscape and horticultural services.* Firms in this segment employ almost half of the wage and salary workers in the industry. These firms provide landscape planning and installation, landscape architecture, lawn care, and landscape and grounds maintenance services. Customers range from individual homeowners to large corporations, institutions, and Federal, State, and local governments. This segment is further subdivided into landscape *architecture* and *landscaping, lawn maintenance, and groundskeeping firms.*

*Landscape architecture firms* plan and design the development of land for projects, such as parks and other recreational facilities, airports, highways, and commercial and residential buildings. They prepare site plans showing landscape features, locations of structures, and roads, walks, and parking areas, as well as specifications and cost estimates for land development. *Landscape contracting firms* actually carry out the plans designed by landscape architecture establishments. They develop a budget for the project in consultation with the client, hire the workers and subcontractors, provide any equipment needed, and obtain the plants to install.

*Landscaping, lawn maintenance, and groundskeeping firms* establish and maintain grounds, lawns, and gardens for homeowners as well as for governments, colleges and universities, real estate and land developers, and other private businesses. These firms are responsible for designing, planting, mulching, watering, fertilizing, mowing, and seeding lawns and grounds; applying pesticides; installing turf and sod; and pruning plants and trees for both new and existing landscapes. They also clear outdoor areas of debris and leaves, remove snow, and maintain all outdoor amenities and decorative features such as pools and other athletic facilities, fountains, benches, and planters. These firms also help maintain and repair roads, walkways, parking lots, and storm drainage systems.

*Veterinary services.* Firms in this segment employ 1 in 5 wage and salary workers in the industry and provide medical care for household pets, horses, livestock, and zoo and sporting animals. The majority of veterinary practices treat companion animals, such as dogs and cats; some practices also treat pigs, goats, sheep, and some nondomestic animals. Veterinarians in such practices diagnose animal health problems, vaccinate against diseases such as distemper and rabies, medicate animals with infections or illnesses, treat and dress wounds, set fractures, perform surgery, and advise owners about feeding, behavior, and breeding. A smaller number of veterinary practices focus exclusively on large animals such as horses or cows, but may care for all kinds of livestock. Large animal veterinarians drive to farms or ranches to provide health services, with an emphasis on preventive care, for herds or individual animals. They test for and vaccinate against diseases, and consult with farm or ranch owners and managers on production, feeding, and housing issues. They also treat and dress wounds, set fractures, and perform surgery—including cesarean sections on birthing animals.

*Agricultural services, not elsewhere classified.* This segment of the industry includes firms that provide *farm labor management services* and *soil preparation and crop services.* *Farm labor and management services* firms account for nearly 16 percent of wage and salary jobs in agricultural services. *Farm labor contractors* or crew leaders provide and manage temporary farm laborers—often migrant workers—who usually work during peak harvesting times. Contractors may place bids with farmers to harvest labor-intensive crops such as fruit, nuts, or vegetables or perform other short-term tasks. Once the bid is accepted, the contractor, or crew leader, organizes and supervises the laborers as they harvest, load, move, and store the crops. *Farm management services* establishments guide and assist farm and ranch land owners, farmers, and ranchers in maximizing the financial returns to their land by managing the day-to-day activities necessary to run a farming operation. Farm management services usually negotiate with the landowner to receive a percentage of any profit resulting from agricultural production on the land. They may employ or contract with a tenant farmer to oversee the actual crop or livestock production.

Companies that provide *soil preparation and crop services* plant, cultivate, and harvest crops by machine and employ only about 1 in 9 wage and salary agricultural services workers. Because some types of farm machinery are highly specialized and very expensive, farms that do not want to invest in machinery often contract with these specialized firms to perform planting, harvesting, or other tasks. For example, farmers or farm managers might contract with crop services firms to do aerial dusting and spraying of pesticides over a large number of acres. Establishments in crop services also perform tasks to prepare crops for market, including shelling, fumigating, cleaning, grading, grinding, and packaging agricultural products.

*Animal services, except veterinary.* This is the smallest segment of the agricultural services industry, accounting for only about 5 percent of wage and salary employment. It is divided into those establishments providing livestock services and those providing services for pets, horses, and other animal specialties. *Nonfarm animal services* include animal shelters, boarding dog kennels and horse stables, dog grooming, and animal training. *Livestock services* include firms that assist in breeding and artificial insemination, do sheep dipping and shearing, and provide herd improvement advice. Breeding services usually monitor herd condition and nutrition, evaluate the quality and quantity of forage, recommend adjustments to feeding when necessary, identify the best cattle or other livestock for breeding and calving, advise on livestock pedigrees, inseminate cattle artificially, and feed and care for sires.

## Working Conditions

The agricultural services industry is attractive to people who enjoy working outdoors or with plants or animals. However, many people in this industry work long hours, and farm managers, crew leaders, agricultural equipment operators, and farmworkers may work a 6- or 7-day week during the planting and harvesting seasons. Workers in these establishments also routinely perform tasks that involve much physical exertion, often requiring strength and manual dexterity, and operate heavy machinery.

Workers in veterinary and animal services may have to lift, hold, or restrain animals of all sizes, and risk being bitten, kicked, or scratched. Evening, night, and weekend or holiday work is common, and some of the tasks of animal caretakers, such as cleaning cages and lifting heavy supplies, may be unpleasant and physically demanding. Many of the jobs in landscape and horticultural services also are physically demanding and repetitive. Laborers do much bending, kneeling, and shoveling, and lift and move supplies as they plant shrubs, trees, flowers, and grass and install decorative features.

Many workers in all segments of the agricultural services industry risk exposure to insecticides, germicides, and other potentially hazardous chemicals that are sprayed on crops and plants or used to treat insect infestation or other conditions in animals.

Also, much of the work in this industry is performed outdoors in all kinds of weather, and adequate sanitation facilities, including drinking water, may not always be available to employees. Some farmworkers and landscaping laborers also must cope with the difficulty in obtaining year-round, full-time employment because of the short-term or seasonal nature of the work. They often must string together as many jobs as possible. Workers also run the risk of injury when working with planting and harvesting equipment, such as combines, chain saws, and electric clippers. In 1999, the rate of injury and illness in agricultural services was 7.1 per 100 full-time workers, compared with 6.3 for all private industry.

## Employment

In 2000, the rapidly growing agricultural services industry comprised almost 1.1 million wage and salary workers, and about 351,000 self-employed and unpaid family workers. The following tabulation shows the distribution of wage and salary employment by industry segment:

| | |
|---|---|
| Landscape and horticultural services | 530,000 |
| Agricultural services, not elsewhere classified | 291,000 |
| Veterinary services | 220,000 |
| Animal services, except veterinary | 58,000 |

About 128,000 establishments employed these wage and salary workers in 2000. Agricultural services establishments are smaller than average—about 85 percent of the establishments employed 9 or fewer workers, compared with about 75 percent of the establishments in all industries combined. In addition, relatively few agricultural services firms employ 50 or more workers (chart).

The median age of agricultural services workers is about 36 years, nearly 4 years younger than the median for workers in all industries. This industry provides employment for many new entrants to the labor market. In 2000, almost 22 percent of the industry's workers were between 16 and 24 years old. More than 47 percent were under age 35, compared with 38 percent of workers in all industries combined—reflecting the high proportion of seasonal and part-time job opportunities.

Nearly 41 percent of all agricultural services workers are employed in California, Florida, and Texas. Other States with a large number of agricultural services workers include Arizona, Illinois, Pennsylvania, Ohio, and New York.

## Occupations in the Industry

The agricultural services industry offers jobs in many occupations requiring specialized skills or the ability to operate agricultural and horticultural equipment (table 1).

Service workers in grounds maintenance occupations include *first-line supervisors and managers of landscaping, lawn service and groundskeeping workers; landscaping and groundskeeping workers; tree trimmers and pruners;* and *pesticide handlers, sprayers and applicators, vegetation.* These workers are employed largely in landscape and horticultural services establishments and account for 32 percent of industry employment. *First-line supervisors and managers of landscaping, lawn service and groundskeeping workers,* also known as *landscape contractors,* coordinate and oversee the installation of trees, flowers, shrubs, sod, benches, and other ornamental features. They implement construction plans at the site, which may involve grading the property, installing lighting or irrigation systems, and building walkways, terraces, patios, and fountains. *Landscaping workers* install and maintain landscaped

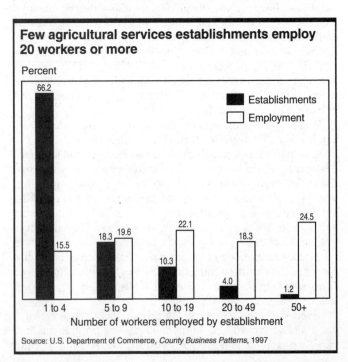

**Few agricultural services establishments employ 20 workers or more**

Percent

Source: U.S. Department of Commerce, *County Business Patterns,* 1997

16

areas by transporting and planting new vegetation; transplanting, mulching, fertilizing, watering, and pruning plants; and mowing and watering lawns. *Groundskeeping workers* perform many of the same tasks as landscaping laborers, but their duties usually are more varied, and encompass snow, leaf, and debris removal, and upkeep and repair of sidewalks, equipment, pools, fences, and benches. *Tree trimmers and pruners* specialize in pruning, trimming, and shaping ornamental trees and shrubs, or cutting away dead or excess branches to maintain rights-of-way for roads, sidewalks, or utilities. *Pesticide handlers, sprayers, and applicators, vegetation* mix and apply pesticides on trees, shrubs, lawns, or botanical crops.

*Landscape architects,* also concentrated in the landscape and horticultural services segment, plan and design the arrangement of flowers, shrubs, trees, walkways, fountains and other decorative features for parks, shopping centers, golf courses, private residences, and industrial parks. They also perform environmental impact studies and work on environmental remediation projects, in addition to urban and community planning.

*Veterinarians* provide healthcare, ranging from preventive medicine to diagnosis and treatment of diseases or injuries, for pets and farm or other animals. They also advise pet owners about feeding, behavior, and breeding, and consult with farm or ranch owners and managers on production, feeding, and disease prevention and eradication. Some inspect livestock at public stockyards and at points of entry into the United States to keep diseased animals out of the country or administer tests for animal diseases, and conduct programs for disease control. *Veterinary technologists and technicians* usually work under the supervision of a veterinarian and assist in providing medical care to animals. They may prepare and administer injections and medications, dress wounds, take vital signs, prepare animals and instruments for surgery, and perform laboratory tests.

*Veterinary assistants and laboratory animal caretakers* also may aid veterinarians, but are more involved in providing basic care for animals, cleaning cages and examination areas, feeding, changing water dishes, and monitoring animals recovering from surgery. *Nonfarm animal caretakers* have similar duties but are less likely to work directly for veterinarians focused on medical care. They provide basic care for animals, and feed, water, bathe, groom, and monitor the exercise activities of those under their charge. Their duties vary depending on the type of establishment in which they work. For example, animal caretakers employed in shelters keep records of the animals received and discharged, answer questions from the public, and euthanize seriously ill or unwanted animals, in addition to providing basic care. Animal caretakers in stables saddle and unsaddle horses, give them rubdowns, polish saddles, and store supplies and feed.

*Animal breeders,* classified under *all other farming, fishing, and forestry workers,* use their knowledge of genetics to select and breed animals, either for show or improved performance or productivity. Responsibilities typically include feeding, watering, and housing breeding animals, and maintaining weight, diet, and pedigree records.

*Farmworkers* perform the manual labor required to plant, cultivate, and harvest crops and horticultural products, and to care for and handle livestock. Crop duties vary with the season. Before seeding, they may prepare the soil by tilling and fertilizing. Once the crops are partially grown, they may return to farms to cultivate fields, transplant, weed, or prune. Often, they spray crops to control weeds, harmful insects, and fungi. Some farms, such as those producing fruit or vegetables, need large numbers of workers to harvest crops. After the harvest, workers

**Table 1. Employment of wage and salary workers in agricultural services by occupation, 2000 and projected change, 2000-2010**

(Employment in thousands)

| Occupation | Employment, 2000 | | Percent change, 2000-2010 |
|---|---|---|---|
| | Number | Percent | |
| **All occupations** | 1,099 | 100.0 | 38.6 |
| **Management, business, and financial occupations** | 43 | 3.9 | 42.1 |
| Farm, ranch, and other agricultural managers | 3 | 0.3 | 45.3 |
| General and operations managers | 18 | 1.6 | 38.5 |
| **Professional and related occupations** | 101 | 9.1 | 43.8 |
| Landscape architects | 7 | 0.7 | 43.2 |
| Veterinarians | 38 | 3.4 | 47.8 |
| Veterinary technologists and technicians | 46 | 4.2 | 41.3 |
| **Service occupations** | 516 | 46.9 | 42.5 |
| First-line supervisors/managers of landscaping, lawn service, and groundskeeping workers | 46 | 4.1 | 24.0 |
| Veterinary assistants and laboratory animal caretakers | 48 | 4.3 | 42.4 |
| Landscaping and groundskeeping workers | 302 | 27.4 | 49.4 |
| Pesticide handlers, sprayers, and applicators, vegetation | 16 | 1.4 | 25.3 |
| Tree trimmers and pruners | 38 | 3.5 | 24.0 |
| Nonfarm animal caretakers | 47 | 4.2 | 37.1 |
| **Sales and related occupations** | 14 | 1.3 | 40.8 |
| **Office and administrative support occupations** | 101 | 9.2 | 32.2 |
| Bookkeeping, accounting, and auditing clerks | 12 | 1.1 | 28.0 |
| Receptionists and information clerks | 36 | 3.2 | 25.8 |
| Office clerks, general | 16 | 1.5 | 49.3 |
| Secretaries, except legal, medical, and executive | 12 | 1.1 | 18.7 |
| **Farming, fishing, and forestry occupations** | 243 | 22.1 | 32.0 |
| First-line supervisors/managers/contractors of farming, fishing, and forestry workers | 15 | 1.4 | 35.6 |
| Farmworkers | 188 | 17.1 | 32.3 |
| Graders and sorters, agricultural products | 19 | 1.7 | 22.9 |
| All other farming, fishing, and forestry workers | 20 | 1.8 | 34.6 |
| **Construction and extraction occupations** | 15 | 1.4 | 41.7 |
| Construction trades and related workers | 14 | 1.3 | 41.3 |
| **Installation, maintenance, and repair occupations** | 12 | 1.1 | 32.6 |
| **Production occupations** | 14 | 1.3 | 25.9 |
| **Transportation and material moving occupations** | 40 | 3.7 | 33.4 |
| Truck drivers, heavy and tractor-trailer | 7 | 0.6 | 41.6 |
| Laborers and freight, stock, and material movers, hand | 11 | 1.0 | 27.2 |
| Packers and packagers, hand | 10 | 0.9 | 35.4 |

NOTE: May not add to totals due to omission of occupations with small employment.

17

are needed to prepare produce for shipment. Farmworkers who work in nurseries and greenhouses help to cultivate the plants used in landscaping projects by preparing nursery acreage or greenhouse beds for planting, and watering, weeding, and spraying trees, shrubs, and plants. They also prepare sod, trees, and other plants for transport to landscaping sites. The duties of farmworkers who care for and handle livestock vary by type of livestock. All livestock must have fresh water and feed. Pests and diseases must be monitored and controlled. Special care must be given to animals when they are giving birth. Dairy cows and other milk-producing animals such as dairy goats must be milked many times a day with close attention to sanitation and cleanliness.

Many of the farmworkers in agricultural services contract for employment with *farm labor contractors,* or *crew leaders,* who contract with farms to provide workers to perform what are often short-term, labor-intensive farm jobs, such as manually harvesting, loading, and moving vegetables. The crew leader also is responsible for transporting the hired workers to the fields or orchards, and for meeting Federal and State regulations regarding the hiring of transient workers, including paying a guaranteed minimum wage, payment for overtime work, and collecting Social Security taxes. Crew leaders, like the workers they hire and supervise, may practice "follow-the-crop" migration, typically recruiting a crew in the southern States, then moving north in a set pattern as crops ripen. Others remain in a single locality.

*Agricultural equipment operators,* classified under *all other farming, fishing, and forestry workers,* drive the heavy machinery used to mechanically harvest and combine crops. *Graders and sorters, agricultural products* sort and classify unprocessed food and other agricultural products by size, weight, color, or condition.

*Farm, ranch, and other agricultural managers* use their knowledge of agriculture and business to make farming management decisions for landowners. Managers may employ a farm operator or contract with a tenant farmer to run the day-to-day activities involved in crop or livestock production. Farm managers help select the type and mix of crops; select practices for tillage and soil conservation as well as methods of irrigation; purchase seed, pesticides, and fertilizers; determine crop transportation and storage requirements; market the crops or livestock; oversee maintenance of the property and equipment; recommend capital improvements; and monitor operating expenses. Farm managers also may hire and assign workers when needed, contract with other firms for specialized services such as chemical spraying of crops, and advise landowners about the purchase or sale of additional farmlands. Managers who work with livestock must know how to maximize animal production by select breeding stock and culling herds, for example. They also must understand animal nutrition, behavior, and handling techniques, as well as how to recognize and control disease and pest problems. Managing an agricultural or livestock production operation is a sophisticated business, and farm managers use computers extensively. Some also use cutting-edge technologies, such as the Global Positioning System and remote sensing.

## Training and Advancement

The skills needed by workers in the agricultural services industry differ widely by occupation. The industry is characterized by an unusually high proportion of workers who have not finished high school: 29 percent as compared with about 13 percent for all industries. These workers qualify for entry-level positions as animal caretakers, farmworkers, and landscaping and groundskeeping workers, which require little or no prior training or experience. The basic tasks associated with many of these jobs usually can be learned in less than a week, and most newly hired workers are trained on the job. Training often is given under the close supervision of an experienced employee or supervisor.

For jobs such as veterinarian, landscape architect, and farm manager, a minimum of 4 years of formal postsecondary training is needed. Aspiring veterinarians generally complete 4 years of preveterinary study, including biology, chemistry, physics, and calculus, before embarking on 4 years of veterinary medical school. They graduate with a Doctor of Veterinary Medicine degree and must obtain a license to practice. Prospective landscape architects must complete a professional program in landscape architecture, and be registered or licensed before they may practice in most States. Farm managers usually obtain a bachelor's degree in a business-related field with a concentration in agriculture. A degree in an agriculture-related discipline with an emphasis on business courses, such as marketing and finance, also is good preparation. Many States require farm managers to carry a real estate license. Farm managers may obtain the designation Accredited Farm Manager through the American Society of Farm Managers and Rural Appraisers after several years of experience and of meeting established standards, although accreditation is not mandatory. College training and professional licensing or certification also may be required for many other jobs in agricultural services, such as grounds manager and landscape contractor. Schools of agriculture are found at many State universities and all State land grant colleges. They offer a variety of programs at the bachelor's, master's, and doctoral levels.

Community colleges and vocational schools also offer an array of programs for people interested in various agricultural services occupations—for example, animal breeder, agricultural equipment operator, and horticultural or landscaping supervisor. Many employers prefer previous work experience, combined with vocational certification or a 2-year degree. Many States have licensing requirements for veterinary technologists, which include 2 years of college-level study in an accredited veterinary technology program culminating in an Associate in Applied Science or related degree, and passing an examination before being allowed to fully assist veterinarians.

Opportunities for advancement for agricultural services workers vary by occupation. Farmworkers have limited opportunities for advancement, but experienced and highly motivated laborers may move into positions as farm labor contractors or crew leaders. Likewise, grounds maintenance workers may advance to supervisory positions after gaining experience, or become managers of landscape operations. Some become self-employed landscape or lawn service contractors, but such positions may require additional formal training. Although many top-level managerial and professional jobs—especially in small companies—are filled by promotion from within, technological innovations in agronomy and animal husbandry have made postsecondary education advantageous for career advancement in agricultural services.

## Earnings

Average earnings in the agricultural services industry are relatively low—nonsupervisory nonfarm workers averaged $10.95 an hour in 2000, compared with $13.74 an hour for workers throughout private industry. Earnings can vary greatly during the year, depending on the season. Many workers in this industry find work only in the growing or harvesting seasons and are unemployed or work in other jobs during the rest of the year. More than 16 percent worked part time in 2000, compared with the industry average of slightly more than 15 percent. Part-time workers are less likely to receive employer-provided benefits. Earnings in selected occupations in agricultural services in 2000 appear in table 2.

Union membership in the agricultural services industry is far below the average for all industries. In 2000, only 2.5 percent of all agricultural services workers were union members or were covered by union contracts, compared with about 14.9 percent of workers in all industries.

**Table 2. Median hourly earnings of the largest occupations in agricultural services, 2000**

| Occupation | Agricultural services | All industries |
|---|---|---|
| Chief executives ..................................... | $ 32.97 | $ 54.72 |
| Veterinarians ......................................... | 29.32 | 29.28 |
| General and operations managers ......... | 22.96 | 29.41 |
| Landscape architects ............................. | 18.18 | 20.93 |
| First-line supervisors/managers of landscaping, lawn service, and groundskeeping workers ..................... | 14.20 | 14.70 |
| Animal trainers ...................................... | 12.43 | 10.54 |
| Pesticide handlers, sprayers, and applicators, vegetation ......................... | 11.66 | 11.11 |
| Tree trimmers and pruners ..................... | 11.27 | 11.41 |
| Veterinary technologists and technicians ........................................... | 10.29 | 10.41 |
| Landscaping and groundskeeping workers ................................................. | 8.63 | 8.80 |

## Outlook

Wage and salary jobs in agricultural services are projected to increase 39 percent through the year 2010, compared with 16 percent for all industries combined. In addition, numerous job openings will arise from the need to replace workers who leave the industry every year. Much of the work in entry-level jobs, which account for a substantial portion of all jobs in the industry, is physically demanding and low paying, making it unattractive for workers over the long term. Turnover is very high among landscaping and groundskeeping workers, animal caretakers, and farmworkers, reflecting the seasonal and part-time nature of the work as well as the low pay and high physical demands.

The agricultural services industry grew very rapidly from the late 1980s through the 1990s, with several segments of the industry experiencing strong employment increases. Job growth was fueled by especially strong increases in two of the largest segments—landscaping and horticultural services, and veterinary services. Although demand for agricultural services is expected to remain strong, the rate of employment growth is expected to slow over the 2000-10 period.

Employment gains in landscaping and horticultural services are tied, in part, to the level of new construction. Construction activity tends to vary depending on the health of the overall economy. Over the long run, the construction industry is expected to grow, though at a slower rate than over the previous 10-year period. Federal, State, and local government budget constraints also may limit demand for services to develop and care for grounds. Nevertheless, the employment outlook should

remain bright. Individuals and businesses are expected to increasingly recognize the value of maintaining and renovating existing landscaping and grounds. As businesses compete to attract customers, enhancing curb appeal by investing in landscaping and lawn services will become an increasingly important marketing consideration. A growing number of homeowners continue to use lawn maintenance and landscaping services to enhance the beauty of their property and to conserve leisure time. Additionally, many land developers and builders who face complex environmental regulations and land-use zoning issues are turning to landscape architecture firms for help in planning sites and integrating buildings and other structures into the natural environment. Overall concern about environmental issues and a growing appreciation for nature will add to the desire for more professional landscaping and horticultural services.

Employment gains in veterinary services, partially attributable to increases in the number of pet owners, are expected to be slower than in the past several years, but still healthy during the projection period. Increases in the pet population, and new technology and better marketing of nontraditional pet medical services, such as preventive dental care, will contribute to demand for veterinary services.

Nonfarm animal services, except veterinary, should be affected by rising trends in pet population growth. Pet owners are expected to increasingly take advantage of grooming services and daily and overnight boarding services.

Slower employment growth is expected of farm-related agricultural services—crop services, soil preparation services, farm labor and management services, and livestock services—that are linked to the health of the agricultural production industry. When agricultural producers face difficult times, such as the recent economic downturns in some Asian countries that reduced the demand for exports of agricultural products from the United States, the demand for farm-related agricultural services also drop. Over the long-run, however, overall employment should increase. Growth in the animal population, emphasis on scientific methods of breeding and raising livestock and poultry, and continued support for public health and disease control programs, will contribute to the demand for farm-related veterinary and livestock animal services. Farmers and agricultural managers should continue to turn to farm labor contracting services to ease their responsibility for meeting labor requirements for workers who are only needed on a temporary basis. Mechanization of the industry is largely in place, and food needs will continue to grow as the population increases. However, agricultural producers are expected to continue to produce more with less labor. The dominance of large producers, food companies, and agribusiness, along with farms that are growing in average size, allows the use of state-of-the-art, more efficient farming practices and technologies, leading to slower demand for contracting services.

## Sources of Additional Information

For general information about agricultural and farming occupations, contact:

➤ National Association of State University and Land Grant Colleges, 1307 New York Avenue NW., Suite 400, Washington, DC 20005-4701.

For information on careers in landscaping and horticulture, contact:

➤ Associated Landscape Contractors of America, Inc., 150 Eldon St., Suite 270, Herndon, VA 20170.
Internet: **http://www.alca.org**

- American Society of Landscape Architects, 636 Eye St. NW., Washington, DC 20001-3736. Internet: **http://www.asla.org**
- Professional Lawn Care Association of America, Suite C-135, 1000 Johnson Ferry Road, NE., Marietta, GA, 30068. Internet: **http://www.plcaa.org**
- National Arborist Association, PO Box 1094, Amherst, NH 03031. Internet: **http://www.natlarb.com**

For information on careers in veterinary science, send a self-addressed, stamped envelope to:

- American Veterinary Medical Association, 1931 N. Meacham Rd., Suite 100, Schaumburg, IL 60173-4360.

For information on careers in animal specialty services, contact:

- National Association of Animal Breeders, 401 Bernadette Dr., P.O. Box 1033, Columbia, MO 65205-1033. Internet: **http://www.naab-css.org**

For a list of State-licensed dog grooming schools, send a self-addressed, stamped envelope to:

- National Dog Groomers Association of America, P.O. Box 101, Clark, PA 16113.

For information on careers in farm management, contact:

- American Society of Farm Managers and Rural Appraisers, 950 S. Cherry St., Suite 508, Denver, CO 80222. Internet: **http://www.agri-associations.org**

Information on these occupations may be found in the 2002-03 edition of the *Occupational Outlook Handbook*:

- Agricultural workers
- Animal care and service workers
- Farmers, ranchers, and agricultural managers
- Grounds maintenance workers
- Landscape architects
- Veterinarians
- Veterinary technologists, technicians, and assistants

# Construction

## SIGNIFICANT POINTS

- Job opportunities are expected to be excellent.

- Workers in construction have relatively high hourly earnings.

- Construction is one of the economy's largest industries.

- More than 8 out of 10 establishments employ fewer than 10 people.

- Construction has a very large number of self-employed workers.

## Nature of the Industry

Houses, apartments, factories, offices, schools, roads, and bridges are only some of the products of the construction industry. This industry's activities include work on new structures as well as additions, alterations, and repairs to existing ones. (Some government establishments do the same work and employ a significant number of people, but information about them is not included in this statement. Information concerning government construction is included in the statements on Federal Government and State and local government, except education and health, in the *Career Guide to Industries*.)

The construction industry is divided into three major segments: General building contractors, heavy construction contractors, and special trade contractors. *General building contractors* build residential, industrial, commercial, and other buildings. *Heavy construction contractors* build sewers, roads, highways, bridges, tunnels, and other projects. *Special trade contractors* are engaged in specialized activities such as carpentry, painting, plumbing, and electrical work.

Construction usually is done or coordinated by *general contractors* who specialize in one type of construction such as residential or commercial building. They take full responsibility for the complete job, except for specified portions of the work that may be omitted from the general contract. Although general contractors may do a portion of the work with their own crews, they often subcontract most of the work to heavy construction or special trade contractors.

Special trade contractors usually do the work of only one trade, such as painting, carpentry, or electrical work, or of two or more closely related trades, such as plumbing and heating. Beyond fitting their work to that of the other trades, special trade contractors have no responsibility for the structure as a whole. They obtain orders for their work from general contractors, architects, or property owners. Repair work is almost always done on direct order from owners, occupants, architects, or rental agents.

## Working Conditions

Most employees in this industry work full time, many over 40 hours a week. In 2000, about 1 in 4 construction workers worked 45 hours or more a week; a large proportion of self-employed individuals also worked over 45 hours a week. Construction workers may sometimes work evenings, weekends, and holidays to finish a job or take care of an emergency. Workers in this industry need physical stamina because the work frequently requires prolonged standing, bending, stooping, and working in cramped quarters. They also may be required to lift and carry heavy objects. Exposure to weather is common because much of the work is done outside or in partially enclosed structures. Construction workers often work with potentially dangerous tools and equipment amidst a clutter of building materials; some work on temporary scaffolding or at great heights and in bad weather. Consequently, they are more prone to injuries than workers in other jobs. In 1999, cases of work-related injury and illness were 8.6 per 100 full-time workers, which is significantly higher than the 6.3 rate for the entire private sector. Workers who do roofing, masonry, stonework, and plastering experienced the highest injury rates. In response, employers increasingly emphasize safe working conditions and work habits that reduce the risk of injuries. To avoid injury, employees wear safety clothing, such as gloves and hard hats, and sometimes devices to protect their eyes, mouth, or hearing.

## Employment

Construction, with 6.7 million wage and salary and 1.6 million self-employed and unpaid family nongovernment jobs in 2000, was one of the Nation's largest industries.

More than 3 out of 5 wage and salary jobs were with special trade contractors, primarily plumbing, electrical, and masonry contractors. More than 1 out of 5 jobs were with general building contractors, mostly in residential and nonresidential construction. The rest were with road and other heavy construction contractors (table 1). Employment in this industry is distributed geographically in much the same way as the Nation's population; the concentration of employment is generally in industrialized and highly populated areas.

There were about 667,000 construction companies in the United States in 1997: 197,091 were general contractors and operative builders; 37,701 were heavy construction or highway contractors; and 431,877 were specialty trade contractors. Most of these establishments tend to be small, the majority employing fewer than 10 workers (chart 1). About 8 out of 10 workers are employed by small contractors.

Construction offers more opportunities than most other industries for individuals who want to own and run their own business. The 1.6 million self-employed and unpaid family workers in 2000 performed work directly for property owners or acted as contractors on small jobs, such as additions, remodeling, and maintenance projects. The large majority of the self-employed work in the construction trades. The rate of self-employment varies greatly by individual occupation in the construction trades (chart 2).

**Table 1. Nongovernment distribution of wage and salary employment in construction by industry, 2000**

(Employment in thousands)

| Industry | Employment | 2000-10 Percent change |
|---|---|---|
| **Total, all industries** | 6,698 | 100.0 |
| **General building contractors** | 1,528 | 22.8 |
| Residential building | 826 | 12.3 |
| Operative builders | 31 | 0.5 |
| Nonresidential building construction | 670 | 10.0 |
| **Heavy construction, except building** | 901 | 13.5 |
| Highway and street construction | 280 | 4.2 |
| Heavy construction, except highway | 621 | 9.3 |
| **Special trade contractors** | 4,269 | 63.7 |
| Plumbing, heating, and air conditioning | 937 | 14.0 |
| Painting and paper hanging | 228 | 3.4 |
| Electrical work | 866 | 12.9 |
| Masonry, stonework, and plastering | 567 | 8.5 |
| Carpentry and floor work | 324 | 4.8 |
| Roofing, siding, and sheet metal work | 253 | 3.8 |

## Occupations in the Industry

Work in construction offers a great variety of career opportunities. People with many different talents and educational backgrounds—managers, clerical workers, skilled craftsworkers, semiskilled workers, and laborers—find job opportunities in construction and related activities (table 2).

Most of the workers in construction are skilled craftsworkers or laborers, helpers, and apprentices who assist the more skilled workers. Most construction workers generally are classified as either structural, finishing, or mechanical workers. *Structural workers* include carpenters; construction equipment operators; brickmasons, blockmasons, and stonemasons; cement masons and concrete finishers; and structural and reinforcing iron and metal workers. *Finishing workers* include carpenters; drywall installers, ceiling tile installers, and tapers; plasterers and stucco masons; segmental pavers; terrazzo workers; painters and

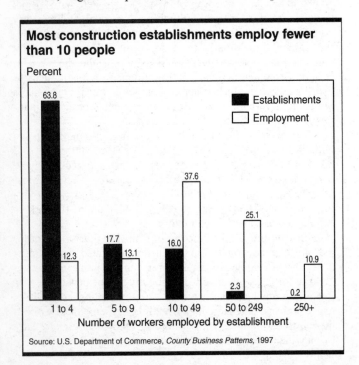

**Most construction establishments employ fewer than 10 people**

Percent

Source: U.S. Department of Commerce, *County Business Patterns*, 1997

**Table 2. Employment of wage and salary workers in construction by occupation, 2000 and projected change, 2000-10**

(Employment in thousands)

| Occupation | Employment, 2000 Number | Percent | Percent change, 2000-2010 |
|---|---|---|---|
| **All occupations** | 6,698 | 100.0 | 12.3 |
| **Management, business, and financial occupations** | 602 | 9.0 | 11.2 |
| Construction managers | 182 | 2.7 | 14.1 |
| General and operations managers | 161 | 2.4 | 7.3 |
| Cost estimators | 105 | 1.6 | 13.8 |
| **Professional and related occupations** | 97 | 1.4 | 7.9 |
| Architecture and engineering occupations | 81 | 1.2 | 3.9 |
| **Service occupations** | 49 | 0.7 | 12.0 |
| **Sales and related occupations** | 109 | 1.6 | 6.2 |
| **Office and administrative support occupations** | 575 | 8.6 | 0.6 |
| Bookkeeping, accounting, and auditing clerks | 126 | 1.9 | -2.3 |
| Office clerks, general | 74 | 1.1 | 13.2 |
| Executive secretaries and administrative assistants | 71 | 1.1 | 2.2 |
| Secretaries, except legal, medical, and executive | 135 | 2.0 | -9.3 |
| **Construction and extraction occupations** | 4,526 | 67.6 | 13.7 |
| First-line supervisors/managers of construction trades and extraction workers | 370 | 5.5 | 13.6 |
| Brickmasons and blockmasons | 98 | 1.5 | 14.1 |
| Carpenters | 681 | 10.2 | 10.0 |
| Carpet, floor, and tile installers and finishers | 64 | 1.0 | 8.6 |
| Cement masons and concrete finishers | 139 | 2.1 | 4.0 |
| Construction laborers | 701 | 10.5 | 15.2 |
| Operating engineers and other construction equipment operators | 198 | 3.0 | 10.4 |
| Drywall and ceiling tile installers | 111 | 1.7 | 13.5 |
| Electricians | 464 | 6.9 | 18.3 |
| Painters, construction and maintenance | 184 | 2.8 | 11.0 |
| Plumbers, pipefitters, and steamfitters | 335 | 5.0 | 11.0 |
| Roofers | 111 | 1.7 | 19.0 |
| Sheet metal workers | 149 | 2.2 | 29.1 |
| Structural iron and steel workers | 70 | 1.0 | 18.2 |
| Helpers—Brickmasons, blockmasons, stonemasons, and tile and marble setters | 56 | 0.8 | 13.7 |
| Helpers—Carpenters | 93 | 1.4 | 5.7 |
| Helpers—Electricians | 109 | 1.6 | 13.0 |
| Helpers—Pipelayers, plumbers, pipe fitters, and steamfitters | 81 | 1.2 | 11.1 |
| **Installation, maintenance, and repair occupations** | 399 | 6.0 | 16.5 |
| Electrical and electronic equipment mechanics, installers, and repairers | 59 | 0.9 | 1.5 |
| Heating, air conditioning, and refrigeration mechanics and installers | 93 | 1.4 | 25.2 |
| **Production occupations** | 101 | 1.5 | 11.3 |
| **Transportation and material moving occupations** | 239 | 3.6 | 14.8 |
| Truck drivers, heavy and tractor-trailer | 99 | 1.5 | 16.0 |
| Material moving occupations | 102 | 1.5 | 14.5 |

NOTE: May not add to totals due to omission of occupations with small employment.

paperhangers; glaziers; roofers; carpet, floor, and tile installers and finishers; and insulation workers. *Mechanical workers* include pipelayers, plumbers, pipefitters, and steamfitters; electricians; sheet metal workers, and heating, air conditioning, and refrigeration mechanics and installers. Other workers, called *hazardous materials removal workers* remove hazardous materials such as asbestos, lead, and radioactive and nuclear materials from buildings, facilities, and the environment to avoid further contamination of natural resources and to promote public health and safety.

The greatest number of construction craftsworkers work as carpenters; electricians; pipelayers, plumbers, pipefitters, and steamfitters; construction equipment operators; painters and paperhangers; sheet metal workers; drywall installers, ceiling tile installers, and tapers; cement masons, concrete finishers, segmental pavers, and terrazzo workers; brickmasons, blockmasons, and stonemasons; and roofers.. The construction industry employs nearly all of the workers in some construction craft occupations—such as plasterers and stucco masons; roofers; structural and reinforcing iron and metal workers; and drywall installers, ceiling tile installers, and tapers. In other construction craft occupations—for example, electricians, painters and paperhangers; plumbers, pipefitters, and steamfitters; and carpet floor, and tile installers and finishers—large numbers also work in other industries (table 3). Other industries employing large numbers of construction workers include transportation equipment manufacturing, transportation, communication and utilities, real estate, wholesale and retail trade, educational services, and State and local government.

Many persons enter the construction crafts through apprenticeship programs. These programs offer on-the-job training under the close supervision of a craftworker, as well as some formal classroom instruction. Depending on the trade, apprentices learn a variety of skills, ranging from laying brick to putting together steel beams.

Many persons advance to construction craft occupations from related, less skilled jobs as *helpers* or *laborers*. They acquire skills while they work. They are first hired as laborers or helpers, performing a variety of unskilled tasks and providing

much of the routine physical labor needed in construction. They erect and dismantle scaffolding, clean up debris, help unload and carry materials and machinery, and operate simple equipment. They work alongside experienced craftworkers, learning the basic skills of a particular craft. After acquiring experience and skill in various phases of the craft, they may become skilled journey level craftworkers.

To develop their skills further after training, construction craftworkers may work on many different projects, such as housing developments, office and industrial buildings, or highways, bridges, and dams. Flexibility and a willingness to adopt new techniques, as well as the ability to get along with people, are essential for advancement. Those skilled in all facets of the trade and who show good leadership qualities may be promoted to *supervisor*. As supervisors, they oversee craftworkers and helpers and ensure work is done well. They plan the job and solve problems as they arise. Those with good organizational skills and exceptional supervisory ability may advance to *superintendent*. Superintendents are responsible for getting a project completed on schedule by working with the architect's plans, making sure materials are delivered on time, assigning work, overseeing craft supervisors, and making sure every phase of the project is completed properly and expeditiously. They also resolve problems and see to it that work proceeds without interruptions. Superintendents may advance to large projects as general managers and top executives. Some go into business for themselves as contractors.

**Table 3. Percent of wage and salary workers in construction craft occupations employed in the construction industry, 2000**

| Occupation | Employed |
| --- | --- |
| Insulation workers | 88.4 |
| Cement masons, concrete finishers, and terrazzo workers | 85.3 |
| Structural iron and steel workers | 83.7 |
| Plasterers and stucco masons | 79.7 |
| Drywall installers, ceiling tile installers, and tapers | 77.6 |
| Roofers | 70.5 |
| Brickmasons, blockmasons, and stonemasons | 67.4 |
| Plumbers, pipefitters, and steamfitters | 66.7 |
| Electricians | 66.5 |
| Glaziers | 64.1 |
| Carpenters | 56.6 |
| Carpet, floor, and tile installers and finishers | 38.4 |
| Painters, construction and maintenance | 37.5 |
| Paperhangers | 27.5 |

## Training and Advancement

Persons may enter most jobs in the construction industry without any formal classroom training after high school. Laborers can learn their job in a few days, but the skills required for many jobs are substantial; they can be learned on the job or through apprenticeships. Skilled workers such as carpenters, bricklayers, plumbers, and other construction trade specialists need either several years of informal on-the-job experience, or apprenticeship training. Workers pick up skills by working alongside more experienced workers, and through instruction provided by their employers. As they demonstrate their ability to perform tasks they are assigned, they move to progressively more challenging work. As they broaden their skills, they are allowed to work more independently, and responsibilities and earnings increase. They may qualify for jobs in related, more highly skilled, occupations. For example, after several years of experience, painters' helpers may become journey level painters.

**Many construction occupations have a substantial percentage of self-employed workers.**

Electricians

Pipelayers, plumbers, pipefitters, and steamfitters

Plasterers and stucco masons

Drywall installers

Roofers

Bricklayers, blockmasons, and stonemasons

Carpenters

Painters and paperhangers

Carpet, floor, and tile installers

0   10   20   30   40   50

**Self-employed as a percent of total occupational employment**

Apprenticeships administered by local employers, trade associations, and trade unions provide the most thorough training. Apprenticeships usually last between 3 and 5 years and consist of on-the-job training and 144 hours or more of related classroom instruction. However, a number of apprenticeship programs are now using competency standards in place of time requirements, making it possible to complete a program in a shorter time. Those who enroll in apprenticeship programs usually are least 18 years old and in good physical condition.

Persons can enter the construction industry with a variety of educational backgrounds. Those entering construction right out of high school start as laborers, helpers, or apprentices. Those who enter construction from technical or vocational schools also may go through apprenticeship training; however, they progress at a somewhat faster pace because they already have had courses such as mathematics, mechanical drawing, and woodworking. Skilled craftworkers may advance to supervisor or superintendent positions, or may transfer to jobs such as construction building inspector, purchasing agent, sales representative for building supply companies, contractor, or technical or vocational school instructor.

Managerial personnel usually have a college degree or considerable experience in their specialty. Individuals who enter construction with college degrees usually start as management trainees or construction managers' assistants. Those who receive degrees in construction science often start as field engineers, schedulers, or cost estimators. College graduates may advance to positions such as assistant manager, construction manager, general superintendent, cost estimator, construction building inspector, general manager or top executive, contractor, or consultant. Although a college education is not always required, administrative jobs usually are filled by people with degrees in business administration, finance, accounting, or similar fields.

Opportunities for workers to form their own firms are better in construction than in many other industries. Construction workers need only a moderate financial investment to become contractors and they can run their businesses from their homes, hiring additional construction workers only as needed for specific projects. The contract construction field, however, is very competitive, and the rate of business failure is high.

## Earnings

Earnings in construction are significantly higher than the average for all industries (table 4). In 2000, production or nonsupervisory workers in construction averaged $17.86 an hour, or about $702 a week. Average earnings of workers in the special trade contractors segment were somewhat higher than those of workers employed by building or heavy construction contractors.

Earnings of workers in the construction industry vary by the education and experience of the worker, type of work, the size and nature of the construction project, geographic location, and economic conditions. Earnings of construction trade workers also are often affected by poor weather. Traditionally, winter is the slack period for construction activity, especially in colder parts of the country. Some workers, such as laborers or roofers, may not work for several months. Heavy rain also may slow or even stop work on a construction project. Because construction trades are dependent on one another—especially on large projects—work delays in one trade delay or stop work in another. Earnings in selected occupations in construction in 2000 appear in table 5.

### Table 4. Average earnings of nonsupervisory workers in construction, 2000

| Industry segment | Weekly | Hourly |
|---|---|---|
| **Total, private industry** | $474 | $13.74 |
| **Construction industry** | 702 | 17.86 |
| **General building contractors** | 655 | 17.20 |
| Residential building contractors | 585 | 15.91 |
| Operative builders | 643 | 17.00 |
| Nonresidential building contractors | 733 | 18.51 |
| **Heavy construction** | 749 | 17.33 |
| Highway and street construction | 769 | 17.59 |
| Heavy construction, except highway | 738 | 17.21 |
| **Special trade contractors** | 706 | 18.20 |
| Plumbing, heating, and air conditioning | 736 | 18.64 |
| Painting and paper hanging | 589 | 15.87 |
| Electrical work | 806 | 20.16 |
| Masonry, stonework, and plastering | 643 | 17.66 |
| Carpentry and floor work | 670 | 18.11 |
| Roofing, siding, and sheet metal work | 551 | 15.73 |

About 20.4 percent of all workers were union members or covered by union contracts, compared with 15 percent of workers throughout private industry. Many different unions represent the various construction trades and form joint apprenticeship committees with local employers to supervise apprenticeship programs.

### Table 5. Median hourly earnings of the largest occupations in construction, 2000

| Occupation | General building contractors | Heavy construction, except building | Special trade contractors | All industries |
|---|---|---|---|---|
| General and operations managers | $ 32.72 | $ 34.02 | $ 31.12 | $ 29.41 |
| Construction managers | 27.23 | 27.89 | 27.40 | 28.00 |
| Cost estimators | 23.38 | 25.14 | 22.57 | 22.02 |
| First-line supervisors/ managers of construction trades and extraction workers | 22.03 | 21.09 | 21.44 | 21.53 |
| Plumbers, pipefitters, and steamfitters | 18.97 | 17.26 | 18.09 | 18.19 |
| Brickmasons and blockmasons | 18.78 | 19.51 | 19.59 | 19.37 |
| Operating engineers and other construction equipment operators | 18.08 | 17.35 | 16.91 | 15.99 |
| Electricians | 16.70 | 17.93 | 19.19 | 19.29 |
| Carpenters | 15.97 | 16.82 | 16.14 | 15.69 |
| Construction laborers | 11.15 | 11.60 | 11.35 | 11.15 |

## Outlook

Job opportunities are expected to be excellent in the construction industry, due largely to the numerous openings arising each year from experienced construction workers who leave jobs. Further, many potential workers may prefer work that is less strenuous and has more comfortable working conditions. The continued shortage of adequate training programs also will contribute to the favorable job market.

The number of wage and salary jobs in the construction industry is expected to grow about 12 percent through the year 2010, compared with 15 percent projected for all industries combined. Employment in this industry depends primarily on the level of construction and remodeling activity. New construction is usually cut back during periods when the economy is not expanding, and the number of job openings in construction fluctuates greatly from year to year. Employment growth in the various segments of the construction industry varies somewhat, depending on the demand for various types of construction. At times, there may be a high demand for new office space or housing, for example, but lower demand for road construction or remodeling work.

Although household growth may slow slightly over the coming decade, the demand for residential construction is expected to continue to grow. The demand for larger homes with more amenities, as well as for second homes, will continue to rise, especially as the baby boomers reach their peak earning years and can afford to spend more on housing. Some older, more affluent baby boomers will want townhouses and condominiums in conveniently located suburban and urban settings. At the same time, as the number of immigrants increases and as the "echo boomers" (the children of the baby boomers) start to replace the smaller "baby bust" generation in the young adult age groups, the demand for manufactured housing, starter homes, and rental apartments also is expected to increase.

Employment in nonresidential construction is expected to grow a little faster than the rest of the industry because industrial construction activity is expected to be stronger as replacement of many industrial plants has been delayed for years, and a large number of structures will have to be replaced or remodeled. Construction of nursing, convalescent homes, and other extended care institutions also will increase due to the aging of the population, the growing use of high-technology medical treatment facilities, and the need for more drug treatment clinics. Construction of schools will increase to accommodate the children of the baby boom generation.

Employment in heavy construction is projected to increase about as fast as the industry average. Growth is expected in highway, bridge, and street construction, as well as in repairs to prevent further deterioration of the Nation's highways and bridges. Poor highway conditions also will result in increased demand for highway maintenance and repair.

Employment in special trades contracting, the largest segment of the industry, should grow at about the same rate as the entire construction industry. Demand for special trades subcontractors in building and heavy construction is rising, and, at the same time, more workers will be needed to repair and remodel existing homes. Home improvement and repair construction is expected to continue to grow faster than new home construction. Remodeling should be the fastest growing sector of the housing industry because of a growing stock of old residential and nonresidential buildings. Many "starter" units will be remodeled to appeal to more affluent, space- and amenity- hungry buyers. Also, some of the trade-up market may result in remodeling and additions rather than the construction of new, larger homes. Remodeling tends to be more labor-intensive than new construction.

Employment growth will differ among various occupations in the construction industry. Employment of construction managers is expected to grow as a result of advances in building materials and construction methods, as well as a proliferation of laws dealing with building construction, worker safety, and environmental issues. Construction managers with a bachelor's degree in construction science with an emphasis on construction management, and who acquire work experience in construction management services firms, should have an especially favorable job outlook. Little change in the employment of administrative support occupations is expected due to increased office automation.

Although employment in construction trades is expected to grow about as fast as the industry average, the rate of growth will vary among the various trades. Employment of brickmasons, blockmasons, and stonemasons; electricians; glaziers; sheet metal workers; and heating, air conditioning, and refrigeration mechanics and installers should grow faster than the industry average because technological changes are not expected to offset employment demand as construction activity grows. Employment of carpenters; carpet, floor, and tile installers and finishers; and cement masons, concrete finishers, segmental pavers, and terrazzo workers is expected to grow more slowly than the construction industry as a whole because the demand for these workers is expected to be offset by a greater use of new materials and equipment. For example, increasing use of prefabricated components in residential construction is expected to reduce the demand for carpenters.

## Sources of Additional Information

Information about apprenticeships and training can be obtained from local construction firms and employer associations, the local office of the State employment service or apprenticeship agency, or the Bureau of Apprenticeship and Training, U.S. Department of Labor.

For additional information on jobs in the construction industry, contact:

➢ Associated Builders and Contractors, 1300 North 17th St., Rosslyn, VA 22209. Internet: **http://www.abc.org**
➢ Associated General Contractors of America, Inc., 1957 E St. NW., Washington, DC 20005. Internet: **http://www.agc.org**
➢ National Association of Home Builders, 15th and M Sts. NW., Washington, DC 20005. Internet: **http://www.nahb.org**

Additional information on occupations in construction may be found in the 2002-03 edition of the *Occupational Outlook Handbook:*

- Brickmasons, blockmasons, and stonemasons
- Carpenters
- Carpet, floor, and tile installers and finishers
- Cement masons, concrete finishers, segmental pavers, and terrazzo workers
- Construction and building inspectors
- Construction equipment operators
- Construction laborers
- Construction managers
- Drywall installers, ceiling tile installers, and tapers
- Electricians
- Elevator installers and repairers
- Glaziers
- Hazardous materials removal workers
- Heating, air conditioning, and refrigeration mechanics and installers
- Insulation workers
- Material moving occupations
- Painters and paperhangers
- Pipelayers, plumbers, pipefitters, and steamfitters
- Plasterers and stucco masons
- Roofers
- Sheet metal workers
- Structural and reinforcing iron and metal workers

# Mining and Quarrying

## SIGNIFICANT POINTS

● Technological innovations, downsizing, environmental regulations, and international competition will continue to reduce employment in mining and quarrying.

● Most production jobs require little or no formal education or training beyond high school.

● Working conditions can be dangerous.

● Earnings are higher than the average for all occupations.

## Nature of the Industry

Mining has played an important role in the development of the United States. In the past, the discovery of minerals such as gold and silver resulted in population shifts and economic growth. Extraction of minerals and coal continues to provide the foundation for local economies in some parts of the country. Products of this industry are used as inputs for consumer goods, processes, and services provided by all other industries, including agriculture, manufacturing, transportation, communication, and construction. Uses of mined materials include coal for energy, copper for wiring, gold for satellites and sophisticated electronic components, and a variety of other minerals as ingredients in medicines and household products.

Besides mining and quarrying coal and metallic and nonmetallic minerals, employers in this industry explore for minerals and develop new mines and quarries. *Metallic minerals* include ores, such as bauxite—from which aluminum is extracted—copper, gold, iron, lead, silver, and zinc. *Nonmetallic minerals* include stone, sand, gravel, clay, and other minerals such as lime and soda ash, used as chemicals and fertilizers. This industry also includes initial mineral processing and preparation activities, because processing plants usually operate together with mines or quarries as part of the extraction process. (A separate section in the *Career Guide* covers careers in oil and gas extraction.)

Mining is the process of digging into the earth to extract naturally occurring minerals. There are two kinds of mining, *surface mining* and *underground mining*. Surface mining, also called open-pit mining or strip mining, is undertaken if the mineral is near the earth's surface. This method usually is more cost-effective and requires fewer workers to produce the same quantity of ore than does underground mining. In surface mining, after blasting with explosives, workers use huge earthmoving equipment, such as power shovels or draglines, to scoop off the layers of soil and rock covering the mineral bed. Once the mineral is exposed, smaller shovels are used to lift it from the ground and load it into trucks. The mineral also can be broken up using explosives, if necessary. In quarrying operations, workers use machines to extract stone used primarily as a building material. Stone, such as marble, granite, limestone and sandstone, is quarried by splitting blocks of rock from a massive rock surface.

Underground mining is used when the mineral deposit lies deep below the surface of the earth. When developing an underground mine, miners first must dig two or more openings, or tunnels, deep into the earth near the place where they believe coal or minerals are located. Depending on where the vein of ore is in relation to the surface, tunnels may be vertical, horizontal, or sloping. One opening allows the miners to move in and out of the mine

with their tools and also serves as a path for transporting the mined rock by small railroad cars or by conveyor belts to the surface. The other opening is used for ventilation.

Entries are constructed so that miners can get themselves and their equipment to the ore and carry it out, while allowing fresh air to enter the mine. Once dug to the proper depth, a mine's tunnels interconnect with a network of passageways going in many directions. Long steel bolts and pillars of unmined ore support the roof of the tunnel. Using the room-and-pillar method, miners remove half of the ore as they work the ore seams from the tunnel entrance to the edge of the mine property, leaving columns of ore to support the ceiling. This process is then reversed, and the remainder of the ore is extracted, as the miners work their way back out. In the case of longwall mining of coal, self-advancing roof supports, made of hydraulic jacks and metal plates, are moved ahead, allowing the ceiling in the mined area to cave in as the miners work back towards the tunnel entrance.

Once all the minerals or coal have been extracted, the mine and its surrounding environment must be restored to the condition that existed before mining began. In surface mining, the layers of topsoil, or overburden, that were removed in order to reach the mineral are used to fill in the mine and reshape the land. This ensures that native plants and animals will be able to thrive once again. Underground mining does not require as extensive a reclamation process; however, mine operators and environmental engineers still must ensure that ground water remains uncontaminated and that abandoned mines will not collapse. The reclamation process is highly regulated by Federal, State, and local laws, and reclamation plans often must be approved before mining permits will be granted.

During the 1990s, production of both minerals and coal increased. Given the more volatile price of metal, its production fluctuated more than that of nonmetallics. However, employment in both sectors declined significantly, as new technology and more sophisticated mining techniques increased productivity, allowing growth in output while employing fewer workers. Most mining machines and control rooms are now automatic or computer-controlled, requiring fewer, if any, human operators. Many mines also operate with other sophisticated technology such as lasers and robotics, which further decrease the number of workers needed to mine materials.

## Working Conditions

The average worker in the coal mining industry worked 44.9 hours a week in 2000; workers in metal mining, and nonmetallic minerals, except fuels, worked an average of 43.7 and 46.2

hours a week, respectively. Work environments vary by occupation. Scientists and technicians work in office buildings and laboratories, while miners and mining engineers spend much of their time in the mine. Geologists who specialize in the exploration of natural resources may have to travel for extended periods to remote locations, in all types of climates, in order to locate mineral or coal deposits.

Working conditions in mines and quarries can be unusual and sometimes dangerous. Underground mines are damp and dark, and some can be very hot. At times, several inches of water may cover tunnel floors. Although underground mines have electric lights, only the lights on miners' caps illuminate many areas. Workers in mines with very low roofs may have to work on their hands and knees, backs, or stomachs, in confined spaces. In underground mining operations, dangers include the possibility of an explosion or cave-in, electric shock, or exposure to harmful gases.

Workers in surface mines and quarries are subject to rugged outdoor work in all kinds of weather and climates. Some surface mines shut down in the winter, because snow and ice covering the mine site makes work too difficult. Physical strength and stamina are necessary, because the work involves lifting, stooping, and climbing. Surface mining, however, usually is less hazardous than underground mining.

In 1999, the rate of work-related injury and illness was 5.0 per 100 full-time workers in metal mining, 4.3 in nonmetallic minerals, and 7.4 in coal mining, compared with 6.3 for the entire private sector. Although mine health and safety conditions have improved dramatically over the years, dust generated by drilling in mines still places miners at risk of developing either of two serious lung diseases: Pneumoconiosis, also called "black lung disease," from coal dust, or silicosis from rock dust. The Federal Coal Mine Health and Safety Act of 1969 regulates dust concentrations in coal mines, and respirable dust levels are closely monitored. Dust concentrations in mines have declined as a result. Underground miners are now required to have their lungs x-rayed when starting a job, with a mandatory follow-up x-ray 3 years later, in order to monitor any development of respiratory illness. Additional x-rays are given every 5 years, on a voluntary basis. Workers who develop black lung disease or silicosis may be eligible for Federal aid.

## Employment

There were approximately 231,000 wage and salary jobs in the mining and quarrying industry in 2000; around 77,000 in coal mining; 41,000 in metal mining; and 114,000 in nonmetallic mineral mining. According to the Energy Information Administration, there were around 1,450 coal mining operations in 28 States in 2000. About three-quarters of all coal mines are located in three States—Kentucky, Pennsylvania, and West Virginia. Metal mining is more prevalent in the West and Southwest, particularly in Arizona, Colorado, Nevada, New Mexico, and Utah. Nonmetallic mineral mining is the most widespread, as quarrying of nonmetallic minerals, such as stone, clay, sand, and gravel, is done in nearly every State. In many rural areas, mining and quarrying operations are the main employer. About 50 percent of mining and quarrying establishments employ fewer than 10 workers (see chart).

## Occupations in the Industry

The mining and quarrying industry requires many kinds of workers. In 2000, 2 out of 3 workers were in *construction and extraction, production,* or *transportation and material-moving* occupations (table 1).

*Mining occupations.* The majority of jobs in the mining and quarrying industry are in construction and extraction occupations. Though most of these jobs can be entered directly from high school, or after acquiring some experience and on-the-job training in an entry-level position, the increasing sophistication of equipment and machinery used in mining means a higher level of technical skill is now required for many positions.

Underground mining primarily includes three methods—conventional, continuous, and longwall mining. Conventional mining, which is being phased out, is the oldest method, requiring the most workers and procedures. In this method, a strip or "kerf" is cut underneath the ore seam to control the direction in which the ore falls after it has been blasted. *Cutting-machine operators* use a huge electric chain saw with a cutter from 6 to 15 feet long to cut the kerf. Next, *drilling-machine operators* drill holes in the ore where the *shot firers* place explosives. This potentially dangerous work requires workers to follow safety procedures, such as making sure everyone is clear of the area before the explosives are detonated. After the blast, *loading-machine operators* scoop up the material and dump it into small rubber-tired cars run by *shuttle-car operators*, who bring the coal or ore to a central location for transportation to the surface.

The continuous mining method eliminates the drilling and blasting operations of conventional mining by using a machine called a continuous miner. Traditionally, a *continuous-mining machine operator* sits or lies in a machine's cab and operates levers that cut or rip out ore and load it directly onto a conveyor or shuttle car. However, the use of remote-controlled continuous mining machines—which have increased safety considerably—now allows an operator to control the machine from a distance.

In longwall mining, which is similar to continuous mining, *longwall-machine operators* run large machines with rotating drums that automatically shear and load ore on a conveyor. At the same time, hydraulic jacks reinforce the roof of the tunnel. As ore is cut, the jacks are hydraulically winched forward, supporting the roof as they move along.

Many other workers are needed to operate safe and efficient underground mines. Before miners are allowed underground, a *mine safety inspector* checks the work area for such hazards as

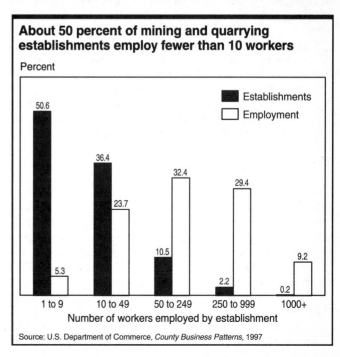

**About 50 percent of mining and quarrying establishments employ fewer than 10 workers**

Percent

- Establishments
- Employment

| Number of workers employed by establishment | Establishments | Employment |
|---|---|---|
| 1 to 9 | 50.6 | 5.3 |
| 10 to 49 | 36.4 | 23.7 |
| 50 to 249 | 10.5 | 32.4 |
| 250 to 999 | 2.2 | 29.4 |
| 1000+ | 0.2 | 9.2 |

Source: U.S. Department of Commerce, *County Business Patterns*, 1997

loose roofs, dangerous gases, and inadequate ventilation. If safety standards are not met, the inspector prohibits the mine from producing until conditions are made safe. *Rock-dust machine operators* spray the mine walls and floor to hold down dust which can interfere with breathing.

*Roof bolters* operate the machines that automatically install roof support bolts to prevent roof cave-ins, the biggest cause of mining injuries. *Brattice builders* construct doors, walls, and partitions in tunnel passageways to force air into the work areas. *Shift bosses*, or *blue-collar worker supervisors*, oversee all operations at the worksite.

In surface mining, most miners operate huge machines that either remove the earth above the ore deposit, or dig and load the ore onto trucks. The number of workers required to operate a surface mine depends on the amount of overburden, or earth, above the ore seam. In many surface mines, the overburden is first drilled and blasted. *Overburden stripping operators* or *dragline operators* then scoop the earth away to expose the coal or metal ore. Some draglines are among the largest land machines on earth.

Next, *loading-machine operators* rip the exposed ore from the seam and dump it into trucks to be driven to the preparation plant. *Tractor operators* use bulldozers to move earth and ore and to remove boulders or other obstructions. *Truckdrivers* haul ore to railroad sidings or to preparation plants and transport supplies to mines.

*Construction, maintenance,* and *repair occupations*. Other workers, who are not directly involved in the extraction process, work in and around mines and quarries. For example, skilled *mechanics* are needed to repair and maintain the wide variety of mining machinery, and skilled *electricians* are needed to check and install electrical wiring. Mechanical and electrical repair work has become increasingly complex, as machinery and other equipment have become computerized. *Carpenters* construct and maintain benches, bins, and stoppings (barricades to prevent air flow through a tunnel). These workers generally need specialized training to work under the unusual conditions found in mines. Mechanics, for example, may have to repair machines while on their knees, with only their headlamps to illuminate the working area.

*Quarrying occupations*. Workers at quarries have duties similar to miners. Using jackhammers and wedges, *rock splitters* remove pieces of stone from a rock mass. *Dredge operators* and *dipper tenders* operate power-driven dredges, or dipper sticks of dredges, to mine sand, gravel, and other materials from beneath the surface of lakes, rivers, and streams. Using power-driven cranes with dragline buckets, *dragline operators* excavate or move sand, gravel, and other materials.

*Processing-plant occupations*. Processing plants often are located next to mines or quarries. In these plants, rocks and other impurities are removed from the ore, which is then washed, crushed, sized, or blended to meet buyer specifications. Methods for physically separating the ore from surrounding material also include more complex processes, such as leaching—mixing the ore with chemical solutions or other liquids in order to separate materials. Most processing plants are highly mechanized and require only a few workers for the washing, separating, and crushing operations. *Processing-plant supervisors* oversee all operations. In plants that are not heavily mechanized, *washbox attendants* operate equipment that sizes and

**Table 1. Employment of wage and salary workers in mining and quarrying by occupation, 2000 and projected change, 2000-2010**

(Employment in thousands)

| Occupation | Employment, 2000 Number | Employment, 2000 Percent | Percent change, 2000-2010 |
|---|---|---|---|
| **All occupations** | 231 | 100.0 | -14.0 |
| **Management, business, and financial occupations** | 15 | 6.3 | -13.0 |
| General and operations managers | 6 | 2.4 | -13.0 |
| **Professional and related occupations** | 9 | 3.7 | -12.0 |
| Mining and geological engineers, including mining safety engineers | 2 | 0.9 | -19.3 |
| Life, physical, and social science occupations | 2 | 0.9 | -9.7 |
| **Office and administrative support occupations** | 17 | 7.4 | -12.3 |
| Bookkeeping, accounting, and auditing clerks | 3 | 1.1 | -19.3 |
| Weighers, measurers, checkers, and samplers, recordkeeping | 2 | 1.1 | -1.3 |
| Office clerks, general | 3 | 1.3 | -5.7 |
| **Construction and extraction occupations** | 75 | 32.2 | -16.9 |
| First-line supervisors/managers of construction trades and extraction workers | 10 | 4.3 | -15.5 |
| Operating engineers and other construction equipment operators | 18 | 7.8 | -19.3 |
| Electricians | 3 | 1.3 | -9.9 |
| Earth drillers, except oil and gas | 4 | 1.7 | -11.4 |
| Helpers—Extraction workers | 7 | 3.2 | -23.1 |
| Continuous mining machine operators | 9 | 3.8 | -16.5 |
| Miscellaneous mining machine operators | 11 | 4.7 | -17.6 |
| All other extraction workers | 8 | 3.3 | -17.7 |
| **Installation, maintenance, and repair occupations** | 30 | 13.1 | -16.2 |
| First-line supervisors/managers of mechanics, installers, and repairers | 2 | 1.1 | -14.8 |
| Mobile heavy equipment mechanics, except engines | 8 | 3.3 | -15.5 |
| Industrial machinery mechanics | 4 | 1.9 | -10.1 |
| Maintenance and repair workers, general | 8 | 3.3 | -23.5 |
| Maintenance workers, machinery | 4 | 1.7 | -15.4 |
| **Production occupations** | 28 | 12.1 | -11.2 |
| First-line supervisors/managers of production and operating workers | 3 | 1.2 | -18.4 |
| Welders, cutters, solderers, and brazers | 3 | 1.3 | -10.3 |
| Separating, filtering, clarifying, precipitating, and still machine setters, operators, and tenders | 3 | 1.4 | -4.8 |
| Crushing, grinding, and polishing machine setters, operators, and tenders | 6 | 2.6 | -4.5 |
| Furnace, kiln, oven, drier, and kettle operators and tenders | 2 | 0.9 | -8.1 |
| Helpers—Production workers | 2 | 0.8 | -20.0 |
| All other production workers | 2 | 1.0 | -20.2 |
| **Transportation and material moving occupations** | 55 | 23.6 | -11.2 |
| Supervisors, transportation and material moving workers | 2 | 0.8 | -8.6 |
| Truck drivers, heavy and tractor-trailer | 15 | 6.6 | -4.2 |
| Conveyor operators and tenders | 3 | 1.5 | -10.7 |
| Excavating and loading machine and dragline operators | 13 | 5.5 | -10.5 |
| Industrial truck and tractor operators | 5 | 2.1 | -18.0 |
| Laborers and freight, stock, and material movers, hand | 4 | 1.6 | -16.6 |
| All other material moving workers | 8 | 3.5 | -20.3 |

NOTE: May not add to totals due to omission of occupations with small employment.

28

separates impurities from ore, and *shake tenders* monitor machinery that further cleans and sizes ore with a vibrating screen. Most jobs in the processing plant are repetitive and, as a result of highly computerized mechanization, are becoming more automated.

*Management, business, and financial* and *professional and related occupations.* Management workers include *top executives*, who are responsible for making policy decisions. Staff specialists (such as *accountants, attorneys*, and *market researchers*) provide information and advice for policymakers.

Professional and related workers in mining and quarrying include engineering, scientific, and technical personnel. *Environmental scientists and geoscientists* search for locations likely to yield coal or mineral ores in sufficient quantity to justify extraction costs. Using sophisticated technologies and equipment, such as the Global Positioning System (GPS)—a satellite system that locates points on the earth using radio signals transmitted by satellites—*surveyors* help map areas for mining. *Mining and geological engineers* examine seams for depth and purity, determine the type of mine to build, and supervise the construction, maintenance, and operation of mines. *Mechanical engineers* oversee the installation of equipment, such as heat and water systems; *electrical engineers* oversee the installation and maintenance of electrical equipment; *civil engineers* oversee the building and construction of mine sites, plants, roads, and other infrastructure; *safety engineers* direct health and safety programs; *chemical engineers* develop the chemical processes for transforming mined products into consumer goods, such as medications and fertilizers; and *materials engineers* determine the usefulness of mined ore and also develop processes for transforming the minerals into products.

*Environmental engineers* play an increasingly important role in mining and quarrying, given environmental concerns and stringent Federal, State, and local regulations imposed on all operations. Restrictions imposed by environmental regulations make obtaining permits for new mine development projects increasingly difficult. Mine owners and operators face substantial penalties should they fail to abide by current regulations. In addition, both Federal regulations, such as the Surface Mining Control and Reclamation Act (SMCRA), and State laws require that land reclamation be part of the mining process. Reclamation plans usually must be approved by both government officials and local interest groups. When a mining operation is closed, the land must be restored to its premine condition, which can include anything from leveling soil and removing waste to replanting vegetation.

Exploration, mine design, impact assessment, and restoration efforts can depend on computer analysis. In addition, rapid technological advancements, particularly in processing-plant operations, are the result of increased computerization. This has led to a growing reliance on computer professionals, such as *systems analysts, computer software engineers*, and *computer scientists.*

## Training and Advancement
Workers in mining and quarrying production occupations must be at least 18 years old, in good physical condition, and able to work in confined spaces. A high school diploma is not necessarily required. Most workers start as helpers to experienced workers and learn skills on the job; however, formal training is becoming more important, as more technologically advanced machinery and mining methods are used. Some employers prefer to hire recent graduates of high school vocational programs in mining or graduates of junior college or technical school programs in mine technology. Such programs usually are found only at schools in mining areas.

Mining companies must offer formal training in either classrooms or training mines for a few weeks before new miners actually begin work. The Federal Mine Safety and Health Act of 1977 mandates that each U.S. mine have an approved worker training program in health and safety issues. Each plan must include at least 40 hours of basic safety training for new miners with no experience in underground mines, and 24 hours for new miners in surface mines. In addition to new miner training, each miner must receive at least 8 hours of refresher safety training a year, and miners assigned to new jobs must receive safety training relating to their new task. The U.S. Mine Safety and Health Administration also conducts classes on health, safety, and mining methods, and some mining machinery manufacturers offer courses in machine operation and maintenance as well.

As production workers gain more experience, they can advance to higher paying jobs requiring greater skill. A mining machine operator's helper, for example, may become an operator. When vacancies occur, announcements are posted, and all qualified workers can bid for the job. Positions are filled on the basis of seniority and ability. Miners with significant experience or special training also can become mine safety inspectors. According to the U.S. Mine Safety and Health Administration, an inspector needs at least 5 years' experience as a miner, or a degree in mining engineering.

For professional and managerial positions in mining and quarrying, a master's degree in engineering, one of the physical sciences, or business administration, is preferred. A number of colleges and universities have mining schools or departments and programs in mining or minerals. Environmental positions require regulatory knowledge and a strong natural science background, or a background in a technical field, such as environmental engineering or hydrology. To date, most environmental professionals have been drawn from the ranks of engineers and scientists who have had experience in the mining and quarrying industry.

Universities and mining schools have introduced more environmental coursework into their programs, and mining and quarrying firms are hiring professionals from existing environment-related disciplines and training them to meet their companies' needs. Additionally, specialized mine technology programs are offered by a few colleges. Enrollment in these programs can lead to a certificate in mine technology after 1 year, an associate degree after 2 years, or a bachelor's degree after 4 years. Courses cover areas such as mine ventilation, roof bolting, and machinery repairs.

## Earnings
Average earnings in mining and quarrying were significantly higher than the average for all industries. In 2000, production workers throughout private industry averaged $13.74 an hour, compared with $19.40 an hour in coal mining, $19.04 an hour in metal mining, and $15.62 an hour in nonmetallic minerals mining (table 2). Workers in underground mines spend time traveling from the mine entrance to their working areas, so their paid workday is slightly longer than that of surface mine workers, 8 hours versus 7¼ hour shifts. Workers in underground mines also tend to earn more per hour than do miners on the surface. Earnings in selected occupations in specified mining and quarrying industries appear in table 3.

**Table 2. Average earnings of nonsupervisory workers in mining and quarrying, 2000**

| Industry segment | Weekly | Hourly |
|---|---|---|
| **Total, private industry** | $474.00 | $13.74 |
| | | |
| **Mining** | 770.00 | 17.14 |
| Coal mining | 871.00 | 19.40 |
| Metal mining | 832.00 | 19.04 |
| Nonmetallic mineral mining | 722.00 | 15.62 |

Around 22.5 percent of mineworkers are union members or are covered by union contracts, compared with about 13.5 percent of workers throughout private industry. About 24 percent of workers in coal and 33 percent in metal mining were union members in 2000, compared with about 16 percent of workers in nonmetallic mineral mining. Union coal miners are primarily represented by the UMWA. The United Steelworkers of America, the International Union of Operating Engineers, and other unions also represent miners.

Workers covered by UMWA contracts receive 11 paid holidays, 12 days of paid vacation each year, 4 additional floating holidays, and 5 days of sick leave; however, coal miners generally must take their vacations during 1 of 3 regular vacation periods, to assure a continuous supply of coal. As length of service increases, UMWA miners get up to 13 extra vacation days after 18 years of continuous employment. Union workers also receive benefits from a welfare and retirement fund.

## Outlook

Wage and salary employment in mining and quarrying is expected to decline by 14 percent through the year 2010, compared with 16 percent growth projected for the entire economy. This continuing long-term decline is due to increased productivity, resulting from technological advances in mining operations, downsizing, stringent environmental regulations, and international competition.

Increasing costs of environmental compliance, investments in new and expensive technology, and low commodity prices have forced mining companies to merge with one another in order to contain costs and expand their business. As a result of these mergers, mines are becoming larger, while employing fewer mining workers.

The ability of U.S mines to remain internationally competitive also will influence the long-term outlook. Currently, U.S. mines are among the most technologically advanced in the world; however, mining operations in other countries have lower labor costs and are subject to fewer government regulations. In addition, pending reform of the Mining Law of 1872, which involves issues such as access to public lands and the payment of royalties, is of particular concern to the mining industry. Changes in policies could have significant long-term implications; and uncertainty over restrictions, regulations, and the future of this law could serve to focus more exploration and investment opportunities elsewhere.

The Internet likely will have an impact on the mining and quarrying industry as well. Mining and quarrying companies and their suppliers are highly localized operations. Business-to-business ("B2B") electronic commerce ("e-commerce") will allow companies to gain access to a larger market for their products, while seeking out the lowest cost suppliers for their needs. B2B e-commerce will likely make the mining and quarrying industry more efficient, while reducing costs. However, companies also would face increased competition from new companies attempting to enter their market. Declining employment will be led by a decline in the coal mining sector. The products of the coal mining industry are used to produce electricity and steel products. Although production of coal is expected to increase, employment should continue to decline, as more efficient and automated production operations require less labor. Advances in longwall and surface mining, which are less labor intensive, have increased productivity, as have improvements in transportation and processing. Additionally, innovations such as roof bolting, self-advancing roof supports, and continuous mining machinery have led to safer, more efficient operations.

The long-term outlook for coal also depends on how electric utility companies—the major consumers of coal—respond to provisions of the Clean Air Act Amendments of 1990, which attempt to limit the emission of sulfur dioxide and other harmful pollutants. Phase I of the Amendments, which took effect in 1995, requires reductions in sulfur emissions from coal combustion. Phase II took effect in 2000, and not only imposes stricter reductions in emissions, but targets the smaller coal-burning plants, not just the largest ones as in Phase I. Compliance involves the installation of costly cleaning and monitoring equipment or increased use of low-sulfur coal. The largest industrial

**Table 3. Median hourly earnings of the largest occupations in metal mining, coal mining, and nonmetallic minerals, except fuels, 2000**

| Occupation | Metal mining | Coal mining | Nonmetallic minerals, except fuels | All industries |
|---|---|---|---|---|
| Mining and geological engineers, including mining safety engineers | $ 27.40 | $ 29.23 | $ 28.08 | $ 29.24 |
| First-line supervisors/managers of construction trades and extraction workers | 26.03 | 25.83 | 20.59 | 21.53 |
| Operating engineers and other construction equipment operators | 18.97 | 17.04 | 13.44 | 15.99 |
| Explosives workers, ordnance handling experts, and blasters | 18.95 | 16.08 | 14.02 | 15.84 |
| Maintenance workers, machinery | 18.47 | 17.37 | 12.31 | 14.89 |
| Electricians | 18.40 | 20.14 | 17.35 | 19.29 |
| Industrial machinery mechanics | 18.39 | 21.35 | 21.93 | 17.30 |
| Continuous mining machine operators | 18.32 | 16.16 | 13.62 | 15.64 |
| Crushing, grinding, and polishing machine setters, operators, and tenders | 18.02 | 18.64 | 12.83 | 11.99 |
| Earth drillers, except oil and gas | 17.34 | 15.67 | 13.75 | 14.68 |
| Excavating and loading machine and dragline operators | 16.05 | 16.05 | 13.24 | 14.94 |
| Laborers and freight, stock, and material movers, hand | 16.04 | 14.70 | 11.28 | 9.04 |

nations also have been pressuring each other to decrease emissions of harmful gases into the atmosphere. As energy plants seek cleaner burning fuel, many new powerplants are being built to run on natural gas. If the demand for coal declines as a result of stricter environmental regulations, employment in mines will decline further, as mine operators are forced to decrease production.

Despite the trend towards cleaner burning fuel, the United States still is highly dependent on coal as a source of energy. Coal accounts for half of the electricity production in this country because it is the cheapest and most abundant fossil fuel. The rising demand for cleaner burning fuel has resulted in regional shifts in coal production and markets. Because of this, lower-sulfur western coal now accounts for an increasing share of output. This trend is resulting in a gradual regional shift in employment from the eastern States to the West. Improvements in clean coal technologies also may help the industry cope with increasingly restrictive regulations through projects such as the Integrated Gasification Combined Cycle (IGCC). This technology combines traditional coal gasification with gas-turbine and steam power to generate electricity more efficiently and reduce carbon and sulfur dioxide emissions.

As in coal mining, continuing productivity increases are expected to cause employment in the metal mining industry to decline through 2010. Because metals are used primarily as raw materials by other industries, such as steel, chemical and drug manufacturing, aerospace, automobile, and telecommunications, the strength of the metal mining industry is greatly affected by the strength of the industries that consume its products. The strength of these industries usually reflects the state of the U.S. and global economies. Employment in the metal mining industry declined during the early 1990s when consumer demand was low, and experienced growth in the late 1990s, when economic growth and consumer demand were high. Thus, the strength of the economy over the next decade will influence employment in the metal mining industry.

Production of certain metals also is affected by the global market prices for those particular metals. For example, despite demand for gold in electronic and telecommunication components, gold prices have fallen in recent years. Gold mines with high costs of operations have been forced either to close or to decrease production, and therefore employ fewer workers.

Like the metal mining industry, the nonmetallic mineral industry is influenced by the strength of the industries that use nonmetals in the manufacture of their products. These nonmetallic minerals are used to make concrete and agricultural chemicals and also are used as materials in residential, nonresidential, and maintenance construction activity. This industry experienced slight employment growth over the past decade, largely attributed to construction. The demand for crushed stone and gravel should remain strong in the next few years because Congress recently increased spending for the building and maintenance of roads and highways. However, employment is sensitive to cyclical swings in the economy. Also, as in the other sectors of the mining industry, technological changes will continue to increase productivity, limiting the need for workers. Despite current levels of demand for minerals used in construction, overall employment in nonmetallic mining is expected to decline through 2010.

## Sources of Additional Information

For additional information about careers and training in the mining and quarrying industry, write to:

➢ American Geological Institute, 4220 King St., Alexandria, VA 22302. Internet: **http://www.agiweb.org**

➢ Mine Safety and Health Administration, 4015 Wilson Blvd., Arlington, VA 22203. Internet: **http://www.msha.gov**

➢ National Mining Association, 1130 17th St. NW., Washington, DC 20036. Internet: **http://www.nma.org**

➢ Society for Mining, Metallurgy, and Exploration, Inc., 8307 Shaffer Parkway, Littleton, CO 80127. Internet: **http://www.smenet.org**

➢ United Mine Workers of America, 8315 Lee Highway, Fairfax, VA 22031. Internet: **http://www.umwa.org**

Information on the following occupations in mining and quarrying may be found in the 2002-03 *Occupational Outlook Handbook:*

● Chemical engineers

● Civil engineers

● Electrical and electronics engineers, except computer

● Environmental engineers

● Environmental scientists and geoscientists

● Industrial machinery installation, repair, and maintenance workers

● Material-moving occupations

● Materials engineers

● Mechanical engineers

● Mining and geological engineers, including mine safety engineers

● Surveyors, cartographers, photogrammetrists, and surveying technicians

● Systems analysts, computer scientists, and database administrators

● Truck drivers and driver/sales workers

# Oil and Gas Extraction

(SIC 13)

## SIGNIFICANT POINTS

- Most establishments employ fewer than 10 workers.

- Over 75 percent of the industry's workforce is concentrated in California, Louisiana, Oklahoma, and Texas.

- Although technological innovations have expanded exploration and development worldwide, employment is expected to decline; however, workers with experience in oilfield operations are in demand.

- Earnings are relatively high.

## Nature of the Industry

Petroleum, commonly referred to as oil, is a natural fuel formed from the decay of plants and animals buried beneath the ground, under tremendous heat and pressure, for millions of years. Formed by a similar process, natural gas often is found in separate deposits and is sometimes mixed with oil. Because oil and gas are difficult to locate, exploration and drilling are key activities in the oil and gas extraction industry. Oil and natural gas furnish about three-fifths of our energy needs, fueling our homes, workplaces, factories, and transportation systems. In addition, they constitute the raw materials for plastics, chemicals, medicines, fertilizers, and synthetic fibers.

Using a variety of methods, on land and at sea, small crews of specialized workers search for geologic formations that are likely to contain oil and gas. Sophisticated equipment and advances in computer technology have increased the productivity of exploration. Maps of potential deposits now are made using remote sensing satellites. Seismic prospecting—a technique based on measuring the time it takes sound waves to travel through underground formations and return to the surface—has revolutionized oil and gas exploration. Computers and advanced software analyze seismic data to provide three-dimensional models of subsurface rock formations. This technique lowers the risk involved in exploring by allowing scientists to locate and identify structural oil and gas reservoirs and the best locations to drill. Four-D, or "time-lapsed," seismic technology tracks the movement of fluids over time and enhances production performance even further. Another method of searching for oil and gas is based on collecting and analyzing core samples of rock, clay, and sand in the earth's layers.

After scientific studies indicate the possible presence of oil, an oil company selects a wellsite and installs a derrick—a towerlike steel structure—to support the drilling equipment. A hole is drilled deep in the earth until oil or gas is found, or the company abandons the effort. Similar techniques are employed in offshore drilling, except that the drilling equipment is part of a steel platform that either sits on the ocean floor, or floats on the surface and is anchored to the ocean floor. Although some large oil companies do their own drilling, most land and offshore drilling is done by contractors.

In rotary drilling, a rotating bit attached to a length of hollow drill pipe bores a hole in the ground by chipping and cutting rock. As the bit cuts deeper, more pipe is added. A stream of

drilling "mud"—a mixture of clay, chemicals, and water—is continuously pumped through the drill pipe and through holes in the drill bit. Its purpose is to cool the drill bit, plaster the walls of the hole to prevent cave-ins, carry crushed rock to the surface, and prevent "blowouts" by equalizing pressure inside the hole. When a drill bit wears out, all drill pipe must be removed from the hole a section at a time, the bit replaced, and the pipe returned to the hole. New materials and better designs have advanced drill bit technology, permitting faster, more cost-effective drilling for longer periods.

Advancements in directional or horizontal drilling techniques, which allow increased access to potential reserves, have had a significant impact on drilling capabilities. Drilling begins vertically, but the drill bit can be turned so that drilling can continue at an angle of up to 90 degrees. This technique extends the drill's reach, enabling it to reach separate pockets of oil or gas. Because constructing new platforms is costly, this technique commonly is employed by offshore drilling operations.

When oil or gas is found, the drill pipe and bit are pulled from the well, and metal pipe (casing) is lowered into the hole and cemented in place. The casing's upper end is fastened to a system of pipes and valves called a wellhead, or "Christmas Tree," through which natural pressure forces the oil or gas into separation and storage tanks. If natural pressure is not great enough to force the oil to the surface, pumps may be used. In some cases, water, steam, or gas may be injected into the oil-producing formation to improve recovery.

Crude oil is transported to refineries by pipeline, ship, barge, truck, or railroad. Natural gas usually is transported to processing plants by pipeline. While oil refineries may be many thousands of miles away from the producing fields, gas processing plants usually are near the fields, so that impurities—water, sulfur, and natural gas liquids—can be removed before the gas is piped to customers. The oil refining industry is considered a separate industry, and its activities are not covered here, even though many oil companies both extract and refine oil.

The oil and gas extraction industry has experienced both "booms" and "busts" over the years, illustrating the cyclical relationship between the price of oil and employment. Generally, the reaction of the labor market lags slightly behind the price fluctuations because oil companies must adjust their production levels accordingly. During the 1970s and early 1980s, the price of crude oil rose sharply, stimulating domestic exploration and

32

production (see chart). Between 1978 and 1982—the year in which industry employment peaked—this industry grew 65 percent, creating 279,000 jobs, while employment in the economy as a whole remained flat during this period. Employment rose one-and-a-half times as fast in the oil and gas field services segment as in the crude petroleum, natural gas, and natural gas liquids segment, reflecting the fact that most exploration and drilling is done on a contract basis. Starting in 1982, oil-producing countries around the world began yielding much larger volumes of crude oil, driving prices down; this culminated in the collapse of oil prices in the mid-1980s. During this time, the industry experienced a sharp decline in domestic exploration and production and an extended period of downsizing and restructuring, losing more than 415,000 jobs from 1982 to 1999. As was the case during the boom period, employment in oil and gas field services changed more than did employment in crude petroleum and natural gas production.

## Working Conditions

Working conditions in this industry vary significantly by occupation. Roustabout and other construction and extraction occupations may involve rugged outdoor work in remote areas in all kinds of weather. For these jobs, physical strength and stamina are necessary. This work involves standing for long periods, lifting moderately heavy objects, and climbing and stooping to work with tools that often are oily and dirty. Executives generally work in office settings, as do most administrators and clerical workers. Geologists, engineers, and managers may split their time between the office and the jobsites, particularly while involved in exploration work.

Only 1 employee in 20 works fewer than 35 hours a week, because opportunities for part-time work are rare. In fact, a higher percentage of workers work overtime in this industry than in all industries combined. The average nonsupervisory worker worked 44.9 hours per week in 2000, compared with 34.5 hours for all workers.

Oil and gas well drilling and servicing can be hazardous. However, in 1999, the rate of work-related injury and illness in the oil and gas extraction industry, as a whole, was 3.5 per 100

full-time workers, somewhat lower than the 6.3 for the entire private sector. The rate for workers in the oil and gas field services segment, 4.8 per 100 full-time workers, was nearly 3 times higher than that for workers in the crude petroleum and natural gas segment, which was only 1.7.

Drilling rigs operate continuously. On land, drilling crews usually work 6 days, 8 hours a day, and then have a few days off. In offshore operations, workers can work 14 days, 12 hours a day, and then have 14 days off. If the offshore rig is located far from the coast, drilling crew members live on ships anchored nearby or in facilities on the platform itself. Workers on offshore rigs are always evacuated in the event of a storm. Most workers in oil and gas well operations and maintenance or in natural gas processing work 8 hours a day, 5 days a week.

Many oilfield workers are away from home for weeks or months at a time. Exploration field personnel and drilling workers frequently move from place to place as work at a particular field is completed. In contrast, well operation and maintenance workers and natural gas processing workers usually remain in the same location for extended periods.

## Employment

The oil and gas extraction industry, with about 311,000 wage and salary jobs in 2000, is the largest industry in the mining division, accounting for more than one-half of employment. The workforce is divided between two segments: Crude petroleum, natural gas, and natural gas liquids, with about 129,000 jobs, and oil and gas field services, with about 182,000 jobs.

Although onshore oil and gas extraction establishments are found in 48 States, over 75 percent of the industry's workers in 2000 were located in just four States—California, Louisiana, Oklahoma, and Texas. While most workers are employed on land, many work at offshore sites. Although they are not included in employment figures for this industry, many Americans are employed by oil companies at locations in Africa, the North Sea, the Far East, the Middle East, South America, and countries of the former Soviet Union.

More than 7 out of 10 establishments employ fewer than 10 workers, although more than half of all workers in this industry work in establishments with 50 or more workers (see chart). As more large domestic oil- and gasfields are depleted, major oil companies are focusing their exploration and production activity in foreign countries. Consequently, smaller companies with less capital for foreign exploration and production are drilling an increasing share of domestic oil and gas. Technology also has significantly decreased the risk and cost for smaller producers.

Relatively few oil and gas extraction workers are in their teens or early 20s. Almost 64 percent of the workers in this industry are between 35 and 54 years of age.

## Occupations in the Industry

People with many different skills are needed to explore for oil and gas, drill new wells, maintain existing wells, and process natural gas. The largest group is construction and extraction workers, accounting for nearly 35 percent of industry employment. Managerial and professional workers account for about 24 percent of employment, while office and administrative support workers make up about 13 percent (table 1).

A *petroleum geologist* or a *geophysicist*, who is responsible for analyzing and interpreting the information gathered, usually heads exploration operations. Other geological specialists, such

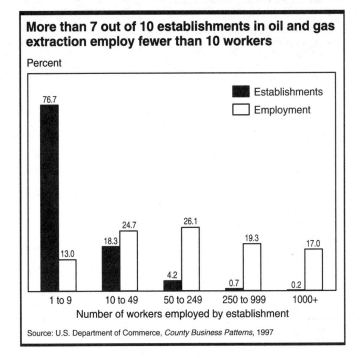

**More than 7 out of 10 establishments in oil and gas extraction employ fewer than 10 workers**

Percent

- Establishments
- Employment

| | 1 to 9 | 10 to 49 | 50 to 249 | 250 to 999 | 1000+ |
|---|---|---|---|---|---|
| Establishments | 76.7 | 18.3 | 4.2 | 0.7 | 0.2 |
| Employment | 13.0 | 24.7 | 26.1 | 19.3 | 17.0 |

Number of workers employed by establishment

Source: U.S. Department of Commerce, *County Business Patterns*, 1997

as *paleontologists*, who study fossil remains to locate oil; *mineralogists*, who study physical and chemical properties of mineral and rock samples; *stratigraphers*, who determine the rock layers most likely to contain oil and natural gas; and *photogeologists*, who examine and interpret aerial photographs of land surfaces, also may be involved in exploration activities. Additionally, exploration parties may include *surveyors* and *drafters*, who assist in surveying and mapping activities.

Some geologists and geophysicists work in district offices of oil companies or contract exploration firms, where they prepare and study geological maps and analyze seismic data. These scientists also may analyze samples from test drillings.

Other workers involved in exploration are *geophysical prospectors*. They lead crews consisting of *gravity* and *seismic prospecting observers*, who operate and maintain electronic seismic equipment; *scouts*, who investigate the exploration, drilling, and leasing activities of other companies to identify promising areas to explore and lease; and *lease buyers*, who make business arrangements to obtain the use of the land or mineral rights from their owners.

*Petroleum engineers* are responsible for planning and supervising the actual drilling operation, once a potential drillsite has been located. These engineers develop and implement the most efficient recovery method, in order to achieve maximum profitable recovery. They also plan and supervise well operation and maintenance. *Drilling superintendents* serve as supervisors of drilling crews, overseeing one or more drilling rigs.

Rotary drilling crews usually consist of four or five workers. *Rotary drillers* supervise the crew and operate machinery that controls drilling speed and pressure. *Rotary-rig engine operators* are in charge of engines that provide the power for drilling and hoisting. Second in charge, *derrick operators* work on small platforms high on rigs to help run pipe in and out of well holes and operate the pumps that circulate mud through the pipe. *Rotary-driller helpers*, also known as *roughnecks*, guide the lower ends of pipe to well openings and connect pipe joints and drill bits.

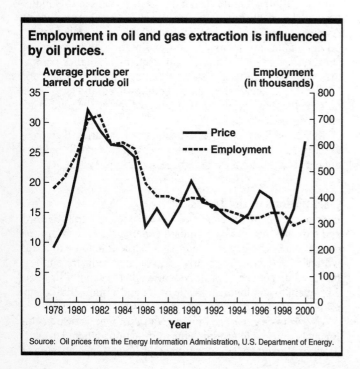

**Employment in oil and gas extraction is influenced by oil prices.**

Source: Oil prices from the Energy Information Administration, U.S. Department of Energy.

**Table 1. Employment of wage and salary workers in oil and gas extraction by occupation, 2000 and projected change, 2000-10**

(Employment in thousands)

| Occupation | Employment, 2000 Number | Employment, 2000 Percent | Percent change, 2000-2010 |
|---|---|---|---|
| **All occupations** | 311 | 100.0 | -7.3 |
| **Management, business, and financial occupations** | 39 | 12.6 | -11.5 |
| Financial managers | 3 | 0.9 | -11.5 |
| General and operations managers | 12 | 3.9 | -9.9 |
| Accountants and auditors | 7 | 2.1 | -14.6 |
| **Professional and related occupations** | 35 | 11.3 | -11.1 |
| Computer specialists | 4 | 1.2 | 4.2 |
| Petroleum engineers | 6 | 1.8 | -17.4 |
| Drafters, engineering, and mapping technicians | 3 | 1.0 | -7.9 |
| Geoscientists, except hydrologists and geographers | 6 | 1.8 | -11.4 |
| Geological and petroleum technicians | 5 | 1.5 | -8.0 |
| **Office and administrative support occupations** | 40 | 13.0 | -17.9 |
| Bookkeeping, accounting, and auditing clerks | 8 | 2.5 | -23.9 |
| Information and record clerks | 4 | 1.4 | -25.0 |
| Material recording, scheduling, dispatching, and distributing occupations | 4 | 1.2 | 0.7 |
| Office clerks, general | 6 | 1.9 | -6.1 |
| Executive secretaries and administrative assistants | 5 | 1.6 | -16.1 |
| Secretaries, except legal, medical, and executive | 8 | 2.6 | -26.6 |
| **Construction and extraction occupations** | 108 | 34.7 | -4.8 |
| First-line supervisors/managers of construction trades and extraction workers | 10 | 3.2 | 0.6 |
| Derrick operators, oil and gas | 12 | 3.7 | 3.1 |
| Rotary drill operators, oil and gas | 12 | 3.8 | -12.6 |
| Service unit operators, oil, gas, and mining | 9 | 3.0 | -4.3 |
| Helpers—Extraction workers | 11 | 3.4 | -12.3 |
| Roustabouts, oil and gas | 33 | 10.6 | -6.6 |
| **Installation, maintenance, and repair occupations** | 19 | 6.0 | 0.2 |
| Vehicle and mobile equipment mechanics, installers, and repairers | 3 | 0.9 | 3.4 |
| Industrial machinery mechanics | 3 | 1.0 | -4.4 |
| Maintenance and repair workers, general | 3 | 0.9 | -12.1 |
| Riggers | 5 | 1.5 | 10.8 |
| **Production occupations** | 28 | 8.9 | -1.3 |
| First-line supervisors/managers of production and operating workers | 3 | 0.9 | -15.8 |
| Welders, cutters, solderers, and brazers | 9 | 2.8 | 9.2 |
| Petroleum pump system operators, refinery operators, and gaugers | 8 | 2.5 | -3.6 |
| **Transportation and material moving occupations** | 38 | 12.2 | -3.6 |
| Truck drivers, heavy and tractor-trailer | 9 | 2.9 | 7.1 |
| Crane and tower operators | 3 | 0.9 | 0.4 |
| Laborers and freight, stock, and material movers, hand | 4 | 1.4 | -13.6 |
| Pump operators, except wellhead pumpers | 3 | 1.0 | -8.5 |
| Wellhead pumpers | 11 | 3.6 | -8.7 |

NOTE: May not add to totals due to omission of occupations with small employment

Though not necessarily part of the drilling crew, *roustabouts*, or general laborers, do general oil field maintenance and construction work, such as cleaning tanks and building roads.

*Pumpers* and their helpers operate and maintain motors, pumps, and other surface equipment that force oil from wells and regulate the flow, according to a schedule set up by petroleum engineers and production supervisors. In fields where oil flows under natural pressure and does not require pumping, *switchers* open and close valves to regulate the flow. *Gaugers* measure and record the flow, taking samples to check quality. *Treaters* test the oil for water and sediment and remove these impurities by opening a drain or using special equipment. In most fields, pumping, switching, gauging, and treating operations are automatic.

Other skilled oilfield workers include *oil well cementers*, who mix and pump cement into the space between the casing and well walls to prevent cave-ins; *acidizers*, who pump acid down the well and into the producing formation to increase oil flow; *perforator operators*, who use subsurface "guns" to pierce holes in the casing to make openings for oil to flow into the well bore; *sample-taker operators*, who take samples of soil and rock formations from wells to help geologists determine the presence of oil; and *well pullers*, who remove pipes, pumps, and other subsurface devices from wells for cleaning, repairing, and salvaging.

Many other skilled workers—such as welders, pipefitters, electricians, and machinists—also are employed in maintenance operations to install and repair pumps, gauges, pipes, and other equipment.

In addition to the types of workers required for onshore drilling, crews at offshore locations also need radio operators, cooks, ships' officers, sailors, and pilots. These workers make up the support personnel who work on or operate drilling platforms, crewboats, barges, and helicopters.

Most workers involved in gas processing are operators. *Gas treaters* tend automatically controlled treating units that remove water and other impurities from natural gas. *Gas-pumping-station operators* tend compressors that raise the pressure of gas for transmission in pipelines. Both types of workers can be assisted by *gas-compressor operators*.

Many employees in large natural gas processing plants—*welders*, *electricians*, *instrument repairers*, and *laborers*, for example—perform maintenance activities. In contrast, many small plants are automated and are checked at periodic intervals by maintenance workers or operators, or monitored by instruments that alert operators if trouble develops. In nonautomated plants, workers usually combine the skills of both operators and maintenance workers.

## Training and Advancement

Workers can enter the oil and gas extraction industry with a variety of educational backgrounds. The most common entry-level field jobs are as roustabouts or roughnecks, jobs that usually require little or no previous training or experience. Applicants for these routine laborer jobs must be physically fit and able to pass a physical examination. Companies also may administer aptitude tests and screen prospective employees for drug use. Basic skills usually can be learned over a period of days through on-the-job training. However, previous work experience or formal training in petroleum technology that provides knowledge of oil field operations and familiarity with computers and other automated equipment can be beneficial. In fact, given the increasing complexity of operations and the sophisticated nature of technology used today, employers now demand a higher level of skill and adaptability, including the ability to work with computers and other sophisticated equipment.

Other entry-level positions, such as engineering technician, usually require at least a 2-year associate degree in engineering technology. Professional jobs, such as geologist, geophysicist, or petroleum engineer, require at least a bachelor's degree, but many companies prefer to hire candidates with a master's degree, and may require Ph.D. for those involved in petroleum research. For well operation and maintenance jobs, companies generally prefer applicants who live nearby, have mechanical ability, and possess knowledge of oilfield processes. Because this work offers the advantage of a fixed locale, members of drilling crews or exploration parties who prefer not to travel may transfer to well operation and maintenance jobs. Training is acquired on the job.

Promotion opportunities for some jobs may be limited due to the general decline of the domestic petroleum industry. Advancement opportunities for oilfield workers remain best for those with skill and experience. For example, roustabouts may move up to become switchers, gaugers, and pumpers. More experienced roughnecks may advance to derrick operator and, after several years, to driller. Drillers may advance to tool pusher. There should continue to be some opportunities for entry-level field crew workers to acquire the skills that qualify them for higher level jobs within the industry. Due to the critical nature of the work, offshore crews, even at the entry level, generally are more experienced than land crews. Many companies will not employ someone who has no knowledge of oilfield operations to work on an offshore rig, so workers who have gained experience as part of a land crew might advance to offshore operations.

As workers gain knowledge and experience, U.S. or foreign companies operating in other countries also may hire them. Although this can be a lucrative and exciting experience, it may not be suitable for everyone, because it usually means leaving family and friends and adapting to different customs and living standards.

Experience gained in many oil and gas extraction jobs also has application in other industries. For example, roustabouts can move to construction jobs, while machinery operators and repairers can transfer to other industries with similar machinery. Geologists and engineers may become involved with environmental activities, especially those related to this industry.

## Earnings

Average earnings in the oil and gas extraction industry were significantly higher than the average for all industries (table 2). Due to the working conditions, employees at offshore operations generally earn higher wages than do workers at onshore oil fields. College-educated workers and technical school graduates in professional and technical occupations usually earn the most. Earnings in selected occupations in oil and gas extraction appear in table 3.

**Table 2. Average earnings of nonsupervisory workers in oil and gas extraction, 2000**

| Industry segment | Weekly | Hourly |
|---|---|---|
| Total, private industry | $474.00 | $13.74 |
| Total, oil and gas extraction | 749.00 | 16.76 |
| Crude petroleum and natural gas | 996.00 | 23.22 |
| Oil and gas field services | 620.00 | 13.61 |

Few industry workers belong to unions. In fact, only about 3 percent of workers were union members or covered by union contracts in 2000, compared with about 13.5 percent of all workers throughout private industry.

**Table 3. Median hourly earnings of the largest occupations in oil and gas extraction, 2000**

| Occupation | Oil and gas extraction | All industries |
|---|---|---|
| Geoscientists, except hydrologists and geographers | $ 43.59 | $ 27.04 |
| Petroleum engineers | 39.74 | 37.94 |
| First-line supervisors/managers of construction trades and extraction workers | 22.44 | 21.53 |
| Petroleum pump system operators, refinery operators, and gaugers | 20.51 | 21.72 |
| Geological and petroleum technicians | 19.64 | 17.55 |
| Wellhead pumpers | 16.05 | 16.35 |
| Rotary drill operators, oil and gas | 14.67 | 14.83 |
| Derrick operators, oil and gas | 12.36 | 12.41 |
| Service unit operators, oil, gas, and mining | 12.04 | 12.12 |
| Roustabouts, oil and gas | 9.79 | 9.83 |

## Outlook

Although worldwide demand for oil and gas is expected to grow, overall wage and salary employment in the oil and gas extraction industry is expected to decline 7 percent through the year 2010, while employment in all industries combined is projected to increase 16 percent. Employment in the crude petroleum, natural gas, and natural gas liquids segment of the industry is expected to decline about 23 percent, while employment in oil- and gasfield services—which includes all contract exploration and drilling services—is expected to increase by about 4 percent. Employment in oil- and gasfield services is subject to greater employment fluctuations than is the crude petroleum, natural gas, and natural gas liquids segment because many workers in the services segment are contractors hired by larger oil companies to drill and operate the wells.

The level of future crude petroleum and natural gas exploration and development and, therefore, employment opportunities, remain contingent upon a number of uncertainties—most importantly, the future price of oil and gas. Sharply higher prices mean that companies, seeking greater profits, can be expected to implement new technologies, expand domestic and international exploration and production, and increase employment. Substantially lower prices, on the other hand, could make exploration and continued production from many existing wells unprofitable, resulting in reduced employment opportunities. Stable and favorable prices are needed to allow companies enough revenue to expand exploration and production projects in order to meet increased global energy demand. Stable oil prices also would allow for more stable employment levels, instead of the boom and bust that has affected the industry for the past few decades. However, maintaining high and stable prices is difficult, especially during economic downturns.

Environmental concerns, accompanied by strict regulation and limited access to protected Federal lands, also continue to have a major impact on this industry. Environmental constraints, especially restrictions on drilling in environmentally sensitive areas, should continue to limit exploration and development, both onshore and offshore. However, changes in policy could expand exploration and drilling for oil and natural gas in currently protected areas, especially in Alaska.

In addition, environmental emissions standards already in place or planned for the future could significantly limit the amount of sulfur and carbon dioxide levels that can be emitted by powerplants. Many new powerplants run on natural gas, as opposed to coal, which emits higher levels of sulfur into the atmosphere. The natural gas exploration and production industry, and its employment, would benefit from the increasing demand for cleaner-burning fuels. However, a lack of proper infrastructure for transporting natural gas, which is found mainly in unpopulated areas or offshore, currently limits natural gas consumption.

While some new oil and gas deposits are being discovered in this country, companies increasingly are moving to more lucrative foreign locations. As companies expand into other areas around the globe, the need for employees in the United States is reduced. However, advances in technology have increased the proportion of exploratory wells that yield oil and gas, enhanced offshore exploration and drilling capabilities, and extended the production of existing wells. As a result, more exploration and development ventures are profitable and provide employment opportunities that otherwise would have been lost.

Despite an overall decline in employment in the oil and gas extraction industry, job opportunities in most occupations should be favorable. The need to replace workers who transfer to other industries, retire, or leave the workforce will be the major source of job openings. Employment opportunities will be best for those with previous experience and with strong technical skills. There is strong demand for qualified professionals and extraction workers who have significant experience in oil field operations and who can work with new technology. As employers develop and implement new technologies—such as 3-D and 4-D seismic exploration methods, horizontal and directional drilling techniques, and deepwater and subsea technologies—more workers capable of using sophisticated equipment will be needed.

## Sources of Additional Information

Information on training and career opportunities for petroleum engineers or geologists is available from:

➤ American Association of Petroleum Geologists, Communications Department, P.O. Box 979, Tulsa, OK 74101. Internet: **http://www.aapg.org**

➤ American Geological Institute, 4220 King St., Alexandria, VA 22302. Internet: **http://www.agiweb.org**

➤ Society of Petroleum Engineers, 222 Palisades Creek Dr., Richardson, TX 75080. Internet: **http://www.spe.org**

Information on some occupations in the oil and gas extraction industry may be found in the 2002-03 *Occupational Outlook Handbook*:

• Construction equipment operators

• Construction laborers

• Engineering and natural sciences managers

• Environmental engineers

• Environmental scientists and geoscientists

• Material-moving occupations

• Petroleum engineers

• Structural and reinforcing iron and metal workers

• Surveyors, cartographers, photogrammetrists, and surveying technicians

• Truck drivers and driver/sales workers

# Manufacturing

# Aerospace Manufacturing

## SIGNIFICANT POINTS

- Skilled production, professional specialty, and technician jobs comprise the bulk of employment.

- Earnings are substantially higher, on average, than in most other manufacturing industries.

### Nature of the Industry

The aerospace industry comprises companies producing aircraft, guided missiles, space vehicles, aircraft engines, propulsion units, and related parts. Aircraft repair and modification and aerospace research and development also are included. The combination of advanced production processes, a highly trained workforce, and significant research and development has allowed U.S. industry to remain dominant in the international market.

The aerospace industry can be divided into two large segments: firms producing aircraft, engines, and parts; and firms producing guided missiles and space vehicles, propulsion units, and parts. The larger employer of the two segments—firms producing aircraft, engines, and parts—can be further divided according to what they produce: civil aircraft or military aircraft.

Firms producing civil transport aircraft make up the largest segment of civil aircraft. Civil transport aircraft are produced for air transportation businesses such as airlines and cargo transportation companies. These craft range from small turbo-props to jumbo jets and are used to move people and goods all over the world. Another segment of civil aircraft is general aviation aircraft. These aircraft are produced for private individuals and corporations. General aviation aircraft range from the small two-seaters designed for leisure use to corporate jets designed for business transport. Civil helicopters, the smallest segment of civil aircraft, are commonly used by police departments, emergency medical services, and businesses such as oil and mining companies that need to transport people to remote worksites.

Military aircraft and helicopters are purchased by governments to meet national defense needs, such as delivering weapons to military targets and transporting troops and equipment around the globe. Some of these aircraft are specifically designed to deliver a powerful array of ordinance to military targets with tremendous maneuverability and low detectability. Research into the materials, electronics, and manufacturing methods used to produce military aircraft has resulted in a vast number of commercial applications. For example, technological innovations discovered in current research can be used to improve or modify an existing design. Aircraft engines used in civil and military aircraft are not produced by the aircraft manufacturers but by aircraft engine manufacturers. These manufacturers design and build engines that match the thrust of the engine to the size and flight characteristics of the aircraft. The type of engine used depends on the initial design of the aircraft or the specifications provided by the buyer. Aircraft manufacturers may use engines designed by different companies on the same type of aircraft.

The smallest segment of the aerospace industry includes firms producing guided missiles and spacecraft. Firms producing guided missiles and missile propulsion units are supported primarily by military and government demand. Although missiles are predominantly viewed as offensive weapons, improved guidance systems have led to their increased use as defensive systems. Applications of missile propulsion units also include their use in launching satellites into orbit.

Space vehicles are predominantly satellites. Firms producing space vehicles also produce craft for space flight and interplanetary scientific exploration. Consumers of spacecraft include the National Aeronautics and Space Administration (NASA), the Department of Defense (DOD), telecommunications companies, television networks, and news organizations. In addition to their military uses, satellites observe weather and the Earth in general, monitor and explore the cosmos, aid in search and navigation, and enable many communications services. Most companies manufacturing satellites also engage in the production of missiles. The businesses that build satellites are usually separate from the businesses that operate them once they are in orbit.

In 1997, about 1,828 establishments made up the aerospace industry. Most were concentrated in the aircraft and parts sector, with about 1,726 establishments, compared with 102 in the guided missiles and space vehicles sector. In the aircraft and parts industry, most establishments were subcontractors that manufacture parts and employ fewer than 50 workers (table 1). In contrast, almost 16 percent of the guided missile and spacecraft establishments employed more than 1,000 workers each, compared with 3 percent of the aircraft and parts firms. Nevertheless, 70 percent of the jobs in both aircraft and parts and guided missiles and spacecraft were in large establishments that employed 1,000 or more workers (chart).

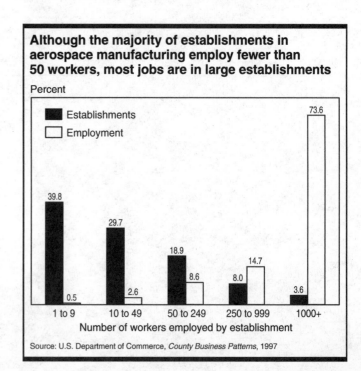

**Although the majority of establishments in aerospace manufacturing employ fewer than 50 workers, most jobs are in large establishments**

Source: U.S. Department of Commerce, *County Business Patterns*, 1997

**Table 1. Percent distribution of establishments in aerospace manufacturing by establishment size, 1997**

| Establishment size (number of workers) | Aerospace manufacturing | Aircraft and parts | Guided missiles and space vehicles |
|---|---|---|---|
| Total ....................................... | 100.0 | 100.0 | 100.0 |
| 1-9 ......................................... | 39.8 | 41.0 | 19.6 |
| 10-49 ..................................... | 29.7 | 29.8 | 28.4 |
| 50-249 ................................... | 18.9 | 18.7 | 21.6 |
| 250-999 ................................. | 8.0 | 7.6 | 14.7 |
| 1,000 or more ........................ | 3.6 | 2.9 | 15.7 |

SOURCE: U.S. Department of Commerce, *County Business Patterns*, 1997

The Federal Government traditionally has been the biggest customer of the aerospace industry, accounting for more than half of industry sales for many years. Because defense purchases have declined substantially in recent years, the value of sales to the Government now accounts for a little over one-third of total industry sales. The vast majority of Government contracts to purchase aerospace equipment are awarded by DOD. NASA also is a major purchaser of the industry's products and services, mainly for space vehicles and launch services.

The aerospace industry is dominated by a few large firms that contract to produce aircraft with Government and private businesses, usually airline and cargo transportation companies. These large firms, in turn, subcontract with smaller firms to produce specific systems and parts for their vehicles. Government purchases are largely related to defense. Typically, DOD announces its need for military aircraft, satellites, or missile systems, specifying a multitude of requirements. Large firms specializing in defense products subsequently submit bids, detailing proposed technical solutions and designs, along with cost estimates, hoping to win the contract. Firms may also research and develop materials, electronics, and components relating to their bid, often at their own expense, in order to enhance their chance of winning the contract. Following a negotiation phase, a manufacturer is selected and a prototype vehicle is developed and built, and then tested and evaluated. If approved by DOD, the program enters production.

Commercial airlines and private businesses typically identify their needs for a particular model of new aircraft based on a number of factors, including the routes they fly. After specifying requirements such as range, size, cargo capacity, and seating arrangements, the airlines invite manufacturers of civil aircraft to submit bids. Selection ultimately is based on a manufacturer's ability to deliver reliable aircraft that best fit the purchaser's stated market needs at the lowest cost and at favorable financing terms.

The way in which commercial and military aircraft are designed, developed, and produced is undergoing significant change in response to the need to cut costs and product development and manufacturing time. Firms producing commercial aircraft have reduced development time drastically through computer-aided design (CAD), which allows firms to design an entire aircraft, including the individual parts, solely by computer. The electronic drawings of these parts are sent to subcontractors who use them to program their machinery. Product development teams are increasingly being used through every phase of development, teaming customers, engineers, and production workers together to make decisions concerning the aircraft. Additionally, the military has changed its design philosophy, using available commercial off-the-shelf technology when appropriate, rather than developing new customized components.

## Working Conditions

The average aerospace production employee worked over 43 hours a week in 2000, compared to less than 42 hours a week throughout manufacturing and less than 35 hours a week across all industries.

Working conditions in aerospace manufacturing facilities vary. Many new factories, in contrast to older facilities, are spacious, well lit, and modern. Specific work environments usually depend on the occupation. Engineers, scientists, and technicians frequently work in office settings or laboratories, although production engineers may spend much of their time with production workers on the factory floor. Production workers, such as welders and other assemblers, may have to cope with high noise levels. Oil, grease, and grime often are present, and some workers may face exposure to volatile organic compounds found in solvents, paints, and coatings. Heavy lifting is required for many production jobs.

Cases of work-related injury and illness in the aircraft and parts sector were 8.2 per 100 full-time workers in 1999, higher than the 2.8 cases per 100 workers in the guided missiles sector. In comparison, cases of work-related injury and illness throughout the private sector averaged 6.3 per 100 workers.

## Employment

Aerospace manufacturing provided more than 551,000 wage and salary jobs in 2000—over 465,000 of them in the aircraft and parts sector and nearly 86,000 in the guided missiles, space vehicles, and parts sector. The largest numbers of aerospace jobs were in Washington and California, although many also were located in Kansas, Texas, Missouri, and Florida.

## Occupations in the Industry

The design and manufacture of the technologically sophisticated products of the aerospace industry require the input and skills of various workers. Skilled production, professional specialty, and technician jobs make up the bulk of employment. A significant number of managerial and administrative support occupations also are employed, stemming from the need to manage the design process and factory operations, coordinate the hundreds of thousands of parts that are assembled into an aircraft, and ensure compliance with Federal recordkeeping regulations. The aerospace industry has a larger proportion of workers with education beyond high school than the average for all industries.

The aerospace industry is on the leading edge of technology and constantly is striving to create new products and improve existing ones. The industry invests a great amount of time and money in research and development, and much of the work is performed by professional and related occupations, who made up about 23 percent of the aerospace workforce in 2000 (table 2). A bachelor's degree in a specialized field, such as engineering, is required for many of these jobs; a master's or doctoral degree is preferred for a few. Two years of technical training after high school is favored for many technician occupations.

Professionals and technicians develop new designs and make improvements to existing designs. Some also do basic aeronautical research. *Aerospace engineers* are integral members of the teams that research, design, test, and produce aerospace vehicles. Some specialize in areas such as structural design, guidance, navigation and control, and instrumentation and communication. Electrical and electronics, industrial, and mechanical engineers also contribute to the research for and development and production of aerospace products. For example, *mechanical engineers* help design mechanical components and develop the specific tools and machines needed to produce aircraft, missile, and space vehicle parts, or they may design jet and rocket engines. *Electrical* and *electronics engineers* specialize in electronic equipment used in aerospace products, such as radar and other transmission and communication equipment. *Engineering technicians* assist engineers, both in the research and development laboratory, and on the manufacturing floor. They may help build prototype versions of newly designed products, run tests and experiments, and perform a variety of other technical tasks. One of the earliest users of computer-aided design software, the aerospace industry continues to use the latest computer technology. *Systems analysts, computer scientists,* and *database administrators*; *computer software engineers; computer programmers;* and *computer support specialists and systems administrators* are responsible for the design, testing, evaluation, and set-up of computer systems that are used throughout the industry for design and manufacturing purposes. A multitude of computer and electronic systems are central to the function of aerospace products, and computer professionals work to integrate the vast array of data these systems provide into useful information for pilots.

Management, business, and financial occupations accounted for 12 percent of industry employment in 2000. Most persons advance to these jobs from professional occupations. Many managers in the aerospace industry have a technical or engineering background, and supervise teams of engineers in activities such as testing and research and development. *Industrial production managers* oversee all workers and lower-level managers in a factory. They also coordinate all activities that relate to production. In addition to technical and production managers, *financial managers; purchasing managers, buyers, and purchasing agents*; *cost estimators*; and *accountants and auditors* are needed to negotiate with customers and subcontractors and to track costs.

Of all aerospace workers, more than 50 percent are employed in production and installation, maintenance and repair, and transportation and material moving occupations. Many of these jobs are not specific to aerospace and can be found in other manufacturing industries. Many production jobs are open to persons with only a high school education; however, special vocational training after high school is preferred for some of the more highly skilled jobs.

*Aircraft structure, surfaces, rigging, and systems assemblers* usually specialize in one assembly task; hundreds of different assemblers may work at various times on producing a single aircraft. Assemblers may put together parts of airplanes, such as wings or landing gear, or install parts and equipment into the airplane itself. Those involved in assembling aircraft or systems must be skilled in reading and interpreting engineering specifications and instructions.

*Machinists* make parts when there are too few needed to be mass-produced. They follow blueprints and specifications and are highly skilled with machine tools and metalworking. *Tool and die makers* are responsible for constructing precision tools and metal forms, called dies, which are used to shape metal. Increasingly, as individual components are designed electronically,

**Table 2. Employment of wage and salary workers in aerospace manufacturing by occupation, 2000 and projected change, 2000-10**

(Employment in thousands)

| Occupation | Employment, 2000 | | Percent change, 2000-2010 |
|---|---|---|---|
| | Number | Percent | |
| **All occupations** | 551 | 100.0 | 18.9 |
| **Management, business, and financial occupations** | 65 | 11.8 | 20.7 |
| Engineering managers | 10 | 1.8 | -0.5 |
| Industrial production managers | 6 | 1.1 | 19.4 |
| Purchasing agents, except wholesale, retail, and farm products | 6 | 1.1 | 21.2 |
| Accountants and auditors | 4 | 0.8 | 26.0 |
| **Professional and related occupations** | 125 | 22.6 | 20.4 |
| Computer systems analysts | 7 | 1.3 | 51.7 |
| Aerospace engineers | 24 | 4.3 | 18.9 |
| Industrial engineers | 8 | 1.5 | 11.7 |
| Materials engineers | 10 | 1.8 | 17.9 |
| Mechanical engineers | 7 | 1.2 | 18.4 |
| **Office and administrative support occupations** | 56 | 10.1 | 15.8 |
| Production, planning, and expediting clerks | 6 | 1.1 | 23.6 |
| Shipping, receiving, and traffic clerks | 8 | 1.4 | 22.0 |
| Executive secretaries and administrative assistants | 6 | 1.1 | 14.3 |
| Secretaries, except legal, medical, and executive | 5 | 1.0 | -0.1 |
| **Construction and extraction occupations** | 12 | 2.1 | 19.6 |
| Sheet metal workers | 7 | 1.2 | 7.3 |
| **Installation, maintenance, and repair occupations** | 35 | 6.3 | 21.4 |
| Aircraft mechanics and service technicians | 12 | 2.2 | 20.1 |
| **Production occupations** | 241 | 43.8 | 17.7 |
| First-line supervisors/managers of production and operating workers | 16 | 3.0 | 18.4 |
| Aircraft structure, surfaces, rigging, and systems assemblers | 12 | 2.2 | 15.6 |
| Fiberglass laminators and fabricators | 6 | 1.0 | 23.5 |
| Team assemblers | 10 | 1.8 | 19.6 |
| Computer-controlled machine tool operators, metal and plastic | 9 | 1.5 | 33.4 |
| Grinding, lapping, polishing, and buffing machine tool setters, operators, and tenders, metal and plastic | 27 | 4.9 | 20.7 |
| Machinists | 16 | 2.9 | 20.5 |
| Foundry mold and coremakers | 26 | 4.6 | 7.4 |
| Molding, coremaking, and casting machine setters, operators, and tenders, metal and plastic | 6 | 1.1 | 20.7 |
| Plating and coating machine setters, operators, and tenders, metal and plastic | 12 | 2.2 | 13.8 |
| Tool and die makers | 5 | 0.8 | 19.5 |
| Welders, cutters, solderers, and brazers | 6 | 1.1 | 33.1 |
| Inspectors, testers, sorters, samplers, and weighers | 22 | 4.0 | 8.8 |

NOTE: May not add to totals due to omission of occupations with small employment

these highly skilled workers must be able to read electronic blueprints and setup and operate computer-controlled machines.

*Inspectors, testers, sorters, samplers, and weighers* perform numerous quality control and safety checks on aerospace parts

40

throughout the production cycle. Their work is vital to ensure the safety of the aircraft.

The remaining jobs in the industry are in office and administrative support, service, and sales occupations. Most of these jobs can be entered without education beyond high school. Workers in office and administrative support occupations help coordinate the flow of materials to the worksite, draw up orders for supplies, keep records, and help with all of the other paperwork associated with keeping a business functioning. Those in service occupations are employed mostly as guards and janitors and other cleaning and maintenance workers. Sales workers are mostly wholesale and manufacturing sales representatives and sales workers supervisors.

## Training and Advancement
Because employers need well-informed, knowledgeable employees who possess the skills needed to keep up with the rapid advancements in technology in aerospace manufacturing, the industry provides substantial support for the education and training of its workers. Firms provide on-site, job-related training to upgrade the skills of technicians, production workers, and engineers. Classes teaching computer skills and blueprint reading are common. Some firms reimburse employees for educational expenses at colleges and universities, emphasizing 4-year degrees and postgraduate studies.

Professionals, such as engineers and scientists, require a bachelor's degree in a specialized field. For some jobs, particularly in research and development, a master's or doctoral degree may be preferred.

Production workers may enter the aerospace industry with minimal skills. Mechanical aptitude and good hand-eye coordination usually are necessary. A high school diploma is preferred, but not required, and some vocational training in electronics or mechanics also is favored.

Unskilled production workers typically start by being shown how to perform a simple assembly task. Through experience, on-the-job instruction provided by other workers, and brief, formal training sessions, they expand their skills. Their pay increases as they advance into more highly skilled or responsible jobs. For example, machinists may take additional training to become numerical tool and process control programmers or tool and die makers. Inspectors are usually promoted from assembly, machine operation, and mechanical occupations.

Due to the reliance on computers and computer-operated equipment, classes in computer skills are common. With training, production workers may be able to advance to supervisory or technician jobs.

To enter some of the more highly skilled production occupations, workers must go through a formal apprenticeship. Machinists and electricians complete apprenticeships that can last up to 4 years. Apprenticeships usually include classroom instruction and shop training.

Entry level positions for technicians usually require a degree from a technical school or junior college. Companies sometimes retrain technicians to upgrade their skills or to teach different specialties. They are taught traditional as well as new production technology skills, such as computer-aided design and manufacturing and statistical process control methods.

## Earnings
Production workers in the aerospace industry earn higher pay than the average for all industries. Weekly earnings for production workers averaged $901 in aircraft and parts manufacturing and $842 in guided missiles, space vehicles, and parts in 2000,

compared with $597 in all manufacturing and $474 in all private industry. Above-average earnings reflect, in part, the high levels of skill required by the industry and the need to motivate workers to concentrate on maintaining high quality standards in their work. Nonproduction workers, such as engineering managers, engineers, and computer specialists, generally command higher pay due to their advanced education and training.

Earnings in selected occupations in aerospace manufacturing appear in table 3.

Table 3. **Median hourly earnings of the largest occupations in aircraft and parts manufacturing, 2000**

| Occupation | Aircraft and parts | All industries |
|---|---|---|
| Engineering managers | $ 42.61 | $ 40.42 |
| Aerospace engineers | 32.80 | 32.66 |
| Materials engineers | 31.45 | 28.41 |
| Computer systems analysts | 31.13 | 28.53 |
| Mechanical engineers | 29.72 | 28.23 |
| Industrial engineers | 28.03 | 28.16 |
| Aircraft structure, surfaces, rigging, and systems assemblers | 21.07 | 19.64 |
| Aircraft mechanics and service technicians | 19.77 | 19.50 |
| Machinists | 16.86 | 14.78 |
| Computer-controlled machine tool operators, metal and plastic | 15.31 | 13.17 |

In 2000, 25 percent of all workers in the aerospace industry were union members or covered by union contracts, compared with 15 percent of all workers throughout private industry. Some of the major aerospace unions include the International Association of Machinists and Aerospace Workers; the United Automobile, Aerospace, and Agricultural Implement Workers of America; the Society of Professional Engineering Employees in Aerospace (SPEEA); and the International Union of Allied Industrial Workers of America.

## Outlook
Employment in the aerospace industry is expected to increase by 19 percent over the 2000-2010 period, compared with the 15 percent growth projected for all industries combined. In the large aircraft and parts sector of the industry, employment is projected to grow by 23 percent, whereas employment in the smaller guided missiles and space vehicles sector is expected to decrease by about 4 percent. Factors affecting the employment outlook in the aerospace industry include Federal defense expenditures, commercial aircraft sales, the growth of telecommunications, and exports.

Federal defense expenditures on the products of the aerospace industry have fallen dramatically since the late 1980s. During most of the 1980s, large defense purchases of aircraft and missiles, together with support of research to develop new military aerospace equipment, kept employment and output at high levels. Large cuts in Federal defense spending have caused an ongoing restructuring of the defense aerospace industry, and significant declines in employment, as firms adjust to the lower spending levels. Some companies are selling their defense-oriented business and others are merging. Although the aerospace industry is less dependent on defense spending than in the past, defense purchases still support a significant number of aerospace workers. Defense spending, although not expected to decline further, is not expected to return to previous levels.

Although new employment opportunities will be limited in the defense-related sector of the aerospace industry, they should be better in the sector supported by civilian aviation. Rapid growth in air travel and environmental and safety concerns have highlighted the benefits of newer aircraft. As a result, airlines are purchasing more planes to meet the increased demand and to upgrade their fleets. Employment growth is expected in the production of commercial aircraft for both domestic and export purposes.

The expanded use of the Internet, direct broadcasting, and wireless communications services, such as cellular telephones and pagers, have increased the need for telecommunications equipment. Because satellites are widely used in telecommunications, this trend should spur further growth in the aerospace manufacturing industry.

Commercial exports have been rising strongly for years, reflecting the growth in overseas markets. Collaboration between domestic and foreign companies is becoming increasingly common as manufacturers seek to win sales in these growing markets and to share the substantial risks and costs of developing and producing new aerospace products. In addition to commercial exports, foreign military sales also are expected to bolster defense contractors, as countries around the world meet their defense needs with U.S. jet fighters, transports, and helicopters.

Due to past reductions in defense expenditures and competition in the commercial aircraft sector, there have been and may continue to be mergers within the industry that sometimes result in layoffs. In the long run, however, these mergers should have relatively little impact on employment. Even though final assemblers of commercial aircraft and major defense aerospace contractors are being reduced to a very small number, hundreds of smaller manufacturers and subcontractors will remain in this industry.

The continuing focus on advanced technology in aerospace manufacturing will lead to significant employment growth among professional specialty workers. Demand for computer specialists is projected to increase by over 60 percent over the 2000-2010 period. However, employment of engineers is expected to grow by about 10 percent, less than the growth rate of the overall industry. Replacement needs for engineers will be sig-nificant because large numbers of engineers who entered the industry in the 1960s are approaching retirement. Overall, professionals in the aerospace industry typically enjoy more employment stability than do other workers. During slowdowns in production, companies prefer to keep technical teams intact to continue research and product development activities, in anticipation of new business. Production workers, on the other hand, are particularly vulnerable to layoffs during downturns in the economy when aircraft orders decline.

## Sources of Additional Information

For additional information about the aerospace industry, write to:

➢ Aerospace Industries Association of America, Communications Department, 1250 Eye St. NW., Washington, DC 20005. Internet: **http://www.aia-aerospace.org**

➢ American Institute of Aeronautics and Astronautics, Inc., Suite 500, 1801 Alexander Bell Dr., Reston, VA 20191-4344. Internet: **http://www.aiaa.org**

➢ Satellite Industry Association, 225 Reinekers Lane, #600, Alexandria, VA 22314. Internet: **http://www.sia.org**

Information on the following occupations may be found in the 2002-03 edition of the *Occupational Outlook Handbook*.

- Aerospace engineers
- Aircraft and avionics equipment mechanics and service technicians
- Assemblers and fabricators
- Electrical and electronics engineers, except computer
- Engineering technicians
- Machinists
- Mechanical engineers
- Machine setters, operators, and tenders—metal and plastic
- Systems analysts, computer scientists, and database administrators
- Tool and die makers
- Welding, soldering, and brazing workers

# Apparel and Other Textile Products

## SIGNIFICANT POINTS

- Nearly half of all workers are sewing machine operators.

- Primarily due to increased imports and new technology, apparel manufacturing is projected to lose 103,000 jobs—more than almost any other industry—over the 2000-10 period.

- Average earnings are below those of other manufacturing industries.

## Nature of the Industry

The range of apparel and other textile products is as broad as their uses—suits, rainwear, fur coats, purses, and curtains are just a few examples. Workers in the apparel industry transform fabrics produced by textile manufacturers into these finished goods and many others that fill the Nation's retail stores. By cutting and sewing fabrics or other materials, such as leather, rubberized fabrics, plastics, and furs, workers in this industry help to keep us warm, dry, and in style.

As in other industries, technological advances, globalization, and changing business practices are affecting the apparel industry. One significant change is that more companies are outsourcing inventory and distribution functions to third-party warehouses, while still emphasizing quick response to customer demand. This system allows businesses to focus on the design and marketing of its garments, without concerns about investments in real estate or building leases for a distribution center, or expenses for materials handling equipment or personnel. Its third-party service can provide all warehousing, packing to customer order, and shipping to stores. Through electronic data interchange, information is instantaneously communicated to and received from trading partners. The electronic sharing of data between corporate offices and warehouses has made it possible for businesses to automate other processes. For example, information can be posted to electronic catalogs and buyers can access these catalogs, identify various items by code, and add these items to their buying assortment.

Other technologies affecting the apparel industry include computerized equipment and material transport systems. Computers and computer-controlled equipment aid in many functions, such as design, marking, and cutting. Overhead conveyor systems transport material between sewing machine operators and between processes. Despite these changes, however, the apparel industry—especially its sewing function—has remained significantly less automated than many other manufacturing industries.

The apparel industry traditionally has consisted of production workers who perform a specific function in an assembly line. This organizational philosophy increasingly is being replaced by a team concept, in which garments are made by a group of sewing machine operators organized into production "modules." Each operator in a module is trained to perform nearly all of the functions required to assemble a garment. Each team is responsible for its own performance, and individuals usually receive compensation based on the team's performance. These changes have greatly altered the atmosphere and responsibilities from those of the traditional assembly line.

Fierce competition from abroad has prompted these changes in work structure and technology. Apparel firms also have responded to growing competition by merging and by employing workers in other countries to perform some production functions. Workers in lower-wage countries increasingly are being hired to assemble garments—the most labor-intensive step in the production process—whereas U.S. workers now perform a greater share of the pre-assembly functions and coordinate the process. Such changes in the nature of the domestic apparel industry will certainly continue as globalization proceeds.

## Working Conditions

Working conditions depend on the age of the facility, the equipment used, and company policies. Sewing machine operators and other production workers work an average of 37.2 hours weekly, but overtime is common during periods of peak production. Some firms in the industry operate several shifts, and may require employees to work nights or weekends. As more expensive machinery is introduced, companies may add shifts to keep expensive machines from being idle.

Factories are generally clean, well lit, and well ventilated, but sewing areas may be noisy. Operators often sit for long periods and lean over machines. New ergonomically designed chairs and machines that allow workers to stand during operation are some of the means that firms use to minimize discomfort for production workers. Another concern for workers is injuries caused by repetitive motions. The implementation of modular units and specially designed equipment reduces potential health problems by lessening the stress of repetitive motions. In 1999, cases of work-related injury and illness in the apparel industry averaged 5.8 per 100 workers, lower than the 9.2 average in all manufacturing industries, and about the same as the rate for all industries.

The movement away from traditional piecework systems often results in a significant change in working conditions. Modular manufacturing involves teamwork, increased responsibility, and greater interaction among coworkers than do traditional assembly lines.

## Employment

The apparel industry provided about 633,000 wage and salary jobs in 2000. As shown in table 1, employment is concentrated in three segments of the industry. Miscellaneous fabricated textile products accounts for about 34 percent of industry employment; women's and misses' outerwear, about 29 percent; and men's and boys' furnishings, about 21 percent. Together, these segments employ 4 out of every 5 workers in the industry.

About two-thirds of jobs in the apparel industry are found in nine States: Alabama, California, Georgia, New Jersey, New York, North Carolina, Pennsylvania, Tennessee, and Texas. The industry had about 23,000 establishments in 2000, with employment concentrated in large firms. Three out of 4 jobs are in establishments with 50 or more workers (chart).

**Table 1. Percent distribution of establishments and employment in apparel and other textile products, 2000**

| Industry segment | Establishments | Employment |
|---|---|---|
| Total ............................................. | 100.0% | 100.0% |
| Miscellaneous fabricated textile products ............................. | 42.7 | 33.9 |
| Womens and misses outerwear .............. | 37.1 | 29.2 |
| Mens and boys furnishings ...................... | 8.4 | 20.8 |
| Miscellaneous apparel and accessories ... | 4.5 | 4.6 |
| Hats, caps, and millinery ........................ | 2.1 | 2.3 |
| Girls and childrens outerwear ................. | 1.8 | 2.5 |
| Womens and childrens undergarments .. | 1.6 | 3.4 |
| Mens and boys suits and coats .............. | 1.1 | 3.2 |
| Fur goods ............................................... | 0.6 | 0.2 |

## Occupations in the Industry

Production workers account for about 70 percent of total employment in the industry. About 42 of all workers are sewing machine operators (table 2). The apparel industry also employs a small number of workers in administrative support, material-moving, and managerial occupations.

*Fashion designers* are the artists of the apparel industry. They create ideas for a range of products including coats, dresses, hats, handbags, and underwear. Some are self-employed and work with individual clients, while others cater to fashion specialty stores or high-fashion department stores. Most fashion designers work for apparel manufacturers or retailers, adapting fashion trends for specific markets.

Before sewing can begin, pattern pieces must be made, layouts determined, and fabric cut. *Fabric and apparel patternmakers* create the "blueprint" or pattern pieces for a particular apparel design. This often involves "grading," or adjusting the pieces for different sized garments. Grading once was a time-consuming job, but now it is quickly completed with the aid of a computer. *Markers* determine the best arrangement of pattern pieces to minimize wasted fabric. Traditionally, markers judged the best arrangement of pieces by eye; today, computers quickly help determine the best layout.

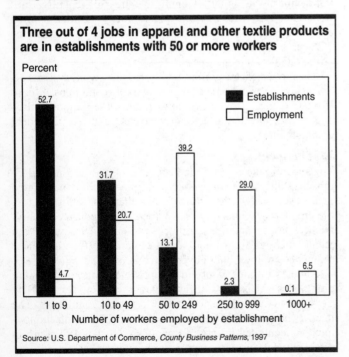

**Three out of 4 jobs in apparel and other textile products are in establishments with 50 or more workers**

Percent

- Establishments
- Employment

| 1 to 9 | 10 to 49 | 50 to 249 | 250 to 999 | 1000+ |
|---|---|---|---|---|
| 52.7 / 4.7 | 31.7 / 20.7 | 13.1 / 39.2 | 2.3 / 29.0 | 0.1 / 6.5 |

Number of workers employed by establishment

Source: U.S. Department of Commerce, *County Business Patterns*, 1997

**Table 2. Employment of wage and salary workers in apparel and other textile products by occupation, 2000 and projected change, 2000-10**

(Employment in thousands)

| Occupation | Employment, 2000 Number | Employment, 2000 Percent | Percent change 2000-2010 |
|---|---|---|---|
| **All occupations** ...................................... | 633 | 100.0 | -16.3 |
| **Management, business, and financial occupations** ........................................ | 33 | 5.1 | -11.3 |
| General and operations managers ........ | 9 | 1.5 | -11.2 |
| Industrial production managers ............ | 5 | 0.8 | -14.1 |
| **Professional and related occupations** .... | 12 | 1.9 | 1.5 |
| Designers ................................................. | 5 | 0.8 | 8.3 |
| **Service occupations** .................................. | 6 | 0.9 | -10.3 |
| Janitors and cleaners, except maids and housekeeping cleaners ................. | 4 | 0.7 | -8.5 |
| **Sales and related occupations** ............... | 15 | 2.3 | -12.5 |
| Sales representatives, wholesale and manufacturing, except technical and scientific products .............................. | 7 | 1.2 | -14.5 |
| **Office and administrative support occupations** ......................................... | 69 | 10.9 | -17.8 |
| Bookkeeping, accounting, and auditing clerks ..................................................... | 6 | 0.9 | -20.6 |
| Customer service representatives ......... | 5 | 0.7 | -10.5 |
| Shipping, receiving, and traffic clerks .... | 14 | 2.2 | -17.0 |
| Stock clerks and order fillers ................. | 8 | 1.3 | -10.6 |
| Office clerks, general .............................. | 8 | 1.2 | -13.2 |
| **Installation, maintenance, and repair occupations** ......................................... | 10 | 1.6 | -9.7 |
| **Production occupations** ............................ | 438 | 69.2 | -17.9 |
| First-line supervisors/managers of production and operating workers ....... | 22 | 3.4 | -17.8 |
| Team assemblers ..................................... | 16 | 2.5 | -8.4 |
| Printing machine operators .................... | 6 | 1.0 | 5.7 |
| Fabric and apparel patternmakers ......... | 7 | 1.2 | -18.5 |
| Pressers, textile, garment, and related materials ................................................ | 12 | 2.0 | -15.5 |
| Sewing machine operators ...................... | 265 | 41.8 | -20.9 |
| Sewers, hand .......................................... | 13 | 2.0 | -11.7 |
| Textile cutting machine setters, operators, and tenders ........................ | 16 | 2.5 | -17.9 |
| All other textile, apparel, and furnishings workers ............................. | 11 | 1.8 | 5.4 |
| Helpers—Production workers ................ | 10 | 1.6 | -14.7 |
| Inspectors, testers, sorters, samplers, and weighers ....................................... | 20 | 3.2 | -27.3 |
| All other production workers .................. | 5 | 0.8 | -10.9 |
| **Transportation and material moving occupations** ......................................... | 50 | 7.8 | -11.2 |
| Laborers and freight, stock, and material movers, hand ....................................... | 18 | 2.8 | -14.7 |
| Packers and packagers, hand ................ | 20 | 3.2 | -6.9 |

NOTE: May not add to totals due to omission of occupations with small employment

The layout arrangement is then given to *cutters*. In less automated companies, cutters may use electric knives or cutting machines to cut pattern pieces. In more automated facilities, markers electronically send the layout to a computer-controlled cutting machine, and *textile cutting machine setters, operators, and tenders* monitor the machine's work.

*Sewing machine operators* assemble or finish clothes or other goods such as curtains and purses. Most sewing functions are specialized and require the operator to receive specific training.

Although operators specialize in one function, the trend toward cross-training requires them to broaden their skills.

*Pressers* receive a garment after it has been assembled. Pressers eliminate wrinkles and give shape to finished products. Most pressers use specially formed, foot-controlled pressing machines to perform their duties. Some pressing machines now have the steam and pressure controlled by computers. *Inspectors, testers, sorters, samplers, and weighers* inspect the finished product to ensure consistency and quality. *Team assemblers* perform all of the assembly tasks assigned to their teams, rotating through the different tasks, rather than specializing in a single task. They also may decide how the work is to be assigned and how different tasks are to be performed.

## Training and Advancement

Most production workers are trained on the job. Although a high school diploma is not required, some employers prefer it. Basic math and computer skills are important for computer-controlled machine operators.

Cutters and pressers are trained on the job, while patternmakers and markers usually have technical or trade school training. All of these workers must understand textile characteristics and have a good sense of three-dimensional space. Traditional cutters need exceptional hand-eye coordination. Computers are becoming a standard tool for these occupations as patternmakers and markers increasingly design pattern pieces and layouts on a computer screen, so new entrants will help themselves by learning computer skills. Those running automatic cutting machines could need technical training, which is available from vocational schools.

Sewing machine operators must have good hand-eye coordination and dexterity, as well as an understanding of textile fabrics. They normally are trained on the job for a period of several weeks to several months, depending on their previous experience and the function for which they are training. Unfortunately, opportunity for advancement is limited because of the repetitive nature of their work. Setting a sleeve, for example, is more complicated and requires more training than sewing a side seam. In general, though, new machinery greatly reduces the skill level and training needed to perform many functions.

Modular manufacturing requires operators to perform more than one function, so they usually are trained to perform several duties. In addition to this functional training, workers in a modular system may also be offered courses in the interpersonal and communication skills necessary to work as part of a team. Further, the added responsibility of self-managing their modules may lead these workers to receive training in problem solving and management.

Designers need a good sense of color, texture, and style. In addition, they must understand the construction and characteristics of specific fabrics, such as durability and stiffness. Many employers seek designers who know how to use computer-assisted design. This specialized training usually is obtained through a university or design school that offers 4-year or 2-year degrees. Beginning designers usually receive on-the-job training. They normally need 1 to 3 years of training before they advance to higher level positions.

Those interested in engineering or production management need a bachelor's degree. Degrees in mechanical, chemical, or industrial engineering are common, but related studies also may be accepted. A few programs offer concentrations in apparel and textile production that focus on the unique characteristics and issues associated with apparel production. Universities offering these specializations generally are found in the South and Northeast.

## Earnings

Average weekly earnings for production workers were $338 in 2000, significantly lower than the overall $597 per week in manufacturing and $474 in the entire private sector. Table 3 shows average weekly and hourly earnings in various segments of the apparel industry.

Table 3. Average earnings of nonsupervisory workers in the apparel and other textile products industry, 2000

| Industry segment | Weekly | Hourly |
|---|---|---|
| **Total, private industry** | $474 | $13.74 |
| | | |
| **Apparel and other textile products** | 338 | 9.09 |
| Miscellaneous fabricated textile products | 390 | 10.13 |
| Men's and boys suits and coats | 341 | 9.32 |
| Miscellaneous apparel and accessories | 331 | 8.68 |
| Girl's and children's outerwear | 325 | 8.61 |
| Men's and boys furnishings | 313 | 8.54 |
| Women's and children's undergarments | 308 | 8.71 |
| Women's and misses' outerwear | 304 | 8.40 |

Earnings in selected occupations in apparel and other textile products appear in table 4. Traditionally, sewing machine operators are paid on a piecework basis determined by the quantity of goods they produce. Many companies are changing to incentive systems based on group performance that consider both the quantity and quality of the goods produced. A few companies pay production workers a salary.

Table 4. Median hourly earnings of the largest occupations in apparel and other textile products, 2000

| Occupation | Apparel and other textile products | All industries |
|---|---|---|
| Industrial production managers | $ 24.54 | $ 29.64 |
| | | |
| Sales representatives, wholesale and manufacturing, except technical and scientific products | 17.96 | 19.40 |
| First-line supervisors/managers of production and operating workers | 14.29 | 19.39 |
| Fabric and apparel patternmakers | 11.30 | 11.57 |
| Printing machine operators | 9.20 | 13.57 |
| Textile cutting machine setters, operators, and tenders | 8.98 | 9.23 |
| Inspectors, testers, sorters, samplers, and weighers | 8.19 | 12.22 |
| Pressers, textile, garment, and related materials | 8.02 | 7.77 |
| Sewers, hand | 7.44 | 8.09 |
| Sewing machine operators | 7.42 | 7.80 |

The apparel industry has a relatively low unionization rate; about 7.1 percent of apparel workers are union members or are covered by a union contract, compared with 14.9 percent for the economy as a whole. The major union in the apparel industry is the Union of Needletrades, Industrial, and Textile

Employees (UNITE), which was formed in 1995 from the International Ladies' Garment Workers Union and the Amalgamated Clothing and Textile Workers Union.

## Outlook

Wage and salary employment in the apparel industry is expected to decline 16 percent through 2010, compared with an increase of 16 percent for all industries combined. The expected decline translates into 103,000 lost jobs over the period—greater than the decrease for almost any other industry. Declining employment will be caused by growing imports, new automation, fierce cost-cutting pressures imposed by retailers, international competition, and mergers and acquisitions. Nevertheless, some job openings will arise as experienced workers transfer to other industries, retire, or leave the workforce.

Changing trade regulations are the single most important factor influencing future employment patterns. Because the apparel industry is labor-intensive, it is especially vulnerable to import competition from nations in which workers receive lower wages. The protection provided to the domestic apparel industry over the past two decades will be significantly reduced in coming years, permitting more apparel imports. For example, the Caribbean Basin Initiative (CBI), which took effect in 2000 and runs through 2008, will eliminate duties and quotas on all garments made up of American components. Because many U.S. firms will continue to move their assembly operations to low-wage countries, this trend is likely to impact lower-skilled machine operators most severely. It will not, however, have as adverse an effect on the demand for some of the presewing functions, such as designing and cutting, because much of the apparel will still be designed and cut in the United States.

New technology will increase the apparel industry's productivity, but unlike other industries, the apparel industry is likely to remain labor-intensive. The variability of cloth and the intricate cuts and seams of the assembly process have been difficult to automate. Machine operators, therefore, will continue to perform most sewing tasks, and automated sewing will be limited to simple functions. In some cases, however, computerized sewing machines will increase the productivity of operators and reduce required training time.

Technology also is increasing the productivity of workers who perform other functions such as designing, marking, cutting, and pressing. Computers and automated machinery will continue to raise productivity and reduce the demand for workers in these areas, but growth in demand for their services generated by offshore assembly sites will help to moderate this decline. These workers also will benefit from the increasing rate at which fashions change, which will produce greater demand for workers employed in those U.S.-based firms that have quick response capabilities.

Continuing changes in the market for apparel goods will exert cost-cutting pressures that affect all workers in the apparel and textile industries. As consumers become more price-conscious, retailers gain bargaining power over apparel producers, and increasing competition limits the ability of producers to pass on costs to consumers, apparel firms are likely to respond by relying more on foreign production and boosting productivity through investments in technology and new work structures. These responses will adversely affect employment of American apparel workers.

The trend today is for apparel firms to merge or consolidate to remain competitive. This trend continues to drive down the number of firms in this industry. In the future, the apparel industry will be dominated by highly efficient, profitable organizations that have developed their dominance through well recognized strategies that enable them to be among the lowest-cost producers of apparel. Consolidation and mergers are likely to result in layoffs of some workers.

## Sources of Additional Information

Information about job opportunities in technical and design occupations can be obtained from colleges offering programs in textile and apparel engineering, production, and design. For information about career opportunities, trade developments, and technology, contact:

➢ American Apparel Manufacturing Association, 2500 Wilson Blvd., Suite 301, Arlington, VA 22201.
  Internet: **http://www.americanapparel.org**

Information on many occupations in apparel manufacturing, including those listed below, appears in the 2002-03 edition of the *Occupational Outlook Handbook*:

- Designers
- Engineers
- Inspectors, testers, sorters, samplers, and weighers
- Textile, apparel, and furnishings occupations

# Chemicals Manufacturing, Except Drugs

(SIC 28, except 283)

## SIGNIFICANT POINTS

- Employment is projected to decline.

- Production and installation, maintenance, and repair workers hold almost 50 percent of all jobs.

- Persons with technical and advanced degrees will have the best opportunities, particularly for research and development work.

- Production workers earn more than in most industries.

## Nature of the Industry

Chemicals are an essential component of manufacturing, vital to industries such as construction, motor vehicles, paper, electronics, transportation, agriculture, and pharmaceuticals. Although some chemical manufacturers produce and sell consumer products such as soap, bleach, and cosmetics, most chemical products are used as intermediate products for other goods.

Chemical manufacturing is divided into eight segments, seven of which are covered here: Plastics materials and synthetics; cleaning preparations; organic chemicals; inorganic chemicals; miscellaneous chemicals; paints and allied products; and agricultural chemicals. The eighth segment, drug manufacturing, is covered in a separate *Career Guide* statement.

The largest employer of the segments included here is the plastics materials and synthetics industry, which produces a wide variety of finished products as well as raw materials. Some of these include polyethylene, polypropylene, polyvinyl chloride (PVC), and polystyrene, which can be made into products such as loudspeakers, toys, PVC pipes, and beverage bottles. Motor vehicle manufacturers are particularly large users of these products.

The cleaning preparations portion of the industry is the only one in which much of the production is geared directly toward consumers. This segment includes firms making soaps, detergents, and cleaning preparations. Cosmetics and toiletries also are included in this segment. Households and businesses use these products in many ways, cleaning everything from babies to bridges.

The industrial organic chemicals segment produces chemicals that contain carbon and hydrogen and are made primarily from petroleum and natural gas, often referred to as petrochemicals. Although organic chemicals are used to make a wide range of products, such as dyes, plastics, and pharmaceutical products, the majority of these chemicals are used in the production of other chemicals.

Industrial inorganic chemicals usually are made from salts, metal compounds, other minerals, and the atmosphere. In addition to solid and liquid chemicals, firms in this segment also produce industrial gases such as oxygen, nitrogen, and helium. Many inorganic chemicals serve as processing ingredients in the manufacture of chemicals, but do not appear in the final products because they are used as reaction aids. Other chemical companies are the largest single customer of this segment.

The miscellaneous chemical products segment includes manufacturers of adhesives and sealants, explosives, printing ink, carbon black, and other miscellaneous chemicals. These products are used by consumers or in the manufacture of other products.

The paints and allied products segment includes firms making paints, varnishes, lacquers, putties, paint removers, sealers, and stains. The construction and furniture industries are large customers of this segment. Other customers range from individuals refurbishing their homes to businesses that need anti-corrosive paints that can withstand high temperatures.

Finally, the segment employing the fewest workers in the chemical industry is agricultural chemicals—which supplies farmers and home gardeners with fertilizers, herbicides, pesticides, and other agricultural chemicals.

Chemicals generally are classified into two groups—commodity chemicals and specialty chemicals. Commodity chemical manufacturers produce large quantities of basic and relatively inexpensive compounds in large plants, often built specifically to make one chemical. Most of these basic chemicals are used to make more highly refined chemicals used in the production of everyday consumer goods by other industries. Specialty chemical manufacturers, on the other hand, produce smaller quantities of more expensive chemicals that are used less frequently. Specialty chemical manufacturers often supply larger chemical companies on a contract basis. Many traditional commodity chemical manufacturers are divided into two separate entities, one focused on commodities and the other on specialty chemicals.

**Table 1. Distribution of wage and salary employment in chemicals manufacturing, except drugs by detailed industry, 2000**

| Industry | Employment | Percent |
|---|---|---|
| Total, all industries ...................................... | 723,000 | 100.0 |
| Soap, cleaners, and toilet goods ................ | 155,000 | 14.9 |
| Plastics materials and synthetics ............... | 154,000 | 14.8 |
| Industrial organic chemicals ....................... | 120,000 | 11.5 |
| Industrial inorganic chemicals ................... | 98,000 | 9.4 |
| Miscellaneous chemical products.............. | 93,000 | 9.0 |
| Paints and allied products ......................... | 52,000 | 5.0 |
| Agricultural chemicals ................................ | 51,000 | 4.9 |

The diversity of products produced by the chemical industry also is reflected in its component establishments. For example, firms producing plastics materials operated relatively large plants in 1997. This segment had 8 percent of the reporting establishments, yet employed almost 21 percent of those working in the chemical manufacturing industry. On the other hand, manufacturers of paints and allied products had a greater number of establishments, each employing a much smaller number of workers. This segment comprised more than 14 percent of the establishments in the chemical industry, yet employed only 8 percent of all workers. The average workplace in the chemical industry ranged from 138 workers in the plastics materials segment to 35 workers in the soaps and cosmetics segment (chart).

The chemical industry segments vary in the degree to which their workers are involved in production activities, administration and management, or research and development. Industries that make products such as cosmetics or paint that are ready for sale to the final consumer employ more administrative and marketing personnel. Industries that market their products mostly to industrial customers generally employ a greater proportion of precision production workers and a lower proportion of unskilled labor.

Chemical firms are concentrated in areas abundant with other manufacturing businesses, such as in the Great Lakes region near the automotive industry, or on the West Coast near the electronics industry. Chemical plants also are located near the petroleum and natural gas production centers along the Gulf Coast in Texas and Louisiana. Because chemical production processes often use water, and chemicals are primarily exported by ship all over the world, major industrial ports are another common location of chemical plants. California, Illinois, New Jersey, New York, Ohio, Pennsylvania, South Carolina, Tennessee, and Texas had about 50 percent of the establishments in the industry.

## Working Conditions

Manufacturing chemicals usually is a continuous process; this means that, once a process has begun, it cannot be stopped when it is time for workers to go home. Split, weekend, and night shifts are common, and workers on such schedules usually are compensated with higher rates of pay. As a result, the average workweek in the chemical industry was 43 hours in 2000, over 2 hours longer than the average for nondurable manufacturing industries, and over 8 hours longer than the average for all private industries. The industry employs relatively few part-time workers.

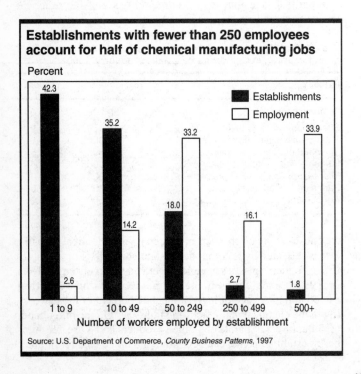

**Establishments with fewer than 250 employees account for half of chemical manufacturing jobs**

Percent

- Establishments
- Employment

| Number of workers employed by establishment | Establishments | Employment |
|---|---|---|
| 1 to 9 | 42.3 | 2.6 |
| 10 to 49 | 35.2 | 14.2 |
| 50 to 249 | 18.0 | 33.2 |
| 250 to 499 | 2.7 | 16.1 |
| 500+ | 1.8 | 33.9 |

Source: U.S. Department of Commerce, *County Business Patterns*, 1997

The plants usually are clean, although the continually running machines sometimes are loud and the interior of many plants can be hot. Hardhats and safety goggles are mandatory and worn throughout the plant.

Hazards in the chemical industry can be substantial, but they generally are avoided through strict safety procedures. Workers require protective gear and extensive knowledge of the dangers associated with the chemicals being handled. Body suits with breathing devices designed to filter out any harmful fumes are mandatory for work in dangerous environments.

In spite of the hazards of working with chemicals, extensive worker training on handling hazardous chemicals and chemical company safety measures have resulted in injury and illness rates for some segments of the chemical industry that are much lower than the average for the manufacturing sector. The chemical industry reported just 4.4 cases of work-related injury or illness per 100 workers, compared with an average of 9.2 cases for all manufacturing industries in 1999.

## Employment

The chemical and allied products industry employed about 723,000 wage and salary workers in 2000, about 4 percent of the total number employed in manufacturing and almost 10 percent of the total number employed in nondurable goods manufacturing. Most segments of the industry had substantial numbers of jobs, as shown in table 1.

## Occupations in the Industry

Nearly three-fifths of those employed in the industry work in production; installation, maintenance, and repair; and transportation and material-moving occupations. More than one-fifth work in management, business, and financial; and office and administrative support occupations. About 14 percent work in professional and related occupations (table 2).

*Production.* Workers in production occupations operate and fix plant machinery, transport raw materials, and monitor the production process. Improvements in technology gradually are increasing the level of plant automation, reducing the number of jobs in production occupations. Although high school graduates qualify for most entry-level production jobs, advancement into better-paying jobs, requiring higher skills or more responsibility, is possible with on-the-job training and work experience or through additional vocational training at a 2-year technical college.

*Chemical plant and system operators* monitor the entire production process. From chemical ingredient ratios to chemical reaction rates, the operator is responsible for the efficient operation of the chemical plant. Chemical plant operators generally advance to these positions from among the most experienced production workers, usually after having acquired extensive experience and technical training in chemical production processes. Experienced operators sometimes advance to senior supervisory positions.

*Industrial machinery mechanics* and *machinery maintenance workers* repair equipment, install machines, or practice preventive maintenance in the plant. Workers advance to these jobs either through apprenticeships or formal vocational training, or by completing in-house training courses.

*Inspectors, testers, sorters, samplers, and weighers* assure that the production process runs efficiently and that products are of acceptable quality. They refer problems to plant operators or management.

**Table 2. Employment of wage and salary workers in chemicals manufacturing, except drugs, by occupation, 2000 and projected change, 2000-10**

(Employment in thousands)

| Occupation | Employment, 2000 | | Percent change, 2000-2010 |
|---|---|---|---|
| | Number | Percent | |
| All occupations | 723 | 100.0 | -4.5 |
| **Management, business, and financial occupations** | 77 | 10.6 | -3.3 |
| Marketing and sales managers | 7 | 1.0 | 12.3 |
| General and operations managers | 12 | 1.7 | -3.6 |
| Industrial production managers | 10 | 1.3 | -7.4 |
| Business operations specialists | 14 | 2.0 | -4.2 |
| **Professional and related occupations** | 99 | 13.7 | -6.1 |
| Computer specialists | 9 | 1.2 | 19.3 |
| Chemical engineers | 12 | 1.6 | -11.1 |
| Chemists | 16 | 2.2 | -3.7 |
| Chemical technicians | 23 | 3.1 | -7.3 |
| **Sales and related occupations** | 24 | 3.3 | -3.7 |
| Sales representatives, wholesale and manufacturing, technical and scientific products | 8 | 1.2 | -5.2 |
| Sales representatives, wholesale and manufacturing, except technical and scientific products | 9 | 1.3 | -4.0 |
| **Office and administrative support occupations** | 84 | 11.7 | -6.3 |
| Bookkeeping, accounting, and auditing clerks | 7 | 1.0 | -10.5 |
| Customer service representatives | 9 | 1.3 | 2.0 |
| Shipping, receiving, and traffic clerks | 12 | 1.7 | -4.1 |
| Executive secretaries and administrative assistants | 9 | 1.2 | -10.7 |
| **Installation, maintenance, and repair occupations** | 56 | 7.8 | -8.2 |
| Industrial machinery mechanics | 13 | 1.8 | -4.3 |
| Maintenance and repair workers, general | 20 | 2.8 | -12.9 |
| **Production occupations** | 300 | 41.6 | -3.8 |
| First-line supervisors/managers of production and operating workers | 28 | 3.8 | -10.5 |
| Team assemblers | 14 | 1.9 | -2.4 |
| Metal workers and plastic workers | 15 | 2.1 | -11.5 |
| Chemical plant and system operators | 56 | 7.8 | -6.0 |
| Extruding and forming machine setters, operators, and tenders, synthetic and glass fibers | 15 | 2.1 | -12.7 |
| Textile winding, twisting, and drawing out machine setters, operators, and tenders | 9 | 1.2 | -13.1 |
| Chemical equipment operators and tenders | 33 | 4.6 | 4.9 |
| Mixing and blending machine setters, operators, and tenders | 29 | 4.1 | 5.4 |
| Helpers—Production workers | 17 | 2.4 | -4.1 |
| Inspectors, testers, sorters, samplers, and weighers | 12 | 1.6 | -19.3 |
| Packaging and filling machine operators and tenders | 28 | 3.9 | 8.2 |
| **Transportation and material moving occupations** | 65 | 8.9 | -2.0 |
| Truck drivers, heavy and tractor-trailer | 10 | 1.4 | -3.5 |
| Industrial truck and tractor operators | 10 | 1.4 | -2.7 |
| Laborers and freight, stock, and material movers, hand | 14 | 1.9 | -6.7 |
| Packers and packagers, hand | 12 | 1.6 | 6.6 |

NOTE: May not add to totals due to omission of occupations with small employment.

*Packaging and filling machine operators and tenders* wrap products and fill boxes to prepare the final product for shipment or sale to the wholesaler or consumer. More than half of these jobs are in the soap and cosmetics industry, due to the amount of packaging needed for this industry's consumer products.

*Transportation and material-moving workers* move materials around the plant using industrial trucks or deliver finished products to customers by truck. For these jobs, employers seek experienced workers with knowledge of chemical hazards, safety procedures, and regulations governing the transport of hazardous chemicals. Operation of industrial trucks and tractors can be learned with on-the-job training, but previous experience driving a truck and a commercial driver's license generally are required to operate a tractor-trailer carrying chemicals. Some jobs in transportation and material movement are open to workers without experience. Workers in these jobs move raw materials and finished products through the chemical plant and assist motor vehicle operators in loading and unloading raw materials and chemicals. They learn safe ways to handle chemicals on the job and develop skills that enable them to advance to other occupations.

**Research, development, and technical.** Most workers in research and development have at least a college degree, and many have advanced degrees. Engineers, scientists, and technicians account for a growing portion of industry employment.

*Chemists and materials scientists* carry out research in a wide range of activities, such as analysis of materials, preparation of new materials or modification of existing ones, study of process chemistry pathways for new or existing products, and formulations of cosmetics, household care products, or paints and coatings. They also try to develop new chemicals for specific applications and new applications for existing chemicals. The most senior chemists sometimes advance to management positions. Although chemical companies hire some chemists with bachelor's degrees, a master's or doctoral degree is becoming more important for chemist jobs.

*Chemical engineers* design equipment and develop processes for manufacturing chemicals on a large scale. Chemical research engineers design and conduct experiments to learn how processes behave and conduct research for potential new chemical products and processes. A bachelor's degree is essential for these jobs, and a master's degree may be preferred or required for some jobs.

*Engineering and science technicians* assist chemists and engineers in research activities and may conduct some research independently. Those with bachelor's degrees in chemistry or graduates of 2-year technical institutes usually fill these positions. Some graduates of engineering programs start as technicians until an opportunity to advance into an engineering position arises.

**Administration and management.** Most managers need a 4-year college degree in addition to experience in the industry. As in other highly technical industries, top managerial positions often are held by those with substantial technical experience. Employment in administrative support and managerial occupations is expected to decline as companies merge and consolidate operations.

*Engineering managers* conduct cost estimations, perform plant design feasibility studies, and coordinate daily operations.

These jobs require a college degree in a technical discipline, such as chemistry or chemical engineering, and experience in the industry. Some employees advance from research and development positions to management positions.

*Advertising, marketing, promotions, public relations,* and *sales managers* promote sales of chemical products by informing customers of company products and services. A bachelor's degree in marketing, chemistry, or chemical engineering usually is required for these jobs.

*Office and administrative support workers* perform office functions such as secretarial duties, bookkeeping, material records processing, and other clerical duties. Training beyond high school and familiarity with computers is preferred for these occupations.

## Training and Advancement

Despite recent reductions in the workforce, the chemical industry offers career opportunities for persons with varying levels of experience and education. Training and advancement differ for the three major categories of occupations.

Production workers may start as laborers or in other unskilled jobs and, with experience and training, advance into better-paying positions that require greater skills or have greater responsibility. Substantial advancement is possible even within a single occupation. For example, chemical plant operators may move up through several levels of responsibility until they reach the highest paying operator job. Advancement in production occupations usually requires mastery of advanced skills. Such skills usually are the result of a combination of on-the-job-training and formal training provided by the employer. Some workers advance into supervisory positions.

Most jobs in research and development require substantial technical education after high school, but opportunities exist for persons with degrees ranging from a 2-year associate degree up to a doctorate. Development of new products and the award of patents bring increases in pay and prestige, but after a point advancement may require moving from research and development into management. Researchers usually are familiar with company objectives and production methods, which, combined with college education, equips them with many of the tools necessary for management positions.

Managerial jobs usually require a 4-year college degree, though some may require only a 2-year technical degree. Managers can usually advance into higher level jobs without additional formal training outside the workplace, although competition is keen. In general, advancement into the highest management ranks depends on experience and proven ability to handle responsibility in several functional areas. Among larger worldwide firms, international experience is important for career advancement. Also, industry restructuring has left fewer layers of management, increasing competition for promotions.

## Earnings

Earnings in the chemical industry are higher than average. The weekly earnings for all production workers in chemical manufacturing averaged $768 in 2000, compared with $597 in all manufacturing industries and $474 throughout private industry. This was due, in part, to more overtime and weekend work, which commands higher hourly rates.

Wages of workers in the chemical industry vary according to occupation, the specific industry segment, and size of the production plant. Earnings for the largest occupations in selected industries are shown in table 3.

Earnings also vary by industry within the chemical industry. Median weekly earnings for production workers were highest in industrial organic chemicals, $962, and lowest in soaps, cleaners, toilet goods, $625.

The principal unions representing chemical workers are the PACE (Paper, Allied-Industrial, Chemical, and Energy Workers) International Union and the International Chemical Workers Union. In 2000, 13.2 percent of chemical manufacturing workers were union members or covered by union contracts, compared with 15 percent of all workers.

## Outlook

Although the chemical industry's output is expected to grow, employment in the chemical and allied products industry, excluding drugs, is projected to decline by about 4 percent over the 2000-10 period, compared with 15 percent growth expected for the entire economy. The expected decline in chemical manufacturing employment can be attributed to trends affecting the U.S. and global economies. There are several factors that will influence chemical industry employment, such as more efficient production processes and increased plant automation, the state of the national and world economy, company mergers and consolidation, increased foreign competition, outsourcing of production, growth of environmental health and safety concerns and legislation, precision farming techniques, and an emphasis on specialty chemicals.

Improvements in production technology have reduced the need for workers in production; installation, maintenance, and repair; and material-moving occupations, which account for a large proportion of jobs in the chemical industry. The growing application of computerized controls in standard production, and the growing manufacture of specialty chemicals requiring precise, computer-controlled production methods, will reduce the need for workers to monitor or directly operate equipment.

**Table 3. Median hourly earnings of the largest occupations in chemicals manufacturing, except drugs, 2000.**

| Occupation | Industrial inorganic chemicals | Soap, cleaners, and toilet goods | Agricultural chemicals | All industries |
|---|---|---|---|---|
| Chemical engineers | $ 29.97 | $ 32.11 | $ 29.76 | $ 31.71 |
| First-line supervisors/managers of production and operating workers | 24.24 | 20.82 | 22.32 | 19.39 |
| Chemists | 23.88 | 24.26 | 25.38 | 24.07 |
| Chemical plant and system operators | 19.80 | 16.88 | 18.38 | 19.59 |
| Industrial machinery mechanics | 19.63 | 18.11 | 18.97 | 17.30 |
| Maintenance and repair workers, general | 19.16 | 18.08 | 17.87 | 13.39 |
| Chemical equipment operators and tenders | 18.20 | 16.44 | 17.62 | 17.21 |
| Chemical technicians | 17.84 | 16.53 | 18.86 | 17.05 |
| Packers and packagers, hand | 17.74 | 8.10 | 8.49 | 7.53 |
| Mixing and blending machine setters, operators, and tenders | 13.91 | 12.79 | 10.84 | 12.58 |

Although production facilities will be easier to run with the increased use of computers, the new production methods will require workers with a better understanding of the use of the systems.

Foreign competition has been intensifying in most industries, and the chemical industry is no exception. Although the U.S. chemical industry has enjoyed a favorable trade balance for quite some time, growing global trade and rapidly expanding foreign production capabilities should increase competition. Pressure to reduce costs and streamline production will result in the continuing mergers and consolidation of companies both within the United States and abroad. Mergers and consolidations are allowing chemical companies to increase profits by eliminating duplicate departments and shifting operations to locations in which costs are lowest. U.S. companies are expected to move some production activities to developing countries—those in East Asia and Latin America, for example—to take advantage of rapidly expanding markets.

To satisfy growing public environmental concerns and to comply with the many government regulations, the chemical industry invests billions of dollars yearly in technology to reduce pollution and clean up existing waste sites. Growing concerns about chemicals and the environment will spur producers to create chemicals with fewer, less dangerous, or useable by-products that can be recycled or disposed of cleanly. This will require greater investment in research and development. As a result, occupations related to environmental compliance, improving product visibility, and promoting consumer confidence should grow.

Precision farming techniques have reduced the demand for agricultural chemicals in this country as farmers use computer technology to determine which chemicals need to be applied in different areas of the farm, rather than simply fertilizing the whole farm. However, this reduced demand will be partially offset by the increase in global demand for agricultural chemicals as other countries become more sophisticated in their farming techniques.

Another trend in the chemical industry is the rising demand for specialty chemicals. Chemical companies are finding that, in order to remain competitive, they must differentiate their products and produce specialty chemicals, such as advanced polymers and plastics designed for customer-specific uses—for example, a durable body panel on an automobile. Because advanced processes often are needed to produce specialty chemicals, this trend should increase employment opportunities for highly trained research and development and production-oriented chemists, chemical engineers, technicians, and production personnel. In these small- to medium-size firms,

responsiveness to customers' chemical needs is imperative, so opportunities for marketing staff such as sales engineers also should be available. An emerging technology within specialty chemicals that will require more research and development is the modeling of chemical reactors and batch and continuous processes.

The factors affecting employment in the chemical manufacturing industry will impact different segments of the industry to varying degrees. The two segments projected to add the most jobs are agricultural chemicals, with an increase of about 4,500 jobs; and paints and allied products, with an increase of around 4,000 jobs. The two largest losers of jobs are plastics materials and synthetics, with about 24,000 fewer jobs projected, and industrial inorganic chemicals, with a projected loss of about 16,000 jobs.

In terms of specific occupations, employment opportunities in the chemical industry can be divided into production and nonproduction occupations. Jobs in production are expected to decline as the increasing automation of the chemical industry improves efficiency and as some production activities are moved overseas, but the outlook is somewhat brighter for certain professional occupations, such as computer specialists. Marketing and sales occupations will decline due to the elimination of personnel as a result of company restructuring and mergers. In general, persons with technical and advanced degrees will have the best opportunities in the chemical industry.

## Sources of Additional Information

Additional information on training and careers in the chemical and allied products industry is available from:

➢ American Chemical Society, 1155 16th St. NW., Washington, DC 20036. Internet: **http://www.acs.org**
➢ American Institute of Chemical Engineers, 3 Park Ave., New York, NY 10016-5991. Internet: **http//www.aiche.org**

Detailed information on many occupations in the chemical industry, including the following, may be found in the 2002-03 edition of the *Occupational Outlook Handbook*.

● Chemical engineers
● Chemists and materials scientists
● Computer programmers
● Engineering technicians
● Industrial production managers
● Material-moving occupations
● Systems analysts, computer scientists, and database administrators

# Drug Manufacturing

## SIGNIFICANT POINTS

- Half of all workers have a bachelor's, master's, professional, or Ph.D. degree—roughly double the proportion for all industries combined.

- More than 40 percent of all jobs are in large establishments employing more than 1,000 workers.

- Drug manufacturing ranks among the faster growing manufacturing industries.

- Earnings are much higher than those in other manufacturing industries.

## Nature of the Industry

The drug manufacturing industry has produced a variety of medicinal and other health-related products undreamed of by even the most imaginative apothecaries of the past. These drugs save the lives of millions of people from various diseases and permit many ill people to lead normal lives.

Thousands of medications are available today for diagnostic, preventive, and therapeutic uses. In addition to aiding in the treatment of infectious diseases such as pneumonia, tuberculosis, malaria, influenza, and sexually transmitted diseases, these medicines also help prevent and treat cardiovascular disease, asthma, diabetes, and cancer. For example, anti-nausea drugs help cancer patients endure chemotherapy; clot-buster drugs help stroke patients avoid brain damage; and psychoactive drugs reduce the severity of mental illness for many people. Antibiotics and vaccines have virtually wiped out such diseases as diphtheria, syphilis, and whooping cough. Discoveries in veterinary drugs have increased animal productivity and controlled various diseases, some of which are transmissible to humans.

At each stage of life—from early infancy through old age—innovative drug discoveries help millions of patients lead longer, healthier, happier, and more productive lives. These longer life spans are due, in large part, to the conquest of diseases by drug research and manufacturing. But modern drugs do even more than save lives and improve the well-being of patients. As they improve health, they also save money by keeping people out of hospitals, emergency rooms, and nursing homes.

Advances in biotechnology and information technology are transforming drug discovery and development. Within biotechnology, scientists have learned a great deal about human genes, but the real work—translating that knowledge into viable new drugs—is just beginning. Thousands of new drugs are expected to be developed in the coming years.

There is a direct relationship between gene discovery and identification of new drugs: the more genes identified, the more paths available for drug discovery. Discovery of new genes also can lead to new diagnostics for the early detection of disease. Among other uses, new genetic technology is being explored to develop vaccines to prevent or treat diseases that have eluded traditional vaccines, such as AIDS, malaria, tuberculosis, and cervical cancer.

The drug industry consists of more than 2,500 places of employment, located throughout the country. These include establishments that make pharmaceutical preparations or finished drugs; biological products, such as serums and vaccines; bulk chemicals and botanicals used in making finished drugs; and diagnostic substances such as pregnancy and blood glucose kits. Pharmaceutical manufacturing firms make up the majority of establishments and employ almost 80 percent of the workers in this industry.

The U.S. drug industry has achieved worldwide prominence through research and development (R&D) of new drugs, and spends a relatively high proportion of its funds on R&D compared with other industries. Each year, drug industry testing involves many thousands of new substances, yet may eventually yield only 10 to 20 new prescription medicines.

For the majority of firms in this industry, the actual manufacture of drugs is the last stage in a lengthy process that begins with scientific research to discover new products and to improve or modify existing ones. The R&D departments in drug manufacturing firms start this process by seeking new chemical compounds with the potential to prevent, combat, or alleviate symptoms of diseases or other health problems. Scientists use sophisticated tools, such as computer simulation and combinatorial chemistry, to hasten and simplify the discovery of potentially useful new compounds.

Most firms devote a substantial portion of their R&D budgets to applied research, using scientific knowledge to develop a drug targeted to a specific use. For example, an R&D unit may focus on developing a compound that will effectively slow the advance of breast cancer. If the discovery phase yields promising compounds, technical teams then attempt to develop a safe and effective product based on the discoveries.

To test new products in development, a research method called "screening" is used. To screen an antibiotic, for example, a sample is first placed in a bacterial culture. If the antibiotic is effective, it is next tested on infected laboratory animals. Laboratory animals also are used to study the safety and efficacy of the new drug. A new drug is selected for testing in humans only if it promises to have therapeutic advantages over drugs already in use, or is safer. Drug screening is an incredibly risky, laborious, and high-cost process—only one in every 5,000 to 10,000 compounds screened eventually becomes an approved drug.

After laboratory screening, firms conduct clinical investigations, or "trials," of the drug on human patients. Human clinical trials normally take place in three phases. First, medical scientists administer the drug to a small group of healthy volunteers to determine and adjust dosage levels, and monitor for side effects. If a drug appears useful and safe, additional tests are conducted in two more phases, each phase using a successively larger group of volunteers or carefully selected patients.

After a drug successfully passes animal and clinical tests, the U.S. Food and Drug Administration (FDA) must review the drug's performance on human patients before approving the substance for commercial use. The entire process, from the first discovery of a promising new compound to FDA approval, can take many years. However, scientific and information technology advances will shorten that process considerably for most drugs. Furthermore, the FDA is becoming more efficient in reviewing and approving drugs.

After FDA approval, problems of production methods and costs must be worked out before manufacturing begins. If the original laboratory process of preparing and compounding the ingredients is complex and too expensive, pharmacists, chemists, chemical engineers, packaging engineers, and production specialists are assigned to develop a manufacturing process economically adaptable to mass production. After marketing the drug, new production methods may be developed to incorporate new technology or to transfer the manufacturing operation to a new production site.

In many production operations, drug manufacturers have developed a high degree of automation. Milling and micronizing machines, which pulverize substances into extremely fine particles, are used to reduce bulk chemicals to the required size. These finished chemicals are combined and processed further in mixing machines. The mixed ingredients may then be mechanically capsulated, pressed into tablets, or made into solutions. One type of machine, for example, automatically fills, seals, and stamps capsules. Other machines fill bottles with capsules, tablets, or liquids, and seal, label, and package the bottles.

Quality control and quality assurance are vital in this industry. Many production workers are assigned full time to quality control and quality assurance functions, whereas other employees may devote part of their time to these functions. For example, although pharmaceutical company sales representatives, often called detailers, primarily work in marketing, they engage in quality control when they assist pharmacists in checking for outdated products.

## Working Conditions

Working conditions in drug plants are better than in most other manufacturing plants. Much emphasis is placed on keeping equipment and work areas clean because of the danger of contamination. Plants usually are air-conditioned, well lighted, and quiet. Ventilation systems protect workers from dust, fumes, and disagreeable odors. Special precautions are taken to protect the relatively small number of employees who work with infectious cultures and poisonous chemicals. With the exception of work performed by material handlers and maintenance workers, most jobs require little physical effort. In 1999, the incidence of work-related injury and illness was 3.8 cases per 100 full-time workers, compared with 9.2 per 100 for all manufacturing industries and 6.3 per 100 for the entire private sector.

Only 4.6 percent of the workers in the drug manufacturing industry are union members or are covered by a union contract, compared with 14.9 percent of workers throughout private industry.

## Employment

Drug manufacturing provided 315,000 wage and salary jobs in 2000. Almost 8 out of 10 jobs were in establishments that made pharmaceutical preparations or finished drugs, such as tranquilizers, antiseptics, and antibiotics. The remaining jobs were in establishments that made biological products, such as serums and vaccines; bulk medicinal chemicals and botanicals used in making finished drugs; or diagnostic substances such as pregnancy and glucose tests.

Drug manufacturing establishments typically employ many workers. More than 40 percent of this industry's employees work for firms with more than 1,000 workers (chart). Most jobs are in California, Illinois, Indiana, New Jersey, New York, North Carolina, and Pennsylvania.

## Occupations in the Industry

About 22 percent of all jobs in the drug manufacturing industry are in professional and related occupations, mostly scientists and science technicians, and about 29 percent are in managerial, administrative support, and sales occupations. Almost half of the jobs in the drug manufacturing industry are in production, maintenance, or material-moving occupations, including both low-skilled and high-skilled jobs (table 1).

Scientists, engineers, and technicians conduct research to develop new drugs. Others work to streamline production methods and improve environmental and quality control. Life scientists are among the largest scientific occupations in this industry. Most of these scientists are *biological* and *medical scientists* who produce new drugs using biotechnology to recombine the genetic material of animals or plants. Biological scientists normally specialize in a particular area. *Biologists* and *bacteriologists* study the effect of chemical agents on infected animals. *Biochemists* study the action of drugs on body processes by analyzing the chemical combination and reactions involved in metabolism, reproduction, and heredity. *Microbiologists* grow strains of microorganisms that produce antibiotics. *Physiologists* investigate the effect of drugs on body functions and vital processes. *Pharmacologists* and *zoologists* study the effect of drugs on animals. *Virologists* grow viruses, and develop vaccines and test them in animals. *Botanists*, with their special knowledge of plant life, contribute to the discovery of

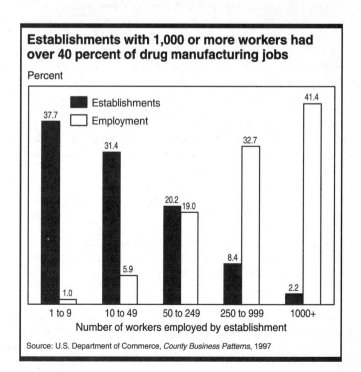

**Establishments with 1,000 or more workers had over 40 percent of drug manufacturing jobs**

Percent

■ Establishments
□ Employment

| 1 to 9 | 10 to 49 | 50 to 249 | 250 to 999 | 1000+ |
|--------|----------|-----------|------------|-------|
| 37.7 / 1.0 | 31.4 / 5.9 | 20.2 / 19.0 | 8.4 / 32.7 | 2.2 / 41.4 |

Number of workers employed by establishment

Source: U.S. Department of Commerce, *County Business Patterns*, 1997

botanical ingredients for drugs. Other biological scientists include *pathologists*, who study normal and abnormal cells or tissues, and *toxicologists*, who are concerned with the safety, dosage levels, and compatibility of different drugs. *Medical scientists*, who also may be physicians, conduct clinical research, test products, and oversee human clinical trials.

Physical scientists, particularly *chemists*, also are important in the research and development of new drugs. *Organic chemists* combine new compounds for biological testing. *Physical chemists* separate and identify substances, determine molecular structure, help create new compounds, and improve manufacturing processes. *Radiochemists* trace the course of drugs through body organs and tissues. *Pharmaceutical chemists* set standards and specifications for the form of products and for storage conditions; they also see that drug labeling and literature meet the requirements of State and Federal laws. *Analytical chemists* test raw and intermediate materials and finished products for quality.

Science technicians, such as *biological* and *chemical technicians*, play an important part in research and development of new medicines. They set up, operate, and maintain laboratory equipment, monitor experiments, analyze data, and record and interpret results. Science technicians usually work under the supervision of scientists or engineers.

Although engineers account for a small fraction of scientific and technical workers, they make significant contributions toward improving quality control and production efficiency. *Chemical engineers* design equipment and devise manufacturing processes. *Bioprocess engineers*, who are similar to chemical engineers, design fermentation vats and various bioreactors for microorganisms that will produce a given product. *Industrial engineers* plan equipment layout and workflow to maintain efficient use of plant facilities.

At the top of the managerial group are executives who make policy decisions concerning matters of finance, marketing, and research. Other managerial workers include *natural sciences managers* and *industrial production managers*.

Office and administrative support employees include *secretaries*, *general office clerks*, and others who keep records on personnel, payroll, raw materials, sales, and shipments.

*Pharmaceutical sales representatives*, often called pharmaceutical detailers, describe their company's products to physicians, pharmacists, dentists, and health services administrators. These sales representatives serve as lines of communication between their companies and clients.

Most plant workers fall into one of three occupational groups: production or processing workers who operate drug-producing equipment and inspect products; maintenance workers who install, maintain, and repair production equipment; and transportation and material-moving workers who package and transport the drugs.

Workers in the largest of the production occupations, *team assemblers*, perform all of the assembly tasks assigned to their teams, rotating through the different tasks, rather than specializing in a single task. They also may decide how the work is to be assigned and how different tasks are to be performed.

Other workers specialize in one part of the production process. *Chemical processing machine setters, operators, and tenders*, such as *pharmaceutical operators* control machines that produce tablets, capsules, ointments, and medical solutions. *Mixing and blending machine setters, operators, and tenders*, such as *granulator machine operators* tend milling and

**Table 1. Employment of wage and salary workers in drug manufacturing by occupation, 2000 and projected change, 2000-10.**

(Employment in thousands)

| Occupation | Employment, 2000 | | Percent change, 2000-2010 |
|---|---|---|---|
| | Number | Percent | |
| **All occupations** | 315 | 100.0 | 23.8 |
| **Management, business, and financial occupations** | 41 | 13.1 | 25.2 |
| Marketing and sales managers | 3 | 1.0 | 42.5 |
| General and operations managers | 4 | 1.2 | 22.4 |
| Industrial production managers | 5 | 1.6 | 20.5 |
| Natural sciences managers | 3 | 0.8 | 18.0 |
| Accountants and auditors | 2 | 0.8 | 29.6 |
| **Professional and related occupations** | 70 | 22.3 | 33.0 |
| Computer specialists | 6 | 1.8 | 59.8 |
| Chemical engineers | 3 | 0.9 | 23.9 |
| Industrial engineers, including health and safety | 4 | 1.2 | 19.0 |
| Drafters, engineering, and mapping technicians | 4 | 1.3 | 20.6 |
| Biological scientists | 11 | 3.4 | 29.6 |
| Medical scientists | 3 | 1.0 | 42.5 |
| Chemists | 14 | 4.6 | 42.5 |
| Biological technicians | 7 | 2.1 | 26.7 |
| Chemical technicians | 8 | 2.5 | 29.6 |
| Healthcare practitioners aand technical occupations | 2 | 0.7 | 27.8 |
| **Service occupations** | 7 | 2.1 | 26.0 |
| Janitors and cleaners, except maids and housekeeping cleaners | 4 | 1.2 | 29.6 |
| **Sales and related occupations** | 6 | 1.8 | 18.5 |
| Sales representatives, wholesale and manufacturing, technical and scientific products | 3 | 1.1 | 16.6 |
| **Office and administrative support occupations** | 43 | 13.7 | 15.2 |
| Bookkeeping, accounting, and auditing clerks | 4 | 1.2 | 11.6 |
| Customer service representatives | 4 | 1.1 | 26.9 |
| Shipping, receiving, and traffic clerks | 6 | 1.8 | 18.7 |
| Office clerks, general | 3 | 1.1 | 23.7 |
| Secretaries, except legal, medical, and executive | 3 | 1.1 | 3.7 |
| **Construction and extraction occupations** | 3 | 1.1 | 32.5 |
| Construction trades and related workers | 3 | 1.0 | 32.9 |
| **Installation, maintenance, and repair occupations** | 17 | 5.4 | 20.6 |
| Industrial machinery mechanics | 3 | 1.1 | 29.6 |
| **Production occupations** | 118 | 37.4 | 21.1 |
| First-line supervisors/managers of production and operating workers | 11 | 3.4 | 16.6 |
| Team assemblers | 33 | 10.6 | 16.6 |
| Chemical plant and system operators | 3 | 0.8 | 29.6 |
| Chemical processing machine setters, operators, and tenders | 9 | 2.9 | 39.5 |
| Mixing and blending machine setters, operators, and tenders | 8 | 2.6 | 29.6 |
| Inspectors, testers, sorters, samplers, and weighers | 11 | 3.6 | 3.7 |
| Packaging and filling machine operators and tenders | 19 | 6.1 | 29.6 |
| **Transportation and material moving occupations** | 9 | 3.0 | 24.5 |
| Packers and packagers, hand | 3 | 0.9 | 29.6 |

NOTE: May not add to totals due to omission of occupations with small employment.

grinding machines that reduce mixtures to particles of designated sizes. *Compounders* tend tanks and kettles in which solutions are mixed and compounded to make up creams, ointments, liquid medications, and powders. *Compressors* operate machines that compress ingredients into tablets. *Pill and tablet coaters*, often called capsule coaters, control a battery of machines that apply coatings that flavor, color, preserve, or add medication to tablets, or control disintegration time. *Ampoule fillers* operate machines that fill small glass containers with measured doses of liquid drug products. Throughout the production process, *inspectors, testers, sorters, samplers, and weighers* ensure consistency and quality. For example, *ampoule examiners* examine ampoules for discoloration, foreign particles, and flaws in the glass. *Tablet testers* inspect tablets for hardness, chipping, and weight to assure conformity with specifications.

After the drug is prepared and inspected, it is bottled or otherwise packaged by *packaging and filling machine operators and tenders*. Semi-skilled workers do most of the packaging and bottle-filling with machines that measure exact amounts of the product and seal containers.

Plant workers who do not operate or maintain equipment perform a variety of other tasks. Some drive industrial trucks or tractors to move materials around the plant, load and unload trucks and railroad cars, or package products and materials by hand.

## Training and Advancement

Training requirements for jobs in the drug industry range from a few hours of on-the-job training to years of formal education plus job experience. About half of all workers have a bachelor's or graduate degree—roughly double the proportion for all industries combined. The drug industry places a heavy emphasis on continuing education for employees, and many firms provide classroom training in safety, environmental and quality control, and technological advances.

For production and maintenance occupations, drug manufacturers usually hire inexperienced workers and train them on the job; high school graduates are generally preferred. Beginners in production jobs assist experienced workers and learn to operate processing equipment. With experience, employees may advance to more skilled jobs in their departments.

Many companies encourage production and maintenance workers to take courses related to their jobs in local schools and technical institutes or to enroll in correspondence courses. College courses in chemistry and related areas are particularly encouraged for highly skilled production workers who operate sophisticated equipment. Some companies reimburse workers for part, or all, of their tuition. Skilled production and maintenance workers with leadership ability may advance to supervisory positions.

For science technicians in the drug industry, most companies prefer to hire graduates of technical institutes or junior colleges or those who have completed college courses in chemistry, biology, mathematics, or engineering. Some companies, however, require science technicians to hold a bachelor's degree in a biological or chemical science. In many firms, newly hired workers begin as laboratory helpers or aides, performing routine jobs, such as cleaning and arranging bottles, test tubes, and other equipment.

The experience required for higher level technician jobs varies from company to company. Usually, employees advance over a number of years from assistant technician, to technician, to senior technician, and then to technical associate, or supervisory technician.

For most scientific and engineering jobs, a bachelor of science degree is the minimum requirement. Scientists involved in research and development usually have a master's or doctoral degree. A doctoral degree is generally the minimum requirement for medical scientists, and those who administer drug or gene therapy to patients in clinical trials must have a medical degree. Because biotechnology is not one discipline, but the interaction of several disciplines, the best preparation for work in biotechnology is training in a traditional biological science, such as genetics, molecular biology, biochemistry, virology, or biochemical engineering. Individuals with a scientific background and several years of industrial experience may eventually advance to managerial positions. Some companies offer training programs to help scientists and engineers keep abreast of new developments in their fields and to develop administrative skills. These programs may include meetings and seminars with consultants from various fields. Many companies encourage scientists and engineers to further their education; some companies provide financial assistance or full reimbursement for this purpose. Publication of scientific papers also is encouraged.

Drug manufacturing companies prefer to hire college graduates, particularly those with strong scientific backgrounds, as pharmaceutical detailers. Newly employed pharmaceutical representatives complete rigorous formal training programs revolving around their company's product lines.

## Earnings

Earnings of workers in the drug industry are higher than the average for all manufacturing industries. In 2000, production or nonsupervisory workers in the drug industry averaged $766 a week, while those in all manufacturing industries averaged $597 a week. Earnings in selected occupations in drug manufacturing appear in table 2.

Some employees work in plants that operate around the clock—three shifts a day, 7 days a week. In most plants, workers receive extra pay when assigned to the second or third shift. Because drug production is subject to little seasonal variation, work is steady.

Table 2. Median hourly earnings of the largest occupations in drug manufacturing, 2000.

| Occupation | Drug manufacturing | All industries |
|---|---|---|
| Industrial production managers | $ 36.32 | $ 29.64 |
| Chemists | 24.43 | 24.07 |
| First-line supervisors/managers of production and operating workers | 23.44 | 19.39 |
| Industrial machinery mechanics | 19.79 | 17.30 |
| Maintenance and repair workers, general | 18.55 | 13.39 |
| Chemical technicians | 17.27 | 17.05 |
| Chemical equipment operators and tenders | 16.91 | 17.21 |
| Biological technicians | 16.78 | 15.16 |
| Inspectors, testers, sorters, samplers, and weighers | 14.11 | 12.22 |
| Team assemblers | 10.86 | 10.32 |

## Outlook

Wage and salary jobs in drug manufacturing are expected to increase by about 24 percent over the 2000-10 period, compared with 16 percent for all industries combined. Drug manufacturing ranks among the faster growing manufacturing industries. Demand for this industry's products is expected to remain strong. Even during fluctuating economic conditions, there will be a market for over-the-counter and prescription drugs, including the diagnostics used in hospitals, laboratories, and homes; the vaccines used routinely on infants and children; analgesics and other symptom-easing drugs; and antibiotics and "miracle" drugs for life-threatening diseases.

Although the use of drugs, particularly antibiotics and vaccines, has helped eradicate or limit a number of deadly diseases, many others, such as cancer, Alzheimer's, and heart disease, continue to elude cures. Ongoing research and the manufacture of new products to combat these diseases will continue to contribute to employment growth.

Because so many of the drug industry's products are related to preventive or routine health care, rather than just illness, demand is expected to increase as the population expands. The growing number of older people who will require more health care services will further stimulate demand—along with the growth of both public and private health insurance programs, which increasingly cover the cost of drugs and medicines.

Another factor propelling demand is the increasing popularity of lifestyle drugs—drugs that are not necessarily vital to one's well being, but help enhance self-confidence or physical appearance. Other factors expected to increase the demand for drugs include a more industry-friendly regulatory environment that has streamlined the FDA approval process, a healthy pipeline of potential new drugs, greater personal income, and the rising health consciousness and expectations of the general public.

Despite the increasing demand for drugs, drug producers and buyers are expected to place more emphasis on cost-effectiveness, due to concerns about the cost of healthcare, including prescription drugs. Growing competition from the producers of generic drugs also may exert cost pressures on many firms in this industry. These factors, combined with continuing improvements in manufacturing processes, are expected to result in slower employment growth over the 2000-10 period than occurred during the previous 10-year period.

Faster-than-average growth is anticipated for professional occupations—especially the biological and medical scientists engaged in research and development, the backbone of the drug industry, and computer specialists such as systems analysts and computer support specialists. Faster-than-average growth also is projected for production occupations. Employment of office and administrative support workers is expected to experience average growth, as companies streamline operations and increasingly rely on computers. In an effort to streamline research and technological development costs, some drug companies have merged. As companies consolidate and grow in size, so do their marketing and sales departments. Drug firms have dramatically increased their pharmaceutical sales forces over the past several years, and this trend is likely to continue.

Unlike many other manufacturing industries, the drug industry is not highly sensitive to changes in economic conditions. Even during periods of high unemployment, work is likely to be relatively stable in this industry.

## Sources of Additional Information

For additional information about careers in drug manufacturing and the industry in general, write to the personnel departments of individual drug manufacturing companies.

For information about careers in biotechnology, contact:

➢ Biotechnology Industry Organization, Suite 1100, 1625 K St. NW., Washington, DC 20006. Internet: **http://www.bio.org**

For information on careers in drug manufacturing, contact:

➢ Pharmaceutical Research and Manufacturers of America (PHRMA), 1100 15th St. NW., Washington, DC 20005. Internet: **http://www.phrma.org**

Information on these key drug-manufacturing occupations may be found in the 2002-03 edition of the *Occupational Outlook Handbook*.

- Assemblers and fabricators
- Biological and medical scientists
- Chemists and materials scientists
- Engineers
- Inspectors, testers, sorters, samplers, and weighers
- Sales representatives, wholesale and manufacturing
- Science technicians
- Systems analysts, computer scientists, and database administrators

# Electronic Equipment Manufacturing

(SIC 357, 365, 366, 367, 381)

## SIGNIFICANT POINTS

- Rapid technological change and intense competition result in some research and development personnel working extensive overtime to meet deadlines.

- Rapid employment growth is expected in the electronic components and accessories segment of this industry, while employment in several other segments remains stable or declines.

- Professional and related personnel account for about 3 out of 10 workers, reflecting the importance of research and development.

- Employment growth among professional and related occupations is expected to outpace overall industry job growth, while employment of production workers is expected to grow more slowly than the industry workforce.

## Nature of the Industry

The electronic equipment manufacturing industry produces computers, television sets, and audio equipment, as well as a wide range of goods used for both commercial and military purposes. In addition, many electronics products or components are incorporated into other industries' products, such as cars, toys, watches, appliances, and a variety of electronic gadgets.

Products manufactured in this industry include computers and computer storage devices, such as disk drives, and computer peripheral equipment, such as printers and scanners; calculating and accounting machines, such as automated teller machines (ATMs); communications equipment, such as telephone switching equipment and cellular telephones and pagers; consumer electronics, such as television and stereo sets; and military electronics, such as radar, sonar, missile guidance systems, and electronic warfare equipment. This industry also includes the manufacture of semiconductors—silicon or computer "chips," or integrated circuits—which constitute the heart of computers and many other advanced electronic products. Two of the most significant types of computer chips are microprocessors, which make up the central processing system of computers, and memory chips, which store information.

Technological innovation characterizes this industry more than most others and, in fact, drives much of the industry's production. Many new products reflect a convergence of technologies. Such products include WebTV that allows for interactive TV viewing, hand-held devices that permit wireless Internet access, and digital cameras that store images digitally rather than recording them on film. On the horizon are many innovative products, including loudspeakers that can be heard but not seen, computers that can recognize voices, and numerous devices used to capture digitized information, such as bar code scanners and computer chips placed on humans that will eliminate the need for forms of identification and credit cards.

The electronic equipment manufacturing industry differs from other manufacturing industries in that production workers account for a much lower proportion of all workers. The unusually rapid pace of innovation and technological advancement requires a high proportion of engineering and technical workers to continually develop and produce new products. Likewise, the importance of promoting and selling the products manufactured by the various sectors of this industry requires knowledgeable marketing and sales workers. American companies manufacture and assemble many products abroad because of lower production costs and new trade agreements. However, the growing complexity of some of the most highly technical production processes—in semiconductor and electronic component manufacturing in particular—is leading to increased demand for a more highly skilled workforce in the United States.

Companies producing intermediate components and finished goods frequently cluster near each other because doing so allows easier access to recent innovations. Electronic products contain many components—and sometimes even major parts, such as integrated circuits—that often are purchased from other manufacturers. As a result of having the skilled workforce that fosters product improvement, some areas of the country have become centers of the electronics industry. The most prominent of these centers is "Silicon Valley," a concentration of integrated circuit and computer firms in California's Santa Clara valley, near San Jose. Other emerging centers are in Texas, Massachusetts, and New York. There are, however, electronics manufacturing plants throughout the country.

To a large extent, electronics manufacturing has become truly global, and it is difficult to characterize many companies and their products as American or foreign. The movement of foreign companies to manufacture some goods in the United States does not change the fact that many products are being designed in one country, manufactured in another, and assembled in a third. Highly sensitive and sophisticated products such as semiconductors and computers are being designed and manufactured in the United States, for example, but it remains likely that other parts of final products, such as the keyboards and outer casings, are made somewhere else and shipped to yet another site for final assembly.

Although some of the companies in this industry are large, most are actually small. The history of innovation in the industry explains the startup of many small firms. Some companies are involved in design or research and development (R&D), whereas others may simply manufacture components, such as computer chips, under contract for others. Often an engineer or physicist will have an innovative idea and set up a new company to develop the product. Although electronic products can be very sophisticated, it has been possible to manufacture many electronic products or components (not necessarily finished products) with a relatively small investment. Furthermore, investors often are willing to put their money behind new companies in this industry because of its history of large paybacks from some very successful companies. Success always will depend on innovation, and, although investment costs are rising, there should continue to be opportunities to develop good ideas.

The rapid pace of innovation in electronics technology makes for a constant demand for newer and faster products and applications. This demand puts a greater emphasis on research and development (R&D) than is typical in most manufacturing operations. Being the first firm to market a new or better product usually determines the success or failure of the product and, often, the company. Even for many relatively commonplace items, R&D continues to result in better, cheaper products with more desirable features. For example, a company that develops a new kind of computer chip to be used in many brands of computers can earn millions of dollars in sales until a competitor is able to copy the technology or develop a better chip. Many employees, therefore, are research scientists, engineers, and technicians, whose job it is to continually develop and improve products.

The product design process includes not only the initial design, but also development work, which ensures that the product functions properly and can be manufactured as inexpensively as possible. When a product is manufactured, the components are assembled, usually by soldering them to a printed circuit board. Often tedious, hand assembly requires both good eyesight and coordination, as many of the parts are very small. However, because of the cost and precision involved, assembly and packaging are becoming highly automated.

## Working Conditions

In general, electronics manufacturing enjoys relatively good working conditions, even for production workers. In contrast to many other manufacturing industries, production workers in this industry usually work in clean and relatively noise-free environments. Computer chips are manufactured in "clean rooms," in which the air is filtered and workers wear special garments to prevent any dust from getting into the air. A speck of dust will ruin a computer chip.

In 1999, the rates of work-related injuries and illness per 100 full-time workers were 2.7 per 100 full-time workers in computer and office equipment, 3.1 in communications equipment, 4.1 in electronic components and accessories, 5.7 in household audio and video equipment, and 2.3 in search and navigation equipment. These rates all were lower than the 6.3 average for the private sector. However, some jobs in this industry may have risks. For example, some workers who fabricate integrated circuits and other components may be exposed to potentially hazardous chemicals, and working with small parts may cause eyestrain.

Most employees work regular 40-hour weeks, but pressure to develop new products ahead of competitors may result in some research and development personnel working extensive overtime to meet deadlines. The competitive nature of the industry makes for an exciting, but sometimes stressful, work environment—especially for those in technical and managerial occupations.

## Employment

The electronic equipment manufacturing industry employed almost 1.6 million wage and salary workers in 2000 (table 1). Few workers were self-employed.

**Table 1. Distribution of wage and salary employment in electronics equipment manufacturing by industry segment, 2000**

| Industry segment | Employment (in thousands) | Percent |
|---|---|---|
| Total, electronic equipment manufacturing ... | 1,553.7 | 100.0 |
| Electronic components and accessories....... | 682.2 | 46.8 |
| Computer and office equipment .................... | 361.4 | 24.8 |
| Communications equipment ........................... | 276.2 | 18.9 |
| Search and navigation equipment................ | 154.3 | 10.6 |
| Household audio and video equipment......... | 79.6 | 5.4 |

The industry comprised about 13,000 establishments in 1997, many of which were small, employing only one or a few workers. Large establishments of 250 workers or more employed the majority—70 percent—of the industry's workforce (see chart).

## Occupations in the Industry

Given the importance of R&D to the industry, it is not surprising that a large proportion—about 3 in 10—of all workers are in professional and related occupations (table 2). About 12 percent of these are engineers—mainly *electrical and electronics engineers* and *computer hardware engineers*. These workers develop new products and devise better, more efficient production methods. Engineers may coordinate and lead teams developing new products. Others may work with customers to help them make the best use of the products. Growing numbers of *computer systems analysts* and *computer scientists* are being employed throughout the industry as both development and production methods become more computerized. Other professionals include *mathematical* and *physical scientists*, and *technical writers*.

About 6 percent of workers are *engineering technicians*, many of whom work closely with engineers. They help develop new products, work in production areas, and sometimes help customers install, maintain, and repair equipment. They also may test new products or processes to make sure everything works correctly.

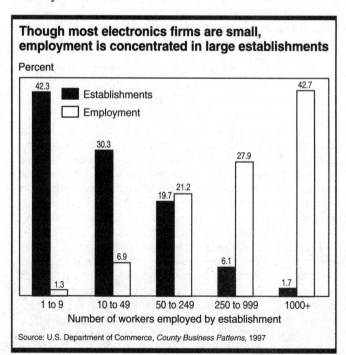

**Though most electronics firms are small, employment is concentrated in large establishments**

Percent

- Establishments
- Employment

| | 1 to 9 | 10 to 49 | 50 to 249 | 250 to 999 | 1000+ |
|---|---|---|---|---|---|
| Establishments | 42.3 | 30.3 | 19.7 | 6.1 | 1.7 |
| Employment | 1.3 | 6.9 | 21.2 | 27.9 | 42.7 |

Number of workers employed by establishment

Source: U.S. Department of Commerce, *County Business Patterns*, 1997

Despite the relatively high proportion of professional and technical workers in electronics manufacturing, almost 4 out of 10 employees are production workers. Many are assemblers, who place and solder components on circuit boards, or assemble and connect the various parts of electronic devices. *Semiconductor processors* initiate and control the many automated steps in the process of manufacturing integrated circuits or computer chips. *Electrical and electronic equipment assemblers* are responsible for putting together products, such as computers and appliances, telecommunications equipment, and even missile control systems. *Assemblers and fabricators* must be able to do accurate work at a rapid pace. Some assemblers are highly skilled and require significant experience and training to assemble major components. A skilled assembler may put together an entire subassembly, or even an entire product, especially when products are made in relatively small numbers. Other, less skilled assemblers often work on a production line, attaching one or a few parts and continually repeating the same operation. Increasingly, as production work becomes more automated, assemblers and other production workers monitor the machinery, which actually does the assembly work. *Inspectors, testers, sorters, samplers,* and *weighers* use sophisticated testing machinery to ensure that devices operate as designed.

About 13 percent of workers in the industry are in management, business, and financial operations occupations. In this industry, top management is much more likely to have a technical background than are its counterparts in other industries. This is especially true in smaller companies, which often are founded by engineers, computer scientists, or other technical professionals.

About 13 percent of workers in this industry hold office and administrative support or sales and related jobs. Sales positions require technical knowledge and abilities and, as a result, engineers and technicians often may find opportunities in sales or sales support.

## Training and Advancement

Workers with different levels of education find employment opportunities in the electronic equipment manufacturing industry. Entry to engineering occupations generally requires at least a bachelor's degree in engineering, although those with 4-year degrees in physical science or computer science or other technical areas can sometimes qualify as well. Some positions, however, may require a master's degree or higher, or relevant work experience. Computer systems analysts or scientists usually need a degree in computer science or a related field and, in many cases, they also must have considerable programming experience. Because companies often are founded by professionals with technical backgrounds, opportunities for advancement into executive or managerial positions may arise for experienced workers who keep up with rapid changes in technology and possess the business expertise necessary to succeed in the rapidly changing economy.

Training for engineering technicians is available from a number of sources. Although most employers prefer graduates of 2-year postsecondary training schools—usually technical institutes or junior colleges—training in the U.S. Armed Forces or through proprietary schools also may meet employer requirements. Engineering technicians, like engineers, should have an aptitude for math and science. Entry-level technicians may begin working with a more experienced technician or engineer. Advancement opportunities for experienced technicians may include supervisory positions or movement into other production and inspection operations.

**Table 2. Employment of wage and salary workers in electronic equipment manufacturing by occupation, 2000 and projected change, 2000-10**

(Employment in thousands)

| Occupation | Employment, 2000 Number | Employment, 2000 Percent | Percent change, 2000-2010 |
|---|---|---|---|
| **All occupations** | 1,554 | 100.0 | 6.6 |
| **Management, business, and financial occupations** | 206 | 13.3 | 6.2 |
| Engineering managers | 29 | 1.9 | -10.0 |
| General and operations managers | 16 | 1.0 | 8.3 |
| Industrial production managers | 18 | 1.2 | 5.6 |
| Purchasing agents, except wholesale, retail, and farm products | 19 | 1.2 | 5.4 |
| Accountants and auditors | 11 | 0.7 | 10.1 |
| **Professional and related occupations** | 464 | 29.9 | 11.4 |
| Computer programmers | 21 | 1.4 | -15.8 |
| Computer systems analysts | 15 | 1.0 | 24.6 |
| Computer software engineers, applications | 29 | 1.9 | 30.5 |
| Computer software engineers, systems software | 48 | 3.1 | 38.7 |
| Computer support specialists | 11 | 0.7 | 53.1 |
| Computer hardware engineers | 20 | 1.3 | 10.2 |
| Electrical engineers | 34 | 2.2 | 1.0 |
| Electronics engineers, except computer | 50 | 3.2 | 9.5 |
| Industrial engineers | 21 | 1.4 | -2.2 |
| Mechanical engineers | 16 | 1.0 | 6.4 |
| All other engineers | 29 | 1.9 | -9.2 |
| Electrical and electronic engineering technicians | 63 | 4.1 | 6.5 |
| **Sales and related occupations** | 40 | 2.6 | 6.4 |
| Sales representatives, wholesale and manufacturing, technical and scientific products | 11 | 0.7 | 0.1 |
| Sales representatives, wholesale and manufacturing, except technical and scientific products | 13 | 0.9 | 9.0 |
| **Office and administrative support occupations** | 157 | 10.1 | 2.3 |
| Bookkeeping, accounting, and auditing clerks | 11 | 0.7 | -1.3 |
| Customer service representatives | 13 | 0.8 | 11.1 |
| Production, planning, and expediting clerks | 18 | 1.1 | 11.0 |
| Shipping, receiving, and traffic clerks | 19 | 1.2 | 6.7 |
| Stock clerks and order fillers | 11 | 0.7 | 16.9 |
| Executive secretaries and administrative assistants | 22 | 1.4 | -1.0 |
| **Installation, maintenance, and repair occupations** | 44 | 2.8 | 8.3 |
| **Production occupations** | 594 | 38.2 | 4.2 |
| First-line supervisors/managers of production and operating workers | 37 | 2.4 | 6.6 |
| Coil winders, tapers, and finishers | 14 | 0.9 | 18.7 |
| Electrical and electronic equipment assemblers | 192 | 12.4 | -6.4 |
| Electromechanical equipment assemblers | 17 | 1.1 | 6.8 |
| Team assemblers | 78 | 5.0 | 3.2 |
| Inspectors, testers, sorters, samplers, and weighers | 59 | 3.8 | -6.2 |
| Semiconductor processors | 51 | 3.3 | 33.1 |
| All other production workers | 27 | 1.7 | 8.2 |

NOTE: May not add to totals due to omission of occupations with small employment.

Though assembly workers generally need only a high school diploma, assemblers in the electronics industry may need more specialized training or experience than do workers in other manufacturing industries. Precision assembly work can be extremely sophisticated and complex, and some precision assembly jobs may even require formal technical training. A 1-year certificate in semiconductor technology is good preparation for semiconductor processor operator positions; for more highly skilled technician positions, an associate degree in electronics technology or a related field is necessary. Again, advancement opportunities depend not only on work experience, but also on the level of technical training and the ability to keep up with changing technology.

## Earnings

In general, earnings in the electronics industry are high, although this is partly because many of the lower wage production jobs have been automated or exported to other countries. Average weekly earnings of all production or nonsupervisory workers in the industry were higher than the average of $474 for all industries in 2000 (table 3).

**Table 3. Average earnings of nonsupervisory workers in the electronic manufacturing industry, 2000**

| Industry segment | Weekly | Hourly |
|---|---|---|
| Total, private industry | $474 | $13.74 |
| Electronics industry | | |
| Computer and office equipment | 732 | 18.45 |
| Search and navigation equipment | 716 | 17.39 |
| Communications equipment | 590 | 14.09 |
| Electronic components and accessories | 587 | 14.11 |
| Household audio and video equipment | 498 | 12.57 |

Earnings in selected occupations in several components of the electronic equipment manufacturing in 2000 appear in table 4.

## Outlook

Wage and salary employment in electronic equipment manufacturing is projected to grow about 7 percent between 2000 and 2010, compared with 16-percent growth for the entire economy.The technological revolutions taking place in computers, semiconductors, and telecommunications should provide many employment opportunities in this industry, especially in research and development. Products of this industry, especially powerful computer chips, will continue to enhance productivity in all areas of research the economy. The electronic equipment manufacturing industry is expected to continue its rapid productivity growth, so that, even though output is expected to increase in most segments as global demand for electronics products rises, employment of production workers will not grow as quickly, and is actually expected to decline in segments.

Expected employment growth varies by industry segment (table 5). Demand for computers should remain relatively strong worldwide, yet, employment is expected to decline due to the introduction of new technology and automated manufacturing processes. This trend also should be seen in household audio and video equipment. Employment in search and navigation equipment is expected to decrease due to technology, which is automating the production of increasingly sophisticated equipment. In addition, labor-intensive manufacturing, assembly, and packaging operations still are being moved to low-wage countries in the Far East or to Mexico, when cost effective, although this strategy grows less attractive as the technical demands of manufacturing become more complex. However, the need for manufacturing to be located near the research site will help to moderate the tendency to move abroad for many segments of this industry.

Employment in electronic components and accessories, on the other hand, is expected to grow faster than the average over the projection period, more than offsetting expected declines in other segments. Despite a recent slowdown, the market for semiconductors has been growing tremendously and, as a result, the need for skilled labor has been increasing worldwide. As chips become smaller and more powerful, and production processes more sophisticated, the size of the U.S. market, coupled with the need for a strong infrastructure and highly skilled workforce, has shifted focus back to the United States in this segment of the industry.

Demand for communications equipment, such as cellular phones, should result in employment growth in this segment. Ownership of cellular phones has grown quickly in recent years; continuing improvements in quality and services should lead to even greater growth between 2000 and 2010. As cellular phones increasingly use digital technology, they will allow users to browse the Internet away from their desks. In addition, a substantial increase in band speeds for these phones will increase their attractiveness to businesses that have relied on desktop

**Table 4. Median hourly earnings of the largest occupations in electronic equipment manufacturing, 2000.**

| Occupation | Computer and office equipment | Household audio and video equipment | Communications equipment | Electronic components and accessories |
|---|---|---|---|---|
| Engineering managers | $ 51.67 | $ 43.21 | $ 46.21 | $ 47.57 |
| Computer hardware engineers | 36.41 | 27.35 | 36.34 | 32.59 |
| Industrial production managers | 36.06 | 29.62 | 34.87 | 34.21 |
| Computer software engineers, systems software | 35.87 | 33.29 | 35.20 | 36.81 |
| Computer software engineers, applications | 35.72 | 31.62 | 33.82 | 34.93 |
| Electronics engineers, except computer | 33.61 | 30.10 | 31.37 | 30.72 |
| Computer programmers | 33.24 | 27.67 | 27.65 | 30.75 |
| Electrical and electronic engineering technicians | 19.52 | 17.26 | 16.95 | 17.07 |
| Inspectors, testers, sorters, samplers, and weighers | 13.36 | 11.41 | 12.73 | 11.55 |
| Electrical and electronic equipment assemblers | 11.68 | 10.32 | 10.23 | 9.93 |
| Team assemblers | 10.36 | 8.71 | 9.45 | 9.66 |

**Table 5. Projected employment change in electronics manufacturing by industry segment, 2000-10**

| Industry segment | Percent Change |
| --- | --- |
| Total, electronic equipment manufacturing | 6.7 |
| Electronic components and accessories | 17.3 |
| Communications equipment | 5.0 |
| Computer and office equipment | -3.2 |
| Household audio and video equipment | -3.3 |
| Search and navigation equipment | -9.3 |

personal computers with their much faster speeds. However, there are some concerns as to whether or not these "wireless" applications will be able to replace conventional computers and office equipment. Also, demand for high-speed Internet access and other forms of Internet connectivity, such as routers, should result in an increase in employment in communications equipment.

Employment growth among professional and related occupations is expected to outpace industry growth. Employment of production occupations is expected to grow more slowly than that of the industry as a whole, as more jobs are lost to technological innovation. However, the numbers of semiconductor processors will grow faster than the industry average. Highly skilled technical personnel should be able to take advantage of the increasingly sophisticated level of manufacturing technology as industries become more integrated and development and manufacturing processes more advanced. Overall, employment of office and administrative support occupations also is expected to grow more slowly than the average.

The electronics industry is characterized by rapid technological advances and has grown faster than most other industries over the past 30 years, although rising capital costs and the rapid pace of innovation continue to pose challenges. Certain segments and individual companies often are subject to problems. For example, the computer industry occasionally undergoes severe downturns, and individual companies can run into trouble—even those in segments of the industry doing well—because they have not kept up with the latest technological developments or because they have erred in deciding which products to manufacture. Such uncertainties can be expected to continue. In addition, the intensity of foreign competition and the future role of imports remain difficult to project. Import competition has wiped out major parts of the domestic consumer electronics industry, and future effects of import competition are dependent on trade policies and market forces. The industry is likely to continue to encounter strong competition from imported electronic goods and components from countries throughout Asia and Europe.

As defense expenditures are expected to increase, sales of military electronics, an important segment of the industry, will likely pick up. Furthermore, firms will continue developing new products, creating large new markets as they have in the past. Smaller, more powerful computer chips are continually being developed and incorporated into an even wider array of products, and the semiconductor content of all electronic products will continue to increase. The growth of digital technology, artificial intelligence, and multimedia applications will continue to create new opportunities. Future developments will lead to a much greater convergence of products and technologies with the expansion of the Internet and demand for global information networking.

## Sources of Additional Information

For information on the electronics industry, contact:

➢ The Electronic Industries Alliance 2500 Wilson Blvd., Arlington, VA 22201. Internet: **http://www.eia.org**

➢ American Electronics Association, The Center for Workforce Excellence, 5201 Great America Pkwy., Suite 520, Santa Clara, CA 95054. Internet: **http://www.aeanet.org**

For information on careers as an electrical, electronics, or computer engineer, contact:

➢ The Institute of Electrical and Electronics Engineers, Inc., 445 Hoes Lane, Piscataway, NJ 08855-1331. Internet: **http://www.ieee.org**

For information on careers and training as an electronics technician, contact:

➢ Electronics Technicians Association, 502 North Jackson, Greencastle, IN 46135. Internet: **http://www.eta-sda.com**

Information on these occupations may be found in the 2002-03 *Occupational Outlook Handbook*:

- Systems analysts, computer scientists, and database administrators
- Computer software engineers
- Electrical and electronics engineers, except computer
- Semiconductor processors
- Engineering and natural sciences managers
- Engineering technicians
- Computer hardware engineers
- Assemblers and fabricators

# Food Processing

- The industry has a high incidence of injury and illness; meatpacking in particular has the highest incidence among all industries.

- Production workers account for nearly 1 out of 2 jobs.

- Most jobs require little formal education or training; many can be learned in a few days.

## Nature of the Industry

Workers in the food processing industry link farmers and other agricultural producers with consumers. They do this by processing raw fruits, vegetables, grains, meats, and dairy products into finished goods ready for the grocer or wholesaler to sell to households, restaurants, or institutional food services.

Food processing workers perform tasks as varied as the many foods we eat. For example, they slaughter, dress, and cut meat or poultry; process milk, cheese, and other dairy products; can and preserve fruits, vegetables, and frozen specialties; manufacture flour, cereal, pet foods, and other grain mill products; make bread, cookies, and other bakery products; manufacture sugar and candy and other confectionery products; process shortening, margarine, and other fats and oils; produce alcoholic and nonalcoholic beverages; prepare packaged seafood, coffee, potato and corn chips, and peanut butter. Although this list is long, it is not exhaustive—food processing workers also play a part in delivering numerous other food products to our tables.

Table 1 shows that about 30 percent of all food processing workers are employed in plants that produce meat products, and another 25 percent work in establishments that make bakery goods and preserved fruits and vegetables. Sugar and confectionery products, the smallest sector of the food processing industry, accounts for only about 5 percent of all jobs.

**Table 1. Employment in food processing by industry segment, 2000 and projected change, 2000-10**

(Employment in thousands)

| Industry segment | 2000 Employment | 2000-2010 Percent change |
|---|---|---|
| Total employment | 1,684 | -3.0 |
| Meat products | 504 | 7.6 |
| Preserved fruits and vegetables | 220 | -11.3 |
| Bakery products | 204 | -6.4 |
| Beverages | 187 | -12.0 |
| Miscellaneous food products | 180 | 3.0 |
| Grain mill products and fats and oils | 152 | -1.1 |
| Dairy products | 146 | -16.8 |
| Sugar and confectionery products | 92 | -7.9 |

## Working Conditions

Many production jobs in food processing involve repetitive, physically demanding work. Food processing workers are highly susceptible to repetitive strain injuries to hands, wrists, and elbows. This type of injury is especially common in meatpacking and poultry processing plants. Production workers often stand for long periods and may be required to lift heavy objects or use cutting, slicing, grinding, and other potentially dangerous tools and machines.

In 1999, there were 12.7 cases of work-related injury or illness per 100 full-time food processing workers, more than double the 6.3 rate for the private sector as a whole. Injury rates vary significantly in specific food processing industries, ranging from a low of 4.5 per 100 workers in wet corn mills to 26.7 per 100 in meatpacking plants, the highest rate among all industries.

In an effort to reduce occupational hazards, many plants have redesigned equipment, increased job rotation, allowed longer or more frequent breaks, and developed training programs in safe work practices. Some workers wear protective hats, gloves, aprons, and shoes. In many industries, uniforms and protective clothing are changed daily for sanitary reasons.

Because of the considerable mechanization in the industry, most food processing plants are noisy, with limited opportunities for interaction among workers. In some highly automated plants, "hands-on" manual work has been replaced by computers and factory automation, resulting in less waste and higher productivity. While much of the basic production—such as trimming, chopping, and sorting—will remain labor intensive for many years to come, automation is increasingly being applied to various functions, including inventory control, product movement, packing, and inspection.

Working conditions also depend on the type of food being processed. For example, some bakery employees work at night or on weekends and spend much of their shift near ovens that can be uncomfortably hot. In contrast, workers in dairies and meat processing plants work typical daylight hours and may experience cold and damp conditions. Some plants, such as those producing processed fruits and vegetables, operate on a seasonal basis, so workers are not guaranteed steady, year-round employment and occasionally travel from region to region seeking work. These plants are increasingly rare, however, as the industry continues to diversify and processing plants produce alternate foods and beverages during otherwise inactive periods.

## Employment

In 2000, the food processing industry provided nearly 1.7 million jobs. Almost all employees are wage and salary workers, but a few food processing workers are self-employed. In 1997, about 11,900 establishments processed food, more than half employing fewer than 20 workers (see chart). Nevertheless, establishments employing 100 or more workers accounted for 80 percent of all jobs.

The employment distribution in this industry is widely varied. The vast majority of employees work in the meat products sector. Employment in this sector has increased over the past 15 years. However, this industry is very dependent on technological advances and the demand for meats in the United States and abroad. The fruits and vegetables, bakery, and beverages sectors also employ a fairly large portion of industry workers, but employment in each of these areas has been declining over the same period.

Food processing workers are found in all States, although some sectors of the industry are concentrated in certain parts of the country. For example, Arkansas, Georgia, Iowa, North Carolina, and Texas employ more than a third of workers in meat-producing industries. Wisconsin has more cheese-processing workers than any other State. Similarly, most workers producing chewing gum work in Illinois and Pennsylvania. California accounts for more than x in x canned, frozen, and preserved fruit, vegetable, and food specialty workers, and together with Illinois, Pennsylvania, and New York, employs a third of all workers who produce bakery products. Employment in raw cane sugar processing is concentrated in Florida, Hawaii, and Louisiana.

## Occupations in the Industry

The food processing industry employs many different types of workers. Nearly 1 out of 2 are production workers, including skilled precision workers and less-skilled machine operators and laborers (table 2). Production jobs require manual dexterity, good hand-eye coordination, and in some sectors of the industry, strength.

Red meat production is the most labor-intensive food processing operation. Animals are not uniform in size, and *slaughterers and meatpackers* must slaughter, skin, eviscerate, and cut each carcass into large pieces. They usually do this work by hand, using large, heavy power saws. They also clean and salt hides and make sausage. *Meatcutters and trimmers* use hand tools to break down the large primary cuts into smaller

sizes for shipment to wholesalers and retailers. *Poultry trimmers and cutters* use knives and other hand tools to eviscerate, split, and bone chickens and turkeys.

*Bakers* mix and bake ingredients according to recipes to produce breads, cakes, pastries, and other goods. Bakers produce goods in large quantities, using mixing machines, ovens, and other equipment.

Many food processing workers use their hands or small hand tools to do their jobs. *Cannery workers* perform a variety of routine tasks—such as sorting, grading, washing, trimming, peeling, or slicing—in canning, freezing, or packing food products. *Hand food decorators* apply artistic touches to prepared foods. *Candy molders* and *marzipan shapers* form fancy shapes by hand.

With increasing levels of automation in the food processing industry, a growing number of workers operate machines. For example, *food batchmakers* operate equipment that mixes, blends, or cooks ingredients used in manufacturing various foods, such as cheese, candy, honey, and tomato sauce. *Dairy processing equipment operators* process milk, cream, cheese, and other dairy products. *Cutting* and *slicing machine operators* slice bacon, bread, cheese, and other foods. *Mixing* and *blending machine operators* produce dough batters, fruit juices, or spices. *Crushing* and *grinding machine operators* turn raw grains into cereals, flour, and other milled grain products, and they produce oils from nuts or seeds. *Extruding* and *forming machine operators* produce molded food and candy, and *casing finishers* and *stuffers* make sausage links and similar products. *Bottle packers* and *bottle fillers* operate machines that fill bottles and jars with beverages, preserves, pickles, and other foodstuffs.

*Cooking machine operators* steam, deep fry, boil, or pressure cook meats, grains, sugar, cheese, or vegetables. *Grain roasters* operate equipment that roasts grains, nuts, or coffee beans, and *drying machine operators* tend ovens, kilns, dryers, and other equipment that removes moisture from macaroni, coffee beans, cocoa, and grain. *Baking equipment operators* tend ovens that bake bread, pastries, and other products. Some foods—ice cream, frozen specialties, and meat, for example—are placed in freezers or refrigerators by *cooling* and *freezing equipment operators*. Other workers tend machines and equipment that clean and wash food or food processing equipment. Some machine operators also clean and maintain machines and perform other duties such as checking the weight of foods.

Many other workers are needed to keep food processing plants and equipment in good working order. *Industrial machinery mechanics* repair and maintain production machines and equipment. *Maintenance repairers* perform routine machinery maintenance, such as changing and lubricating parts. Specialized mechanics include *heating, air-conditioning* and *refrigeration technicians, farm equipment mechanics*, and *diesel engine specialists*.

Still other workers directly oversee the quality of the work and of final products. *Supervisors* direct the activities of production workers. *Graders* and *sorters* of agricultural products, *production inspectors,* and *quality control technicians* evaluate foodstuffs before, during, or after processing.

Food may spoil if not properly packaged and promptly delivered, so packaging and transportation employees play a vital role in the industry. Among these are *freight, stock,* and *material movers*, who manually move materials; *hand packers* and *packagers*, who pack bottles and other items as they come off the production line; and *machine feeders and offbearers*, who feed materials into machines and remove goods from the end of the production line. *Industrial truck* and *tractor operators* drive

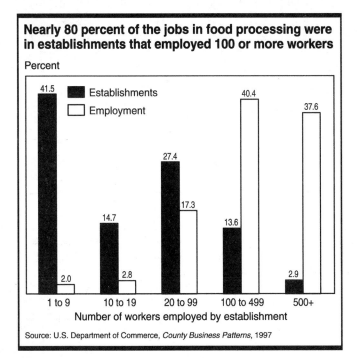

**Nearly 80 percent of the jobs in food processing were in establishments that employed 100 or more workers**

Percent

| Number of workers employed by establishment | Establishments | Employment |
|---|---|---|
| 1 to 9 | 41.5 | 2.0 |
| 10 to 19 | 14.7 | 2.8 |
| 20 to 99 | 27.4 | 17.3 |
| 100 to 499 | 13.6 | 40.4 |
| 500+ | 2.9 | 37.6 |

Source: U.S. Department of Commerce, *County Business Patterns*, 1997

gasoline or electric-powered vehicles equipped with forklifts, elevated platforms, or trailer hitches to move goods around a storage facility. *Truckdrivers* transport and deliver livestock, materials, or merchandise, and may load and unload trucks. *Driver/sales workers* drive company vehicles over established routes to deliver and sell goods, such as bakery items, beverages, and vending machine products.

The food processing industry also employs a variety of managerial and professional workers. Managers include *top executives*, who make policy decisions; *industrial production managers*, who organize, direct, and control the operation of the manufacturing plant; and *advertising, marketing, promotions, public relations* and *sales managers*, who direct advertising, sales promotion, and community relations programs.

Engineers, scientists, and technicians are becoming increasingly important as the food processing industry implements new automation. These workers include *industrial engineers,* who plan equipment layout and workflow in manufacturing plants, emphasizing efficiency and safety. Also, *mechanical engineers* plan, design, and oversee the installation of tools, equipment, and machines. *Chemists* perform tests to develop new products and maintain quality of existing products. *Computer programmers* and *systems analysts* develop computer systems and programs to support management and scientific research. Food scientists, such as *food technicians* and *technologists* and *chemical technicians*, work in research laboratories or on production lines to develop new products, test current ones, and control food quality.

Finally, many sales workers, including *manufacturers' representatives* and *demonstrators*, are needed to sell the manufactured goods to wholesale and retail establishments. *Bookkeeping* and *accounting clerks*, *procurement clerks*, and *traffic clerks* keep track of the food products going into and out of the plant. *Janitors* and *cleaners* keep buildings clean and orderly.

## Training and Advancement

Most workers in production-line food processing jobs require little formal education or training. Graduation from high school is preferred but not always required. In general, inexperienced workers start as helpers to experienced workers and learn skills on the job. Many of these entry-level jobs can be learned in a few days. Typical jobs include operating a bread-slicing machine, washing fruits and vegetables before processing begins, hauling carcasses, or packing bottles as they come off the production line. Even though it may not take long to learn to operate a piece of equipment, employees may need several years of experience to enable them to keep the equipment running smoothly, efficiently, and safely.

Some food processing workers need specialized training and education. Inspectors and quality control workers, for example, often are trained in food safety and may need a certificate to be employed in a food processing plant. Formal educational requirements for managers in food processing plants range from 2-year degrees to master's degrees. Those who hold research positions, such as food technologists and scientists, usually need a master's or doctoral degree.

In addition to specialized training, a growing number of workers receive broader training to perform a number of jobs. The need for flexibility in more-automated workplaces has meant that many food processing workers are learning new tasks and being trained to effectively work in teams.

Advancement may come in the form of higher earnings or more responsibility. Helpers usually progress to jobs as machine

**Table 1. Employment of wage and salary workers in food processing by occupation, 2000 and projected change, 2000-10**
(Employment in thousands)

| Occupation | Employment, 2000 Number | Employment, 2000 Percent | Percent change, 2000-2010 |
|---|---|---|---|
| **All occupations** | 1,684 | 100.0 | -3.0 |
| **Management, business, and financial occupations** | 102 | 6.0 | -2.2 |
| General and operations managers | 18 | 1.1 | -4.2 |
| Industrial production managers | 14 | 0.8 | -4.9 |
| **Professional and related occupations** | 38 | 2.3 | 0.3 |
| **Service occupations** | 56 | 3.3 | -2.3 |
| Janitors and cleaners, except maids and housekeeping cleaners | 30 | 1.8 | 1.4 |
| **Sales and related occupations** | 51 | 3.1 | -7.5 |
| **Office and administrative support occupations** | 131 | 7.8 | -8.5 |
| Shipping, receiving, and traffic clerks | 21 | 1.2 | -7.2 |
| **Farming, fishing, and forestry occupations** | 25 | 1.5 | 4.9 |
| **Installation, maintenance, and repair occupations** | 106 | 6.3 | -3.9 |
| Industrial machinery mechanics | 24 | 1.4 | 3.5 |
| Maintenance and repair workers, general | 42 | 2.5 | -9.7 |
| **Production occupations** | 832 | 49.4 | -1.7 |
| First-line supervisors/managers of production and operating workers | 54 | 3.2 | -6.6 |
| Team assemblers | 29 | 1.7 | -10.2 |
| Bakers | 34 | 2.0 | -1.5 |
| Meat, poultry, and fish cutters and trimmers | 115 | 6.8 | 8.6 |
| Slaughterers and meat packers | 116 | 6.9 | 2.0 |
| Food and tobacco roasting, baking, and drying machine operators and tenders | 15 | 0.9 | -8.8 |
| Food batchmakers | 58 | 3.5 | -1.1 |
| Food cooking machine operators and tenders | 29 | 1.8 | -1.7 |
| All other food processing workers | 41 | 2.4 | -15.6 |
| Mixing and blending machine setters, operators, and tenders | 24 | 1.4 | 0.8 |
| Helpers—Production workers | 52 | 3.1 | -7.7 |
| Inspectors, testers, sorters, samplers, and weighers | 24 | 1.4 | -17.6 |
| Packaging and filling machine operators and tenders | 127 | 7.5 | -1.1 |
| **Transportation and material moving occupations** | 335 | 19.9 | -4.4 |
| Driver/sales workers | 23 | 1.4 | -14.3 |
| Truck drivers, heavy and tractor-trailer | 41 | 2.4 | -2.5 |
| Industrial truck and tractor operators | 48 | 2.8 | -8.6 |
| Laborers and freight, stock, and material movers, hand | 58 | 3.4 | -8.3 |
| Machine feeders and offbearers | 15 | 0.9 | -17.2 |
| Packers and packagers, hand | 93 | 5.5 | 0.6 |

NOTE: May not add to totals due to omission of occupations with small employment.

operators, but the speed of this progression can vary considerably. Some workers who perform exceptionally well on the production line, or those with special training and experience, may advance to supervisory positions. Plant size and the existence of formal promotion tracks may influence advancement opportunities.

Requirements for other jobs are similar to requirements for the same types of jobs in other industries. Employers usually hire high school graduates for secretarial and other clerical work. Graduates of 2-year associate degree or other postsecondary programs often are sought for science technician and related positions. College graduates or highly experienced workers are preferred for middle management or professional jobs in personnel, accounting, marketing, or sales.

## Earnings

Table 3 shows that production workers in food processing averaged $12.41 an hour, compared with $13.74 per hour for all workers in private industry in 2000. Weekly earnings among food processing workers, however, were higher than average, $514 compared with $474, reflecting more hours of work. Food processing workers averaged about 41.4 hours a week, compared with only 34.5 for all workers in the private sector. Weekly earnings ranged from $425 in meat products manufacturing plants to $708 in beverages manufacturing plants. Hours worked play a large part in determining earnings. For example, fats and oils manufacturing workers, who averaged 42.0 hours a week, had higher hourly and weekly earnings than did bakery products manufacturing workers, who averaged 40.8 hours a week. Earnings in selected occupations in food processing appear in table 4.

Table 3. Average earnings of production or nonsupervisory workers in food processing by industry segment, 2000

| Industry segment | Weekly | Hourly |
|---|---|---|
| **Total, private industry** | $474 | $13.74 |
| **Food processing** | 514 | 12.41 |
| Beverages | 708 | 16.39 |
| Grain mill products | 685 | 15.26 |
| Dairy products | 606 | 14.43 |
| Sugar and confectionery products | 594 | 14.42 |
| Fats and oils | 575 | 13.68 |
| Bakery products | 534 | 13.10 |
| Preserved fruits and vegetables | 489 | 12.11 |
| Miscellaneous foods | 439 | 11.25 |
| Meat products | 425 | 10.24 |

Table 4. Median hourly earnings of the largest occupations in food processing, 2000

| Occupation | Food and kindred products | All industries |
|---|---|---|
| Industrial machinery mechanics | $16.10 | $17.30 |
| Maintenance and repair workers, general | 14.89 | 13.39 |
| Mixing and blending machine setters, operators, and tenders | 12.55 | 12.58 |
| Inspectors, testers, sorters, samplers, and weighers | 10.92 | 12.22 |
| Bakers | 10.75 | 9.48 |
| Packaging and filling machine operators and tenders | 10.51 | 9.45 |
| Food cooking machine operators and tenders | 10.47 | 9.92 |
| Food batchmakers | 10.46 | 10.09 |
| Slaughterers and meat packers | 9.34 | 9.33 |
| Meat, poultry, and fish cutters and trimmers | 7.99 | 8.06 |

In 2000, about 23.3 percent of workers in the food processing industry belonged to a union or were covered by a union contract, compared with 14.9 percent of all workers in the private sector. Prominent unions in the industry include the United Food and Commercial Workers, Teamsters, Bakery and Confectionery Workers, Grain Millers, and Distillery Workers.

## Outlook

Overall wage and salary employment in food processing is expected to decline by about 3 percent over the 2000-2010 period. Despite the rising demand for processed food products by a growing population, automation and increasing productivity are limiting the need for workers. Nevertheless, numerous job openings will arise in many segments of food processing as experienced workers transfer to other industries, retire, or leave the laborforce.

Job growth will vary by occupation but will be concentrated among food processing workers—the largest group of workers in the industry. Because many of the sorting, cutting, and chopping tasks performed by these workers have proven difficult to automate, employment among handworkers will rise along with the growing demand for food products. Handworking occupations include meat, poultry, and fish cutters and trimmers, whose employment will rise as the consumption of meat, poultry and fish climbs and more processing takes place at the manufacturing level. Other production workers also will benefit from the recent rise in the share of processing that occurs in food processing plants instead of in retail establishments.

Although automation has had little effect on most handworkers, it is having a broader impact on numerous other occupations in the industry. Fierce competition has led food processing plants to invest in technologically advanced machinery to be more productive. These machines have been applied to tasks as varied as packaging, inspection, and inventory control. As a result, employment has fallen among some machine operators, such as packaging machine operators, but has risen for industrial machinery mechanics who repair and maintain the new machinery. Computers also are being widely implemented throughout the industry, reducing employment levels of some mid-level managers and administrative support workers, but increasing the demand for workers with excellent technical skills. Taken as a whole, automation will continue to have a significant impact on workers in the industry as competition becomes even more intense in coming years.

Food processing firms will be able to use this new automation to better meet the changing demands of the American marketplace. As convenience becomes more important, consumers increasingly demand highly processed foods such as prepeeled and cut carrots and microwaveable soups or "ready-to-heat" dinners. Such a shift in consumption will contribute to the demand for food processing workers and will lead to the development of thousands of new processed foods. Domestic producers will also attempt to market these goods abroad as international trade continues to grow. The combination of growing export markets and shifting domestic consumption will help employment among food processing workers to rise slightly over the next decade and will lead to significant changes throughout the food processing industry.

## Sources of Additional Information

For information on job opportunities in food processing, contact individual manufacturers, locals of the unions listed above, and State employment service offices. Information on occupations in the industry is available from:

➤ United Food and Commercial Workers International Union, 1775 K St. NW., Washington, DC 20006. Internet: **http://www.ufcw.org**

Detailed information on many occupations in food processing, including the following, appears in the 2002-03 *Occupational Outlook Handbook*.

- Food processing occupations
- Industrial production managers
- Industrial machinery installation, repair, and maintenance workers
- Inspectors, testers, sorters, samplers, and weighers
- Material-moving occupations
- Truck drivers and driver/sales workers
- Science technicians

# Motor Vehicle and Equipment Manufacturing

## SIGNIFICANT POINTS

- Nearly one-third of all the industry's jobs are located in Michigan.

- Larger manufacturers are turning toward independent parts and component makers.

- Average earnings are very high compared with those in other industries.

- Employment is highly sensitive to cyclical swings in the economy, but generally is expected to grow.

## Nature of the Industry

The motor vehicle is an intricate series of systems, subsystems, and components assembled into a final product. Each manufactured part or component is integrated into the vehicle—none is developed to exist separately. Vehicles are constantly changing as new technology or reengineered components are incorporated, and as new and updated models are designed to keep abreast of the constantly changing tastes of buyers. Like their products, motor vehicle and equipment manufacturers are complex organizations that constantly evolve to maximize their efficiency and maintain a continuing stream of commercially viable products in a highly competitive market.

Motor vehicles play a central role in our society. Most U.S. residents rely on them every day to get to work or school, to go shopping, or to visit family and friends. Businesses depend on motor vehicles to transport people and goods. The United States is the world's largest marketplace for motor vehicles due to the size and affluence of its population. According to the U.S. Department of Transportation, more than 210 million motor vehicles—over 131 million passenger cars and 79 million trucks—were registered in the United States in 1998. The number of light trucks has shown especially steady growth since the mid- to late 1980s.

The motor vehicle and equipment manufacturing industry in the United States has become increasingly integrated into the international economy. In fact, "domestic" vehicles often are produced using the components, manufacturing plants, and distribution methods of other nations around the world, as U.S. and foreign manufacturers of motor vehicles benefit from competitive cooperation in the design, production, and distribution of vehicles and parts. Collaboration in manufacturing practices has dramatically increased productivity and improved efficiency. These cooperative practices have also caused manufacturers from the United States, Europe, and the Pacific Rim to locate production plants in the countries in which they plan to sell their vehicles, to reduce distribution time and costs. Foreign motor vehicle and parts makers with production sites in the United States are known as "transplants," and account for a growing share of U.S. production and employment.

Globalization of the industry has boosted competition among U.S. motor vehicle manufacturers, prompting innovations in product design and in the manufacturing process. One result of these product innovations is a proliferation of rapidly designed and produced new models aimed at niches in the market. Firms also must be fast and flexible in implementing new production techniques. Smaller production runs and mass customization result from attempts to reduce waste in the production cycle,

develop more adaptive production facilities, and allow customer demand to drive changes in design and marketing. Customer-driven markets force manufacturers to replace traditional assembly lines with modern systems using computers, robots, and interchangeable tools. Customized plants put resources in the right place at the right time, allowing manufacturers to change production inputs quickly and accurately.

Competition has led manufacturers to adopt innovative approaches to research and development, often in response to evolving consumer and regulatory demands. For example, demand for vehicles that can run on alternative fuels derived from batteries or solar power will put pressure on manufacturers to develop a great deal of new technology, a challenge that likely will necessitate cooperation among both domestic and foreign manufacturers.

The vehicles we drive are only a small part of the story in motor vehicle and equipment manufacturing. In 2000, about 6,500 establishments manufactured motor vehicles and equipment; these ranged from small parts plants with only a few workers to huge assembly plants that employ thousands. Table 1 shows that nearly 7 out of 10 establishments in the industry manufactured motor vehicle parts and accessories—including axles, brakes, camshafts, defrosters, engines, frames, manifolds, radiators, steering mechanisms, transmissions, and windshield wiper systems. Other establishments specialized in assembling finished motor vehicles—passenger cars, sport utility vehicles, pickup trucks and vans, heavy-duty trucks, buses, and special purpose motor vehicles ranging from limousines to garbage trucks. Still others manufacture truck trailers, motor homes, and special bodies placed on separately purchased truck or bus chassis.

Motor vehicle and equipment manufacturers have a major influence on other industries in the economy. They are major consumers of steel, rubber, plastics, glass, and other basic materials, thus creating jobs in industries that produce those materials. The production of motor vehicles also spurs employment growth in other industries, including motor vehicle dealerships, automotive repair shops, gasoline service stations, highway construction companies, and public transit companies.

## Working Conditions

In 2000, 38 percent of workers in the motor vehicle and equipment manufacturing industry worked, on average, more than 40 hours per week. Overtime is especially common during periods of peak demand. Most employees, however, typically work an 8-hour shift: either from 7:00 a.m. to 3:30 p.m. or from 4:00 p.m. to 12:30 a.m., with two breaks per shift and a half-hour for meals. A third shift often is reserved for maintenance and cleanup.

**Table 1. Percent distribution of establishments in motor vehicle and equipment manufacturing by detailed industry sector, 2000**

| Industry sector | Establishments |
|---|---|
| Total | 100.0 |
| Motor vehicle parts and accessories | 66.1 |
| Truck and bus bodies | 11.0 |
| Motor vehicles and car bodies | 12.2 |
| Truck trailers | 8.5 |
| Motor homes | 2.2 |

Although working conditions have improved in recent years, some production workers are still subject to uncomfortable conditions. Heat, fumes, noise, and repetition are not uncommon in this industry. In addition, many workers come into contact with oil and grease and may have to lift and fit heavy objects. Employees also may operate powerful, high-speed machines that can be dangerous. Accidents and injuries usually are avoided when protective equipment and clothing are worn and safety practices are observed.

Newer plants are more automated and have safer, more comfortable conditions. For example, these plants may have ergonomically designed work areas and job tasks that accommodate the worker's physical size and eliminate awkward reaching and bending and unnecessary heavy lifting. Workers may function as part of a team, doing more than one job and thus reducing the repetitiveness of assembly line work.

Workers in the motor vehicle and equipment manufacturing industry experience higher rates of injury and illness than do workers in most other industries. In 1999, cases of work-related injury and illness averaged 16.8 per 100 full-time workers in motor vehicle and equipment manufacturing, compared with 9.2 in all manufacturing industries and 6.3 in the entire private sector.

As in other industries, professional and managerial workers normally have clean, comfortable offices, and are not subject to the hazards of assembly line work. Improved ergonomics help clerical support workers avoid repetitive strain injuries, but employees using computer terminals for long periods may develop eye strain and fatigue.

## Employment

Motor vehicle and equipment manufacturing was among the largest of the manufacturing industries in 2000, providing 1.0 million jobs. The majority of jobs, 54 percent, were in firms that make motor vehicle parts and accessories. About 35 percent of workers in the industry were employed in firms assembling motor vehicles and car bodies, while 11 percent worked in firms producing truck and bus bodies, truck trailers, and motor homes.

Although motor vehicle and equipment manufacturing jobs are scattered throughout the Nation, certain States account for the greatest numbers of jobs. Michigan, for example, accounts for nearly one-third of all jobs. Combined, Michigan, Ohio, and Indiana include about half of all the jobs in this industry. Other States that account for significant numbers of jobs are California, New York, Illinois, Missouri, North Carolina, Tennessee, and Kentucky.

Employment is concentrated in a relatively small number of very large establishments. More than 51 percent of motor vehicle and equipment manufacturing jobs are in firms with over 1,000 workers (chart). Motor vehicle and car body manufacturing employment in particular is concentrated in large firms,

whereas many motor vehicle parts and accessories jobs are found in small and medium-sized firms.

Workers in motor vehicle and equipment manufacturing tend to be somewhat older than those in other industries. In 2000, the median age was 41.0 years, compared with 39.6 years for all workers.

## Occupations in the Industry

Prior to assembling components in the manufacturing plant, extensive design, engineering, testing, and production planning goes into the manufacture of motor vehicles. These tasks often require years and millions of dollars.

Using artistic talent, computers, and information on product use, marketing, materials, and production methods, *designers* create designs they hope will make the vehicle competitive in the marketplace. Designers use sketches and computer-aided design techniques to create computer models of proposed vehicles. These computer models eliminate the need for physical body mockups in the design process because they give designers complete information on how each piece of the vehicle will work with others. Workers may repeatedly modify and redesign models until the models meet engineering, production, and marketing specifications. Designers working in parts and accessory production increasingly collaborate with manufacturers in the initial design stages to integrate motor vehicle parts and accessories into the design specifications for each vehicle.

*Engineers*—the largest professional occupation in the industry—play an integral role in all stages of motor vehicle manufacturing. They oversee the building and testing of the engine, transmission, brakes, suspension, and other mechanical and electrical components. Using computers and assorted models, instruments, and tools, engineers simulate various parts of the vehicle to determine whether each part meets cost, safety, performance, and quality specifications. *Mechanical engineers* design improvements for engines, transmissions, and other working parts. *Electrical and electronics engineers* design the vehicle's electrical system, including the ignition system and accessories, and industrial robot control systems used to

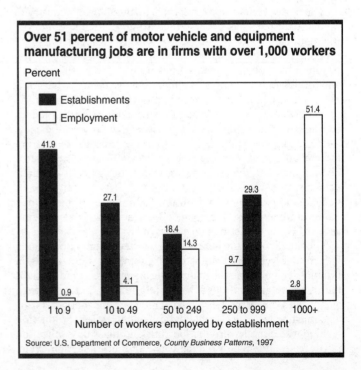

**Over 51 percent of motor vehicle and equipment manufacturing jobs are in firms with over 1,000 workers**

Percent

- ■ Establishments
- □ Employment

| Number of workers employed by establishment | Establishments | Employment |
|---|---|---|
| 1 to 9 | 41.9 | 0.9 |
| 10 to 49 | 27.1 | 4.1 |
| 50 to 249 | 18.4 | 14.3 |
| 250 to 999 | 9.7 | 29.3 |
| 1000+ | 2.8 | 51.4 |

Source: U.S. Department of Commerce, *County Business Patterns*, 1997

assemble the vehicle. *Industrial engineers* concentrate on plant layout, including the arrangement of assembly line stations, material-moving equipment, work standards, and other production matters.

Under the direction of engineers, *engineering technicians* prepare specifications for materials, devise and run tests to ensure product quality, and study ways to improve manufacturing efficiency. For example, testing may reveal how metal parts perform under conditions of heat, cold, and stress, and whether emissions control equipment meets environmental standards. Finally, prototype vehicles incorporating all the components are built and tested on test tracks, on road simulators, and in test chambers that can duplicate almost every driving condition, including crashes.

*Computer programmers* write detailed instructions for computers, and *computer systems analysts* work with computer systems to improve manufacturing efficiency. When the many details are worked out, the machinery and tools required for assembly line production of the vehicle are set in place.

*Management* workers establish guidelines for the design of motor vehicles to provide direction for the teams of experts in engineering, design, marketing, sales, finance, and production. From the earliest stages of planning and design, these specialists help to assess whether the vehicle will satisfy consumer demand, meet safety and environmental regulations, and prove economically practical to make. These executives also serve as public representatives for the company—they are the face of the company.

*Industrial production managers* oversee *first-line supervisors and managers of production and operating workers*. These supervisors oversee inspectors, precision workers, machine setters and operators, assemblers, fabricators, and plant and system operators. They coordinate a variety of manufacturing processes and production activities, including scheduling, staffing, equipment, quality control, and inventory control. For example, metal parts are welded, plastic and glass parts are molded and cut, seat cushions are sewn, and many parts are painted. Many manufacturing processes are highly automated; robots, computers, and programmable devices are an integral part of motor vehicle manufacturing. Throughout the manufacturing process, "statistical process control" (teamwork and quality control) is emphasized. From initial planning and design to final assembly, numerous tests and inspections ensure that vehicles meet quality and safety standards. Modern manufacturing facilities integrate interchangeable tools on the assembly line so that they can quickly be changed to meet the needs of various models and specifications.

*Production workers* account for more than 3 out of 5 motor vehicle and equipment manufacturing jobs (table 2). *Assemblers and fabricators* and *metal workers and plastic workers* put together various parts to form subassemblies, and then put the subassemblies together to build a complete motor vehicle. Some may perform other routine tasks such as mounting and inflating tires; adjusting brakes; and adding gas, oil, brake fluid, and coolant. Although robots perform most of the welding, *welding, soldering, and brazing workers* still are needed for some welding and for maintenance and repair duties. *Machinists* produce precision metal parts that are made in numbers too small to produce with automated machinery. *Tool and die makers* produce tools, dies, and special guiding and holding devices used in machines. *Computer-controlled machine tool operators* use computer-controlled machines or robots that can be programmed to manufacture parts of different dimensions automatically.

Table 2. Employment of wage and salary workers in motor vehicle and equipment manufacturing by occupation, 2000 and projected change, 2000-10

(Employment in thousands)

| Occupation | Employment, 2000 Number | Employment, 2000 Percent | Percent change, 2000-2010 |
|---|---|---|---|
| All occupations | 1,013 | 100.0 | 8.6 |
| **Management, business, and financial occupations** | 73 | 7.2 | 12.7 |
| Industrial production managers | 9 | 0.9 | 9.7 |
| **Professional and related occupations** | 110 | 10.9 | 9.6 |
| Industrial engineers | 14 | 1.4 | 2.4 |
| Mechanical engineers | 10 | 1.0 | 11.5 |
| Engineering technicians, except drafters | 7 | 0.7 | 10.4 |
| **Service occupations** | 7 | 0.7 | 16.3 |
| **Sales and related occupations** | 12 | 1.1 | 7.9 |
| **Office and administrative support occupations** | 52 | 5.2 | 7.1 |
| Shipping, receiving, and traffic clerks | 9 | 0.9 | 8.0 |
| **Construction and extraction occupations** | 25 | 2.4 | 23.9 |
| Electricians | 14 | 1.3 | 29.7 |
| **Installation, maintenance, and repair occupations** | 60 | 5.9 | 10.1 |
| Industrial machinery mechanics | 10 | 1.0 | 17.9 |
| Maintenance and repair workers, general | 21 | 2.1 | 4.7 |
| **Production occupations** | 629 | 62.1 | 7.2 |
| First-line supervisors/managers of production and operating workers | 29 | 2.8 | 6.1 |
| Engine and other machine assemblers | 25 | 2.5 | 7.8 |
| Team assemblers | 170 | 16.8 | 6.1 |
| All other assemblers and fabricators | 74 | 7.3 | 6.1 |
| Computer-controlled machine tool operators, metal and plastic | 11 | 1.1 | 18.6 |
| Cutting, punching, and press machine setters, operators, and tenders, metal and plastic | 21 | 2.1 | -5.7 |
| Machinists | 14 | 1.4 | 8.5 |
| Multiple machine tool setters, operators, and tenders, metal and plastic | 15 | 1.5 | 17.6 |
| Tool and die makers | 13 | 1.3 | 6.1 |
| Welders, cutters, solderers, and brazers | 35 | 3.4 | 17.9 |
| Welding, soldering, and brazing machine setters, operators, and tenders | 10 | 1.0 | 17.9 |
| Helpers—Production workers | 8 | 0.8 | 8.1 |
| Inspectors, testers, sorters, samplers, and weighers | 29 | 2.9 | -5.7 |
| Painters, transportation equipment | 10 | 1.0 | 17.9 |
| **Transportation and material moving occupations** | 45 | 4.5 | 9.6 |
| Industrial truck and tractor operators | 14 | 1.4 | 8.8 |
| Laborers and freight, stock, and material movers, hand | 13 | 1.3 | 6.1 |

NOTE: May not add to totals due to omission of occupations with small employment.

Workers in other production occupations—who run various machines that produce the array of motor vehicle bodies and parts—account for almost 10 percent of jobs in the industry. These workers set up and operate machines and make adjustments according to their instructions. In computer-controlled systems, they monitor computers that control the machine processes and may have little interaction with the machinery or materials. Some workers specialize in one type of machine; others operate more than one type.

*Grinding and polishing workers* use handtools or hand-held power tools to sand and polish metal surfaces, and *painting workers* paint surfaces of motor vehicles. *Sewing machine operators* sew together pieces of material to form seat covers and other parts.

Throughout the manufacturing process, *inspectors, testers, sorters, samplers, and weighers* ensure that motor vehicles and parts meet quality standards. They inspect raw materials, check parts for defects, check the uniformity of subassemblies, and test drive vehicles. *Helpers* supply or hold materials or tools, and clean work areas and equipment.

Keeping the plant running smoothly requires motor vehicle operators and material-moving workers. *Industrial truck and tractor operators* carry materials and equipment around and between factories, warehouses, and outdoor storage areas. *Truckdrivers* carry raw materials to plants, equipment and materials between plants, and finished motor vehicles to dealerships for sale to consumers. *Laborers and hand freight, stock, and material movers* manually move materials to and from storage areas, loading docks, delivery vehicles, and containers. *Machine feeders* and *offbearers* feed materials into, or remove materials from, machines or equipment on the assembly line, and *hand packers and packagers* manually package or wrap materials.

Workers in construction, installation, maintenance, and repair occupations account for 1 out of 12 jobs in the motor vehicle and equipment manufacturing industry. These skilled workers set up, maintain, and repair equipment. *Electricians* service complex electrical equipment. *Pipelayers, plumbers, pipefitters, and steamfitters* install and repair piping, valves, pumps, and compressors. *Industrial machinery mechanics* and *machinery maintenance workers* maintain machinery and equipment to prevent costly breakdowns and, when necessary, perform repairs. *Millwrights* install and move machinery and heavy equipment according to the factory's layout plans. *Vehicle and mobile equipment mechanics, installers, and repairers* repair bodies, engines, and other parts of motor vehicles, industrial trucks, and other mobile heavy equipment.

## Training and Advancement

Faced with technological advances and the continued need to cut costs, manufacturers increasingly emphasize continuing education and cross-train many workers—that is, they train workers to do more than one job. This has led to a change in the profile of the industry's workers. Standards for new hires are much higher now than in the past. Employers increasingly require at least a high school diploma as the number of unskilled jobs declines. Manual dexterity will continue to be necessary for many production jobs, but employers also look for employees with good communication and math skills, as well as an aptitude for computers, problem-solving and critical thinking. Because many plants now emphasize the team approach, employees interact more with coworkers and supervisors to determine the best way to get the job done. They are expected to work with much less supervision than in the past and to be responsible for ensuring that their work conforms to guidelines.

Opportunities for training and advancement vary considerably by occupation, plant size, and sector. Training programs in larger auto and light truck assembly plants usually are more extensive than those in smaller parts and accessories, truck trailer, and motor home factories. Production workers receive most of their training on the job or through more formal apprenticeship programs. Training normally takes from a few days to several months and may combine classroom with on-the-job training under the guidance of more experienced workers. Attaining the highest level of skill in some production jobs requires several years, however. Training often includes courses in health and safety, teamwork, and quality control. With advanced training and experience, production workers can advance to inspector or more skilled production, craft, operator, or repair jobs.

Skilled production workers—such as tool and die makers, millwrights, machinists, pipefitters, and electricians—normally are hired on the basis of previous experience and, in some cases, a competitive examination. Alternatively, the company may train inexperienced workers in apprenticeship programs that last up to 5 years, and combine on-the-job training with classroom instruction. Typical courses include mechanical drawing, tool designing and programming, blueprint reading, shop mathematics, hydraulics, and electronics. Training also includes courses on health and safety, teamwork, quality control, computers, and diagnostic equipment. With training and experience, workers who excel can advance to become supervisors or managers.

Motor vehicle manufacturers provide formal training opportunities to all workers, regardless of educational background. Manufacturers offer some classes themselves and pay tuition for workers who enroll in colleges, trade schools, or technical institutes. Workers sometimes can get college credit for training received on the job. Subjects of company training courses range from communication skills to computer science. Formal educational opportunities at postsecondary institutions range from courses in English, basic mathematics, electronics, and computer programming languages to work-study programs leading to associate, bachelor's, and graduate degrees in engineering and technician specialties, management, and other fields.

## Earnings

Average weekly earnings of production or nonsupervisory workers in the motor vehicle and equipment manufacturing industry are relatively high. In 2000, workers in the industry earned $865 per week, compared with $597 for workers in all manufacturing industries, and $474 for those in the entire private sector. At $1,093 per week, earnings of production workers in establishments that manufacture complete motor vehicles and car bodies were among the highest in the Nation. Workers in establishments that make motor vehicle parts and accessories averaged $795 weekly; those in truck and bus body manufacturing earned $679, while truck trailer manufacturing workers earned $502. Earnings in selected occupations in motor vehicle and equipment manufacturing appear in table 3.

These hourly earnings may increase during overtime or special shifts. Workers generally are paid 1-1/2 times their normal wage rate for working more than 8 hours a day or 40 hours a week, or for working on Saturdays. They may receive double their normal wage rate for working on Sundays and holidays. The largest manufacturers and suppliers often offer other benefits, including paid vacations and holidays; life, accident, and health insurance; education allowances; nonwage cash payment plans, such as performance and profit-sharing bonuses; and pension plans. Some laid-off workers in the motor vehicle and equipment manufacturing industry have access to supplemental unemployment benefits, which can provide them with nearly full pay and benefits for up to 3 years, depending on the worker's seniority.

In 2000, 36.7 percent of workers in motor vehicle and equipment production were union members or were covered by union

**Table 3. Median hourly earnings of the largest occupations in motor vehicle and equipment manufacturing, 2000**

| Occupation | Motor vehicles and equipment | All industries |
|---|---|---|
| Industrial engineers ....................................... | $ 30.29 | $ 28.16 |
| Electricians ..................................................... | 26.71 | 19.29 |
| Tool and die makers ....................................... | 25.76 | 19.76 |
| First-line supervisors/managers of production and operating workers ........... | 22.26 | 19.39 |
| Multiple machine tool setters, operators, and tenders, metal and plastic ................. | 22.09 | 12.96 |
| Inspectors, testers, sorters, samplers, and weighers ............................................. | 21.50 | 12.22 |
| Maintenance and repair workers, general ..... | 21.11 | 13.39 |
| Engine and other machine assemblers ......... | 14.39 | 13.47 |
| Welders, cutters, solderers, and brazers ...... | 13.43 | 13.13 |
| Team assemblers ........................................... | 13.15 | 10.32 |

contracts, compared with 14.9 percent of workers throughout private industry. Unionization rates are higher in motor vehicle production than in parts and accessories producers. The primary union in the industry is the United Automobile, Aerospace, and Agricultural Implement Workers of America, also known as the United Auto Workers (UAW). Nearly all production workers in motor vehicle assembly plants, and most in motor vehicle parts plants, are covered by collective bargaining agreements negotiated by the UAW. Other unions—including the International Association of Machinists and Aerospace Workers of America, the United Steelworkers of America, and the International Brotherhood of Electrical Workers—cover certain plant locations or specified trades in the industry.

## Outlook

Employment in the motor vehicle and equipment manufacturing industry is expected to increase 9 percent over the 2000-10 period. In addition to job openings due to growth, the need to replace workers who transfer to jobs in other industries or retire will also generate job openings. A substantial number of job openings is expected from this source because more than one-third of the motor vehicle manufacturing workforce is over 44 years of age and positioned to retire in the near future.

Not all the workers who retire or transfer to other occupations will be replaced, and many of the new workers will be hired for occupations different from those vacated by departing employees. Employment in the motor vehicle and equipment manufacturing industry is expected to grow with demand for motor vehicles and parts, but jobs will be lost due to downsizing and productivity increases. The growing intensity of international and domestic competition has increased cost pressures on manufacturers. In response, they have sought to improve productivity and quality through the application of high-technology production techniques, including robots, computers, and programmable equipment. Increasing productivity should mostly offset the increasing output of the motor vehicle and equipment manufacturing industry, resulting in slow job growth. In addition, the industry is increasingly turning to contract employees in an effort to reduce costs. Contract workers are less costly to hire and lay off than permanent employees; contract jobs also serve as a screening tool for candidates for permanent jobs that are more complex and require more skills.

Growth in demand for domestically manufactured motor vehicles could be limited by a number of factors. A slowdown in the growth of the driving-age population, as the smaller post baby-boom generation comes of age may curb demand for cars

and trucks. Also, foreign motor vehicle and parts producers will continue to control a substantial share of the U.S. market and, should they increasingly meet demand with imported vehicles and parts instead of products manufactured in U.S. transplant factories, domestic motor vehicle and parts output would be lower. Other factors that may limit growth of domestic motor vehicle production include improvements in vehicle quality and durability, which extend longevity, and more stringent safety and environmental regulations, which increase the cost of producing and operating motor vehicles.

Employment in motor vehicle and equipment manufacturing is highly sensitive to cyclical swings in the economy. A 10- to 20-percent change in employment from one year to the next is not unusual. During periods of economic prosperity, consumers are more willing and able to purchase expensive goods such as motor vehicles, which may require large down payments and extended loan payments. During recessions, however, consumers are more likely to delay such purchases. Motor vehicle manufacturers respond to these changes in demand by hiring or laying off workers.

Expanding factory automation, robotics, efficiency gains, and the need to cut costs are expected to keep employment from growing as fast as output. The movement towards efficiency and automation will force employment declines in machine setter, operator, and tender occupations. Employment of office and administrative support workers will grow slowly due to expanding office and warehouse automation. Automation and continued global competition, however, are expected to produce job growth for engineers, industrial production managers, business operations specialists, and computer specialists. These workers will increasingly be relied upon for further innovation in reducing costs and enhancing competitive advantage.

## Sources of Additional Information

Information on employment and training opportunities in the motor vehicle and equipment manufacturing industry is available from local offices of the State employment service, employment offices of motor vehicle and equipment manufacturing firms, and locals of the unions mentioned above.

Detailed information on most occupations in this industry, including the following, appears in the 2002-03 *Occupational Outlook Handbook:*

- Designers
- Drafters
- Electricians
- Engineers
- Engineering technicians
- Industrial machinery installation, repair, and maintenance workers
- Industrial production managers
- Inspectors, testers, sorters, samplers, and weighers
- Machine setters, operators, and tenders—metal and plastic
- Machinists
- Material moving occupations
- Material recording, scheduling, dispatching, and distributing occupations, except postal workers
- Mechanical engineers
- Painting and coating workers, except construction and maintenance
- Tool and die makers
- Welding, soldering, and brazing workers

71

# Printing and Publishing

## SIGNIFICANT POINTS

- Twenty-four percent of the jobs in the industry were in managerial and professional occupations, a higher proportion than in any other manufacturing industry.

- Most firms are small, employing fewer than 10 people.

- Computerization is changing or eliminating occupations, resulting in a slight decline in projected employment.

## Nature of the Industry

The printing and publishing industry produces items ranging from newspapers, magazines, and books to brochures, labels, newsletters, postcards, memo pads, business order forms, checks, maps, and even T-shirts.

This industry includes a number of segments (table 1). Commercial printing establishments, which print newspaper inserts, catalogs, pamphlets, and advertisements, make up the largest segment of the industry, accounting for 36 percent of employment and 50 percent of total establishments. Newspapers are the next largest sector, with 29 percent of industry employment. The greeting card segment is the smallest, accounting for only 2 percent of employment and less than 1 percent of total establishments.

Printing and publishing is a large industry composed of many shops which vary in size. Almost 7 of every 10 printing shops employ 10 or fewer workers (see chart). These small printing shops often are referred to as "job shops," because what they print is determined by the needs of their customers.

There are five printing methods that use plates or some other form of image carrier— lithography, letterpress, flexography, gravure, and screen-printing. Plateless or nonimpact processes, such as electronic, electrostatic, or inkjet printing, are mainly used for copying, duplicating, and specialty printing, usually in quick or in-house print shops.

Lithography, which uses the basic principle that water repels oil, remains the dominant printing process in the industry. Lithography lends itself to computer composition and the economical use of color, accounting for its dominance. In the future, flexography and gravure are expected to be more widely used. Flexography produces vibrant colors with little ruboff, qualities valued for newspapers, directories, and books, which are its biggest markets. Gravure's high-quality reproduction, flexible pagination and formats, and consistent print quality has won it a significant share of packaging and product printing and a growing share of periodical printing. In response to environmental concerns, printers increasingly use alcohol-free solutions, water-based inks, and recycled paper.

The printing industry, like many other industries, continues undergoing technological change, as computers and technology alter the manner in which work is performed. Many of the processes that were once done by hand are becoming more automated. Technology's influence can be seen in all three stages of printing: *prepress*, preparation of materials for printing; *press*, the actual printing process; and *postpress* or *finishing*, the folding, binding, and trimming of printed sheets into final form. The most notable changes have occurred in the prepress stage. Instead of cutting and pasting articles by hand, entire publications

Table 1. Establishments and wage and salary employment in printing and publishing by detailed industry, 2000

| Industry segment | Establishments | Employment |
|---|---|---|
| **Total** | 100.0 | 100.0 |
| **Printing** | 59.3 | 48.5 |
| Commercial printing | 50.1 | 36.3 |
| Blankbooks and bookbinding | 2.5 | 3.8 |
| Book printing | 0.9 | 2.5 |
| Manifold business forms | 1.4 | 2.8 |
| Typesetting | 2.3 | 1.2 |
| Platemeking services | 2.0 | 1.9 |
| **Publishing** | 40.7 | 51.1 |
| Newspapers | 15.3 | 28.6 |
| Periodicals | 10.7 | 9.1 |
| Book publishing | 5.3 | 5.6 |
| Miscellaneous publishing | 9.0 | 6.2 |
| Greeting cards | 0.3 | 1.6 |

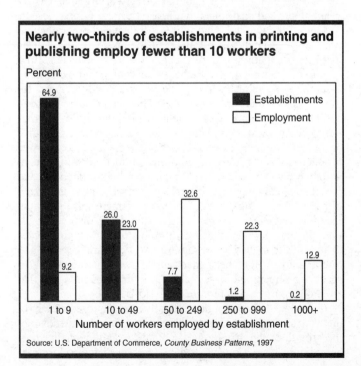

**Nearly two-thirds of establishments in printing and publishing employ fewer than 10 workers**

Percent

| Number of workers employed by establishment | Establishments | Employment |
|---|---|---|
| 1 to 9 | 64.9 | 9.2 |
| 10 to 49 | 26.0 | 23.0 |
| 50 to 249 | 7.7 | 32.6 |
| 250 to 999 | 1.2 | 22.3 |
| 1000+ | 0.2 | 12.9 |

Source: U.S. Department of Commerce, *County Business Patterns*, 1997

now are produced on a computer, complete with artwork and graphics. Columns can be displayed and arranged on the computer screen exactly as they will appear in print, and then printed. Nearly all prepress work is expected to be computerized by 2010, and workers will need more training in electronics, computers, and mathematics.

Many segments of the publishing industry produce their products electronically. For example, many periodicals, books, and promotional materials can be found on the Internet, on CD-ROM, and on audio and videotapes. This expansion into nonprint media is expected to continue as the Internet heralds a new era in the printing and publishing industry. Individuals now design their own work on the Internet and, consequently, have a reader base of millions. As a result, the market for the design and development of Internet pages and publications is growing significantly.

## Working Conditions

The average nonsupervisory worker in the printing and publishing industry worked 38.1 hours per week in 2000, compared with 41.5 hours per week across all manufacturing industries. Workers in the industry generally put in an 8-hour day, but overtime often is required to meet publication deadlines. Some employees, particularly those employed by newspapers, work nights, weekends, and holidays. Larger companies tend to have shiftwork. There is a fair amount of flexibility with shift schedules and overtime options, which are largely based on seniority.

Working conditions vary by occupation. For example, press operators work in noisy environments and often wear ear protectors. On the other hand, typesetters and compositors usually work in quiet, clean, air-conditioned offices. Most printing work involves dealing with fine detail, which can be tiring both mentally and physically. Fortunately, with the advanced technology in machinery, there is not as much strain on the eyes as in the past.

Even with more safety enhanced machinery, some workers still are subject to occupational hazards. Platemakers, for example, may work with toxic chemicals that can cause skin irritations, and press operators work with rapidly moving machinery that can cause injuries. In 1999, work-related injuries and illnesses were 5.0 per 100 full-time workers, much lower than the 9.2 percent rate for manufacturing as a whole. Blankbooks, such as ledgers and notebooks, and bookbinding had the highest incidence of injury and illness, with 6.3 cases per 100 full-time employees. In recent years, however, working conditions have become less hazardous as the industry has become more automated. Also, companies are using fewer chemicals and solutions than in the past and are experiencing fewer equipment-related accidents.

## Employment

In 2000, the printing and publishing industry had about 1.5 million wage and salary jobs, in addition to 76,000 self-employed workers, ranking it among the largest manufacturing industries. Nearly two-thirds of wage and salary jobs were in establishments employing fewer than 10 workers (see chart); nearly 70 percent were in the two largest sectors—commercial printing and newspapers (table 1). Printing plants are widely dispersed throughout the country; however, more specialized types of printing tend to be regionally concentrated. For example, financial printing is concentrated in New York City.

## Occupations in the Industry

Printing and publishing occupations range from writers, editors, and sales workers to specialized production occupations rarely found in other industries (table 2). The printing sectors that perform press preparation or printing and binding work, such as commercial printing plants, blankbook and bookbinding shops, and printing trade services, account for the majority of specialized printing occupations.

Specialized printing occupations comprise 23 percent of industry employment and are located in the prepress, press, and binding or postpress stages of printing. Almost all jobs in the printing industry require at least a high school education. Additional training and cross training is becoming increasingly necessary as the industry continues to automate. It often is beneficial to receive training in mathematics, electronics, and computers.

Prepress technicians and workers—including *typesetting* and *composing machine operators*, and *photoengraving* and *lithographic machine operators*—prepare material for printing presses. Included among their tasks are composing text, designing page layout, photographing text and pictures, and making printing plates. *Precision compositors* and *typesetters* set up and arrange type by hand or by computer into a galley for printing. *Job printers* set type according to copy, read proof copy for errors and clarity, and correct mistakes. *Desktop publishers*, using computer software, format and combine text, numerical data, photographs, charts, and other visual graphic elements to produce publication-ready material. Depending on the nature of a particular project, desktop publishers may write and edit text, create graphics to accompany text, convert photographs and drawings into digital images and then manipulate those images, design page layouts, typeset and do color separation, and translate electronic information onto film or other traditional forms for production.

Traditionally, *camera operators*—who are classified as line camera operators, halftone operators, or color separation photographers—start the process of making a lithographic plate by photographing and developing negatives of the material to be printed. *Scanner operators* employ electronic or computerized scanning equipment to produce and screen film separations of photographs or art to use in lithographic printing plates. Operators review all work and adjust the equipment if they need to make corrections to the original. *Lithographic dot etchers* retouch negatives by sharpening or reshaping the images on the negatives. They work by hand, using chemicals, dyes, and special tools. *Film strippers* cut the film to required size and arrange and tape the pieces of negatives onto "flats," or layout sheets, used to make press plates. *Platemakers* produce printing plates by exposing sensitized metal sheets to special light through a photographic negative. Some platemakers operate machines that process the plates automatically. In letterpress and gravure printing, *photoengravers* photograph copy, develop negatives, and prepare photosensitized metal plates for use.

When the material is ready, *printing machine operators* install and adjust the printing plate, mix fountain solution, adjust pressure, ink the presses, load paper, and adjust the presses to paper size. Operators also must correct any problems that might occur during a press run.

Technology is rapidly changing the nature of many traditional press and prepress occupations. Manual film handling is quickly becoming the exception rather than the rule. Typesetters, platemakers, paste up workers, and film strippers are being replaced with workers who have mastered desktop publishing and the electronic aspects of the various printing processes. While a camera negative was used in the past to produce plates of images, those images are increasingly being recorded by computerized photographic devices.

**Table 2. Employment of wage and salary workers in printing and publishing by occupation, 2000 and projected change, 2000-10**

(Employment in thousands)

| Occupation | Employment, 2000 Number | Employment, 2000 Percent | Percent change, 2000-2010 |
|---|---|---|---|
| **All occupations** | 1,547 | 100.0 | -0.2 |
| **Management, business, and financial occupations** | 147 | 9.5 | 2.3 |
| Marketing and sales managers | 16 | 1.0 | 14.8 |
| General and operations managers | 35 | 2.3 | -2.3 |
| Business operations specialists | 22 | 1.4 | 1.6 |
| **Professional and related occupations** | 224 | 14.5 | 12.8 |
| Computer specialists | 32 | 2.1 | 25.4 |
| Graphic designers | 36 | 2.3 | 6.3 |
| News analysts, reporters and correspondents | 41 | 2.6 | -4.4 |
| Editors | 62 | 4.0 | 25.4 |
| Writers and authors | 12 | 0.8 | 19.0 |
| **Sales and related occupations** | 152 | 9.8 | 3.5 |
| Advertising sales agents | 51 | 3.3 | 14.2 |
| Sales representatives, wholesale and manufacturing, except technical and scientific products | 43 | 2.8 | -6.9 |
| Telemarketers | 21 | 1.3 | 5.4 |
| **Office and administrative support occupations** | 344 | 22.2 | -3.8 |
| Customer service representatives | 52 | 3.3 | 1.0 |
| Production, planning, and expediting clerks | 14 | 0.9 | 0.0 |
| Shipping, receiving, and traffic clerks | 22 | 1.5 | -5.2 |
| Data entry and information processing workers | 13 | 0.9 | -25.9 |
| Desktop publishers | 26 | 1.7 | 54.6 |
| Office clerks, general | 29 | 1.9 | -1.0 |
| Executive secretaries and administrative assistants | 16 | 1.0 | -5.0 |
| **Installation, maintenance, and repair occupations** | 20 | 1.3 | -5.1 |
| **Production occupations** | 506 | 32.7 | -3.7 |
| First-line supervisors/managers of production and operating workers | 39 | 2.5 | -8.3 |
| Bindery workers | 81 | 5.2 | 2.5 |
| Job printers | 42 | 2.7 | 6.7 |
| Prepress technicians and workers | 85 | 5.5 | -19.0 |
| Printing machine operators | 126 | 8.1 | 1.9 |
| All other printing workers | 19 | 1.2 | -8.1 |
| Cutting and slicing machine setters, operators, and tenders | 14 | 0.9 | -3.0 |
| Helpers—Production workers | 31 | 2.0 | -6.1 |
| Paper goods machine setters, operators, and tenders | 11 | 0.7 | -6.5 |
| **Transportation and material moving occupations** | 140 | 9.1 | -5.1 |
| Laborers and freight, stock, and material movers, hand | 31 | 2.0 | -7.4 |
| Machine feeders and offbearers | 26 | 1.7 | -18.7 |
| Packers and packagers, hand | 29 | 1.9 | 4.2 |

NOTE: May not add to totals due to omission of occupations with small employment.

Pre-flight technicians examine and edit the work of desktop publishers. They ensure that the design, format, settings, quality and all other aspects of the automated desktop work are acceptable, and the finished product is completed according to the client's specifications before it is delivered.

During the binding or postpress stage, the printed sheets are transformed into products such as books, catalogs, magazines, or directories. *Bookbinders* assemble books from large, flat, printed sheets of paper. They cut, saw, and glue parts to bind new books and perform other finishing operations, such as decorating and lettering, often using handtools.

A small number of bookbinders work in hand binderies. These highly skilled workers design original or special bindings for publications with limited editions, or restore and rebind rare books. In many shops, *bindery workers* do much of the work. They fasten sheets or signatures together using a machine stapler and feed signatures into various machines for stitching, folding, or gluing.

In addition to these specialized printing occupations, office and administrative support workers, marketing and sales workers, professional and related occupations, and management, business, and financial operations workers also are employed in significant numbers in the printing and publishing industry. One occupation becoming more common is customer service representative, who tracks the various processes of production and acts as liaison between clients and technicians. The representative ensures the customer's satisfaction with the timely delivery of a high-quality product.

Establishments engaged in publishing newspapers, periodcals, books, and other miscellaneous items employ the greatest numbers of professional and related occupations, particularly reporters, writers, editors, artists, and sales occupations. These positions usually require a college education.

*News analysts, reporters,* and *correspondents* gather information and prepare stories that inform us about local, State, National, and international events. They collect and analyze facts about events by interview, investigation, or observation and write stories for newspapers and magazines. *Writers* develop fiction and nonfiction for books, magazines, trade journals, and newspapers. *Editors* supervise writers and select, plan, and prepare the contents of books, magazines, or newspapers. *Graphic designers* use a variety of print and film media to create and execute art that meets a client's needs. They increasingly use computers to lay out and test various designs, patterns, and colors before printing a final design. Finally, *sales workers* promote and sell a printer's or publisher's product.

## Training and Advancement

Workers enter the industry with various educational backgrounds. In general, job applicants must be high school graduates with mathematical, verbal, and written communication skills, and be computer literate.

Helpers generally have a high school or vocational school background, and management trainees may have a college background. Formal graphic arts programs, offered by community and junior colleges and some 4-year colleges, provide an introduction to the industry. Training in desktop publishing is particularly useful. Bachelor's degree programs in graphic arts prepare persons who may want to enter management, and 2-year programs provide technical skills. A bachelor's degree in journalism, communications, or English provides a good background for those wishing to become reporters or writers. Experience on school newspapers and internships with news organizations are also beneficial.

As the industry continues to become more computerized, most workers will need a working knowledge of computers. Courses in electronics and computer technology are beneficial for anyone entering the industry, and some employers will offer tuition assistance or continuing education classes.

In the past, apprenticeships were quite common for specialized printing occupations. Now, workers usually are trained informally on the job. Hand bookbinders are one exception. These workers usually need a 4-year apprenticeship to learn the craft of restoring rare books and producing valuable collector items.

The length of on-the-job training needed to learn skills varies by occupation and shop. For example, press operators begin as helpers and advance to press operators after years of training. Bindery workers begin by doing simple tasks such as moving paper from cutting machines to folding machines. Workers learn how to operate more complicated machinery within a few months. Training often is given under the close supervision of an experienced or senior employee. Through experience and training, workers may advance to more responsible positions. Workers usually begin as helpers, advance to skilled craft jobs, and eventually may be promoted to supervisor. Reporters and writers may advance to editors or supervising reporters.

Opportunities for advancement depend on the specific plant or shop. Technological changes will continue to introduce new types of computerized equipment or dictate new work procedures. Workers with computer and mechanical aptitude are especially in demand, so proper training or retraining will be essential to careers in printing and publishing.

## Earnings

In 2000, average weekly earnings for production workers in the printing and publishing industry were $545, compared with $597 for all production workers in manufacturing. Weekly wages in the printing and publishing industry can vary significantly by sector, ranging from $442 in blankbooks and bookbinding, to $696 in printing trade services.

The principal union in this industry is the Graphic Communications International Union. About 8.6 percent of employees are union members or are covered by a union contract, compared with 14.9 percent of workers throughout the economy, but this proportion varies greatly from city to city.

**Table 3. Median hourly earnings of the largest occupations in printing and publishing, 2000**

| Occupation | Printing and publishing | All industries |
|---|---|---|
| Editors | $18.55 | $18.93 |
| Printing machine operators | 14.94 | 13.57 |
| Advertising sales agents | 14.94 | 17.24 |
| Graphic designers | 14.86 | 16.62 |
| Prepress technicians and workers | 14.82 | 14.57 |
| Job printers | 14.30 | 13.61 |
| Desktop publishers | 14.26 | 14.71 |
| Customer service representatives | 13.21 | 11.83 |
| News analysts, reporters and correspondents | 13.11 | 14.00 |
| Bindery workers | 10.54 | 10.05 |

## Outlook

Wage and salary employment in the printing and publishing industry is projected to decline very slightly—less than 1 percent—over the 2000-10 period, compared with the 16 percent growth projected for the economy as a whole. This decline reflects competition from nonprint media, such as the Internet, and increasing computerization of printing processes. Nonetheless, predictions that computers will turn us into a paperless society have not yet come true. The printing industry will continue to supply products for education, business, and leisure for a long time to come. Although technological innovation and automation, mergers and acquisitions of small to medium-size printing firms, and partnering services offered among printing firms will result in fewer jobs, certain sectors of the industry will experience growth.

Employment in printing trade services is expected to decline because more companies are preparing printing and post-press in-house. Employment in newspapers also is expected to decline as more people choose to receive their news from non-print sources. Newspapers also will continue to face strong competition for advertising dollars from direct-mail advertising, which targets specific types of consumers in a more cost-effective manner. Many newspapers are responding by featuring specialized products and services for specific segments of the population. Employment in commercial printing and business forms companies is projected to decline as digital-printing technology allows more work to be produced in-house. Declining employment in blankbooks and bookbinding firms also reflects increasing productivity as binding operations become more mechanized.

Eleven percent growth, however, is expected in periodicals, spurred by increasing interest in professional, scientific, and technical journals, as well as special interest publications, such as health and fitness magazines. Similarly, employment in book publishing and greeting cards also should experience relatively slow growth, spurred by an increasing and aging population. Employment in miscellaneous publishing is expected to grow as the popularity of catalogs and mail order shopping fuel this sector. However, increased paper costs, consumer preferences, and the growth of online catalogs will result in fewer jobs than in past years.

Employment growth will differ among the various occupations in the printing and publishing industry, largely due to technological advances. Processes currently performed manually will be automated in the future, causing a shift from craft occupations to related occupations that perform the same function using electronic equipment. For example, employment of desktop publishing specialists is expected to increase much faster than the average for all occupations over the 2000-10 period as the elements of print production, including layout, design, and printing, increasingly are performed electronically. In contrast, demand for prepress technicians and workers who perform these tasks manually, including paste-up workers, photoengravers, camera operators, film strippers, and platemakers, is expected to decline. Job printers, however, are expected to experience growth as some firms contract out typesetting and composition work to small shops, where job printers are primarily employed. In response to the growth in electronic printing, employment of press operators is expected to grow very little, as are bookbinders and bindery workers.

New technology and equipment will require workers to update their skills to remain competitive in the job market. For example, paste-up workers will have to learn how to lay out pages using a computer. The concepts and principles behind page layout and design are the same, but the workers will have to learn how to perform their work using different tools. As the industry continues to modernize and delivery of content takes on new forms, a greater diversity of workers will be needed, including engineers, marketing specialists, graphic artists, and computer specialists. Workers who develop content—writers and editors, reporters and correspondents, photographers, artists, and designers—as well as those who sell advertising, are less likely to be affected by advances in printing technology and competition from nonprint media such as the Internet. In fact, because Web site content is updated more often than that in print media, employment requirements may increase for workers who develop content.

## Sources of Additional Information

Information on apprenticeships and other training opportunities may be obtained from local employers such as newspapers and printing shops, local offices of the Graphic Communications International Union, local affiliates of the Printing Industries of America, or local offices of the State employment service.

For general information on careers and training programs in printing, contact:

➢ Bindery Industries Association, 70 East Lake St., #300, Chicago, IL 60601.

➢ Graphic Communications Council, 1899 Preston White Dr., Reston, VA 20191.
  Internet: **http://www.npes.org/edcouncil/index.htm**

➢ Graphic Arts Technical Foundation, 200 Deer Run Rd., Sewickley, PA 15143.
  Internet: **http://www.gatf.org**

➢ Graphic Communications International Union, 1900 L St. NW., Washington, DC 20036. Internet: **http://www.gciu.org**

➢ National Association of Printers and Lithographers, 75 W. Century Rd., Paramus, NJ 07652.
  Internet: **http://www.napl.org**

➢ Printing Industries of America, 100 Daingerfield Rd., Alexandria, VA 22314. Internet: **http://www.gain.org/servlet/gateway/PIA_GATF/non_index.html**

Information on most occupations in the printing and publishing industry, including the following, may be found in the 2002-03 *Occupational Outlook Handbook*:

- Artists and related workers
- Bookbinders and bindery workers
- Desktop publishers
- News analysts, reporters, and correspondents
- Prepress technicians and workers
- Printing machine operators
- Writers and editors

# Steel Manufacturing

(SIC 331)

SIGNIFICANT POINTS

- Employment is expected to continue to decline.

- Opportunities will be best for adaptable individuals with technical skills and training in complex manufacturing processes.

## Nature of the Industry

Faced with international competition and a complex global market, the United States steel industry responded by modernizing manufacturing processes to increase productivity. Despite successful efforts to reduce costs and an improving competitive position, steel manufacturing firms still face stiff competition—and employment is expected to continue to decline. However, investment in modern equipment and worker training has transformed the U.S. steel industry from one of the Nation's most moribund to one of the world's leaders in worker productivity and lowest cost producer for some types of steel.

Establishments in this industry smelt and refine metals from iron ore and scrap. The molten metal output is solidified into semifinished shapes before it is rolled, drawn, and extruded to make sheet, rod, bar, tubing, and wire.

New investment has sparked fundamental changes in the nature of this industry. The most significant change is the development of the electric arc furnace (EAF), sometimes called the "minimill," which converts scrap metal from many sources—such as old bridges, refrigerators, and automobiles—into steel. The term "minimill" originated from the relatively small size of these mills when they first appeared, compared with traditional integrated mills. Today, many EAFs or minimills are larger than integrated mills producing steel from raw materials. The smaller initial capital investment required to start and operate an EAF has helped drive its growth. Moreover, scrap metal is found in all parts of the country, so EAFs are not tied as closely to raw material deposits as are integrated mills and can locate closer to consumers. EAFs now comprise about half of American steel production and their share is expected to continue to grow in coming years.

The growth of EAFs comes partly at the expense of integrated mills. Integrated mills reduce iron ore to molten pig iron in blast furnaces. The iron is then sent to the oxygen furnace, where it is combined with scrap to make molten steel. The steel produced by integrated mills generally is considered to be of higher quality than steel from EAFs but, because more steps are involved in the production process, it also is more costly. The initial step in the integrated mill process is to prepare coal for use in a blast furnace by converting it to coke. Coal is heated in coke ovens to remove impurities and to reduce it to nearly pure carbon.

At the other end of the steel manufacturing process, semifinished steel from either EAFs or integrated mills is converted into finished products. Some of the goods produced in finishing mills are steel wire, pipe, bars, rods, and sheets. Products also may be coated with chemicals, paints, or other metals that give the steel desired characteristics for various industries and consumers. Also involved in steel manufacturing are firms that produce alloys, by adding materials like silicon and manga-

nese to the steel. Varying the amounts of carbon and other elements contained in the final product can produce thousands of different types of steel, each with specific properties suited for a particular use.

For workers, modernization of integrated and EAF steel mills often has meant learning new skills to operate sophisticated equipment. Competition also has resulted in increasing specialization of steel production, as various producers attempt to capture different niches in the market. With these changes has come a growing emphasis on flexibility and adaptability for both workers and production technology. As international and domestic competition continue for U.S. steel producers, the nature of the industry and the jobs of its workers are expected to continue to change.

## Working Conditions

Steel mills evoke images of strenuous, hot, and potentially dangerous work. While many dangerous and difficult jobs remain in the steel industry, modern equipment and facilities have helped to change this. The most strenuous tasks were among the first to be automated. For example, computer-controlled machinery helps to monitor and move iron and steel through the production processes, reducing the need for heavy labor. In some cases, workers now monitor and control the equipment from air-conditioned rooms.

Nevertheless, large machinery and molten metal can be hazardous, unless safety procedures are observed. Hard hats, safety shoes, protective glasses, earplugs, and protective clothing are required in most production areas.

Cases of occupational injury and illness in the industry were 9.6 per 100 full-time workers in 1999, higher than the 6.3 cases per 100 workers for the entire private sector and slightly higher than the 9.2 cases per 100 for all manufacturing.

The expense of plant and machinery and significant production startup costs force most mills to operate around the clock. Workers averaged 44.7 hours per week in 2000, and only about 5 percent of workers are employed part time. Night and weekend shifts are common, as is overtime work during peak production periods.

## Employment

Employment in the steel industry declined to about 225,000 wage and salary jobs in 2000, less than half its 1980 level. The rate of decline, however, has slowed in recent years. The steel industry traditionally has been located in the eastern and midwestern regions of the country, where iron ore, coal, or one of the other natural resources required for steel are found. Even today, about 47 percent of all steelworkers are employed in Pennsylvania, Ohio, and Indiana. The growth of EAFs has

77

allowed steelmaking to spread to virtually all parts of the country, although many firms find lower cost rural areas the most attractive. Large firms employ most workers in the steel industry. More than 9 out of 10 work in establishments employing at least 50 workers, and almost half work in establishments employing 1,000 or more persons (chart 1).

## Occupations in the Industry

Opportunities exist in a variety of occupations, but the largest group of workers—45 percent—are employed in production occupations (table 1). Installation, maintenance, repair, and construction workers accounted for about 18 percent of jobs; and transportation and material-moving workers accounted for about 16 percent. About 20 percent of jobs were in managerial, professional, sales, and administrative support occupations.

Although the steel making procedure varies with the type of furnace used, the jobs associated with the various processes are similar. At integrated mills, production begins when *material-moving workers* load iron ore, coke, and limestone into the top of a blast furnace. As the materials are heated, a chemical reaction frees the iron from other elements in the ore. *Metal-refining furnace operators and tenders*, also known as *blowers* and *melters*, direct the overall operation of the furnace to melt and refine metal before casting or to produce specific types of steel. They gather information on the characteristics of the raw materials they will use and the type and quality of steel they are expected to produce. They direct the loading of the furnace with raw materials and supervise the taking of samples, to ensure that the steel has the desired qualities. They may also coordinate the loading and melting of raw materials with the steel molding or casting operation to avoid delays in production.

Generally, either a basic oxygen or an electric arc furnace is used to make steel. Operators and tenders use controls to tilt the furnace to receive the raw materials. Once they have righted the furnace, they use levers and buttons to control the flow of oxygen and other materials into the furnace. During the production process, assistants routinely take samples to be analyzed. Based on this analysis, operators determine how much

longer they must process the steel or what materials they must add to meet specifications. Operators also pay close attention to conditions within the furnace and correct any problems that arise during the production process.

Traditionally, liquid steel was moved from the furnaces into a ladle from which it was poured into ingots. Steel producers now use a process known as "continuous casting" almost exclusively. Continuous casting allows firms to produce steel ready for the next step in processing directly from liquid steel, thus eliminating many of the steps involved in pouring and rolling ingots. *Metal pourers and casters* tend machines that release the molten steel from the ladle into water-cooled molds at a controlled rate where it solidifies into semifinished shapes. These shapes are then cut to desired lengths, as they emerge from the caster. During this process, operators monitor the flow of raw steel and the supply of water to the mold.

The "rolling" method shapes most steel processed in steel mills. In this method, hot steel is squeezed between two cylinders, or "rollers," which flatten or shape the steel. *Rolling machine setters, operators, and tenders* operate the rolling mills that produce the finished product; the quality of the product and the speed at which the work is completed depend on the roller's skills. Placing the steel and positioning the rollers are very important, for they control the product's final shape. Improperly adjusted equipment may damage the rolling mill or gears.

*Extruding and drawing machine setters, operators, and tenders* operate equipment to extrude or draw metal materials into tubes, rods, hoses, wire, bars, or structural shapes. *Cutting, punching, and press machine setters, operators, and tenders* operate machines to saw, cut, shear, slit, punch, crimp, notch, bend, or straighten metal. *Welding, soldering, and brazing workers* join metal components or fill holes, indentations or seams of fabricated metal products. *Multiple machine tool setters, operators, and tenders* operate more than one type of cutting or forming machine tool or robot.

*Team assemblers and leaders* work as part of a team responsible for assembling an entire product or component of a product. Team assemblers can perform all tasks conducted by the team in the assembly process and rotate through all or most of them rather than being assigned to a specific task on a permanent basis. They may participate in making management decisions affecting the work. *Machinists* operate a variety of machine tools to produce precision parts and instruments. They may fabricate and modify parts to make or repair machine tools or maintain industrial machines. *Inspectors, testers, sorters, samplers, and weighers* check parts or products for defects, wear, and deviations from specifications.

*Millwrights* are employed to install and maintain much of the sophisticated machinery in steel mills. As the technology becomes more advanced, they work more closely with *electricians*, who help repair and install electrical equipment like computer controls for machine tools.

With more sophisticated technology and demands for specialized products, *computer specialists, engineers, and engineering technicians* have a significant role in the steel industry. For example, *industrial engineers* design, test, and evaluate integrated systems for managing production including quality control, inventory control, logistics and material flow, cost analysis, and production coordination.

## Training and Advancement

Many jobs in steel manufacturing require only a high school diploma. However, as machinery becomes more complex, employers

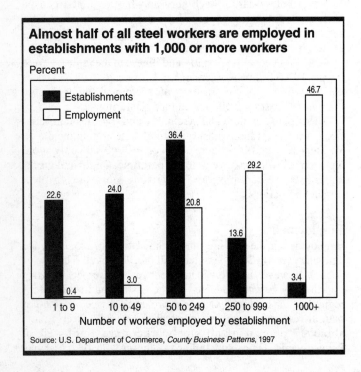

**Almost half of all steel workers are employed in establishments with 1,000 or more workers**

Percent

■ Establishments
□ Employment

| | 1 to 9 | 10 to 49 | 50 to 249 | 250 to 999 | 1000+ |
|---|---|---|---|---|---|
| Establishments | 22.6 | 24.0 | 36.4 | 13.6 | 3.4 |
| Employment | 0.4 | 3.0 | 20.8 | 29.2 | 46.7 |

Number of workers employed by establishment

Source: U.S. Department of Commerce, *County Business Patterns*, 1997

**Table 1. Employment of wage and salary workers in steel manufacturing by occupation, 2000 and projected change, 2000-10**

(Employment in thousands)

| Occupation | Employment, 2000 Number | Percent | Percent change, 2000-2010 |
|---|---|---|---|
| **All occupations** | 225 | 100.0 | -21.6 |
| **Management, business, and financial occupations** | 14 | 6.1 | -18.5 |
| General and operations managers | 2 | 1.1 | -20.3 |
| Industrial production managers | 2 | 0.8 | -21.5 |
| **Professional and related occupations** | 11 | 4.8 | -17.0 |
| Computer specialists | 2 | 0.8 | 1.8 |
| Industrial engineers, including health and safety | 2 | 0.7 | -24.6 |
| Drafters, engineering, and mapping technicians | 3 | 1.2 | -18.0 |
| **Service occupations** | 2 | 1.0 | -18.9 |
| **Sales and related occupations** | 3 | 1.2 | -23.8 |
| Sales representatives, wholesale and manufacturing, except technical and scientific products | 2 | 0.9 | -24.0 |
| Office and administrative support occupations | 17 | 7.6 | -22.7 |
| Secretaries, administrative assistants, and other office support occupations | 4 | 1.7 | -25.8 |
| **Construction and extraction occupations** | 9 | 4.1 | -12.7 |
| Electricians | 4 | 1.8 | -7.1 |
| **Installation, maintenance, and repair occupations** | 31 | 13.9 | -21.8 |
| First-line supervisors/managers of mechanics, installers, and repairers | 3 | 1.2 | -15.6 |
| Industrial machinery mechanics | 4 | 1.7 | -15.6 |
| Maintenance and repair workers, general | 9 | 3.9 | -25.0 |
| Millwrights | 5 | 2.0 | -35.5 |
| **Production occupations** | 102 | 45.3 | -23.1 |
| First-line supervisors/managers of production and operating workers | 10 | 4.4 | -24.0 |
| Team assemblers | 3 | 1.5 | -24.0 |
| Cutting, punching, and press machine setters, operators, and tenders, metal and plastic | 10 | 4.6 | -32.5 |
| Extruding and drawing machine setters, operators, and tenders, metal and plastic | 7 | 3.1 | -21.5 |
| Machinists | 3 | 1.5 | -22.3 |
| Metal-refining furnace operators and tenders | 3 | 1.4 | -8.3 |
| Pourers and casters, metal | 3 | 1.1 | -15.6 |
| Multiple machine tool setters, operators, and tenders, metal and plastic | 3 | 1.3 | -15.8 |
| Rolling machine setters, operators, and tenders, metal and plastic | 10 | 4.6 | -24.0 |
| Welders, cutters, solderers, and brazers | 4 | 1.8 | -15.6 |
| Inspectors, testers, sorters, samplers, and weighers | 4 | 2.0 | -32.5 |
| **Transportation and material moving occupations** | 36 | 15.9 | -21.7 |
| Crane and tower operators | 8 | 3.7 | -19.1 |
| Laborers and freight, stock, and material movers, hand | 9 | 3.9 | -24.0 |

NOTE: May not add to totals due to omission of occupations with small employment.

increasingly prefer to hire graduates from formal postsecondary technical and trade schools for highly skilled operating positions.

After production workers are hired, they receive specific training on the job. New workers entering the production process as lower skilled operators and maintenance personnel generally assist more experienced workers, beginning with relatively simple tasks. As workers acquire experience, they specialize in a particular process and acquire greater skill in that area. The time required to become a skilled worker depends upon individual abilities, acquired skills, and available job openings. It generally takes at least 2 to 5 years, and sometimes longer, to advance to a skilled position. At times, workers change their specialization to increase their opportunities for advancement. Workers are continuously trained to perform a variety of tasks and provide more flexibility to the firm, as company needs change. Computers have become important, as companies have modernized. Workers must learn to operate computers and other advanced equipment.

To work as an engineer, scientist, or in some other technical occupations in the steel industry, a college education is necessary. Many workers in administrative and managerial occupations have degrees in business or possess a combination of technical and business degrees. A master's degree may give an applicant an advantage in getting hired or help an employee advance. Managers need strong problem-solving, planning, and supervisory skills.

## Earnings

Earnings in the steel industry vary by occupation and experience but are higher than average earnings in private industry. Average weekly earnings of nonsupervisory production workers in 2000 were $870 in the steel industry, compared with $597 in all manufacturing and $474 throughout private industry. Weekly earnings in blast furnaces and steel mills, at $967, were significantly higher than those in steel pipes and tubes, at $645. Earnings in selected occupations in steel manufacturing appear in table 2.

**Table 2. Median hourly earnings of the largest occupations in steel manufacturing, 2000**

| Occupation | Blast furnace and basic steel products | All industries |
|---|---|---|
| First-line supervisors/managers of production and operating workers | $ 22.25 | $ 19.39 |
| Industrial machinery mechanics | 18.96 | 17.30 |
| Millwrights | 18.85 | 19.33 |
| Maintenance and repair workers, general | 16.81 | 13.39 |
| Crane and tower operators | 16.30 | 15.89 |
| Rolling machine setters, operators, and tenders, metal and plastic | 14.98 | 12.85 |
| Welders, cutters, solderers, and brazers | 13.51 | 13.13 |
| Extruding and drawing machine setters, operators, and tenders, metal and plastic | 13.36 | 11.66 |
| Cutting, punching, and press machine setters, operators, and tenders, metal and plastic | 12.88 | 11.03 |
| Laborers and freight, stock, and material movers, hand | 12.67 | 9.04 |

Union membership, geographic location, and plant size affect earnings and benefits of workers. In most firms, earnings or bonuses are linked to output. Workers receive standard benefits, including health insurance, paid vacation, and pension plans.

The iron and steel industry traditionally has been highly unionized. In 2000, 40.3 percent of steel workers were covered by union contracts, compared with 16.2 percent in durable goods manufacturing and 14.9 percent in all industries. In some instances, companies are closed shops—that is, workers must belong to the union in order to work there. EAFs, though, typically are nonunion. The overall decline of employment in traditional integrated steel mills and the growth of EAFs, together, have caused union membership to decline in recent years.

## Outlook

Employment in the steel industry is expected to decline by about 22 percent over the 2000-10 period, primarily due to increased use of labor-saving technologies and machinery. Other factors affecting employment in the industry include foreign trade, overall economic conditions, growth of EAFs, and environmental regulations. Despite the continuing decline in employment, qualified workers still will be needed to replace workers who retire or leave the industry. In production occupations, opportunities will be best for individuals with the technical skills and training to handle technologically advanced machinery.

Employment levels in coming years will be greatly affected by the ability of steel makers located in the United States to compete with imports from abroad. Worker productivity has increased in U.S. firms in recent years, leaving the domestic steel industry better able to compete with imports. The unintended consequence of productivity gains and growing foreign competition has been a glut of steel on the international market. Overcapacity stemming from increased output and slowing demand for steel has reduced the market price of steel to all-time lows. Many American steel producers complain that these low prices are the result of unfair competition from abroad and that foreign producers subsidize their operations through government intervention. This "dumping" of steel in the U.S. market puts further pressure on domestic producers to decrease costs and increase productivity. Efforts currently are underway to improve trade relations in steel and help provide security for a historically significant domestic industry. If successful, the most efficient American firms could take advantage of an increasingly attractive trade market that will result in export opportunities. It also would hasten the demise of inefficient plants trying to compete with low-priced imports.

Employment in the steel industry varies with overall economic conditions and the demand for goods produced with steel. For example, as the automotive industry produces more cars and light trucks, it will purchase more steel. In this way, much of the demand for steel is derived from the demand for other products. Other industries that are significant users of steel include structural metal products, motor vehicle parts and equipment, and household appliances. As many of these goods require a large outlay, consumers are more likely to purchase them in good economic times.

Steel companies, like most businesses, have entered the era of sophisticated technology. Taking several forms, this technology has improved both product quality and worker productivity. Computers are essential to most technological advances in steel production, from production scheduling and machine control to metallurgical analysis. Computerized systems change the nature of many jobs, while they eliminate or reduce the demand for others. For example, computers allow one worker to perform duties that previously took the efforts of several workers. However, computer-controlled equipment often requires operators to have greater skills. Hence, workers who are comfortable with computers and other high-tech equipment—as well as those willing and able to learn—will be more widely sought after by employers. This automation will contribute to better opportunities for engineers and other professionals, while causing significant declines for lower skilled machine operators and inspectors.

Environmental issues also have affected the steel industry. Past decades have seen technological changes spurred by environmental emission regulations. Emission standards, under the present Clean Air Act, will likely result in costly modifications or shutdowns in many coal-processing facilities that employ a dirty, heavily polluting process. Necessary furnace modifications will require major investments and increase the overall cost of production for coke-producing plants. These modifications are, therefore, likely to raise costs in integrated mills that use coke to produce steel.

The emergence of EAFs is perhaps the most important factor in transforming the steel industry. This trend will continue in the foreseeable future, as EAFs dominate the new capacity expected to begin operation in the next few years. Integrated mills are expected to maintain a major share of the market in higher grade steel and are also entering areas like residential construction, but EAFs will continue to account for a larger share of the international steel market. Growth of EAFs is driven by many factors, including relatively low startup costs, flexibility, and the ability to locate close to the consumer. This is especially important in the construction industry. Because the scrap steel they need to operate is widely available, EAFs have provided job opportunities in the steel industry in additional geographic areas. However, because they generally have higher worker productivity, as EAFs capture more of the domestic steel market, fewer workers will be employed to meet the existing demand for steel products.

## Sources of Additional Information

For additional information about careers and training in the steel industry, contact:

➢ American Iron and Steel Institute, 1101 17th St. NW., Suite 1300, Washington, DC 20036-4700.
Internet: **http://www.steel.org**

➢ Steel Manufacturers Association, 1150 Connecticut Ave., NW., Suite 715, Washington, DC 20036.
Internet: **http://www.steelnet.org**

Information on the following occupations may be found in the 2002-03 *Occupational Outlook Handbook*:

- Assemblers and fabricators
- Electricians
- Engineering technicians
- Engineers
- Industrial machinery installation, repair, and maintenance workers
- Inspectors, testers, sorters, samplers, and weighers
- Machine setters, operators, and tenders—metal and plastic
- Machinists
- Material-moving occupations

# Textile Mill Products

(SIC 22)

## SIGNIFICANT POINTS

- About 3 out of 5 jobs are in three States—North Carolina, South Carolina, and Georgia.

- Production workers account for more than 3 out of 5 jobs.

- Employment is expected to decline, due to technological advances and an open trading environment.

- Average earnings are low.

## Nature of the Industry

Textile mills make yarn and fabric for clothing and many other items that keep us warm, safe, and in style. Although most people associate textiles with cloth for apparel, the industry also manufactures such products as carpeting, towels, cord and twine, automotive upholstery, reinforcing materials, bulletproof vests, and decorative braids and ribbons.

A textile mill takes natural and synthetic fibers, such as cotton and polyester, and blends them to create yarn and fabric used in the production of finished products like clothing and upholstered furniture. A few products—sheets, towels, and hosiery, for example—are ready for the retail market when they leave the textile mill. Although a large share of textile products is used in the production of apparel, nontraditional uses, such as in highway construction and the manufacture of fire resistant housing panels, are growing rapidly.

Textile mills are classified by type of product or process. The major processes of textile production include yarn spinning, weaving, knitting, and tufting. Some textiles are "nonwoven" and are produced by fusing fibers with heat or bonding fibers by using a type of glue. Two or more of these processes often can be found in the same facility. For example, one mill may spin yarn and also weave it into fabric.

*Weaving, finishing, yarn, and thread mills* employed more than half of all workers in the industry. Workers in weaving mills use looms to transform yarns into cloth, a process that has been known for centuries. Looms weave or interlace two yarns, so they cross each other at right angles to form fabric. Although modern looms are complex, automated machinery, the principle remains the same as in ancient times.

Yarns are strands of fibers in a form ready for weaving, knitting, or otherwise intertwining to form a textile fabric. They form the basis for most textile production and commonly are made of cotton, wool, or synthetic fiber. Yarns also can be made of thin strips of plastic, paper, or metal. To produce spun yarn, natural fibers, such as cotton and wool, must first be processed to remove impurities and give products the desired texture and durability, as well as other characteristics. After this initial cleaning stage, the fibers are spun into yarn.

*Knitting* is another method of transforming yarn into fabric. Knitting interlocks a series of loops of one or more yarns to form familiar goods, such as sweaters. However, unlike the knitting done with hand-held needles, knitting in the textile industry is performed on automated machines. Many consumer items, such as socks, panty hose, and underwear, are produced from knitted fabric. Knitting mills account for one-fourth of employment in the industry.

*Tufting*, used by carpeting and rug mills, is a process by which a cluster of soft yarns is drawn through a backing fabric. These yarns project from the backing's surface in the form of cut yarns or loops to form the familiar texture of many carpets and rugs. Tufting mills employ about 12 percent of textile workers.

Finally, *nonwoven textile products* are produced by fusing fibers or bonding fibers with a cementing medium or heat. A familiar example of a nonwoven fabric is felt. This segment of the industry is among the fastest growing, because of the medical and sanitary uses for its products.

Regardless of the process used, mills in the textile industry are rapidly modernizing, as new investments in automation and information technology have been made necessary by growing domestic and international competition. Firms also have responded to competition by developing new products and services. For example, some manufacturers are producing textiles developed from fibers made from recycled materials. These innovations have had a wide effect across the industry. Advanced machinery is boosting productivity levels in textiles, costing some workers their jobs, while fundamentally changing the nature of work for others. New technology also has led to broad and increasingly technical training for workers throughout the industry.

The emphasis in the industry continues to shift from mass production to flexible manufacturing, as textile mills aim to supply customized markets. Firms are concentrating on systems that allow small quantities to be produced with minimum leadtime. This flexibility brings consumer goods to retailers significantly faster than before. Information technology allows the retail industry to rapidly assess its needs and communicate them back through the apparel manufacturer to textile firms.

## Working Conditions

Working conditions vary greatly. Production workers, including front-line managers and supervisors, spend most of their shift on or near the production floor. Some factories are noisy and can have airborne fibers and odors; but most modern textile facilities are relatively clean, well lit, and ventilated.

In 1999, work-related injuries and illnesses in the textile mill products industry averaged 6.4 per 100 full-time workers, compared with 9.2 percent for all manufacturing and 6.3 percent for the entire private sector. This record has been achieved in part by requiring, when appropriate, the use of protective shoes, clothing, facemasks, and earplugs. Also, new machinery is designed with additional protection, such as noise shields. Still, many workers in production occupations must stand for long periods while bending over machinery, and noise and dust still are a problem in some plants. Some workers are occasionally

81

exposed to the fumes and odors of coolants and lubricants used in machines. Quality control inspectors may endure some stress on the job because of tensions resulting when they inspect for problems.

Because many mills run 24 hours a day, production workers may work evenings and weekends. Many operators work on rotating schedules, which can cause sleep disorders and other stress from constant changes in work hours. Production workers in textile mills averaged 4.3 overtime hours per week in 2000. Overtime is common for these workers during periods of peak production. Managerial and administrative support personnel typically work a 5-day, 40-hour week in an office setting, although some of these employees also may significant overtime.

## Employment

Most of the 529,000 wage and salary workers employed in textile mills in 2000 were found in southeastern States. North Carolina accounted for about 27 percent of textile jobs. South Carolina and Georgia combined to provide employment for another 32 percent of the workers in this industry. The remaining jobs primarily were found in other areas of the South, California, and the Northeast.

Most textile production is concentrated in large mills. In fact, establishments employing more than 250 persons accounted for almost 60 percent of all textile workers (chart).

## Occupations in the Industry

The textile industry offers employment opportunities in a variety of occupations, but production occupations accounted for almost 65 percent of all jobs. Some of these production occupations are unique to the industry. (See table 1.) Additional opportunities also exist in material-moving, administrative support, maintenance, repair, management, and professional occupations. The industry also employs a small number of workers in service and sales occupations.

Many workers enter the textile industry as *machine setters and operators*, the largest occupational group in the industry. They are responsible for setting each machine and monitoring

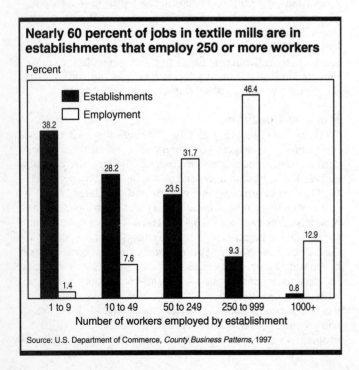

### Nearly 60 percent of jobs in textile mills are in establishments that employ 250 or more workers

Percent

- Establishments
- Employment

| | 1 to 9 | 10 to 49 | 50 to 249 | 250 to 999 | 1000+ |
|---|---|---|---|---|---|
| Establishments | 38.2 | 28.2 | 23.5 | 9.3 | 0.8 |
| Employment | 1.4 | 7.6 | 31.7 | 46.4 | 12.9 |

Number of workers employed by establishment

Source: U.S. Department of Commerce, *County Business Patterns*, 1997

its operation. Usually, operators work with one type of less complex machine, but they can advance to jobs operating more sophisticated machinery or several machines simultaneously. They often specialize in a particular type of machine. For example, experienced operators may work with machinery that processes raw cotton, spins fibers into thread, or weaves fabric. Additionally, they must diagnose problems when the machinery stops and restart it as soon as possible, to reduce costly machine idle time. Traditionally, operators tended a small number of machines; however, as production processes have become more automated, the number of machines each operator monitors has increased. *Team assemblers* perform all of the assembly tasks assigned to their teams, rotating through the different tasks, rather than specializing in a single task. They also may decide how the work is to be assigned and how different tasks are to be performed.

Skilled production occupations also include *inspectors, testers, sorters, samplers, and weighers*, who use precision measuring instruments and complex testing equipment to detect product defects, wear, or deviations from specifications. Among installation, maintenance, and repair occupations, *industrial machinery mechanics* account for about 3 percent of industry employment.

Plant workers who do not operate or maintain equipment mostly perform a variety of other material-moving tasks. Some drive industrial trucks or tractors to move materials around the plant, load and unload trucks and railroad cars, or package products and materials by hand.

*Engineers and engineering technicians*, although a vital part of the textile industry, account for less than 1 percent of employment in the industry. Some engineers are *textile engineers*, who specialize in the design of textile machinery, the study of fibers, and textile production. The industry also employs other types of engineers, particularly *industrial* and *mechanical engineers*.

## Training and Advancement

As the textile industry becomes increasingly automated, production workers need to be prepared. A high school diploma may be necessary for many entry-level positions, and extensive postsecondary training is required for more technical jobs. This training may be obtained at technical schools and community colleges. More and more often, job applicants are screened through the use of tests, to ensure that they have the necessary skills.

Extensive on-the-job training has become an integral part of working in today's textile mills. This training may be provided by experienced workers at the firm or by outside contractors and vendors. Technical training is designed to help workers understand complex, automated machinery, recognize problems, and restart machinery when the problem is solved. Installation, maintenance, and repair workers, such as industrial machinery mechanics, also require extensive training, often through a combination of classroom and apprenticeship programs. Training may help experienced workers advance to supervisory positions.

Increasingly, training is offered to enable people to work well in a team-oriented environment. Many firms have established training centers or hosted seminars that encourage employee self-direction and responsibility and the development of interpersonal skills. Because of the emphasis on teamwork and the small number of management levels in modern textile mills, firms place a premium on workers who show initiative and communicate effectively.

Engineering applicants generally need a bachelor's or advanced degree in a field of engineering or production

**Table 1. Employment of wage and salary workers in textile mill products by occupation, 2000 and projected change, 2000-10**

(Employment in thousands)

| Occupation | Employment, 2000 Number | Employment, 2000 Percent | Percent change, 2000-2010 |
|---|---|---|---|
| All occupations | 529 | 100.0 | -5.4 |
| **Management, business, and financial occupations** | 27 | 5.2 | -4.8 |
| General and operations managers | 5 | 1.0 | -6.8 |
| Industrial production managers | 5 | 0.9 | -9.2 |
| **Professional and related occupations** | 11 | 2.1 | -1.2 |
| Engineers and engineering technicians | 4 | 0.7 | -9.8 |
| **Service occupations** | 6 | 1.1 | -5.1 |
| Janitors and cleaners, except maids and housekeeping cleaners | 4 | 0.8 | -2.8 |
| **Sales and related occupations** | 6 | 1.1 | -4.3 |
| **Office and administrative support occupations** | 43 | 8.2 | -9.7 |
| Customer service representatives | 4 | 0.7 | 0.3 |
| Production, planning, and expediting clerks | 5 | 0.9 | -3.7 |
| Shipping, receiving, and traffic clerks | 7 | 1.4 | -10.0 |
| Stock clerks and order fillers | 4 | 0.8 | -2.0 |
| **Installation, maintenance, and repair occupations** | 40 | 7.6 | -7.8 |
| Industrial machinery mechanics | 14 | 2.6 | -3.7 |
| Maintenance and repair workers, general | 13 | 2.4 | -12.4 |
| Maintenance workers, machinery | 6 | 1.0 | -12.2 |
| **Production occupations** | 341 | 64.6 | -4.4 |
| First-line supervisors/managers of production and operating workers | 20 | 3.7 | -12.0 |
| Team assemblers | 7 | 1.3 | -8.6 |
| Extruding and forming machine setters, operators, and tenders, synthetic and glass fibers | 15 | 2.9 | 18.4 |
| Pressers, textile, garment, and related materials | 7 | 1.3 | -3.8 |
| Sewing machine operators | 27 | 5.0 | -12.4 |
| Textile bleaching and dyeing machine operators and tenders | 27 | 5.1 | -3.1 |
| Textile cutting machine setters, operators, and tenders | 8 | 1.6 | -11.6 |
| Textile knitting and weaving machine setters, operators, and tenders | 60 | 11.3 | -2.1 |
| Textile winding, twisting, and drawing out machine setters, operators, and tenders | 73 | 13.8 | -4.4 |
| All other textile, apparel, and furnishings workers | 32 | 6.0 | 6.1 |
| Helpers—Production workers | 10 | 1.9 | -11.8 |
| Inspectors, testers, sorters, samplers, and weighers | 20 | 3.8 | -22.2 |
| All other production workers | 6 | 1.2 | -8.5 |
| **Transportation and material moving occupations** | 50 | 9.6 | -8.6 |
| Industrial truck and tractor operators | 10 | 1.8 | -7.0 |
| Laborers and freight, stock, and material movers, hand | 15 | 2.9 | -11.0 |
| Machine feeders and offbearers | 8 | 1.6 | -19.7 |
| Packers and packagers, hand | 11 | 2.1 | -1.1 |

NOTE: May not add to totals due to omission of occupations with small employment.

management. Degrees in mechanical or industrial engineering are common, but concentrations in textile-specific areas of engineering are especially useful. For example, many applicants take classes in textile engineering, textile technology, textile materials, and design. These specialized programs usually are found in engineering and design schools in the South and Northeast. As in other industries, a technical degree with an advanced degree in business can lead to opportunities in management.

## Earnings

Average weekly earnings of nonsupervisory textile production workers were $450 in 2000, compared with $597 for production workers in all manufacturing and $474 for workers throughout private industry. Wages within the textile industry depend upon skill level and type of mill. At $516, average weekly earnings in miscellaneous textile goods were the highest in the industry, whereas workers in narrow fabric mills earned an average of $400 per week, the lowest in the industry. In addition to typical benefits, employees often are eligible for discounts in factory merchandise stores. Earnings in the largest occupations in textile mill products appear in table 2.

**Table 2. Median hourly earnings of the largest occupations in textile mill products, 2000**

| Occupation | Textile mill products | All industries |
|---|---|---|
| Industrial machinery mechanics | $ 13.06 | $ 17.30 |
| Maintenance and repair workers, general | 12.75 | 13.39 |
| Maintenance workers, machinery | 12.08 | 14.89 |
| Extruding and forming machine setters, operators, and tenders, synthetic and glass fibers | 11.32 | 12.66 |
| Textile knitting and weaving machine setters, operators, and tenders | 10.35 | 10.32 |
| Industrial truck and tractor operators | 10.19 | 11.74 |
| Inspectors, testers, sorters, samplers, and weighers | 9.89 | 12.22 |
| Textile winding, twisting, and drawing out machine setters, operators, and tenders | 9.82 | 9.89 |
| Textile bleaching and dyeing machine operators and tenders | 9.79 | 9.42 |
| Sewing machine operators | 8.31 | 7.80 |

The industry has a low unionization rate; only 5.6 percent of textile workers were union members or were covered by a union contract in 2000, compared with 14.9 percent for the economy as a whole. The most prominent union in the industry is the Union of Needletrades, Industrial and Textile Employees (UNITE), which was formed in 1995 by the merger of the Amalgamated Clothing and Textile Workers Union and the International Ladies' Garment Workers Union.

## Outlook

Wage and salary employment in the textile mill products industry is expected to decline by about 5 percent through 2010, compared with an increase of 16 percent for all industries combined. Employment decreases will result from increasing worker productivity, international trade, and the decline of the textile industry's primary buyer—the American apparel industry. Despite the expected overall employment decline, some occupations within the industry—such as extruding machine operators—will show some growth because these occupations are not highly automated. Nevertheless, most job openings will arise as experienced workers transfer to other industries, retire, or leave the workforce for other reasons.

Textiles manufacturing has evolved into a high-tech industry, keeping pace with scientific advancements in chemistry, engineering, and materials science. In order to remain competitive, industry professionals and research organizations continue to look for ways to produce goods of high quality while increasing productivity. For example, biotechnology research is expected to lead to new sources of fibers and improved varieties of existing fibers, and continuing improvements in machinery will allow faster production. These technologies and engineering advancements, along with the application of computers to various processes in textile production, will be implemented at a growing rate in coming years, as textile mills merge to consolidate capital and make their operations as efficient as possible. As this happens, demand for textile machine operators and material handlers will continue to decline.

Jobs also will be affected by the relatively open trading environment, resulting from ratification of the North American Free Trade Agreement and the Agreement on Textiles and Clothing of the World Trade Organization. These agreements will open additional markets to textiles made in the United States, but they will also expose U.S. textile producers to increasing competition from abroad. Some segments of the textile industry, like industrial fabrics, carpets, and specialty yarns, are highly automated, innovative, and competitive on a global scale, so they will be able to expand exports as a result of more open trade. Other sectors, such as fabric for apparel, will be negatively impacted, as a number of textile and apparel manufacturers relocate production to other countries. On balance, textile mills are likely to lose employment as a result of this open trade because of its effect on the American apparel industry. The expected increase in apparel imports and the decline in apparel production will adversely affect demand for domestically produced textiles.

## Sources of Additional Information

For additional information concerning career opportunities, technological advances, and legislative developments in the textile industry, contact:

➢ American Textile Manufacturing Institute, 1130 Connecticut Ave. NW., Suite 1200, Washington, DC 20036-3954. Internet: **http://www.atmi.org**

➢ Institute of Textile Technology, 2551 Ivy Rd., Charlottesville, NC 22903-4614. Internet: **http://www.itt.edu**

Information on the following occupations employed in the textile industry can be found in the 2002-03 edition of the *Occupational Outlook Handbook*.

- Engineers
- Engineering technicians
- Industrial machinery installation, maintenance, and repair workers
- Inspectors, testers, sorters, samplers, and weighers
- Machinists
- Material moving occupations
- Textile, apparel, and furnishings occupations

# Transportation, Communications, and Public Utilities

# Air Transportation

## SIGNIFICANT POINTS

- Although flight crews—pilots and flight attendants—are the most visible occupations, more than three-fourths of this industry's employees work in ground occupations.

- Senior pilots for major airlines are among the highest paid workers in the Nation.

- Except for pilots, most workers in this industry are trained to do their jobs after they are hired.

- More than 40 percent of workers are members of unions or covered by union contract.

## Nature of the Industry

The rapid development of air transportation has increased the mobility of the population and created thousands of job opportunities. The air transportation industry involves many activities. Most familiar are the major airlines, which provide transportation for passengers and cargo; and airports, which provide the many ground support services required by aircraft, passengers, and cargo. Air taxi companies and commuter airlines also provide commercial transportation, such as passenger and cargo service, often to and from small airports not serviced by the major airlines. Other companies provide air courier services, which furnish air delivery for individually addressed letters, parcels, and packages, and helicopter and sightseeing airplane services for tourists. This industry also includes services related to air transportation, such as aircraft repair, cleaning, and storage.

The air transportation industry has been through a period of adjustment and turmoil since the start of Federal deregulation in the late 1970s. Nonetheless, most of the 1980s was a prosperous period for the industry, marked by high earnings and by rapid job growth as new carriers entered the industry. The reduction in air travel that accompanied the recession of the early 1990s exposed many companies to problems of overcapacity and high labor costs. Intense competition—including destructive fare cutting—created a great deal of instability, causing many airlines to go out of business and many persons to lose their jobs.

The air transportation industry has recovered from the severe financial losses it suffered during the early 1990s. Smaller regional and commuter airlines, which have lower costs than larger airlines, have emerged in recent years to primarily serve shorter routes. Major airlines are regaining profitability and hope to achieve long-term stability by curbing excess capacity and distribution and marketing costs, using their aircraft and crews more efficiently, and reducing their labor costs through negotiations with the major labor unions that represent air transportation workers.

## Working Conditions

Working conditions vary widely, depending on the occupation. Although most employees work in fairly comfortable surroundings, such as offices, terminals, or airplanes, mechanics and others who service aircraft are subject to noise, dirt, and grease and sometimes work outside in bad weather.

In 1999, the air transportation industry had 13.3 injuries and illnesses per 100 full-time workers, compared with 6.3 through-

out private industry. Virtually all work-related fatalities resulted from transportation accidents.

Because airlines operate flights at all hours of the day and night, some workers often have irregular hours or schedules. Flight and ground personnel may have to work at night or on weekends or holidays. Flight personnel may be away from their home bases frequently. When they are away from home, the airlines provide hotel accommodations, transportation between the hotel and airport, and an allowance for meals and expenses. Pilots and flight attendants employed outside the major airlines also may have irregular schedules.

Flight crews, especially those on international routes, often suffer jet lag—disorientation and fatigue caused by flying into different time zones. Because employees must report for duty well rested, they must allow ample time to rest during their layovers.

## Employment

The air transportation industry provided 1.3 million wage and salary jobs in 2000. Most employment is found in larger establishments—nearly 9 out of 10 jobs are in establishments with 50 or more workers. However, more than half of all establishments employ fewer than 10 workers (chart).

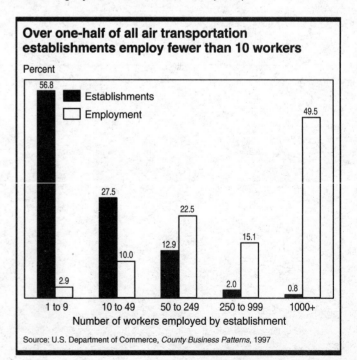

**Over one-half of all air transportation establishments employ fewer than 10 workers**

Percent

| | Establishments | Employment |
|---|---|---|
| 1 to 9 | 56.8 | 2.9 |
| 10 to 49 | 27.5 | 10.0 |
| 50 to 249 | 12.9 | 22.5 |
| 250 to 999 | 2.0 | 15.1 |
| 1000+ | 0.8 | 49.5 |

Number of workers employed by establishment

Source: U.S. Department of Commerce, *County Business Patterns*, 1997

Most air transportation employees work at major airports located close to cities. A substantial proportion of these employees work at airports that serve as central hubs for major airlines, such as New York, Chicago, Los Angeles, Atlanta, San Francisco, Dallas-Fort Worth, and Miami.

## Occupations in the Industry

Although pilots and flight attendants are the most visible occupations in this industry, more than 40 percent of all employees in air transportation work in ground occupations (table 1). For example, *aircraft mechanics and service technicians* service, inspect, and repair planes, and *reservation and transportation ticket agents and travel clerks* make and confirm reservations and sell tickets to passengers.

*Aircraft mechanics and service technicians* may work on several different types of aircraft, such as jet transports, small propeller-driven airplanes, or helicopters. Many, however, specialize in one section of a particular type of aircraft, such as the engine or the hydraulic or electrical systems. In small, independent repairshops, mechanics and technicians usually inspect and repair many different types of aircraft.

Many mechanics and technicians specialize in scheduled maintenance required by the Federal Aviation Administration (FAA). Following a schedule based on the number of hours flown, calendar days, cycles of operation, or a combination of these factors, mechanics inspect the engines, landing gear, instruments, and other parts of aircraft and perform necessary maintenance and repairs.

Other employees interact with the public. *Reservation and transportation ticket agents and travel clerks* answer telephones, sell tickets, and make reservations for passengers on scheduled airlines. *Customer service representatives* assist passengers, check tickets when passengers board or disembark an airplane, and check luggage at the reception area and ensure that it is placed on the proper carrier. They also assist elderly or handicapped persons and unaccompanied children in claiming personal belongings and baggage, and in getting on and off the plane. They also may provide assistance to passengers who become ill or injured. *Airline security representatives* screen passengers and visitors to ensure that weapons and illegal or forbidden articles are not carried into restricted areas.

*Airplane cargo agents* take orders from shippers and arrange for transportation of their goods. *Baggage handlers*, classified under *laborers and freight, stock, and material movers, hand* are responsible for loading and unloading passengers' baggage. They stack baggage on specified carts or conveyors to see that it gets to the proper destination and also return baggage to passengers at airline terminals upon receipt of their claim check. *Aircraft cleaners* clean aircraft interiors after each flight. Firms supplying air courier services that deliver individually addressed packages, letters, and parcels employ many *truck drivers, light or delivery services* to deliver and pick up merchandise or to deliver packages within a specified area. The airline industry also relies on many management, professional, and administrative support workers to keep operations running smoothly.

Flight crewmembers make up the remainder—about one-fifth—of air transportation employment, and include pilots and flight attendants. Pilots are highly trained professionals who fly airplanes and helicopters to carry out a wide variety of tasks. Although most are *airline pilots, copilots, and flight engineers* who transport passengers and cargo, others are *commercial pilots* involved in more unusual tasks, such as dusting crops, spreading seed for reforestation, testing aircraft, flying passengers and cargo

**Table 1. Employment of wage and salary workers in air transportation by occupation, 2000 and projected change, 2000-10**

(Employment in thousands)

| Occupation | Employment, 2000 | | Percent change, 2000-2010 |
|---|---|---|---|
| | Number | Percent | |
| **All occupations** | 1,281 | 100.0 | 24.9 |
| **Management, business, and financial occupations** | 67 | 5.2 | 32.7 |
| Transportation, storage, and distribution managers | 10 | 0.8 | 36.3 |
| **Professional and related occupations** | 37 | 2.8 | 35.1 |
| Engineers | 10 | 0.8 | 24.1 |
| **Service occupations** | 152 | 11.9 | 19.6 |
| Baggage porters and bellhops | 13 | 1.0 | 21.2 |
| Flight attendants | 124 | 9.7 | 18.4 |
| **Sales and related occupations** | 12 | 1.0 | 27.6 |
| **Office and administrative support occupations** | 307 | 23.9 | 18.4 |
| First-line supervisors/managers of office and administrative support workers | 14 | 1.1 | 36.0 |
| Customer service representatives | 48 | 3.8 | 40.9 |
| Order clerks | 11 | 0.9 | -11.2 |
| Reservation and transportation ticket agents and travel clerks | 126 | 9.8 | 10.0 |
| Cargo and freight agents | 18 | 1.4 | 7.3 |
| Stock clerks and order fillers | 9 | 0.7 | 35.1 |
| Office clerks, general | 12 | 0.9 | 18.9 |
| **Installation, maintenance, and repair occupations** | 165 | 12.9 | 23.4 |
| First-line supervisors/managers of mechanics, installers, and repairers | 9 | 0.7 | 32.7 |
| Aircraft mechanics and service technicians | 110 | 8.6 | 21.1 |
| Maintenance and repair workers, general | 10 | 0.8 | 19.5 |
| **Production occupations** | 12 | 0.9 | 19.7 |
| **Transportation and material moving occupations** | 528 | 41.2 | 29.0 |
| First-line supervisors/managers of helpers, laborers, and material movers, hand | 11 | 0.9 | 24.0 |
| First-line supervisors/managers of transportation and material-moving machine and vehicle operators | 18 | 1.4 | 34.1 |
| Airline pilots, copilots, and flight engineers | 92 | 7.2 | 7.7 |
| Commercial pilots | 11 | 0.9 | 35.4 |
| Truck drivers, heavy and tractor-trailer | 20 | 1.6 | 61.1 |
| Truck drivers, light or delivery services | 143 | 11.2 | 41.9 |
| Cleaners of vehicles and equipment | 14 | 1.1 | 33.4 |
| Industrial truck and tractor operators | 12 | 0.9 | 25.3 |
| Laborers and freight, stock, and material movers, hand | 146 | 11.4 | 22.7 |

NOTE: May not add to totals due to omission of occupations with small employment

to areas not serviced by regular airlines, directing firefighting efforts, tracking criminals, monitoring traffic, and rescuing and evacuating injured persons.

Except on small aircraft, two pilots usually constitute the cockpit crew. Generally, the most experienced pilot, or captain, is in command and supervises all other crewmembers. The pilot and copilot split flying and other duties such as communicating with air traffic controllers and monitoring the instruments. Some aircraft have a third pilot in the cockpit—the *flight engineer* or second officer—who assists the other pilots by monitoring and operating many of the instruments and systems and watching for other aircraft. Most newer aircraft are designed to be flown without a flight engineer.

Most airline flights have one or more *flight attendants* on board. Their most important function is assisting passengers in the event of an emergency. This may range from reassuring passengers during occasional encounters with strong turbulence to opening emergency exits and inflating escape chutes. More routinely, flight attendants instruct passengers in the use of safety and emergency equipment. Once in the air, they serve meals and snacks, answer questions about the flight, distribute magazines and pillows, and help care for small children and elderly and disabled persons. They also may administer first aid to passengers who become ill.

## Training and Advancement

The skills and experience needed by workers in the air transportation industry differ by occupation. Some jobs may be entered directly from high school, while others require extensive specialized training. Mechanics and pilots must be certificated by the FAA; skills for many other air transportation occupations can be learned on the job.

Pilots must have a commercial pilot's license with an instrument rating, and must be certified to fly the types of aircraft their employer operates. For example, helicopter pilots must hold a commercial pilot's certificate with a helicopter rating. Pilots receive their flight training from the military or from civilian flying schools. Physical requirements are strict. With or without glasses, pilots must have 20/20 vision and good hearing, and be in excellent health. In addition, airlines generally require 2 years of college and increasingly prefer or require a college degree. Pilots who work for smaller airlines may advance to flying for larger companies. They also can advance from flight engineer to copilot to captain and, by becoming certified, to fly larger planes.

Applicants for flight attendant jobs must be in excellent health. Employers prefer those who have completed some college and have experience in dealing with the public. Speaking a foreign language also is an asset. Applicants are trained for their jobs at company schools; the length of training usually lasts from 2 to 7 weeks, depending on the size and the type of carrier. Training may include crew resource management, which emphasizes teamwork and safety. After completing initial training, flight attendants must go through additional training and pass an FAA safety exam each year in order to continue flying. Advancement opportunities are limited, although some attendants become customer service directors, instructors, or recruiting representatives.

When hiring aircraft mechanics, employers prefer graduates of aircraft mechanic trade schools who are in good physical condition. After being hired, aircraft mechanics must keep up-to-date on the latest technical changes and improvements in aircraft and associated systems. Most mechanics remain in the maintenance field, but they may advance to head mechanic and, sometimes, to supervisor. Most other workers in ground occupations learn their job through a combination of company classroom and on-the-job training. At least a high school education is required for most jobs.

A good speaking voice and a pleasant personality are essential for reservation and transportation ticket agents and customer service representatives. Reservation agents also need some keyboard skills. Airlines prefer applicants with experience in sales or in dealing with the public and most require a high school education, but some college is preferred. Some agents and service representatives advance to supervisor or other administrative positions.

Some entry-level jobs in this industry, such as baggage handler and aircraft cleaner, require little or no previous training. The basic tasks associated with many of these jobs are learned in less than a week, and most newly hired workers are trained on the job under the guidance of an experienced employee or a manager. However, promotional opportunities for many ground occupations are limited due to the narrow scope of the duties and the specialized skills of some occupations. Some may advance to supervisor or other administrative positions.

## Earnings

Earnings in selected occupations in air transportation appear in table 2.

**Table 2. Median hourly earnings of the largest occupations in air transportation, 2000**

| Occupation | Transportation by air | All industries |
|---|---|---|
| First-line supervisors/managers of transportation and material-moving machine and vehicle operators | $ 23.21 | $ 19.37 |
| Aircraft mechanics and service technicians | 19.99 | 19.50 |
| Truck drivers, heavy and tractor-trailer | 18.97 | 15.25 |
| Truck drivers, light or delivery services | 16.58 | 10.74 |
| Cargo and freight agents | 13.75 | 13.73 |
| Baggage porters and bellhops | 13.03 | 7.80 |
| Customer service representatives | 12.85 | 11.83 |
| Reservation and transportation ticket agents and travel clerks | 11.66 | 10.87 |
| Laborers and freight, stock, and material movers, hand | 10.46 | 9.04 |
| Cleaners of vehicles and equipment | 10.00 | 7.55 |

Most employees in the air transportation industry receive standard benefits, such as life and health insurance and retirement plans. Some airlines provide allowances to employees for purchasing and cleaning their company uniforms. A unique benefit—free or reduced-fare transportation for airline employees and their immediate families—attracts many jobseekers.

In 2000, 41.3 percent of all workers in the air transportation industry were union members or were covered by union contracts, compared with 14.9 percent of all workers throughout the economy.

## Outlook

Wage and salary jobs in the air transportation industry are projected to increase by 25 percent over the 2000-10 period, compared with 16 percent for all industries combined. Passenger and cargo traffic is expected to expand in response to increases in population, income, and business activity. Employment in other air transportation activities also is expected to rise as more aircraft are purchased for business, agricultural, and recreational purposes.

Air travel has become an affordable means of transportation for more and more people. Demographic and income trends indicate favorable conditions for leisure travel in the United States and abroad over the next decade. An aging population, in combination with growing disposable income among the elderly, should increase the demand for air transportation services. Also, business travel will contribute to demand as world trade expands, companies continue to go global, and the economies in many foreign countries expand. However, growth in business travel will be somewhat restricted as U.S. corporations continue to downsize and automate operations, eliminating many middle management positions and reducing the base of both current and future business travelers. In addition, communication technologies—such as fax machines, computer networks, and teleconferencing—have somewhat reduced the need for business travel.

Besides job openings created by employment growth, many openings also will arise as experienced workers retire or transfer to other industries. Job opportunities may vary from year to year, however, because the demand for air travel—particularly pleasure travel, a discretionary expense—fluctuates with ups and downs in the economy.

New technology is not expected to have any significant effect on air transportation occupations over the 2000-10 period; most laborsaving technology already has been introduced and should have minimal impact on future employment. Job opportunities in the air transportation industry are expected to vary depending on the occupation.

Pilots are expected to face strong competition for jobs through the year 2010. The number of job openings resulting from the need to replace pilots who retire or leave the occupation traditionally has been very low. Aircraft pilots usually have a strong attachment to their occupation because it requires a substantial investment in specialized training that is not transferable to other fields, and it commonly offers very high earnings. However, many of the pilots who were hired in the late 1960s are approaching the age for mandatory retirement and, thus, several thousand job openings are expected to be generated each year.

Customer service representatives and reservation and transportation ticket agents also are expected to face keen competition for available positions because the jobs offer reasonably good pay and the opportunity to travel, and require little education beyond high school.

Opportunities should be favorable for persons seeking flight attendant jobs because the number of applicants is expected to be roughly the same as the number of job openings. Those with at least 2 years of college and experience in dealing with the public should have the best chance of being hired. The majority of job openings for flight attendants should be due to the need to replace flight attendants who transfer to other occupations or who leave the labor force. Many flight attendants are attracted to the occupation by the glamour of the airline industry and the opportunity to travel, but some eventually leave in search of jobs that offer higher earnings and require fewer nights away from their families.

Opportunities also should be favorable for aircraft and avionics equipment mechanics and service technicians. The likelihood of fewer entrants from the military and a large number of retirements, points to favorable opportunities for students just beginning technician training. Opportunities will be somewhat better for mechanics working in general aviation than for commercial airlines; mechanics will face competition for jobs at the commercial airlines because these jobs tend to pay more. Opportunities should be better with rapidly growing commuter and regional airlines and at FAA repair stations.

Opportunities also are expected to be good among unskilled entry-level positions, such as baggage handler and aircraft cleaner, because the turnover rate of these jobs usually is high.

## Sources of Additional Information

Information about specific job opportunities and qualifications required by a particular airline may be obtained by writing to personnel managers of the airlines.

For information about job opportunities in companies other than airlines, consult the classified section of aviation trade magazines or apply to companies that operate aircraft at local airports.

Information on these key air transportation occupations may be found in the 2002-03 *Occupational Outlook Handbook*:

- Aircraft and avionics equipment mechanics and service technicians
- Aircraft pilots and flight engineers
- Flight attendants
- Reservation and transportation ticket agents and travel clerks

# Cable and Other Pay Television Services

**(SIC 484)**

- Administrative support and installation, maintenance, and repair occupations comprise most jobs.

- Most jobs are in establishments with more than 50 workers.

- Opportunities will be best for applicants with technical skills and an understanding of the new telecommunications services provided by this industry.

## Nature of the Industry

Establishments in this industry provide television and other services on a subscription or fee basis. These establishments include both cable networks and distributors. Cable networks produce or acquire television programming and deliver it to distributors. The distributors then transmit the programming to customers. Cable networks produce some original television programs in their studios. Although the amount of original programming is growing, much of the programming is acquired from the motion picture industry. (See the statement on motion picture production and distribution elsewhere in the *Career Guide*.)

Distributors of pay television services transmit programming through two basic types of systems. Cable systems transmit programs over fiber optic and coaxial cables. Fiber optic cables are made of glass strands and can carry more information than conventional coaxial cables, made of wire. Direct broadcasting satellite (DBS) operators constitute a rapidly growing segment of the pay television industry. DBS operators transmit programming from orbiting satellites to customer receivers, known as mini-dishes. The dishes are about 18 inches in diameter, although newer dishes that provide Internet access are slightly larger.

Establishments in this industry generate revenue through subscriptions, special service fees, and advertising sales. Pay television systems charge installation and subscription fees to set up and provide service. They also charge fees for special services, such as the transmission of specialty pay-per-view programs; these often are popular movies or sporting events. Some cable networks sell advertising time during selected programs. Rates paid by advertisers depend on the size and characteristics of the program's audience and the time of day the program is shown.

Subscription television services are widely used. In 2000, more than 70 percent of households with television sets received pay television services. Most of these customers subscribed to cable service; however, subscriptions to satellite services are growing rapidly. The number of national cable networks has expanded rapidly, from 87 in 1992 to 214 in 1999.

Changes in technology and regulation are transforming the industry. An important change has been the rapid increase in two-way communications capacity. Conventional pay television services provided communications only from the distributor to the customer. These services could not provide effective communications from the customer back to other points in the system, due to signal interference and the limited capacity of conventional cable systems. Encouraged by the increasing need for communications services, cable operators have implemented new technologies to reduce signal interference. The capacity of distribution systems also has increased, due to the installation of fiber optic cables and improved data compression. As a result, pay television systems now offer two-way telecommunications services, such as telephone service and high-speed Internet access. Cable subscribers can access the Internet by installing cable modems that connect customers' personal computers to the cable system.

The upgraded systems also facilitate the transmission of digital television signals. Digital signals consist of simple electronic code that can carry more information than conventional television signals. Digital transmission creates higher resolution television images and improved sound quality. It also allows the transmission of a variety of other information. Another feature of digital television is more channels, thanks to compression technology. Viewers of football games will be able to decide which camera angle they want to watch. Commercials will become interactive, as consumers will be able to find out additional information about a product, and even order it, simply by using buttons on their remote control.

Another major change is the rapid growth of satellite-based systems, with more than 13 million subscribers in 2000. The growth of the satellite subscription industry stems from several major factors. Prices for mini-dish subscriptions have dropped dramatically, and are now competitive with cable. Regulatory changes allowed satellite services to begin carrying local network channels. The most recent change has been the offering of high-speed Internet access by satellite services.

The Telecommunications Act of 1996 reduced barriers to competition across all communications industries. As a result, operators of pay television systems are competing with telephone companies and public utilities to provide video, telephone, and high-speed Internet services. Consolidations have increased, as companies acquire facilities that allow them to offer their customers multiple services. Such combined offerings are popular with customers seeking to simplify their purchase of communications services. (A statement on the telecommunications industry appears elsewhere in the *Career Guide*.)

## Working Conditions

Working conditions in cable and other pay television services vary by occupational group. Most professional, clerical, and sales employees work indoors in comfortable, well lighted surroundings. However, installation, maintenance, and repair workers must travel to various locations to perform their duties. These responsibilities often require outdoor work under a variety of weather conditions.

Workers who install pay television services travel to the customers' premises to perform the installation. Cable service installers sometimes must climb telephone poles or access underground cables to connect a customer's television set to the cable system. Antenna and satellite dish installers must climb ladders and attach the receiving equipment to rooftops or the sides of houses.

Cable television line installers and repairers travel to locations in the cable system that are malfunctioning. They often travel in vehicles equipped with aerial buckets so that they can do repair work on cables carried on telephone poles. Technicians responsible for monitoring signal quality sometimes work on outdoor equipment, such as transmission towers and satellite dishes.

Cases of work-related injury and illness in cable and other pay television services in 1999 were approximately 6.4 per 100 full-time workers, slightly higher than the 6.3 per 100 full-time workers throughout private industry. Many installation, maintenance, and repair jobs in the industry pose hazards that can result in injuries—for example, falls or electric shock from contact with high-voltage power lines.

## Employment

Cable and other pay television services provided about 216,000 wage and salary jobs in 2000. Most jobs were in establishments that employed more than 50 workers (chart 1). However, more than half of the establishments in the industry employed fewer than 10 workers. Pay television establishments are found throughout the country, but jobs with large employers are concentrated in large cities.

## Occupations in the Industry

Administrative support and installation, maintenance, and repair occupations account for most jobs. The remaining employees are found in variety of occupations (table 1). In small cable establishments, employees are less specialized and may have a wide range of responsibilities.

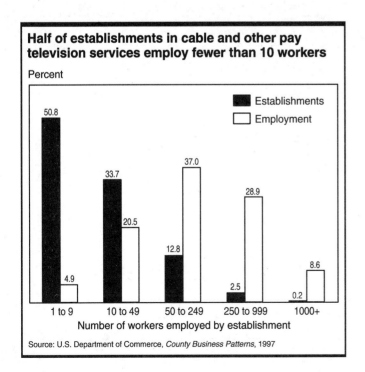

**Half of establishments in cable and other pay television services employ fewer than 10 workers**

Percent

Source: U.S. Department of Commerce, *County Business Patterns*, 1997

*Office and administrative support occupations.* About 35 percent of all jobs in this industry are in office and administrative support occupations. *Customer service representatives* talk with customers by phone or in person and receive orders for installation, turn-on, discontinuance, or change in services. They often work at a computer, so they can quickly access customer records and authorize the provision of new services. As the industry begins to offer new services—such as telephone and high-speed Internet access—customer service representatives also must respond to technical questions about the operation of these services. Some customer service representatives are expected to sell services and may work on a commission basis. They also investigate customer questions about pay television services, including billing questions. They determine responsibility for a customer complaint and notify customers of any adjustments, such as refunds or other changes to customers' bills. *Dispatchers* schedule work crews and service vehicles for installation of pay television service. Duties can include transmitting assignments via radio or telephone, and compiling statistics and reports on work progress.

*Installation, maintenance, and repair occupations.* Installation, maintenance, and repair occupations include 30 percent of the workers in the industry. The largest occupation in this group, *telecommunications line installers and repairers*, lay fiber optic and coaxial cable and install equipment, such as repeaters and amplifiers, which maintain signal strength. Maintenance and repair duties include periodic monitoring of the cable system to identify malfunctions. When a problem is detected, the technicians travel to the location of the malfunction and repair or replace the defective cable or equipment. Construction duties related to line installation, such as erecting supports and digging underground trenches, are often contracted to employees working in other industries.

*Installers* travel to customers' premises to set up pay television service so that customers can receive programming. Cable service installers connect a customer's television set to the cable serving the entire neighborhood. Satellite service installers attach antennas or satellite dishes to the sides of customers' houses. These devices must be positioned to provide clear lines of sight with satellite locations. (Satellite installation may be handled by employees of electronic retail stores that sell satellite dishes.)

Installers check the strength and clarity of the television signal before completing the installation. They may need to explain to the subscriber how pay television services operate. As these services expand to include telephone and high-speed Internet access, an understanding of the basic technology and an ability to communicate that knowledge are increasingly important.

A new occupation employed by cable operators is *cable modem installer*. These workers install cable modems, which allow customers to connect their personal computers to the cable line. Cable modem installers connect the modem to the cable line and configure the modem so that it is compatible with the customer's personal computer.

*Other occupations.* The remaining employees, who make up 35 percent of employment in this industry, work in a variety of occupations. Many are employed by cable networks that produce television programs, such as news or talk shows. *Television camera operators* set up and operate television cameras to photograph scenes for cable television broadcasts. *Producers* plan and develop live or taped productions, determining how the show will look and sound. (The motion picture industry produces many programs seen on cable television. Actors and directors working on these prerecorded programs are not employed by cable or other pay television services.)

*Electrical* and *electronics engineers* design cable and wireless distribution systems for pay television services. Engineers determine the physical layout and requirements of the system, test equipment, solve operating problems, and estimate the time and cost of engineering projects. In wireless cable systems, engineers determine where operators need to install repeaters and towers in the distribution systems.

*Network and computer systems administrators* and *network systems and data communications analysts* design, set up, and maintain systems of computer servers. These servers store customer data for billing and authorization purposes. Network administrators set up connections between servers, so that customer service agents and other employees can efficiently access customer data for billing and authorization purposes. Other computer specialists include *computer hardware and software engineers*, who work with the hardware and software aspects of systems design and development, and *computer support specialists*, who provide assistance and advice to users.

*Broadcast technicians*, also known as *cable technicians*, set up, operate, and maintain the electronic equipment used to transmit television programming. In cable services, they insure that incoming signals from satellites are clearly received and transmitted along cable lines to the customer. *Engineering technicians* assist engineers by designing, building, and testing electrical equipment. In cable networks that produce television programming, *master control engineers* ensure that the scheduled program elements—such as on-location feeds, prerecorded segments, and commercials—are smoothly transmitted.

## Training and Advancement

Many jobs in the cable and other pay television services industry do not require a college degree. Applicants with a high school diploma generally qualify for entry-level positions in administrative support or installation, maintenance, and repair occupations. However, a college degree usually is required for managerial and professional jobs.

Customer service representatives require a high school degree and good communication skills. Familiarity with personal computers and a clear speaking voice are helpful. These workers receive on-the-job training to familiarize them with company services.

Installers require a high school degree, mechanical ability, and some technical knowledge. Newly hired installers receive on-the-job training and, after several years, may advance to line technician positions and work on complex maintenance and installation tasks. Cable modem installers should have experience working with computers or an associate degree in computer information systems.

Telecommunications line installers and repairers working on large feeder and trunk lines require several years' experience with cable technology. A 2-year associate degree is helpful, as is knowledge of basic electronics and good mathematical aptitude. Experienced line technicians may advance to broadcast technicians, operating and maintaining electronic equipment used to transmit cable programming.

The Society of Cable Telecommunications Engineers (SCTE) offers certification programs for a variety of technician positions. Applicants for certification must be employed in the industry and attend training sessions at local SCTE chapters. Applicants must pass both written and hands-on exams to receive certification.

**Table 1. Employment of wage and salary workers in cable and other pay television services by occupation, 2000 and projected change, 2000-10**

(Employment in thousands)

| Occupation | Employment, 2000 Number | Percent | Percent change, 2000-2010 |
|---|---|---|---|
| **All occupations** | 216 | 100.0 | 50.6 |
| **Management, business, and financial occupations** | 21 | 9.7 | 52.4 |
| Marketing and sales managers | 2 | 0.9 | 69.9 |
| General and operations managers | 4 | 2.0 | 45.9 |
| Human resources, training, and labor relations specialists | 2 | 0.7 | 47.1 |
| Accountants and auditors | 2 | 0.8 | 54.4 |
| **Professional and related occupations** | 24 | 11.1 | 73.8 |
| Computer support specialists | 4 | 1.8 | 131.7 |
| Network systems and data communications analysts | 2 | 0.8 | 108.5 |
| Electrical and electronic engineering technicians | 2 | 0.7 | 39.0 |
| Producers and directors | 2 | 1.0 | 54.4 |
| Media and communication occupations | 2 | 0.9 | 52.0 |
| Broadcast technicians | 3 | 1.2 | 54.4 |
| **Sales and related occupations** | 25 | 11.4 | 52.4 |
| Advertising sales agents | 3 | 1.2 | 69.9 |
| Door-to-door sales workers, news and street vendors, and related workers | 3 | 1.3 | 42.6 |
| Sales representatives, wholesale and manufacturing, except technical and scientific products | 2 | 1.1 | 39.0 |
| Supervisors, sales workers | 2 | 0.7 | 46.2 |
| Telemarketers | 12 | 5.5 | 54.4 |
| **Office and administrative support occupations** | 75 | 34.6 | 50.2 |
| First-line supervisors/managers of office and administrative support workers | 4 | 2.0 | 54.4 |
| Bill and account collectors | 2 | 0.8 | 46.0 |
| Bookkeeping, accounting, and auditing clerks | 3 | 1.4 | 33.0 |
| Customer service representatives | 41 | 18.9 | 59.4 |
| Dispatchers, except police, fire, and ambulance | 5 | 2.1 | 50.7 |
| Office clerks, general | 4 | 1.8 | 36.1 |
| Executive secretaries and administrative assistants | 3 | 1.2 | 39.0 |
| Secretaries, except legal, medical, and executive | 3 | 1.2 | 23.6 |
| **Construction and extraction occupations** | 2 | 0.9 | 56.7 |
| Construction trades and related workers | 2 | 0.8 | 57.1 |
| **Installation, maintenance, and repair occupations** | 66 | 30.4 | 41.5 |
| First-line supervisors/managers of mechanics, installers, and repairers | 6 | 2.6 | 54.4 |
| Electrical and electronics repairers, commercial and industrial equipment | 3 | 1.4 | 49.2 |
| Telecommunications equipment installers and repairers, except line installers | 11 | 5.1 | 23.6 |
| Telecommunications line installers and repairers | 39 | 18.2 | 43.0 |
| Maintenance and repair workers, general | 2 | 0.8 | 37.1 |
| **Transportation and material moving occupations** | 2 | 0.9 | 42.6 |

NOTE: May not add to totals due to omission of occupations with small employment.

**Table 2. Average earnings of nonsupervisory workers in cable and other pay television services, 2000**

| Industry segment | Weekly | Hourly |
|---|---|---|
| Total, private industry ...................................... | $474 | $13.74 |
| Communications industries ............................ | 715 | 17.79 |
| Cable and other pay television services ......... | 624 | 15.45 |

Similar training for cable technicians is available from private trade schools and organizations.

Professional positions in pay television services normally require a college degree. Employees in program production, such as producers and news analysts, often receive degrees in communications or broadcast journalism. Camera operator positions may require only a vocational school degree or equivalent experience. Competition for program production positions is strongest in large metropolitan areas. As a result, entry-level applicants often must look for work in small markets. Internships while in school are recommended for employment in program production; experience gained at college television stations also is helpful.

Engineering positions require a college degree, usually in electrical and electronic engineering. Useful specializations include communications, radio frequency systems, and signal processing. Positions as computer specialists, such as network and computer systems administrators, also require a college degree. These employees generally need knowledge of the Internet and familiarity with different computer operating systems. Positions as market researchers and advertising sales representatives usually require a degree in business, communications, or related fields. Experience gained through college internships is also useful.

## Earnings

Earnings in 2000 averaged $624 a week in cable and other pay television services. This was higher than the average for all private industry; however, it was lower than average for communications industries as a whole, which includes telecommunications; radio and television broadcasting; and cable and other pay television services (table 2). Earnings in selected occupations in cable and other pay television services appear in table 3.

**Table 3. Median hourly earnings of the largest occupations in cable and other pay television services, 2000**

| Occupation | Cable and other pay TV services | All industries |
|---|---|---|
| First-line supervisors/managers of mechanics, installers, and repairers .......... | $ 23.40 | $ 21.27 |
| Advertising sales agents ................................ | 20.71 | 17.24 |
| Telecommunications equipment installers and repairers, except line installers ............ | 16.17 | 21.17 |
| Telecommunications line installers and repairers ................................................. | 14.86 | 18.32 |
| Computer support specialists ........................ | 14.58 | 17.53 |
| Dispatchers, except police, fire, and ambulance ................................................. | 13.74 | 13.66 |
| Bookkeeping, accounting, and auditing clerks.................................................. | 13.05 | 12.34 |
| Broadcast technicians .................................... | 12.87 | 12.96 |
| Customer service representatives ................. | 12.59 | 11.83 |
| Telemarketers ................................................. | 8.74 | 9.06 |

## Outlook

Employment in cable and other pay television services is expected to increase 51 percent between 2000 and 2010, much faster than the 15 percent projected for all industries combined. Job growth will be driven by advances in technology that allow the industry to expand beyond pay television services. The delivery of new telecommunications services—such as high-speed Internet access, telephone communications, and digital television programming—will increase demand for subscriptions to pay television services. Industry employment will grow, as companies expand and upgrade their equipment to efficiently provide these new services, and as they add to their marketing capacity to compete for increased customer demand. The need for employees in a variety of occupations should create openings for both high school and college graduates. Opportunities will be best for those with technical skills and an understanding of the new telecommunications services offered in this industry. Some jobs will be lost as a result of consolidation in this industry; however, these losses will be more than offset by employment gains stemming from increased customer demand for additional or improved services.

A variety of occupations will experience employment growth. Operators of cable systems will need workers to lay fiber optic cable, deploy new technologies to increase line capacity, and maintain the growing networks of cable lines. As cable systems become more competitive, there may be more overbuilding—new companies laying cables adjacent to existing cables in an attempt to compete for service. These trends should contribute to an increase in the employment of line installers.

Employment of installers who set up service also will increase, as residential and business customers are drawn to high-speed Internet access and telephone services. The increasing complexity of home installations will make each individual installation a more involved and longer process, stimulating demand for installers. More DBS installers will be need to setup and maintain home mini-satellite dishes, as self-installation will become nearly impossible with broadcasters using multiple satellites and providing broadband Internet access.

All distributors of pay television services will need more customer service representatives. Customers are unfamiliar with the new services offered in this industry and need help understanding their operation. In this increasingly competitive industry, providing easily accessible customer service representatives will be a priority for all distributors.

Finally, the introduction of digital technology, resulting in an increase in the number of cable networks and pay television service providers, will create opportunities in program production occupations, such as producers, newscasters, and camera operators. As distributors of pay television services install networks of computer servers, employment of computer specialists, such as network and computer systems administrators, will increase. Computer servers not only will track customer information for authorization and billing, but will also house digital information, such as movies that customers can access on demand. With additional networks attempting to sell advertising, the demand for market researchers and advertising sales staff should increase as well.

## Sources of Additional Information

Information on the cable industry is available from:

➢ National Cable Television Association, 1724 Massachusetts Ave. NW., Washington, DC 20036. Internet: **http://www.ncta.com**

For information on training and certification programs in the cable industry, contact:

➤ Society of Cable Telecommunications Engineers, Certification Department, 140 Philips Rd., Exton, PA 19341. Internet: **http://www.scte.org**

For information on training for satellite service installers, contact:

➤ Satellite Broadcasting & Communications Association, 225 Reinekers Lane, Suite 600, Alexandria, VA 22314. Internet: **http://www.sbca.com**

Information on the following occupations can be found in the 2002-03 edition of the *Occupational Outlook Handbook*.

- Actors, producers, and directors
- Advertising, marketing, promotions, public relations, and sales managers
- Announcers
- Broadcast and sound engineering technicians and radio operators
- Engineers
- Line installers and repairers
- News analysts, reporters, and correspondents
- Television, video, and motion picture camera operators and editors
- Writers and editors

# Public Utilities

## SIGNIFICANT POINTS

- Persons with college training in advanced technology will have the best opportunities.

- Employment growth and opportunities vary among segments of the industry.

- Production workers' earnings are significantly higher than in most other industries.

## Nature of the Industry

The simple act of walking into a restroom, turning on the light, and washing your hands, uses the products of perhaps four different utilities. Electricity powers the light, water supply systems provide water for washing, wastewater treatment plants treat the sewage, and natural gas or electricity heats the water. Some government establishments do the same work and employ a significant number of workers; however, information about them is not included in this statement. Information concerning government employment in public utilities is included in the *Career Guide to Industries* statements on Federal Government and State and local government, excluding education and hospitals. Each of the various segments within the public utilities sector is distinctly different.

*Electric services.* This segment includes firms engaged in the generation, transmission, and distribution of electricity for sale. Electric plants harness highly pressurized steam or some force of nature to spin the blades of a turbine, which is attached to an electric generator. Coal is by far the dominant fuel used to generate steam in electric power plants, followed by nuclear power, natural gas, petroleum, and other energy sources. Hydroelectric generators are powered by the release of the tremendous pressure of water existing at the bottom of a dam or near a waterfall. Scientists also are conducting considerable research into renewable sources of electric power—geothermal, wind, and solar energy. Some municipalities capture combustible gases or burn waste materials at landfills to generate electricity.

Legislative changes have created new classes of firms that generate and sell electricity. Industrial plants often have their own electricity generating facilities, usually capable of producing more than they require. They are called nonutility generators (NUG) and sell their excess power to utilities or to other industrial plants. A type of NUG, termed an independent power producer, is an electricity generating plant designed to take advantage of both industry deregulation and the latest generating technology to compete directly with utilities for industrial and other wholesale customers.

Transmission or high voltage lines supported by huge towers connect generating plants with industrial customers and substations. At substations, the electricity's voltage is reduced and made available for household and small business use via distribution lines, which usually are carried by telephone poles.

*Gas production and distribution.* Natural gas, a clear odorless gas, is found underground, often near or associated with crude oil reserves. Exploration and extraction of natural gas is part of the oil and gas extraction industry, covered elsewhere in the *Career Guide to Industries*. Once found and brought to the surface, it is transported throughout the United States, Canada,

and Mexico by gas transmission companies using pressurized pipelines. Local distribution companies take natural gas from the pipeline, depressurize it, add its odor, and operate the system that delivers the gas from transmission pipelines to industrial, residential, and commercial customers. Industrial customers, such as chemical and paper manufacturing firms, account for nearly half of natural gas consumption. Residential customers who use gas for heating and cooking, electric utilities, and commercial businesses—such as hospitals and restaurants—account for most of the remaining consumption.

*Water supply.* Water utilities provide over 100 gallons of fresh, treated water every day for each person in this country, or about 40 billion gallons per day nationwide. Water is collected from various sources such as rivers, lakes, and wells. After collection, water is filtered, treated, and sold for residential, industrial, commercial, and public use. Depending on the population served by the water system, the utility may be a small plant in a rural area that requires the occasional monitoring of a single operator or a huge system of reservoirs, dams, pipelines, and treatment plants, requiring the coordinated efforts of hundreds of people.

*Sanitary services.* This segment includes sewage and refuse systems. Sewage systems collect wastewater from homes and industries, treat it, and return clean water to the surface water supply. Wastewater treatment plants are similar to water treatment plants, although the treatment processes and regulatory requirements are generally more complicated, especially in the case of industrial wastes.

Refuse systems collect and dispose of household garbage—called municipal solid waste—and refuse from commercial and industrial establishments by processing or destroying it through the operation of waste treatment plants, landfills, recycling plants, and incinerators. An increasing proportion of refuse is either recycled or burned to generate electricity.

*Other utilities* include steam and air-conditioning supply utilities, which produce and sell steam and cooled air; and irrigation systems, which operate water supply systems primarily for irrigation.

*Combination utility services.* Utilities are classified as combination utilities when they are involved in both the production of electricity and the distribution of natural gas, telecommunications, or some other utility service. They are considered either electric-combined or gas-combined services, depending on which service makes up the majority of their business. Combination utilities usually are located in large metropolitan areas.

Utilities and the services they provide are so vital to everyday life that they are considered "public goods" and are typically heavily regulated. Formerly, utility companies operated as "regulated monopolies," meaning that in return for having no competition, they were subject to control by public utility commissions that ensured utilities acted in the public interest and regulated the rates they were allowed to charge. However, legislative changes in recent years have established and promoted competition in the utilities industry. The electric utilities industry, for example, is currently restructuring in an effort to promote efficiency, lower costs to customers, and provide users with an increased number of service options.

Many utility companies are municipally owned. For example, of the roughly 2,000 gas distribution companies in the United States, about 1,000 are municipally owned. In general, utilities serving large cities have sufficient numbers of customers to justify the large expenditures necessary for building plants, and are run by private, investor-owned companies. In rural areas, where the small number of customers in need of services would not provide an adequate return for private investors, the State or local government funds the plant construction and operates the utility.

The various segments of the utilities industry vary in the degree to which their workers are involved in production activities, administration and management, or research and development. Industries such as water supply that employ relatively few workers employ more production workers and plant operators. On the other hand, electric utilities and combination utilities generally operate larger plants using very expensive, high technology equipment, and thus employ more professional and technical personnel.

A unique feature of the utilities industry is that urban areas with many inhabitants generally have relatively few utility companies. For instance, there were about 54,000 community water systems in the United States in 2000 serving roughly 264 million people. The 45,900 small water systems served only 26 million people while the 8,100 largest systems served almost 238 million. Alaska, with a 2000 population about 10 percent of that of Massachusetts, had about 3 times more electric generating plants than Massachusetts. These examples show that economies of scale in the utilities industry allow one or two large companies to serve large numbers of customers in metropolitan areas more efficiently than many smaller companies.

Unlike most industries, the utilities industry imports and exports only a small portion of its product. In the natural gas industry, this reflects the fact that the country has a sizable, proven resource base that can be used economically to meet the country's needs. This is the result of a National policy that utilities should be self-sufficient, without dependence on imports for the basic services our country requires. However, easing trade restrictions, increased pipeline capacity, and shipping natural gas in liquefied form have made importing and exporting natural gas more economical. In 2000, about 16 percent of the natural gas consumed was imported, mostly from Canada. A small portion of natural gas is exported in liquefied form, primarily to Japan.

## Working Conditions

Electricity, gas, and water are produced and used continuously throughout each day. As a result, split, weekend, and night shifts are common for utility workers. The average workweek in utilities was 41.7 hours in 2000, compared with 34.5 hours for all industries, and 38.5 hours for all transportation and public utilities. Employees often must work overtime to accommodate peaks in demand and to repair damage caused by storms, cold weather, accidents, and other occurrences. The industry employs relatively few part-time workers.

The hazards of working with electricity, natural gas, treatment chemicals, and wastes can be substantial, but generally are avoided by following rigorous safety procedures. Protective gear such as rubber gloves with long sleeves, nonsparking maintenance equipment, and body suits with breathing devices designed to filter out any harmful fumes are mandatory for work in dangerous environs. Employees also undergo extensive training on working with hazardous materials and utility company safety measures.

In 1999, the electric, gas, and sanitary services industries reported just 6.1 cases of work-related injury or illness per 100 full-time workers, compared with an average of 6.3 cases for all industries, and 9.2 cases for manufacturing industries. Sanitary services, however, had injury and illness rates higher than the average for all industries, with 9.9 cases per 100 full-time workers, reflecting the physically demanding nature of refuse collection and disposal.

## Employment

Public utilities employed about 851,000 workers in 2000. Electric services provided about 42 percent of all jobs, as shown in table 1.

**Table 1. Distribution of wage and salary employment in nongovernment public utilities, 2000**

(Employment in thousands)

| Industry | Employment | Percent |
|---|---|---|
| Total, all utilities | 851 | 100.0 |
| Electric services | 357 | 42.0 |
| Water supply and sanitary services | 214 | 25.1 |
| Combination utility services | 152 | 17.9 |
| Gas production and distribution | 128 | 15.0 |

Although electric utilities are among the biggest customers of natural gas utilities, the processes used to produce their services are largely unrelated. This diversity of production processes is reflected in the size of the establishments that make up the utilities industry. The combination utility industry consists of relatively large plants. In 2000, it accounted for less than 7 percent of the reporting establishments, yet employed an average of more than 90 workers per establishment. On the other hand, water supply utilities accounted for 16 percent of workplaces, yet employed only an average of 8 workers per establishment (table 2).

**Table 2. Nongovernment establishments in electric, gas, and sanitary services and average employment per establishment, 2000**

| Industry | Number of establishments | Employment per establishment |
|---|---|---|
| Total, all utilities | 25,369 | 34 |
| Sanitary services | 8,157 | 21 |
| Electric services | 6,440 | 56 |
| Gas production and distribution | 4,491 | 28 |
| Water supply | 3,966 | 8 |
| Combination utility services | 1,674 | 91 |
| Irrigation systems | 514 | 6 |
| Steam and air-conditioning supply | 128 | 16 |

Although many establishments are small, almost half of public utility workers are employed in establishments with 250 or more workers (chart).

## Occupations in the Industry

About one-third of those employed in the public utilities industry work in production or installation, maintenance, and repair occupations (table 3). About 20 percent work in office and administrative support occupations; about 13 percent are employed in management, business, and financial occupations; and the remaining workers primarily are in professional or transportation and material moving occupations.

Workers in production and installation, maintenance, and repair occupations install and maintain pipelines and powerlines, operate and fix plant machinery, and monitor treatment processes. For example, *electrical power-line installers and repairers* install and repair cables or wires used in electrical power or distribution systems. They install insulators, wooden poles, and light- or heavy-duty transmission towers. *First-line supervisors and managers* directly supervise and coordinate the activities of production and repair workers. These supervisors ensure that workers use and maintain equipment and materials properly and efficiently to maximize productivity.

Production occupations include *power plant operators, power distributors and dispatchers*, and *water and liquid waste treatment plant operators. Power plant operators* control or operate machinery, such as stream-driven turbine generators, to generate electric power, often using control boards or semi-automatic equipment. *Power distributors and dispatchers* coordinate, regulate, or distribute electricity or steam in generating stations, over transmission lines to substations, and over electric power lines. *Water and liquid waste treatment plant and system operators* control the process of treating water or liquid waste, take samples of water for testing, and may perform maintenance of treatment plants.

*Industrial machinery mechanics* install, repair, and maintain machinery in power generating stations, gas plants, and water treatment plants. They repair and maintain the mechanical components of generators, waterwheels, water-inlet controls, and piping in generating stations; steam boilers, condensers, pumps, compressors, and similar equipment in gas manufacturing plants; and equipment used to process and distribute water for public and industrial uses.

*General maintenance and repair workers* perform work involving a variety of maintenance skills to keep machines, mechanical equipment, and the structure of an establishment in repair. Generally found in small establishments, these workers have duties that may involve pipefitting, boilermaking, electrical work, carpentry, welding, and installing new equipment.

Office and administrative support occupations account for about one-fifth of the jobs in the utilities industry. *Customer service representatives* interview applicants for water, gas, and electric service. They talk with customers by phone or in person and receive orders for installation, turn-on, discontinuance, or change in service. *General office clerks* may do bookkeeping, typing, stenography, office machine operation, and filing. *Utilities meter readers* read electric, gas, water, or steam consumption meters visually or remotely using radio transmitters and record the volume used by residential and industrial customers. Financial clerks, such as *bookkeeping, accounting, and auditing clerks*, compute, classify, and record numerical data to keep financial records complete. They perform any combination of routine calculating, posting, and verifying duties to obtain primary financial data for use in maintaining accounting records.

Transportation and material-moving occupations include *refuse and recyclable material collectors* and *truck drivers. Refuse and recyclable material collectors* collect and dump refuse and recyclable materials from containers into a truck. *Truck drivers* operate refuse collection trucks that are either self-loading or loaded by refuse collectors.

Managers and administrators in the utilities industry plan, organize, direct, and coordinate management activities. They often are responsible for maintaining an adequate supply of electricity, gas, water, steam, or sanitation service.

Professional and related occupations in this industry include *engineers* and *computer specialists. Engineers* develop technologies that allow, for example, utilities to produce and transmit gas and electricity more efficiently and water more cleanly. They also may develop improved methods of landfill or wastewater treatment operations in order to maintain compliance with government regulations. *Computer specialists* develop computer systems to automate utility processes; provide plant simulators for operator training; and improve operator decision making. *Engineering technicians* assist engineers in research activities and may conduct some research independently.

## Training and Advancement

Public utilities provide career opportunities for persons with varying levels of experience and education. However, because the utilities industry consists of many different companies and products, skills developed in one industry may not be transferable to other industries.

High school graduates qualify for most entry-level production jobs. Production workers may start as laborers or in other unskilled jobs and, by going through an apprenticeship program and gaining on-the-job experience, advance into better-paying positions that require greater skills or have greater responsibility. Substantial advancement is possible even within a single occupation. For example, power plant operators may move up through several levels of responsibility until they reach the highest-paying operator jobs. Advancement in production

**Although many establishments are small, almost half of public utilities workers are employed in establishments with 250 or more workers**

Percent

Legend:
- Establishments
- Employment

| Number of workers employed by establishment | Establishments | Employment |
|---|---|---|
| 1 to 9 | 55.8 | 5.0 |
| 10 to 49 | 29.7 | 18.0 |
| 50 to 99 | 7.3 | 13.6 |
| 100 to 249 | 4.7 | 18.7 |
| 250+ | 2.5 | 44.7 |

Source: U.S. Department of Commerce, *County Business Patterns*, 1997

**Table 3. Employment of wage and salary workers in public utilities by occupation, 2000 and projected change, 2000-10**

(Employment in thousands)

| Occupation | Employment, 2000 Number | Employment, 2000 Percent | Percent change, 2000-2010 |
|---|---|---|---|
| All occupations ........................................ | 851 | 100.0 | 4.9 |
| **Management, business, and financial occupations** .................................. | 110 | 13.0 | 4.6 |
| General and operations managers ....... | 18 | 2.1 | 13.9 |
| Accountants and auditors ..................... | 9 | 1.1 | 3.5 |
| **Professional and related occupations** ... | 101 | 11.9 | 2.1 |
| Computer specialists ............................ | 15 | 1.8 | 20.2 |
| Electrical engineers .............................. | 10 | 1.2 | -11.9 |
| Nuclear engineers ................................ | 8 | 0.9 | -9.3 |
| Engineering technicians ....................... | 13 | 1.5 | -1.4 |
| **Service occupations** ............................... | 15 | 1.7 | 18.2 |
| Building and grounds cleaning and maintenance occupations .................. | 10 | 1.1 | 24.2 |
| **Sales and related occupations** .............. | 15 | 1.8 | 9.7 |
| **Office and administrative support occupations** ...................................... | 170 | 20.0 | -5.9 |
| First-line supervisors/managers of office and administrative support workers .... | 12 | 1.5 | 8.0 |
| Bookkeeping, accounting, and auditing clerks ................................................... | 9 | 1.1 | -0.4 |
| Customer service representatives ........ | 44 | 5.2 | 4.4 |
| Meter readers, utilities ......................... | 25 | 2.9 | -34.3 |
| Office clerks, general ........................... | 17 | 2.0 | -2.9 |
| Executive secretaries and administrative assistants .................... | 11 | 1.3 | -6.4 |
| **Construction and extraction occupations** ...................................... | 71 | 8.4 | 11.7 |
| Electricians .......................................... | 10 | 1.1 | 7.2 |
| Plumbers, pipefitters, and steamfitters ........................................ | 12 | 1.4 | 6.4 |
| Hazardous materials removal workers ................................... | 9 | 1.1 | 46.3 |
| **Installation, maintenance, and repair occupations** ...................................... | 181 | 21.3 | -0.9 |
| First-line supervisors/managers of mechanics, installers, and repairers ... | 21 | 2.4 | -2.0 |
| Electrical and electronics repairers, powerhouse, substation, and relay ..... | 14 | 1.6 | -5.5 |
| Vehicle and mobile equipment mechanics, installers, and repairers ... | 9 | 1.0 | 11.5 |
| Control and valve installers and repairers, except mechanical door ..... | 19 | 2.2 | -1.8 |
| Industrial machinery mechanics ........... | 10 | 1.2 | 3.4 |
| Electrical power-line installers and repairers ............................................ | 62 | 7.3 | -5.8 |
| Maintenance and repair workers, general ................................................ | 18 | 2.1 | 8.0 |
| **Production occupations** .......................... | 96 | 11.2 | 5.4 |
| First-line supervisors/managers of production and operating workers ...... | 16 | 1.9 | -0.9 |
| Power distributors and dispatchers ....... | 6 | 0.7 | -12.7 |
| Power plant operators .......................... | 24 | 2.8 | -4.6 |
| Water and liquid waste treatment plant and system operators ............... | 11 | 1.2 | 57.5 |
| **Transportation and material moving occupations** ...................................... | 90 | 10.6 | 31.1 |
| Truck drivers, heavy and tractor-trailer ....................................... | 18 | 2.1 | 50.5 |
| Refuse and recyclable material collectors ............................................ | 38 | 4.4 | 24.3 |

NOTE: May not add to totals due to omission of occupations with small employment.

occupations generally requires mastery of advanced skills on the job, usually with some formal training provided by the employer or through additional vocational training at a 2-year technical college. Additional formal education from an outside source is sometimes needed.

Most computer, engineering, and technician jobs require technical education after high school, although opportunities exist for persons with degrees ranging from an associate degree to a doctorate. These workers are usually familiar with company objectives and production methods which, combined with college education, equips them with many of the tools necessary for advancement to management positions. Graduates of 2-year technical institutes usually fill technician positions. Sometimes, graduates of engineering programs will start as technicians until an opportunity to advance into an engineering position arises.

Managerial jobs generally require a 4-year college degree, although a 2-year technical degree may be sufficient in smaller plants. Managers usually can advance into higher-level management jobs without additional formal training outside the workplace. Competition is expected to be keen for management positions, as industry restructuring is forcing utility companies to shed excess layers of management to improve productivity and competitiveness in the new deregulated environment.

## Earnings

Overall, nonsupervisory workers in the industry had average weekly earnings of $895 in 2000. Earnings varied by industry segment within public utilities (table 4). Average weekly earnings for production workers were highest in combination utilities ($1,084) and electric services ($941), and lowest in sanitary services ($758).

**Table 4. Average earnings and hours of nonsupervisory workers in public utilities by industry segment, 2000**

| Industry segment | Earnings Weekly | Earnings Hourly | Weekly hours |
|---|---|---|---|
| **Total, private industry** ......................... | $474 | $13.74 | 34.5 |
| **Public utilities** ...................................... | 895 | 21.47 | 41.7 |
| Combination utility services .................. | 1084 | 25.57 | 42.4 |
| Electric services ................................... | 941 | 22.50 | 41.8 |
| Gas production and distribution ............ | 812 | 19.67 | 41.3 |
| Sanitary services ................................... | 758 | 18.17 | 41.7 |

Earnings in public utilities are generally higher than earnings in other industries. The hourly earnings for production workers in public utilities averaged $21.47 in 2000, compared with $13.74 in all private industry. This was due in part to more overtime and weekend work—as utility plant operations must be monitored 24 hours a day—which commands higher hourly rates. Earnings in selected occupations in public utilities appear in table 5.

More than 30 percent of workers in public utilities are union members or are covered by a union contract, more than double the 14.9 percent for all industries.

## Outlook

Wage and salary employment in public utilities is expected to increase only 5 percent between 2000 and 2010, slower than the 16 percent growth projected for all industries combined.

**Table 5. Median hourly earnings of the largest occupations in public utilities, 2000**

| Occupation | Electric, gas, and sanitary services | All industries |
|---|---|---|
| Electrical and electronics repairers, powerhouse, substation, and relay .......... | $ 23.95 | $ 23.34 |
| Industrial machinery mechanics ................. | 23.93 | 17.30 |
| Electrical power-line installers and repairers ...................................... | 23.52 | 22.01 |
| Power plant operators ............................. | 23.44 | 22.16 |
| Control and valve installers and repairers, except mechanical door .......................... | 22.37 | 19.87 |
| Customer service representatives .............. | 15.55 | 11.83 |
| Truck drivers, heavy and tractor-trailer ....... | 15.31 | 15.25 |
| Meter readers, utilities ........................... | 15.27 | 13.32 |
| Water and liquid waste treatment plant and system operators ........................... | 14.74 | 15.09 |
| Refuse and recyclable material collectors ............................................. | 12.27 | 11.83 |

Projected employment change, however, varies by industry segment, as shown in table 6. Although electric power and natural gas are essential to everyday life, employment declines will result from improved production methods and technology, energy conservation by consumers and more efficient appliances, and a more competitive regulatory environment.

**Table 6. Projected employment growth in public utilities by industry segment, 2000-10**

| Industry segment | Percent change |
|---|---|
| Total, all public utilities ................................. | 4.9 |
| Electric services ........................................... | -9.2 |
| Gas production and distribution ................... | -6.3 |
| Combination utility services ......................... | -9.2 |
| Water supply and sanitary services ........... | 45.1 |

Reorganization of electric and gas utilities has increased competition and provided incentives for improved efficiency. For example, nonutility generators of electricity, such as a major industrial plant operating its own power generators, are permitted to sell their excess electricity to utilities at competitive rates. Also, independent power producers can build electric power generating plants for the sole purpose of selling their power to utilities. These producers generally build gas-turbine generating plants, which have lower construction and environmental costs, employ fewer workers, and usually can sell electric power more cheaply than the coal-powered steam-turbine generator plants.

In the gas transmission and distribution industry, regulatory changes now allow wholesale buyers to purchase gas at competitive rates from any producer and to use the gas pipeline transmission network to transport the gas. This process also is occurring at the distribution level. These changes have caused an increase in gas and electric utility mergers, workforce reductions, and the redesign and reallocation of job duties in a process that will continue through the projection period.

New and continuing energy policies also provide investment tax credits for research on and development of renewable sources of energy and improving the efficiency of equipment used in electric utilities. As a result, electric utilities will continue to increase the productivity of their plants and workers, resulting

in a slowdown in employment opportunities. However, highly trained technical personnel with the education and experience to take advantage of new developments in electric utilities should face good prospects for employment.

In the water supply and sanitary services industries, regulatory changes have had the opposite impact. Regulations in these industries have not been designed to increase competition, but to increase the number of contaminants that must be monitored and treated and to tighten the environmental impact standards of these industries, resulting in increased employment.

Two nonregulatory competing trends affect gas production and distribution utilities. Although natural gas is an increasingly popular choice among homeowners, businesses, and electric utilities, the efficiency of natural gas furnaces has increased dramatically, significantly reducing average home consumption. These energy-conserving technologies will likely continue to minimize the relative use of natural gas by most industries and by individual homes. In addition, utilities in colder climates have begun to automate meter reading and billing procedures. Combined, these developments are projected to result in a decrease in employment in natural gas transmission and distribution services.

Water supply and sanitation services are projected to be the fastest growing segment of public utilities, with employment projected to increase 45 percent from 2000 to 2010. This segment is expected to grow due to an increase in the amount of waste generated per person, growth of the population, increasing disposal requirements for different materials, and a rise in the percentage of refuse that is recycled. Also, newly constructed housing developments are more likely to have community water supplies and wastewater treatment facilities, increasing demand for these services.

About 28,000 new jobs in this industry will be created in transportation and material-moving occupations, such as truck drivers and refuse and recyclable material collectors. Despite automation and other improvements in production technology in this industry, expanding hazardous waste regulations and the increasing number of contaminants that must be monitored are expected to contribute to fast growth in occupations such as hazardous materials removal workers and water and liquid waste treatment plant and system operators.

In general, persons with college training in advanced technology will have the best opportunities in public utilities industries. Computer specialists, including *computer systems analysts* and *computer programmers,* are expected to be among the fastest growing occupations in the professional and related occupations group. With emphasis on improving plant automation and productivity, employment of these college-educated workers is projected to grow by 20 percent. Sales and related occupations are expected to increase in number and importance as competition for wholesale customers, who can now buy power from the lowest bidder, increases and utilities begin to rely on their sales staff to expand their customer base. Some office and administrative support workers, such as utilities meter readers and bookkeeping, accounting, and auditing clerks, are among those affected by increasing automation. Technologies including radio-transmitted meter reading and computerized billing procedures are expected to decrease employment.

## Sources of Additional Information

General information on the public utilities industry and employment opportunities often is available from local utilities, the unions to which their workers belong, and from:

➤ American Gas Association, 400 N. Capitol St. NW., Washington, DC 20001. Internet: **http://www.aga.org**

➤ Utility Workers Union of America, 815 16th St. NW., Suite 605, Washington, DC 20006.

➤ American Water Works Association, 6666 West Quincy, Denver, CO 80235.

➤ International Brotherhood of Electrical Workers, 1125 15th St. NW., Washington, DC 20005.

➤ American Public Gas Association, 11094 Lee Highway, Suite 102, Fairfax, VA 22030. Internet: **http://www.apga.org**

Detailed information on many key occupations in the public utilities industry, including the following, may be found in the 2002-03 edition of the *Occupational Outlook Handbook*.

• Construction laborers

• Electrical and electronics engineers, except computer
• Engineering technicians
• Hazardous materials removal workers
• Industrial machinery installation, repair, and maintenance workers
• Line installers and repairers
• Material-moving occupations
• Nuclear engineers
• Power plant operators, distributors and dispatchers
• Stationary engineers and boiler operators
• Systems analysts, computer scientists and database administrators
• Water and liquid waste treatment plant and system operators

# Radio and Television Broadcasting

(SIC 483)

## SIGNIFICANT POINTS

- Keen competition is expected for many jobs, particularly in large metropolitan areas, due to the large number of jobseekers attracted by the glamour of this industry.

- Job prospects will be best for applicants with a college degree in broadcasting or a related field, as well as relevant work experience.

- Many entry-level positions are at broadcast stations serving smaller markets.

- Because many radio and television stations are small, workers often must change employers, and sometimes relocate, to advance.

## Nature of the Industry

This industry consists of radio and television stations that broadcast programs free of charge to the public. Broadcast signals travel over the airwaves from a station's transmission tower to the antennas of television sets and radios; personal computers can also be equipped to receive the transmissions. Anyone in the signal area with a radio, television, or properly equipped personal computer can receive the programming. Television broadcasts carried on cable and other pay television systems are classified in a separate industry. (The statement on cable and other pay-television services appears elsewhere in the *Career Guide*.)

Radio and television stations broadcast a variety of programs, such as national and local news, talk shows, music programs, movies, other entertainment, and advertisements. Broadcast stations produce some of these programs, most notably news programs, in their own studios; however, much of the programming is produced outside the broadcast industry. Establishments that produce programming for radio and television stations—but do not broadcast the programming—are classified in the amusement and recreation services industry and in the motion picture industry. (Statements on amusement and recreation services and motion picture production and distribution appear elsewhere in the *Career Guide*).

Cable and pay television providers are required to compensate local television stations for rebroadcast rights. Revenue for commercial radio and television stations comes from the sale of advertising time during selected programs. The rates paid by advertisers depend on the size and characteristics of a program's audience. Revenue for educational and noncommercial stations primarily comes from donations, foundations, government, and corporations. These stations are generally owned and managed by public-broadcasting organizations, religious institutions, or school systems.

Changes in government regulation and technology are affecting the broadcast industry. The Telecommunications Act of 1996 relaxed ownership restrictions, an action that has had a tremendous impact on the industry. Instead of owning only one radio station per market, companies now can purchase up to eight radio stations in a single market. In television, owners are permitted two stations in a single market. These changes have led to a large-scale consolidation of radio stations. In some areas, five FM and three AM radio stations are owned by the same company and share the same offices. Independently owned commercial radio stations are increasingly rare.

The U.S. Federal Communications Commission (FCC) is a proponent of digital television (DTV), a technology that uses digital signals to transmit television programs. Digital signals consist of pieces of simple electronic code that can carry more information than conventional analog signals. A growing number of television stations are implementing digital broadcasting. This allows for the transmission of higher-resolution pictures, referred to as high-definition television (HDTV).

Broadcasters can use digital technology to transmit a single HDTV broadcast, or they can multi-cast several conventional broadcasts. Multi-casting is the transmission of more than one signal on a given channel. For example, a broadcast station could transmit a sporting event from several different camera angles on the same channel. Viewers would then be able to select which view their television set receives.

Digital broadcasting can transmit a variety of information besides television programming. For example, viewers with access to DTV could obtain electronic newspapers, computer software, telephone directories, and any other information that can be translated into digital code.

## Working Conditions

Most employees in this industry work in clean, comfortable surroundings in broadcast stations and studios. Some employees work in the production of shows and broadcasting while other employees work in advertising, sales, promotions, and marketing.

Television news teams made up of reporters, camera operators, and technicians travel in electronic news gathering trucks to various locations to cover news stories. Although such location work is exciting, some assignments, such as reporting on natural disasters, may present danger. These assignments may also require outdoor work under adverse weather conditions.

Camera operators working on such news teams must have the physical stamina to carry and set up their equipment. Broadcast technicians on electronic news gathering trucks must ensure that the mobile unit's antenna is correctly positioned in order to avoid electrocution from power lines. Field service engineers work on outdoor transmitting equipment and may have to climb poles or antenna towers; their work can take place under a variety of weather conditions. Broadcast technicians who maintain and set up equipment may have to do heavy lifting. Technological changes have enabled camera operators to also fulfill the tasks of broadcast technicians, operating the transmission and editing equipment on a remote broadcasting

101

truck. News operations, programming, and engineering employees work under a great deal of pressure in order to meet deadlines. As a result, these workers are likely to experience varied or erratic work schedules, often working on early morning or late evening news programs.

Sales workers may face stress meeting sales goals. Aside from sometimes erratic work schedules, management and administrative workers work in an environment similar to any other office.

For many people, the excitement of working in broadcasting compensates for the demanding nature of the jobs. Although this industry is noted for its high pressure and long hours, the work is generally not hazardous. The rate of occupational illness and injury in broadcasting is much lower than the average for all industries. In 1998, cases of work-related injury and illness averaged only 2.1 per 100 full-time workers in radio and television broadcasting, significantly lower than the rate of 6.3 per 100 for all private industry.

## Employment

The radio and television broadcasting industry provided 255,000 wage and salary jobs in 2000. Most jobs were in large establishments; more than 60 percent of all jobs were in establishments with at least 50 employees in 1997 (chart 1). Radio and television broadcasting establishments are found throughout the country, but jobs in larger stations are concentrated in large cities.

## Occupations in the Industry

Occupations at large broadcast stations fall into five general categories: program production, news-related, technical, sales, and general administration. At small stations, jobs are less specialized, and employees often perform several functions. Although on-camera or on-air positions are the most familiar occupations in broadcasting, the majority of employment opportunities are behind the scenes (table 1).

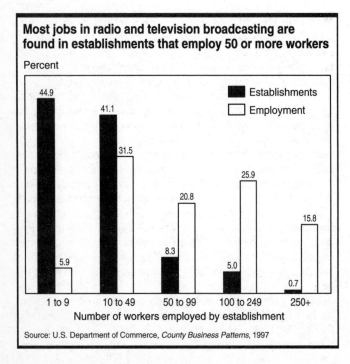

**Most jobs in radio and television broadcasting are found in establishments that employ 50 or more workers**

Percent

Legend: ■ Establishments ☐ Employment

| Number of workers employed by establishment | Establishments | Employment |
| --- | --- | --- |
| 1 to 9 | 44.9 | 5.9 |
| 10 to 49 | 41.1 | 31.5 |
| 50 to 99 | 8.3 | 20.8 |
| 100 to 249 | 5.0 | 25.9 |
| 250+ | 0.7 | 15.8 |

Source: U.S. Department of Commerce, *County Business Patterns*, 1997

*Program production occupations.* Most television programs are produced by the motion picture industry; actors, directors, and producers working on these prerecorded programs are not employed by the television and radio broadcast industry. Program production occupations at television and radio stations create programs such as news, talk, and music shows.

*Assistant producers* provide clerical support and background research; assist with the preparation of musical, written, and visual materials; and time the production to make sure it does run over schedule. They also may operate cameras and other audio and video equipment.

*Video editors* select and assemble pretaped video to create a finished program, applying sound and special effects as necessary. Conventional editing requires assembling pieces of videotape to create a finished product in a linear fashion. The editor first assembles the beginning of the program, and then works sequentially towards the end. Newer computerized editing allows an editor to electronically cut and paste video segments. This technique is known as nonlinear editing because the editor is no longer restricted to working sequentially; a segment may be moved at any time to any location in the program.

*Producers* plan and develop live or taped productions, determining how the show will look and sound. They select the script, talent, sets, props, lighting, and other production elements. They also coordinate the activities of on-air personalities, production staff, and other personnel. *Website or Internet producers*, a relatively new occupation in the broadcast industry, plan and develop Internet sites that provide news updates, program schedules, and information about popular shows. The producer decides what will appear on the site and is responsible for its overall design and maintenance.

*Announcers* read news items and provide other information, such as program schedules and station breaks for commercials or public service information. Many radio announcers are referred to as disc jockeys, playing recorded music on radio stations. They may take requests from listeners; interview guests; and comment on the music, weather, or traffic. Most stations now have placed all of their advertisements, sound bites, and music on a computer, which is used to select and play or edit the items. Technological advances have simplified the monitoring and adjusting of the transmitter, leaving disc jockeys responsible for all of the tasks associated with keeping a station on the air. Traditional tapes and CD-ROMs are used only as backups in case of a computer failure. Announcers and disc jockeys need a good speaking voice; the latter also need a significant knowledge of music.

*Program directors* are in charge of on-air programming in radio stations. Program directors decide what type of music will be played, supervise on-air personnel, and often select the specific songs and the order in which they will be played. Considerable experience, usually as a disc jockey, is required, as well as a thorough knowledge of music.

*News-related occupations.* News, weather, and sports reports are important to many television stations because they attract a large audience and account for a large proportion of revenue. Many radio stations depend on up-to-the-minute news for a major share of their programming. Program production occupations, such as producers and announcers, also work on the production of news programs.

*Reporters* gather information from various sources, analyze and prepare news stories, and report on-the-air. *Correspondents* report on news occurring in the large U.S. and foreign cities where they are stationed. *Newswriters* write and edit the news stories from information collected by reporters. Newswriters may advance to positions as reporters or correspondents.

*Broadcast news analysts*, also known as news anchors, analyze, interpret, and broadcast news received from various sources. News anchors present news stories and introduce videotaped news or live transmissions from on-the-scene reporters. Newscasters at large stations may specialize in a particular field. Weathercasters, also called weather reporters, report current and forecasted weather conditions. They gather information from national satellite weather services, wire services, and local and regional weather bureaus. Some weathercasters are trained *atmospheric scientists* and can develop their own weather forecasts. Sportscasters are responsible for reporting sporting events. They usually select, write, and deliver the sports news for each newscast.

*Assistant news directors* supervise the newsroom; they coordinate wire service reports, tape or film inserts, and stories from individual newswriters and reporters. *Assignment editors* assign stories to news teams, sending them on location if necessary.

*News directors* have overall responsibility for the news team of reporters, writers, editors, and newscasters, as well as studio and mobile unit production crews. This senior administrative position entails responsibilities that include determining what events to be covered, and how and when they will be presented in a news broadcast.

*Technical occupations.* Employees in these occupations operate and maintain the electronic equipment that records and transmits radio or television programs. The titles of some of these occupations use the terms "engineer," "technician," and "operator" interchangeably.

*Radio operators* manage equipment that regulates the signal strength, clarity, and range of sounds and colors of broadcasts. They also monitor and log outgoing signals and operate transmitters. *Audio and video equipment technicians* operate equipment to regulate the volume, sound quality, brightness, contrast, and visual quality of a broadcast. *Broadcast technicians* set up and maintain electronic broadcasting equipment. Their work can extend outside the studio, as when they set up portable transmitting equipment or maintain stationary towers.

*Television and video camera operators* set up and operate studio cameras, which are used in the television studio; and electronic news gathering cameras, which are mobile and used outside the studio when a news team is pursuing a story at another location. Camera operators need training in video, as well as some experience in television production.

*Master control engineers* ensure that all of the radio or television station's scheduled program elements, such as on-location feeds, prerecorded segments, and commercials, are smoothly transmitted. They also are responsible for ensuring that transmissions meet Federal Communications Commission (FCC) requirements.

*Technical directors* direct the studio and control room technical staff during the production of a program. They need a thorough understanding of both the production and technical aspects of broadcasting, acquired as a lighting director or camera operator, or as another type of broadcast worker.

*Assistant chief engineers* oversee the day-to-day technical operations of the station. *Chief engineers* or *directors of engineering* are responsible for all of the station's technical facilities and services. These workers need a bachelors' degree in electrical engineering, technical training in broadcast engineering, and years of broadcast engineering experience acquired in less responsible positions.

**Table 1. Employment of wage and salary workers in radio and television broadcasting by occupation, 2000 and projected change, 2000-10**

(Employment in thousands)

| Occupation | Employment, 2000 Number | Employment, 2000 Percent | Percent change, 2000-2010 |
|---|---|---|---|
| **All occupations** | 255 | 100.0 | 9.7 |
| **Management, business, and financial occupations** | 28 | 11.0 | 14.8 |
| Advertising and promotions managers .. | 3 | 1.3 | 26.7 |
| Sales managers | 3 | 1.3 | 26.7 |
| Engineering managers | 2 | 0.7 | -5.9 |
| General and operations managers | 8 | 3.0 | 8.8 |
| Business and financial operations occupations | 3 | 1.1 | 16.6 |
| **Professional and related occupations** | 156 | 61.2 | 7.3 |
| Computer specialists | 3 | 1.1 | 43.2 |
| Engineers | 2 | 0.7 | 2.3 |
| Multi-media artists and animators | 2 | 0.9 | 9.7 |
| Producers and directors | 16 | 6.5 | 27.2 |
| Announcers | 43 | 17.0 | -7.9 |
| News analysts, reporters and correspondents | 21 | 8.4 | 8.7 |
| Public relations specialists | 2 | 0.8 | 26.7 |
| Editors | 4 | 1.6 | 12.8 |
| Writers and authors | 4 | 1.5 | 15.1 |
| All other media and communication workers | 2 | 0.9 | 15.1 |
| Audio and video equipment technicians | 4 | 1.7 | 7.8 |
| Broadcast technicians | 23 | 9.1 | 3.6 |
| Photographers | 6 | 2.5 | 15.1 |
| Camera operators, television, video, and motion picture | 10 | 3.8 | 15.1 |
| Film and video editors | 3 | 1.3 | 15.1 |
| **Sales and related occupations** | 36 | 14.1 | 23.8 |
| Advertising sales agents | 29 | 11.3 | 26.7 |
| First-line supervisors/managers of retail sales workers | 2 | 0.7 | 16.3 |
| **Office and administrative support occupations** | 31 | 12.0 | 0.5 |
| First-line supervisors/managers of office and administrative support workers | 2 | 0.7 | 15.1 |
| Bookkeeping, accounting, and auditing clerks | 3 | 1.3 | -0.9 |
| Receptionists and information clerks | 3 | 1.2 | 15.1 |
| Material recording, scheduling, dispatching, and distributing occupations | 2 | 0.7 | 6.7 |
| Office clerks, general | 5 | 2.1 | 1.5 |
| Executive secretaries and administrative assistants | 3 | 1.3 | 3.6 |
| Secretaries, except legal, medical, and executive | 3 | 1.0 | -7.9 |

NOTE: May not add to totals due to omission of occupations with small employment.

*Sales, promotions, and marketing occupations.* Most workers in this category are *advertising sales agents*, sometimes known as *account executives*. They sell advertising time to sponsors, advertising agencies, and other buyers. Sales representatives must have a thorough knowledge of the size and characteristics of their station's audience, including income levels, gender, age, and consumption patterns. Sales work has expanded beyond the traditional role of simply selling advertising to a wide range of marketing efforts. Stations earn additional revenue through broadcasting from a business, such as a dance club. Businesses also sponsor concerts or other promotions that are organized by a station. In return for sponsorship, the business may set up a booth or post large signs.

*Continuity directors* schedule and produce commercials. Continuity directors carefully schedule commercials, taking into account both the timeslot in which a commercial is to be played, as well as competing advertisements. For example, two car dealership advertisements should not be played during the same commercial break. Continuity directors also create and produce advertisements for clients who do not produce their own.

Large stations generally have several workers who spend all of their time handling sales. *Sales worker supervisors*, who may handle a few large accounts personally, supervise these workers. In small stations, part-time sales personnel or announcers often handle sales responsibilities during hours they are not on-the-air.

*General administration.* *General managers* or *station managers* coordinate all radio and television station activities. In very small stations, the manager and a bookkeeper may handle all the accounting, purchasing, hiring, and other routine office work. In larger stations, the general administrative staff includes business managers, accountants, lawyers, personnel workers, public relations workers, and others. They are assisted by office and administrative support workers such as secretaries, word processors, typists, and financial clerks.

## Training and Advancement
Professional, management, and sales occupations generally require a college degree; technical occupations often do not. It is easier to obtain employment and gain promotions with a degree, especially in larger, more competitive markets. Advanced schooling is generally required for supervisory positions—including technical occupations—having greater responsibility and higher salaries.

Entry-level jobs in news or program production increasingly require a college degree and some broadcast experience. Approximately 450 colleges offer formal programs in journalism and mass communications, including radio and television broadcasting. Some community colleges offer 2-year programs in broadcasting. Broadcast trade schools offer courses that last 6 months to a year and teach radio and television announcing, writing, and production.

Individuals pursuing a career in broadcasting often gain initial experience through work at college radio and television stations or through internships at professional stations. Although these positions are usually unpaid, they sometimes provide college credit or tuition. More importantly, they provide hands-on experience and a competitive edge when applying for jobs. In this highly competitive industry, broadcasters are less willing to provide on-the-job training, and instead seek candidates who can perform the job immediately.

Some technical positions require only a high school diploma. However, many broadcast stations seek individuals with training in broadcast technology, electronics, or engineering from a technical school, community college, or 4-year college. An understanding of computer networks and software will become more important as the industry introduces more digital technology. Supervisory technical positions and jobs in large stations generally require a college degree.

The Society of Broadcast Engineers (SBE) issues certification to technicians who pass a written examination. Several classes of certification are available, requiring increasing levels of experience and knowledge for eligibility. The Telecommunications Act of 1996 mandated that the FCC drop its licensing requirements for transmitter maintenance; SBE certification has filled the void left by the elimination of this license.

Employees in the radio and television broadcasting industry often find their first job in broadcast stations serving smaller markets. Competition for positions in large metropolitan areas is stronger, and these stations usually seek highly experienced personnel. Because many radio and television stations are small, workers in this industry often must change employers to advance. Relocation to other parts of the country frequently is necessary.

## Earnings
Weekly earnings of nonsupervisory workers in radio and television broadcasting averaged $670 in 2000, higher than the average of $474 for all private industry. As a common rule, earnings of broadcast personnel are highest in large metropolitan areas. Earnings in selected occupations in radio and television broadcasting for 2000 appear in table 2.

Table 2. Median hourly earnings of the largest occupations in radio and television broadcasting, 2000

| Occupation | Radio and television broadcasting | All industries |
|---|---|---|
| General and operations managers | $ 31.81 | $ 29.41 |
| Advertising sales agents | 17.53 | 17.24 |
| News analysts, reporters and correspondents | 16.13 | 14.00 |
| Editors | 14.81 | 18.93 |
| Film and video editors | 14.46 | 16.42 |
| Photographers | 14.37 | 10.72 |
| Audio and video equipment technicians | 11.70 | 14.57 |
| Broadcast technicians | 11.41 | 12.96 |
| Camera operators, television, video, and motion picture | 11.28 | 13.40 |
| Announcers | 9.54 | 9.52 |

The principal unions representing employees in radio and TV broadcasting are the National Association of Broadcast Employees and Technicians (NABET), the International Brotherhood of Electrical Workers (IBEW), the International Alliance of Theatrical Stage Employees (IATSE), and the American Federation of Television and Radio Artists (AFTRA).

## Outlook
Employment in radio and television broadcasting is expected to increase only 10 percent over the 2000-10 period, slower than the 15 percent projected for all industries combined. Factors contributing to the relatively slow rate of growth include industry consolidation, introduction of new technologies, greater use of prepared programming, and competition from other media. Keen

competition is expected for many jobs due to the large number of jobseekers attracted by the glamour of this industry. Job prospects will be best for applicants with a college degree in broadcasting or a related field, as well as relevant work experience.

Consolidation of individual broadcast stations into large networks, especially in the radio sector, has increased due to relaxed ownership regulations. This trend will limit employment growth as networks use workers more efficiently. For example, a network can run eight radio stations from one office, producing news programming at one station and then using the programming for broadcast from other stations, thus eliminating the need for multiple news staffs. Similarly, technical workers, upper-level management, and marketing and advertising sales workers are pooled to work for several stations simultaneously. In the consolidation of the radio industry, several major companies purchased scores of stations nationwide, leaving many of these companies with large debts to pay off. Consequently, some radio stations will be forced to reduce costs, including staff.

The introduction of new technology also is slowing employment growth. Conventional broadcast equipment used to be relatively specialized; each piece of equipment served a separate function and required an operator with specialized knowledge. Newer computerized equipment often combines the functions of several older pieces of equipment and does not require specialized knowledge for operation. This reduces the need for certain types of workers, including those responsible for editing, recording, and creating graphics. In addition, increased use of remote-monitoring equipment allows technical workers in one location to operate and monitor transmissions at a remote station.

Employment growth also is being constrained by the increasing use of radio and television programming created by services outside the broadcasting industry. These establishments provide prepared programming, including music, news, weather, sports, and professional announcer services. The services can easily be accessed through satellite hookups and reduce the need for program production and news staff at radio and television stations.

Finally, employment growth will remain relatively slow because television broadcasters anticipate increased competition from cable systems, satellite and other pay television services, and growing use of the Internet. Radio broadcasters expect continued growth in revenues as consumers spend more time driving. The major threat to the radio industry, especially smaller, marginal stations, is from satellite radio, which functions like cable television with subscribers paying a monthly fee.

One area in which broadcasting may experience faster employment growth is data services. The introduction of digital transmission will allow broadcasters to start transmitting data such as electronic publications, software, and interactive educational materials. Although the broadcasters who enter the data services market will face much competition from other industries, such as telecommunications and cable and other pay television services, strong consumer demand could lead to employment growth in this area. Digital broadcasting will allow television stations to broadcast several channels, instead of one, possibly producing minor gains in employment as well.

## Sources of Additional Information

For a list of schools with accredited programs in broadcast journalism, send a request to:

➤ Accrediting Council on Education in Journalism and Mass Communications, University of Kansas, School of Journalism, Stauffer-Flint Hall, Lawrence, KS 66045.
Internet: **http://www.ukans.edu/~acejmc**

For career information, contact:

➤ National Association of Broadcast Employees and Technicians, Communications Workers of America (NABET/CWA) International, 501 Third St. NW., Washington, DC 20001.
Internet: **http://union.nabetcwa.org/nabet/front.html**
➤ National Association of Broadcasters, Career Center, 1771 N St. NW., Washington, DC 20036.
Internet: **http://www.nab.org**

Information on the following occupations may be found in the 2002-03 *Occupational Outlook Handbook*:

- Actors, producers, and directors
- Advertising, marketing, promotions, public relations, and sales managers
- Announcers
- Broadcast and sound engineering technicians and radio operators
- News analysts, reporters, and correspondents
- Television, video, and motion picture camera operators and editors
- Writers and editors

# Telecommunications

## SIGNIFICANT POINTS

- Telecommunications are rapidly expanding beyond traditional voice telephone service.

- The demand for greater telecommunications capacity—or bandwidth—will create jobs that require technical skills.

- Average earnings in telecommunications greatly exceed average earnings throughout private industry.

## Nature of the Industry

Changes in technology and government regulation continue to transform the telecommunications industry. Whereas voice telephone communication was once the primary service of the industry, the transmission of a variety of materials, including data, graphics, and video, is now commonplace. The widespread installation of fiber optic cables, which transmit light signals along glass strands, permits faster, higher capacity transmissions than those that are possible with traditional copper wirelines. In addition, networks of radio towers provide rapidly expanding wireless telecommunications services.

Changes in government regulation have introduced competition into an industry that was once dominated by a single company. Competition from outside the industry is increasing as cable companies and public utilities expand their own communications networks.

The principal sector of the telecommunications industry is telephone communications. Establishments in this sector operate both wireline and wireless networks. Wireline networks use wires and cables to connect customers' premises to central offices maintained by telecommunications companies. Central offices contain switching equipment that routes content to its final destination or to another switching center. For example, switching equipment may route local phone calls directly from the central office to their final destination; long distance calls are routed to larger switching centers that determine the most efficient route for the call to take.

Wireless networks are rapidly expanding; they operate through the transmission of signals over networks of radio towers. For example, a wireless cellular telephone transmits radio signals to an antenna located on a radio tower. The signal is then transmitted through the antenna into the wireline network. Other wireless services include beeper, paging, and limited Internet access. Because these devices require no wireline connection, they are popular with customers who need to communicate as they travel, residents of areas with inadequate wireline service, and those who simply desire the convenience of portable communications.

Wireless providers are developing additional technology called third generation (3G) wireless access. Conventional wireless Internet access is slow, and allows cellular phones to display only limited amounts of text-based information. A 3G system allows high-speed data transmission and better Internet access. Wireless service is expanding into homes through fixed cellular service, which involves connecting the telephone system in a house to an antenna, instead of a telephone line. It should become increasingly common, because 3G wireless will provide a level of service similar to that of wireline systems.

The wireline and wireless sectors also include resellers of telecommunications services who compete with traditional local telephone service providers. These resellers lease transmission facilities, such as telephone wirelines, from existing telecommunications networks, and then resell the service to other customers. Other sectors in the industry include message communications services, such as e-mail and facsimile services, and operators of other communication services, ranging from radar stations to radio networks used by taxicab companies.

Voice telephone communications have long been the predominant service offered by telephone companies. With the rising popularity of the Internet, however, customers increasingly use their telephone service to transmit data and other electronic materials. The transmission of such content relies on digital technologies that use telecommunications networks more efficiently than do conventional systems. Digital signals consist of separate pieces of electronic code that can be broken apart during transmission and then reassembled at the destination without loss of clarity. Telecommunications providers have built networks of computerized switching equipment, called packet switched networks, to route digital signals. Packet switches break the signals into small segments or "packets" and provide each with the necessary routing information. Segments may take separate paths to their destination and may share the paths with transmissions from other users. At the destination, the segments are reassembled, and the transmission is complete. Because packet switching considers alternate routes, and allows multiple transmissions to share the same route, it results in a more efficient use of telecommunications capacity.

The transmission of voice signals requires relatively small amounts of capacity on telecommunications networks. By contrast, the transmission of data, video, and graphics requires much higher capacity. This transmission capacity is referred to as bandwidth. As the demand increases for high-capacity transmissions—especially with the rising volume of Internet data—telecommunications companies are continually expanding and upgrading their networks to increase the amount of available bandwidth.

Wireline providers are expanding their networks by laying additional fiber optic cable, which provides higher bandwidth and transmission speed than does copper wire. The capacity of fiber optic cables is increasing due to a technology known as wavelength division multiplexing (WDM). WDM divides each glass strand within a cable into different colors of the spectrum; each color can carry a separate stream of data, increasing overall capacity. Providers have also begun offering upgraded service on the copper wirelines that connect most residential customers with the central offices. Technologies such as digital subscriber lines (DSL) allow simultaneous transmission of voice and data communications at relatively high speeds. Additionally, satellite communications providers are expanding a network of satellites that competes with wireline providers for high-bandwidth data communication services.

The Telecommunications Act of 1996 allowed competition in all sectors of the communications industry, from local and long-distance telephone services to cable television and broadcasting. The Act also opened the telecommunications market to sectors outside the industry, such as public utilities. As a result of this latest round of industry deregulation, telecommunications companies are able to compete across traditionally separate markets. For example, a single provider might offer both local and long-distance telephone service. Providers from other industries also are entering the telecommunications market, offering cable TV and high-speed Internet access, as well as telephone service. Such convergent services are popular with customers seeking to consolidate their purchase of communication services. To meet this demand for combined services, mergers are taking place as companies seek to acquire the services they need to compete in the marketplace.

## Working Conditions

The telecommunications industry offers steady, year-round employment. Overtime sometimes is required, especially during emergencies such as floods or hurricanes when workers may need to report to work with little notice.

Telecommunications line installers and repairers work in a variety of places, both indoors and outdoors, and in all kinds of weather. Their work involves lifting, climbing, reaching, stooping, crouching, and crawling. They must work in high places such as rooftops and telephone poles, or below ground when working with buried lines. Their jobs bring them into proximity with electrical wires and circuits, so they must take precautions to avoid shocks. These workers must wear safety equipment when entering manholes, and test for the presence of gas before going underground.

Telecommunications equipment installers and repairers, except line installers, generally work indoors—most often in a telecommunication company's central office or a customer's place of business. They may have to stand for long periods; climb ladders; and do some reaching, stooping, and light lifting. Adherence to safety precautions is essential to guard against work injuries such as minor burns and electrical shock.

Most communications equipment operators, such as telephone operators, work at video display terminals in pleasant, well-lighted, air-conditioned surroundings. If the worksite is not well designed, however, operators may experience eye strain and back discomfort. The rapid pace of the job and close supervision may cause stress. Some workplaces have introduced innovative practices among their operators to reduce job-related stress.

The number of disabling injuries in telephone communications, the principal sector of the telecommunications industry, has been well below the average for all industries in past years. In 1999, cases of work-related injury and illness were 2.8 per 100 full-time workers, significantly lower than the 6.3 per 100 full-time workers for the entire private sector.

## Employment

The telecommunications industry provided almost 1.2 million wage and salary jobs in 2000. Most jobs were concentrated in telephone communications. Only 34,000 worked in the other sector of the telecommunications industry—telegraph and communications services, not elsewhere classified.

Most telephone employees work in large establishments. About 77 percent of employment is in establishments with 50 or more employees (chart). With continuing deregulation, however, the number of small contractors has been increasing. Telecommunications jobs are found in almost every community, but most telephone employees work in cities that have large concentrations of industrial and business establishments.

## Occupations in the Industry

Although the telecommunications industry employs workers in many different occupations, about 55 percent of all workers are employed in either office and administrative support occupations or installation, maintenance, and repair occupations (table 1).

Telephone craftworkers install, repair, and maintain telephone equipment, cables and access lines, and telecommunications systems. These workers can be grouped by the type of work they perform. *Telecommunications line installers and repairers* connect telephone central offices to customers' telephone systems. They install poles and terminals, and place wires and cables that lead to a consumer's premises. They use power-driven equipment to dig holes and set telephone poles. Line installers climb the poles or use truck-mounted buckets (aerial work platforms) and attach the cables using various hand tools. After line installers place cables on poles, or towers or in underground conduits and trenches, they complete the line connections.

*Telecommunications equipment installers and repairers, except line installers,* install, repair, and maintain the array of increasingly complex and sophisticated communications equipment and cables. Their work includes setting up, rearranging, and removing the complex switching and dialing equipment used in central offices. They may also solve network-related problems and program equipment to provide special features.

Some telecommunications equipment installers are referred to as telephone station installers and repairers. They install, service, and repair telephone systems and other communications

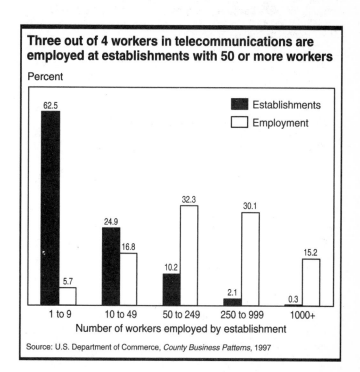

**Three out of 4 workers in telecommunications are employed at establishments with 50 or more workers**

Percent

Legend: ■ Establishments □ Employment

| Number of workers employed by establishment | Establishments | Employment |
|---|---|---|
| 1 to 9 | 62.5 | 5.7 |
| 10 to 49 | 24.9 | 16.8 |
| 50 to 249 | 10.2 | 32.3 |
| 250 to 999 | 2.1 | 30.1 |
| 1000+ | 0.3 | 15.2 |

Source: U.S. Department of Commerce, *County Business Patterns*, 1997

**Table 1. Employment of wage and salary workers in telecommunications by occupation, 2000 and projected change, 2000-10**

(Employment in thousands)

| Occupation | Employment, 2000 Number | Employment, 2000 Percent | Percent change, 2000-2010 |
|---|---|---|---|
| All occupations | 1,168 | 100.0 | 12.2 |
| Management, business, and financial occupations | 235 | 20.2 | 15.8 |
| Marketing and sales managers | 11 | 1.0 | 30.6 |
| Computer and information systems managers | 9 | 0.7 | 48.0 |
| General and operations managers | 23 | 1.9 | 12.1 |
| Human resources managers | 10 | 0.8 | 8.9 |
| Management analysts | 19 | 1.6 | 16.9 |
| Financial specialists | 17 | 1.4 | 22.5 |
| Professional and related occupations | 137 | 11.7 | 33.3 |
| Computer software engineers, systems software | 15 | 1.3 | 60.4 |
| Computer support specialists | 14 | 1.2 | 77.9 |
| Electrical and electronics engineers | 8 | 0.7 | 15.6 |
| Electrical and electronic engineering technicians | 10 | 0.8 | 6.5 |
| Sales and related occupations | 143 | 12.3 | 14.3 |
| Retail salespersons | 11 | 0.9 | 18.8 |
| Sales representatives, wholesale and manufacturing, technical and scientific products | 33 | 2.9 | 14.6 |
| Sales representatives, wholesale and manufacturing, except technical and scientific products | 19 | 1.6 | 6.8 |
| First-line supervisors/managers of non-retail sales workers | 21 | 1.8 | 7.0 |
| Telemarketers | 9 | 0.8 | 18.9 |
| Office and administrative support occupations | 374 | 32.0 | 6.8 |
| First-line supervisors/managers of office and administrative support workers | 30 | 2.6 | 18.9 |
| Telephone operators | 41 | 3.5 | -40.5 |
| Bill and account collectors | 8 | 0.7 | 12.4 |
| Bookkeeping, accounting, and auditing clerks | 10 | 0.8 | 2.2 |
| Customer service representatives | 141 | 12.1 | 22.7 |
| Material recording, scheduling, dispatching, and distributing occupations | 21 | 1.8 | 14.5 |
| Office clerks, general | 30 | 2.6 | 4.8 |
| Executive secretaries and administrative assistants | 13 | 1.1 | 6.7 |
| Installation, maintenance, and repair occupations | 265 | 22.7 | 4.7 |
| First-line supervisors/managers of mechanics, installers, and repairers | 18 | 1.5 | 18.9 |
| Telecommunications equipment installers and repairers, except line installers | 126 | 10.8 | -4.9 |
| Electrical power-line installers and repairers | 10 | 0.9 | 18.9 |
| Telecommunications line installers and repairers | 68 | 5.8 | 10.1 |

NOTE: May not add to totals due to omission of occupations with small employment.

equipment on customers' property. When customers move or request new types of service, such as a high-speed internet connection, a fax, or an additional line, installers relocate telephones or make changes in existing equipment. They assemble equipment and install wiring. They also connect telephones to outside service wires and sometimes must climb poles or ladders to make these connections.

*Telephone operators*, including central office operators and directory assistance operators, make telephone connections; assist customers with specialized services such as reverse-charge calls; provide telephone numbers; and may provide emergency assistance.

*Customer service representatives* help customers understand the new and varied types of services offered by telecommunications providers. Some customer service representatives also are expected to sell services and may work on a commission basis. Other administrative support workers include *financial, information, and records clerks*; *secretaries and administrative assistants*; and *first-line supervisors/managers of office and administrative support workers*. These workers perform a variety of duties including keeping service records, compiling and sending bills to customers, and preparing statistical and other company reports.

About 12 percent of the industry's employees are professional workers. Many of these are scientific and technical personnel such as engineers and computer specialists. *Engineers* plan cable and microwave routes, central office and PBX equipment installations, and the expansion of existing structures, and solve other engineering problems. Some engineers also engage in research and development of new equipment. specializing in telecommunications design voice and data communications systems, and integrate communications equipment with computer networks. They work closely with clients, who may not understand sophisticated communications systems, and design systems that meet their customers' needs. *Computer software engineers* and *network systems and data communications analysts* design, develop, test, and debug software products. These include computer-assisted engineering programs for schematic cabling projects; modeling programs for cellular and satellite systems; and programs for telephone options, such as voice mail, electronic mail, and call waiting. Telecommunications specialists coordinate the installation of these systems and may provide follow-up maintenance and training. In addition, the industry employs many other managerial, professional, and technical workers, such as *financial information and record clerks*; *accountants and auditors*; *human resources, training, and labor relations managers; engineering technicians*; and *computer programmers*.

About 12 percent of the industry's employees are in sales and related occupations. These workers sell telecommunications services, such as long-distance service, personal answering services, voice mail, electronic mail, and call-waiting telephone options.

New occupational specialties have emerged based on the industry's new innovations and technologies. For example, some engineers research, design, and develop gas lasers and related equipment needed to send messages via fiber optic cable transmission. They study the limitations and uses of lasers and fiber optics; find new applications for them; and oversee the building, testing, and operations of the new applications.

## Training and Advancement

The telecommunications industry offers employment in jobs requiring a variety of skills and training. Many jobs require a high school education in addition to on-the-job training. Other jobs require particular skills that may take several years of experience to learn completely. For some managerial and professional jobs, employers require a college education.

Line installers often are hired initially as helpers, ground workers, or tree trimmers who clear branches from telephone lines. Because the work entails a lot of climbing, applicants should have physical stamina and be unafraid of heights. The ability to distinguish colors is necessary because wires and cables are coded by color. Although line installers usually do not complete a formal apprenticeship, they generally receive several years of on-the-job training. Line installers may transfer to other highly skilled jobs, such as engineering assistant, or may move into other kinds of work, such as sales. Promotion to crew supervisor, technical staff, or instructor of new employees also is possible.

Most companies prefer to hire telecommunications equipment installers and repairers with postsecondary training in electronics; familiarity with computers is also important. Training sources include 2- and 4- year college programs in electronics or communications, trade schools, and training provided by equipment and software manufacturers. Telecommunications equipment installers and repairers may advance to jobs maintaining more sophisticated equipment or to engineering technician positions.

Communications equipment operators should have clear speech and good hearing; computer literacy and typing skills also are important. New operators learn equipment operation and procedures for maximizing efficiency. Instructors monitor both the time and quality of trainees' responses to customer requests. Formal classroom instruction and on-the-job training may last several weeks.

A bachelor's degree in engineering usually is required for entry-level jobs as electrical and electronics engineers. Continuing education is important for these engineers; those who fail to keep up with the rapid changes in technology risk technological obsolescence, which makes them more susceptible to layoffs or, at a minimum, more likely to be passed over for advancement.

While there is no universally accepted way to prepare for a job as a computer professional, most employers place a premium on some formal college education. Computer software engineers usually hold a degree in computer science or in software engineering. For systems analyst, computer scientist, or database administrator positions, many employers seek applicants who have a bachelor's degree in computer science, information science, or management information systems.

Due to the rapid introduction of new technologies and services, the telecommunications industry is among the most rapidly changing in the economy. This means workers must keep their job skills up to date. From managers to telephone operators, increased knowledge of both computer hardware and software is of paramount importance. Several major companies and the telecommunications unions have created a website that provides free training for current employees, enabling them to keep their knowledge current and helping them to advance. Telecommunications industry employers now look for workers with skills, abilities, and knowledge in the following areas: computer programming and software design; voice telephone technology, known as telephony; laser and fiber optic technology; wireless technology; data compression skills; and sales ability enhanced by interpersonal skills and a knowledge of telecommunications terminology.

## Earnings

Average weekly earnings of nonsupervisory workers in telephone communications, the principal sector of the telecommunications industry, were $743 in 2000, significantly higher than average earnings of $474 in private industry. Earnings in selected occupations in telephone communications for 2000 appear in table 2.

Table 2. Median hourly earnings of the largest occupations in telecommunications, 2000

| Occupation | Telephone communications | All industries |
|---|---|---|
| General and operations managers | $ 38.88 | $ 29.41 |
| Computer software engineers, systems software | 33.14 | 33.43 |
| Telecommunications line installers and repairers | 22.88 | 18.32 |
| First-line supervisors/managers of non-retail sales workers | 22.86 | 23.54 |
| First-line supervisors/managers of office and administrative support workers | 22.56 | 17.51 |
| Telecommunications equipment installers and repairers, except line installers | 22.52 | 21.17 |
| Sales representatives, wholesale and manufacturing, technical and scientific products | 19.09 | 25.30 |
| Customer service representatives | 16.58 | 11.83 |
| Sales representatives, wholesale and manufacturing, except technical and scientific products | 15.97 | 19.40 |
| Telephone operators | 14.79 | 13.46 |

About 26.7 percent of employees in the industry are union members or covered by union contracts, compared with 15 percent for all industries. Most telecommunications employees belong to one of two unions—the Communications Workers of America or the International Brotherhood of Electrical Workers.

## Outlook

Employment in the telecommunications industry is expected to increase 12 percent over the 2000-10 period, somewhat less than the 15 percent projected for all industries combined. Increases in both residential and business demand for high-capacity communications will lead to the expansion of telecommunications networks. Rapidly increasing wireless demand, and the construction of a new generation of wireless systems, will contribute to the continued rapid growth of the wireless portion of the industry. However, technological improvements, such as fiber-optic lines and advanced switching equipment, have massively increased the data transmission capacity of telecommunications networks, thus limiting employment growth due to productivity gains. The best employment opportunities will be for individuals with strong technical skills.

Residential demand will increase as technology and competition lower the price of today's premium services, such as high-speed Internet access, wireless telephone service, and cable television. Demand also will increase as deregulation allows providers to offer combined services, making it easier for households to obtain a wide variety of telecommunications services. Wireless carriers will enter into the residential service business, providing fixed systems and high-speed Internet service. Therefore, the lines between cable TV, wireless, and wireline telephone systems will become blurred.

Business demand will rise as companies increasingly rely on their telecommunications systems to conduct electronic commerce. In order to remain competitive, businesses will require higher-speed access to the Internet for a variety of purposes including purchasing, marketing, sales, and customer service. Some employment loss will result from improved labor-saving technologies, such as self-monitoring equipment, and from lay-offs resulting from mergers and consolidation in the deregulated industry.

Technology will continue to transform the industry. The installation and upgrading of fiber optic networks will bring ever-faster communications closer to residential customers. Internet telephony, which transmits voice, video, fax, and electronic mail communications over the World Wide Web, will blur the boundaries between telecommunications providers and Internet service providers. Wireless providers will increase the capacity of their radio networks and introduce portable, lightweight devices capable of transmitting voice, data, and video. Undersea cables and orbiting satellites will integrate wireline and wireless customers into a global system of high bandwidth communications. The installation of computerized switching systems designed for digital content makes transmitting data, video, and graphics as easy as making voice telephone calls.

The removal of competitive barriers increased competition from providers outside the traditional telecommunications industry. Cable TV providers are using their wireline networks to offer customers a combination of services including telephone service, Internet access, and cable TV programming.

Employment growth will differ among the various occupations in the telecommunications industry, largely as a result of technology. Employment of telephone operators is expected to decline due to increasing automation. Computer voice recognition technology lessens the need for central office operators, as customers can obtain help with long distance calls from automated systems. This technology, which also enables callers to request numbers from a computer instead of a person, is expected to reduce the number of directory assistance operators. Their numbers may drop further as the increasing use of the Internet leads customers to use automated directory assistance resources on the Web.

Employment of line installers and repairers is expected to increase as telecommunications providers expand their networks in response to customer demand. New fiber optic networks will be installed and existing ones expanded to provide customers with high-speed access to data, video, and graphics. Businesses will request more wireline installations to provide increased connections to suppliers and customers. Residential customers who are not able to obtain upgrades to their copper wirelines will install additional wirelines in order to use voice and data communications simultaneously.

Employment of telecommunications equipment installers and repairers is expected to decrease because newer, more reliable technologies will decrease the need for equipment maintenance. However, there still will be many openings available for individuals with the necessary technical skills.

Employment of engineers and computer professionals is expected to increase. The expansion of communications networks, and the need for telecommunications providers to invest in research and development, will create job opportunities for electrical and electronics engineers. The use of increasingly sophisticated computer technology will increase employment of computer professionals, including computer software engineers, computer support specialists, and computer systems analysts. Growth among these occupations will, in turn, create employment opportunities for engineering and computer and information systems managers.

## Sources of Additional Information

For more details about employment opportunities, contact your local telephone company or write to:

➤ International Brotherhood of Electrical Workers, Telecommunications Department, 1125 15th St. NW., Washington, DC 20005.

➤ Communications Workers of America, 501 3rd St. NW., Washington, DC 20001. Internet: **http://www.cwa-union.org**

For more information on the telephone industry, write:

➤ United States Telecom Association, 1401 H St. NW., Suite 600, Washington, DC 20005-2164. Internet: **http://www.usta.org**

More information about the following occupations in the telecommunications industry appears in the 2002-03 edition of the *Occupational Outlook Handbook*.

- Communications equipment operators
- Line installers and repairers
- Office clerks, general
- Radio and telecommunications equipment installers and repairers

# Trucking and Warehousing

## SIGNIFICANT POINTS

- Truckdrivers hold one-half of all trucking and warehousing jobs.

- Job opportunities are expected to be good for qualified truckdrivers and service technicians.

- A growing proportion of the Nation's freight is being transported by truck, but business in the industry is prone to rise and fall with upswings and downturns in the overall economy.

## Nature of the Industry

Firms in the trucking and warehousing industry provide a link between manufacturers and consumers. Businesses, and occasionally individuals, contract with trucking and warehousing companies to pick up, transport, store, and deliver a variety of goods. This industry includes two segments, *local and long-distance trucking and terminals* and *public warehousing and storage*. However, the trend towards full-service logistical companies is blurring the distinction between trucking and warehousing.

*Local and long-distance trucking and terminals* provide over-the-road transportation of cargo using motor vehicles, such as trucks and tractor trailers. This industry segment is further subdivided based on distance traveled and type of goods delivered. Local trucking establishments primarily carry goods within a single metropolitan area and its adjacent nonurban areas. Long-distance trucking establishments carry goods between distant areas. Courier service establishments handle individual letters and light packages.

*Local trucking* comprised almost 65,000 trucking establishments in 2000. The work of local trucking firms varies depending on the products transported. Produce truckers usually pick up loaded trucks early in the morning and spend the rest of the day delivering produce to many different grocery stores. Lumber truckdrivers, on the other hand, make several trips from the lumber yard to one or more construction sites. Some local truck transportation firms also take on sales and customer relations responsibilities, in addition to delivering the firm's products. Some local trucking firms specialize in local furniture moving, garbage collection and trash removal, or hauling dirt and debris.

*Long-distance trucking* firms account for a majority of the jobs in the trucking and warehousing industry. Numbering more than 51,000 establishments, this sector comprises establishments primarily engaged in providing long-distance trucking between distant areas and sometimes between the United States and Canada and Mexico. These establishments handle a wide variety of commodities, transported in numerous types of equipment—from refrigerated trailers to flatbeds. Included in this industry are establishments operating as truckload (TL) or less than truckload (LTL) carriers.

*Truckload carriers* move large amounts of goods directly to their destination usually with no stops in between. These long-distance carrier establishments provide full truck movement of freight from the shipment's origin to its destination. The shipment of freight is a full single load not combined with other shipments.

*Less-than-truckload carriers* pick up multiple shipments and bring them to a terminal, where they are unloaded and then reloaded by destination. The combined shipment is carried to a terminal near the shipments' destination, and each shipment is delivered from there. Through a national or regional network of terminals, activities of LTL carriers include local pickup, local sorting and terminal operations, line-haul of freight, destination sorting, terminal operations, and local delivery.

Some goods are carried across country using intermodal transportation to save time and money. Intermodal transportation encompasses any combination of truck, train, plane, or ship. Typically, trucks perform at least one leg in the intermodal transportation of goods. For example, a shipment of cars from an assembly plant begins its journey when they are loaded onto rail cars. Next, trains haul the cars across country to a depot where the shipments are broken into smaller lots, loaded onto tractor-trailers, and sent off on the final leg of their journey to dealerships. Each of these steps is carefully orchestrated and timed so that the cars arrive just in time to be shipped on their next leg of their journey. Goods can be transported at lower cost this way, but they cannot be highly perishable—such as fresh produce—nor have strict delivery time schedules. Trucking still dominates the transportation of perishable and time-sensitive goods.

*Courier services* establishments deliver letters, parcels, and small packages under 100 pounds, usually within the confines of a metropolitan area. In the past, they were one of the fastest growing segments of the industry. (Companies that use aircraft to deliver small items to distant destinations are part of the air transportation industry, covered elsewhere in the *Career Guide*.)

*Motor freight transportation terminals* are mostly operated by large trucking companies. However, there were about 473 independent terminals not affiliated with trucklines in 2000. Many of these independent terminals break down truckloads of produce and other foods into shipments to area wholesalers. Many terminals also offer truck maintenance and repair services.

*Public warehousing and storage* facilities comprised more than 15,000 establishments in 2000. These firms were primarily engaged in operating warehousing and storage facilities for general merchandise and refrigerated goods. They provided facilities to store goods; self-storage mini-warehouses that rent to the general public are also included in this segment of the industry.

Deregulation of interstate trucking in 1980 encouraged many firms to add a wide range of customer-oriented services to complement trucking and warehousing services and led to innovations in the distribution process. Increasingly, trucking and warehousing firms provide businesses full-service logistical services encompassing the entire transportation process, including inventory management, materials handling, and warehousing. Firms that offer these services are often referred to as third-party logistics providers. Logistical services manage all

111

aspects of the movement of goods between producers and consumers, such as sorting bulk goods into customized lots, packaging and repackaging goods, inventory control and management, order entry and fulfillment, labeling, light assembly, and price marking. Logistical services such as computerized inventory information on the location, age, and quantity of goods available have improved the efficiency of relationships between manufacturers and customers. Just-in-time shipping—where trucking companies deliver goods from suppliers just in time for their use—allows recipients to reduce costly inventories but requires constant communication and accurate inventory information. Packaging, labeling, and small assembly of manufacturers' products are other services that warehousing establishments use to attract potential customers. Some full-service companies even perform warranty repairwork and serve as local parts distributors for manufacturers.

## Working Conditions

In the trucking and warehousing industry in 2000, workers averaged 40.5 hours a week, compared with an average of 34.5 hours for all private industries.

The U.S. Department of Transportation governs work hours and other working conditions of truckdrivers engaged in interstate commerce. For example, a long-distance driver generally cannot work more than 60 hours in any 7-day period. Many drivers, particularly on long runs, work close to the maximum time permitted because employers usually compensate them based on the number of miles or hours they drive. Drivers frequently travel at night, on holidays, and weekends to avoid traffic delays and to deliver cargo on time.

Truckdrivers must cope with a variety of working conditions including variable weather and traffic conditions, boredom, and fatigue. Many truckdrivers, however, enjoy the independence and lack of supervision found in long-distance driving. Local truckdrivers often have regular routes or assignments that allow them to return home in the evenings.

Improvements in roads and trucks are reducing stress and increasing the efficiency of long-distance drivers. Many advanced trucks are equipped with refrigerators, televisions, and beds for the driver's convenience. Included in some of these state-of-the-art vehicles is a satellite link with the company headquarters. Drivers can get directions, weather reports, and other important communications in a matter of seconds. In the event of bad weather or mechanical problems, truckers can communicate with dispatchers to discuss delivery schedules and courses of action. Dispatchers can also track the location of the truck and monitor fuel consumption and engine performance.

*Vehicle and mobile equipment mechanics, installers, and repairers* usually work indoors, although they occasionally make repairs on the road. Minor cuts, burns, and bruises are common, but serious accidents can be avoided when the shop is kept clean and orderly and safety practices observed. Service technicians and mechanics handle greasy and dirty parts and may stand or lie in awkward positions to repair vehicles and equipment. They usually work in well-lighted, heated, and ventilated areas, but some shops are drafty and noisy.

*Freight, terminal, and warehouse workers* usually work indoors, though they may do occasional work on trucks and forklifts outside. Some occasions warrant heavy lifting and other physical labor.

Safety is a major concern of the trucking and warehousing industry. The operation of trucks, lifts, and other technically advanced equipment can be dangerous without proper training and supervision. Efforts are underway to standardize the training programs to make drivers more efficient and effective truck operators. Truckdrivers already must adhere to federally mandated certifications and regulations. Federal mandates require drivers to submit to drug and alcohol tests as a condition of employment and more employers require periodic checks while on the job.

In 1999, work-related injuries and illnesses in the trucking and warehousing industry averaged 8.7 per 100 full-time workers, higher than the 6.3-incidence rate for the entire private sector. About 2 out of 3 on-the-job fatalities in the trucking and warehousing industry resulted from motor vehicle accidents.

## Employment

The trucking and warehousing industry provided more than 1.8 million wage and salary jobs in 2000. About half of the salaried jobs in the industry, 926,000, were for truckdrivers and driver/sales workers. Other transportation and material-moving jobs numbered 350,000, and another 314,000 jobs were in various office and administrative support occupations. There were about 99,000 managers; 57,000 bus and truck mechanics and diesel engine specialists; and 31,000 sales and related workers. In addition to wage and salary workers, an estimated 289,000 workers in the industry were self-employed in 2000.

Most employees in the trucking and warehousing industry work in small establishments. Over 3 out of 4 trucking and warehousing establishments employ fewer than 10 workers (chart). Consolidation in the industry has reduced the number of small, specialized firms. About 8 percent of truckdrivers operate their own business. Although these owner-operators constantly enter the industry each year, intense competition has caused many to fail.

Trucking and warehousing establishments are found throughout the United States, with a higher concentration around the major interstate highways and in heavily industrialized regions of the country such as in California, New Jersey, and Texas.

**Over 3 out of 4 trucking and warehousing companies employ fewer than 10 workers**

Percent

■ Establishments
□ Employment

| Number of workers employed by establishment | Establishments | Employment |
|---|---|---|
| 1 to 9 | 75.7 | 13.2 |
| 10 to 49 | 19.5 | 28.6 |
| 50 to 249 | 4.3 | 28.1 |
| 250 to 999 | 0.4 | 12.1 |
| 1000+ | 0.1 | 17.9 |

Source: U.S. Department of Commerce, *County Business Patterns*, 1997

112

## Occupations in the Industry

Transportation and material moving occupations account for 69 percent of all jobs in the industry (table 1). *Truckdrivers and driver/sales workers,* who hold one-half of all trucking and warehousing jobs, transport goods from one location to another. They ensure safe delivery of cargo to a specific destination, often by a designated time. Drivers also perform some minor maintenance work on their vehicles and make routine safety checks.

The length of trips varies according to the type of merchandise and its final destination. Local drivers provide regular service while other drivers make inter-city and interstate deliveries that take longer and may vary from job to job. The driver's responsibilities and assignments change according to the time spent on the road and the type of payloads transported.

Local drivers usually work more normal schedules and return home at the end of the day. They may deliver goods to stores or homes, or haul away dirt and debris from excavation sites. Many local drivers cover the same routes daily or weekly. Long-distance truckdrivers often are on the road for long stretches of time. Their trips vary from an overnight stay to a week or more. On longer trips, drivers sometimes sleep in bunks in their cabs or share driving with another driver.

*Laborers, and hand freight, stock, and material movers* help load and unload freight and move it around warehouses and terminals. Often these unskilled employees work together in groups of three or four. They may use conveyor belts, hand trucks, or forklifts to move freight. They may place heavy or bulky items on wooden skids or pallets and have industrial truck and tractor operators move them.

*Office and administrative support workers* perform the daily record keeping operations for the trucking and warehousing industry. *Dispatchers* coordinate the movement of freight and trucks. They provide the main communication link that informs the truckdrivers of their assignments, schedules, and routes. Often dispatchers receive new shipping orders on short notice and must juggle drivers' assignments and schedules to accommodate a client. *Shipping, receiving, and traffic clerks* keep records of shipments arriving and leaving. They verify the contents of trucks' cargo against shipping records. They may also pack and move stock. *Billing and posting clerks and machine operators* maintain company records of the shipping rates negotiated with customers and shipping charges incurred; they also prepare customer invoices.

Workers in *installation, maintenance, and repair occupations* generally enter these jobs only after acquiring experience in related jobs or after receiving specialized training. Most *vehicle and mobile equipment mechanics, installers, and repairers* require special vocational training. Service technicians and mechanics in trucking and warehousing firms perform preventive safety checks as well as routine service and repairs. Service technicians and mechanics sometimes advance to parts manager positions. *Parts managers* keep the supply of replacement parts needed to repair vehicles. Parts managers monitor the parts inventory using a computerized system, and purchase new parts to replenish supplies. These employees need mechanical knowledge and must be familiar with computers and purchasing procedures.

*Sales and related workers* sell trucking and warehousing services to shippers of goods. They meet with prospective buyers,

Table 1. **Employment of wage and salary workers in trucking and warehousing by occupation, 2000 and projected change, 2000-10**
(Employment in thousands)

| Occupation | Employment, 2000 Number | Employment, 2000 Percent | Percent change, 2000-2010 |
|---|---|---|---|
| **All occupations** | 1,856 | 100.0 | 21.9 |
| **Management, business, and financial occupations** | 99 | 5.3 | 31.4 |
| General and operations managers | 38 | 2.0 | 24.7 |
| Transportation, storage, and distribution managers | 18 | 1.0 | 46.2 |
| **Sales and related occupations** | 31 | 1.7 | 29.8 |
| **Office and administrative support occupations** | 314 | 16.9 | 17.1 |
| First-line supervisors/managers of office and administrative support workers | 21 | 1.1 | 33.2 |
| Billing and posting clerks and machine operators | 19 | 1.0 | 3.1 |
| Bookkeeping, accounting, and auditing clerks | 21 | 1.2 | 12.3 |
| Customer service representatives | 22 | 1.2 | 38.1 |
| Couriers and messengers | 41 | 2.2 | -6.0 |
| Dispatchers, except police, fire, and ambulance | 40 | 2.1 | 24.3 |
| Shipping, receiving, and traffic clerks | 19 | 1.0 | 35.0 |
| Office clerks, general | 46 | 2.5 | 16.4 |
| **Installation, maintenance, and repair occupations** | 96 | 5.2 | 12.4 |
| Bus and truck mechanics and diesel engine specialists | 57 | 3.0 | 1.7 |
| Maintenance and repair workers, general | 15 | 0.8 | 24.0 |
| **Transportation and material moving occupations** | 1,276 | 68.7 | 22.5 |
| First-line supervisors/managers of helpers, laborers, and material movers, hand | 16 | 0.9 | 23.3 |
| First-line supervisors/managers of transportation and material-moving machine and vehicle operators | 32 | 1.7 | 24.4 |
| Truck drivers, heavy and tractor-trailer | 795 | 42.8 | 23.3 |
| Truck drivers, light or delivery services | 124 | 6.7 | 13.7 |
| Industrial truck and tractor operators | 79 | 4.2 | 25.1 |
| Laborers and freight, stock, and material movers, hand | 148 | 8.0 | 20.0 |
| Packers and packagers, hand | 17 | 0.9 | 41.4 |
| Refuse and recyclable material collectors | 28 | 1.5 | 26.8 |

NOTE: May not add to totals due to omission of occupations with small employment.

discuss the customer's needs, and suggest appropriate services. Travel may be required, and many analyze sales statistics, prepare reports, and handle some administrative duties.

*Managerial* staff provide general direction to the firm. They staff, supervise, and provide safety and other training to workers in the various occupations. They also resolve logistical problems such as forecasting transportation demand, mapping out the most efficient traffic routes, order processing, parts and equipment service support, and transportation of goods to the right place at the right time.

## Training and Advancement

Many jobs in the trucking and warehousing industry require only a high school education, although an increasing number of workers have at least some college education. Increased emphasis on formal education stems from increased complexity in the industry. Nearly all operations involve computers and information management systems. Many occupations require detail-oriented persons with computer skills. A growing number of employers recommend some form of formal training either in-house or through trade or union programs. Although, the Federal Government does not mandate these programs, the trend is toward certification and standardized competency.

Whereas many States allow those who are 18 years old to drive trucks within State borders, the U.S. Department of Transportation establishes minimum qualifications for truckdrivers engaged in interstate commerce. Federal Motor Carrier Safety Regulations require truckdrivers to be at least 21 years old, have at least 20/40 vision and good hearing, and be able to read and speak English. They must also have good driving records. In addition, drivers must have a State commercial driver's license, for which they must pass a written examination and a skills test operating the type of vehicle they will be driving. Individual companies often have additional requirements applicants must meet.

Some truckdrivers enter the occupation by attending training schools for truckdrivers. Schools vary greatly in the quality of training they provide, but they are becoming more standardized. Many employers and some States support these programs.

Some large trucking companies have formal training programs that prospective drivers attend. Other companies assign experienced drivers to teach and mentor newer drivers. Local trucking firms often start drivers as truckdriver helpers. As they gain experience and demonstrate their reliability, they receive assignments with greater earnings or preferred work schedules. Because of increased competition for experienced drivers, some larger companies lure these drivers with increased pay and preferred assignments. Some trucking firms hire only experienced drivers.

Some long-distance truckdrivers purchase a truck and go into business for themselves. Although many of these owner-operators are successful, some fail to cover expenses and eventually go out of business. Owner-operators should have good business sense as well as truckdriving experience. Courses in accounting, business, and business mathematics are helpful, and knowledge of truck mechanics can enable owner-operators to perform their own routine maintenance and minor repairs.

Unskilled employees may work as helpers, laborers, and material-movers in their first job. They must be in good physical condition because the work often involves a great deal of physical labor and heavy lifting. They acquire skills on the job and often advance to more skilled jobs, such as industrial truck operator, truckdriver, shipping and receiving clerk, or supervisor.

Office and administrative support jobs in the trucking and warehousing industry require good typing skills and familiarity with computers. Shipping and receiving clerks watch and learn the skills of the trade from more experienced workers while on the job. Stock clerks and truckdrivers often advance to dispatcher positions after becoming familiar with company operations and procedures.

While some vehicle and mobile equipment mechanics, installers, and repairers learn the trade on the job, most employers prefer to hire graduates of programs in diesel mechanics offered by community and junior colleges or vocational and technical schools. Those with no training often start as helpers to mechanics, doing basic errands and chores such as washing trucks or moving them to different locations. Experience as an automotive service technician is helpful because many of the skills relate to diesel technology. Experienced technicians may advance to shop supervisor or parts manager positions.

For managerial jobs in the trucking and warehousing industry, employers prefer persons with bachelor's degrees in business, marketing, accounting, industrial relations, or economics. Good communication, problem-solving, and analytical skills are valuable in entry level jobs. Although most managers must learn logistics through extensive training on the job, several universities offer graduate and undergraduate programs in logistics. These programs emphasize the tools necessary to manage the distribution of goods and are sometimes associated with the business departments of schools. Managers hired for entry-level positions sometimes advance to top level managerial jobs.

Some college graduates and persons without a college degree enter sales or administrative positions. Marketing and sales workers must be familiar with their firm's products and services and have strong communication skills.

## Earnings

Average earnings in the trucking and warehousing industry are higher than the average for all private industry, as shown in table 2. The average wage in the trucking sector of the industry was higher than the average wage in warehousing. Earnings in selected occupations in trucking and warehousing appear in table 3.

Table 2. Average earnings of nonsupervisory workers in trucking and warehousing, 2000

| Industry segment | Weekly | Hourly |
|---|---|---|
| **All private industry** | $474 | $13.74 |
| **Trucking and warehousing** | 579 | 14.29 |
| Trucking and courier services, except air | 588 | 14.51 |
| Public warehousing and storage | 490 | 12.25 |

Most employers compensate truckdrivers with an hourly rate or a rate-per-mile system. Truckdrivers who operate heavy tractor-trailers generally have higher earnings than those who drive light delivery trucks. Benefits, including performance related bonuses, health insurance, and sick and vacation leave are common in the trucking industry.

The major union in the trucking and warehousing industry is the International Brotherhood of Teamsters. About 19.0 percent of trucking and warehousing workers are union members or are covered by union contracts, compared to 14.9 percent of workers in all industries combined. Some trucking companies use "double breasting" in an attempt to lower labor costs. This involves employing union as well as nonunion operating divisions. Other companies use multi-tier wage scales and pay lower wages for new hires. Pay increases after predetermined periods and safe driving records.

## Outlook

The number of wage and salary jobs in the trucking and warehousing industry is expected to grow 22 percent from 2000 through 2010, compared with projected growth of 16 percent for all industries combined. Because the industry is large, many job openings will result—not only from employment growth—but also from the need to replace the large number of workers who transfer to other industries or retire. Opportunities in this industry should be good for qualified workers at all levels, especially in truckdriving and service technician occupations.

Table 3. Median hourly earnings of the largest occupations in trucking and warehousing, 2000

| Occupation | Trucking and warehousing | All industries |
|---|---|---|
| General and operations managers | $ 27.11 | $ 29.41 |
| Transportation, storage, and distribution managers | 23.61 | 26.07 |
| First-line supervisors/managers of transportation and material-moving machine and vehicle operators | 20.18 | 19.37 |
| Truck drivers, heavy and tractor-trailer | 16.32 | 15.25 |
| Dispatchers, except police, fire, and ambulance | 15.33 | 13.66 |
| Bus and truck mechanics and diesel engine specialists | 14.66 | 15.55 |
| Laborers and freight, stock, and material movers, hand | 10.37 | 9.04 |
| Truck drivers, light or delivery services | 12.57 | 10.74 |
| Industrial truck and tractor operators | 11.72 | 11.74 |
| Couriers and messengers | 9.01 | 8.96 |

One of the main factors influencing the growth of the trucking and warehousing industry is the state of the national economy. Growth in the industry parallels economic upswings and downturns. As the national economy grows, production and sales of goods increase, thus increasing demand for transportation services to move goods from producers to consumers. In a recession, this industry is one of the first to slow down as orders for goods and shipments decline. Competition in the trucking and warehousing industry is intense, both among trucking companies and, in some long-haul truckload segments, with the railroad industry. Nevertheless, trucking has been accounting for an increasingly large share of freight transportation revenue.

Additional employment growth will result from manufacturers' willingness to concentrate more on their core competencies—producing goods—and outsource their distribution functions to trucking and warehousing companies. As firms in other industries increasingly employ this industry's logistical services, such as inventory management and just-in-time shipping, many new jobs will be created. Also, the expansion of electronic commerce as more consumers and businesses make purchases over the Internet will continue to increase demand for the transportation and logistical services of the trucking and warehousing industry.

Opportunities for qualified truckdrivers are expected to be favorable. In some areas, companies have experienced difficulties recruiting adequately skilled drivers. Truckdriving pays relatively well, but many persons leave the career because of the lengthy periods away from home, long hours of driving, and the negative public image drivers face. Stricter requirements for obtaining—and keeping—a commercial driver's license also make truckdriving less attractive as a career. Opportunities for diesel service technicians and mechanics also are expected to be favorable, especially for applicants with formal postsecondary training.

Growth in the trucking and warehousing industry should prompt an increase in office and administrative support employment. More dispatchers, stock clerks, and shipping, receiving, and traffic clerks will be needed to support expanded logistical services across the country. However, fewer secretaries, bookkeepers, and file clerks will be needed because computers and other automated equipment will make workers in these occupations more efficient and productive.

Courier and delivery services has been one of the most rapidly growing segments of the industry. Employment is expected to continue to increase even as competition from overnight air-courier firms, and business use of fax machines and e-mail moderates growth.

## Sources of Additional Information

For additional information about careers and training in the trucking and warehousing industry, write to:

➤ American Trucking Associations, 2200 Mill Rd., Alexandria, VA 22314. Internet: **http://www.truckline.com**

➤ International Warehouse Logistics Association, 1300 W. Higgins, Suite 111, Park Ridge, IL 60068. Internet: **http://www.warehouselogistics.org**

➤ International Association of Refrigerated Warehouses, 7315 Wisconsin Ave., Suite 1200N, Bethesda, MD 20814.

➤ Professional Truck driver Institute, 2200 Mill Rd., Alexandria, VA 22314; or by calling (703) 838-8842. Internet: **http://www.ptdi.org**

Detailed information on the following occupations can be found in the 2002-03 *Occupational Outlook Handbook*:

- Diesel service technicians and mechanics
- Dispatchers
- Material moving occupations
- Sales representatives, wholesale and manufacturing
- Shipping, receiving, and traffic clerks
- Truckdrivers and driver/sales workers

# Wholesale and Retail Trade

# Department, Clothing, and Accessory Stores

**(SIC 53 and 56)**

## SIGNIFICANT POINTS

- There are no formal educational requirements for most sales and administrative support jobs; many people get their first jobs in this industry.

- The industry offers many part-time jobs.

- Despite relatively slow employment growth, turnover will produce numerous job openings in this large industry.

- Earnings are relatively low.

## Nature of the Industry

Department, clothing, and accessory stores are located in all regions of the country. Department stores generally carry apparel; home furnishings, such as furniture, floor coverings, curtains, draperies, linens, and major household appliances; and housewares, such as table and kitchen appliances, dishes, and utensils. Different types of merchandise normally are arranged in separate sections or departments, under a single management. Department stores commonly provide their own charge accounts, deliver merchandise, and have 50 or more employees.

Discount and variety stores carry a wide variety of merchandise, from lawn rakes to dinnerware to motor oil. They emphasize self-service and low prices, and their numbers have grown rapidly in recent years. Warehouse clubs—which carry a more limited variety of merchandise than department stores, often in bulk quantities—also are included in this industry.

Clothing and accessory stores specialize in men's, women's, or children's clothing and related products, such as ties and shoes. Furriers and custom tailors carrying stocks of materials also are included in this industry. In contrast to department stores, clothing and accessory stores usually are much smaller, may concentrate on a limited type or style of clothing, and employ fewer workers.

## Working Conditions

Most employees in department, clothing, and accessory stores work under clean, well-lighted conditions. Many jobs are part time, and employees are on duty during peak selling hours, including nights, weekends, and holidays. Because weekends are busy days in retailing, almost all employees work at least one of these days and have a weekday off. During busy periods, such as holidays and back-to-school season, longer than normal hours may be scheduled, and vacation time is limited for most workers, including buyers and managers.

Retail salespersons and cashiers often stand for long periods, and stock clerks may perform strenuous tasks such as moving heavy, cumbersome boxes.

The incidence of work-related illnesses and injuries varied greatly among segments of the industry. In 1999, workers in general merchandise and apparel and accessory stores had 8.5 and 3.2 cases of injury and illness per 100 full-time workers, respectively, compared with an average of 6.3 throughout private industry.

## Employment

Department, clothing, and accessory stores—one of the largest employers in the Nation—had about 4.0 million wage and salary jobs in 2000. Department stores accounted for most jobs in the industry, but only about 7 percent of establishments. In 1997, about 2 of 3 workers were employed in department, clothing, and accessory stores with more than 50 workers (chart 1). In contrast to many industries, this industry employs workers in all sections of the country, from the largest cities to all but the smallest towns.

Many of the industry's workers are young—35 percent were under 24 years old in 2000, compared with 15 percent for all industries. About 31 percent of the workers were employed part time.

## Occupations in the Industry

Sales and related occupations accounted for almost 65 percent of workers in this industry in 2000 (table 1). *Retail salespersons*, who comprised 42 percent of employment in the industry,

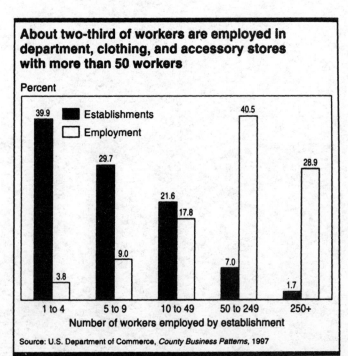

**About two-third of workers are employed in department, clothing, and accessory stores with more than 50 workers**

Percent

- Establishments
- Employment

| 1 to 4 | 5 to 9 | 10 to 49 | 50 to 249 | 250+ |
|--------|--------|----------|-----------|------|
| 39.9 / 3.8 | 29.7 / 9.0 | 21.6 / 17.8 | 7.0 / 40.5 | 1.7 / 28.9 |

Number of workers employed by establishment

Source: U.S. Department of Commerce, *County Business Patterns*, 1997

help customers select and purchase merchandise. A salesperson's primary job is to interest customers in the merchandise and to answer any questions customers may have. In order to do this, the worker may describe the product's various models, styles, and colors, or demonstrate its use. To sell expensive and complex items, an indepth knowledge of the products is necessary.

In addition to selling, most retail salespersons electronically register the sale on a cash register or terminal; receive cash, checks, and charge payments; and give change and receipts. Depending on the hours they work, they may open or close their cash registers or terminals. This may include counting the money in the cash register; separating charge slips, coupons, and exchange vouchers; and making deposits at the cash office. Salespersons are held responsible for the contents of their register, and repeated shortages are often a cause for dismissal.

Salespersons may be responsible for handling returns and exchanges of merchandise, wrapping gifts, and keeping their work areas neat. In addition, they may help stock shelves or racks, arrange for mailing or delivery of a purchase, mark price tags, take inventory, and prepare displays. They also must be familiar with the store's security practices to help prevent theft of merchandise. *Cashiers* total bills, receive money, make change, fill out charge forms, and give receipts. Retail salespersons and cashiers often have similar duties.

Office and administrative support occupations make up the next largest group of employees, accounting for 17 percent of total employment in the industry. *Stock clerks and order fillers* bring merchandise to the sales floor and stock shelves and racks. They may also mark items with identifying codes or prices so that they can be recognized quickly and easily, although many items today arrive preticketed. *Customer service representatives* investigate and resolve customers' complaints about merchandise, service, billing, or credit ratings. The industry also employs administrative occupations found in most industries, such as general office clerks and bookkeepers.

Management and business and financial operations occupations accounted for 3.5 percent of industry employment. *Department managers* oversee sales workers in a department or section of the store. They set the work schedule, supervise employee performance, and are responsible for the overall sales and profitability of their departments.

*Buyers* purchase merchandise for resale from wholesalers or manufacturers. Using historical records, market analysis, and their sense of consumer demand, they buy merchandise with the most appropriate style, quality, and selection at the lowest price. Wrong decisions mean that the store will mark down slow-selling merchandise, thus losing profits. Buyers for larger stores or chains usually buy one classification of merchandise, such as casual menswear or home furnishings; those working for smaller stores may buy all the merchandise sold in the store. They also plan and implement sales-promotion plans for their merchandise, such as arranging for advertising and ensuring that the merchandise is displayed properly.

*Merchandise managers* are in charge of a group of buyers and department managers; they plan and supervise the purchase and marketing of merchandise in a broad area, such as women's apparel or appliances. In department store chains, which have many stores, many of the buying and merchandising functions are centralized in one location. Some local managers might decide which merchandise, among that bought centrally, would be best for their own stores.

*Department store managers* direct and coordinate the activities in these stores. They may set pricing policies to maintain profitability and notify senior management of concerns or problems. Department store managers usually supervise department managers directly, and indirectly oversee other department store workers.

Because they may be the only managers in smaller stores, *clothing and accessory store managers* combine many of the duties of department managers, department store managers, and buyers. *Retail chain store area managers* or *district managers* oversee the activities of clothing and accessory store managers in an area. They hire managers, ensure that company policies are carried out, and coordinate sales and promotional activities.

Various other store-level occupations in this diversified industry include interior designers, hairdressers, material-moving workers, food-preparation and serving workers, and security guards.

## Training and Advancement

There are no formal educational requirements for most sales and administrative support jobs; in fact, many people get their first jobs in this industry. A high school education is preferred, especially by larger employers. Because many of the new workers in this industry are recent immigrants, employers may require English proficiency and may even offer language training to employees.

Salespersons should enjoy working with people. Among other desirable characteristics are a pleasant personality, a neat appearance, and the ability to communicate clearly. Because of the trend toward providing more service, it is becoming increasingly important for salespersons to be knowledgeable about the products and merchandise available. Some employers may conduct a background check of applicants—especially of those seeking work selling high-priced items.

In most small stores, an experienced employee or the manager instructs newly hired sales personnel on making out sales checks and operating the cash register. In larger stores, training programs are more formal and usually are conducted over several days. Some stores conduct periodic training seminars to refresh and improve the customer service and selling skills of their sales workers. Initially, trainees are taught how to make cash, check, and charge sales and eventually are instructed on returns and special orders. Other topics usually covered are customer service, security, and store policies and procedures. Depending on the type of product they are selling, sales workers may be given specialized training in their area. For example, those working in cosmetic sales receive instruction on the types of products available and the types of customers for whom these would be most beneficial.

Some salespersons are hired for a particular department, and others are placed after they have completed training. Placement usually is based on where positions are available. There are some salespersons, often called "floaters," who are not assigned to a particular department; instead, they work where needed.

Advancement opportunities for salespersons vary. As those who work full time gain experience and seniority, they usually move to positions of greater responsibility or to positions with potentially higher commissions. Salespersons who are paid on a commission basis—that is, they earn a percentage of the value of what they sell—may advance to selling more expensive items. The most experienced, and highest paid, salespersons sell big-ticket items. This work requires the most knowledge of the product and the greatest talent for persuasion. In some establishments, advancement opportunities are limited because one

Table 1. Employment of wage and salary workers in department, clothing, and accessory stores by occupation, 2000 and projected change, 2000-10.

(Employment in thousands)

| Occupation | Employment, 2000 | | Percent change, 2000-2010 |
|---|---|---|---|
| | Number | Percent | |
| All occupations | 4,030 | 100.0 | 4.2 |
| Management, business, and financial occupations | 140 | 3.5 | -0.5 |
| General and operations managers | 66 | 1.6 | -0.8 |
| Business operations specialists | 33 | 0.8 | -3.6 |
| Professional and related occupations | 73 | 1.8 | 29.5 |
| Healthcare practitioners and technical occupations | 46 | 1.2 | 43.8 |
| Service occupations | 180 | 4.5 | -0.5 |
| Security guards | 32 | 0.8 | -5.8 |
| Food preparation and serving related occupations | 38 | 0.9 | -8.5 |
| Janitors and cleaners, except maids and housekeeping cleaners | 41 | 1.0 | 7.5 |
| Hairdressers, hairstylists, and cosmetologists | 33 | 0.8 | -0.9 |
| Sales and related occupations | 2,637 | 65.4 | 5.0 |
| Cashiers, except gaming | 494 | 12.3 | 4.5 |
| Retail salespersons | 1,697 | 42.1 | 5.0 |
| First-line supervisors/managers of retail sales workers | 328 | 8.1 | 4.2 |
| Office and administrative support occupations | 698 | 17.3 | 3.1 |
| First-line supervisors/managers of office and administrative support workers | 49 | 1.2 | 8.4 |
| Financial clerks | 34 | 0.8 | -11.4 |
| Customer service representatives | 63 | 1.6 | 9.6 |
| Shipping, receiving, and traffic clerks | 99 | 2.5 | -1.7 |
| Stock clerks and order fillers | 311 | 7.7 | 6.9 |
| Office clerks, general | 31 | 0.8 | 5.6 |
| Installation, maintenance, and repair occupations | 40 | 1.0 | -7.3 |
| Production occupations | 90 | 2.2 | -0.8 |
| Textile, apparel, and furnishings occupations | 33 | 0.8 | -7.3 |
| Transportation and material moving occupations | 172 | 4.3 | -0.8 |
| Laborers and freight, stock, and material movers, hand | 121 | 3.0 | -3.0 |

NOTE: May not add to totals due to omission of occupations with small employment.

person, often the owner, is the only manager, but sales experience may be useful in finding a higher level job elsewhere. Retail selling experience is an asset when one is applying for sales positions with larger retailers or in other kinds of sales, such as motor vehicles, financial services, or wholesale merchandise.

Traditionally, capable salespersons with good leadership skills, yet without a college degree, could advance to management positions; however, a college education is becoming increasingly important for managerial positions such as department manager, store manager, or buyer. Computer skills are extremely important in all parts of the industry, especially in areas such as inventory control, human resources, sales forecasting, and electronic commerce. Many retailers prefer to hire persons with associate or bachelor's degrees in marketing, merchandising, or business as management trainees or assistant managers. Despite this trend, capable employees without a college degree may still be able to advance to administrative or supervisory work.

## Earnings

Hourly earnings of nonsupervisory workers in department, clothing, and accessory stores are well below the average for all workers in private industry. This reflects both the high proportion of part-time and less experienced workers in these stores, and the fact that even experienced workers receive relatively low pay compared with experienced workers in many other industries (table 2). Earnings in selected occupations in department, clothing, and accessory stores appear in table 3.

Table 2. Average earnings of nonsupervisory workers in department, clothing, and accessory stores, 2000.

| Industry segment | Weekly | Hourly |
|---|---|---|
| Total, private industry | $474 | $13.74 |
| Total, general merchandise stores | 274 | 9.47 |
| Department stores | 278 | 9.59 |
| Variety stores | 207 | 7.62 |
| Miscellaneous general merchandise stores | 272 | 9.10 |
| Total, apparel and accessory stores | 241 | 9.31 |
| Men's and boys' clothing stores | 298 | 10.90 |
| Women's clothing stores | 220 | 9.32 |
| Family clothing stores | 242 | 9.15 |
| Shoe stores | 239 | 8.79 |

Many employers permit workers to buy merchandise at a discount. Smaller stores usually offer limited employee benefits. In larger stores, benefits are more comparable with those offered by employers in other industries and can include vacation and sick leave, health and life insurance, profit-sharing, and pension plans.

Unionization in this industry is limited. Only 3.7 percent of workers were union members or covered by union contracts, compared with 15 percent in all industries.

Table 3. Median hourly earnings of the largest occupations in department, clothing, and accessory stores, 2000

| Occupation | General merchandise Stores | Apparel and accessory stores | All industries |
|---|---|---|---|
| General and operations managers | $ 18.45 | $ 20.28 | $ 29.41 |
| First-line supervisors/managers of retail sales workers | 11.10 | 12.48 | 13.23 |
| First-line supervisors/managers of office and administrative support workers | 9.80 | 14.86 | 17.51 |
| Security guards | 9.12 | 10.53 | 8.45 |
| Hairdressers, hairstylists, and cosmetologists | 8.44 | 12.44 | 8.49 |
| Customer service representatives | 8.41 | 8.52 | 11.83 |
| Laborers and freight, stock, and material movers, hand | 8.07 | 8.39 | 9.04 |
| Retail salespersons | 7.56 | 7.30 | 8.02 |
| Stock clerks and order fillers | 7.79 | 7.56 | 8.75 |
| Cashiers, except gaming | 6.87 | 6.88 | 6.95 |

## Outlook

Numerous job openings will result from turnover in this large industry. Jobs will be available for young workers, first-time job seekers, persons with limited job experience, senior citizens, and people seeking part-time work, such as those with young children or those who wish to supplement their income from other jobs. Persons with a college degree or computer skills will be sought for managerial positions in human resources, data management, logistics, management information systems, and finance.

Overall, the number of wage and salary jobs in department, apparel, and accessory stores is expected to increase 4 percent over the 2000-10 period, slower than the 15 percent increase projected for all industries combined. The relatively slow growth is due mainly to the employment decline in clothing and accessory stores, stemming from the increasing popularity of discount stores and "mega-retailers." Besides stressing low prices, the latter types of stores also stress self-service; they tend to be less labor-intensive than the traditional retailers. Employment in department stores, on the other hand, is expected to increase, but more slowly than the average for all industries.

There will continue to be keen competition among retailers; new stores will continually open, and others will close. Alternative retail outlets—such as mail-order companies, home shopping, and electronic commerce—have taken customers away from traditional retail stores. Many retailers provide their products on the Internet to expand their customer base and to remain competitive. Electronic commerce allows self-service in selecting and purchasing goods, which may lead to sales of more goods at lower prices than in traditional retail stores. Although online sales are expected to grow rapidly, sales at traditional "bricks and mortar" stores probably will remain a major portion of total retail sales. Although electronic commerce is expected to limit growth of some retail jobs, it is increasing opportunities for Internet sales managers, webmasters, technical support workers, and other related workers.

Even large, well-established department stores are subject to mergers, acquisitions, and sometimes bankruptcy. Some companies are moving towards obtaining goods directly from the manufacturer, bypassing the wholesale level completely, reducing costs, and increasing profits. This trend may further limit job growth in this industry, particularly among administrative and managerial workers.

Worker productivity is increasing because of technological advances, particularly among clerks, managers, and buyers. For example, computerized systems allow companies to streamline purchasing and obtain customer information and preferences, reducing the need for buyers. However, because direct customer contact also will remain important, employment of sales workers who interact personally with customers will be less affected by technological advances.

## Sources of Additional Information

General information on careers in retail establishments is available from:

➤ National Retail Federation, 325 7th St. NW., Suite 1100, Washington, DC 20004. Internet: **http://www.nrf.com**

➤ International Council of Shopping Centers, 665 5th Ave., New York, NY 10022. Internet: **http://www.icsc.org**

➤ Retail, Wholesale, and Department Store Union, 30 East 29th St., 4th Floor, New York, NY 10016. Internet **http://www.rwdsu.org**

Information on these occupations may be found in the 2002-03 *Occupational Outlook Handbook*:

- Advertising, marketing, promotions, public relations, and sales managers
- Cashiers
- Customer service representatives
- Designers
- Purchasing managers, buyers, and purchasing agents
- Retail salespersons
- Sales worker supervisors
- Security guards and gaming surveillance officers
- Stock clerks and order fillers

# Eating and Drinking Places

(SIC 58)

SIGNIFICANT POINTS

- Eating and drinking places provide many young people with their first jobs—in 2000, 25 percent of all workers in these establishments were aged 16 to 19, 5 times the average for all industries.

- Cooks, waiters and waitresses, and other food preparation and serving workers held almost 9 out of 10 jobs.

- Thirty-eight percent of all employees work part time, more than double the overall average.

- Job opportunities will be plentiful due to high turnover; there are few or no formal education or training requirements, and earnings tend to be relatively low.

## Nature of the Industry

So fundamental are the services provided by eating and drinking places, that this may be the world's most widespread and familiar industry. In the United States, the eating and drinking places industry comprises about 458,000 places of employment in large cities, small towns, and rural areas. These establishments include all types of restaurants, from fast food to elegant and expensive. They also include drinking places—establishments that primarily sell alcoholic beverages for consumption on the premises.

Restaurants make up the majority of establishments in this industry. The most common type is a franchised operation of a nationwide restaurant chain that sells fast food. According to the National Restaurant Association, the fast-food component accounted for 1 out of every 3 eating and drinking places in 2000; the number of these establishments has grown steadily from 20 percent of the industry in 1970. A limited menu, lack of waiters and waitresses, and emphasis on self-service characterize these restaurants. Menu selections usually are prepared by workers with limited cooking skills. Because the food typically is served in disposable, take-out containers that retain the food's warmth, it often is prepared prior to a customer's request. A growing number of fast-food restaurants are providing drive-through and delivery services.

Full-service restaurants, in contrast, offer broader menus with a variety of choices, including appetizers, entrées, salads, side dishes, desserts, and beverages. Waiters and waitresses usually serve meals at a leisurely pace, in comfortable surroundings. Although the number of full-service restaurants that are part of national chains is growing, the typical restaurant is independently owned and locally operated. Recently, many full-service restaurants have begun to focus on design, décor, and atmosphere to differentiate themselves from growing competition. The physical setting of the restaurant has become the primal focal point. However, the National Restaurant Association has found that the physical setting is of less importance at midscale or family-type restaurants. Customers frequenting these restaurants generally spend less time dining and are more interested in getting something to eat quickly. In upscale dining places, customers tend to linger for longer periods and, therefore, setting becomes quite important.

Cafeterias open to the general public and those operated under contract by commercial food service companies make up another major segment of this industry. Like fast-food restaurants, cafeterias usually offer a somewhat limited selection, which varies from day to day. Yet, like full-service restaurants, their selections may require more culinary skills to prepare. Selections usually are prepared ahead in large quantities, and seldom are cooked to the customer's order.

Drinking places comprise about 11 percent of all establishments in this industry. Although considered drinking places, some bars and nightclubs offer patrons limited dining services in addition to alcoholic beverages. In some States, they also sell packaged alcoholic beverages for consumption off the premises. Establishments selling alcoholic beverages are closely regulated by State and local alcoholic beverage control authorities.

Finally, the eating and drinking places industry includes a wide variety of specialized businesses, such as catering firms, concession stands at sports events, ice cream stores, and even dinner theaters.

## Working Conditions

Jobs in eating and drinking places are far more likely to be part time than are those in other industries; about 38 percent of the workers in eating and drinking establishments worked fewer than 35 hours a week in 2000, compared with 15 percent in the workforce as a whole. Full-time employees often are on the job during evenings, weekends, and holidays. Some employees are required to work split shifts—they work for several hours during one busy period, are off duty for a few hours, and then go back to work during the next busy period. Some employees work rotating shifts on a daily, weekly, or monthly basis.

Although many eating and drinking places have well-designed kitchens and dining areas with state-of-the-art equipment, kitchens usually are noisy, and may be very hot near stoves, grills, ovens, or steam tables. Dining areas also are noisy when customers are present and servers are waiting on patrons.

Workers directly involved in food preparation and services spend most of the time on their feet. Upper body strength often is needed to lift heavy items, such as trays of dishes or cooking pots. Work during peak dining hours can be very hectic and stressful.

Employees who have direct contact with customers should have a professional and pleasant manner, which may be difficult to maintain over the course of a long shift. Excellent food

122

that is poorly served can result in the failure of a restaurant, while average food served in an outstanding manner often results in success. Therefore, professional hospitality is required from the moment guests enter until the time they leave.

In 1999, the rate of work-related injuries and illnesses was 5.6 per 100 full-time workers in eating and drinking places, slightly less than the average of 6.3 for the private sector. Work hazards include the possibility of burns from hot equipment, sprained muscles, and wrenched backs from heavy lifting and falls on slippery floors.

## Employment

The eating and drinking places industry, with about 8.1 million wage and salary jobs in 2000, ranks among the Nation's leading employers. Eating and drinking places tend to be small; about 54 percent of the establishments in the industry employ fewer than 10 paid workers (see chart). As a result, this industry often is considered attractive to individuals who want to own and run their own businesses. An estimated 233,000 self-employed people worked in the industry, representing about 3 percent of total employment.

This industry, particularly fast-food establishments, is a leading employer of teenagers—aged 16 through 19—providing first jobs for many new entrants to the labor force. In 2000, nearly 25 percent of all workers in eating and drinking places were teenagers, 5 times the proportion in all industries (table 1). About 45 percent were under age 25, triple the proportion in all industries.

## Occupations in the Industry

Workers in this industry perform a variety of tasks. They prepare menu items, keep food preparation and service areas clean, wait on and take payment from customers, and provide support services to the establishment. Cooks, waiters and waitresses, and other food preparation and serving workers account for almost 9 out 10 jobs (table 2).

Employees in the various food preparation and serving and related occupations deal with customers in a dining area or at a

service counter. *Waiters* and *waitresses* take customers' orders, serve food and beverages, and prepare itemized checks. In finer restaurants, they may describe chef's specials and suggest wines. In some establishments, they escort customers to their seats, accept payments, and set up and clear tables. In many larger restaurants, however, these tasks are assigned to other workers.

**Table 1. Percent distribution of employment in eating and drinking places by age group, 2000**

| Age group | Eating and drinking places | All industries |
|---|---|---|
| Total | 100.0 | 100.0 |
| 16-19 | 25.2 | 5.4 |
| 20-24 | 19.8 | 9.9 |
| 25-34 | 21.1 | 22.6 |
| 35-44 | 17.7 | 27.1 |
| 45-54 | 10.1 | 22.0 |
| 55-64 | 4.4 | 10.1 |
| 65 and older | 1.6 | 3.0 |

**Table 2. Employment of wage and salary workers in eating and drinking places by occupation, 2000 and projected change, 2000-10.**

(Employment in thousands)

| Occupation | Employment, 2000 Number | Employment, 2000 Percent | Percent change, 2000-2010 |
|---|---|---|---|
| **All occupations** | 8,114 | 100.0 | 18.3 |
| **Management, business, and financial occupations** | 387 | 4.8 | 16.8 |
| Food service managers | 237 | 2.9 | 24.7 |
| General and operations managers | 104 | 1.3 | 3.6 |
| **Service occupations** | 7,178 | 88.5 | 19.3 |
| Chefs and head cooks | 100 | 1.2 | 17.0 |
| First-line supervisors/managers of food preparation and serving workers | 414 | 5.1 | 9.6 |
| Cooks, fast food | 493 | 6.1 | -1.3 |
| Cooks, restaurant | 560 | 6.9 | 26.9 |
| Cooks, short order | 140 | 1.7 | -0.9 |
| Food preparation workers | 356 | 4.4 | 14.5 |
| Bartenders | 253 | 3.1 | 9.6 |
| Combined food preparation and serving workers, including fast food | 1,793 | 22.1 | 38.4 |
| Counter attendants, cafeteria, food concession, and coffee shop | 217 | 2.7 | 9.6 |
| Food servers, nonrestaurant | 62 | 0.8 | 9.6 |
| Waiters and waitresses | 1,664 | 20.5 | 24.8 |
| Dining room and cafeteria attendants and bartender helpers | 273 | 3.4 | -12.3 |
| Dishwashers | 372 | 4.6 | -12.3 |
| Hosts and hostesses, restaurant, lounge, and coffee shop | 277 | 3.4 | 18.7 |
| Building cleaning workers | 66 | 0.8 | 9.6 |
| **Sales and related occupations** | 234 | 2.9 | 9.6 |
| Cashiers, except gaming | 209 | 2.6 | 9.6 |
| **Office and administrative support occupations** | 87 | 1.1 | 0.4 |
| **Transportation and material moving occupations** | 166 | 2.0 | 6.5 |
| Driver/sales workers | 118 | 1.4 | 9.6 |

NOTE: May not add to totals due to omission of occupations with small employment.

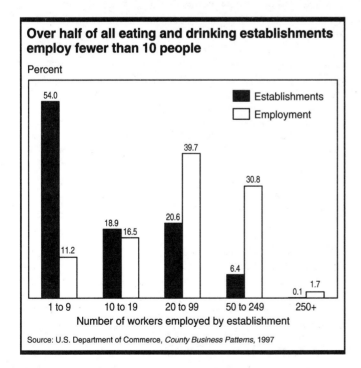

**Over half of all eating and drinking establishments employ fewer than 10 people**

Percent

- Establishments
- Employment

| 1 to 9 | 54.0 / 11.2 |
| 10 to 19 | 18.9 / 16.5 |
| 20 to 99 | 20.6 / 39.7 |
| 50 to 249 | 6.4 / 30.8 |
| 250+ | 0.1 / 1.7 |

Number of workers employed by establishment

Source: U.S. Department of Commerce, *County Business Patterns*, 1997

Other food service occupations include *hosts* and *hostesses,* who welcome customers, show them to their tables, and give them menus. *Bartenders* fill drink orders for waiters and waitresses and from customers seated at the bar. *Dining room attendants* and *bartender helpers* assist waiters, waitresses, and bartenders by clearing, cleaning, and setting up tables, as well as keeping service areas stocked with supplies. *Counter attendants* take orders and serve food at counters, cafeteria steam tables, and fast-food counters. Depending on the size and type of establishment, attendants also may operate the cash register.

Workers in the various food preparation occupations prepare food in the kitchen. *Institutional* and *cafeteria cooks* work in the kitchens of schools, hospitals, industrial cafeterias, and other institutions, where they prepare large quantities of a small variety of menu items. *Restaurant cooks* usually prepare a wider selection of dishes for each meal, cooking individual servings to order. *Bread* and *pastry bakers* typically produce small quantities of baked goods for sale or use in the establishment. *Short-order cooks* prepare grilled items and sandwiches in establishments that emphasize fast service. *Fast-food cooks* prepare a limited selection of items in fast-food restaurants, cooking and packaging batches of food that are either prepared to order or kept warm until sold. *Food preparation workers* shred lettuce for salads, cut up food, keep work areas clean, and perform simple cooking tasks under the direction of the chef or head cook. *Dishwashers* clean dishes, glasses, and kitchen accessories by hand or by machine.

*Food service managers* hire, train, supervise, and discharge workers in eating and drinking establishments. They also purchase supplies, deal with vendors, keep records, and help whenever an extra worker is needed in the kitchen or dining room. The *executive chef* oversees the kitchen, selects the menu, instructs the food preparation workers, and directs the preparation of food. In fine dining establishments, the *maitre d'* serves as host or hostess while overseeing the dining room. Larger establishments may employ a *general manager*, as well as a number of assistant managers. Many managers are part owners of the establishments they manage.

Eating and drinking places employ a wide range of other workers, including accountants, advertising and public relations workers, bookkeepers, dietitians, mechanics and other maintenance workers, musicians and other entertainers, human resources workers, and various clerks.

## Training and Advancement

Although the skills and experience required by workers in eating and drinking places differ by occupation, many entry-level positions, such as waiter and waitress or food preparation worker, require little or no formal education or previous training. These jobs are most commonly held by young workers; for many youths, this is their first job. On-the-job training, typically under the close supervision of an experienced employee or manager, often lasts less than a week. Some large chain operations require formal training sessions for new employees and may use video training programs.

Formal training of managers is common. Training seminars often can offer a variety of solutions to the many complex issues faced by food service managers. They can be a useful tool in helping to find motivated, quality employees and can improve retention rates. Training also can assist in improving morale, profitability, and customer service. As more restaurants use computers to keep track of sales and inventory, computer training is becoming increasingly integrated into management training programs.

In smaller, independent restaurants, assistant managers learn their duties on the job, while most chain-affiliated establishments provide formal programs that introduce new managers to company procedures. Increasingly, establishments use video and satellite TV training programs to educate newly hired staff about quality and daily operational standards. Nationwide restaurant chains often operate their own schools for managers, where people nominated for assistant manager jobs attend training seminars before acquiring additional responsibilities. Eventually, successful assistant managers may advance to general manager of one of the chain's establishments, or even to a top management position in a large chain operation.

Completion of postsecondary training in culinary arts, restaurant and food service management, or a related field is increasingly important for advancement in the eating and drinking places industry. Completion of such a program often enables graduates to start as trainee chefs or assistant managers. Management programs last from 18 months to 4 years; upon completion, a bachelor's degree is awarded. Programs are available through junior and community colleges, 4-year colleges and universities, trade schools, hotel or restaurant associations, and trade unions. The Armed Forces are another source of training and experience in food service work.

Training for chefs has changed radically in the past 10 years, as chefs assume greater leadership and managerial roles in the industry. Today, most culinary programs offer more business courses, along with computer training, to better prepare chefs to manage a large operation.

Promotion opportunities in eating and drinking places vary by occupation and the size of individual establishments. As in other industries, larger establishments and organizations usually offer better advancement opportunities. As beginners gain experience and basic skills, those who choose to pursue careers in eating and drinking places transfer to other jobs that require greater skill and offer higher earnings. Many workers earn progressively larger incomes as they gain experience by switching to jobs in other establishments offering higher compensation or requiring greater service skills and managerial responsibilities. For example, waiters and waitresses may transfer to jobs in more expensive or busier restaurants that offer larger tips.

Advancement opportunities are better for food preparation workers, particularly for those who work in full-service restaurants. Starting as unskilled food preparation workers, some advance to cook jobs as they pick up skills in the kitchen, and from those jobs to more challenging chef positions. As chefs improve their culinary skills, their opportunities for professional recognition and higher earnings improve.

Many managers of eating and drinking places obtain their positions through hard work and experience. Chefs often advance to executive chef positions, and food service workers often are promoted to *maitre d'* or other managerial jobs. Many managers of fast-food restaurants have advanced from the ranks of hourly workers. Managers with access to the necessary capital may even open their own eating and drinking places.

## Earnings

Earnings in eating and drinking places usually are much lower than the average for all industries (table 3). However, these low earnings are supplemented for many workers by tips from customers. Waiters, waitresses, and bartenders, for example, often derive the majority of their earnings from tips, which depend on menu prices and the volume of customers served. In some establishments, workers who receive tips share a portion of their gratuities with other workers in the dining room and kitchen.

**Table 3. Average earnings of nonsupervisory workers in eating and drinking places, 2000**

| Industry segment | Weekly | Hourly |
|---|---|---|
| Total, private industry ......................................... | $474.00 | $13.74 |
| Eating and drinking places ................................. | 177.00 | 6.93 |

Earnings vary by occupation and by location, type, and size of establishment. Usually skilled workers, such as chefs, have the highest wages, and workers who receive tips have the lowest. Many workers in the industry earn the Federal minimum wage of $5.15 an hour, or less if tips are included as a substantial part of earnings. A number of employers provide free or discounted meals and uniforms to full- and part-time employees. Earnings in the largest occupations employed in eating and drinking places appear in table 4.

**Table 4. Median hourly earnings of the largest occupations in eating and drinking places, 2000**

| Occupation | Eating and drinking places | All industries |
|---|---|---|
| Food service managers ................................. | $ 15.09 | $ 15.25 |
| First-line supervisors/managers of food preparation and serving workers ................ | 10.50 | 10.91 |
| Cooks, restaurant ........................................... | 8.57 | 8.72 |
| Food preparation workers ............................. | 6.88 | 7.38 |
| Hosts and hostesses, restaurant, lounge, and coffee shop ........................................ | 6.87 | 6.95 |
| Dishwashers .................................................. | 6.62 | 6.69 |
| Cooks, fast food ............................................ | 6.52 | 6.53 |
| Combined food preparation and serving workers, including fast food ........................ | 6.43 | 6.52 |
| Waiters and waitresses ................................. | 6.38 | 6.42 |
| Dining room and cafeteria attendants and bartender helpers ...................................... | 6.38 | 6.53 |

Unionization is not widespread in the eating and drinking places industry. Only 1.7 percent of all employees are union members or are covered by union contracts, compared with 14.9 percent for all industries.

## Outlook

Job opportunities in eating and drinking places should be plentiful. Wage and salary jobs in eating and drinking places are expected to increase by 18 percent over the 2000-10 period, slightly faster than the 16-percent growth projected for all industries combined. In addition to employment growth, vast numbers of job openings will stem from replacement needs in this large industry, as experienced workers find other jobs or stop working. The high job turnover reflects the large number of young, part-time workers in this industry. Thus, numerous jobs will be available for people with limited job skills, first-time job seekers, senior citizens, and those seeking part-time work.

Increases in population, personal incomes, leisure time, and dual-income families will contribute to job growth. With a growing proportion of the population concentrated in the older age groups, moderately-priced restaurants that offer table service and that appeal to families should be the fastest growing segment of the eating and drinking places industry. Fine dining establishments, which appeal to affluent, often older, customers, also should grow as the 45-and-older population increases rapidly. The numbers of limited-service and fast-food restaurants that appeal to younger diners should increase more slowly than in the past. As schools, hospitals, and company cafeterias contract out institutional food services, jobs should shift to firms specializing in these services. Also, an aging population should drive up the demand for managerial and food service workers in nursing homes and assisted-living facilities through the year 2010. Some of the increased demand for food services will be met through more supermarket food service options, self-service facilities such as salad bars, untended meal stations, and automated beverage stations.

Occupational projections reflect different rates of growth among the various segments of the eating and drinking places industry (table 2). Employment of occupations concentrated in full-service restaurants—including skilled restaurant cooks and chefs, waiters and waitresses, and hosts and hostesses—is expected to increase faster than overall employment in the eating and drinking places industry. On the other hand, employment of occupations concentrated in limited-service and fast-food restaurants—including fast-food, cafeteria, and short-order cooks—is expected to increase more slowly than overall employment in the eating and drinking places industry or decline. Those who qualify—either through experience or formal culinary training—for skilled head cook, chef, and baker positions should be in demand. The greatest number of job openings will be in the largest occupations—waiters and waitresses, and combined food preparation and serving workers.

Employment of salaried managers is projected to grow as a result of rapid growth of chain and franchised establishments. Graduates of college hospitality programs, particularly those with good computer skills, should have especially good opportunities. The growing dominance of chain-affiliated eating and drinking places also should enhance opportunities for advancement from food service manager positions into general manager and corporate administrative jobs. Employment of self-employed managers of independent eating and drinking places is expected to increase more slowly.

## Sources of Additional Information

For additional information about careers and training in the eating and drinking places industry, write to:

➤ National Restaurant Association, 1200 17th St. NW., Washington, DC 20036. Internet: **http://www.restaurant.org**

➤ The American Culinary Federation, 10 San Bartola Dr., St. Augustine, FL 32086. Internet: **http://www.acfchefs.org**

For a list of educational programs in the eating and drinking industry, write to:

➤ The International Council on Hotel, Restaurant, and Institutional Education, 3205 Skipwith Rd., Richmond, VA 23294-4442. Internet: **http://www.chrie.org**

Information on vocational education courses for food preparation and service careers may be obtained from your State or local director of vocational education or superintendent of schools.

Information on these and other occupations found in eating and drinking places appears in the 2002-03 *Occupational Outlook Handbook*:

• Cashiers

• Chefs, cooks, and food preparation workers

• Food and beverage serving and related workers

• Food service managers

# Grocery Stores

## SIGNIFICANT POINTS

- Numerous job openings—many of them part-time—should be available due to the industry's large size and high rate of turnover.

- Grocery stores provide a large number of jobs to young workers who have little or no work experience.

- Cashiers and stock clerks account for half of all jobs.

- College graduates will fill most new management positions.

## Nature of the Industry

Grocery stores, also known as supermarkets, are familiar to everyone. They sell an array of fresh and preserved foods, primarily for preparation and consumption at home. They often sell prepared food, such as hot entrees or salads, for take-out meals. Stores range in size from supermarkets, which may employ hundreds of workers and sell numerous food and non-food items, to convenience stores with small staffs and limited selections. However, convenience stores often sell fuel, including gasoline, kerosene, and propane. (Specialty grocery stores—meat and fish markets; fruit and vegetables markets; candy, nut, and confectionery stores; dairy products stores; retail bakeries; and health and dietetic food stores, for example—are not covered in this section. Also excluded are eating and drinking establishments that sell food and beverages for consumption on the premises. The latter are discussed elsewhere in the *Career Guide*.)

Grocery stores are found everywhere, although the size of the establishment and range of goods and services offered varies. Traditionally, inner-city stores are small and offer a limited selection, although larger stores are now being built in many urban areas; suburban stores tend to be large supermarkets with a more diverse stock. Many supermarkets include several specialty departments that offer the products and services of seafood stores, bakeries, delicatessens, pharmacies, or florist shops. Household goods, health and beauty care items, automotive supplies, greeting cards, and clothing also are among the growing range of non-food items sold. Some of the largest supermarkets even house cafeterias or food courts, and a few feature convenience stores. In addition, grocery stores may offer basic banking services and automatic-teller machines; postal services; onsite film processing; dry cleaning; video rentals; and catering services.

## Working Conditions

Working conditions in most grocery stores are pleasant, with clean, well-lighted, climate-controlled surroundings. Work can be hectic, and dealing with customers can be stressful.

Grocery stores are open more hours and days than most work establishments, so workers are needed for early morning, late night, weekend, and holiday work. With employees working fewer than 30 hours a week, on average, these jobs are particularly attractive to workers who have family or school responsibilities or another job.

Most grocery store workers wear some sort of clothing, such as a jacket or apron, that identifies them as store employees and keeps their personal clothing clean. Health and safety regulations require some workers, such as those who work in the delicatessen or meat department, to wear head coverings, safety glasses, or gloves.

In 1999, cases of work-related injury and illness averaged 8.4 per 100 full-time workers in grocery stores, compared with 6.3 per 100 full-time workers in the entire private sector. Some injuries occur while workers transport or stock goods. Persons in food processing occupations, such as butchers and meatcutters, as well as cashiers working with computer scanners or traditional cash registers, may be vulnerable to cumulative trauma and other repetitive motion injuries.

## Employment

Grocery stores ranked among the largest industries in 2000, providing 3.1 million wage and salary jobs. More than 30 percent of all grocery store employees worked part time, and the average workweek was less than 30 hours. Some self-employed workers also worked in grocery stores, mostly in smaller establishments.

In 1997, about 131,000 grocery stores operated throughout the Nation. Most grocery stores are small; more than 60 percent employ fewer than 10 workers. Most jobs, however, are found in the largest stores. About two-thirds of workers were employed in grocery stores with more than 50 workers (chart 1).

Many grocery store workers are young, with persons 16 to 24 years old holding 34 percent of the jobs. This reflects the large number of jobs in this industry open to young workers who have little or no work experience.

## Occupations in the Industry

Grocery store workers stock shelves on the sales floor; prepare food and other goods; assist customers in locating, purchasing, and understanding the content and uses of various items; and provide support services to the establishment. If the store is part of a chain, many important tasks—such as marketing and promotion, inventory control and management, and financing—are done at a centralized corporate headquarters. However, 49 percent of all grocery store employees are cashiers or stock clerks.

*Cashiers* make up the largest occupation in grocery stores, accounting for about one-third of all workers (table 1). They scan the items being purchased by customers, total the amount due, accept payment, and produce a cash register receipt that shows the quantity and price of the items. In most supermarkets, the cashier passes the universal product code on the item's label across a computer scanner that identifies the item and its price, which is automatically relayed to the cash register. In some grocery stores, customers scan and bag their purchases, and pay using an automatic payment terminal. Cashiers verify that the items have been paid for before the customer leaves. In other grocery stores, the cashier reads a hand-stamped price on the item and keys that price directly into the cash register. Cashiers then place items in bags for customers; accept cash, personal check, credit card, or electronic debit card payments; and make change. When cashiers are not needed to check out customers, they sometimes assist other workers.

*Stock clerks and order fillers* are the second largest occupation in grocery stores, accounting for almost 1 of every 6 workers. They fill the shelves with merchandise and arrange displays to attract customers. In stores without computer scanning equipment, stock clerks may have to manually mark prices on individual items and count stock for inventory control.

Many office clerical workers—such as *secretaries and administrative assistants*; *general office clerks*; and *bookkeeping, accounting, and auditing clerks*—prepare and maintain the records necessary to keep grocery stores running smoothly.

*Butchers and other meat, poultry, and fish processing workers* prepare meat, poultry, and fish for purchase by cutting up and trimming carcasses and large sections into smaller pieces, which they package, weigh, price, and place on display. They also prepare ground meat from other cuts and fill customers' special orders. These workers also may prepare ready-to-heat foods by filleting or cutting meat, poultry, or fish into bite-sized pieces, preparing and adding vegetables, or applying sauces or breading. Butchers and other meat, poultry, and fish processing workers often work from a central facility from which smaller packages are sent to area stores.

Some specialty workers prepare food for sale in the grocery store and work in kitchens that may not be located in the store. *Bakers* produce breads, rolls, cakes, cookies, and other baked goods. *Chefs, cooks, and food preparation workers* make salads—such as coleslaw or potato, macaroni, or chicken salad—

**Table 1. Employment of wage and salary workers in grocery stores by occupation, 2000 and projected change, 2000-10.**

(Employment in thousands)

| Occupation | Employment, 2000 Number | Percent | Percent change, 2000-2010 |
|---|---|---|---|
| **All occupations** | 3,107 | 100.0 | 5.6 |
| **Management, business, and financial occupations** | 99 | 3.2 | 0.0 |
| General and operations managers | 56 | 1.8 | 0.3 |
| **Professional and related occupations** | 56 | 1.8 | 40.2 |
| Pharmacists | 22 | 0.7 | 52.3 |
| **Service occupations** | 385 | 12.4 | 7.1 |
| First-line supervisors/managers of food preparation and serving workers | 29 | 0.9 | 6.2 |
| Food preparation workers | 119 | 3.8 | 23.0 |
| Combined food preparation and serving workers, including fast food | 133 | 4.3 | -3.3 |
| Janitors and cleaners, except maids and housekeeping cleaners | 22 | 0.7 | 6.2 |
| **Sales and related occupations** | 1,320 | 42.5 | 14.1 |
| Cashiers, except gaming | 1,026 | 33.0 | 16.8 |
| Retail salespersons | 63 | 2.0 | -4.4 |
| First-line supervisors/managers of retail sales workers | 185 | 5.9 | 7.3 |
| **Office and administrative support occupations** | 674 | 21.7 | -11.1 |
| First-line supervisors/managers of office and administrative support workers | 22 | 0.7 | 6.2 |
| Bookkeeping, accounting, and auditing clerks | 31 | 1.0 | -8.5 |
| Customer service representatives | 48 | 1.5 | 7.7 |
| Stock clerks and order fillers | 500 | 16.1 | -15.0 |
| Office clerks, general | 26 | 0.8 | 6.2 |
| **Production occupations** | 201 | 6.5 | -1.4 |
| Bakers | 47 | 1.5 | 27.5 |
| Butchers and meat cutters | 102 | 3.3 | -15.0 |
| **Transportation and material moving occupations** | 357 | 11.5 | 4.8 |
| Laborers and freight, stock, and material movers, hand | 39 | 1.2 | -4.4 |
| Packers and packagers, hand | 286 | 9.2 | 6.2 |

NOTE: May not add to totals due to omission of occupations with small employment.

and other entrees, and they prepare ready-to-heat foods—such as burritos, marinated chicken breasts, or chicken stir-fry—for sale in the delicatessen or in the gourmet food or meat department. Other food preparation workers arrange party platters or prepare various vegetables and fruits that are sold at the salad bar.

*Demonstrators and product promoters* may offer samples of various products to entice customers to purchase them.

In supermarkets that serve food and beverages for consumption on the premises, *food and beverage serving workers* take orders and serve customers at counters. They may prepare short-order items, such as salads or sandwiches, to be taken out and consumed elsewhere. *Janitors and cleaners* keep the stores clean and orderly.

In the warehouses and stockrooms of large supermarkets, *laborers and freight, stock, and material movers* move stock and goods in storage and deliver them to the sales floor; they also help load and unload delivery trucks. *Hand packers and*

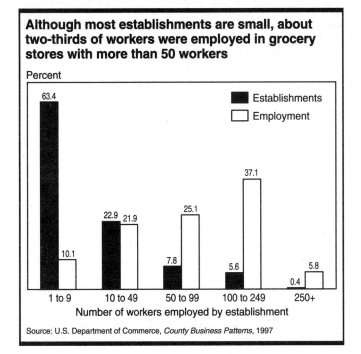

**Although most establishments are small, about two-thirds of workers were employed in grocery stores with more than 50 workers**

Percent

- Establishments
- Employment

| Number of workers employed by establishment | Establishments | Employment |
|---|---|---|
| 1 to 9 | 63.4 | 10.1 |
| 10 to 49 | 22.9 | 21.9 |
| 50 to 99 | 7.8 | 25.1 |
| 100 to 249 | 5.6 | 37.1 |
| 250+ | 0.4 | 5.8 |

Source: U.S. Department of Commerce, *County Business Patterns*, 1997

*packagers*, also known as courtesy clerks or baggers, perform a variety of simple tasks, such as bagging groceries, loading parcels in customers' cars, and returning unpurchased merchandise from the checkout counter to shelves.

*First-line supervisors/managers of retail sales workers*, usually called *department managers*, supervise mostly entry-level employees at the grocery, produce, meat, and other specialty departments. Department managers train employees and schedule their hours; oversee ordering, inspection, pricing, and inventory of goods; monitor sales activity; and make reports to store managers. *Store managers* are responsible for the efficient and profitable operation of grocery stores. Working through their department managers, store managers may set store policy, hire and train employees, develop merchandising plans, maintain good customer and community relations, address customer complaints, and monitor the store's profits or losses.

*Purchasing managers* plan and direct the activities of *buyers*, who purchase goods for resale to consumers. Purchasing managers and buyers must thoroughly understand grocery store foods, other items, and each stores' customers. They must select the best suppliers and maintain good relationships with them. Purchasing managers and buyers evaluate their store's sales reports to determine what products are in demand and plan purchases according to their budget.

Because of the expansion of the industry to meet the consumers' desire for "one-stop shopping," grocery stores have begun to employ an array of workers to help meet that need. For example, *marketing managers* forecast sales and develop a marketing plan based on demographic trends, sales data, community needs, and consumer feedback. *Dietitians and nutritionists* provide information to help consumers choose among the many food and nonfood products, and develop nutrition education programs. *Pharmacists* fill customers' drug prescriptions and advise them on over-the-counter medicines. *Inspectors, testers, sorters, samplers, and weighers* assess whether products and facilities meet quality, health, and safety standards. *Human resources, training, and labor relations managers and specialists* are responsible for making sure that employees maintain and, if necessary, improve their skill levels.

## Training and Advancement

Most grocery store jobs are entry-level and can be learned in a short time. Employers generally prefer high school graduates for occupations such as cashier, stock clerk, or food preparation workers. In large supermarket chains, prospective employees are matched with available jobs, hours, and locations and are sent to a specific store for on-the-job training. Many cashiers are trained in a few days, with some stores offering formal classroom training to familiarize workers with the equipment with which they will work. Meat cutters and bakers are more skilled. Trade schools and industry associations offer training for these jobs, but the skills also can be learned on the job.

College graduates will fill most new management positions. Employers increasingly seek graduates of college and university, junior and community college, and technical institute programs in food marketing, food management, and supermarket management. Many supermarket chains place graduates of these programs, or of bachelor's or master's degree programs in business administration, in various professional positions or management training programs in areas such as logistics, replenishment, food safety, human resources, and strategic planning. Management trainees start as assistant or department managers and, depending on experience and performance, may advance

to positions of greater responsibility. It is not unusual for managers to supervise a large number of employees early in their careers.

Courtesy clerks sometimes advance to work as service clerks in the delicatessen or bakery, stock clerks, or perhaps cashiers. Sometimes workers rotate assignments in a supermarket; for example, a cashier might occasionally wrap meat. Union contracts, however, may have strict occupational definitions in some stores, making movement among departments difficult.

Entry-level workers may advance to management positions, depending on experience and performance. Grocery store management has become increasingly complex and technical. Managers of some large supermarkets are responsible for millions of dollars in yearly revenue and hundreds of employees. They use computers to manage budgets, schedule work, track and order products, price goods, manage shelf space, and assess product profitability. Many stores that promote from within have established tracks by which workers move from department to department, gaining broad experience, until they are considered ready for an entry-level management position. Opportunities for advancement to management jobs exist in both large supermarket chains and in small, independent grocery stores.

Grocery store jobs call for various personal attributes. Almost all workers must be in good physical condition. Because managers, cashiers, stock clerks, and other workers on the sales floor constantly deal with the public, a neat appearance and a pleasant, businesslike manner are important. Cashiers and stock clerks must be able to do repetitive work accurately while under pressure. Cashiers need basic arithmetic skills, good hand-eye coordination, and manual dexterity. Stock clerks, especially, must be in good physical condition because of the lifting, crouching, and climbing they do. For managers, good communication skills and the ability to solve problems quickly and to perform well under pressure are important.

## Earnings

Average weekly earnings in grocery stores are considerably lower than the average for all industries, reflecting the large proportion of entry-level, part-time jobs. In 2000, nonsupervisory workers in grocery stores averaged $284 a week, compared with $474 a week for all workers in the private sector. Earnings in selected occupations in grocery stores appear in table 2.

Managers receive a salary, and often a bonus based on store or department performance. Managers in highly profitable stores generally earn more than those in less profitable stores.

Full-time workers generally receive typical benefits, such as paid vacations, sick leave, and health and life insurance. Part-time workers who are not unionized may receive few benefits. Unionized part-time workers sometimes receive partial benefits. Grocery store employees may receive a discount on purchases.

About 20.5 percent of all employees in grocery stores belong to a union or are covered by union contracts, compared with about 15 percent in all industries. Workers in chain stores are more likely to be unionized or covered by contracts than are workers in independent grocery stores. In independent stores, wages often are determined by job title, and increases are tied to length of job service and job performance. The United Food and Commercial Workers International Union is the primary union representing grocery store workers.

## Outlook

Employment in grocery stores is expected to increase about 6 percent by the year 2010, compared with the 15-percent growth projected for all industries combined. Many additional job openings will arise from the need to replace workers who transfer to jobs in other industries, retire, or stop working for other reasons. Replacement needs are particularly significant due to the industry's large size and the high rate of turnover among cashiers and other workers who do not choose to pursue grocery industry careers.

**Table 2. Median hourly earnings of the largest occupations in grocery stores, 2000**

| Occupation | Grocery stores | All industries |
|---|---|---|
| General and operations managers | $ 21.21 | $ 29.41 |
| First-line supervisors/managers of retail sales workers | 13.16 | 13.23 |
| Butchers and meat cutters | 12.34 | 11.60 |
| Bakers | 9.24 | 9.48 |
| Stock clerks and order fillers | 7.94 | 8.75 |
| Retail salespersons | 7.92 | 8.02 |
| Food preparation workers | 7.90 | 7.38 |
| Combined food preparation and serving workers, including fast food | 7.32 | 6.52 |
| Cashiers, except gaming | 6.99 | 6.95 |
| Packers and packagers, hand | 6.48 | 7.53 |

Employment will grow as the population increases and as more grocery stores offer a wider array of goods and services that include prescription drugs, flowers, liquor, and carryout food, as well as banking, postal, and catering services. Grocery stores are adding and enhancing delicatessens, bakeries, and meat and seafood departments to counter the trend toward eating away from home, as well as adding ready-to-eat-meals to compete with fast-food restaurants. These expansions are expected to create many new jobs.

Some technological advances—such as computer scanning cash registers and automated warehouse equipment—have boosted productivity, but these innovations are not expected to adversely affect employment levels. In fact, past technological improvements like scanners and electronic data interchange are expected to improve opportunities in areas such as category management and distribution. Increasing competition from large discount department stores will encourage the industry to continue to improve its efficiency by adopting new technologies and procedures and by reducing redundancies, especially in the supply chains. Some stores even let customers process their own transaction with almost no interaction with a cashier. However, many tasks, such as stocking shelves on the sales floor or helping a customer find a product, cannot be performed effectively by machines. In addition, many consumers have demonstrated their strong desire for personal services. For example, consumers want managers to answer questions about store policy and services; they want cashiers and courtesy clerks to answer questions, bag goods, or help them bring groceries to their cars;

and they want workers in specialty departments to advise them on their purchases and fill personal orders by providing special cuts of meat, fish, or poultry.

Projected growth for some grocery store occupations differs from the 6 average growth projected for the industry as a whole. Employment of bakers and food preparation workers is expected to grow faster than average because of the popularity of fresh baked breads and pastries, carryout food, and catering services. Employment of retail sales worker supervisors and managers is expected to grow more slowly than average as new service departments and stores are built. A decline in employment of butchers and other meat, poultry, and fish processing workers is expected as more meatcutting and processing shifts from the retail store to the manufacturing plant.

Electronic shopping currently is gaining in popularity across the country. Its impact on industry employment could be significant within the near future, depending on how fast consumers adopt the new technology.

## Sources of Additional Information

For information on job opportunities in grocery stores, contact individual stores or the local office of the State employment service.

General information on careers in retail establishments is available from:

➢ United Food and Commercial Workers International Union, Education Office, 1775 K St. NW., Washington, DC 20006-1502. Internet: **http://www.ufcw.org**

➢ Food Marketing Institute, 655 15th St., NW., Suite 700, Washington, DC 20005. Internet: **http://www.fmi.org**

➢ National Association of Convenience Stores, 1605 King St., Alexandria, VA 22314. Internet: **http://www.cstorecentral.com**

➢ National Retail Federation, 325 7th St., NW., Suite 1100, Washington, DC 20004. Internet: **http://www.nrf.com**

Information on most occupations in grocery stores, including the following, appears in the 2002-03 *Occupational Outlook Handbook*:

- Advertising, marketing, promotions, public relations, and sales managers
- Cashiers
- Chefs, cooks, and food preparation workers
- Demonstrators, product promoters, and models
- Food processing occupations
- Pharmacists
- Pharmacy aides
- Pharmacy technicians
- Purchasing managers, buyers, and purchasing agents
- Retail salespersons
- Stock clerks and order fillers

# Motor Vehicle Dealers

## SIGNIFICANT POINTS

- Most jobs in motor vehicle dealerships offer above-average earnings, but require only 2 years of postsecondary training or less.

- Motor vehicle dealerships are expected to decline in number but increase in size, as consolidation continues in the industry.

- Employment growth is expected to be average but sensitive to downturns in the economy.

## Nature of the Industry

Motor vehicle dealers are the bridge between automobile manufacturers and the U.S. consumer. Most dealerships offer one-stop shopping for customers who wish to buy, finance, and service their next vehicle.

Full-service motor vehicle dealerships generally have four departments: new vehicle sales, used vehicle sales, aftermarket sales, and service. These departments employ a wide range of occupations including those involving management, administrative support, sales, service, and repair. In addition to full-service dealerships, some motor vehicle dealers specialize in used vehicle sales only.

The *new vehicle sales department* in a full-service dealership accounts for over half of total dealership sales, making it the cornerstone and lifeblood of the dealership. Although profit margins on new vehicle sales are quite small in comparison with those of other departments, these sales spawn additional revenue for more profitable departments of the dealership. By putting new vehicles on the road, dealerships can count on aftermarket additions, new repair and service customers, and future used vehicle trade-ins.

Sales of new cars, trucks, and vans depend on changing consumer tastes, popularity of the manufacturers' vehicle models, and the intensity of competition with other dealers. The business cycle greatly affects automobile sales—when the economy of the Nation is declining, car buyers may postpone purchases of new vehicles and, conversely, when the economy is growing and consumers feel more financially secure, vehicle sales increase.

Car and truck leasing is included in the new vehicle sales department. Leasing services have grown in recent years to accommodate changing consumer purchasing habits. As vehicles have become more costly, growing numbers of consumers are unable or reluctant to make the long-term investment entailed in the purchase of a new car or truck. Leasing provides an alternative to high initial investment costs while typically yielding lower monthly payments.

The *used vehicle sales department* sells trade-ins and former rental and leased cars, trucks, and vans. Because new vehicle prices continue to increase faster than used vehicle prices, used vehicles have become more popular among customers. Also, innovative technology has increased the durability and longevity of new vehicles, resulting in higher quality used vehicles. In recent years, the sale of used vehicles has become a major source of profits for many dealers in the wake of decreasing margins for new vehicles. In fact, some luxury vehicle manufacturers promote "certified pre-owned" vehicles to customers who may be unable to afford new vehicles of a particular make. In economic downturns, the demand for these and other used vehicles often increases as sales of new vehicles decline.

The *aftermarket sales department* sells additional services and merchandise after the new vehicle salesperson has closed a deal. Aftermarket sales workers sell service contracts and insurance to new and used vehicle buyers and arrange financing for their purchase. Representatives offer extended warranties and additional services, such as undercoat sealant and environmental paint protection packages, to increase the revenue generated for each vehicle sold.

The *service department* provides automotive repair services and sells accessories and replacement parts. Most service only cars and small trucks, but a small number service large trucks, buses, and tractor-trailers. Some dealerships also have bodyshops to do collision repair, refinishing, and painting. The work of the service department has a major influence on customers' satisfaction and willingness to purchase future vehicles from the dealership.

As is the case in the used vehicle department of a traditional full-service dealership, stand-alone *used vehicle dealers* sell trade-ins and former rental and leased vehicles. These dealers range from small, one-location stores to large, nationwide superstores. Each one capitalizes on the increased demand for used vehicles and relatively large profits on sales of previously owned cars, trucks, and vans. Some of the larger stores offer low-hassle sales on large inventories of these popular vehicles. Such dealers typically contract out warranty and other service-related work to other dealers or to satellite service facilities. Growth in leasing agreements and rental companies will continue to provide quality vehicles to these dealers, thus providing for future employment growth in the used vehicle market.

## Working Conditions

Employees in motor vehicle dealerships work longer hours than do those in most other industries. About 86 percent of motor vehicle dealership employees worked full time in 2000; nearly 42 percent worked more than 40 hours a week. To satisfy customer service needs, many dealers provide evening and weekend service. The 5-day, 40-hour week usually is the exception, rather than the rule, in this industry.

Most automobile salespersons and administrative workers spend their time in dealer showrooms; individual offices are a rarity. Multiple users share limited office space that may be cramped and sparsely equipped. The competitive nature of selling is stressful to automotive salespersons, as they try to meet company sales quotas and personal earnings goals. Compared with that for all occupations in general, the proportion of workers who transfer from automotive sales jobs to other occupations is relatively high.

Service technicians and automotive body repairers generally work indoors in well-ventilated and well-lighted repairshops. However, some shops are drafty and noisy. Technicians and repairers frequently work with dirty and greasy parts, and in awkward positions. They often lift heavy parts and tools. Minor cuts, burns, and bruises are common, but serious accidents are avoided when the shop is kept clean and orderly and safety practices are observed. Despite hazards, precautions taken by dealers to avoid and prevent injuries have kept the workplace relatively safe. In 1999, there were 6.3 cases of work-related injuries and illnesses per 100 full-time workers in the new and used motor vehicle dealers industry, equivalent to the national average of 6.3 cases. Separately, stand-alone used motor vehicle dealers reported only 2.3 cases of work-related injuries and illnesses per 100 full-time workers—well below the national average.

## Employment

Motor vehicle dealers provided about 1.2 million wage and salary jobs in 2000. An additional 50,000 self-employed persons worked in this industry. Sales, installation, maintenance, and repair workers shared two-thirds of industry employment. The remaining third primarily were management, administrative support, transportation, and material-moving positions.

Workers in motor vehicle dealerships tend to be somewhat older than those in other retail trade industries. The median age of workers in dealerships was 38.7, with 26 percent between the ages of 35 and 44.

Since 1950, the trend in this industry has been toward consolidation. Franchised dealers have decreased in number while their sales volume has increased. Larger dealerships can offer more services, typically at lower costs to the dealership and the customer. More than 75 percent of motor vehicle dealerships

employ at least 10 workers, compared with about 32 percent for retail trade establishments in general. Dealerships with 10 or more workers employ about 98 percent of the workers in the industry, whereas such establishments account for fewer than 85 percent of all retail trade employment (chart). On average, motor vehicle dealers employ nearly 24 employees per establishment, compared with an average of 16 employees in all retail businesses.

## Occupations in the Industry

The number of workers employed by motor vehicle dealers varies significantly depending on dealership size, location, makes of vehicles handled, and distribution of sales among departments. Table 1 indicates that the majority of workers in this industry are sales workers, automotive service technicians and mechanics, and administrative support personnel.

*Sales and related occupations* are among the most important occupations in the dealership. Their success in selling vehicles and services determines the success of the dealership. *Automotive retail salespersons* usually are the first to greet customers and determine their interests through a series of questions. Before entering the dealership, many customers use the Internet to research and compare vehicle prices, features, and options. Salespersons then explain and demonstrate the vehicle's features in the showroom and on the road. Working closely with *automotive sales worker supervisors* and their customers, they negotiate the final terms and price of the sale. Automotive salespersons must be tactful, well-groomed, and able to express themselves well. Their success in sales depends upon their ability to win the respect and trust of prospective customers.

In support of the service and repair department, *parts salespersons* supply vehicle parts to technicians and repairers. They also sell replacement parts and accessories to the public.

*Installation, maintenance, and repair occupations* are another integral part of dealerships. *Automotive service technicians and mechanics* diagnose, adjust, and repair automobiles and light trucks with gasoline engines, such as vans and pickups. *Automotive body and related repairers* repair and finish vehicle bodies, straighten bent body parts, remove dents, and replace crumpled parts that are beyond repair.

*Office and administrative support workers* handle the paperwork of motor vehicle dealers. *Bookkeeping, accounting, and auditing clerks; general office clerks;* and *secretaries and administrative assistants* prepare reports on daily operations, inventory, and accounts receivable. They gather, process, and record information; and perform other administrative support and clerical duties. Dealership *office managers* organize, supervise, and coordinate administrative operations. Many office managers also are responsible for collecting and analyzing information on each department's financial performance.

*Transportation and material-moving occupations* account for 1 out of 10 jobs in motor vehicle dealers. *Cleaners of vehicles and equipment* prepare new and used vehicles for display in the showroom or parking lot and for delivery to customers. They may wash and wax vehicles by hand and perform simple services such as changing a tire or battery. *Truckdrivers* operate light delivery trucks to pick up and deliver automotive parts. Some drive tow trucks that bring damaged vehicles to the dealership for repair.

*Management* jobs often are filled by promoting workers with years of related experience. For example, most *sales managers* start as automotive salespersons. *Shop managers* usually are among the most experienced service technicians. They super-

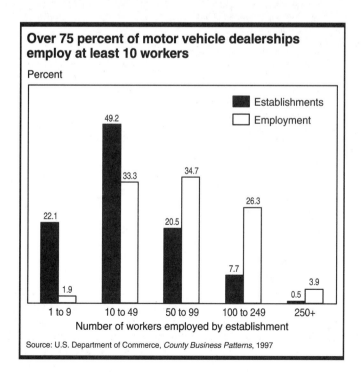

**Over 75 percent of motor vehicle dealerships employ at least 10 workers**

Percent

Legend: ■ Establishments □ Employment

1 to 9: 22.1, 1.9
10 to 49: 49.2, 33.3
50 to 99: 20.5, 34.7
100 to 249: 7.7, 26.3
250+: 0.5, 3.9

Number of workers employed by establishment

Source: U.S. Department of Commerce, *County Business Patterns*, 1997

vise and train other technicians to make sure that service work is performed properly. *Parts managers* run the parts department and keep the automotive parts inventory. They display and promote sales of parts and accessories and deal with garages and other repairshops seeking to purchase parts. *Service managers* oversee the entire service department and are responsible for the department's reputation, efficiency, and profitability. Increasingly, service departments use computers to increase productivity and improve service workflow by scheduling customer appointments, troubleshooting technical problems, and locating service information and parts.

*Service advisors* handle the administrative and customer relations part of the service department. They greet customers, listen to their description of problems or service desired, write repair orders, and estimate the cost and time needed to do the repair. They also handle customer complaints, contact customers when technicians discover new problems while doing the work, and explain to customers the work performed and the charges associated with the repairs.

*Sales managers* hire, train, and supervise the dealership's sales force. They are the lead negotiators in all transactions between sales workers and customers. Most advance to their positions after success as salespersons. They review market analyses to determine consumer needs, estimate volume potential for various models, and develop sales campaigns to accomplish dealership goals.

*General and operations managers* are in charge of all of the dealership's operations. They need extensive business and management skills, usually acquired through experience as a manager in one or more of the dealership departments. Dealership performance and profitability ultimately are up to them. General managers sometimes have an ownership interest in the dealership.

## Training and Advancement

Requirements for many jobs vary from dealer to dealer. To find out exactly how to qualify for a specific job, ask the dealer or manager in charge. The majority of positions do not require postsecondary education—more than half of those employed have not received any formal education past high school. In today's competitive job market, however, nearly all dealers demand a high school diploma. Courses in automotive technology are important for service jobs, as well as a basic background in business, electronics, mathematics, computers, and science. Sales workers require strong communication skills to deal with the public because they represent the dealership.

Most new sales workers receive extensive on-the-job training, beginning with mentoring from sales managers and experienced sales workers. In large dealerships, beginners receive several days of classroom training to learn the models for a sale, methods for approaching prospective customers, negotiation techniques, and ways to close sales. Some manufacturers furnish training manuals and other informational materials for sales workers. Managers continually guide and train sales workers, both on the job and at periodic sales meetings.

Some service technicians and repairers may begin as apprentices or trainees, helpers, or lubrication workers. They work under close supervision of experienced technicians, repairers, and service managers. Even though beginners may be able to perform routine service tasks and make simple repairs after a few months on the job, they usually need 1 to 2 years of experience to acquire enough skills to become a certified service technician.

**Table 1. Employment of wage and salary workers in motor vehicle dealers by occupation, 2000 and projected change, 2000-10**

(Employment in thousands)

| Occupation | Employment, 2000 Number | Percent | Percent change, 2000-2010 |
|---|---|---|---|
| **All occupations** | 1,221 | 100.0 | 11.9 |
| **Management, business, and financial occupations** | 106 | 8.7 | 15.2 |
| Sales managers | 22 | 1.8 | 28.5 |
| Financial managers | 10 | 0.8 | 16.8 |
| General and operations managers | 33 | 2.7 | 10.3 |
| Financial specialists | 11 | 0.9 | 17.5 |
| **Service occupations** | 19 | 1.6 | 14.8 |
| Janitors and cleaners, except maids and housekeeping cleaners | 14 | 1.1 | 16.8 |
| **Sales and related occupations** | 444 | 36.4 | 13.1 |
| Cashiers, except gaming | 21 | 1.8 | 16.8 |
| Counter and rental clerks | 26 | 2.1 | 16.8 |
| Parts salespersons | 66 | 5.4 | -6.6 |
| Retail salespersons | 261 | 21.4 | 16.8 |
| First-line supervisors/managers of retail sales workers | 50 | 4.1 | 18.0 |
| **Office and administrative support occupations** | 189 | 15.5 | 5.4 |
| First-line supervisors/managers of office and administrative support workers | 17 | 1.4 | 16.8 |
| Switchboard operators, including answering service | 11 | 0.9 | -24.1 |
| Billing and posting clerks and machine operators | 11 | 0.9 | -6.6 |
| Bookkeeping, accounting, and auditing clerks | 35 | 2.8 | 0.6 |
| Customer service representatives | 9 | 0.7 | 18.5 |
| Material recording, scheduling, dispatching, and distributing occupations | 19 | 1.6 | 11.5 |
| Office clerks, general | 38 | 3.1 | 16.8 |
| Secretaries and administrative assistants | 13 | 1.1 | -2.3 |
| **Installation, maintenance, and repair occupations** | 328 | 26.9 | 14.3 |
| First-line supervisors/managers of mechanics, installers, and repairers | 31 | 2.5 | 16.8 |
| Automotive body and related repairers | 46 | 3.8 | 19.3 |
| Automotive service technicians and mechanics | 218 | 17.8 | 12.5 |
| Helpers—Installation, maintenance, and repair workers | 13 | 1.1 | 23.4 |
| **Transportation and material moving occupations** | 127 | 10.4 | 7.6 |
| Truck drivers, light or delivery services | 19 | 1.5 | 15.4 |
| All other motor vehicle operators | 12 | 1.0 | 12.4 |
| Cleaners of vehicles and equipment | 68 | 5.6 | 3.7 |
| Laborers and freight, stock, and material movers, hand | 9 | 0.8 | 5.1 |

NOTE: May not add to totals due to omission of occupations with small employment.

Automotive technology is rapidly increasing in sophistication, and dealerships increasingly prefer to hire graduates of postsecondary automotive training programs for trainee positions. Graduates of such programs often earn promotion to the journey level after only a few months on the job. Most

132

community and junior colleges and vocational and technical schools offer postsecondary automotive training programs leading to an associate's degree in automotive technology or auto body repair. They generally provide intense career preparation through a combination of classroom instruction and hands-on practice. Good reading and basic math skills also are required to study technical manuals, keep abreast of new technology, and learn new service and repair techniques.

Various automotive manufacturers and their participating dealers sponsor 2-year associate degree programs at postsecondary schools across the Nation. Students in these programs typically spend alternate 10- to 12-week periods attending classes full time and working full time in the service departments of sponsoring dealers. Dealers increasingly send experienced technicians to factory training centers to receive special training in the repair of components, such as electronic fuel injection or air-conditioning. Factory representatives also visit many shops to conduct short training sessions.

Workers need years of experience in sales, service, or administration to advance to management positions in dealerships. Employers increasingly prefer persons with 4-year college degrees in business administration and marketing, particularly in dealerships that are larger, more competitive, and more efficient. Some motor vehicle manufacturers offer management training classes and seminars.

## Earnings

Average weekly earnings of nonsupervisory workers in full-service motor vehicle dealerships were $599 in 2000, higher than the average for retail trade, as well as that for all private industry. Earnings vary depending on occupation, experience, and the dealer's geographic location and size. Earnings in selected occupations in motor vehicle dealers appear in table 2.

Most automotive sales workers are paid on a commission-only basis. Commission systems vary, but dealers often guarantee new salespersons a modest salary for the first few months until they learn how to sell vehicles. Many dealers also pay experienced, commissioned sales workers a modest weekly or monthly salary to compensate for the unstable nature of sales. Dealerships, especially larger ones, also pay bonuses and have special incentive programs for exceeding sales quotas. With increasing customer service requirements, some dealerships and manufacturers have adopted a noncommissioned sales force paid entirely by salary.

Most automotive service technicians and mechanics receive a commission related to the labor cost charged to the customer. Their earnings depend on the amount of work available and completed.

Relatively few workers in motor vehicle dealerships, 4.0 percent, are union members or are covered by union contracts, compared with 14.9 percent of all workers in private industry.

## Outlook

Wage and salary jobs in motor vehicle dealerships are projected to increase 12 percent over the 2000-10 period, compared with projected growth of about 16 percent for all industries combined. Growth in the automobile industry strongly reflects consumer confidence and purchasing habits. The structure of dealerships, the strength of the Nation's economy, and trends in consumer preferences will influence the employment outlook for this industry.

Over the 2000-10 period, population growth will increase demand for motor vehicles and employment in motor vehicle

dealerships. Growth of the labor force and in the number of families in which both spouses need vehicles to commute to work will contribute to increased vehicle sales and employment in this industry. As personal incomes continue to grow, greater numbers of persons will be able to afford the luxury of owning multiple vehicles, which also should increase sales. However, the penchant for the public to keep vehicles for many more years than in the past may have a dampening effect on motor vehicle sales.

**Table 2. Median hourly earnings of the largest occupations in motor vehicle dealers, 2000**

| Occupation | New and used car dealers | Used car dealers | All industries |
|---|---|---|---|
| General and operations managers | $ 39.11 | $ 25.39 | $ 29.41 |
| Sales managers | 38.79 | 32.97 | 32.94 |
| First-line supervisors/managers of retail sales workers | 28.23 | 21.06 | 13.23 |
| First-line supervisors/managers of mechanics, installers, and repairers | 21.66 | 17.96 | 21.27 |
| Retail salespersons | 17.81 | 13.03 | 8.02 |
| Automotive service technicians and mechanics | 16.87 | 11.69 | 13.70 |
| Automotive body and related repairers | 15.76 | 12.57 | 15.00 |
| Counter and rental clerks | 14.90 | 9.32 | 7.87 |
| Parts salespersons | 13.47 | 12.84 | 10.85 |
| Cleaners of vehicles and equipment | 8.02 | 7.65 | 7.55 |

The trend towards dealership consolidation should have a minimal effect on the industry because of continued demand for vehicles and related services. Dealerships will always need well-qualified people to work in the various departments of the dealership. In an effort to achieve greater financial and operational efficiency and flexibility, greater emphasis will be placed on after-sales services, such as financing and vehicle service and repair. For larger dealerships, this will also include onsite body repair facilities.

Opportunities in the service and repair sectors of this industry should be plentiful, especially for persons who complete formal automotive service technician training. The growing complexity of automotive technology increasingly requires highly trained service technicians to service vehicles. Most persons who enter service and repair occupations may expect steady work because changes in economic conditions have little effect on this part of the dealership's business.

Opportunities for sales positions will depend largely on the state of the economy, which will continue to play a dominant role in motor vehicle sales. Replacement needs will be a greater source of job openings than will overall dealership expansion. The high turnover of sales jobs, characteristic of this industry, will ensure many job openings for sales workers in motor vehicle dealerships. In addition, as consumers' expectations and demands continue to increase, dealerships will seek more highly educated salespersons. Persons who have a college degree and previous sales experience should have the best opportunities. If alternative sales techniques and compensation systems, such as using salaried noncommissioned sales professionals, become more common, the greater income stability may lead to less turnover of sales jobs.

Opportunities in management occupations will be best for persons with college degrees and those with considerable industry experience. However, consolidation of dealerships will slow the growth of managerial jobs. Competition for managerial positions will remain relatively keen.

## Sources of Additional Information

For more information about work opportunities, contact local motor vehicle dealers or the local offices of the State employment service. The latter also may have information about training programs.

For additional information about careers and training in the motor vehicle dealers industry, write to:

➢ National Automobile Dealers Association, 8400 Westpark Dr., McLean, VA 22102. Internet: **http://www.nada.org**

More information on the following occupations may be found in the 2002-03 *Occupational Outlook Handbook:*

• Advertising, marketing, promotions, public relations, and sales managers
• Automotive body and related repairers
• Automotive service technicians and mechanics
• Retail salespersons
• Sales worker supervisors

# Wholesale Trade

(SIC 50, 51)

## SIGNIFICANT POINTS

- Most workplaces are small, employing fewer than 10 workers.

- Two-thirds work in office and administrative support, sales, or transportation and material-moving occupations.

- While some jobs require a college degree, a high school education is sufficient for most jobs.

- E-commerce, consolidation, and new technology should slow employment growth in some occupations, but many new jobs will be created in other occupations.

## Nature of the Industry

When consumers purchase goods, they usually buy them from a retail establishment such as a supermarket, department store, gas station, or cybershop. When retail establishments, other businesses, governments, or institutions—such as universities or hospitals—need to purchase goods for resale, equipment, office supplies, or any other items, they normally buy them from wholesale trade establishments.

Wholesale trade firms are essential to the economy. They buy large lots of goods, usually from manufacturers, and sell them in smaller quantities to businesses, governments, other wholesalers, or institutional customers. They simplify product, payment, and information flows by acting as intermediaries between the manufacturer and the final customer. They store goods that neither manufacturers nor retailers can store until consumers require them. In so doing, they fill several roles in the economy. They provide businesses a nearby source of goods made by many different manufacturers; they provide manufacturers with a manageable number of customers, while allowing their products to reach a large number of users; and they allow manufacturers, businesses, institutions, and governments to devote minimal time and resources to transactions by taking on some sales and marketing functions—such as customer service, sales contact, order processing, and technical support—that manufacturers otherwise would have to perform.

There are three types of wholesale trade firms. *Wholesaler-distributors*, sometimes known as merchant wholesalers, purchase goods from manufacturers in large quantities, store them, and then sell them to retailers, manufacturers, other wholesalers, or other customers. They are by far the most common type of wholesaling business. Wholesalers are companies that resell products to another intermediary; distributors resell to the final customer.

*Sales branches and offices* of manufacturing operations are local offices of manufacturers. They market their own products and coordinate distribution directly from the producer to the buyer. They rarely handle stock during a sale.

*Wholesale agents or brokers* coordinate the sale of goods from one party to another—usually from manufacturers to retailers. This category includes auction companies and commission merchants. They seldom take title to or handle goods in the process.

Only firms that sell most of their wares to businesses, institutions, and governments are considered part of wholesale trade. As a marketing ploy, many retailers that sell mostly to the general public present themselves as wholesalers. For example, "wholesale" price clubs, factory outlets, and other organizations are retail establishments, even though they sell their goods to the public at "wholesale" prices.

The size and scope of firms in the wholesale trade industry vary greatly. They sell any and every type of good. Customers buy goods to use in making other products, such as a bicycle manufacturer that purchases steel tubing, wire cables, and paint; for use in the course of daily operations, such as a corporation that buys office furniture, paper clips, or computers; or for resale to the public, such as a department store that purchases socks, flatware, or televisions. Wholesalers may offer only a few items for sale, perhaps all made by one manufacturer, or they may offer thousands of items produced by hundreds of different manufacturers. Wholesalers may sell only a narrow range of goods, such as very specialized machine tools, or a broad range of goods, such as all the supplies necessary to open a new store, including shelving, light fixtures, wall paper, floor coverings, signs, cash registers, accounting ledgers, and perhaps even some merchandise for resale.

Besides selling and moving goods to their customers, wholesaler-distributors may provide other services to clients, such as the financing of purchases, customer service and technical support, marketing services such as advertising and promotion, technical or logistical advice, and installation and repair services. After customers buy equipment, such as cash registers, copiers, computer workstations, or various types of industrial machinery, assistance often is needed to integrate the products into the customers' workplace. Wholesale trade firms often employ workers to visit customers, install or repair equipment, train users, troubleshoot problems, or advise on how to use the equipment most efficiently.

## Working Conditions

Working conditions and physical demands of wholesale trade jobs vary greatly. Moving stock and heavy equipment can be strenuous, but freight, stock, and material movers may be aided by forklifts in large warehouses. Workers in some automated warehouses use computer-controlled storage and retrieval systems that further reduce labor requirements. Employees in refrigerated meat warehouses work in a cold environment, and those in chemical warehouses often wear protective clothing to avoid harm from toxic chemicals. Outside sales workers are away from the office for much of the workday and may spend a considerable amount of time traveling. On the other hand, most management, administrative support, and marketing staff work in offices.

Overall, work in wholesale trade is relatively safe. In 1999, there were 5.6 work-related injuries or illnesses per 100 full-time workers, less than the 6.3 incidence rate for the entire private sector. Not all wholesale trade sectors are equally safe, however. Occupational injury and illness rates were considerably higher than the national average for wholesale trade workers who dealt with lumber and construction materials (9.8 per 100 workers); metals and minerals (11.5); groceries (10.6 per 100 workers); and beer, wine, and distilled beverages (10.4 per 100 workers).

Most workers put in long shifts, particularly during peak times, and others, such as produce wholesalers, work unusual hours. The latter group of workers must be on the job early in the morning to receive shipments of vegetables and fruits, and they must be ready to deliver goods to local grocers at dawn.

## Employment

Wholesale trade accounted for about 7 million wage and salary jobs in 2000, about 5 percent of all jobs in the economy. Firms that employed 10 or more workers provided about 83 percent of the jobs in wholesale trade; nevertheless, roughly 7 out of 10 establishments in the industry are small, employing fewer than 10 workers (chart 1) in 1997. Although some large firms employ many workers, when compared with other industries, wholesale trade is characterized by a large number of relatively small establishments. Wholesale trade workers are spread fairly evenly throughout the country, have relatively low union membership, and are more likely to work full time than are workers in most other industries.

## Occupations in the Industry

Many occupations are involved in wholesale trade, but not all are employed in every type of wholesale trade firm. For example, manufacturers' sales branch offices do not employ *wholesale buyers*, because they do not purchase goods for resale; and

brokers employ few *stock clerks* or *truck drivers*, because they keep little stock. Wholesaler-distributors—by far the largest part of the industry—employ workers in most of the occupations that appear in table 1.

The activities of wholesale-distribution firms commonly center on storing, selling, and transporting goods. As a result, the three largest occupational groups in the industry are *office and administrative support* workers, many of whom work in inventory management; *sales and related workers*; and *transportation and material-moving occupations*, most of whom are truck drivers and material movers. In 2000, two-thirds of wholesale trade workers were concentrated in these three groups.

Most office and administrative support workers need to have at least a high school diploma, and some related experience or additional schooling is an asset. As in most industries, many *secretaries* and *bookkeeping, accounting,* and *general office clerks* are employed in wholesale trade. Most of the other administrative support workers are needed to control inventory. *Shipping receiving, and traffic clerks* check the contents of all shipments, verifying condition, quantity, and sometimes shipping costs. They may use computer terminals or bar code scanners and, in small firms, may pack and unpack goods. *Order clerks* handle order requests from customers or from the firm's regional branch offices in the case of a large, decentralized wholesaler. These workers take and process orders, and route them to the warehouse for packing and shipment. Often, they must be able to answer customer inquiries about products and monitor inventory levels or record sales for the accounting department. *Stock clerks* code or price goods and store them in the appropriate warehouse sections. They also retrieve from stock the appropriate type and quantity of goods ordered by customers. In some cases, they also may perform tasks similar to those performed by shipping and receiving clerks.

Like office and administrative support workers, many sales and related workers need no postsecondary training, but many employers seek applicants with prior sales experience. Generally, workers in marketing and sales occupations try to interest customers and assist them in purchasing a wholesale firm's goods. There are three primary types of sales people in wholesale firms, and their duties vary considerably.

*Counter sales workers* wait on customers who come to the firm to make a purchase. These workers must be knowledgeable about product lines and able to use computer terminals to check on the availability of particular goods in inventory.

*Inside sales workers* usually are more experienced and more knowledgeable about specific products, prices, and the lead times required for delivery. Like order clerks, they take phone orders but may also solicit new business over the phone or the Internet.

*Outside sales workers*, also called *wholesale sales representatives* or *sales engineers*, are the most skilled workers and one of the largest occupations in wholesale trade. They travel to customers' places of business—whether manufacturers, retailers, or institutions—to maintain current customers or to attract new ones. They make presentations to buyers and management or may demonstrate items to production supervisors. Sales representatives must be very knowledgeable about product operation, prices, maintenance needs, and capabilities and must be thoroughly familiar with customers' needs and business goals so that they can suggest how customers can use products to their greatest advantage. For example, sales representatives sometimes advise manufacturers on how to use a new piece of equipment to make production more efficient or may train workers to use the equipment. In the case of complex equipment, sales engineers may need a great deal of highly technical knowledge.

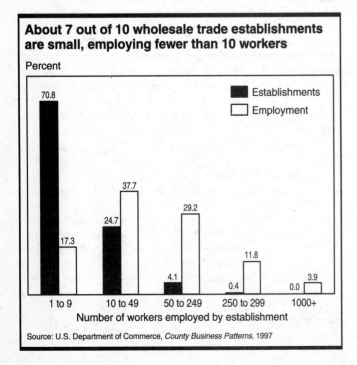

**About 7 out of 10 wholesale trade establishments are small, employing fewer than 10 workers**

Percent

- Establishments
- Employment

| 1 to 9 | 10 to 49 | 50 to 249 | 250 to 299 | 1000+ |
|---|---|---|---|---|
| 70.8 / 17.3 | 24.7 / 37.7 | 4.1 / 29.2 | 0.4 / 11.8 | 0.0 / 3.9 |

Number of workers employed by establishment

Source: U.S. Department of Commerce, *County Business Patterns*, 1997

For this reason, some outside sales workers need to have postsecondary technical education.

*Sales worker supervisors* monitor and coordinate the work of the sales staff and often do outside sales work themselves.

Transportation and material-moving workers move goods around the warehouse, pack and load goods for shipment, and transport goods to buyers. *Laborers and freight, stock, and material movers* manually move goods to or from storage and help load delivery trucks. *Hand packers and packagers* also prepare items for shipment. *Industrial truck and tractor operators* use forklifts and tractors with trailers to transport goods within the warehouse, to outdoor storage facilities, or to trucks for loading. *Truck drivers* transport goods between the wholesaler and the purchaser or between distant warehouses. Drivers of medium and heavy trucks need a State Commercial Driver's License (CDL). *Driver/sales workers* deliver goods to customers, unload goods, set up retail displays, and take orders for future deliveries. They are responsible for maintaining customer confidence and keeping clients well-stocked. Sometimes these workers visit prospective clients, in hopes of generating new business.

Management and business and financial operations workers direct the operations of firms and include *general and operations managers* and *chief executives*, as well as *middle managers*, who supervise workers and ensure that operations meet standards and goals set by top management. Managers with ownership interest in smaller firms often also have some sales responsibilities.

Two large occupations are *wholesale buyers* and *purchasing managers*. Wholesale buyers purchase goods from manufacturers for resale, based on price and what they think customers want. Purchasing managers coordinate the activities of buyers and determine when to purchase what types and quantities of goods.

*Installation, maintenance, and repair* workers set up, service, and repair equipment sold by wholesalers. Others maintain vehicles and other equipment. For these jobs, firms usually hire workers with maintenance and repair experience or mechanically inclined individuals who can be trained on the job. Supervising warehouse workers—such as clerks, material movers, and truck drivers—and seeing that standards of efficiency are maintained is the work of *first-line supervisors*.

## Training and Advancement

Although some workers need a college degree, most jobs in wholesale trade can be entered without education beyond high school. New workers usually receive training after they begin work—for instance, in operation of inventory management databases, on-line purchasing systems, or electronic data interchange systems. Technological advances and market forces are rapidly altering this industry. Even workers in small firms need to keep informed about new selling techniques, management methodologies, and information systems. In addition, these technological advances affect the skill requirements for occupations across the entire industry—from warehouse workers to truck drivers to those in management. As a result, numerous firms devote significant resources to worker training.

Many firms offer on-the-job training. However, as providing training is becoming more costly and complex, the industry is increasingly using third-party training organizations and trade associations to reduce this burden. To increase productivity, many companies make their employees responsible for more than one function and cross-train them by familiarizing them with many aspects of the company.

**Table 1. Employment of wage and salary workers in wholesale trade by occupation, 2000 and projected change, 2000-10**

(Employment in thousands)

| Occupation | Employment, 2000 Number | Employment, 2000 Percent | Percent change, 2000-2010 |
|---|---|---|---|
| **All occupations** | 7,024 | 100.0 | 11.1 |
| **Management, business, and financial occupations** | 757 | 10.8 | 14.6 |
| Sales managers | 62 | 0.9 | 30.5 |
| General and operations managers | 251 | 3.6 | 12.1 |
| Wholesale and retail buyers, except farm products | 67 | 1.0 | -5.1 |
| Financial specialists | 64 | 0.9 | 19.6 |
| **Professional and related occupations** | 389 | 5.5 | 26.6 |
| Computer programmers | 57 | 0.8 | -3.2 |
| **Sales and related occupations** | 1,649 | 23.5 | 8.9 |
| Cashiers, except gaming | 64 | 0.9 | 18.8 |
| Parts salespersons | 91 | 1.3 | -5.9 |
| Retail salespersons | 127 | 1.8 | 18.7 |
| Sales representatives, wholesale and manufacturing, technical and scientific products | 211 | 3.0 | 7.1 |
| Sales representatives, wholesale and manufacturing, except technical and scientific products | 845 | 12.0 | 6.8 |
| First-line supervisors/managers of retail sales workers | 53 | 0.8 | 19.7 |
| First-line supervisors/managers of non-retail sales workers | 122 | 1.7 | 6.8 |
| **Office and administrative support occupations** | 1,720 | 24.5 | 6.4 |
| First-line supervisors/managers of office and administrative support workers | 112 | 1.6 | 13.6 |
| Bookkeeping, accounting, and auditing clerks | 167 | 2.4 | 2.2 |
| Customer service representatives | 129 | 1.8 | 15.1 |
| Order clerks | 126 | 1.8 | -22.8 |
| Shipping, receiving, and traffic clerks | 226 | 3.2 | 8.7 |
| Stock clerks and order fillers | 273 | 3.9 | 18.5 |
| Office clerks, general | 196 | 2.8 | 13.6 |
| Executive secretaries and administrative assistants | 75 | 1.1 | 6.9 |
| Secretaries, except legal, medical, and executive | 79 | 1.1 | -5.1 |
| **Installation, maintenance, and repair occupations** | 492 | 7.0 | 13.8 |
| Computer, automated teller, and office machine repairers | 79 | 1.1 | 6.1 |
| Heavy vehicle and mobile equipment service technicians and mechanics | 78 | 1.1 | 11.1 |
| Maintenance and repair workers, general | 67 | 1.0 | 5.2 |
| **Production occupations** | 497 | 7.1 | 9.5 |
| Team assemblers | 124 | 1.8 | 6.9 |
| Metal workers and plastic workers | 90 | 1.3 | 11.7 |
| Other production occupations | 132 | 1.9 | 9.5 |
| **Transportation and material moving occupations** | 1,350 | 19.2 | 12.3 |
| Supervisors, transportation and material moving workers | 56 | 0.8 | 25.5 |
| Driver/sales workers | 121 | 1.7 | 4.7 |
| Truck drivers, heavy and tractor-trailer | 225 | 3.2 | 22.2 |
| Truck drivers, light or delivery services | 234 | 3.3 | 14.6 |
| Industrial truck and tractor operators | 112 | 1.6 | 11.8 |
| Laborers and freight, stock, and material movers, hand | 398 | 5.7 | 6.7 |
| Packers and packagers, hand | 120 | 1.7 | 11.4 |

NOTE: May not add to totals due to omission of occupations with small employment.

Wholesale trade has historically offered good advancement opportunities from the lowest skilled jobs up through management positions. For example, unskilled workers can start in the warehouse or stock room. After they become familiar with the products and procedures of the firm, workers may be promoted to counter sales or even to inside sales positions. Others may be trained to install, service, and repair the products sold by the firm. Eventually, workers may advance to outside sales positions or to managerial positions. Wholesale trade firms often emphasize promotion from within, especially in the numerous small businesses in the industry. Even in some of the largest firms, it is not uncommon to find top executives who began as part-time warehouse help.

As the wholesale trade industry changes in the coming years, advancement opportunities could become more limited. New technologies and changing management techniques are placing increasing demands on managers, so it will become more difficult to promote less-educated workers from within. However, consolidations have resulted in larger companies with more opportunities for those with the appropriate skills to advance. Currently, several large firms in this industry have formal management training programs that train college graduates for management positions, and the number of these programs will probably grow. There are also a growing number of industrial distribution programs at universities providing students with both business and technical training.

In addition to advancement opportunities within a firm, there also are opportunities for self-employment. For example, because brokers match buyers with sellers and never actually own goods, those with the proper connections can establish wholesale brokerage businesses with only a small investment—perhaps working out of their home. Moreover, establishing a wholesale-distribution business can be easier than establishing many other kinds of businesses. Wholesalers who get exclusive distribution rights to popular items can become profitable quickly; although wholesale-distribution firms usually require a substantial investment, obtaining rights to a successful product can be the foundation of a successful new business.

All workers should expect to periodically take classes and seminars to learn new skills as the industry adapts to new technology and business practices.

## Earnings

Nonsupervisory wage and salary workers in wholesale trade averaged $584 a week in 2000, higher than the average of $474 a week for the entire workforce. Earnings varied greatly between wholesale trade sectors. For example, in the sector with the highest earnings—professional and commercial equipment—workers averaged $785 a week; but in the sector with the lowest earnings—farm-product raw materials—workers made $354 a week. Earnings in selected occupations in wholesale trade appear in table 2.

Part of the earnings of some workers is based on performance, especially in the case of outside sales workers, who frequently receive commissions on their sales. Although many sales workers receive a base salary in addition to commission, some receive compensation based solely on sales revenue. Performance-based compensation may become more common among other occupations as wholesaling firms attempt to offer more competitive compensation packages.

Like earnings, benefits vary widely from firm to firm. Some small firms offer few benefits. Benefits in larger firms include life insurance, partially or fully paid health insurance, and a pension. Other benefits may include profit sharing, savings or investment plans, and fully or partially paid dental insurance.

Only 5.6 percent of workers in the wholesale trade industry were union members or covered by union contracts in 2000, compared with 15 percent of the entire workforce.

Table 2. Median hourly earnings of the largest occupations in wholesale trade, 2000

| Occupation | Wholesale trade, durable goods | Wholesale trade, nondurable goods | All industries |
|---|---|---|---|
| General and operations managers ... | $ 35.94 | $ 31.46 | $ 29.41 |
| Sales representatives, wholesale and manufacturing, technical and scientific products ... | 25.80 | 26.98 | 25.30 |
| Sales representatives, wholesale and manufacturing, except technical and scientific products ... | 19.98 | 18.66 | 19.40 |
| Truck drivers, heavy and tractor-trailer ... | 13.46 | 14.77 | 15.25 |
| Customer service representatives .... | 13.31 | 12.52 | 11.83 |
| Bookkeeping, accounting, and auditing clerks ... | 12.76 | 12.11 | 12.34 |
| Shipping, receiving, and traffic clerks ... | 10.85 | 10.81 | 10.52 |
| Stock clerks and order fillers ... | 10.16 | 9.72 | 8.75 |
| Truck drivers, light or delivery services ... | 9.86 | 10.98 | 10.74 |
| Laborers and freight, stock, and material movers, hand ... | 9.45 | 9.34 | 9.04 |

## Outlook

Wage and salary jobs in wholesale trade are projected to grow by 11 percent over the 2000-10 period, compared with the 15-percent rate of growth projected for all industries combined. Industry trends will change the composition and nature of much wholesale trade employment. Electronic commerce (usually called e-commerce), consolidation of the industry into larger firms, and the spread of new technology should slow growth in some occupations. However, many new jobs will be created in other fields as firms provide a growing array of support services. In addition, the roles of many other workers will change.

Wholesale trade will undoubtedly feel the effects of e-commerce. E-commerce allows people and companies to instantly obtain price quotes and product information, make and process transactions, track product delivery, and share marketing information. Demand for some occupations will decline as e-commerce dramatically improves worker productivity, although previous technological improvements have already refined the distribution system in many areas of ordering, fulfillment, and purchasing.

The two largest occupational groups in wholesale trade—office and administrative support, and sales and related occupations—will be the most affected. As customers purchase goods and track their delivery electronically, more of the sales activities as well as customer service will be done without sales or customer service workers. As retailers and manufacturers electronically integrate their systems to inform each other of products, availability, and prices, more goods may be ordered and shipped directly from manufacturers to retailers.

The increasing use of brokers and electronic business exchanges will limit growth in the numbers of sales and administrative workers. The work of sales workers also will change, both as the selling process becomes more automated and as customer service becomes more important. Work related to most of the sales that are not automated or transacted electronically will fall to inside sales workers. They will field calls and solicit new business by phone or over the Internet, and assist buyers with computerized purchases. However, more of outside sales workers' responsibilities will involve complex customer service work, such as visiting customers to solicit new business and to maintain good relations, aiding with installation and maintenance, and advising on the most efficient use of purchases.

Consolidation will continue due to globalization and cost pressures. International competition will heat up as domestic firms expand sales to other countries and as foreign firms export more to the United States, adding to the cost pressures on manufacturers. This should continue to force distributors to merge with other firms, or to acquire smaller firms. In addition, the largest retail operations will continue to grow, increasing the demand for large, national wholesale-distributor firms to supply them. But small, geographically isolated wholesalers may continue to form national alliances that will be more versatile in fulfilling customer orders. The differences between large and small firms will become more pronounced as they compete less for the same customers and emphasize their area of expertise. The resulting consolidation of wholesale trade among fewer, larger firms will reduce demand for some workers, as merged companies eliminate duplicated staff. At the same time, the expansion of customer services should increase demand for related workers. Office and administrative workers and sales workers will advance to many of these new customer service and marketing jobs. New workers with the necessary education and training will be needed for financial, logistical, or technical positions. Further automation of record keeping, ordering, and processing will result in slower growth for office and administrative support occupations, compared with most other wholesale trade occupations. Use of computerized labels with bar codes allows stock clerks with scanners to immediately record locations, quantities, and types of goods in a computerized inventory management system. Customers frequently order and pay for goods electronically through the Internet or other special systems. Therefore, fewer bookkeeping, accounting, and auditing clerks will be needed as fewer paper transactions are conducted. Despite this new technology, some office and administrative support workers will still be needed to oversee the process and make adjustments when problems occur. These workers will need to be proficient with new computerized systems.

## Sources of Additional Information

For information about job opportunities in wholesale trade, contact local firms.

For general information on the wholesale trade industry, contact:

➢   National Association of Wholesale-Distributors, 1725 K St. NW., Washington, DC 20006. Internet: **http://www.naw.org**

Information on careers in the wholesale trade industry is available from:

➢   Retail, Wholesale, and Department Store Union, 30 East 29th St., 4th floor, New York, NY 10016. Internet: **http://www.rwdsu.org**

For training and other information on wholesale distributors in the plumbing, heating, cooling, and piping industry, contact:

➢   American Suppliers Association Education Foundation, 222 Merchandise Mart Plaza, Suite 1400, Chicago, IL 60654. Internet: **http://www.asa.net**

For information on wholesale distributors in the food industry, contact:

➢   Food Distributors International, 201 Park Washington Ct., Falls Church, VA 22046. Internet: **http://www.fdi.org**

Information on many key occupations in wholesale trade may be found in the 2002-03 *Occupational Outlook Handbook*:

● Bookkeeping, accounting, and auditing clerks

● Computer, automated teller, and office machine repairers

● Order clerks

● Purchasing managers, buyers, and purchasing agents

● Sales engineers

● Sales representatives, wholesale and manufacturing

● Shipping, receiving, and traffic clerks

● Stock clerks and order fillers

● Truck drivers and driver/sales workers

# Finance and Insurance

# Banking

## SIGNIFICANT POINTS

- Office and administrative support workers constitute almost 2 out of 3 jobs; tellers account for nearly 1 out of 4 jobs.

- Banking employment is projected to decline as mergers and automation make banks more efficient.

- Employment of tellers will decrease, while growth is expected for customer service representatives and for securities and financial services sales representatives.

- Job openings for tellers arising from replacement needs should be plentiful because turnover is high and the occupation is large.

### Nature of the Industry

Banks safeguard money and valuables and provide loans, credit, and payment services, such as checking accounts, money orders, and cashier's checks. With the passage of the Financial Modernization Act in 1999, banks also may offer investment and insurance products, which they were once prohibited from selling. Although other "nonbank" financial companies increasingly provide many of the same depository and payment services, a major difference between banks and other financial institutions is that deposits in banks are insured by the Federal Deposit Insurance Corporation. This ensures that depositors will get their money back, up to a stated limit, if a bank should fail.

There are several types of banks, also called depository institutions, which differ in the number of services they provide and the clientele they serve. *Commercial banks*, which dominate this industry, offer a full range of services for individuals, businesses, and governments. These banks come in a wide range of sizes, from large global banks to regional and community banks. Global banks are involved in international lending and foreign currency trading, in addition to the more typical banking services. Regional banks have numerous branches and automated teller machine (ATM) locations throughout a multistate area that provide banking services to individuals. Community banks are based locally and offer more personal attention, which many individuals and small businesses prefer. In recent years, online banks—which provide all services entirely over the Internet—have entered the market.

*Savings banks* and *savings and loan associations*, sometimes called thrift institutions, are the second largest group of depository institutions. They were first established as community-based institutions to finance mortgages for people to buy homes and still cater mostly to the savings and lending needs of individuals.

*Credit unions* are another kind of depository institution. Most credit unions are formed by people with a common bond, such as those who work for the same company or belong to the same labor union or church. Members pool their savings and, when they need money, they may borrow from the credit union, often at a lower interest rate than that demanded by other financial institutions.

*Federal Reserve banks* are Government agencies that perform many financial services for the Government. Their chief responsibilities are to regulate the banking industry and to control the Nation's money supply—the total quantity of money in the country, including cash and bank deposits. Federal Reserve banks also perform a variety of services for other banks. For example, they make emergency loans to banks that are short of cash and clear checks that are drawn and paid out by different banks.

Interest on loans is the principal source of revenue for most banks, making their various lending departments critical to their success. The commercial lending department loans money to companies to start or expand a business or to purchase inventory and capital equipment. The consumer lending department handles student loans, credit cards, and loans for home improvements, debt consolidation, and automobile purchases. Finally, the mortgage lending department loans money to individuals and businesses to purchase real estate.

The money to lend comes primarily from deposits in checking and savings accounts, certificates of deposit, money market accounts, and other deposit accounts that consumers and businesses set up with the bank. These deposits often earn interest for the owner, and accounts that offer checking provide an easy method for making payments safely without using cash.

The bank's trust department performs a number of other services. For example, it may act as executor and administrator of a will, assembling and distributing assets to the beneficiaries. It also may serve as guardian of assets for minors or incompetent people. One of the department's most important functions is to manage assets entrusted to it, such as a pension or endowment fund, and to distribute the proceeds. Some trust departments also act as stock transfer agents for corporations. As agents, they record the transfer of ownership of stock. They also distribute dividend checks, annual reports, and other mailings to stockholders.

Technology is having a major impact on the banking industry. For example, many routine bank services that once required a teller, such as making a withdrawal or deposit, are now available through ATMs that allow people to access their accounts 24 hours a day. Also, direct deposit allows companies and governments to electronically transfer payments into various accounts. Further, debit cards and "smart cards" instantaneously deduct money from an account when the card is swiped across a machine at a store's cash register. Electronic banking by phone or computer allows customers to pay bills and transfer money from one account to another. Finally, the availability and growing use of credit scoring software allows loans to be approved in minutes—rather than days—making lending departments more efficient.

Other fundamental changes are occurring in the industry as banks diversify their services to become more competitive. Many banks now offer their customers financial planning and asset management services, as well as brokerage and insurance services, often through a subsidiary or third party. Others are beginning to provide investment banking services that help companies and governments raise money through the issuance of stocks and bonds, also usually through a subsidiary. As banks respond to deregulation and as competition in this sector grows, the nature of the banking industry will continue to undergo significant change.

## Working Conditions

The average workweek for nonsupervisory workers in banking was 35.6 hours in 2000. Supervisory and managerial employees, however, usually work substantially longer hours. Eleven percent of employees in 2000, mostly tellers, worked part-time.

Working conditions also vary according to where the employee works. Employees in a typical branch work weekdays, some evenings if the bank is open late, and Saturday mornings. Hours may be longer for workers in bank branches located in grocery stores and shopping malls, which are open most evenings and weekends. Branch office jobs, particularly teller positions, require continual communication with customers, repetitive tasks, and a high level of attention to security. Tellers also must stand for long periods in a confined space.

To improve customer service and provide greater access to bank personnel, banks are establishing centralized phone centers, staffed mainly by customer service representatives. Employees of phone centers spend most of their time answering phone calls from customers and must be available to work evening and weekend shifts.

Administrative support employees may work in large processing facilities, in the banks' headquarters, or in other administrative offices. Most support staff work a standard 40-hour week; some may work overtime. Those support staff located in the processing facilities may work evening shifts.

Commercial and mortgage loan officers often work out of the office, visiting clients, checking out loan applications, and soliciting new business. Loan officers may be required to travel if a client is out of town, or to work evenings if that is the only time at which a client can meet. Financial service sales representatives also may visit clients in the evenings and on weekends to go over the client's financial needs.

The remaining employees located primarily at the headquarters or other administrative offices usually work in comfortable surroundings and put in a standard workweek. In general, banks are relatively safe places to work. In 1999, cases of work-related injury and illness averaged 1.5 per 100 full-time workers, among the lowest in the private sector, where the rate was 6.3.

## Employment

The banking industry employed more than 2.0 million wage and salary workers in 2000. More than 7 out of 10 jobs were in commercial banks; the remainder were concentrated in savings and loan associations and credit unions (table 1).

**Table 1. Percent distribution of employment in banking by type of institution, 2000**

| Establishment | Percent |
| --- | --- |
| Depository institutions ........................................................ | 100.0 |
| Commercial banks .............................................................. | 70.5 |
| Savings institutions ............................................................ | 12.5 |
| Credit unions ...................................................................... | 9.5 |
| Banking and closely related functions, nec ......................... | 7.5 |

In 1997, nearly 95 percent of establishments in banking employed fewer than 50 workers (chart). However, these small establishments, mostly bank branch offices, employed only half of all employees. The other half worked in establishments with 50 or more workers. Banks are found everywhere in the United States, but most bank employees work in heavily populated States such as New York, California, Illinois, Pennsylvania, and Texas.

## Occupations in the Industry

Office and administrative support occupations account for about 2 out of 3 jobs in the banking industry (table 2). *Bank tellers*, the largest individual banking occupation, provide routine financial services to the public. They handle customers' deposits and withdrawals, change money, sell money orders and travelers checks, and accept payment for loans and utility bills. Increasingly, tellers also are selling bank services to customers. *New accounts clerks* and *customer service representatives* answer questions from customers, and help them open and close accounts and fill out forms to apply for banking services. They are knowledgeable about a broad array of bank services and must be able to sell those services to potential clients.

*Loan* and *credit clerks* assemble and prepare paperwork, process applications, and complete the documentation after a loan or line of credit has been approved. They also verify applications for completeness. *Bill and account collectors* attempt to

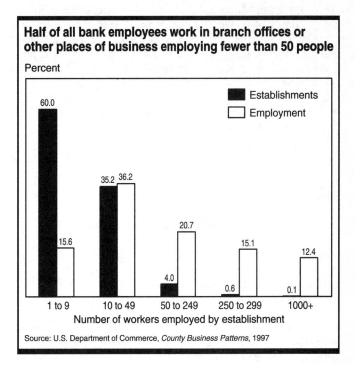

Source: U.S. Department of Commerce, *County Business Patterns*, 1997

143

collect payments on overdue loans. Many *general office clerks* and *bookkeeping, accounting, and auditing clerks* are employed to maintain financial records, enter data, and process the thousands of deposit slips, checks, and other documents that banks handle daily. Banks also employ many *secretaries, data entry keyers, receptionists*, and other administrative support workers. *First-line supervisors/managers of office and administrative support workers* oversee the activities and training of workers in the various administrative support occupations.

Management, business, and financial occupations account for about 23 percent of employment in the banking industry. *Financial managers* direct bank branches and departments, resolve customers' problems, ensure that standards of service are maintained, and administer the institutions' operations and investments. *Loan officers* evaluate loan applications, determine an applicant's ability to pay back a loan, and recommend approval of loans. They usually specialize in commercial, consumer, or mortgage lending. When loans become delinquent, loan officers, or *loan counselors*, may advise borrowers on the management of their finances or take action to collect outstanding amounts. Loan officers also play a major role in bringing in new business and spend much of their time developing relationships with potential customers. *Trust officers* manage a variety of assets that were placed in trust with the bank for other people or organizations; these assets can include pension funds, school endowments, or a company's profit-sharing plan. Sometimes, trust officers act as executors of estates upon a person's death. They also may work as accountants, lawyers, and investment managers.

*Securities, commodities, and financial services sales agents*, who make up the majority of sales positions in banks, sell complex banking services. They contact potential customers to explain their services and to ascertain the customer's banking and other financial needs. They also may discuss services such as deposit accounts, lines of credit, sales or inventory financing, certificates of deposit, cash management, or investment services. These sales agents also solicit businesses to participate in consumer credit card programs. At most small and medium-size banks, however, branch managers and commercial loan officers are responsible for marketing the bank's financial services.

Other occupations used widely by banks to maintain financial records and ensure the bank's compliance with Federal and State regulations are *accountants and auditors*, and *lawyers*. In addition, *computer engineers* and *specialists* are needed to maintain and upgrade the bank's computer systems and to implement the bank's entry into the world of electronic banking and paperless transactions.

## Training and Advancement

Bank tellers and other clerks usually need only a high school education. Most banks seek people who have good basic math and communication skills, enjoy public contact, and feel comfortable handling large amounts of money. Through a combination of formal classroom instruction and on-the-job training under the guidance of an experienced worker, tellers learn the procedures, rules, and regulations that govern their jobs. Banks encourage upward mobility by providing access to higher education and other sources of additional training.

Tellers, clerks, and mid-level banking personnel can increase their job skills and enhance their knowledge by taking courses accredited by the American Institute of Banking (AIB), an educational affiliate of the American Bankers Association, and by the Institute of Financial Education (IFE), an affiliate of the Bank

**Table 2. Employment of wage and salary workers in banking by occupation, 2000 and projected change, 2000-10**

(Employment in thousands)

| Occupation | Employment, 2000 Number | Percent | Percent change, 2000-2010 |
|---|---|---|---|
| **All occupations** | 2,029 | 100.0 | -1.5 |
| **Management, business, and financial occupations** | 476 | 23.4 | -0.1 |
| Marketing and sales managers | 16 | 0.8 | 12.4 |
| Chief executives | 21 | 1.1 | -2.3 |
| Financial managers | 85 | 4.2 | -7.4 |
| General and operations managers | 43 | 2.1 | -3.3 |
| Human resources, training, and labor relations specialists | 15 | 0.7 | -4.3 |
| All other business operations specialists | 17 | 0.9 | 3.0 |
| Accountants and auditors | 20 | 1.0 | 2.2 |
| Credit analysts | 17 | 0.9 | 2.7 |
| Financial analysts | 17 | 0.8 | 15.8 |
| Loan officers | 104 | 5.1 | -4.9 |
| All other financial specialists | 23 | 1.1 | 12.9 |
| **Professional and related occupations** | 127 | 6.3 | 30.2 |
| Computer software engineers, systems software | 28 | 1.4 | 37.0 |
| Computer support specialists | 28 | 1.4 | 53.1 |
| **Service occupations** | 17 | 0.8 | -1.9 |
| **Sales and related occupations** | 99 | 4.9 | 9.8 |
| Securities, commodities, and financial services sales agents | 39 | 1.9 | 22.3 |
| All other sales and related workers | 30 | 1.5 | 2.0 |
| **Office and administrative support occupations** | 1,304 | 64.2 | -6.0 |
| First-line supervisors/managers of office and administrative support workers | 97 | 4.8 | 2.1 |
| Bill and account collectors | 33 | 1.6 | -0.6 |
| Bookkeeping, accounting, and auditing clerks | 64 | 3.2 | -11.6 |
| Tellers | 484 | 23.9 | -12.4 |
| Credit authorizers, checkers, and clerks | 22 | 1.1 | -18.4 |
| Customer service representatives | 160 | 7.9 | 37.4 |
| Loan interviewers and clerks | 70 | 3.5 | -34.0 |
| New accounts clerks | 82 | 4.0 | 1.4 |
| Receptionists and information clerks | 15 | 0.8 | -8.7 |
| All other financial, information, and record clerks | 22 | 1.1 | 1.1 |
| Data entry keyers | 18 | 0.9 | -24.0 |
| Office clerks, general | 60 | 3.0 | -19.8 |
| Executive secretaries and administrative assistants | 44 | 2.2 | -8.1 |
| Secretaries, except legal, medical, and executive | 19 | 0.9 | -18.6 |

NOTE: May not add to totals due to omission of occupations with small employment.

Administration Institute. These organizations have several hundred chapters in cities across the country and numerous study groups in small communities. Most banks use the facilities of these organizations, which assist local banks in conducting cooperative training programs or developing independent programs. Some community colleges also offer courses for employed tellers and those seeking to become tellers. Taking these courses can give applicants an advantage over other jobseekers.

Some banks have their own training programs, which result in teller certification. Experienced tellers qualify for certification by taking required courses and passing examinations. Experienced tellers and clerks may advance to head teller, new accounts clerk, or customer service representative. Outstanding tellers who have had some college or specialized training offered by the banking industry are sometimes promoted to managerial positions.

Workers in management, business, and financial occupations usually have at least a college degree. A bachelor's degree in business administration or a liberal arts degree with business administration courses is suitable preparation, as is a bachelor's degree in any field followed by a Master of Business Administration (MBA) degree. Many financial management positions are filled by promoting experienced, technically skilled professional personnel—for example, accountants, auditors, budget analysts, credit analysts, or financial analysts—or accounting or related department supervisors in large banks.

Financial services sales agents usually need a college degree; a major or courses in finance, accounting, economics, marketing, or related fields serve as excellent preparation. Experience in sales also is very helpful. These workers learn on the job under the supervision of bank officers. Sales agents selling securities need to be licensed by the National Association of Securities Dealers.

Advancement to higher level executive, administrative, managerial, and professional positions may be accelerated by special study. Banks often provide opportunities for workers to broaden their knowledge and skills, and they encourage employees to take classes offered by the AIB and IFE, as well as courses at local colleges and universities. In addition, financial management and banking associations, often in cooperation with colleges and universities, sponsor numerous national or local training programs. Each of their schools deals with a different phase of financial management and banking, such as accounting management, budget management, corporate cash management, financial analysis, international banking, and data processing systems procedures and management. Employers also sponsor seminars and conferences, and provide textbooks and other educational materials. Many employers pay all or part of the costs for those who successfully complete courses.

In recent years, the banking field has been revolutionized by technological improvements in computer and data processing equipment. Learning how to apply these improvements is a vital upgrade to managerial skills that enhances advancement opportunities.

## Earnings

Earnings of nonsupervisory bank employees averaged $417 a week in 2000, compared with $547 for all workers in finance, insurance, and real estate industries, and $474 for workers throughout the private sector. Relatively low pay in the banking industry reflects the high proportion of low-paying administrative support jobs.

Earnings in the banking industry vary significantly by occupation. Earnings in the largest occupations in banking appear in table 3.

In general, greater responsibilities result in a higher salary. Experience, length of service, and, especially, the location and size of the bank also are important. In addition to typical benefits, equity sharing and performance-based pay increasingly are part of compensation packages for some bank employees. As in other industries, part-time workers do not enjoy the same benefits that full-time workers do.

Very few workers in the banking industry are unionized—only 1.3 percent are union members or are covered by union contracts, compared with 14.9 percent of workers throughout private industry.

**Table 3. Median hourly earnings of the largest occupations in banking, 2000**

| Occupation | Depository institutions | All industries |
|---|---|---|
| Computer software engineers, systems software | $ 31.51 | $ 33.43 |
| General and operations managers | 30.36 | 29.41 |
| Financial managers | 26.23 | 32.22 |
| Financial analysts | 22.85 | 25.20 |
| Loan officers | 19.55 | 19.92 |
| Credit analysts | 18.23 | 19.32 |
| Securities, commodities, and financial services sales agents | 17.62 | 26.96 |
| Customer service representatives | 11.33 | 11.83 |
| New accounts clerks | 11.05 | 11.10 |
| Tellers | 9.21 | 9.21 |

## Outlook

Wage and salary employment in banking is projected to decline 2 percent between 2000 and 2010, compared with the 16-percent growth projected for the economy as a whole. The combined effects of technology, deregulation, mergers, and population growth will continue to affect total employment growth and the mix of occupations in the banking industry. Overall declines in office and administrative support occupations will be offset by growth in professional, managerial, and sales occupations. Although a decline in employment is expected, job opportunities should be plentiful, particularly among tellers and other administrative support staff, who make up a large proportion of bank employees and often transfer to other occupations or leave the labor force.

Bank mergers contributed significantly to employment declines throughout the 1990s. Merger activity—at a slower pace—is expected to continue over the projection period, dampening employment growth. At the same time, many banks will open more branch offices in areas in which the population is growing. However, because of widespread automation of many banking services, fewer employees will be hired to staff new branches than in the past.

Advances in technology should continue to have the most significant effect on employment in the banking industry. Demand for computer specialists will grow as more banks make their services available electronically and eliminate much of the paperwork involved in many banking transactions. On the other hand, these changes in technology will reduce the need for several office and administrative support occupations. Employment of tellers will decline as customers increasingly use ATMs, direct deposit, debit cards, and electronic banking to perform routine transactions. Other technological improvements, such as digital imaging and computer networking, will adversely affect employment of the "back-office" clerical workers who process checks and other bank statements. Employment of customer service representatives, however, is expected to increase as banks hire more of these workers to staff phone centers and sell banking products to branch customers.

Recent deregulation of the banking industry now allows banks to offer a variety of financial and insurance products that they were once prohibited from selling. The need to develop, analyze, and sell these new services will spur demand for securities

145

and financial services sales representatives, financial analysts, and personal financial advisors. Demand for "personal bankers" and trust officers to manage the assets of and advise wealthy clients, as well as the aging baby-boom generation, also will grow. However, banks will face continued competition—particularly in lending—from nonbank establishments, such as consumer credit companies and mortgage brokers. Companies and individuals now are able to obtain loans and credit and raise money through a variety of means other than bank loans. Therefore, employment of loan officers will grow only slowly, as financial services sales representatives, who sell loans along with other bank services, take their place.

## Sources of Additional Information

State bankers' associations can furnish specific information about job opportunities in their State. Individual banks can provide detailed information about job openings and the activities, responsibilities, and preferred qualifications of banking personnel.

Information about careers with the Federal Reserve System is available from the Web site or human resources department of the regional Federal Reserve Bank of interest.

Information on many of the occupations in banking, including the following, may be found in the 2002-03 edition of the *Occupational Outlook Handbook*:

- Accountants and auditors
- Bill and account collectors
- Bookkeeping, accounting, and auditing clerks
- Computer support specialists and systems administrators
- Credit authorizers, checkers, and clerks
- Customer service representatives
- Financial managers
- Information and record clerks
- Loan counselors and officers
- Securities, commodities, and financial services sales agents
- Systems analysts, computer scientists, and database administrators
- Tellers

# Insurance

(SIC 63, 64)

## SIGNIFICANT POINTS

- Office and administrative occupations usually require a high school diploma, while employers prefer college graduates for sales, managerial, and professional jobs.

- Medical service and health insurance is the fastest growing sector of the insurance industry.

- While corporate downsizing, computerization, and changes in business practices will limit job growth, numerous job openings are expected in this large industry to replace those who leave and to accommodate the insurance industry's expansion into the broader financial services field.

## Nature of the Industry

The insurance industry provides protection against financial losses resulting from a variety of perils. By purchasing insurance policies, individuals and businesses can receive reimbursement for losses due to car accidents, theft of property, and fire and storm damage; medical expenses; and loss of income due to disability or death.

The insurance industry consists mainly of *insurance carriers*, or *"insurers,"* and *insurance sales agents*. In general, insurance carriers are large companies that provide insurance and assume the risks covered by the policy. Insurance sales agents sell insurance policies for the carriers and work either for themselves or directly as employees of the insurer. While the majority of sales agents are independent and are free to market policies of a variety of insurance carriers, others may work exclusively for one insurance carrier, selling only that carrier's policies. Some carriers market without agents, using the telephone, mail, and—increasingly—the Internet.

Insurance carriers offer a variety of insurance policies. *Life insurance* policies provide financial protection to beneficiaries—usually spouses and dependent children—upon the death of the insured. *Disability insurance* provides income if a person is unable to work, and *health insurance* pays the expenses resulting from accidents and sickness. *Annuities* (contracts that provide a periodic income at regular intervals for a specified period) provide a steady income during retirement for the remainder of one's life. *Property-casualty insurance* protects against loss or damage to property resulting from hazards such as fire, theft, and natural disasters. *Liability insurance* shields policyholders from financial responsibility for injuries to others or damage to other people's property. Most policies, such as automobile and homeowner's insurance combine both property-casualty and liability coverage. Companies that write this kind of insurance are called property-casualty carriers.

Some insurance policies cover groups of people, ranging from a few to thousands of individuals. These policies usually are issued to employers for the benefit of their employees. Among the most common of these policies are group life and health plans. Insurance carriers also write a variety of specialized types of insurance, such as real estate title insurance and employee surety and fidelity bonding. A recent act of Congress has allowed insurance carriers and other financial institutions, such as banks and securities firms, to sell one another's products. As a result, more insurance carriers now sell financial products such as securities, mutual funds, options and derivatives, and various retirement plans. This is most common in life insurance companies that already sell annuities; however, property and casualty companies also sell financial products. In order to expand into one another's markets, insurance carriers, banks, and securities firms have recently engaged in numerous mergers. This allows the merging companies access to each other's client base and geographical markets.

In the last few years, insurance carriers have discovered that the Internet can be a powerful tool for reaching potential and existing customers. Most carriers use the Internet simply to post company information such as sales brochures and product information, financial statements, and a list of local agents. However, an increasing number of carriers are starting to expand their websites to include online access to accounts and billing information. A few even allow customers to submit claims online, and also provide insurance quotes from information submitted by customers on the website. In the future, carriers' websites will allow customers to purchase policies through the Internet without ever speaking to a live agent.

In addition to individual carrier-sponsored websites, several "lead-generating" sites have emerged. These sites allow potential customers to input information about their insurance policy needs. For a fee, these websites forward customer information to insurance companies, which review the information and, if they decide to take on the policy, contact the customer with their offer. This gives consumers the freedom to accept the best rate.

The insurance industry also includes a number of independent organizations that provide a wide array of insurance-related services to carriers and their clients. One such service is the processing of medical claims forms for medical practitioners. Other services include loss prevention and risk management. Also, insurance companies hire independent claims adjusters to investigate accidents and claims for property damage and assign a dollar estimate to the claim.

Other organizations are formed by groups of insurance companies to perform functions that would result in a duplication of effort if each company carried them out individually. For example, service organizations are supported by insurance companies to provide loss statistics, which the companies use to set their rates. Information institutes produce and distribute relevant statistics and educational materials on the different lines of insurance to teachers and schools, and prepare news releases concerning developments of general interest to the public. Trade associations actively work with regulators and legislators to develop or amend the many rules and laws that affect this highly

147

regulated industry. This segment of the industry also is supported by numerous educational institutions that grant certifications and designations to insurance industry employees, as well as provide a source of continuing education that is required by many State licensing bureaus.

## Working Conditions

Many workers in the insurance industry, especially those in administrative support positions, work a 5-day, 40-hour week. Those in executive and managerial occupations may often put in more than 40 hours. Many insurance sales agents and claims adjusters and investigators work irregular hours outside of office settings. Often, sales agents and adjusters arrange their own hours, scheduling evening and weekend appointments for the convenience of clients. This accommodation may result in sales agents and claims adjusters working 50 to 60 hours per week.

Insurance sales agents often visit prospective and existing customers' homes and places of business to market new products and provide services. Claims adjusters and auto damage appraisers frequently leave the office to inspect damaged property. Occasionally, claims adjusters are away from home for days when they travel to the scene of a disaster—such as a tornado, flood, or hurricane—to work with local adjusters and government officials. Insurance investigators often work irregular hours to conduct surveillance or to contact people who are not available during normal working hours.

A small but increasing number of insurance employees spend most of their time on the telephone working in call centers, answering questions and providing information to prospective clients or current policyholders. These jobs may include selling insurance, taking claims information, or answering medical questions. Because these centers operate 24 hours a day, 7 days a week, some of their employees must work evening and weekend shifts. The irregular business hours in the insurance industry provide some workers with the opportunity for part-time work. Part-time employees make up 8.1 percent of the workforce. As would be expected in an industry dominated by office and sales employees, the incidence of occupational injuries and illnesses among insurance workers is low. In 1999, only 1.9 and 0.9 cases per 100 full-time workers were reported in the insurance carriers and agents and brokers segments, respectively, compared with an average of 6.3 for all private industry.

## Employment

The insurance industry employed about 2.3 million wage and salary workers in 2000. Insurance carriers provided 2 out of 3 jobs in the insurance industry; insurance sales agents and providers of other insurance-related services accounted for 1 out of 3 jobs. In addition, there were about 150,000 self-employed workers in 2000, most of whom were insurance sales agents.

Insurance carriers are mostly large employers, as shown in chart. Over half of their employment is in establishments with 250 or more employees, and 80 percent is in establishments with 50 or more workers. Conversely, small establishments dominate the agents and brokers segment of the industry, with nearly all employing fewer than 50 workers (see chart on next page). Approximately 40 percent work in establishments with fewer than 10 employees, and another 30 percent work in establishments with 10 to 49 employees.

Many insurance carriers' home and regional offices are located near large urban centers. Insurance workers who deal directly with the public—sales agents and claims adjusters—are located throughout the country. Almost all insurance sales agents work out of local company offices or independent agencies. Many claims adjusters work for independent firms located in small cities and towns throughout the country.

## Occupations in the Industry

Almost 1 in 2 insurance workers are in office and administrative support jobs found in every industry, including jobs such as secretaries, typists, word processors, bookkeepers, and other clerical workers (table 1). Many office and administrative support positions in the insurance industry, however, require skills and knowledge unique to the industry.

*Customer service representatives*, for example, process insurance policy applications, changes, and cancellations. They review applications for completeness, compile data on policy changes, and verify the accuracy of insurance company records. They may also process claims and sell new policies to existing clients. These workers are taking on increased responsibilities in insurance offices, such as handling most of the continuing contact with clients. An increasing number of customer service representatives work in call centers that are open 24 hours a day, 7 days a week, answering clients' questions, updating policy information, and providing potential clients with information regarding types of policies issued.

About 3 in 10 insurance workers have a job in a management and business and financial operations occupation. *Marketing and sales managers* constitute the majority of managers in carriers' local sales offices and in the insurance sales agents segment. They sell insurance products, work with clients, and supervise staff. Other managers who work in their companies' home offices are in charge of departments such as actuarial calculations, policy issuance, accounting, and investments.

*Claims adjusters, examiners,* and *investigators* decide whether claims are covered by the customer's policy, confirm payment, and, when necessary, investigate the circumstances surrounding a claim. *Claims adjusters* work for property and liability insurance carriers or for independent adjusting firms.

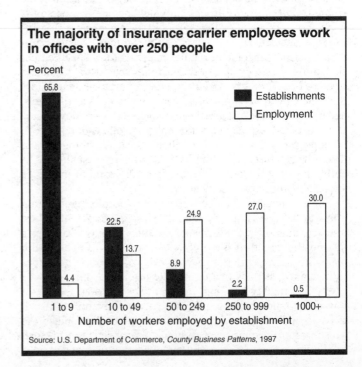

**The majority of insurance carrier employees work in offices with over 250 people**

Percent

Source: U.S. Department of Commerce, *County Business Patterns*, 1997

They plan and schedule the work required to process claims, which includes interviewing the claimant and witnesses, consulting police and hospital records, and inspecting property damage to determine the extent of the insurance company's liability.

In life and health insurance carriers, the counterpart of the claims adjuster is the *claims examiner*. Examiners in the health insurance field review health-related claims to see if costs are reasonable based on the diagnosis. Examiners check claim applications for completeness and accuracy, interview medical specialists, and consult policy files to verify information on a claim. Claims examiners in the life insurance field review causes of death, and also may review new applications for life insurance to make sure applicants have no serious illnesses that would prevent them from qualifying for insurance. Claims examiners in property and casualty insurance review claims to ensure that payments and settlements have been made in accordance with company practices and procedures. They ensure that adjusters have followed proper methods when investigating claims. Examiners may consult with lawyers on claims requiring legal action.

*Insurance investigators* handle claims in which companies suspect there might be fraudulent or criminal activity, such as arson cases, false workers' disability claims, staged accidents, or unnecessary medical treatments. Investigators usually perform database searches on suspects to determine whether they have a history of attempted insurance fraud. Then, investigators may visit claimants and witnesses to obtain a recorded statement, take photographs, inspect facilities, and conduct surveillance on suspects. Investigators often consult with legal counsel and are expert witnesses in court cases as well.

*Auto damage appraisers* usually are hired by insurance companies and independent adjusting firms to inspect auto damage after an accident and provide unbiased repair cost estimates. Claims adjusters and auto damage appraisers can work for insurance companies, or they can be independent or public adjusters. Insurance companies hire independent adjusters to represent their interests while assisting the insured, whereas public adjusters are hired to represent the insured's interests against insurance carriers.

*Loss control representatives* assess various risks faced by insurance companies. They inspect insurance applicants and business operations and analyze historical data regarding workplace injuries, automobile accidents, natural hazards, and conditions that may result in catastrophic physical and financial loss. They might then recommend, for example, that a factory add safety equipment, that a house be built to withstand environmental catastrophes, or that incentives be implemented to encourage automobile owners to install air bags in their cars. Because these standards can greatly reduce the probability of loss, loss control representatives are increasingly important to both insurance companies and the insured.

Another important management and business and financial occupation in insurance is that of *underwriter*. These professionals evaluate insurance applications to determine the risk involved in issuing a policy. They decide whether to accept or reject an application and determine the appropriate premium rate for each policy.

About 13 percent of wage and salary employees are sales staff, who sell policies to individuals and businesses. *Insurance sales agents* may work as exclusive agents, or captive agents, selling for one company or as independent agents selling for several companies. Through regular contact with clients, agents are able to update coverage, assist with claims, ensure customer satisfaction, and obtain referrals. Insurance sales agents may sell many types of insurance, including life, annuities, property-casualty, health, or disability. Also, many insurance sales agents are involved in "cross-selling" or "total account development," which means that, besides insurance, they have become licensed to sell mutual funds, annuities, and other securities. These agents usually find their own customers and ensure that policies they sell meet the specific needs of their policyholders.

The insurance industry employs relatively few people in professional or related occupations; however, these professionals are essential to company operations. For example, lawyers representing insurance companies are needed to defend clients who are sued, especially when potentially large claims are involved. They also review regulations and policy contracts. Nurses and other medical professionals advise clients on wellness issues and on medical procedures covered by their managed-care plan. *Computer systems analysts, computer programmers,* and *computer support specialists* are needed to analyze, design, develop, and program the systems that support the day-to-day operations of the insurance company.

*Actuaries* represent a relatively small proportion of insurance employment, but they are vital to the industry's profitability. Actuaries study the probability of an insured loss and determine premium rates. They must set rates so that there is a high probability that premiums paid by customers will cover claims, but not so high that their company loses business to competitors.

### Training and Advancement
A few jobs in the insurance industry, especially in office and administrative support occupations, require no more than a high school diploma. However, for most jobs, including sales, managerial, and professional jobs, employers prefer to hire workers with a college education. When specialized training is required, it usually is obtained on the job or through independent study during work or after-work hours.

Graduation from high school or business school is adequate preparation for most beginning office and administrative support jobs. Courses in word processing and business math

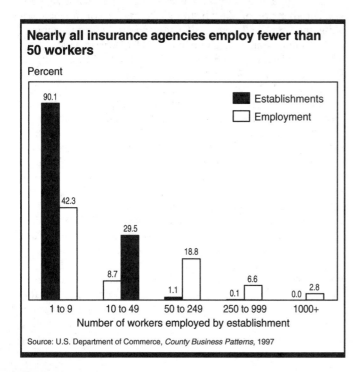

**Nearly all insurance agencies employ fewer than 50 workers**

Percent

Number of workers employed by establishment

Source: U.S. Department of Commerce, *County Business Patterns*, 1997

**Table 1. Employment of wage and salary workers in insurance by occupation, 2000 and projected change, 2000-10**

(Employment in thousands)

| Occupation | Employment, 2000 | | Percent change, 2000-2010 |
|---|---|---|---|
| | Number | Percent | |
| All occupations | 2,346 | 100.0 | 6.4 |
| **Management, business, and financial occupations** | 666 | 28.4 | 8.7 |
| Marketing and sales managers | 27 | 1.2 | 19.7 |
| Chief executives | 23 | 1.0 | 5.8 |
| Computer and information systems managers | 18 | 0.8 | 33.5 |
| Financial managers | 23 | 1.0 | 9.3 |
| General and operations managers | 51 | 2.2 | 3.8 |
| Claims adjusters, examiners, and investigators | 163 | 7.0 | 13.2 |
| Insurance appraisers, auto damage | 11 | 0.5 | 13.7 |
| Human resources, training, and labor relations specialists | 27 | 1.1 | 4.1 |
| Management analysts | 25 | 1.0 | 5.0 |
| All other business operations specialists | 41 | 1.7 | 10.0 |
| Accountants and auditors | 37 | 1.6 | 9.0 |
| Insurance underwriters | 99 | 4.2 | -0.1 |
| **Professional and related occupations** | 246 | 10.5 | 18.3 |
| Computer programmers | 31 | 1.3 | -13.2 |
| Computer systems analysts | 35 | 1.5 | 29.6 |
| Computer support specialists | 20 | 0.9 | 65.1 |
| Title examiners, abstractors, and searchers | 19 | 0.8 | -14.2 |
| Health diagnosing and treating practitioners | 20 | 0.9 | 14.2 |
| Actuaries | 10 | 0.4 | -3.8 |
| **Sales and related occupations** | 303 | 12.9 | 2.3 |
| Insurance sales agents | 237 | 10.1 | 1.2 |
| First-line supervisors/managers of non-retail sales workers | 19 | 0.8 | -1.8 |
| **Office and administrative support occupations** | 1,103 | 47.0 | 3.6 |
| First-line supervisors/managers of office and administrative support workers | 78 | 3.3 | 9.8 |
| Bookkeeping, accounting, and auditing clerks | 50 | 2.1 | -4.7 |
| Customer service representatives | 260 | 11.1 | 49.4 |
| Insurance claims and policy processing clerks | 248 | 10.6 | -28.4 |
| Office clerks, general | 98 | 4.2 | 9.7 |
| Executive secretaries and administrative assistants | 54 | 2.3 | -1.1 |
| Secretaries, except legal, medical, and executive | 77 | 3.3 | -11.1 |

NOTE: May not add to totals due to omission of occupations with small employment.

are assets, and the ability to operate computers is essential. These and other special skills also help beginners advance to higher paying positions. On-the-job training usually is provided for clerical jobs such as customer service representatives. Because customer service representatives in call centers must be knowledgeable about insurance products in order to provide advice to clients, more States are requiring customer service representatives to become licensed like agents are.

Management, business, financial, and professional jobs require the same college training as similar jobs in other industries. Managerial positions usually are filled by promot-

ing college-educated employees within the company. For beginning underwriting jobs, many insurance companies prefer college graduates who have a degree in business administration or a related field. However, some companies prefer to hire liberal arts graduates at a lower cost and many insurers send them to company schools or enroll them in outside institutes for professional training. As an underwriter's career develops, it is beneficial to earn the specialty designation, Associate in Commercial Underwriting (AU). This certification, which is administered by the Insurance Institute of America, typically takes 1 to 2 years to earn and requires the completion of a series of courses and examinations. More advanced certification includes the Chartered Property and Casualty Underwriter (CPCU) designation which takes about 5 years and requires passing 10 exams covering topics in insurance, economics, finance, law, accounting, ethics, management, and risk management. Those working in the life and health sectors of the insurance industry can earn the Chartered Life Underwriter (CLU) or Registered Health Underwriter (RHU) designations. (Additional information on these designations is available in the *Handbook* statement on insurance underwriters).

Most companies prefer to hire college graduates for claims adjuster and examiner positions. No specific college major is required, although most workers in these positions have a business, accounting, engineering, legal, or medical background. Some States require independent, or public, adjusters to be licensed. Most adjusters also find it beneficial to earn one or more professional designations, such as the Associate in Claims (AIC); Registered Professional Adjuster (RPA); Certified Professional Public Adjuster (CPPA) or Senior Professional Public Adjuster (SPPA); and the Associate, Life and Health Claims (ALHC) or the Fellow, Life and Health Claims (FLHC). Many State licenses and professional designations require continuing education for renewal. Continuing education is important because adjusters and examiners must be knowledgeable about changes in the laws, recent court decisions, and new medical procedures. (Additional information on these designations is available in the *Handbook* statement on claims adjusters, appraisers, examiners, and investigators).

Auto damage appraisers typically begin as auto body repairers, and then are hired by insurance companies or independent adjusting firms. While auto damage appraisers do not require a college education, most companies require them to have at least a bachelor's degree. Only four States—Florida, Massachusetts, Rhode Island, and Wyoming—require auto damage appraisers to be licensed. As for adjusters and examiners, continuing education is very important for appraisers because of the new car models and repair techniques that are introduced each year.

Most insurance companies prefer to hire former law enforcement or private investigators as insurance investigators. Many experienced claims adjusters or examiners also can become investigators. Licensing requirements vary among States. Most employers look for individuals with ingenuity and who are persistent and assertive. Investigators must not be afraid of confrontation, should communicate well, and should be able to think on their feet. Good interviewing and interrogation skills also are important and usually are acquired in earlier careers in law enforcement.

For actuarial jobs, companies prefer candidates to have degrees in actuarial science, mathematics, or statistics. However, candidates with degrees in business, finance, or economics also are becoming more common. Actuaries must pass a series of national examinations to become fully qualified. Completion of all the exams takes from 5 to 10 years. Some of the exams may be taken while an individual is in college, but most require extensive home study. Many companies grant study time to their actuarial students to prepare for the exams.

Although some employers hire high school graduates with potential or proven sales ability for entry-level sales positions, most prefer to hire college graduates. All insurance sales agents must obtain a license in the States in which they plan to sell insurance. In most States, licenses are issued only to applicants who complete specified courses and pass written examinations covering insurance fundamentals and State insurance laws. New agents receive training from their employer either at work or at the insurance company's home office. Sometimes, entry-level employees attend company-sponsored classes to prepare for examinations. Others study on their own and, as on-the-job training, accompany experienced agents when they meet with prospective clients. After obtaining a license, agents must earn continuing education credits throughout their careers in order to remain a licensed insurance sales agent.

Insurance sales agents wishing to sell securities and other financial products must also meet State licensing requirements, which include passing an examination. Before agents can qualify as securities representatives, they must pass the General Securities Registered Representative Examination (Series 7 exam), administered by the National Association of Securities Dealers (NASD). This test measures the prospective representative's knowledge of the securities business, customer protection requirements, and recordkeeping procedures. To further demonstrate competency in the area of financial planning, many agents also find it worthwhile to obtain a Certified Financial Planner (CFP) or Chartered Financial Consultant (ChFC) designation.

Advancement opportunities are relatively good in the insurance industry. Office and administrative support workers can advance to higher paying claims adjusting positions and entry-level underwriting jobs. Sales workers may advance by handling greater numbers of accounts and more complex commercial insurance policies. Having a master's degree, particularly in business administration or a related field, helps advancement into higher levels of management. Many insurance companies expect their employees to take continuing education courses to improve their professionalism and their knowledge of the industry.

## Earnings

Weekly earnings of nonsupervisory workers in the insurance carriers segment of the industry averaged $675 in 2000, considerably higher than the average of $474 for all private industry. Earnings for the largest occupations in insurance for 1999 appear in table 2.

Most independent sales agents, who own their own business, are paid by commission only. Sales agents who are employees of an agency may be paid by salary only, salary plus commission, or salary plus bonus. An agent's earnings usually increase rapidly with experience. Many agencies also pay an agent's expenses for automobiles and transportation, travel to conventions, and continuing education.

Insurance carriers offer attractive benefits packages, as often is the case with large companies. Yearly bonuses, retirement investment plans, insurance, and paid vacation often are standard. Insurance agencies, which generally are smaller, offer less extensive benefits.

Unionization is not widespread in the insurance industry. In 2000, 2.3 percent of all insurance workers were union members or were covered by union contracts, compared with 13.5 percent of workers throughout private industry.

**Table 2. Median hourly earnings of the largest occupations in insurance, 2000**

| Occupation | Insurance carriers | Insurance agents, brokers, and service | All industries |
|---|---|---|---|
| General and operations managers | $ 40.23 | $ 38.38 | $ 29.41 |
| Computer systems analysts | 28.10 | 26.33 | 28.53 |
| Computer programmers | 27.06 | 25.77 | 27.69 |
| Insurance underwriters | 20.97 | 20.26 | 20.74 |
| Accountants and auditors | 20.77 | 20.30 | 20.91 |
| Claims adjusters, examiners, and investigators | 20.37 | 18.73 | 19.75 |
| Insurance sales agents | 19.23 | 18.50 | 18.63 |
| Title examiners, abstractors, and searchers | 15.82 | 14.55 | 14.40 |
| Insurance claims and policy processing clerks | 14.24 | 12.65 | 13.47 |
| Customer service representatives | 12.77 | 12.70 | 11.83 |

## Outlook

Wage and salary employment in the insurance industry is projected to increase 6 percent between 2000 and 2010, more slowly than the 16 percent average for all industries combined. While demand for insurance is expected to rise, downsizing, productivity increases due to new technology, and a trend towards direct mail, telephone, and Internet sales will limit job growth. Nevertheless, thousands of openings are expected to arise in this large industry to replace workers who leave and to accommodate the industry's expansion into the broader financial services field.

Medical service and health insurance is the fastest growing sector of the insurance industry. Laws to help people purchase health insurance should boost demand. As the population ages, more people are expected to buy health and long-term care insurance, as well as annuities and other types of pension products sold by insurance sales agents. Population growth will stimulate demand for auto and homeowners insurance. Population growth also will create demand for businesses to service its needs, and these businesses will need insurance as well. Moreover, large liability awards are motivating many individuals and businesses to purchase liability policies to cover lawsuits brought by people claiming damage or injury by a particular person or product.

Many successful insurance companies will recognize the Internet's potential as a powerful marketing tool. Not only might this reduce costs for insurance companies, but it could also enable many clients to first turn to the Internet as a source of information on their policies, to obtain quotes, or to submit claims. As insurance companies begin to offer more information and services on the Internet, some occupations such as insurance sales agents could experience slower employment growth.

Sales agents working in the property and casualty market, particularly in auto insurance, will be most affected by increasing reliance on the Internet. Auto policies are relatively straightforward and can be issued more easily without the involvement of a live agent. Also, auto premiums tend to cost more per year than do other types of policies, so people are more likely to shop around for the best price. The Internet makes it easier to compare rates between companies. As a result, the Internet will create more competition among carriers, and rates could fall.

Faced with more competition and a greater need to contain costs, companies could begin to reduce employment of agents.

Insurance companies will continue to face increased competition from banks and securities firms entering the insurance markets. As more banks and securities firms begin to sell insurance policies, increasing numbers of insurance sales agents will be employed in such firms, rather than in insurance companies. In order to stay competitive, some insurance companies will need to either expand their financial service offerings, or establish a partnership with a bank or brokerage firm.

Productivity gains caused by the greater use of computer software will continue to limit the growth of certain jobs within the insurance industry. For example, the use of underwriting software that automatically analyzes and rates insurance applications will limit growth of underwriters. Also, computers that are linked directly to the databases of insurance carriers and other organizations have greatly facilitated communications among sales agents, adjusters, and insurance carriers, making employees much more productive. Furthermore, efforts to contain costs have led to an increasing reliance on customer service representatives to deal with the day-to-day processing of policies and claims.

Sales agents and adjusters still are needed to meet face-to-face with clients. Many clients prefer to talk directly with an agent, especially regarding complicated policies. Opportunities will be best for sales agents who sell more than one type of insurance or financial service. Adjusters will still be needed to inspect damage and interview witnesses. Many adjusters are now getting investigators' licenses to make themselves more attractive to employers. Insurance investigators should be in strong demand due to increases in the number of claims in litigation and in the number and complexity of insurance fraud cases.

## Sources of Additional Information

General information on employment opportunities in the insurance industry may be obtained from the human resources departments of major insurance companies or from insurance agencies in local communities. Information about licensing requirements for insurance sales agents and claim adjusters may be obtained from the department of insurance in each State.

For information on the property and casualty insurance industry, contact:

➤ Insurance Information Institute, 110 William St., New York, NY 10038. Internet: **http://www.iii.org**

For information about careers in the life insurance industry, contact:

➤ LIMRA International, P.O. Box 203, Hartford, CT 16141-0208. Internet: **http://www.limra.com**

For information about the health insurance industry, contact:

➤ Health Insurance Association of America, 555 13th St. NW., Suite 600 East, Washington, DC 20004. Internet: **http://www.hiaa.org**

➤ National Association of Health Underwriters, 2000 North 14th St., Suite 450, Arlington, VA 22201. Internet: **http://www.nahu.org**

For information about insurance sales careers and training, contact:

➤ The American Institute for CPCU/Insurance Institute of America, 720 South Providence Rd., Malvern, PA 19355. Internet: **http://www.aicpcu.org**

➤ Independent Insurance Agents of America, 127 South Peyton St., Alexandria, VA 22314. Internet: **http://www.iiaa.org**

➤ Insurance Vocational Education Student Training (InVEST), 127 South Peyton St., Alexandria, VA 22314. Internet: **http://www.investprogram.org**

➤ National Association of Professional Insurance Agents, 400 North Washington St., Alexandria, VA 22314. Internet: **http://www.pianet.com**

For information on insurance education and training, contact:

➤ The American College, 270 Bryn Mawr Ave., Bryn Mawr, PA 19010. Internet: **http://www.amercoll.edu**

➤ The National Alliance for Insurance Education and Research, P.O. Box 27027, Austin, TX 78755. Internet: **http://www.scic.com**

Information on the following insurance occupations may be found in the 2002-03 *Occupational Outlook Handbook*:

- Actuaries
- Claims adjusters, appraisers, examiners, and investigators
- Insurance sales agents
- Insurance underwriters

# Securities and Commodities

## SIGNIFICANT POINTS

- Half of all jobs in the industry are held by securities sales agents and management and financial operations workers, who generally have a college degree; the rest are mainly office and administrative support.

- Strong employment growth is projected to result from increasing investment in securities and commodities, along with the growing need for investment advice.

- The high earnings of successful securities sales agents will cause keen competition for these positions—particularly in larger firms.

### Nature of the Industry

The securities and commodities industry is made up of a variety of firms and organizations that bring together buyers and sellers of securities and commodities, manage investments, and offer financial advice. The industry is undergoing substantial change because of technology improvements, financial services deregulation, the globalization of the marketplace, and demographics. The Internet, along with high-speed computer systems, have dramatically altered the way in which securities and commodities are bought and sold, almost completely automating the transaction process. At the same time, the number of financial services being offered is rising as firms look for new ways to attract the business of an increasingly wealthy and investment-savvy public.

One of the most important functions of the industry is to facilitate the trading of securities and commodities by bringing together buyers and sellers. Brokerage firms typically provide this function. In these firms, investors place their buy and sell orders for a particular security or commodity by phone, online, or through a broker. The firm fills the order in one of three ways. If the stock or commodity is sold on an exchange, such as the New York Stock Exchange (NYSE) or the Chicago Mercantile Exchange (CME), the firm will send the order electronically to the company's floor broker at the exchange, who will post the order and execute the trade by finding a seller or buyer who offers the best price for the client. Alternatively, if a security is sold through a dealer network, such as Nasdaq, the broker can access a computer network that lists the prices that dealers in that security are willing to buy or sell it for. If a price that the client agrees with is found, then a purchase or sale is made. Large investors and brokerage firms also can buy and sell securities and commodities on "electronic communications networks," or ECNs. ECNs are very powerful computers that automatically list, match, and execute trades, eliminating the middleman. ECNs commonly are used for stocks that trade frequently and in large numbers.

Brokerage firms generally are classified as full-service, discount, or online. Investors who do not have time to research investments on their own will likely rely on a full-service broker to manage their investments or make recommendations on which investments to buy. Full-service brokers have access to a wide range of reports and analyses from the company's large staff of financial analysts. These analysts research companies and make recommendations on which investments are best for people with different savings and investment needs. Discount and online brokerage firms do not offer advice about specific securities; rather, they encourage clients to make their trades over the Internet or through other electronic means in order to keep costs down and fees low. Discount brokerage firms usually have branch offices, while online firms do not. Most brokerage firms now have call centers staffed with both licensed sales agents and customer service representatives to take orders and answer questions at all hours of the day.

Brokerage firms also provide investment banking services; that is, they act as an intermediary between those companies or governments that would like to raise money and those with money or capital to invest. Investment banking usually involves the firm buying initial stock or bond offerings from private companies or from Federal, State, and local governments, and in turn selling them to investors for a potential profit. This service can be risky, especially when it involves a new company selling stock to the public for the first time. Investment bankers must try to determine the value of the company based on a number of factors, including projected growth and sales, and decide what price investors are willing to pay for the new stock. Investment bankers also advise businesses on merger and acquisition strategies and may arrange for the transfer of ownership.

Companies that specialize in providing investment advice and portfolio management also are included in this industry. These companies range from very large mutual fund management companies to self-employed personal financial advisors, or financial planners. They also include managers of pension funds, commodity pools, trust funds, and other investment accounts. Portfolio or asset management companies direct the investment decisions for investors who have chosen to pool their assets in order to have them professionally managed. Many brokerage firms also provide these services. Personal financial advisors also can manage investments for individuals, but their main objective is to provide a formal financial plan that meets a wide range of financial needs.

A relatively small number of professionals in the industry work in the exchanges, where the actual trading of securities and commodities takes place. Computers and their applications have made brokers in the exchanges much more productive and capable of handling ever-increasing volumes of trades.

Firms in this industry offer a number of other services. Many offer cash-management accounts that allow account holders to deposit money into a money market fund against which they can write checks, take out margin loans, or use a debit card. Some brokerage firms offer mortgages and other types of loans and lines of credit. They also may offer trust services and help businesses set up benefit plans for their employees. They may sell annuities and other life insurance products.

The securities and commodities industry has invested heavily in technology, which is allowing firms to handle larger volumes of trades with fewer people. The growth of online trading, in particular, has produced a number of online trading firms that did not exist just a few years ago. In order to compete, many full-service brokerage firms are now offering online trading to their customers. This explosion in technology is changing the nature of many of the jobs and the mix of people employed by securities firms. Some companies are more likely to resemble information technology (IT) companies than securities firms, with most of the employees working in computer-related occupations. Across the industry, computer professionals are accounting for a greater proportion of the workforce. And with so much business now being conducted online and through call centers, traditional sales agents are spending less time processing orders and more time seeking out new clients and offering detailed advice.

Employment in each of the segments of the securities and commodities industry is directly affected by the activity of the stock and futures markets and the savings and investment goals of individuals. Because these factors are largely determined by the strength of the economy, the industry prospers during good times and when interest rates are low, but is more adversely affected by downturns than many other industries.

## Working Conditions

Most people in this industry work in comfortable offices; however, long hours, including evenings and weekends, are common. Nearly 1 in 4 employees worked 50 hours per week or more in 2000. Even when not working, professionals in this industry must keep abreast of events that may affect the markets in which they specialize. Opportunities for part-time work are limited—only 8 percent work part time. In 1999, the industry had only 0.6 injuries and illnesses per 100 full-time workers. Working conditions vary by occupation.

Securities sales agents who deal mostly with individual investors and small businesses often work in branch offices of regional or national brokerage firms, or for a small brokerage or financial planning firm. New sales agents work long hours, mostly soliciting customers. During the day, they are on the phone continually with prospective customers, while at night they may attempt to generate new business by giving classes or seminars or by attending community functions. New sales agents also spend many hours studying to pass a variety of tests that will qualify them to sell other investment products, such as commodities or insurance. Although established agents work more regular hours, all agents meet with clients in the evenings and on weekends, as needed.

Sales agents who actually perform the buying and selling of securities and commodities may have one of the most hectic jobs of any profession. Often called traders, market makers, dealers, or floor brokers, they work on the floors of exchanges or at a computer that is linked to other traders. They not only take orders from clients and try to get the best price for them, but must also constantly keep an eye on market activity and stay in touch with other traders and brokers to know what prices are being offered.

Increasingly, sales agents for many of the brokerage and mutual fund companies work in call centers, opening accounts for individuals, entering trades, and providing advice over the phone on different investment products. Although many simply respond to inquiries and do not actively solicit customers, others may be required to contact potential clients. Call centers also employ a large number of customer service representatives, who answer questions for current clients about their accounts and make any needed changes or transfers. All workers in call centers must maintain a professional and courteous attitude and be able to speak for long periods of time. Many call centers operate 24 hours a day, 7 days a week, and employees may be required to work evenings and weekends.

Jobs in investment banking, including those of financial managers, analysts, or assistants, generally require the longest hours—often 70 to 80 hours per week—in addition to extensive travel. In this area, there is a great deal of pressure to meet deadlines and acquire new business. Researchers, financial analysts, and investment managers working for brokerage and mutual fund firms also work long hours, researching and evaluating companies and their markets. Frequent travel to visit companies is common.

Personal financial advisors work in offices or out of their homes. Most work regular business hours, but many accommodate clients by visiting them at their homes in the evenings or on weekends. Administrative support workers usually work a 40-hour week, but overtime may be necessary during times of heavy trading.

## Employment

The securities and commodities industry employed 748,000 wage and salary workers in 2000. An additional 125,000 workers were self-employed. With their large networks of retail sales representatives located in branch offices throughout the country, the large nationally known brokerage companies employ the majority of workers in this industry (see chart). The headquarters of many of these firms, in which most executives and administrative support personnel are employed, are located in New York City. Many people also work for mutual fund management companies and smaller regional brokerage firms. As a consequence of deregulation, banks have been either acquiring securities firms or adding securities and commodities business to their list of services, and are becoming a factor in the industry. A relatively small number of employees work at securities or commodities exchanges—primarily the New York Stock Exchange, the Chicago Board of Trade, the Chicago Mercantile Exchange, and a number of regional exchanges.

## Occupations in the Industry

*Securities, commodities, and financial services sales agents* account for 1 in 4 wage and salary jobs in this industry (table 1). Although the occupation encompasses a variety of job titles and activities, all of them involve placing orders or buying and selling securities, commodities, or other financial services. The most common types of sales agents deal directly with the public and often are called *retail brokers*, *account executives*, *registered representatives*, *or financial consultants*. Securities brokers typically buy and sell stocks, bonds, mutual funds, and other financial services, while commodities brokers primarily deal with futures contracts on metals, energy supplies, agricultural products, and financial instruments.

When a client places an order for one of these items, brokers relay the order through the firm's computers to the floor of an exchange, to a dealer, or to an ECN. Upon confirmation of the trade, the broker notifies clients of the final price. As part of

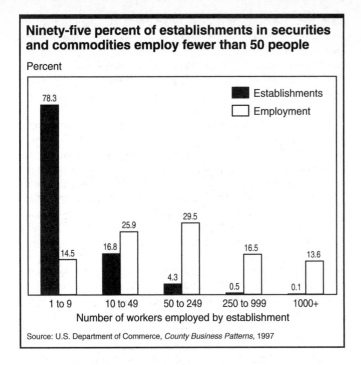

**Ninety-five percent of establishments in securities and commodities employ fewer than 50 people**

Percent

- Establishments
- Employment

| Number of workers employed by establishment | Establishments | Employment |
|---|---|---|
| 1 to 9 | 78.3 | 14.5 |
| 10 to 49 | 16.8 | 25.9 |
| 50 to 249 | 4.3 | 29.5 |
| 250 to 999 | 0.5 | 16.5 |
| 1000+ | 0.1 | 13.6 |

Source: U.S. Department of Commerce, *County Business Patterns*, 1997

their job, brokers often provide advice to clients about possible investments, taking into consideration the client's financial situation, tolerance for risk, and savings needs. Because sales is one of their major responsibilities, brokers also spend a considerable amount of time soliciting new business.

A small number of sales agents deal exclusively with large investors, such as insurance companies, pension funds, and mutual funds. They typically are called institutional representatives or institutional brokers and provide many of the same services as a retail broker, but on a larger scale.

Sales agents referred to as *traders, market makers, and floor brokers* actually make the trades on the exchange floor or over the computer. They match buyers and sellers of a particular security or commodity, sometimes using their own or their firm's money to close the deal.

Keeping track of transactions and paperwork constitutes a large portion of the work in this industry, which is why its largest occupational group is office and administrative support workers. *Brokerage clerks,* the largest occupation in this category, handle much of the day-to-day operations within a brokerage firm. The largest group of brokerage clerks, called *sales assistants*, take calls from brokers' clients, write up order tickets and enter them into the computer, handle the paperwork for new accounts, inform clients of stock prices, and perform other tasks as needed. Some sales assistants obtain licenses to sell securities. This allows them to call brokers' clients with recommendations from the broker on specific investments. Other brokerage clerks may compute transfer taxes and dividends and keep daily records of transactions and holdings. At some companies, a number of brokerage clerk positions are considered entry level, with promotion potential to securities sales agent jobs or other higher level jobs.

Because more clients are choosing to trade without the use of sales agents or brokers, *customer service representatives* are playing a larger role in securities firms. While some may have licenses to sell securities or other financial products, most are not in the business of sales or offering advice, but mainly take questions from current customers. Customer service represen-

tatives usually work in central call centers, where they handle account transfers, redemptions, and address changes; answer tax questions; and help clients navigate the website, among other services.

Management, business, and financial occupations account for 31 percent of total employment, a larger proportion than in most industries. This category includes a myriad of people with expertise in finance and investment policy, *accountants and auditors*, who prepare the firm's financial statements; and *general managers*, who run the business. *Financial analysts* generally work in the research and investment banking departments. They review financial statements of companies, evaluate economic and market trends, and make recommendations concerning the potential profits from investments in specific companies. They may also attempt to determine fair market values for companies wishing to trade their stocks publicly or for those firms involved in mergers or acquisitions. Analysts in large firms usually specialize in a certain industry sector, such as transportation or utilities, or in a market, such as government financing.

*Personal financial advisors,* also called *financial planners*, provide advice to both individuals and businesses on a broad range of financial subjects, such as investments, retirement planning, tax management, and employee benefits. They may take a comprehensive approach to the client's financial needs or address only a specific issue. Advisors also may buy and sell financial products, such as stocks, bonds, mutual funds, and insurance, for their clients.

*Financial managers* are employed throughout the industry, preparing financial documents for the regulatory authorities or directing a firm's investment policies. In many departments, managers act as senior advisors and oversee teams of junior analysts or brokers while continuing to be actively involved in working out deals with clients.

*Portfolio managers* and *commodity trading advisors* are responsible for making investment decisions for clients with large sums of money to invest. These clients include mutual funds, pension funds, trust funds, commodity pools, and high net worth individuals. Portfolio managers must know the investment goals of the client and ensure that the investments they make meet those goals.

The increasingly computerized environment in this industry requires the expertise of *computer software engineers*, *database administrators*, *Web developers*, and other computer professionals to develop and operate the communications networks that provide online trading.

## Training and Advancement

This industry has one of the most highly educated and skilled workforces of any industry, and the requirements for entry are high—even brokerage clerks often have a college degree. The most successful workers at all levels have an aptitude for numbers and a very keen interest in investing. In addition, most people in this industry are required to be licensed by the National Association of Securities Dealers (NASD) before they can sell securities or recommend specific investments. To be licensed, brokers and assistants must pass an examination that reflects their knowledge of investments. Various licenses are available for different investment products. However, the one most brokers and broker's assistants receive is the "Series 7" license, which requires a passing score on the General Securities Registered Representative Examination administered by the NASD. Since 1995, the NASD has also required all registered persons to undergo a continuing education program approxi-

**Table 1. Employment of wage and salary workers in securities and commodities by occupation, 2000 and projected change, 2000-10**

(Employment in thousands)

| Occupation | Employment, 2000 | | Percent change, 2000-2010 |
|---|---|---|---|
| | Number | Percent | |
| **All occupations** | 748 | 100.0 | 0.3 |
| **Management, business, and financial occupations** | 230 | 30.7 | 6.9 |
| Administrative services managers | 8 | 1.0 | 5.3 |
| Sales managers | 6 | 0.8 | 2.7 |
| Chief executives | 10 | 1.3 | 5.8 |
| Financial managers | 41 | 5.5 | 0.4 |
| General and operations managers | 18 | 2.4 | 4.3 |
| Human resources, training, and labor relations specialists | 5 | 0.7 | 2.4 |
| Management analysts | 7 | 0.9 | 9.5 |
| Accountants and auditors | 13 | 1.8 | 0.9 |
| Financial analysts | 37 | 4.9 | 5.8 |
| Personal financial advisors | 37 | 4.9 | 0.9 |
| All other financial specialists | 15 | 2.0 | 2.7 |
| **Professional and related occupations** | 47 | 6.3 | 2.4 |
| Computer programmers | 8 | 1.0 | -2.0 |
| Computer software engineers, applications | 8 | 1.0 | 3.2 |
| Social scientists and related occupations | 5 | 0.7 | 1.9 |
| **Sales and related occupations** | 219 | 29.2 | 8.8 |
| Securities, commodities, and financial services sales agents | 191 | 25.6 | 9.0 |
| First-line supervisors/managers of non-retail sales workers | 5 | 0.7 | 8.6 |
| Telemarketers | 9 | 1.1 | 0.9 |
| All other sales and related workers | 6 | 0.8 | 0.6 |
| **Office and administrative support occupations** | 244 | 32.6 | 1.2 |
| First-line supervisors/managers of office and administrative support workers | 13 | 1.7 | 0.8 |
| Bill and account collectors | 7 | 0.9 | 5.1 |
| Bookkeeping, accounting, and auditing clerks | 12 | 1.7 | 4.3 |
| Brokerage clerks | 53 | 7.1 | -2.9 |
| Customer service representatives | 25 | 3.3 | 2.8 |
| Receptionists and information clerks | 8 | 1.1 | 8.3 |
| Office clerks, general | 27 | 3.6 | 0.8 |
| Executive secretaries and administrative assistants | 41 | 5.5 | 8.9 |
| Secretaries, except legal, medical, and executive | 19 | 2.5 | -3.4 |
| All other secretaries, administrative assistants, and other office support workers | 7 | 0.9 | 2.0 |

NOTE: May not add to totals due to omission of occupations with small employment.

mately every 3 years in order to retain their licenses. Classes consist of computer-based training in regulatory matters and training on new investment products.

A number of professionals in this industry begin their careers as brokerage clerks. Depending on the actual job, brokerage clerks can be high school or college graduates. Positions dealing with the public, such as broker's or sales assistant, and those dealing with more complicated financial records, are increasingly held by college graduates. In addition, these jobs require good organizational ability, phone skills, and attention to detail. A Series 7 brokerage license can make a clerk more valuable to the broker because it gives the assistant the ability to answer more of a client's questions and to pass along securities recommendations from the broker. Clerks may be promoted to sales representative positions or other professional positions. Some of the larger firms have training programs, especially for their college graduates, to provide clerks with the skills needed for advancement.

A college education, although not essential, is increasingly important for securities, commodities, and financial services sales agents because it helps them to understand economic conditions and trends. In fact, the overwhelming majority of entrants to this occupation are college graduates. Still, many employers consider personal qualities and skills more important than academic training. Employers seek applicants with good communication skills, a professional appearance, and a strong desire to succeed. Securities, commodities, and financial services sales workers must meet Federal and State licensing requirements, which generally include passing an examination and a background investigation and, in some cases, furnishing a personal bond. Most of the large brokerage firms provide formal classroom training for new brokers that can last a couple of weeks to several months. Smaller firms usually rely on informal on-the-job training.

Although there are no specific licensure requirements to be a personal financial advisor, most advisors must be knowledgeable about economic trends, finance, budgeting, and accounting. Therefore, a college education is important. Personal financial advisors must possess excellent communication and interpersonal skills to be able to explain complicated issues to their clients. Many personal financial advisors earn a Certified Financial Planning (CFP) designation issued by the CFP Board of Standards in Denver, Colorado, or a Chartered Financial Consultant (ChFC) designation offered by the American College in Bryn Mawr, Pennsylvania. To receive these designations, a person must pass a series of exams on insurance, investments, tax planning, employee benefits, and retirement and estate planning; have the required experience in related jobs; and, in the case of the CFP, agree to abide by the rules and regulations issued by the Board of Standards. It may take from 2 to 3 years of study to complete these programs.

Entry-level analyst and other managerial support positions usually are filled by college graduates who have majored in business administration, marketing, economics, accounting, industrial relations, or finance. Many of the large companies have management training programs for college graduates in which trainees work for brief periods in various departments to get a broad picture of the industry before they are assigned to a particular department. Those working as financial analysts are encouraged to obtain the Chartered Financial Analyst designation sponsored by the Association of Investment Management and Research. To qualify, applicants must have at least 3 years of qualifying experience and pass a series of rigorous essay exams requiring an extensive knowledge of many areas, including accounting, economics, and securities.

Advancement opportunities in the securities and commodities industry vary by occupation. To advance into the managerial ranks or to get some of the more lucrative and prestigious jobs on Wall Street, a master's degree is increasingly becoming essential. In investment banking, for example, most firms select the top candidates from the Nation's most prestigious business schools. However, because many business schools accept master's degree candidates only if they have some job experience, many securities firms hire analysts with a bachelor's degree and provide them with the experience they need, assuming that they will eventually obtain their master's degree.

The principal form of advancement for securities, commodities, and financial services sales agents is an increase in the number and size of the accounts they handle. Some eventually manage the assets of clients. Although beginners usually service the accounts of individual investors, a select few eventually may handle very large institutional accounts. Administrative support workers such as brokerage clerks may advance to sales agent positions or to other professional positions. Financial analysts may advance to positions in management, in which they may manage investment portfolios or negotiate investment banking deals.

## Earnings

Most workers in the securities and commodities industry are paid a salary on an annual or weekly basis. In 2000, the average weekly earnings of nonsupervisory workers in the security and commodity services industry were $841, compared with $474 in all industries combined. Median earnings for the largest occupations in the securities and commodities industry in 2000 are presented in table 2.

Table 2. Median hourly earnings of the largest occupations in securities and commodities, 2000

| Occupation | Security and commodity brokers | All industries |
| --- | --- | --- |
| Financial managers | $ 53.85 | $32.22 |
| General and operations managers | 46.85 | 29.41 |
| Computer software engineers, applications | 35.29 | 32.53 |
| Securities, commodities, and financial services sales agents | 33.47 | 26.96 |
| Computer programmers | 32.22 | 27.69 |
| Personal financial advisors | 30.77 | 26.60 |
| Financial analysts | 27.76 | 25.20 |
| Accountants and auditors | 23.17 | 20.91 |
| Brokerage clerks | 15.04 | 14.93 |
| Customer service representatives | 13.59 | 11.83 |

Earnings of securities, commodities, and financial services sales agents, especially those working for full-service brokerage firms, depend in large part on commissions from the sale or purchase of stocks, bonds, and other securities or futures contracts. Commission earnings are likely to be lower when there is a slump in market activity. Earnings also can be based on the amount of assets that a broker or portfolio manager has under management, with the broker or portfolio manager receiving a small percentage of the value of the assets.

Personal financial advisors are compensated in a number of ways. Those who manage client's assets usually collect a percent of the assets as their fee. Others charge hourly fees and some charge different rates depending on the type of plan requested. Many receive commissions based on the financial products they sell. Those who work for financial services firms may receive a salary.

For many in this industry, a large part of earnings come from annual bonuses based on the success of the firm. Profit-sharing and stock options also are common. Salaried employees are more likely to receive typical benefits, such as paid vacations, sick leave, and pension plans, than are self-employed workers.

## Outlook

Wage and salary employment in the securities and commodities industry is projected to rise 20 percent from 2000 to 2010, faster than the 16-percent increase expected for all industries in the economy. Job growth will be fueled primarily by the increasing levels of investment in securities and commodities in the global marketplace. So long as interest rates remain low and the stock market performs adequately, people will continue to seek higher rates of return by investing in stocks, mutual funds, and other investments. In addition to the many new job openings stemming from this growth, a large number of openings will arise as people retire or leave the industry for other reasons.

Several trends bode well for the industry through the next decade. Baby boomers are in the middle of their peak savings years and are putting money into a number of tax-favorable retirement plans, such as the 401(k) and the Roth IRA. These plans have been one of the major causes of huge inflows of money into the stock market and into mutual funds, and this trend towards saving for retirement is expected to continue.

Also, although online trading will grow and reduce the need for direct contact with an actual broker, the number of securities sales agents is still expected to grow fast, as many people still are willing to pay for the advice that a full-service representative can offer. Competition for securities sales agent jobs, though, usually is keen because the job attracts a large number of qualified applicants. Job opportunities for sales agents should be best for mature individuals with successful work experience. Employment of personal financial advisors will grow faster than average. As the number of self-directed retirement plans increases and as the number and complexity of investments rises, individuals will require more help in managing their money.

Another factor contributing to projected employment growth is the "globalization" of securities and commodities markets—the expansion of traditional exchange and trading boundaries into new markets in foreign countries. This, in turn, has provided an expanding array of investment opportunities and access to markets in which new financial products are now available to domestic investors. These new products and markets encourage trading and prompt firms to hire more workers.

Demand for financial analysts should remain strong in the investment banking field, where they will be needed to assist new high-technology companies in raising money. In addition, the number of mergers and acquisitions taking place in the economy is not expected to slow down appreciably, so financial analysts will be needed to assist with these types of activities. Competition for entry-level analyst positions in investment banking typically is intense, as the number of applicants usually far exceeds the number of vacancies.

Due to advances in telecommunications and computer technology, the securities and commodities industry has become highly automated. This automation is expected to cause rapid growth in employment of computer software engineers, systems analysts, database administrators, and other computer support specialists. On the other hand, automation has resulted in computerized recordkeeping of transactions, more productive administrative support staffs, and enhanced communications among foreign firms. Accordingly, employment of brokerage clerks and secretaries will decline, and employment of bookkeeping, accounting, and auditing clerks is projected to grow more slowly than the average for this industry.

## Sources of Additional Information

For general information on the securities industry, contact:

➤ Securities Industry Association, 120 Broadway, New York, NY 10271.  Internet: **http://www.sia.com**

Detailed information on many key occupations in the securities and commodities industry, including the following, may be found in the 2002-03 edition of the *Occupational Outlook Handbook*:

- Brokerage clerks

- Financial managers

- Financial analysts and personal financial advisors

- Securities, commodities, and financial services sales agents

Services

# Advertising

## SIGNIFICANT POINTS

- Employment is concentrated in large cities, especially New York.

- Competition for many jobs will be keen because the glamour of the industry traditionally attracts many more jobseekers than there are job openings.

- Layoffs are common when accounts are lost, major clients cut advertising budgets, or agencies merge.

## Nature of the Industry

Firms in the advertising industry prepare advertisements for other companies and organizations and might also arrange to place them in print, broadcast, interactive, and other media. This industry also includes firms that sell advertising space for publications, radio, television, and the Internet. Divisions of companies that produce and place their own advertising are not considered part of this industry.

Companies often look to advertising as a way of boosting sales by increasing the public's exposure to a product. Most companies do not have the staff with the necessary skills or experience to create effective advertisements; furthermore, many advertising campaigns are temporary, so employers would have difficulty maintaining their own advertising staff. Instead, companies commonly solicit bids from ad agencies to develop advertising for them. Next, ad agencies offering their services to the company often make presentations. The real work for ad agencies begins when they win an account. Various departments within an agency—such as creative, production, media, and research—work together to meet the client's goal of increasing sales.

There are more than 21,000 advertising establishments in the United States. About 6 out of 10 write, copy, and prepare artwork, graphics, and other creative work, and then place the resulting ads on television, radio, or the Internet or in periodicals, newspapers, or other advertising media. Within the industry, only these full-service establishments are known as *advertising agencies*. Many of the largest agencies are international, with a substantial proportion of their revenue coming from abroad.

About 3 out of 10 advertising firms specialize in a particular market niche. Some companies produce and solicit outdoor advertising, such as billboards and electric displays. Others place ads in buses, subways, taxis, airports, and bus terminals. A small number of firms produce aerial advertising, while others distribute circulars, handbills, and free samples.

Groups within agencies have been created to serve their clients' electronic advertising needs on the Internet. Online advertisements link users from one website to a company's or product's website, where information such as new product announcements, contests, and product catalogs appears, and where purchases may be made.

Some firms are not involved in the creation of ads at all; instead, they sell advertising time or space on radio and television stations or in publications. Because these firms do not produce advertising, their staffs are mostly sales workers.

In an effort to attract and maintain clients, advertising agencies are diversifying their services, offering advertising as well as sales, marketing, public relations, and interactive media services. Advertising firms have found that highly creative work is particularly suitable for their services, resulting in a better product and increasing their clients' profitability.

## Working Conditions

Most advertising employees work in comfortable offices; however, long hours, including evenings and weekends, are common. There are fewer opportunities for part-time work than in many other industries; in 2000, 11.4 percent of advertising employees worked part time, compared with 15.3 percent of all workers.

Advertising work is fast-paced and exciting, but it can also be stressful. Being creative on a tight schedule can be emotionally draining. In addition, frequent meetings with clients and media representatives may involve substantial travel. Among all full-time advertising workers, one-sixth work 50 or more hours per week.

## Employment

The advertising industry employed 302,000 workers in 2000. Although advertising firms are located throughout the country, they are concentrated in the largest cities. New York has the most firms; other top cities include Chicago, Detroit, Los Angeles, San Francisco, Boston, Minneapolis, and Dallas. Firms vary in size, ranging from one-person shops to international agencies employing thousands of workers. About 4 of 5 advertising firms employ fewer than 10 employees, somewhat higher than the proportion for all industries combined (chart 1).

The small size of the average advertising firm demonstrates the opportunities for self-employment. It is relatively easy to open a small ad agency; in fact, many successful agencies began as one- or two-person operations. In 2000, more than 8 percent of all advertising workers were self-employed or unpaid family workers.

The median age of advertising workers is 38, compared with nearly 40 for all workers. More than 59 percent of advertising employees are 25 to 44 years of age, compared with 50 percent of all workers in the economy. Very few advertising workers are below the age of 20, which reflects the need for postsecondary training or work experience.

## Occupations in the Industry

Management, business, and financial workers; professionals and related workers; sales and related workers; and office and administrative support workers account for more than 9 of every 10 jobs in the industry (table 1). Employees have varied responsibilities in agencies with only a few workers, and the specific job duties of each worker often are difficult to distinguish. Workers in relatively large firms specialize more, so the distinctions among occupations are more apparent.

Advertising agencies have five categories of jobs—account management, creative, media, research, and support services and administration. The account management department links the agency and the client. It represents the agency to the client, as well as the client to the agency. Account management brings business to the agency and ultimately is responsible for the quality of the advertisement. Account management workers carefully monitor the activities of the other areas to ensure that everything runs smoothly. *Account managers* and their assistants analyze competitive activity and consumer trends, report client billing, forecast agency income, and combine the talents of the creative, media, and research areas.

Working with the marketing idea that account management obtains from the client, the creative department brings the idea to life. Staff work together to transform a blank piece of paper into an advertisement. As the idea takes shape, *copywriters* and their assistants write the words of ads—both the written part of print ads as well as the scripts of radio and television spots. *Art directors* and their assistants develop the visual concepts and designs of advertisements. They prepare paste-ups and layouts for print ads and television storyboards, cartoon style summaries of how an advertisement will appear. They also oversee the filming of television commercials and photo sessions. Once completed, the ad is shown to the client. At this point, the job of the creative department could be over; however, based on the client's response, it is likely that the creative department staff will have to modify their ideas or develop an entirely different approach.

The media department is responsible for placing advertisements in the right place at the right time, so that the ads will reach the desired audience for the least amount of money.

*Media planners* gather information on the public's viewing and reading habits, and evaluate editorial content and programming to determine the potential use of media such as newspapers, magazines, radio, television, or the Internet. The media staff calculate the numbers and types of people reached by different media, and how often they are reached. *Media buyers* track the media space and times available for purchase, negotiate and purchase time and space for ads, and make sure ads appear exactly as scheduled. Additionally, they calculate rates, usage, and budgets.

*Advertising sales agents* sell air time on radio and television, and page space in print media. They work in firms representing radio stations, television stations, and publications.

Workers in the research department try to understand the desires, motivations, and ideals of consumers, in order to produce and place the most effective advertising in the most effective media. *Research executives* compile data, monitor the progress of internal and external research, develop research tools, and interpret and provide explanations of the data gathered. Research executives often specialize in specific research areas and perform supervisory duties.

Support services and administration includes jobs ranging from janitors to administrative assistants to accountants, and the occupational composition of this group varies widely among agencies.

## Training and Advancement

Most entry-level professional and managerial positions in the advertising industry require a bachelor's degree, preferably with broad liberal arts exposure. Beginners usually enter the industry in the account management or media department. Occasionally, entry-level positions are available in the market research or creative departments of an agency, but these positions usually require some experience.

Completing an advertising-related internship while in school provides an advantage when applying for an entry-level position; in fact, internships are becoming a necessary step to obtaining permanent employment. In addition to an internship, courses in marketing, psychology, accounting, statistics, and creative design can help prepare potential entrants for careers in this field.

Assistant account executive, the entry-level account management position in most firms, requires a bachelor's degree in marketing or advertising. At some agencies, a master's degree in business administration may be required.

Bachelor's degrees are not required for entry-level positions in the creative department. Assistant art directors usually need at least a 2-year degree from an art or design school. Although assistant copywriters do not need a degree, obtaining one helps to develop the superior communication skills and abilities required for this job.

Assistant media planner or assistant media buyer also are good entry-level positions, but almost always require a bachelor's degree, preferably with a major in marketing or advertising. Experienced applicants who possess at least a master's degree usually fill research positions. Often, they have a background in marketing or statistics and years of experience. Requirements for support services and administrative positions depend on the job and vary from firm to firm.

Employees in the advertising industry should have good people skills, common sense, creativity, communication skills,

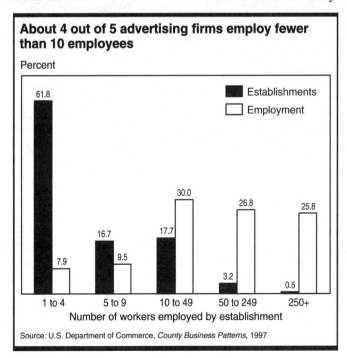

**About 4 out of 5 advertising firms employ fewer than 10 employees**

Percent

- Establishments
- Employment

61.8
7.9
16.7
9.5
17.7
30.0
3.2
26.8
0.5
25.8

1 to 4    5 to 9    10 to 49    50 to 249    250+

Number of workers employed by establishment

Source: U.S. Department of Commerce, *County Business Patterns*, 1997

**Table 1. Employment of wage and salary workers in advertising by occupation, 2000 and projected change, 2000-10**

(Employment in thousands)

| Occupation | Employment, 2000 Number | Employment, 2000 Percent | Percent change, 2000-2010 |
|---|---|---|---|
| All occupations .......................................... | 302 | 100.0 | 32.5 |
| **Management, business, and financial occupations** .......................................... | 66 | 22.0 | 33.5 |
| Advertising and promotions managers .......................................... | 16 | 5.4 | 37.2 |
| Marketing managers ............................... | 5 | 1.6 | 29.9 |
| Chief executives ..................................... | 4 | 1.2 | 28.9 |
| Financial managers ................................ | 3 | 1.1 | 34.7 |
| General and operations managers ...... | 13 | 4.4 | 27.3 |
| Purchasing agents, except wholesale, retail, and farm products ................... | 4 | 1.5 | 34.7 |
| Accountants and auditors ..................... | 3 | 1.1 | 34.7 |
| **Professional and related occupations** .......................................... | 73 | 24.2 | 46.5 |
| Computer programmers ....................... | 3 | 0.9 | 9.5 |
| Art directors .......................................... | 9 | 2.9 | 48.2 |
| Multi-media artists and animators ....... | 4 | 1.5 | 52.4 |
| Graphic designers ................................. | 18 | 5.9 | 61.7 |
| Producers and directors ....................... | 2 | 0.8 | 24.8 |
| Public relations specialists .................. | 4 | 1.3 | 48.2 |
| Writers and editors ............................... | 10 | 3.2 | 33.9 |
| Photographers ....................................... | 4 | 1.2 | 34.7 |
| **Sales and related occupations** .............. | 72 | 23.8 | 30.6 |
| Advertising sales agents ...................... | 37 | 12.3 | 34.7 |
| Demonstrators and product promoters .......................................... | 15 | 4.8 | 34.7 |
| Sales representatives, wholesale and manufacturing, except technical and scientific products ...................... | 5 | 1.6 | 5.2 |
| First-line supervisors/managers of non-retail sales workers ................... | 5 | 1.6 | 21.3 |
| Telemarketers ....................................... | 4 | 1.2 | 15.2 |
| **Office and administrative support occupations** .......................................... | 69 | 22.9 | 19.5 |
| First-line supervisors/managers of office and administrative support workers .......................................... | 6 | 1.9 | 2.5 |
| Bookkeeping, accounting, and auditing clerks ................................... | 8 | 2.7 | 16.0 |
| Customer service representatives ....... | 6 | 2.0 | 27.4 |
| Receptionists and information clerks .... | 4 | 1.2 | 34.7 |
| Production, planning, and expediting clerks ............................... | 7 | 2.4 | 29.8 |
| Office clerks, general .......................... | 7 | 2.4 | 34.7 |
| Executive secretaries and administrative assistants ................... | 9 | 2.9 | 21.3 |
| Secretaries, except legal, medical, and executive ................................... | 5 | 1.6 | 7.8 |
| **Construction and extraction occupations** .......................................... | 5 | 1.6 | 34.7 |
| **Production occupations** ......................... | 7 | 2.2 | 24.4 |
| **Transportation and material moving occupations** .......................................... | 6 | 2.1 | 30.7 |

NOTE: May not add to totals due to omission of occupations with small employment.

and problem-solving ability. Foreign language skills have always been important for those wanting to work abroad for domestic firms or to represent foreign firms domestically. However, these skills are increasingly vital to reach linguistic minorities in U.S. cities such as Los Angeles, New York, Miami, Houston, and Phoenix. New media, such as the Internet, are creating opportunities to market products, but also increasing the need for additional training for those already employed. Keeping pace with technology is fundamental to success in the industry. Besides staying abreast of new technology, advertisers must keep in tune with the changing values, cultures, and fashions of the Nation.

Success in progressively responsible staff assignments usually leads to advancement to supervisory positions. As workers climb the organizational ladder, broad vision and planning skills become extremely important. Another way to get to the top in this industry is to open one's own firm. In spite of the difficulty and high failure rate, many find starting their own business to be personally and financially rewarding. Among the self-employed, advancement takes the form of increasing the size and strength of the company.

## Earnings

In 2000, nonsupervisory workers in advertising averaged $712 a week—significantly higher than the $474 a week for all nonsupervisory workers in private industry. Earnings of workers in selected occupations in advertising appear in table 2.

**Table 2. Median hourly earnings of the largest occupations in advertising, 2000**

| Occupation | Advertising | All industries |
|---|---|---|
| Marketing managers ............................... | $ 34.90 | $ 34.25 |
| Art directors .......................................... | 30.53 | 27.35 |
| Advertising and promotions managers ... | 28.31 | 25.66 |
| Writers and authors ............................... | 24.76 | 20.32 |
| Sales representatives, wholesale and manufacturing, except technical and scientific products ...................... | 20.86 | 19.40 |
| Public relations specialists ..................... | 20.44 | 19.03 |
| Multi-media artists and animators ........... | 20.08 | 19.77 |
| Advertising sales agents ......................... | 19.81 | 17.24 |
| Graphic designers .................................. | 17.83 | 16.62 |
| Demonstrators and product promoters ... | 8.90 | 9.51 |

## Outlook

Competition for many jobs will be keen because the glamour of the advertising industry traditionally attracts many more jobseekers than there are job openings. Employment in the advertising industry is projected to grow 32 percent over the 2000-10 period, compared with 15 percent for all industries combined. New jobs will be created as an expanding economy generates more products and services to advertise. Increased demand for advertising services also will stem from growth in the number and types of media outlets used to reach consumers, creating opportunities for people skilled in preparing material for presentation on the Internet.

On the other hand, employment growth may be tempered by the increased use of more efficient technologies that could replace some workers. Employment also may be adversely affected if legislation further restricts advertising for specific products such as alcoholic beverages and tobacco or via specific media such as billboards. In addition to those generated by job growth, openings also will arise as workers transfer to other jobs or stop working.

## Sources of Additional Information
For information about careers or training contact:

➤ American Association of Advertising Agencies, 405 Lexington Ave., New York, NY 10174. Internet: **http://www.aaaa.org**

Information on these occupations can be found in the 2002-03 *Occupational Outlook Handbook*:

- Artists and related workers

- Advertising, marketing, promotions, public relations, and sales managers

- Demonstrators, product promoters, and models

- Economists and market and survey researchers

- Public relations specialists

- Television, video, and motion picture camera operators and editors

- Writers and editors

# Amusement and Recreation Services

## SIGNIFICANT POINTS

- More than 40 percent of all workers have no formal education beyond high school.

- Employment growth, along with high turnover, should create numerous job opportunities.

- Earnings are relatively low, reflecting the large number of part-time and seasonal jobs.

## Nature of the Industry

As leisure time and personal incomes have grown across the Nation, so has the amusement and recreation services industry. This industry includes more than 102,000 establishments, ranging from theme parks to fitness centers. Practically any activity that occupies a person's leisure time, excluding the viewing of motion pictures and videotape rentals, is part of the amusement and recreation services industry. The diverse range of activities offered by this industry can be categorized into three broad groups—sports, performing arts, and amusement, including gaming.

*Sports.* This segment of the industry includes professional sports, as well as establishments providing sports facilities and services to amateurs. Commercial sports clubs operate professional and amateur athletic clubs and promote athletic events. Every possible type of sport can be found in these establishments, including baseball, basketball, boxing, football, ice hockey, soccer, wrestling, and even auto racing. Professional and amateur companies involved with sports promotion also are part of this industry segment, as are sports establishments in which gambling is allowed, such as auto, dog, and horse racetracks.

This segment of the industry also includes physical fitness facilities that feature exercise and weight loss programs, gyms, health clubs, and day spas. These establishments also frequently offer aerobic dance, yoga, and exercise classes. Other amusement and recreation businesses include bowling centers that rent lanes and equipment for tenpin, duckpin, or candlepin bowling.

These facilities may be open to the public or available on a membership basis. Sports and recreation clubs open only to members and their guests include some golf, yacht, tennis, racquetball, hunt, and gun clubs. Public golf courses, unlike private clubs, offer facilities to the general public on a fee basis.

*Performing arts.* A variety of businesses and groups involved in live theatrical and musical performances are included in this segment. Theatrical production companies, for example, coordinate all aspects of producing a play or theater event, including employing actors and actresses. Agents represent actors and assist them in finding jobs. Booking agencies line up performance engagements for theatrical groups. Costume design management companies design costumes for productions. Also included are lighting and stage crews that handle the technical aspects of productions.

Performers of live musical entertainment include popular music artists, dance bands, orchestras, jazz musicians, and rock-and-roll bands. Orchestras range from major professional orchestras with million dollar budgets to community orchestras, often with part-time schedules. The performing arts segment also includes dance studios, schools, and halls, which provide places for professional and amateur dancers to practice, perform, and learn. The majority of these dance troupes perform ballet or modern dance.

*Amusement.* A variety of establishments provide amusement for a growing number of customers. Some of these businesses provide video game, pinball, and gaming machines to amusement parks, arcades, and casinos. Casinos and other gaming establishments offering off-track betting are a rapidly growing part of this industry segment. This segment also includes amusement and theme parks, which range in size from local carnivals to multi-acre parks. These establishments may have mechanical rides, shows, and refreshment stands. Other amusement and recreation services include day camps, fireworks display services, go-cart rentals, rodeos, riding stables, waterslides, skating rinks, ski lifts, and establishments offering rental sporting goods.

## Working Conditions

Jobs in amusement and recreation services are more likely to be part time than are those in other industries. In fact, the average nonsupervisory worker in the amusement and recreation industry worked 25.9 hours a week in 2000. Entertainers, actors, and musicians were most likely to work part time, due to the large number of performers competing for a limited number of positions. The majority of performers are unable to support themselves in this profession alone and are forced to supplement their income through other jobs.

Many types of amusement and recreation establishments dramatically increase employment during the summer and either scale back employment during the winter or close down completely. Workers may be required to work nights and holidays because most establishments are busiest during major holidays. Some jobs require extensive travel. Music and dance troupes, for example, frequently tour or travel to major metropolitan areas across the country, in hopes of attracting large audiences.

Many in this industry work outdoors, whereas others may work in hot, crowded, or noisy conditions. Some jobs, such as those at fitness facilities or in amusement parks, involve some manual labor and, thus, require physical strength and stamina. Also, athletes, dancers, and many other performers must be in particularly good physical condition. Many jobs include customer-service responsibilities, so employees must be able to work well with the public.

In 1999, cases of work-related illness and injury averaged 6.7 for every 100 full-time workers, higher than the average of 6.3 for the entire private sector. Risks of injury are high in some jobs, especially those of athletes. Although most injuries are minor, including sprains and muscle pulls, they may prevent an employee from working for a period.

## Employment

The amusement and recreation services industry provided more than 1.7 million jobs in 2000. Miscellaneous amusement and recreation services—which includes amusement parks, coin-operated amusement devices, public golf courses, membership sports and recreation clubs, and physical fitness facilities—accounted for 3 out of 4 jobs (table 1).

**Table 1. Employment in amusement and recreation services by industry segment, 2000**

(Employment in thousands)

| Industry segment | Employment |
|---|---|
| Amusement and recreation services | 1,728 |
| Miscellaneous amusement and recreation services | 1,287 |
| Producers, orchestras, and entertainers | 181 |
| Commercial sports | 153 |
| Bowling centers | 81 |
| Dance studios, schools, and halls | 27 |

Although most establishments in the amusement and recreation industry are small, over half of all jobs were in establishments that employ more than 50 workers (chart).

The amusement and recreation services industry is characterized by a large number of seasonal and part-time positions and by workers who are younger than the average for all industries. The majority of workers are under the age of 35. Many businesses in the industry increase hiring during the summer, often employing high school- and college-age workers.

## Occupations in the Industry

About 56 percent of workers in the industry are employed in service occupations (table 2). *Amusement and recreation attendants*, the largest occupation in amusement and recreation services, perform a variety of duties depending on where they

are employed. Common duties include setting up games, handing out sports equipment, providing caddy services for golfers, collecting money, and operating amusement park rides.

*Fitness trainers and aerobics instructors* instruct or coach groups or individuals in exercise activities and in the fundamentals of sports.

**Table 2. Employment of wage and salary workers in amusement and recreation services by occupation, 2000 and projected change, 2000-10**

(Employment in thousands)

| Occupation | Employment, 2000 Number | Employment, 2000 Percent | Percent change, 2000-2010 |
|---|---|---|---|
| **All occupations** | 1,728 | 100.0 | 34.5 |
| **Management, business, and financial occupations** | 112 | 6.5 | 35.1 |
| General and operations managers | 41 | 2.4 | 34.0 |
| Business operations specialists | 13 | 0.7 | 37.2 |
| **Professional and related occupations** | 227 | 13.1 | 32.5 |
| Self-enrichment education teachers | 20 | 1.2 | 29.9 |
| Actors | 34 | 2.0 | 36.9 |
| Coaches and scouts | 23 | 1.3 | 31.3 |
| Dancers and choreographers | 20 | 1.2 | 16.8 |
| Musicians and singers | 39 | 2.2 | 34.5 |
| **Service occupations** | 972 | 56.2 | 34.8 |
| Security guards | 37 | 2.1 | 22.3 |
| Bartenders | 36 | 2.1 | 35.3 |
| Combined food preparation and serving workers, including fast food | 39 | 2.3 | 8.0 |
| Counter attendants, cafeteria, food concession, and coffee shop | 23 | 1.3 | 41.9 |
| Waiters and waitresses | 82 | 4.7 | 3.6 |
| Dining room and cafeteria attendants and bartender helpers | 20 | 1.1 | 18.8 |
| Building cleaning workers | 66 | 3.8 | 42.0 |
| Landscaping and groundskeeping workers | 108 | 6.2 | 45.0 |
| Ushers, lobby attendants, and ticket takers | 28 | 1.6 | 26.6 |
| Amusement and recreation attendants | 121 | 7.0 | 41.2 |
| First-line supervisors/managers, gaming workers | 18 | 1.0 | 34.2 |
| Gaming services workers | 43 | 2.5 | 45.6 |
| Fitness trainers and aerobics instructors | 100 | 5.8 | 52.1 |
| Recreation workers | 19 | 1.1 | 48.0 |
| **Sales and related occupations** | 152 | 8.8 | 41.2 |
| Cashiers, except gaming | 60 | 3.5 | 42.2 |
| Gaming change persons and booth cashiers | 19 | 1.1 | 48.8 |
| Counter and rental clerks | 25 | 1.4 | 32.6 |
| **Office and administrative support occupations** | 157 | 9.1 | 30.8 |
| Gaming cage workers | 14 | 0.8 | 33.1 |
| Receptionists and information clerks | 35 | 2.0 | 48.6 |
| Office clerks, general | 23 | 1.4 | 41.3 |
| Executive secretaries and administrative assistants | 16 | 0.9 | 24.9 |
| **Installation, maintenance, and repair occupations** | 56 | 3.2 | 29.3 |
| Maintenance and repair workers, general | 32 | 1.8 | 20.6 |
| **Transportation and material moving occupations** | 35 | 2.0 | 33.9 |

NOTE: May not add to totals due to omission of occupations with small employment.

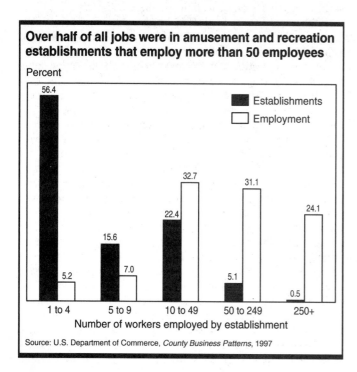

**Over half of all jobs were in amusement and recreation establishments that employ more than 50 employees**

Percent

| | Establishments | Employment |
|---|---|---|
| 1 to 4 | 56.4 | 5.2 |
| 5 to 9 | 15.6 | 7.0 |
| 10 to 49 | 22.4 | 32.7 |
| 50 to 249 | 5.1 | 31.1 |
| 250+ | 0.5 | 24.1 |

Number of workers employed by establishment

Source: U.S. Department of Commerce, *County Business Patterns*, 1997

*Recreation workers* organize and promote activities such as arts and crafts, sports, games, music, dramatics, social recreation, camping, and hobbies. They generally are employed by schools; theme parks and other tourist attractions; or health, sports, and other recreational clubs. Recreation workers schedule organized events to structure leisure time.

*Gaming services workers* assist in the operation of games such as keno, bingo, and gaming table games. They may calculate and pay off the amount of winnings, or collect players' money or chips.

Other service workers include *waiters* and *waitresses*, who serve food in entertainment establishments; *counter attendants* and *food preparation and serving workers,* who serve and sometimes prepare food for patrons; and *bartenders,* who mix and serve drinks in amusement establishments.

Building, grounds cleaning, and maintenance occupations include *building cleaning workers*, who clean up after shows or sporting events and are responsible for the daily cleaning and upkeep of facilities. *Landscaping and groundskeeping workers* care for athletic fields and golf courses. These workers maintain artificial and natural turf fields, mark boundaries, and paint team logos. They also mow, water, and fertilize natural athletic fields and vacuum and disinfect synthetic fields. Protective service occupations include *security guards and gaming surveillance officers*, who patrol the property and guard against theft, vandalism, and illegal entry. At sporting events, guards maintain order and direct patrons to various facilities.

Professional and related occupations account for 13 percent of all jobs in this industry. Members of one of the most well-known, *athletes and sports competitors,* perform in a variety of sports. Professional athletes compete in events for compensation, either through salaries or prize money. Organizations such as the Women's National Basketball Association (WNBA) and the National Football League (NFL) sanction events for professionals. Few athletes are able to make it to the professional level, where high salaries are common. In some professional sports, minor leagues offer lower salaries with a chance to develop skills through competition before advancing to major league play.

*Coaches and scouts* train athletes to perform at their highest level. Often, they are experienced athletes who have retired and are able to provide insight from their own experiences to players. *Umpires, referees, and other sports officials*, even in professional sports, usually work part time and often have other full-time jobs. For example, many professional sport referees and umpires officiate at amateur games, as well.

*Musicians and singers* may play musical instruments, sing, compose, arrange music, or conduct groups in instrumental or vocal performances. The specific skills and responsibilities of musicians vary widely by type of instrument, size of ensemble, and style of music. For example, musicians can play jazz, classical, or popular music, either alone or in groups ranging from small rock bands to large symphony orchestras.

*Actors* entertain and communicate with people through their interpretation of dramatic and other roles. They can belong to a variety of performing groups, ranging from those appearing in community and local dinner theaters to those playing in full-scale Broadway productions. *Dancers* express ideas, stories, rhythm, and sound with their bodies through different types of dance, including ballet, modern dance, tap, and jazz. Dancers usually perform in a troupe, although some perform solo. Many become teachers when their performing careers end. *Producers and directors* select and interpret plays or scripts, and give directions to actors and dancers. They conduct rehearsals, audition cast members, and approve choreography. They also ar-

range financing, hire production staff members, and negotiate contracts with personnel.

About 9 percent of all jobs in this industry are in sales and related occupations. The largest of these, *cashiers*, often use a cash register to receive money and give change to customers. In casinos, *gaming change persons and booth cashiers* exchange coins and tokens for patrons' money. *Counter and rental clerks* check out rental equipment to customers, receive orders for service, and handle cash transactions.

Another 9 percent of jobs in this industry are in office and administrative support occupations. *Receptionists and information clerks*, one of the larger occupations in this category, answer questions and provide general information to patrons. Other large occupations in this group include *general office clerks* and *secretaries and administrative assistants*.

Management, business, and financial operations occupations make up 6 percent of employment in this industry. Managerial duties in the performing arts include marketing, business management, event booking, fundraising, and public outreach. *Recreation supervisors* and *park superintendents* oversee personnel, budgets, grounds and facility maintenance, and land and wildlife resources. Some common administrative jobs in sports are *tournament director, health club manager,* and *sports program director*.

Installation, maintenance, and repair occupations make up 3 percent of industry employment. *General maintenance and repair workers* are the largest occupation in this group.

## Training and Advancement

About half of all workers in the amusement and recreation industry have no formal education beyond high school. In the case of performing artists or athletes, talent and years of training are more important than education. However, upper level management jobs usually require a college degree.

Most service jobs require little or no previous training or education beyond high school. Many companies hire young, unskilled workers, such as students, to perform low-paying, seasonal jobs. Amusement parks prefer workers who are at least 17 years old. Employers look for people with the interpersonal skills necessary to work with the public.

In physical fitness facilities, fitness trainer and aerobic instructor positions usually are filled by persons who develop an avid interest in the activity and then become certified. Certification from a professional organization may require knowledge of CPR; experience as an instructor at a health club; and successful completion of written and oral exams covering a variety of areas, including anatomy, nutrition, and fitness testing. Sometimes fitness workers become health club managers or owners. To advance to a management position, a degree in physical education, sports medicine, or exercise physiology is useful.

In the arts, employment in professional and related occupations usually requires a great deal of talent. There are many highly talented performers, creating intense competition for every opening. Performers such as musicians, dancers, and actors often study their professions most of their lives, taking private lessons and spending hours practicing. Usually, performers have completed some college or related study. Musicians, dancers, and actors often go on to become teachers after completing the necessary requirements for at least a bachelor's degree. Musicians who complete a graduate degree in music sometimes move on to a career as a conductor. Dancers often become choreographers, and actors can advance into producer and director jobs.

Almost all arts administrators have completed 4 years of college, and the majority possess a master's degree or a doctorate.

Experience in marketing and business is helpful because promoting events is a large part of the job.

Entry-level supervisory or professional jobs in recreation sometimes require completion of a 2-year associate degree in parks and recreation at a junior college. Completing a 4-year bachelor's degree in this field is necessary for high-level supervisory positions. Students can specialize in such areas as aquatics, therapeutic recreation, aging and leisure, and environmental studies. Those who obtain graduate degrees in the field and have years of experience usually can obtain administrative or university teaching positions. The National Recreation and Parks Association certifies individuals who meet eligibility requirements for professional and technical jobs. Certified Leisure Professionals must pass an exam; earn a bachelor's degree with a major in recreation, park resources, or leisure services; and have at least 2 years of relevant full-time experience.

## Earnings

Earnings in amusement and recreation services generally are low, reflecting the large number of part-time and seasonal jobs. Nonsupervisory workers in amusement and recreation services averaged $262 a week in 2000, compared with $474 throughout private industry.

Earnings vary according to occupation and segment of the industry. For example, some professional athletes earn millions, but competition for these positions is intense, and most athletes are unable to reach even the minor leagues. Many service workers make the minimum wage or a little more. Actors often go long periods with little or no income from acting, so they are forced to work at second jobs. Earnings in selected occupations in amusement and recreation services appear in table 3.

**Table 3. Median hourly earnings of the largest occupations in amusement and recreation services, 2000**

| Occupation | Amusement and recreation services | All industries |
|---|---|---|
| Fitness trainers and aerobics instructors ... | $ 12.20 | $ 10.96 |
| Self-enrichment education teachers .......... | 11.97 | 13.44 |
| Security guards .......................................... | 8.80 | 8.45 |
| Landscaping and groundskeeping workers ...................................................... | 8.35 | 8.80 |
| Receptionists and information clerks ......... | 7.78 | 9.63 |
| Cashiers, except gaming ........................... | 7.11 | 6.95 |
| Waiters and waitresses .............................. | 6.83 | 6.42 |
| Ushers, lobby attendants, and ticket takers ...................................................... | 6.81 | 6.61 |
| Amusement and recreation attendants ...... | 6.63 | 6.72 |
| Gaming dealers .......................................... | 6.54 | 6.41 |

Because many amusement and theme parks dramatically increase employment during vacation periods, employment for a number of jobs in the industry is seasonal. Theme parks, for example, frequently hire young workers, often students, for summer employment. Also, many sports are not played all year, so athletes and people in the service jobs associated with those sports often are seasonally employed.

Employers in some segments of this industry offer benefits not available in other industries. For example, benefits for workers in some theme parks include free passes to the park, transportation to and from work, housing, scholarships, and discounts on park merchandise.

Although unions are not common in most segments of this industry, they are important in the performing arts sector. Virtu-ally all actors, actresses, and performers are members of a union. Consequently, earnings of most performers are determined by union contracts that specify minimum salary rates and working conditions.

## Outlook

Wage and salary jobs in amusement and recreation services are projected to increase about 35 percent over the 2000-10 period, more than double the rate of growth projected for the entire economy. Growing participation in amusement and recreation activities—reflecting increasing incomes, leisure time, and awareness of the health benefits of physical fitness—will provide a large market for establishments providing amusement and recreational facilities and services.

Changing demographics of the Nation also will have a major impact on industry employment. For example, amusement and recreation services are expected to increasingly target the growing elderly population. Consequently, employment opportunities may be better in those establishments, such as cruise ships and golf courses, that serve active adults between 50 and 75 years old. Continued growth in hospital and hotel fitness centers and instructional exercise programs, especially those designed and marketed for retirees, also should lead to more job openings. Growth also is expected in those amusement and recreation services, such as health spas and fitness centers, that cater to younger adults in their 20s and 30s with steadily rising incomes.

In addition to these increases, employment in the performing arts will grow rapidly, along with demand for entertainment from a growing population. However, the supply of workers in this segment also will grow, because of the appeal of these jobs, ensuring continued intense competition. Additionally, amusement and theme parks should experience steady growth and offer many seasonal and part-time job opportunities.

The amusement and recreation services industry has relied heavily on workers under the age of 25 to fill seasonal and unskilled positions. Although the pool of these workers will grow in coming years, opportunities should be good for young, seasonal, part-time, and unskilled workers. In addition, the industry is expected to hire a growing number of workers in other age groups.

## Sources of Additional Information

For additional information about careers in the amusement and recreation services industry and a listing of colleges and universities offering accredited programs in parks and recreation studies, write to:

➤ National Recreation and Parks Association, 22377 Belmont Ridge Rd., Ashburn, VA 20148.
Internet: **http://www.activeparks.org**

Information on the following occupations found in amusement and recreation services appears in the 2002-03 *Occupational Outlook Handbook*:

- Actors, producers, and directors
- Athletes, coaches, umpires, and related workers
- Dancers and choreographers
- Gaming cage workers
- Gaming services occupations
- Ground maintenance workers
- Musicians, singers, and related workers
- Recreation and fitness workers
- Security guards and gaming surveillance officers

# Childcare Services

## SIGNIFICANT POINTS

- Preschool teachers, teacher assistants, and childcare workers account for about 3 out of 4 wage and salary jobs.

- Training requirements for most jobs are minimal.

- Job openings should be numerous due mostly to high turnover—reflecting few benefits, low pay, and occasionally stressful working conditions.

## Nature of the Industry

Obtaining affordable, quality childcare, especially for children under age 5, is a major concern for many parents. Childcare needs are met in many different ways. Care in a child's home, care in an organized childcare facility, or care in a provider's home are all common arrangements for preschool-age children. Older children may receive childcare services when they are not in school, generally through before- and after-school programs. With the increasing number of women in the workforce, the provision of childcare services has been one of the most talked about and fastest growing industries in the U.S. economy.

This industry consists of establishments that provide paid care for infants, prekindergarten or preschool children, or older children in after-school programs. Formal childcare centers include nursery schools, preschool centers, Head Start centers, and group daycare centers. Self-employed workers in this industry often provide care from their home for a fee. Private household workers in this industry provide care for children in the child's home. This industry does not include occasional babysitters or persons who provide unpaid care in their homes for the children of relatives or friends. (Social services, except childcare is covered in a separate *Career Guide* statement.)

The for-profit sector of this industry includes centers that operate independently or are part of a local or national chain, whereas nonprofit childcare organizations include religious institutions, YMCA's, colleges, employers, public schools, social service agencies, and State and Federal Government agencies. For-profit establishments have grown rapidly in response to demand for childcare services. Within the nonprofit sector, there has been strong growth in Head Start, the federally funded childcare program designed to provide disadvantaged children with social, educational, and health services.

Childcare shifted in the past from unpaid to paid caregivers, particularly childcare centers. Center-based care has increased, substituting for unpaid care by relatives, as fewer families have access to relatives who were willing or able to keep their children.

Some employers offer childcare benefits to employees. They recognize that the lack of childcare benefits is a barrier to the employment of qualified women, and that the cost of the childcare is offset by increased employee morale and reduced absenteeism. Some employers sponsor childcare centers in or near the workplace; others offer direct financial assistance, vouchers, or discounts for childcare, after-school or sick childcare services, or a dependent care option in a flexible benefits plan.

## Working Conditions

Watching children grow, learn, and gain new skills can be very rewarding. Preschool teachers and childcare workers often improve their own communication, learning, and other personal skills by working with children. The work is never routine; new activities and challenges mark each day. However, childcare can be physically and emotionally taxing, as workers constantly stand, walk, bend, stoop, and lift to attend to each child's interests and problems. They must be constantly alert, anticipate and prevent trouble, deal effectively with disruptive children, and provide fair but firm discipline. Nonetheless, this is a relatively safe industry; in 1999, childcare services had an injury and illness rate of 2.6 per 100 full-time workers, compared with a rate of 6.3 throughout private industry.

The hours of childcare workers vary. Many centers are open 12 or more hours a day and cannot close until all the children are picked up by their parents or guardians. Unscheduled overtime, traffic jams, and other types of emergencies can cause parents or guardians to be late. Nearly half of the full-time employees in the childcare services industry work more than 40 hours per week. Self-employed workers tend to work longer hours than do their salaried counterparts. The industry also offers many opportunities for part-time work—around 40 percent of all employees work part time.

Many childcare workers are faced with stressful conditions, low pay, and few benefits. Turnover among childcare workers is high.

## Employment

About 712,000 workers held wage and salary jobs in childcare services in 2000. Also, about 487,000 self-employed persons worked in the industry. Most of the self-employed were family childcare providers, and some were self-employed managers of childcare centers. Employment estimates understate the total number of people working in this industry because family childcare homes run by relatives often are not counted, and because many other family childcare providers operate illegally without a license to avoid the expense of licensing and taxation.

Jobs in childcare are found across the country, mirroring the distribution of the population. Childcare operations vary in size, from the self-employed person caring for a few children in a private home to the large corporate-sponsored center employing a large staff. More than 2 out of 10 wage and salary jobs in 1997 were located in establishments with fewer than 10 employees. Nearly all have less than 50 workers (chart 1).

Opportunities for self-employment in this industry are among the best in the economy. More than 40 percent of all workers in the industry are self-employed, compared with only 8 percent in all industries. This reflects the ease of entering the childcare business.

The median age of childcare providers is 37.1 compared with 39.6 for all workers. About 20 percent of all care providers are 24 years of age or younger (table 1). More than 7 percent of these workers are below the age of 20, reflecting the minimal training requirements for many childcare positions.

**Table 1. Percent distribution of employment in childcare services by age group, 2000**

| Age group | Childcare services | All industries |
|---|---|---|
| Total ......................................... | 100.0 | 100.0 |
| 16 to 19............................................ | 7.4 | 5.4 |
| 20 to 24............................................ | 12.9 | 9.9 |
| 25 to 34............................................ | 24.4 | 22.6 |
| 35 to 44............................................ | 26.6 | 27.1 |
| 45 to 54............................................ | 17.6 | 22.0 |
| 55 to 64............................................ | 8.0 | 10.1 |
| 65 and older ................................... | 3.2 | 3.0 |

## Occupations in the Industry

There is far less occupational diversity in the childcare services industry than in most other industries. Three occupations—*preschool teachers, teacher assistants,* and *childcare workers*—account for 74 percent of all wage and salary jobs (table 2).

*Preschool teachers* make up the largest occupation in the childcare industry, accounting for about 39 percent of wage and salary jobs. They teach pupils basic physical, mental, and developmental skills in public or private schools. *Teacher assistants* account for 13 percent of employment. They give teachers more time for teaching by assuming a variety of tasks. For example, they may set up and dismantle equipment or prepare instructional materials.

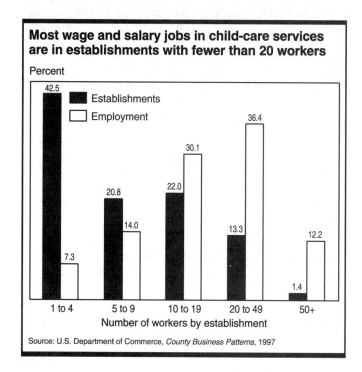

**Most wage and salary jobs in child-care services are in establishments with fewer than 20 workers**

Percent

Establishments / Employment

1 to 4: 42.5 / 7.3
5 to 9: 20.8 / 14.0
10 to 19: 22.0 / 30.1
20 to 49: 13.3 / 36.4
50+: 1.4 / 12.2

Number of workers by establishment

Source: U.S. Department of Commerce, *County Business Patterns,* 1997

**Table 2. Employment of wage and salary workers in childcare services by occupation, 2000 and projected change, 2000-10**

(Employment in thousands)

| Occupation | Employment, 2000 Number | Employment, 2000 Percent | Percent change, 2000-2010 |
|---|---|---|---|
| **All occupations** ....................................... | 712 | 100.0 | 41.9 |
| **Management, business, and financial occupations** ....................................... | 59 | 8.3 | 45.7 |
| Education administrators ..................... | 19 | 2.7 | 53.0 |
| General and operations managers ...... | 13 | 1.8 | 44.5 |
| **Professional and related occupations** ....................................... | 422 | 59.3 | 37.0 |
| Social and human service assistants ....................................... | 6 | 0.9 | 53.0 |
| Child, family, and school social workers ....................................... | 7 | 1.0 | 53.0 |
| Preschool teachers, except special education ....................................... | 280 | 39.3 | 28.7 |
| Kindergarten teachers, except special education ....................................... | 9 | 1.3 | 53.0 |
| Elementary school teachers, except special education ....................................... | 6 | 0.8 | 53.0 |
| Other teachers and instructors ........... | 5 | 0.7 | 59.3 |
| Teacher assistants ............................. | 96 | 13.4 | 53.0 |
| **Service occupations** ............................. | 194 | 27.3 | 51.4 |
| Cooks, institution and cafeteria ........... | 16 | 2.3 | 40.8 |
| Janitors and cleaners, except maids and housekeeping cleaners ............... | 7 | 1.0 | 53.0 |
| Child care workers .............................. | 148 | 20.8 | 53.0 |
| **Office and administrative support occupations** ....................................... | 26 | 3.6 | 37.7 |
| Financial clerks .................................. | 6 | 0.8 | 30.9 |
| Office clerks, general ........................... | 7 | 0.9 | 53.0 |
| Secretaries and administrative assistants ....................................... | 7 | 1.0 | 31.0 |
| **Transportation and material moving occupations** ....................................... | 8 | 1.2 | 52.5 |
| Bus drivers, school .............................. | 5 | 0.8 | 53.0 |

NOTE: May not add to totals due to omission of occupations with small employment.

*Childcare workers* account for about 21 percent of wage and salary jobs. Large proportions of the self-employed who keep children in their homes also are childcare workers. In a home setting, they are known as *family childcare providers*. Some parents hire *private household workers*, such as *nannies*, to care for their children in their own home. Regardless of the setting, these workers feed, diaper, comfort, and play with infants. When dealing with older preschoolers, they attend to the children's basic needs and organize activities that stimulate physical, emotional, intellectual, and social development.

*Managers*, who account for about 8 percent of wage and salary workers, establish overall objectives and standards for their center and provide day-to-day supervision of their staff. They bear overall responsibility for program development as well as for marketing, budgeting, staffing, and all other administrative tasks.

In addition to the above occupations, childcare centers also employ a variety of *office and administrative support workers, building cleaning workers, cooks,* and *bus drivers.*

## Training and Advancement

Most States do not impose training requirements for family childcare providers. However, many local governments offer training and require family childcare providers to obtain licenses. Home safety inspections and criminal background checks are usually required of an applicant. In the case of childcare centers, however, staffing requirements are imposed primarily by the States and by insurers. Although requirements vary, in most cases a minimum age of 18 is required for teachers, and directors or officers must be at least 21. In some States, assistants may work at age 16, and in several States, at 14.

Most States have established minimum educational or training requirements. Training requirements are most stringent for directors, less so for teachers, and minimal for childcare workers and teacher assistants. In many centers, directors must have a college degree, often with experience in childcare and specific training in early childhood development. Teachers must have a high school diploma and, in many cases, a combination of college education and experience. Assistants and childcare workers usually need a high school diploma, but it is not always a requirement. Some employers prefer to hire workers who have received credentials from a nationally recognized childcare organization, including the Council for Professional Recognition.

Many States also mandate other types of training for staff members, such as health and first aid, fire safety, and child abuse detection and prevention. In nearly all States, licensing regulations require criminal record checks for all childcare staff. This screening requirement protects children from abuse and reduces liability risks, making insurance more available and affordable.

State governments also have established requirements for other childcare center personnel involved in food preparation, transportation of children, provision of medical services, and other services. Most States have defined minimum staff-to-children ratios. These vary depending on the State and the age of the children involved.

## Earnings

In 2000, hourly earnings of nonsupervisory workers in the childcare services industry averaged $8.69, much less than the average of $13.74 for all industries combined. On a weekly basis, earnings in childcare services averaged only $258 in 2000, compared with the average of $474 for all industries. Weekly earnings, in part, reflect hours worked—salaried workers in childcare services averaged 29.7 hours a week, compared with about 34.5 throughout private industry. Earnings in selected occupations in childcare services in 2000 appear in table 3.

**Table 3. Median hourly earnings of the largest occupations in childcare services, 2000**

| Occupation | Childcare services | All industries |
|---|---|---|
| General and operations managers | $ 15.92 | $ 29.41 |
| Executive secretaries and administrative assistants | 11.49 | 14.95 |
| Social and human service assistants | 11.36 | 10.74 |
| Child, family, and school social workers | 11.09 | 15.13 |
| Office clerks, general | 8.25 | 10.16 |
| Preschool teachers, except special education | 8.16 | 8.56 |
| Bus drivers, school | 8.12 | 10.05 |
| Janitors and cleaners, except maids and housekeeping cleaners | 7.66 | 8.26 |
| Cooks, institution and cafeteria | 7.52 | 8.22 |
| Childcare workers | 6.74 | 7.43 |

Employee benefits often are minimal as well. A substantial number of childcare centers offer no healthcare benefits to any teaching staff. Reduced childcare fees for workers' children, however, is a common benefit. Wage levels, employee benefits, and resulting turnover depends in part on the type of childcare center. Nonprofit and religiously affiliated centers generally pay higher wages and offer more generous benefits than for-profit establishments.

Only about 3.5 percent of all workers in childcare services are union members or are covered by union contracts, compared with 15 percent of workers in all industries.

## Outlook

Wage and salary jobs in the childcare services industry are projected to grow 42 percent over the 2000-10 period, compared with the 15 percent employment growth projected for all industries combined. An unusually large number of job openings will also result each year from the need to replace experienced workers who leave this industry. Turnover is very high, reflecting the low wages and relatively meager benefits. Faster than average employment growth, when coupled with high turnover should create numerous employment opportunities.

The rising demand for childcare services reflects demographic trends. Over the 1988-98 period, the population of women of childbearing age (widely considered to be ages 15 to 44) increased by almost 2 million, accompanied by a rise in their labor force participation. As a result, the number of women in the labor force with children young enough to require childcare increased very rapidly. These demographic changes are projected to slow over the 2000-10 period, so projected employment growth in the childcare services industry will slow down accordingly. Although the number of women of childbearing age is expected to grow very slowly, the number of children under age 5 still will increase during this period.

The demand for childcare services will remain high. As the labor force participation of women between the ages of 16 and 44 increases, more parents of preschool and school-age children will seek suitable daycare arrangements. As more parents work during weekends, evenings, and late nights, the demand will increase significantly for childcare programs that can provide care during nontraditional hours. School-age children, who generally require childcare only before and after school, increasingly are being cared for in centers.

Center-based care should continue to expand its share of the industry as government increases its involvement in promoting and funding childcare services. Increased funding for Head Start and other national childcare programs would result in more children being served in centers. Demand for preschool teachers could increase if many States implement mandatory preschool for 4-year-old children. Another factor that could result in more children being cared for in centers is the greater involvement of employers in funding and operating daycare centers. Welfare reform legislation requiring more welfare recipients to work also could contribute to demand for childcare services.

## Sources of Additional Information

For additional information about careers in early childhood education, contact:

➤ National Association for the Education of Young Children, 1509 16th St. NW., Washington, DC 20036-1426.
Internet: **http://www.naeyc.org**

State Departments of Human Services or Social Services can supply State regulations concerning childcare programs, childcare workers, teacher assistants, and preschool teachers.

Detailed information on the following key occupations in the childcare services industry appears in the 2002-03 *Occupational Outlook Handbook*:

- Childcare workers

- Teacher assistants

- Teachers—preschool, kindergarten, elementary, middle, and secondary

# Computer and Data Processing Services

## SIGNIFICANT POINTS

- Computer and data processing services is projected to be the fastest growing industry in the economy, with employment expected to increase 86 percent between 2000 and 2010.

- Job opportunities will be excellent for most workers; professional and related workers enjoy the best prospects, reflecting continuing demand for higher level skills needed to keep up with changes in technology.

- Computer specialists account for almost half of all employees in this industry.

## Nature of the Industry

All organizations today rely on computer and information technology to conduct business and operate more efficiently. Often, however, these institutions do not have the resources to effectively implement new technologies or satisfy their changing needs. When this happens, they turn to the computer and data processing services industry to meet their specialized needs on a contract or customer basis. Firms may enlist the services of one of over 178,000 establishments in the computer and data processing services industry for help with a particular project or problem, such as setting up a secure website or establishing a marketplace online. Alternatively, they may choose to "outsource" one or more activities, such as the management of their entire data center or help-desk support, to a computer and data processing services firm.

Services provided by this industry include prepackaged software; customized computer programming services and applications and systems software design; data processing, preparation, and information retrieval services, including online databases and Internet services; integrated systems design and development and management of databases; onsite computer facilities management; rental, leasing, and repair of computers and peripheral equipment; and a variety of specialized consulting services. Computer training contractors, however, are grouped with educational services, and establishments that manufacture and sell computer equipment are included with electronic equipment manufacturing. Telecommunications services, including cable Internet providers, also are classified separately.

Software and professional services offered within this industry include prepackaged software, custom programming, integrated systems design, and other specialized consulting. Prepackaged software establishments develop operating system software as well as word processing and spreadsheet packages, games and graphics packages, data storage software, and Internet-related software tools such as search engines and Web browsers—the software that permits browsing, retrieval, and viewing of content from the World Wide Web. Some may install the software package on a user's system and customize it to the user's specific needs. Programming service firms may be hired to code large programs or to get new systems up and running. Programming service firms also may update or reengineer existing systems.

Electronic business ("e-business") is any process that a business organization conducts over a computer-mediated network. Electronic commerce ("e-commerce") is that part of e-business that involves the buying and selling of goods and services. With the growth of the Internet and the expansion of electronic commerce, some service firms specialize in developing and maintaining websites for client companies. Others create and maintain corporate Intranets or self-contained internal networks linking multiple users within an organization by means of Internet technology. These firms design sophisticated computer networks, assist with upgrades or conversions, and engage in continual maintenance. They help clients select the right hardware and software products for a particular project, and then develop, install, and implement the system, as well as train the client's users. Service firms also offer consulting services for any stages of development throughout the entire process, from design and content development to administration and maintenance of site security.

This widespread use of the Internet and Intranets also has resulted in an increased focus on security. The robust growth of electronic commerce highlights this concern, as firms seek to attract as many potential customers as possible to their websites. Security threats range from damaging computer viruses to online credit card fraud. Services outsourced to security consulting firms include analyzing vulnerability, managing firewalls, and providing intrusion and antivirus protection.

Information services include data preparation and processing services, as well as information retrieval services. Establishments may provide payroll processing, credit reporting, data entry services, and optical scanning services, as well as the leasing of computer time. Usually, information is collected from the client's databases, processed, and passed to other online subscribers, to contracted users, or back to the client. With the Internet and electronic business creating tremendous volumes of data, there is growing need to be able to store, manage, and extract data effectively. Establishments in these sectors also include a number of Internet service providers. These companies provide access to end users of the Internet who usually subscribe for a set fee.

Hardware services for computers and other data processing equipment include facilities management and operation, rental and leasing, maintenance and repair of computers and peripheral equipment. Such services usually are offered on the customer's site, although, in the case of maintenance and repair work, equipment may be taken to repair shops and replacements left for temporary use. Miscellaneous services establishments include database development firms engaged in building and maintaining databases of critical information. Miscellaneous services also include disk and diskette conversions, hardware requirements analysis, and consulting on a contract or fee basis.

## Working Conditions

Most workers in this industry work in clean, quiet offices. Those in facilities management or maintenance and repair may work in computer operations centers or repairshops. Given the technology available today, however, more work can be done from remote locations using modems, fax machines, e-mail, and especially the Internet. For example, systems analysts may work from home, with their computers linked directly to computers at a financial services firm. Although they often relocate to a customer's place of business while working on a project, programmers and consultants may actually perform work from locations offsite. Even technical support personnel can tap into a customer's computer remotely in order to identify and fix problems.

About 6.2 percent of the workers in computer and data processing services firms work part time, compared with 15.3 percent of workers throughout all industries. For some professionals or technical specialists, evening or weekend work may be necessary to meet deadlines or solve problems. Professionals working for large establishments may have less freedom in planning their schedule than do consultants for very small firms, whose work may be more varied.

Data entry and information processing workers and others who work at video terminals for extended periods may experience musculoskeletal strain, eye problems, stress, or repetitive motion illnesses, such as carpal tunnel syndrome.

## Employment

Employment in computer and data processing services grew by more than 1.3 million jobs from 1990 to 2000. In 2000, there were about 2.1 million wage and salary jobs, and an additional 164,000 self-employed workers, making the industry one of the largest in the economy. Most self-employed workers are independent consultants. Since the late 1980s, employment has grown most rapidly in the computer programming services, information retrieval services, and prepackaged software segments of the industry. From 1990 to 2000, about 368,000 jobs were created in programming services, 196,000 in information retrieval services, and another 187,000 in prepackaged software.

While the industry has both large and small firms, the average establishment in computer and data processing services is relatively small; approximately 80 percent of establishments employed fewer than 10 workers. The majority of jobs, however, are found in establishments that employ 50 or more workers (see chart). Many small establishments in the industry are startup firms that hope to capitalize on a market niche.

Relative to the rest of the economy, there are significantly fewer workers 45 years of age and older in computer and data processing establishments; this industry's workforce remains younger than most, with large proportions of workers in the 25 to 44 age range (table 1). This reflects the industry's explosive growth in employment since the early 1980s. The huge increase in employment afforded thousands of opportunities to younger workers possessing the newest technological skills.

## Occupations in the Industry

Providing a wide array of information services to clients requires a diverse and well-educated workforce. The majority of workers in computer and data processing services are professional and related workers, such as computer systems analysts, computer engineers, and computer programmers (table 2). This occupational group accounts for 53 percent of the jobs in the industry, reflecting the emphasis on high level technical skills and creativity. By 2010, the share of professional and related occupations is expected to be even greater, while the employment share of office and administrative support jobs, currently accounting for 20 percent of industry employment, is projected to fall.

**Table 1. Percent distribution of employment in computer and data processing services by age group, 2000**

| Age group | Computer and data processing services | All Industries |
|---|---|---|
| Total ............................................... | 100.0% | 100.0% |
| 16-19................................................. | 1.4 | 5.4 |
| 20-24................................................. | 9.3 | 9.9 |
| 25-34................................................. | 36.9 | 22.6 |
| 35-44................................................. | 30.0 | 27.1 |
| 45-54................................................. | 16.0 | 22.0 |
| 55-64................................................. | 5.7 | 10.1 |
| 65 and older ..................................... | 0.7 | 3.0 |

*Programmers* write, test, and maintain the detailed instructions, called programs or software, that computers must follow to perform their functions. These programs tell the computer what to do, such as which information to identify and access, how to process it, and what equipment to use. Programmers write these commands by breaking down each step into a logical series, converting specifications into a language the computer understands. While some still work with traditional programming languages like COBOL, object-oriented programming languages, such as C++ and Java, computer-aided software engineering (CASE) tools, and artificial intelligence shells now are being used to create and maintain programs. These

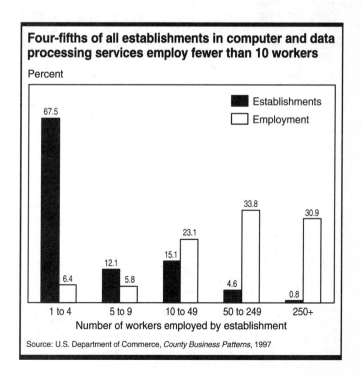

**Four-fifths of all establishments in computer and data processing services employ fewer than 10 workers**

Percent

- Establishments
- Employment

| | 1 to 4 | 5 to 9 | 10 to 49 | 50 to 249 | 250+ |
|---|---|---|---|---|---|
| Establishments | 67.5 | 12.1 | 15.1 | 4.6 | 0.8 |
| Employment | 6.4 | 5.8 | 23.1 | 33.8 | 30.9 |

Number of workers employed by establishment

Source: U.S. Department of Commerce, *County Business Patterns*, 1997

languages and tools allow portions of code to be reused in programs that require similar routines. Many programmers also customize a package to clients' specific needs or create better packages.

Computer engineers design, develop, test, and evaluate computer hardware and related equipment, software programs, and systems. Although programmers write and support programs in new languages, much of the design and development now is the responsibility of *software engineers* or *software developers*. Software engineers must possess strong programming skills, but are more concerned with developing algorithms and analyzing and solving programming problems than with actually writing code. These professionals develop many types of software, including operating systems software, network distribution software, and a variety of applications software. *Computer systems software engineers* coordinate the construction and maintenance of a company's computer systems, and plan their future growth. They develop software systems for control and automation in manufacturing, business, and other areas. They research, design, and test operating system software, compilers—software that converts programs for faster processing—and network distribution software. *Computer applications software engineers* analyze users' needs and design, create, and modify general computer applications software or specialized utility programs. They analyze user needs and develop software solutions. *Computer hardware engineers*, on the other hand, usually design, develop, and test computer hardware, such as computer chips, and supervise its manufacture and installation. One of the goals of computer hardware engineering is to design and produce computing devices that function efficiently and economically.

Professionals involved in analyzing and solving problems include *systems analysts*, who study business, scientific, or engineering data processing problems and design new flows of information. Computers need to be connected to each other and to a control server to allow communication among users, thus enhancing use of their computing power. Systems analysts tie together hardware and software to give an organization the maximum benefit from its investment in machines, personnel, and business processes. To do this, they may design entirely new systems or add a single new software application to harness more of the computer's power. They use data modeling, structured analysis, information engineering, and other methods. Systems analysts prepare charts for programmers to follow for proper coding and also perform cost-benefit analyses to help management evaluate the system. They ensure that the system performs to its specifications and test it thoroughly.

*Database administrators* determine ways to organize and store data and work with database management systems software. They set up computer databases and test and coordinate changes to them. Because they also may be responsible for design implementation and system security, database administrators often plan and coordinate security measures.

*Computer and information scientists* work as theorists, researchers, or inventors. They apply a higher level of theoretical expertise and innovation and develop solutions to complex problems relating to computer hardware and software.

*Computer support specialists* provide technical assistance, support, and advice to customers and users. This group of occupations includes workers with a variety of titles, such as *technical support specialists* and *help-desk technicians*. These troubleshooters interpret problems, and provide technical support for hardware, software, and systems. Support specialists may work either within a company or other organization or directly for a computer hardware and software vendor. They

**Table 2. Employment of wage and salary workers in computer and data processing services by occupation, 2000 and projected change, 2000-10**

(Employment in thousands)

| Occupation | Employment, 2000 Number | Percent | Percent change, 2000-2010 |
|---|---|---|---|
| **All occupations** | 2,095 | 100.0 | 86.2 |
| **Management, business, and financial occupations** | 370 | 17.6 | 78.4 |
| Marketing and sales managers | 28 | 1.3 | 87.5 |
| Computer and information systems managers | 62 | 3.0 | 81.3 |
| Engineering managers | 18 | 0.9 | 48.2 |
| Financial managers | 16 | 0.8 | 81.3 |
| General and operations managers | 54 | 2.6 | 71.3 |
| Management analysts | 30 | 1.4 | 113.8 |
| Accountants and auditors | 16 | 0.8 | 81.3 |
| **Professional and related occupations** | 1,118 | 53.3 | 105.7 |
| Computer programmers | 231 | 11.0 | 43.2 |
| Computer and information scientists, research | 9 | 0.4 | 73.8 |
| Computer systems analysts | 135 | 6.5 | 99.4 |
| Computer software engineers, applications | 194 | 9.3 | 144.8 |
| Computer software engineers, systems software | 124 | 5.9 | 144.8 |
| Computer support specialists | 137 | 6.5 | 144.8 |
| Database administrators | 25 | 1.2 | 103.6 |
| Network and computer systems administrators | 55 | 2.6 | 144.8 |
| Network systems and data communications analysts | 36 | 1.7 | 117.6 |
| All other computer specialists | 41 | 2.0 | 120.0 |
| Computer hardware engineers | 15 | 0.7 | 63.4 |
| **Sales and related occupations** | 113 | 5.4 | 54.5 |
| Sales representatives, wholesale and manufacturing, technical and scientific products | 29 | 1.4 | 24.9 |
| **Office and administrative support occupations** | 412 | 19.7 | 52.5 |
| First-line supervisors/managers of office and administrative support workers | 29 | 1.4 | 38.0 |
| Bookkeeping, accounting, and auditing clerks | 29 | 1.4 | 56.1 |
| Information and record clerks | 95 | 4.5 | 67.0 |
| Customer service representatives | 60 | 2.9 | 71.5 |
| Computer operators | 22 | 1.0 | 8.6 |
| Data entry keyers | 69 | 3.3 | 34.7 |
| Office clerks, general | 33 | 1.6 | 81.3 |
| Executive secretaries and administrative assistants | 35 | 1.6 | 63.2 |
| Secretaries, except legal, medical, and executive | 16 | 0.7 | 45.0 |
| **Installation, maintenance, and repair occupations** | 40 | 1.9 | 67.5 |
| Computer, automated teller, and office machine repairers | 24 | 1.1 | 61.3 |
| **Production occupations** | 18 | 0.9 | 62.5 |

NOTE: May not add to totals due to omission of occupations with small employment.

answer phone calls, analyze problems using automated diagnostic programs, and resolve recurrent difficulties encountered by users.

Other computer specialists include a wide range of related professionals who specialize in operation, analysis, education, application, or design for a particular piece of the system. Many are involved in the design, testing, and evaluation of network systems such as local area networks (LAN), wide area networks (WAN), Internet, and other data communications systems. Specialty occupations reflect an emphasis on client-server applications and end-user support; however, occupational titles shift rapidly to reflect new developments in technology.

*Network systems and data communications analysts*, for example, design, and evaluate network systems, such as local area networks, wide area networks, and the Internet. They perform network modeling, analysis, and planning and may deal with the interfacing of computer and communications equipment. With the explosive growth of the Internet, this group includes a variety of occupations relating to design, development, and maintenance of websites and their servers. *Web developers* are responsible for day-to-day site design and creation while *webmasters* are responsible for the technical aspects of the website, including performance issues such as speed of access, and for approving site content.

*Network* or *computer systems administrators* install, configure, and support an organization's LAN, WAN, network segment, or Internet system. They maintain network hardware and software, analyze problems, and monitor the network to ensure availability to system users. Administrators also may plan, coordinate, and implement network security measures. In some organizations, *computer security specialists* are responsible for the organization's information security.

*Computer and information systems managers* direct the work of systems analysts, computer programmers, and other computer-related workers. They analyze the computer and information needs of their organization and determine personnel and equipment requirements. These managers plan and coordinate activities such as the installation and upgrading of hardware and software; programming and systems design; the development of computer networks; and the implementation of Internet and Intranet sites.

Traditionally, the role of *computer operators* has been to ensure that computer systems run as efficiently as possible. Depending upon the size of the computer installation, they may work with mainframes, minicomputers, or networks of personal computers. They oversee regular operations and solve problems that surface within the system. Peripheral equipment, such as printers and tape drives, and the console of the computer itself must be correctly accessed and controlled. As errors arise, operators respond by resetting controls or terminating the run. In some establishments, they keep logs of malfunctions, suggest the acquisition of new equipment, or supervise and train other operators or peripheral equipment operators.

*Data entry and information processing workers* transfer information from audio or printed forms to a computer system. Many also manipulate or edit existing data or proofread entries to an existing database. Increasingly, data are entered into computer systems at the point of origin, as in the case of automatic teller machines and sophisticated optical character readers, which scan a document and copy the information to the computer.

*Computer repairers* maintain mainframe and personal computers, printers, and other peripheral equipment. They install new equipment for clients, do preventive maintenance, and correct emergency problems. Workers may also install operating software and peripheral equipment, checking that all components are configured to correctly function together. Repairers may work in both repairshops and customer locations. When equipment breaks down, many repairers travel to custom-ers' workplaces or other locations to make the necessary repairs. As the amount of computer equipment increases, more installation, maintenance, and repairwork will become necessary.

Due, in part, to the robust growth in electronic commerce, a growing number of other workers in this industry are in sales and related occupations. In order to compete successfully and gain customers and clients in the online world, the presentation and features of websites and other web-related content becomes increasingly important. The marketing and sales workers employed in this industry are responsible for promoting and selling the products and services provided by the various sectors of this industry.

**Training and Advancement**
Occupations in the computer and data processing services industry require varying levels of education. The level of education and type of training required depend on employers' needs. One factor affecting these needs is changes in technology. As demonstrated by the current demand for workers with skills related to the Internet, employers often scramble to find workers capable of implementing "hot" new technologies. Another factor driving employers' needs is the timeframe within which a project must be completed.

Entry-level positions such as data entry and information processing workers generally need a high school diploma. Most jobs are awarded to those applicants with the greatest keyboarding speed and some business education. Computer operators usually receive on-the-job training in order to become acquainted with their employer's equipment and routines but may need some postsecondary education. Some computer operator positions may require an associate degree or even a bachelor's degree. More commonly, however, a high school diploma, previous experience with an operating system, and familiarity with the latest technologies are the minimum requirements. Completion of vocational training also is an asset.

Computer programmers commonly hold a bachelor's degree; however, there are no universal educational requirements. Some hold a degree in computer science, mathematics, or information systems while others have taken special courses in computer programming to supplement their study in fields such as accounting, inventory control, or other areas of business. Because employers' needs are so varied, a 2-year degree or certificate may be sufficient for some positions so long as applicants possess the right technical skills.

Most computer systems analysts and computer engineers, on the other hand, usually have a bachelor's or higher degree and work experience. Many hold advanced degrees in technical fields or a master's degree in business administration (MBA) with a concentration in information systems, and are specialists in their fields. For systems analyst, programmer-analyst, or even database administrator positions, many employers seek applicants who have a bachelor's degree in computer science, information science, or management information systems (MIS). Computer hardware engineers generally need at least a bachelor's degree in computer engineering or electrical engineering, whereas software engineers are more likely to hold a degree in computer science. For computer and information scientists, a doctoral degree generally is required due to the highly technical nature of their work. For some networks systems and data communication analysts, such as webmasters, an associate degree or certificate generally is sufficient, although more advanced positions might require a computer-related bachelor's degree.

Persons interested in becoming a computer support specialist generally need only an associate degree in a computer-related field, as well as significant hands-on experience with computers. They also must possess strong problem-solving and analytical skills as well as excellent communication skills because troubleshooting and helping others are such a vital part of the job. And because there is constant interaction on the job with other computer personnel, customers, or employees, computer support specialists must be able to communicate effectively on paper, using e-mail, or in person. They also must possess strong writing skills when preparing manuals for employees and customers. As technology continues to improve, computer support specialists must constantly strive to stay up to date and acquire new skills if they wish to remain in the field.

Computer and information systems managers usually require a bachelor's degree in a computer-related occupation combined with work experience. Employers, though, often prefer a graduate degree, especially a master's degree in business administration (MBA) with technology as a core component.

The size of the firm and the local demand for workers also may influence training requirements for specific jobs. Smaller firms may be willing to train informally on the job, whereas larger organizations may pay for formal training or higher education. For example, many of the marketing and sales workers are able to secure entry-level jobs with little technical knowledge but quickly learn the technical knowledge necessary for their company and product. With more formal education, employees may advance to completely different jobs within the industry. Education or training in a specialty area may provide new opportunities for the worker and allow the establishment to offer new services.

As technological advances in the computer field continue, employers in all areas demand a higher level of skill and expertise. Employers, hardware and software vendors, colleges and universities, private training institutions, or professional computing societies offer continuing education and professional development seminars. Technical or professional certification is a way by which employers ensure the competency or quality of computer professionals. Certification can be obtained voluntarily, though many vendors now offer or even require professionals who work with their products to be certified.

Voluntary certification also is available through organizations such as the Institute of Certification and Computing Professionals (ICCP) and the Institute of Electrical and Electronics Engineers (IEEE) Computer Society. Although professional certification is not mandatory, it may provide a jobseeker a competitive advantage. ICCP offers the Certified Computing Professional (CCP) designation to those who have at least 2 years of experience and a college degree. Candidates must pass a core examination testing general knowledge, plus exams in two specialty areas, or in a specialty area and two computer programming languages. The IEEE Computer Society recently announced plans to certify software engineers who pass an examination.

The computer and data processing services industry offers advancement opportunities for all workers who keep up with changing technology. Beginning data entry and information processing workers may move to project leader, and then to first-line supervisor or to office manager. This advancement may result from work experience or from continued training and education.

Computer operators may begin on small computer installations or supervise one aspect of operations. They may move to larger systems that run a greater number of jobs and require more complex problem-solving skills. They also may advance to become operations analysts, or move into computer operations management. These employees apply available computing power to business situations, and they research and suggest upgrades or modifications to the operation of the computer system. Some operators may even become system supervisors. Because they work closely with computer operating languages and systems, computer operators may gain the necessary experience to become programmers or customer support liaisons within their specialty. Many also seek formal education to advance to emerging occupations, such as operations analysts or network administrators.

Entry-level computer programmers usually start working with an experienced programmer updating existing code, generating lines of one portion of a larger program, or writing relatively simple programs. They then advance to more difficult programming and may become project supervisors, or move into higher management positions within the organization. Many programmers who work closely with systems analysts advance to systems analyst positions.

Systems analysts may begin working with experienced analysts or may deal with only small systems or one aspect of a system. They also may move into supervisory positions as they gain further education or work experience. Systems analysts, who work with one type of system, or one aspect or application of a system, can become specialty consultants or move into management positions. Computer engineers and scientists who show leadership ability can also become project managers or advance into management positions, such as manager of information systems or chief information officer. Technical support specialists may advance by developing expertise in an area that leads to other opportunities. For example, those responsible for network support may advance into network administration or network security.

Consulting is an attractive option for experienced workers who do not wish to advance to management positions, or who would rather continue to work with hands-on applications or in a particular specialty. These workers may market their services on their own, under contract as specialized consultants, or with an organization that provides consulting services to outside clients. Many of the largest firms today have subsidiaries that offer specialized services to the host company and to outside clients. Large consulting and computer firms often will hire inexperienced college graduates and put them through intensive, company-based programs that train them to provide such services.

Many experienced workers also have opportunities to move into sales positions as they gain knowledge of specific products. Data entry and information processing workers, for example, may represent an organization in contracting with clients to ensure proper completion of a data entry project. The emergence of various forms of electronic commerce has resulted in efforts by technical workers to make websites and content appealing to potential customers so that they become comfortable conducting transactions over the Internet. Computer programmers who adapt prepackaged software for accounting organizations may use their specialized knowledge to sell such products to similar firms.

## Earnings

Employees in the computer and data processing services industry generally command higher earnings than the national average. All production or nonsupervisory workers in the industry averaged $897 a week in 2000, significantly higher than the average of $474 for all industries. This reflects the concentration of professionals and specialists who often are highly compensated for their specialized skills or expertise. Given the pace at which technology advances in this industry, earnings can be driven by demand for specific skills or experience. Workers in segments of the industry that offer only professional services have even higher average earnings because there are fewer less skilled, lower paid workers in these segments. Earnings in selected occupations in computer and data processing services appear in table 3.

As one might expect, education and experience influence earnings as well. For example, annual earnings of computer software engineers ranged from less than $42,710 for the lowest 10 percent to more than $106,680 for the highest 10 percent in 2000. Managers usually earn more because they have been on the job longer and are more experienced than their staffs, but their salaries, too, can vary by level and experience. Accordingly, annual earnings of computer and information systems managers ranged from less than $44,090 for the lowest 10 percent to more than $127,460 for the highest 10 percent in 2000. Earnings also are affected by other factors such as size, location, and type of establishment, hours and responsibilities of the employee, and level of sales.

Table 3. Median hourly earnings of the largest occupations in computer and data processing services, 2000

| Occupation | Computer and data processing services | All Industries |
|---|---|---|
| Computer and information systems managers | $ 42.50 | $ 37.90 |
| Computer software engineers, systems software | 33.72 | 33.43 |
| Computer software engineers, applications | 33.43 | 32.53 |
| Computer systems analysts | 30.82 | 28.53 |
| Computer programmers | 29.33 | 27.69 |
| Network systems and data communications analysts | 28.44 | 26.20 |
| Network and computer systems administrators | 26.16 | 24.65 |
| Computer support specialists | 18.20 | 17.53 |
| Customer service representatives | 11.97 | 11.83 |
| Data entry keyers | 9.84 | 10.24 |

Unionization is rare in the computer and data processing services industry; fewer than 2 percent of all workers are union members or are covered by union contracts, compared with 14.9 percent of workers throughout private industry.

## Outlook

The computer and data processing services industry has grown dramatically over the past decade and wage and salary employment is expected to grow about 86 percent by the year 2010, making this the fastest growing industry in the U.S. economy. Given the rate at which the computer and data processing services industry is expected to grow and the increasing complexity of technology available, job opportunities will be excellent for most workers. The best opportunities will be for professional and related occupations, reflecting their rapid growth and the continuing demand for higher level skills to keep up with changes in technology.

An increasing reliance on information technology, combined with falling prices of computers and related hardware, means

that individuals and organizations will continue to turn to computer and data processing service firms to maximize the return on their investments in equipment and to fulfill their growing computing needs. Such needs include the expansion of electronic commerce, a growing reliance on the Internet, faster and more efficient internal and external communication, and the development of new technologies and applications. With increasing global competition and rising costs, organizations must be able to obtain and manage the latest information in order to make business decisions.

Within the industry, projected growth varies by sector. Among the fastest growing sectors should be client-server applications, consulting and integration services, prepackaged software, and end-user support. The demand for networking and the need to integrate new technologies will drive the demand for consulting and integration. Advances in software technology and expanding Internet usage will increase the need for software support and services. Prepackaged software has historically grown very rapidly, and will continue to grow as individuals and establishments try to capitalize on the latest improvements. Demand for support services should spur growth in areas such as help-desk outsourcing. And, as more individuals and organizations are conducting business electronically, the importance of maintaining system and network security will increase.

New growth areas will continue to arise from rapidly evolving technologies and business forces. The rate at which the Internet has expanded demonstrates the potential effects of as yet unknown technological developments and the tremendous room for growth. The expansion of the Internet and the proliferation of websites have created a demand for a wide variety of new products and related services, including Internet and Web software, online services, Internet design services, website development, and a range of specialized consulting. Yet, the way the Internet is used is constantly changing, and so are the products, services, and personnel required to support new applications. Expanding electronic commerce, for example, has changed the way companies transact business, enabling markets to expand and an increasing array of services to be provided to customers. Business-to-business commerce is automating many steps in the transaction of business between companies, allowing many firms involved to operate more efficiently. And as the amount of computer-stored information grows, organizations will continue to look for ways to tap the full potential of their vast stores of data. Demand for an even wider array of services should increase as companies continue to expand their capabilities, integrate new technologies, and develop new applications.

Given the increasingly widespread use of information technologies and the overall rate of growth expected for the entire industry, most occupations should grow very rapidly, although some much faster than others. As firms continue to install sophisticated computer networks, set up Internet and Intranet sites, and engage in electronic commerce, the most rapid growth will occur among computer specialists such as computer software engineers, systems analysts, and network and computer systems administrators. This group of workers also includes computer support specialists needed to provide technical assistance, support, and advice to customers and users. Rapid growth also is expected among computer hardware engineers and computer and information systems managers. Employment of computer repairers also will grow rapidly due to increasing dependence of business and residential customers on computers and sophisticated office machines.

Employment of programmers should continue to expand, but more slowly than that of other occupations, as the proportion of

177

programmers decreases in relation to computer software engineers and other computer specialists. Employment of administrative support occupations, including data entry and information processing workers, also is expected to grow more slowly than the rest of the industry. And, as client-server environments and automation continue to increase productivity, automated operating packages and robotic equipment should continue to reduce the need for computer operators.

## Sources of Additional Information

Information regarding certification of computer professionals is available from:

➤ Institute for Certification of Computing Professionals (ICCP), 2350 E. Devon Ave., Suite 115, Des Plaines, IL 60018. Internet: **http://www.iccp.org**

Further information about computer careers is available from:

➤ Association for Computing Machinery (ACM), 1515 Broadway, New York, NY 10036. Internet: **http://www.acm.org**

➤ IEEE Computer Society, Headquarters Office, 1730 Massachusetts Ave. NW., Washington, DC 20036-1992. Internet: **http://www.computer.org**

➤ National Workforce Center for Emerging Technologies, 3000 Landerholm Circle SE., Bellevue, WA 98007. Internet: **http://www.nwcet.org**

Information on the following occupations can be found in the 2002-03 *Occupational Outlook Handbook*:

- Computer, automated teller, and office machine repairers
- Computer and information systems managers
- Computer operators
- Computer programmers
- Computer software engineers
- Computer support specialists and systems administrators
- Data entry and information processing workers
- Systems analysts, computer scientists, and database administrators

# Educational Services

## SIGNIFICANT POINTS

- With about 1 in 4 Americans enrolled in educational institutions, educational services is the largest industry, accounting for nearly 12 million jobs.

- Most teaching positions—which constitute almost half of all educational services jobs—require at least a bachelor's degree, and some require a master's or doctoral degree.

- Retirements in a number of education professions will create many job openings.

## Nature of the Industry

Education is an important part of life. The type and level of education that an individual attains often influences occupational choice and earnings potential. Lifelong learning is important to acquire new knowledge and upgrade skills, particularly in this age of rapid technological and economic changes. The educational services industry includes a variety of institutions that offer academic instruction, vocational and technical instruction, and other education and training to millions of students each year.

Because school attendance is compulsory until age 16 to 18 in all 50 States and the District of Columbia, elementary, middle, and secondary schools are the most numerous of all educational establishments. Elementary, middle, and secondary schools provide academic instruction to students in kindergarten through grade 12, in public schools, parochial schools, boarding and other private schools, and military academies. Some secondary schools provide a mixture of academic and vocational instruction.

Postsecondary institutions provide academic or technical courses or both in colleges, universities, professional schools, community or junior colleges, and technical institutes. Universities offer bachelor's, master's, and doctoral degrees, while colleges generally offer only the bachelor's degree. Professional schools offer graduate degrees in fields such as law, medicine, business administration, and engineering. The undergraduate bachelor's degree typically requires 4 years of study, while graduate degrees require additional years of study. Community colleges and technical institutes offer associate degrees, certificates, or diplomas, typically involving 2 years of study or less.

Establishments that make up the remainder of the educational services industry include libraries; vocational schools, including computer training, business and secretarial, commercial art, practical nursing, and correspondence schools; and institutions providing a variety of specialized training and services, such as curriculum development, student exchange programs, and art, music, automobile driving, and cooking schools.

In recent decades, the Nation has focused attention on the educational system because of the growing importance of producing a trained and educated workforce. Many institutions, including government, private industry, and research organizations, are involved in improving the quality of education. States have introduced performance standards in an effort to raise academic achievement among students and set standards for graduation. Additionally, a growing number of States are requiring prospective teachers to pass basic skills tests before they are allowed to teach. In an effort to promote innovation in public education, many local and State governments have authorized the creation of public charter schools, in the belief that presenting students and their parents a greater range of instructional options provides greater incentives for students—and schools—to strive for excellence. Charter schools, which usually are run by teachers and parents, or, increasingly, by private firms, operate independently of the school system, setting their own standards and practicing a variety of innovative teaching methods. Businesses strive to improve education by donating instructional equipment, lending personnel for teaching and mentoring, hosting worksite visits, and providing job shadowing and internship opportunities. Businesses also collaborate with educators to develop curriculums that will provide students with the skills they need to cope with new technology in the workplace.

Quality improvements also are being made to vocational, or career and technical, education at secondary and postsecondary schools. Academics are playing a more important role in vocational curriculums, and programs are more relevant to the local job market. Often, students must meet rigorous standards set in consultation with private industry before receiving a certificate or degree. Vocational programs are emphasizing general workplace skills such as problem solving, teamwork, and customer service. Many high schools offer tech-prep programs, which are developed jointly by high schools and community colleges to provide a continuous course of study leading to an associate's degree or other postsecondary credential.

Computer technology continues to affect the education industry. Computers simplify administrative tasks and make it easier to track student performance. Teachers use the Internet in classrooms and to communicate with colleagues around the country; students use the Internet for research projects. Distance learning continues to expand as more postsecondary institutions use Internet-based technology to post lessons and coursework electronically, allowing students in distant locations access to virtual classrooms.

Despite these quality improvements, dropout rates have not declined over the decade and many high school students still lack many of the math and communication skills needed in today's workplace, according to employers. School budgets often are not sufficient to meet the many goals that schools are trying to meet, particularly in the inner cities, where aging facilities and chronic teacher shortages make teaching difficult.

## Working Conditions

School conditions can vary from town to town. Some schools in poorer neighborhoods may be rundown, have few supplies and equipment, and lack air-conditioning. Other schools may be new and well equipped and maintained. Conditions at postsecondary institutions are generally very good. Despite conditions, seeing students develop and enjoy learning can be rewarding for teachers and other education workers. However, dealing with unmotivated students, or those with social or behavioral problems, can be stressful, and requires patience and understanding.

Most educational institutions operate 10 months a year, but summer sessions for remedial or adult students are not uncommon. Education administrators, office and administrative support workers, and janitors and cleaners often work the entire year. Night and weekend work is common for adult literacy and remedial and self-enrichment education teachers, postsecondary teachers, and library workers in postsecondary institutions. Part-time work is common for schoolbus drivers, adult literacy and remedial and self-enrichment education teachers, postsecondary teachers, teacher assistants, and some library workers. Schoolbus drivers often work a split shift, driving one or two routes in the morning and afternoon; drivers who are assigned field trips, athletic and other extracurricular activities, or midday kindergarten routes work additional hours during or after school. Many teachers spend significant time outside of school preparing for class, doing administrative tasks, conducting research, writing articles and books, and pursuing advanced degrees.

Despite occurrences of violence in some schools, educational services is a relatively safe industry. There were 2.9 cases of occupational injury and illness per 100 full-time workers in private educational establishments in 1999, compared with 6.3 in all industries combined.

## Employment

Educational services was the largest industry in the economy in 2000, providing jobs for nearly 11.9 million workers—about 11.8 million wage and salary workers, and 116,000 self-employed workers. The majority of wage and salary workers are employed in the public sector, because most students attend public educational institutions. According to the Department of Education's National Center for Education Statistics, public elementary, middle, and secondary schools accounted for more than three-fourths of all nonpostsecondary schools in 1999.

Employees in this industry are older than average; 46 percent are over the age of 45, compared with 35 percent of employees in all industries combined (table 1).

Table 1. Percent distribution of employment in educational services by age group, 2000

| Age group | Educational services | All industries |
|---|---|---|
| Total ................................................................ | 100.0% | 100.0% |
| 16-24 ............................................................. | 10.6 | 15.3 |
| 25-34 ............................................................. | 18.7 | 22.6 |
| 35-44 ............................................................. | 24.5 | 27.1 |
| 45-54 ............................................................. | 30.2 | 22.0 |
| 55-64 ............................................................. | 13.2 | 10.1 |
| 65 and older .................................................. | 2.8 | 3.0 |

## Occupations in the Industry

Workers in this industry take part in all aspects of education, from teaching and counseling students to driving schoolbuses and serving cafeteria lunches. Although most occupations are professional, the industry employs many administrative support, managerial, service, and other workers (table 2).

Teachers account for almost half of all workers in the educational services industry. Their duties depend on the age group and subject they teach and on the type of institution in which they work. Teachers should have a sincere interest in helping students and the ability to inspire respect, trust, and confidence. Strong speaking and writing skills, inquiring and analytical minds, and a desire to pursue and disseminate knowledge are vital for teachers.

*Preschool, kindergarten* and *elementary school teachers* play a critical role in the early development of children. They usually instruct one class in a variety of subjects, introducing the children to mathematics, language, science, and social studies. They use games, artwork, music, computers, and other tools to teach basic skills.

*Middle* and *secondary school teachers* help students delve more deeply into subjects introduced in elementary school. Middle and secondary school teachers specialize in a specific academic subject, such as English, mathematics, or history, or a vocational area, such as automobile mechanics, business education, or computer repair. Some supervise extracurricular activities after school and help students deal with academic problems and choose courses, colleges, and careers.

*Special education teachers* work with students—from toddlers to those in their early 20s—who have a variety of learning and physical disabilities. Most special education teachers are found at the elementary school level. Using the general education curriculum, special education teachers modify instruction to meet a student's special needs. They also help special education students develop emotionally, be comfortable in social situations, and be aware of socially acceptable behavior.

*Postsecondary teachers*, or *faculty* as they are usually called, generally are organized into departments or divisions, based on subject or field. They teach and advise college students and perform a significant part of our Nation's research. They also consult with government, business, nonprofit, and community organizations. They prepare lectures, exercises, and laboratory experiments; grade exams and papers; and advise and

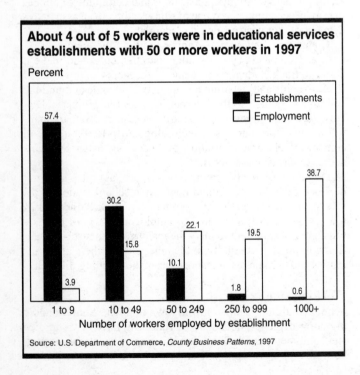

**About 4 out of 5 workers were in educational services establishments with 50 or more workers in 1997**

Percent

Legend: ■ Establishments □ Employment

| Number of workers employed by establishment | Establishments | Employment |
|---|---|---|
| 1 to 9 | 57.4 | 3.9 |
| 10 to 49 | 30.2 | 15.8 |
| 50 to 249 | 10.1 | 22.1 |
| 250 to 999 | 1.8 | 19.5 |
| 1000+ | 0.6 | 38.7 |

Source: U.S. Department of Commerce, *County Business Patterns*, 1997

**Table 2. Employment of wage and salary workers in educational services by occupation, 2000 and projected change, 2000-10**

(Employment in thousands)

| Occupation | Employment, 2000 Number | Employment, 2000 Percent | Percent change, 2000-2010 |
|---|---|---|---|
| All occupations | 11,797 | 100.0 | 13.6 |
| **Management, business, and financial occupations** | 722 | 6.1 | 11.4 |
| Education administrators | 369 | 3.1 | 13.0 |
| **Professional and related occupations** | 7,802 | 66.1 | 18.7 |
| Computer specialists | 131 | 1.1 | 44.1 |
| Educational, vocational, and school counselors | 160 | 1.4 | 24.3 |
| Postsecondary teachers | 1,256 | 10.6 | 24.3 |
| Preschool teachers, except special education | 53 | 0.5 | 10.1 |
| Kindergarten teachers, except special education | 161 | 1.4 | 13.0 |
| Elementary school teachers, except special education | 1,502 | 12.7 | 13.0 |
| Middle school teachers, except special and vocational education | 568 | 4.8 | 9.6 |
| Secondary school teachers, except special and vocational education | 1,000 | 8.5 | 18.6 |
| Vocational education teachers, secondary school | 106 | 0.9 | 13.0 |
| Special education teachers, preschool, kindergarten, and elementary school | 228 | 1.9 | 36.3 |
| Special education teachers, middle school | 94 | 0.8 | 24.3 |
| Special education teachers, secondary school | 121 | 1.0 | 24.3 |
| Adult literacy, remedial education, and GED teachers and instructors | 40 | 0.3 | 17.6 |
| Self-enrichment education teachers | 60 | 0.5 | 16.6 |
| All other teachers, primary, secondary, and adult | 399 | 3.4 | 19.7 |
| Librarians | 92 | 0.8 | 1.7 |
| Library technicians | 59 | 0.5 | 24.3 |
| Teacher assistants | 1,023 | 8.7 | 22.0 |
| Instructional coordinators | 56 | 0.5 | 24.3 |
| Registered nurses | 81 | 0.7 | 13.0 |
| Speech-language pathologists | 46 | 0.4 | 35.6 |
| **Service occupations** | 1,396 | 11.8 | 5.3 |
| Cooks, institution and cafeteria | 213 | 1.8 | -7.5 |
| Food preparation workers | 106 | 0.9 | 9.1 |
| Janitors and cleaners, except maids and housekeeping cleaners | 469 | 4.0 | 1.7 |
| Child care workers | 111 | 0.9 | 35.6 |
| **Office and administrative support occupations** | 1,216 | 10.3 | -3.7 |
| Library assistants, clerical | 43 | 0.4 | 13.0 |
| Office clerks, general | 257 | 2.2 | -9.6 |
| Executive secretaries and administrative assistants | 164 | 1.4 | 3.7 |
| Secretaries, except legal, medical, and executive | 339 | 2.9 | 0.7 |
| **Installation, maintenance, and repair occupations** | 154 | 1.3 | 5.0 |
| **Transportation and material moving occupations** | 379 | 3.2 | 2.4 |
| Busdrivers, school | 328 | 2.8 | 1.7 |

NOTE: May not add to totals due to omission of occupations with small employment.

work with students individually. Postsecondary teachers keep abreast of developments in their field by reading current litera-ture, talking with colleagues and businesses, and participating in professional conferences. They also do their own research to expand knowledge in their field, often publishing their findings in scholarly journals, books, and electronic media.

*Adult literacy and remedial and self-enrichment education teachers* provide courses in "English as a Second Language" (ESL), preparation sessions for the General Educational Development (GED) exam, and basic instruction courses to out-of-school youths and adults, and may also teach classes that students take for personal enrichment, such as cooking or dancing.

*Education administrators* provide vision, direction, leadership, and day-to-day management of educational activities in schools, colleges and universities, businesses, correctional institutions, museums, and job training and community service organizations. They set educational standards and goals and aid in establishing the policies and procedures to carry them out. They develop academic programs; monitor students' educational progress; hire, train, motivate, and evaluate teachers and other staff; manage guidance and other student services; administer recordkeeping; prepare budgets; and handle relations with staff, parents, current and prospective students, employers, and the community.

*Instructional coordinators* evaluate school curriculums and recommend changes. They research the latest teaching methods and coordinate and provide training to teachers. They also coordinate equipment purchases and assist in the use of new technology in schools.

*Educational, vocational, and school counselors*—who work at the elementary, middle, secondary, and postsecondary school levels—help students evaluate their abilities, talents, and interests so that the student can develop realistic academic and career options. They also help students understand and deal with their social, behavioral, and personal problems. Secondary school counselors use interviews, counseling sessions, tests, or other methods when advising and evaluating students. They advise on college majors, admission requirements, and entrance exams, and on trade, technical school, and apprenticeship programs. Elementary school counselors do more social and personal counseling and less vocational and academic counseling than do secondary school counselors. School counselors work with students individually or in small groups, or with entire classes.

*Librarians* help people to find information and to use it effectively in their scholastic, personal, and professional pursuits. They manage staff and develop and direct information programs and systems for the public, as well as oversee the selection and organization of library materials. Librarians may supervise *library technicians*—who help librarians acquire, prepare, and organize material; direct library users to standard references; and retrieve information from computer databases—and *library assistants, clerical*—who check out and receive library materials, collect overdue fines, and shelve materials.

*Teacher assistants*, also called teacher aides or instructional aides, provide instructional and clerical support for classroom teachers, allowing teachers more time for lesson planning and teaching. Teacher assistants tutor and assist children, particularly special education students, in learning class material using the teacher's lesson plans, providing students with individualized attention. Assistants also aid and supervise students in the cafeteria, schoolyard, or school discipline center, or on field trips. They record grades, set up equipment, and prepare materials for instruction.

*Schoolbus drivers* transport students to and from school and related events.

The educational services industry employs many other workers who are found in a wide range of industries. For example, administrative support workers such as *secretaries, administrative assistants, and general office clerks* account for about 1 out of 10 jobs in educational services.

## Training and Advancement

The educational services industry employs some of the most highly educated workers in the labor force. Postsecondary teachers, particularly college and university faculty, generally need a doctoral degree for full-time, tenure-track employment, but sometimes can teach with a master's degree, particularly at 2-year colleges. Most faculty members are hired as instructors or assistant professors and may advance to associate professor and full professor. Some faculty advance to administrative and managerial positions, such as department chairperson, dean, or president.

Kindergarten, elementary, middle, and secondary school teachers must have a bachelor's degree and complete an approved teacher training program, with a prescribed number of subject and education credits and supervised practice teaching. All States require public school teachers to be licensed; licensure requirements vary by State. Many States offer alternate licensure programs for people who have bachelor's degrees in the subject they will teach, but lack the necessary education courses required for a regular license. With additional education or certification, teachers may become school librarians, reading specialists, curriculum specialists, or guidance counselors. Some teachers advance to administrative or supervisory positions—such as department chairperson, assistant principal, or principal—but the number of these jobs is limited. In some school systems, highly qualified, experienced elementary and secondary school teachers can become senior or mentor teachers, with higher pay and additional responsibilities.

Vocational education teachers normally need work or other experience in their field—and a license or certificate, when required by the field—for full professional status. Most States require vocational education teachers and adult literacy and remedial education teachers to have a bachelor's degree and some States also require teacher certification. Self-enrichment teachers need only practical experience in the field to teach.

School counselors generally need a master's degree in a counseling specialty or a related field. All States require school counselors to hold State school counseling certification; however, certification procedures vary from State to State. Some States require public school counselors to have both counseling and teaching certificates. Depending on the State, a master's degree in counseling and 2 to 5 years of teaching experience may be required for a counseling certificate. Experienced school counselors may advance to a larger school; become directors or supervisors of counseling, guidance, or student personnel services; or, with further graduate education, become counseling psychologists or school administrators.

Training requirements for education administrators depend on where they work. Principals, assistant principals, and school administrators usually have held a teaching or related job before entering administration, and they generally need a master's or doctoral degree in education administration or educational supervision, as well as State teacher certification. Academic deans usually have a doctorate in their specialty. Education administrators may advance up an administrative ladder or transfer to larger schools or school systems. They also may become superintendent of a school system or president of an educational institution.

Training requirements for teacher assistants range from a high school diploma to some college training. Districts that assign teaching responsibilities to teacher assistants usually have higher training requirements than those that do not. Teacher assistants who obtain a bachelor's degree, usually in education, may become certified teachers.

Librarians normally need a master's degree in library science. Many States require school librarians to be licensed as teachers and have courses in library science. Experienced librarians may advance to administrative positions, such as department head, library director, or chief information officer. Training requirements for library technicians range from a high school diploma to specialized postsecondary training; a high school diploma is sufficient for library assistants. Library workers can advance—from assistant, to technician, to librarian—with experience and the required formal education. Schoolbus drivers, who need a commercial driver's license, have limited opportunities for advancement; some become supervisors or dispatchers.

## Earnings

Earnings of occupations concentrated in the educational services industry—education administrators, teachers, counselors, and librarians—are significantly higher than the average for all occupations, because the workers tend to be older and have higher levels of educational attainment. Among teachers, earnings increase with higher educational attainment and more years of service. Full-time postsecondary teachers earn the most, followed by elementary, middle, and secondary school teachers. Most teachers are paid a salary, but part-time instructors in postsecondary institutions usually are paid a fixed amount per course. Educational services employees who work the traditional school year can earn additional money during the summer in jobs related to, or outside of, education. Benefits generally are good but, as in other industries, part-time workers often do not receive the same benefits that full-time workers do. Earnings in selected occupations in educational services appear in table 3.

**Table 3. Median hourly earnings of the largest occupations in educational services, 2000**

| Occupation | Educational services | All industries |
|---|---|---|
| Educational, vocational, and school counselors | $ 21.31 | $ 20.24 |
| Librarians | 20.60 | 20.05 |
| Registered nurses | 19.27 | 21.56 |
| Self-enrichment education teachers | 14.81 | 13.44 |
| Secretaries, except legal, medical, and executive | 11.57 | 11.47 |
| Janitors and cleaners, except maids and housekeeping cleaners | 10.04 | 8.26 |
| Office clerks, general | 10.00 | 10.16 |
| Bus drivers, school | 9.96 | 10.05 |
| Child care workers | 8.48 | 7.43 |
| Cooks, institution and cafeteria | 7.71 | 8.22 |

Almost 40 percent of workers in the educational services industry—the largest number being in elementary, middle, and secondary schools—are union members or are covered by union contracts, compared with only 14.9 percent of workers in all

182

industries combined. The American Federation of Teachers and the National Education Association are the largest unions representing teachers and other school personnel.

## Outlook

Overall growth in student enrollments is expected to slow over the next 10 years, resulting in wage and salary employment growth of 14 percent in the educational services industry between 2000-10, slightly less than the 16 percent increase projected for all industries combined. However, because a greater than average number of workers in nearly all the major occupations that make up this industry—from janitors to education administrators—are over the age of 45, it is likely that a surge in baby-boomer retirements will create many job openings in addition to those due to employment growth.

A growing number of school districts, particularly those in urban and rural areas, are finding it harder to recruit all the teachers, administrators, and support personnel they need. Many schools in fast-growing areas of the country—including several States and cities in the South and West—also are experiencing difficulty recruiting education workers, especially teachers. As retirements increase over the projection decade, the number of students graduating with education degrees may not be sufficient to meet this industry's growing needs, making job opportunities for graduates in many education fields very good to excellent. Currently, alternative licensing programs are helping to attract noneducation majors into teaching. Still, math, science, and bilingual teachers should continue to have excellent opportunities. At the postsecondary level, a smaller number of Ph.D's is projected to graduate, making the market for postsecondary teachers more favorable than it has been in years. Candidates applying for tenured positions, though, will continue to face keen competition as many colleges and universities reduce the number of these positions in favor of adjunct or part-time faculty.

A growing emphasis on improving education and making it available to more children and young adults will increase overall demand for workers in education services. Reforms, such as universal preschool, all-day kindergarten, and reduced class sizes, if enacted, will require more preschool and elementary school teachers. However, flat enrollment projections at the preschool and elementary school level will reduce demand and a moderate increase in enrollment at the secondary school level will lead to average employment growth for preschool, elementary, middle, and secondary school teachers. As children of the baby boom reach college age, postsecondary student enrollments are expected to increase, spurring faster than average employment growth for postsecondary teachers.

The numbers of counselors, speech-language pathologists and audiologists, and special education teachers are projected to grow faster than average through 2010, because of increasing enrollment of special education students, continued emphasis on inclusion of disabled students in general education classrooms, and the effort to reach students with problems at younger ages. Employment of teacher assistants also will grow faster than average. School reforms call for more individual attention to students, and many teacher assistants will be needed in general, special education, and English as a Second Language classrooms.

Despite expected increases in education expenditures, budget constraints at all levels of government may place restrictions on educational services, particularly in light of the rapidly escalating cost of college tuition, special education, construction costs for new schools, and other services. Cuts in funding could affect student services—such as school busing, library and educational materials, and extracurricular activities—and employment of administrative, instructional, and support staff. Budget considerations also may affect attempts to expand school programs, such as increasing the number of counselors and teacher assistants in elementary schools

## Sources of Additional Information

Information on unions and education-related issues can be obtained from:

➢ American Federation of Teachers, 555 New Jersey Ave. NW., Washington, DC 20001. Internet: **http://www.aft.org**

➢ National Education Association, 1201 16th St. NW., Washington, DC 20036. Internet: **http://www.nea.org**

Information on most occupations in the educational services industry, including the following, appears in the 2002-03 edition of the *Occupational Outlook Handbook*:

- Busdrivers
- Counselors
- Education administrators
- Librarians
- Library assistants, clerical
- Library technicians
- Teacher assistants
- Teachers—adult literacy and remedial and self-enrichment education
- Teachers—postsecondary
- Teachers—preschool, kindergarten, elementary, middle, and secondary
- Teachers—special education

# Health Services

- Health services is one of the largest industries in the country, with more than 11 million jobs, including the self-employed.

- About 13 percent of all wage and salary jobs created between 2000 and 2010 will be in health services.

- Nine out of 20 occupations projected to grow the fastest are concentrated in health services.

- Most jobs require less than 4 years of college education.

## Nature of the Industry

Combining medical technology and the human touch, the health services industry administers care around the clock, responding to the needs of millions of people—from newborns to the critically ill.

More than 469,000 establishments make up the health services industry; all vary greatly in terms of size, staffing patterns, and organizational structures. Two-thirds of all private health services establishments are offices of physicians or dentists. Although hospitals constitute less than 2 percent of all private health services establishments, they employ nearly 40 percent of all workers (table 1). When government hospitals are included, the proportion rises to 45 percent of the workers in the industry.

**Table 1. Percent distribution of wage and salary employment and establishments in private health services, 2000**

| Establishment type | Establishments | Employment |
|---|---|---|
| Total, health services ............................. | 100.0 | 100.0 |
| Hospitals, private ..................................... | 1.6 | 39.3 |
| Offices of physicians including osteopaths ......................................... | 41.1 | 19.7 |
| Nursing and personal care facilities ............................................... | 4.5 | 17.9 |
| Offices and clinics of dentists ................ | 23.8 | 6.8 |
| Home healthcare services ..................... | 3.1 | 6.3 |
| Offices of other health practitioners ...................................... | 19.2 | 4.4 |
| Health and allied services, not elsewhere classified ................... | 3.3 | 3.5 |
| Medical and dental laboratories ...................................... | 3.5 | 2.1 |

The health services industry includes establishments ranging from small-town private practice physicians who employ only one medical assistant to busy inner city hospitals that provide thousands of diverse jobs. More than half of all non-hospital health services establishments employ fewer than 5 workers (see chart). On the other hand, almost two-thirds of hospital employees were in establishments with more than 1,000 workers (see chart on next page).

The health services industry consists of the following eight segments:

*Hospitals.* Hospitals provide complete healthcare, ranging from diagnostic services to surgery and continuous nursing care. Some hospitals specialize in treatment of the mentally ill, cancer patients, or children. Hospital-based care may be on an inpatient (overnight) or outpatient basis. The mix of workers needed varies, depending on the size, geographic location, goals, philosophy, funding, organization, and management style of the institution. As hospitals work to improve efficiency, care continues to shift from an inpatient to outpatient basis whenever possible. Many hospitals have also expanded into long-term and home healthcare services, providing a continuum of care for the communities they serve.

*Nursing and personal care facilities.* Nursing facilities provide inpatient nursing, rehabilitation, and health-related personal care to those who need continuous healthcare, but do not require hospital services. Nursing aides provide the vast majority of direct care. Other facilities, such as convalescent homes, help patients who need less assistance.

*Offices and clinics of physicians, including osteopaths.* Physicians and surgeons practice privately or in groups of practitio-

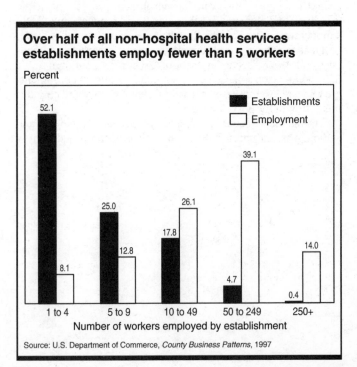

**Over half of all non-hospital health services establishments employ fewer than 5 workers**

Source: U.S. Department of Commerce, *County Business Patterns,* 1997

ners who have the same or different specialties. Group practice has become the recent trend, including clinics, freestanding emergency care centers, and ambulatory surgical centers. Physicians and surgeons are increasingly working as salaried employees of group medical practices, clinics, or integrated healthcare systems.

*Home healthcare services.* Skilled nursing or medical care is sometimes provided in the home, under a physician's supervision. Home healthcare services are provided mainly to the elderly. The development of in-home medical technologies, substantial cost savings, and patients' preference for care in the home have helped make this once small segment of the industry into one of the fastest growing in the U.S. economy.

*Offices and clinics of dentists.* Almost 1 out of every 4 healthcare establishments is a dentist's office. Most employ only a few workers, who provide general or specialized dental care, including dental surgery.

*Offices and clinics of other health practitioners.* This segment includes offices of chiropractors, optometrists, and podiatrists, as well as occupational and physical therapists, psychologists, audiologists, speech-language pathologists, dietitians, and other miscellaneous health practitioners. Demand for the services of this industry is related to the ability of patients to pay, either directly or through health insurance. Hospitals and nursing facilities may contract out for these services. This industry also includes alternative-medicine practitioners, such as acupuncturists, homeopaths, hypnotherapists, and naturopaths.

*Health and allied services, not elsewhere classified.* Among the diverse establishments in this group are kidney dialysis centers, drug treatment clinics and rehabilitation centers, blood banks, and providers of childbirth preparation classes.

*Medical and dental laboratories.* Medical laboratories provide analytic or diagnostic services to the medical profession or di-

rectly to patients following a physician's prescription. Workers may analyze blood, take x rays, or perform other clinical tests. In dental laboratories, workers make dentures, artificial teeth, and orthodontic appliances. Medical and dental laboratories provide the fewest number of jobs in health services.

In the rapidly changing health services industry, technological advances have made many new procedures and methods of diagnosis and treatment possible. Clinical developments such as organ transplants, less invasive surgical techniques, skin grafts, and gene therapy for cancer treatment continue to increase longevity and improve the quality of life for many Americans. Advances in medical technology also have improved the survival rates of trauma victims and the severely ill, who then need extensive care from therapists and social workers, among other support personnel.

Advances in information technology also continue to improve patient care and worker efficiency with devices such as hand-held computers that record notes on each patient. Information on vital signs and orders for tests are electronically transferred to a main database, eliminating paper and reducing record-keeping errors.

Cost containment also is shaping the healthcare industry, as shown by the growing emphasis on providing services on an outpatient, ambulatory basis; limiting unnecessary or low-priority services; and stressing preventive care that reduces the eventual cost of undiagnosed, untreated medical conditions. Enrollment in managed healthcare programs—predominantly Preferred Provider Organizations (PPOs), Health Maintenance Organizations (HMOs), and hybrid plans such as Point-of-Service (POS) programs—continues to grow. These prepaid plans provide comprehensive coverage to members and control health insurance costs by emphasizing preventive care. Cost effectiveness also is improved with the increased use of Integrated Delivery Systems (IDS). An IDS combines two or more segments of the industry to increase efficiency through the streamlining of functions, primarily financial and managerial. According to a 2000 Deloitte & Touche survey, only 48 percent of surveyed hospitals expect to be stand-alone, independent facilities in 2005, as compared with 61 percent in 2000. These changes will continue to reshape not only the nature of the health services workforce, but also the manner in which health services are provided.

## Working Conditions

Nonsupervisory workers in private health services averaged 33.1 hours per week in 2000, compared with 34.5 for all private industry. Hours varied somewhat among the different segments of the industry. Workers in home healthcare averaged only 29.5 hours per week; those in nursing and personal care facilities worked 32.6 hours; and hospital workers averaged 35.0 hours.

Many workers in the health services industry are on part-time schedules. Part-time workers made up 15.3 percent of the workforce as a whole in 2000, but accounted for 36.8 percent of workers in offices and clinics of dentists and 18.8 percent of those in offices of physicians. Students, parents with young children, dual jobholders, and older workers make up much of the part-time workforce.

Many health services establishments operate around the clock and need staff at all hours. Shift work is common in some occupations, such as registered nurses. Numerous health service workers hold more than one job, particularly in hospitals and in nursing and personal care facilities.

**Unlike other segments of the health services industry, almost two-thirds of hospital employees work in establishments with 1,000 or more workers**

Percent

■ Establishments
□ Employment

| Number of workers employed by establishment | Establishments | Employment |
|---|---|---|
| 1 to 9 | 2.8 | 0.0 |
| 10 to 49 | 3.5 | 0.1 |
| 50 to 249 | 33.5 | 6.7 |
| 250 to 999 | 37.7 | 27.6 |
| 1000+ | 22.5 | 65.5 |

Source: U.S. Department of Commerce, *County Business Patterns*, 1997

In 1999, the incidence rate for occupational injury and illness in hospitals was 9.2 cases per 100 full-time workers, compared with an average of 6.3 for the private sector. Nursing and personal care facilities had a much higher rate, 13.5. Healthcare workers involved in direct patient care must take precautions to guard against back strain from lifting patients and equipment, exposure to radiation and caustic chemicals, and infectious diseases such as AIDS, tuberculosis, and hepatitis. Home care personnel who make house calls are exposed to the possibility of being injured in highway accidents, all types of overexertion when assisting patients, and falls inside and outside homes.

## Employment

The health services industry provided more than 11 million wage and salary jobs in 2000. Almost one-half of all salaried health services jobs were in hospitals; another one-third were in either nursing and personal care facilities or offices of physicians including osteopaths. About 91 percent of wage and salary jobs were in the private sector; the remainder, in State and local government hospitals.

In 2000, there were about 383,000 self-employed workers in the health services industry. Of these, more than two-thirds were in offices of physicians, dentists, and other health practitioners. Health services jobs are found throughout the country, but are concentrated in large States, specifically California, New York, Florida, Texas, and Pennsylvania.

Workers in health services tend to be older than workers in other industries. They are also more likely to remain employed in the same occupation due, in part, to the high level of education and training required for many health occupations.

## Occupations in the Industry

Health services firms employ large numbers of workers in professional and service occupations. Together, these two occupational groups cover nearly 3 out of 4 jobs in the industry. The next largest share of jobs is in office and administrative support. Management, business, and financial operations occupations account for only 4.9 percent of employment. Other occupations in health services comprise only 2.5 percent of the total (table 2).

Professional occupations such as *physicians and surgeons, dentists, registered nurses, social workers,* and *physical therapists*, usually require at least a bachelor's degree in a specialized field or higher education in a specific health field, although *registered nurses* also enter through associate degree or diploma programs. Professional workers often have high levels of responsibility and complex duties. They may supervise other workers or conduct research, as well as provide services.

Other health professionals and technicians work in many fast growing occupations, such as *medical records and health information technicians* and *dental hygienists*. These workers may operate technical equipment and assist health diagnosing and treating practitioners. Graduates of 1- or 2-year training programs often fill these positions; these jobs usually require specific formal training beyond high school, but less than 4 years of college.

Service occupations attract many workers with little or no specialized education or training. This group includes *nursing aides, home health aides, maids and housekeeping cleaners, dental assistants, medical assistants,* and *personal and home care aides*. Service workers may advance to higher level positions or transfer to new occupations, with experience and, in some cases, further education and training.

Most jobs in health services provide clinical services, but there also are many in occupations with other functions as well. Numerous workers in management and administrative support jobs keep organizations running smoothly. Although many *medical and health services managers* have a background in a clinical specialty or training in health services administration, some enter these jobs with a general business education.

Each segment of the health services industry employs a different mix of health-related occupations and other workers.

*Hospitals.* Hospitals employ workers with all levels of education and training to provide a wider variety of services than other segments of the health services industry. About 1 in 4 hospital workers is a *registered nurse*. Hospitals also employ many *physicians and surgeons, therapists,* and *social workers*. About 1 in 5 jobs is in a service occupation, such as *nursing, psychiatric, and home health aide,* or *building cleaning worker*. Hospitals also employ large numbers of office and administrative support workers.

*Nursing and personal care facilities.* More than three-fifths of all nursing facility jobs are in service occupations, primarily *nursing, psychiatric, and home health aides*. Professional and administrative support occupations are a much smaller percentage of employment in nursing facilities than in other parts of the health services industry. Federal law requires nursing facilities to have licensed personnel on hand 24 hours a day, and to maintain an appropriate level of care.

*Offices and clinics of physicians, including osteopaths.* Many of the jobs in offices of physicians are in professional and related occupations, primarily *physicians and surgeons* and *registered nurses*. A large number of jobs, however, are in office and administrative support occupations, such as *receptionists and information clerks*, who comprise one-third of the workers in physicians' offices.

*Home health care services.* More than half of the jobs in home health care are in service occupations, mostly *home health aides* and *personal and home care aides*. Nursing and therapist jobs also account for substantial shares of employment in this industry.

*Offices and clinics of dentists.* More than one-third of the jobs in this segment are in service occupations, mostly *dental assistants*. The typical staffing pattern in dentists' offices consists of one professional with a support staff of *dental hygienists* and *dental assistants*. Larger practices are more likely to employ office managers and administrative support workers, as well as *dental laboratory technicians*.

*Offices and clinics of other health practitioners.* Professional and related occupations accounted for about 2 in 5 jobs in this segment, including *physical therapists*, *occupational therapists*, *dispensing opticians*, and *chiropractors*. Office and administrative support occupations also accounted for a significant portion of all jobs, almost one-third.

*Medical and dental laboratories.* Professional and related workers account for more than one-third of all jobs in this industry segment, primarily *clinical laboratory* and *radiologic technologists and technicians*. Unlike the case in other segments of the health services industry, many jobs also are in production occupations—most notably, *dental laboratory technicians*.

**Table 2. Employment of wage and salary workers in health services by occupation, 2000 and projected change, 2000-10**

(Employment in thousands)

| Occupation | Employment, 2000 Number | Employment, 2000 Percent | Percent change, 2000-2010 |
|---|---|---|---|
| **All occupations** | 11,065 | 100.0 | 25.5 |
| **Management, business, and financial occupations** | 546 | 4.9 | 27.3 |
| Medical and health services managers | 167 | 1.5 | 34.9 |
| Business operations specialists | 87 | 0.8 | 19.2 |
| **Professional and related occupations** | 4,975 | 45.0 | 26.9 |
| Social workers | 110 | 1.0 | 37.2 |
| Dentists | 86 | 0.8 | 13.7 |
| Physicians and surgeons | 459 | 4.1 | 27.8 |
| Registered nurses | 1,774 | 16.0 | 25.3 |
| Physical therapists | 109 | 1.0 | 36.7 |
| Medical and clinical laboratory technologists | 133 | 1.2 | 18.0 |
| Medical and clinical laboratory technicians | 121 | 1.1 | 18.9 |
| Dental hygienists | 142 | 1.3 | 37.1 |
| Radiologic technologists and technicians | 159 | 1.4 | 23.5 |
| Health diagnosing and treating practitioner support technicians | 210 | 1.9 | 23.9 |
| Licensed practical and licensed vocational nurses | 552 | 5.0 | 18.8 |
| Medical records and health information technicians | 118 | 1.1 | 54.1 |
| **Service occupations** | 3,275 | 29.6 | 29.5 |
| Dental assistants | 237 | 2.1 | 37.8 |
| Home health aides | 261 | 2.4 | 59.6 |
| Nursing aides, orderlies, and attendants | 1,053 | 9.5 | 21.7 |
| Medical assistants | 301 | 2.7 | 59.8 |
| Medical transcriptionists | 87 | 0.8 | 30.3 |
| Food preparation workers | 98 | 0.9 | 15.4 |
| Food and beverage serving workers | 97 | 0.9 | 3.9 |
| Janitors and cleaners, except maids and housekeeping cleaners | 93 | 0.8 | 21.9 |
| Maids and housekeeping cleaners | 245 | 2.2 | 12.4 |
| Personal and home care aides | 160 | 1.4 | 66.8 |
| **Office and administrative support occupations** | 1,987 | 18.0 | 16.0 |
| First-line supervisors/managers of office and administrative support workers | 147 | 1.3 | 3.3 |
| Billing and posting clerks and machine operators | 166 | 1.5 | 29.0 |
| Bookkeeping, accounting, and auditing clerks | 96 | 0.9 | 15.6 |
| Receptionists and information clerks | 288 | 2.6 | 26.6 |
| Office clerks, general | 264 | 2.4 | 12.2 |
| Medical secretaries | 280 | 2.5 | 20.0 |
| Secretaries, except legal, medical, and executive | 144 | 1.3 | 2.1 |
| **Installation, maintenance, and repair occupations** | 80 | 0.7 | 9.8 |
| **Production occupations** | 118 | 1.1 | 13.7 |

NOTE: May not add to totals due to omission of occupations with small employment.

*Health and allied services, not elsewhere classified.* This segment of the health services industry employs the highest percentage of professional and related workers, including *counselors*, *social workers*, and *registered nurses*.

## Training and Advancement

A variety of programs after high school provide specialized training for jobs in health services. Students preparing for healthcare careers can enter programs leading to a certificate or a degree at the associate, baccalaureate, professional, or graduate level. Two-year programs resulting in certificates or associate degrees are the minimum standard credential for occupations such as *dental hygienist* or *radiologic technologist*. Most *therapists* and *social workers* have at least a bachelor's degree; *physicians and surgeons*, *optometrists*, and *podiatrists* have significant additional education and training beyond college. Persons considering careers in healthcare should have a strong desire to help others, genuine concern for the welfare of patients and clients, and an ability to deal with diverse people and stressful situations.

The health services industry provides many job opportunities for people without specialized training beyond high school. In fact, 56 percent of the workers in nursing and personal care facilities have a high school diploma or less, as do 25 percent of the workers in hospitals.

Some health services establishments provide on-the-job or classroom training, as well as continuing education. For example, in all certified nursing facilities, nursing aides must complete a State-approved training and competency evaluation program and participate in at least 12 hours of in service education annually. Hospitals are more likely than other segments of the industry to have the resources and incentive to provide training programs and advancement opportunities to their employees. In other segments, staffing patterns tend to be more fixed and the variety of positions and advancement opportunities more limited. Larger establishments usually offer a broader range of opportunities.

Some hospitals provide training or tuition assistance in return for a promise to work for a particular length of time in the hospital after graduation. Many nursing facilities have similar programs. Some hospitals have cross-training programs that train their workers—through formal college programs, continuing education, or in-house training—to perform functions outside their specialties.

Health specialists with clinical expertise can advance to department head positions or even higher level management jobs. *Medical and health services managers* can advance to more responsible positions, all the way up to chief executive officer.

## Earnings

Average earnings of nonsupervisory workers in health services are slightly higher than the average for all private industry, with hospital workers earning considerably more than the average, and those in nursing and personal care facilities and home healthcare services earning less (table 3). Average earnings often are higher in hospitals because the percentage of jobs requiring higher levels of education and training is greater than in other segments. Segments of the industry with lower earnings employ large numbers of part-time service workers.

As in most industries, professionals and managers working in health services typically earn more than other workers do. Earnings in individual health services occupations vary as widely

**Table 3. Average earnings and hours of nonsupervisory workers in private health services by industry segment, 2000**

| Industry segment | Earnings Weekly | Earnings Hourly | Weekly hours |
|---|---|---|---|
| Total, private industry | $474 | $13.74 | 34.5 |
| Health services | 488 | 14.75 | 33.1 |
| Hospitals | 577 | 16.49 | 35.0 |
| Offices and clinics of medical doctors | 507 | 15.46 | 32.8 |
| Offices and clinics of dentists | 436 | 15.58 | 28.0 |
| Offices and clinics of other health practitioners | 401 | 13.15 | 30.5 |
| Home health care services | 367 | 12.44 | 29.5 |
| Nursing and personal care facilities | 349 | 10.72 | 32.6 |

as their duties, level of education and training, and amount of responsibility (table 4). Some establishments offer tuitionreimbursement, paid training, child daycare services, and flexible work hours. Healthcare establishments that must be staffed around the clock to care for patients and handle emergencies often pay premiums for overtime and weekend work, holidays, late shifts, and time spent on call. Bonuses and profit-sharing payments also may add to earnings.

Earnings vary not only by type of establishment and occupation, but also by size. Salaries are often higher in larger hospitals and group practices. Geographic location also can affect earnings.

**Table 4. Median hourly earnings of the largest occupations in health services, 2000**

| Occupation | Health services | All industries |
|---|---|---|
| Medical and health services managers | $ 27.12 | $ 27.10 |
| Dental hygienists | 24.70 | 24.68 |
| Registered nurses | 21.56 | 21.56 |
| Radiologic technologists and technicians | 17.25 | 17.31 |
| Licensed practical and licensed vocational nurses | 13.96 | 14.15 |
| Dental assistants | 12.47 | 12.49 |
| Medical assistants | 11.07 | 11.06 |
| Receptionists and information clerks | 10.15 | 9.63 |
| Nursing aides, orderlies, and attendants | 8.83 | 8.89 |
| Home health aides | 8.10 | 8.23 |

Unionization is more common in hospitals, although most segments of the health services industry are not heavily unionized. In 2000, 13.8 percent of hospital workers and 10.1 percent of workers in nursing and personal care facilities were members of unions or covered by union contracts, compared with 13.5 percent of all workers in private industry.

## Outlook

Wage and salary employment in the health services industry is projected to increase more than 25 percent through 2010, compared with an average of 16 percent for all industries (table 5). Employment growth is expected to account for about 2.8 million new jobs—13 percent of all wage and salary jobs added to

the economy over the 2000-10 period. Projected rates of employment growth for the various segments of this industry range from 10 percent in hospitals, the largest and slowest growing industry segment, to 68 percent in the much smaller home healthcare services.

**Table 5. Employment of wage and salary workers in health services by industry segment, 2000 and projected change 2000-10**

(Employment in thousands)

| Occupation | Employment, 2000 | Percent change, 2000- 2010 |
|---|---|---|
| All industries | 133,718 | 16.5 |
| Health services | 11,065 | 25.5 |
| Hospitals, public and private | 4,960 | 9.8 |
| Offices of physicians including osteopaths | 1,973 | 43.8 |
| Nursing and personal care facilities | 1,796 | 21.9 |
| Offices and clinics of dentists | 686 | 25.6 |
| Home health care services | 643 | 68.0 |
| Offices of other health practitioners | 439 | 46.8 |
| Health and allied services, not elsewhere classified | 358 | 53.6 |
| Medical and dental laboratories | 209 | 29.2 |

Many of the occupations projected to grow fastest are concentrated in the health services industry. For example, by 2010, employment within the health services industry of *personal and home care aides* is projected to increase by 67 percent, *medical assistants* by 60 percent, *physician assistants* by 57 percent, and *medical records and health information technicians* by 54 percent.

Employment in health services will continue to grow for a number of reasons. The elderly population, a group with much greater than average healthcare needs, will grow faster than the total population between 2000 and 2010, increasing the demand for health services, especially for home healthcare and nursing and personal care. Advances in medical technology will continue to improve the survival rate of severely ill and injured patients, who will then need extensive therapy and care. In addition, new technologies enable the identification and treatment of conditions not previously treatable. Medical group practices and integrated healthcare systems will become larger and more complex, increasing the need for office and administrative support workers. Also contributing to industry growth will be the shift from inpatient to less expensive outpatient care, made possible by technological improvements and Americans' increasing awareness of and emphasis on all aspects of health. Various combinations of all these factors will ensure robust growth in this massive, diverse industry.

Employment growth in the hospital segment will be the slowest within the health services industry, as the segment consolidates to control costs and as clinics and other alternate care sites become more common. Hospitals will streamline healthcare delivery operations, provide more outpatient care, and rely less on inpatient care. Job opportunities, however, will remain plentiful because hospitals employ a large number of people. Besides job openings due to employment growth, additional openings will result as workers leave the labor force or transfer to other occupations. Occupations with the most replacement openings are usually large, with high turnover due to low pay and status, poor benefits, low training requirements, and a high proportion of young and part-time workers, such as *nursing, psychiatric, and home health aides*. Occupations with relatively few replacement openings, on the other hand, are those with high pay and status, lengthy training requirements, and a high proportion of full-time workers, such as *physicians and surgeons*.

The fastest growth is expected for workers in occupations concentrated outside the inpatient hospital sector, such as *medical assistants* and *personal and home care aides*. Because of cost pressures, many healthcare facilities will adjust their staffing patterns to lower bottom-line labor costs. Where patient care demands and regulations allow, healthcare facilities will substitute lower-paid providers and cross-train their workforce. Many facilities have cut the number of middle managers, while simultaneously creating new managerial positions as they diversify. Because traditional inpatient hospital positions are no longer the only option for many future healthcare workers, persons seeking a career in the field must be flexible and forward-looking (see chart).

The demand for dental care will increase due to population growth, greater retention of natural teeth by middle-aged and older persons, and greater awareness of the importance of dental care and ability to pay for services.

For some management, business, and financial operations occupations, rapid growth will be countered by restructuring to reduce administrative costs and streamline operations. The effects of office automation and other technological changes will slow employment growth in office and administrative support occupations but, because the employment base is large, replacement needs will continue to create substantial numbers of job openings. Slower growing service occupations also will have job openings due to replacement needs.

Technological changes, such as increased laboratory automation, will negatively affect the demand for other occupations as well. For example, the use of robotics in blood analysis may limit job growth of *medical and clinical laboratory technologists and technicians*, although the nature of healthcare precludes wholesale productivity gains in many instances.

Health services workers at all levels of education and training will continue to be in demand. In many cases, it may be easier for job seekers with health-specific training to obtain jobs and advance. Specialized clinical training is a requirement for many jobs in health services and is an asset even for many administrative jobs that do not specifically require it.

## Sources of Additional Information

For referrals to hospital human resource departments about local opportunities in healthcare careers, contact:

➢ American Hospital Association/American Society for Hospital Human Resources Administrators, One North Franklin, Chicago, IL 60606.

For additional information on specific health-related occupations, contact:

➢ American Medical Association/Health Professions Career and Education Directory, 515 N. State St., Chicago, IL 60610. Internet:
**http://www.ama-assn.org/ama/pub/category/2322.html**

There is also a wealth of information on health careers and job opportunities available through the Internet, schools, libraries, associations, and employers.

Information on the following occupations may be found in the 2002-03 *Occupational Outlook Handbook*:

- Cardiovascular technologists and technicians
- Chiropractors
- Clinical laboratory technologists and technicians
- Dental assistants
- Dental hygienists
- Dental laboratory technicians
- Dentists
- Diagnostic medical sonographers
- Dietitians and nutritionists
- Emergency medical technicians and paramedics
- Licensed practical and licensed vocational nurses
- Medical and health services managers
- Medical assistants
- Medical records and health information technicians
- Medical secretaries
- Medical transcriptionists
- Nuclear medicine technologists
- Nursing, psychiatric, and home health aides
- Occupational therapist assistants and aides
- Occupational therapists
- Ophthalmic laboratory technicians
- Opticians, dispensing
- Optometrists
- Personal and home care aides
- Pharmacists

**The proportion of health services jobs in public and private hospitals will decrease by 2010.**

Percent

| | Hospitals, public and private | Offices of physicians, including osteopaths | Nursing and personal care facilities | Home health care services | All other health services |
|---|---|---|---|---|---|
| 2000 | 45 | 18 | 16 | 6 | 15 |
| 2010 | 39 | 20 | 16 | 8 | 17 |

- Pharmacy aides
- Pharmacy technicians
- Physical therapist assistants and aides
- Physical therapists
- Physician assistants
- Physicians and surgeons
- Podiatrists
- Psychologists
- Radiologic technologists and technicians
- Receptionists and information clerks
- Recreational therapists
- Registered nurses
- Respiratory therapists
- Social and human service assistants
- Social workers
- Speech-language pathologists and audiologists
- Surgical technologists
- Veterinarians

# Hotels and Other Lodging Places

(SIC 70)

## SIGNIFICANT POINTS

- Service occupations, by far the largest occupational group, account for 66 percent of the industry's employment.

- Hotels employ many young workers and others in part-time and seasonal jobs.

- Average earnings are lower than in most other industries.

## Nature of the Industry

Hotels and lodging places are as diverse as the many families and business travelers they accommodate. The industry includes all types of lodging, from upscale hotels to campgrounds. Motels, spas, inns, and boarding houses also are included. In fact, nearly 60,000 establishments provided overnight accommodations to suit many different needs and budgets in 2000.

Establishments vary greatly in size and in the services they provide. *Hotels* and *motels* make up the majority of establishments and tend to provide more services than other lodging places. There are four basic types of hotels—*commercial, resort, residential,* and *extended-stay.* Most hotels and motels are *commercial* properties that cater mainly to business people, tourists, and other travelers who need accommodations for a brief stay. Commercial hotels and motels usually are located in cities or suburban areas and operate year round. Larger properties offer a variety of services for their guests, including coffee shops, restaurants, and cocktail lounges with live entertainment. Some even provide gift shops, newsstands, barber and beauty shops, laundry and valet services, theater and airline counters, swimming pools, and fitness centers and health spas.

Larger hotels and motels often have banquet rooms, exhibit halls, and spacious ballrooms to accommodate conventions, business meetings, wedding receptions, and other social gatherings. Conventions and business meetings are major sources of revenue for these hotels and motels. Some commercial hotels are known as *conference hotels*—fully self-contained entities specifically designed for meetings. They provide physical and recreational facilities for meetings in addition to state-of-the-art audiovisual and technical equipment.

*Resort hotels* and *motels* offer luxurious surroundings with a variety of recreational facilities like swimming pools, golf courses, tennis courts, gamerooms, and health spas, as well as planned social activities and entertainment. Resorts are located primarily in vacation destinations near mountains, the seashore, or other attractions. As a result, the business of many resorts fluctuates with the season. Some resort hotels and motels provide additional convention and conference facilities to encourage customers to combine business with pleasure. During their off season, they solicit conventions, sales meetings, and incentive tours to fill their otherwise empty rooms.

*Residential hotels* provide living quarters for permanent and semipermanent residents. They combine the comfort of apartment living with the convenience of hotel services. Many have dining rooms and restaurants that also are open to the general public.

*Extended-stay hotels* combine features of a resort and a residential hotel. Typically guests use these hotels for a minimum of 5 consecutive nights. These facilities usually provide rooms with fully equipped kitchens, entertainment systems, ironing boards and irons, office spaces with computer and telephone lines, access to fitness centers, and other amenities.

In addition to hotels and motels, *inns, campgrounds*, and *spas* provide lodging for overnight guests. *Inns* vary greatly in size, appearance, type of operation, and cost. Some inns are very large and provide services similar to those found in hotels, while others are quite small and often run by families. Their appeal is quaintness, with unusual service and decor. *Campgrounds,* including *trailer and recreational vehicle (RV) parks,* cater to people who enjoy recreational camping at moderate prices. Some campgrounds provide service stations, general stores, shower and toilet facilities, and coin-operated laundries. Although some are designed for overnight travelers only, others are for vacationers who stay longer. *Spas* may offer an all-inclusive package with lodging, food, and various programs for health-conscious guests, such as massage and exercise classes. Most spas are small, with fewer than 80 guestrooms.

In recent years, hotels, motels, camps, and RV parks affiliated with national chains have been growing rapidly. To the traveler, familiar chain establishments represent dependability and quality at predictable rates. National corporations own many chains, although several others are independently owned, but affiliated with a chain through a franchise agreement.

Increased competition and more sophisticated travelers have induced the chains to provide lodging to serve a variety of customer budgets and accommodation preferences. In general, these lodging places may be grouped into properties that offer luxury, all-suite, moderately priced, and economy accommodations. The numbers of limited service or economy chain properties—economy lodging without lobbies, restaurants, lounges, and meeting rooms—has been growing. These properties are not as costly to build and operate. They appeal to budget-conscious family vacationers and travelers who are willing to sacrifice amenities for lower room prices.

While economy chains have become more important, the movement in the hotel and lodging industry is towards more extended-stay properties. In addition to fully equipped kitchenettes and laundry services, the extended-stay market offers guest amenities like inroom access to the Internet and grocery shopping. This segment has eliminated traditional hotel lobbies and 24-hour personnel, and housekeeping is usually only done about once a week. This helps keep costs to a minimum.

All-suite facilities, especially popular with business travelers, offer a living room and a bedroom. These accommodations are aimed at travelers who require lodging for extended stays, families traveling with children, and business people needing to conduct small meetings without the expense of renting an additional room.

Increased competition among establishments in this industry has spurred many independently owned and operated hotels and other lodging places to join national or international reservation systems, which allow travelers to make multiple reservations for lodging, airlines, and car rentals with one telephone call. Nearly all hotel chains operate online reservation systems through the Internet.

## Working Conditions

Work in hotels and other lodging places can be hectic, particularly for those providing check-in and checkout services. Hotel desk clerks must quickly, accurately, and cordially process large numbers of sometimes impatient and irate guests. Hotel managers often experience pressure and stress when coordinating a wide range of events such as conventions, business meetings, and social gatherings. Further, large groups of tourists can present unusual problems requiring extra work and long hours.

Because hotels are open around the clock, employees frequently work varying shifts. Employees who work the late shift generally receive additional compensation. Although managers who live in the hotel usually have regular work schedules, they may be called at any time in the event of an emergency. Those who are self-employed tend to work long hours and often live at the establishment.

Food preparation and food service workers in hotels must withstand the strain of working during busy periods and being on their feet for many hours. Kitchen workers lift heavy pots and kettles and work near hot ovens and grills. Job hazards include slips and falls, cuts, and burns, but injuries are seldom serious. Food service workers often carry heavy trays of food, dishes, and glassware. Many of these workers work part time, including evenings, weekends, and holidays.

In 1999, work-related injuries and illnesses averaged 7.8 for every 100 full-time workers in hotels and other lodging places, compared with 6.3 for workers throughout private industry. Work hazards include burns from hot equipment, sprained muscles and wrenched backs from heavy lifting, and falls on wet floors.

## Employment

Hotels and other lodging places provided 1.9 million wage and salary jobs in 2000. In addition, there were about 56,000 self-employed workers in the industry, who were found mostly in lodging places other than hotels and motels, such as inns, campgrounds, and spas.

Employment is concentrated in densely populated cities and resort areas. Compared with establishments in other industries, hotels, motels, and other lodging places tend to be small. Over 90 percent employed fewer than 50 people; about 60 percent employ fewer than 10 workers (see chart). As a result, lodging establishments offer opportunities for those who are interested in owning and running their own business. Although establishments tend to be small, most jobs are in large hotels and motels with more than 50 employees.

Many of the industry's workers are young because hotels and other lodging places provide first jobs to many new entrants to the labor force. Almost 21 percent of the workers were younger than age 25, compared with about 15 percent across all industries (table 1).

Table 1. Percent distribution of employment in hotels and other lodging places by age group, 2000

| Age group | Hotels and other lodging services | All industries |
|---|---|---|
| Total | 100.0 | 100.0 |
| 16-19 | 7.4 | 5.4 |
| 20-24 | 13.5 | 9.9 |
| 25-34 | 23.2 | 22.6 |
| 35-44 | 16.7 | 22.0 |
| 55-64 | 9.1 | 10.1 |
| 65 and older | 4.0 | 3.0 |

## Occupations in the Industry

The vast majority of workers in this industry—over 4 out of 5 in 2000—were employed in service and office and administrative support occupations (table 2). Workers in these occupations usually learn their skills on the job. Postsecondary education is not required for most entry-level positions; however, college training may be helpful for advancement in some of these occupations. For many administrative support and service occupations, personality traits and special abilities may be more important than formal schooling. Traits most important for success in the hotel and motel industry are good communication skills; the ability to get along with people in stressful situations; a neat, clean appearance; and a pleasant manner.

*Service occupations*, by far the largest occupational group, account for 66 percent of the industry's employment. Most service jobs are in housekeeping and building service occupations—including maids, housekeepers, janitors, linenroom attendants, and laundry workers—and in food preparation and service jobs—including chefs and cooks, waiters and waitresses, bartenders, food counter workers, and various kitchen workers.

Workers in *cleaning* and *housekeeping occupations* ensure that the lodging facility is clean and in good condition for the comfort and safety of guests. *Maids and housekeepers* clean lobbies, halls, guestrooms, and bathrooms. They make sure

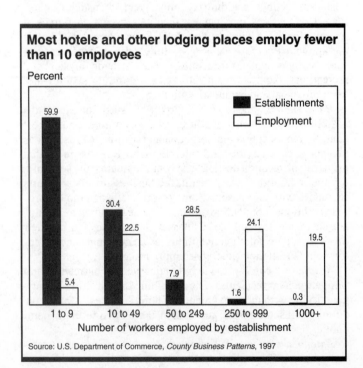

**Most hotels and other lodging places employ fewer than 10 employees**

Percent

Number of workers employed by establishment

Source: U.S. Department of Commerce, *County Business Patterns*, 1997

**Table 1. Employment of wage and salary workers in hotels and other lodging places by occupation, 2000 and projected change, 2000-10.**

(Employment in thousands)

| Occupation | Employment, 2000 Number | Employment, 2000 Percent | Percent change, 2000-2010 |
|---|---|---|---|
| **All occupations** | 1,912 | 100.0 | 13.3 |
| **Management, business, and financial occupations** | 126 | 6.6 | 14.8 |
| Food service managers | 15 | 0.8 | -8.5 |
| General and operations managers | 20 | 1.1 | 15.6 |
| Lodging managers | 29 | 1.5 | 7.3 |
| **Service occupations** | 1,260 | 65.9 | 10.2 |
| Security guards | 33 | 1.7 | 7.7 |
| Chefs and head cooks | 16 | 0.8 | -14.8 |
| First-line supervisors/managers of food preparation and serving workers | 20 | 1.0 | 24.3 |
| Cooks, restaurant | 58 | 3.0 | -12.2 |
| Food preparation workers | 21 | 1.1 | 19.6 |
| Bartenders | 42 | 2.2 | 12.2 |
| Combined food preparation and serving workers, including fast food | 16 | 0.8 | -6.5 |
| Food servers, nonrestaurant | 44 | 2.3 | 24.6 |
| Waiters and waitresses | 152 | 8.0 | -27.7 |
| Dining room and cafeteria attendants and bartender helpers | 53 | 2.8 | -0.4 |
| Dishwashers | 47 | 2.5 | -0.5 |
| Hosts and hostesses, restaurant, lounge, and coffee shop | 25 | 1.3 | -30.6 |
| First-line supervisors/managers of housekeeping and janitorial workers | 36 | 1.9 | 24.3 |
| Janitors and cleaners, except maids and housekeeping cleaners | 61 | 3.2 | 24.0 |
| Maids and housekeeping cleaners | 405 | 21.2 | 24.5 |
| Landscaping and groundskeeping workers | 21 | 1.1 | 20.8 |
| Gaming supervisors | 18 | 0.9 | 9.7 |
| Gaming dealers | 48 | 2.5 | 19.8 |
| Baggage porters and bellhops | 26 | 1.4 | 12.1 |
| **Sales and related occupations** | 58 | 3.0 | 22.9 |
| Cashiers, except gaming | 20 | 1.0 | 23.1 |
| Gaming change persons and booth cashiers | 16 | 0.8 | 24.8 |
| **Office and administrative support occupations** | 306 | 16.0 | 21.8 |
| Bookkeeping, accounting, and auditing clerks | 25 | 1.3 | 6.7 |
| Hotel, motel, and resort desk clerks | 167 | 8.7 | 34.1 |
| **Installation, maintenance, and repair occupations** | 76 | 4.0 | 12.0 |
| Maintenance and repair workers, general | 61 | 3.2 | 9.4 |
| **Production occupations** | 38 | 2.0 | 23.7 |
| Laundry and dry-cleaning workers | 30 | 1.6 | 24.7 |
| **Transportation and material moving occupations** | 32 | 1.7 | 16.5 |

NOTE: May not add to totals due to omission of occupations with small employment.

guests not only have clean rooms, but all the necessary furnishings and supplies. They change sheets and towels, vacuum carpets, dust furniture, empty wastebaskets, and mop bathroom floors. In large hotels, the housekeeping staff may include assistant housekeepers, floor supervisors, housekeepers, and executive housekeepers. *Janitors* help with the cleaning of the facility and perform minor maintenance work. They may fix leaky faucets, do some painting and carpentry, see that heating and air conditioning equipment works properly, empty trash, mow lawns, and exterminate pests.

Workers in the various *food service* occupations deal with customers in the dining room or at a service counter. *Waiters and waitresses* take customers' orders, serve meals, and prepare checks. In restaurants, they may describe chef's specials and suggest appropriate wines. In small establishments, they often set tables, escort guests to their seats, accept payments, and clear tables. They also may deliver room service orders to guests. In large restaurants, some of these tasks are assigned to other workers.

*Hosts and hostesses* welcome guests, show them to their tables, and give them menus. *Bartenders* fill beverage orders that waiters and waitresses take from the customers at tables and seated at the bar. *Dining room and cafeteria attendants* and *bartender helpers* assist waiters, waitresses, and bartenders by clearing, cleaning, and setting up tables, and by keeping the serving areas stocked with linens, tableware, and other supplies. *Counter attendants* take orders and serve food at fast-food counters and in coffee shops. They also may operate the cash register.

Workers in the various *food preparation* occupations prepare food in the kitchen. Beginners may advance to more skilled food preparation jobs with experience or specialized culinary training. *Food preparation workers* shred lettuce for salads, cut up food for cooking, and perform simple cooking under the direction of the chef or head cook. *Chefs* and *cooks* generally prepare a wide selection of dishes, often cooking individual servings to order. Large hotels employ cooks who specialize in the preparation of many different kinds of food. They may have titles such as salad chef, roast chef, sauce chef, or dessert chef. Chef positions generally are attained after years of experience and, sometimes, formal training, including apprenticeships. Large establishments also have *chief stewards* and *assistant stewards* who plan menus, purchase food, and supervise various kitchen personnel.

Many full-service hotels employ a uniformed staff to assist arriving and departing guests. *Baggage porters and bellhops* carry bags and escort guests to their rooms. *Concierges* arrange special or personal services for guests. They may take messages, arrange for babysitting, make hotel reservations in other cities, arrange for or give advice on entertainment, and monitor requests for housekeeping and maintenance. *Doorkeepers* help guests into and out of their cars or taxis, summon taxis, and carry baggage into the hotel lobby.

Hotels also employ the largest percentage of *gaming services* workers because many hotels have casinos. Some positions are associated with oversight and direction—supervision, surveillance, and investigation—while others involve working with the games or patrons themselves, such as tending the slot machines, handling money, writing and running tickets, and dealing cards.

*Office and administrative support* positions account for 16 percent of the jobs in hotels and other lodging places. Hotel desk clerks, secretaries, bookkeeping and accounting clerks, and telephone operators ensure that the front office operates smoothly. The majority of these workers are *hotel, motel, and resort desk clerks*. They process reservations and guests' registration and checkout, monitor arrivals and departures, handle complaints, and receive and forward mail. The duties of hotel desk clerks depend on the size of the facility. In small lodging places, one clerk or a manager may do everything. In large hotels, the duties are divided among several types of clerks. Although hotel desk clerks sometimes are hired from the outside, openings usually are filled by promoting other hotel employees such as bellhops and porters, credit clerks, and other administrative support workers.

*Public relations workers* must be completely familiar with all hotel operations and policies and act as spokespersons for the hotel. They may handle press, community, and consumer relations, and prepare radio or television announcements as well as newspaper and magazine articles. Some hotels combine the public relations functions with advertising or sales. *Advertising workers* design and coordinate advertising campaigns and oversee the production of promotional literature.

Hotels and other lodging places employ many different types of *managers* to direct and coordinate the activities of the front office, kitchen, dining room, and other departments, such as housekeeping, accounting, personnel, purchasing, publicity, sales, and maintenance. Managers make decisions on room rates, establish credit policy, and have ultimate responsibility for resolving problems. In small establishments, the manager also may perform much of the front office clerical work. In the smallest establishments, the owners—sometimes a family team—do all the work necessary to operate the business.

*Lodging managers* or *general and operations managers* in large hotels often have several assistant managers, each responsible for a phase of operations. For example, *food service managers* oversee restaurants, lounges, and catering operations. Large hotels and conference centers also employ *public relations* and *sales managers* to promote their image as well as to bring in business. Large hotels have many different sales managers, including convention managers, merchandise managers, foreign sales managers, and tour and agency managers. They often travel around the country selling their meeting, banquet, and convention facilities.

Hotels employ a variety of workers found in many other industries. Among these are cashiers, accountants, personnel workers, entertainers, recreation workers, and maintenance workers, such as stationary engineers, plumbers, and painters. Still others include guards and security officers, barbers, cosmetologists, valets, gardeners, and parking attendants.

## Training and Advancement
Although the skills and experience needed by workers in this industry depend on the specific occupation, most entry-level jobs require little or no previous training. Basic tasks usually can be learned in a short time. Almost all workers in the hotel and other lodging places industry undergo on-the-job training, which usually is provided under the supervision of an experienced employee or manager. Some large chain operations have formal training sessions for new employees, and others have video training programs.

Hotel operations are becoming increasingly complex, with a greater emphasis being placed on specialized training. Therefore, the demand is increasing for people with special skills obtained in colleges, junior colleges, technical institutes, vocational schools, and high schools. Vocational courses and apprenticeship programs in food preparation, catering, and hotel and restaurant management, offered through restaurant associations and trade unions, provide training opportunities. Programs range in length from a few months to several years. Nearly 200 community and junior colleges offer 2-year degree programs in hotel and restaurant management. The U.S. Armed Forces also offer experience and training in food service.

Traditionally, many hotels filled first-level manager positions by promoting administrative support and service workers—particularly those with good communication skills, a solid educational background, tact, loyalty, and a capacity to endure hard work and long hours. People with these qualities still advance to manager jobs, but more recently lodging chains have primarily been hiring persons with 4-year college degrees in the liberal arts or other fields and starting them in trainee or junior management positions. Bachelor's and master's degree programs in hotel and restaurant management provide the strongest background for a career as a hotel manager, with nearly 150 colleges and universities offering programs. Graduates of these programs are highly sought by employers in this industry. New graduates often go through on-the-job training programs before being given much responsibility. Eventually, they may advance to a top management position in a large chain operation.

Upper management positions, such as general manager, lodging manager, food service manager, or sales manager, generally require considerable formal training and job experience. Some department managers, such as comptrollers, purchasing managers, executive housekeepers, and executive chefs, generally require some specialized training and extensive on-the-job experience. To advance to positions with more responsibilities, managers frequently change employers or relocate to a chain property in another area.

For office and administrative support and service workers, advancement opportunities in the hotel industry vary widely. Some workers, such as housekeepers and janitors, generally have few opportunities for advancement. In large properties, however, some janitors may advance to supervisory positions. Hotel desk clerks, hospitality workers, and chefs sometimes advance to managerial positions. Promotional opportunities from the front office often are greater than from any other department, because one has an excellent opportunity to learn the establishment's overall operation from this vantage point. Front office jobs are excellent entry-level jobs and can serve as a stepping stone to jobs in hospitality, public relations, advertising, sales, and management.

Advancement opportunities for chefs and cooks are better than those for most other service occupations. Cooks often advance to chef or to supervisory and management positions, such as executive chef, restaurant manager, or food service manager. Some transfer to jobs in clubs, go into business for themselves, or become instructors of culinary arts.

## Earnings
Earnings in hotels and other lodging places generally are much lower than the average for all industries. In 2000, average earnings for all nonsupervisory workers in this industry were $9.65 an hour, or $298 a week, compared with $13.75 an hour, or $474 a week, for workers throughout private industry. Many workers in this industry earn the Federal minimum wage of $5.15 an hour. Some States have laws that establish a higher minimum wage. Federal laws, however, allow employers to pay below the minimum wage when an employee is expected to receive tips.

Food and beverage service workers as well as hosts and hostesses, maids and housekeeping cleaners, concierges, and baggage porters and bellhops derive their earnings from a combination of hourly earnings and customer tips. Waiters and waitresses often derive the majority of their earnings from tips, which vary greatly depending on menu prices and the volume of customers served. Many employers also provide free meals and furnish uniforms. Food service personnel may receive extra pay for banquets and other special occasions. In general, workers with the greatest skills, such as restaurant cooks, have the highest earnings, and workers who receive tips have the lowest. Earnings in the largest occupations in hotels and other lodging places appear in table 3.

Salaries of lodging managers are dependent upon the size and sales volume of the establishment and their specific duties and responsibilities. Managers may earn bonuses ranging up to 20 percent of their basic salary. In addition, they and their families may be furnished with lodging, meals, parking, laundry, and other services. Some hotels offer profit-sharing plans, tuition reimbursement, and other benefits to their employees.

About 10.9 percent of the workers in hotels and other lodging places are union members or are covered by union contracts, compared with 14.9 percent of workers in all industries combined.

**Table 3. Median hourly earnings of the largest occupations in hotels and other lodging places, 2000**

| Occupation | Hotels and other lodging places | All industries |
|---|---|---|
| Lodging managers ................................. | $ 14.95 | $ 14.79 |
| Maintenance and repair workers, general ................................. | 9.98 | 13.39 |
| Cooks, restaurant ................................. | 9.96 | 8.72 |
| Security guards ................................. | 9.61 | 8.45 |
| Hotel, motel, and resort desk clerks ..... | 7.84 | 7.87 |
| Laundry and dry-cleaning workers ........ | 7.48 | 7.59 |
| Maids and housekeeping cleaners ........ | 7.09 | 7.41 |
| Baggage porters and bellhops ............. | 6.74 | 7.80 |
| Waiters and waitresses ........................ | 6.60 | 6.42 |
| Gaming dealers ................................. | 6.26 | 6.41 |

## Outlook

Wage and salary employment in hotels and other lodging places is expected to increase 13 percent over the 2000-10 period, slower than the 16-percent growth projected for all industries combined. Job growth reflects rising personal income, an increase in the number of two-income families, low-cost airfares, emphasis on leisure activities, and growth of foreign tourism in the United States. In addition, special packages for short vacations and weekend travel should stimulate employment growth and, as more States legalize some form of gambling, the hotel industry will increasingly invest in gaming, further fueling job growth.

Job opportunities should be concentrated in the largest hotel occupations, such as building cleaning workers and hotel, motel and resort desk clerks. Many of these openings will arise in full-service hotels and resorts and spas. Because all-suite properties as well as extended stay and budget hotels and motels do not have restaurants, dining rooms, lounges, or kitchens, these limited-service establishments offer a narrower range of employment opportunities.

Employment outlook varies by occupation. Employment of hotel, motel, and resort desk clerks is expected to grow rapidly as some of these workers assume responsibilities previously reserved for managers. However, the spread of computer technology will cause employment of other clerical workers—bookkeeping, accounting, and auditing clerks and secretaries, for example—to grow more slowly than the industry as a whole. Employment of waiters and waitresses is projected to decline—reflecting the trend toward hotels and other lodging places that do not offer full-service restaurants. Similarly, employment of lodging managers is expected to increase more slowly than the overall hotel industry due to the growth of economy-class establishments with fewer departments to manage. However, the trend toward chain-affiliated lodging places should provide managers with opportunities for advancement into general manager positions and corporate administrative jobs. Opportunities should be more limited for self-employed managers or owners of small lodging places.

Job turnover is relatively high in this industry, particularly in lodging places other than hotels and motels. To attract and retain workers, the lodging industry is placing more emphasis on hiring and training. Nevertheless, many young people and others—who are only looking for seasonal or part-time work, not a career—take food service and other jobs that require little or no previous training. Therefore, job opportunities exist for first-time jobseekers and people with a wider range of experience and skills, including those with limited skills.

## Sources of Additional Information

For information on hospitality careers, write to:

➤ International Council on Hotel, Restaurant, and Institutional Education, 3205 Skipwith Rd., Richmond, VA 23294-4442. Internet: **http://www.chrie.org**

➤ American Hotel and Lodging Association, 1201 New York Ave. NW, #600, Washington, DC 20005-3931. Internet: **http://www.ahlaonline.org**

General information on food and beverage service jobs is available from:

➤ National Restaurant Association, 1200 17th St. NW., Washington, DC 20036-3097. Internet: **http://www.restaurant.org**

Information about housekeeper and janitorial jobs may be obtained from a local State employment service office or from:

➤ Service Employees International Union, 1313 L St. NW., Washington, DC 20005. Internet: **http://www.seiu.org**

Information on housekeeping management may be obtained from:

➤ International Executive Housekeepers Association, 1001 Eastwind Dr., Suite 301, Westerville, OH 43081. Phone: (800) 200-6342. Internet: **http://www.ieha.org**

For information on the American Culinary Federation's apprenticeship and certification programs for cooks, write to:

➤ American Culinary Federation, 10 San Bartola Dr., St. Augustine, FL 32086. Internet: **http://www.acfchefs.org**

Detailed information on the following occupations employed in hotels and other lodging places may be found in the 2002-03 *Occupational Outlook Handbook*:

● Building cleaning workers

● Chefs, cooks, and other food preparation workers

● Food and beverage serving and related workers

● Food service managers

● Lodging managers

● Hotel, motel, and resort desk clerks

● Gaming cage workers

● Gaming services occupations

● Security guards and gaming surveillance officers

# Management and Public Relations Services

(SIC 874)

## SIGNIFICANT POINTS

- This industry is projected to be one of the fastest growing through the year 2010.

- Nearly one-fifth of all workers are self-employed.

- About 70 percent of workers have a bachelor's degree or higher; half of all jobs are in managerial, business, financial, and professional occupations.

- This industry is one of the highest paying.

## Nature of the Industry

Widespread management and public relations services firms influence how businesses, governments, and institutions make decisions and, in so doing, affect the lives of all Americans. Often working behind the scenes, these firms have a variety of functions. For example, a management consulting team could recommend that a pharmaceutical company take a brand of pain reliever off the market. A construction management firm might oversee the building of a new airport. A facilities support services firm might manage the daily operations of a local hospital. A traffic consultant could conclude that a major highway should be widened. Or, a public relations firm might issue a press release that is printed in newspapers across the country.

Firms in management and public relations services offer one or more resources that clients cannot provide themselves. Usually this resource is expertise—in the form of knowledge, experience, special skills, or creativity—but sometimes the resource is time or personnel that the client cannot spare. Clients are large and small for-profit firms in the private sector; bodies of State, local, or Federal Government; institutions, such as hospitals, universities, unions, and trade groups; and foreign governments or businesses.

The management and public relations services industry is diverse. In general, firms in management or other business consulting offer operational advice, those in public relations services advise and implement public exposure strategies, and firms in facility support management services furnish administrative services. Management services and management consulting are by far the largest sectors, together accounting for most of the industry's revenue. The facility support, business consulting, and public relations segments bring in the remaining revenue.

Management consulting firms advise on almost any aspect of corporate operations, including marketing; finance; corporate strategy and organization; manufacturing and technology; information systems and data processing; electronic commerce ("e-commerce") or business; and human resources, benefits, and compensation. Depending on the nature of clients' problems and needs, management consulting firms might advise how best to enter a new market or increase the client's share in an existing market. They might suggest how to get the most out of a computer network or which department or subsidiary should be sold, shut down, or merged. They might recommend how to adhere to Federal environmental regulations or when to issue a new public offering of stock. Occasionally, management consulting firms also help implement their own advice.

Management consulting has grown rapidly over the past several decades, as businesses increasingly use consulting services. Using consultants is advantageous, because these experts are experienced, welltrained, and abreast of the latest technologies, government regulations, and management and production techniques. In addition, consultants are cost effective because they can be hired temporarily and can objectively perform their duties, free of the influence of company politics.

Miscellaneous business consulting firms offer a variety of services similar to those of management consultants, but the former primarily offer technical expertise or advise clients on nonmanagement issues. For example, an economic consultant might be hired to help a business project future product sales, or a traffic consultant might be retained to advise a city government on how much a proposed new tunnel would alleviate traffic congestion. This group of businesses includes sociological research firms, architectural consultants, educational consulting firms, city planners, and many others. In fact, there are highly specialized consultants with expertise in almost every business and government-related activity.

Public relations firms help secure favorable public exposure for their clients, advise them in the case of a sudden public crisis, and design strategies to help them attain a certain public image. Toward these ends, public relations firms analyze public or internal sentiment about clients; establish relationships with the media; write speeches and coach clients for interviews; issue press releases; and organize client-sponsored publicity events, such as contests, concerts, exhibits, symposia, and sporting and charity events. Clients of public relations firms include all types of businesses, institutions, trades, and public interest groups, and even some high-profile individuals.

Lobbying firms, a special type of public relations firm, differ somewhat. Instead of attempting to secure favorable public opinion about their clients, they attempt to influence legislators in favor of their clients' special interests. Lobbyists often work for large businesses, industry trade organizations, unions, or public interest groups.

Management services and facility support services firms are similar to each other, but differ in one important respect. Management services firms administer other firms' properties, businesses, or projects and provide management personnel but not operating staff. In contrast, facility support services firms provide both management and staff. For example, a common type of management service is construction management. A corporation, real estate developer, or group of investors might hire a construction management firm to oversee a construction project to ensure that it is completed within certain time and cost constraints. The construction management firm prepares estimates of building costs and a project schedule; coordinates the work of designers, contractors, workers, and suppliers; and inspects the work as it progresses, to ensure that it conforms to plans, budget, quality standards, and the completion schedule. However, the construction management firm employs none of the construction workers, designers, or contractors; it only coordinates and administers the process.

Facility management firms, on the other hand, might administer and staff various services at airports, military installations, universities, hospitals, or corporate headquarters. Unlike management services firms, facility management firms employ many of the workers necessary to run these facilities—managers, guards, maintenance and custodial staff, groundskeepers, and other workers. Facility management firms do not provide all of the staffing, particularly management. Many times, there is an in-house facility manager that oversees the department but may choose to outsource trades and custodial workers through a facility management firm.

The vast majority of firms in the management and public relations services industry are small, primarily because new firms, particularly those engaged in consulting and public relations, can easily enter the industry. Licensing, certification, and large capital outlays seldom are necessary to become a management or business consultant, public relations specialist, or construction manager; and the work can be quite lucrative for those with the right education, experience, and contacts. As a result, many wage and salary workers in management and public relations services eventually leave established firms to go into business for themselves. In addition, after developing specialized expertise, people working in other industries often start their own consulting businesses, and some experienced workers perform consulting work after retiring.

## Working Conditions

For most employees, working conditions in management and public relations services are similar to those for most office workers operating in a teamwork environment. The work is rarely hazardous, except in a few cases—such as for facility support workers contracted to run correctional institutions or construction management workers who must inspect construction sites. In 1999, the industry had only 1.9 injuries and illnesses per 100 full-time workers, compared with an average of 6.3 throughout private industry.

Most firms encourage employees to attend employer-paid time-management classes. This helps reduce the stress sometimes associated with working under strict time constraints. Also, with today's hectic lifestyle, many firms in this industry offer or provide health facilities or clubs for employees to maintain good health.

Not all employees in this industry work under identical conditions. In 2000, workers in the industry averaged 35.9 hours per week, a little above the national average. However, some must work long hours in stressful environments, as often is the case with lobbyists, consultants, construction managers, and public relations writers, who frequently must meet hurried deadlines. Workers whose services are billed hourly—such as many business and management consultants and public relations specialists—are often under pressure to manage their time very carefully. Occasionally, weekend work also is necessary, depending upon the job that is being performed. In addition, the increasing globalization of the marketplace compels many executives and consultants to travel extensively or live away from home for extended periods.

## Employment

The management and public relations services industry had about 1.1 million wage and salary workers in 2000; about 232,000 were self-employed. Management services and management consulting firms were the largest employers in the industry, accounting for 68 percent of wage and salary jobs. Public relations services accounted for 5 percent.

The vast majority of establishments in this industry were fairly small, employing fewer than 5 workers (see chart). Self-employed individuals operated many of these small firms. Despite the prevalence of small firms and self-employed workers, large firms tend to dominate the industry. Nearly 60 percent of jobs are found in only about 3 percent of the establishments, and some of the largest firms in the industry employ several thousand people.

Although employees in this industry work in all parts of the country, many workers are concentrated near large urban centers.

## Occupations in the Industry

Although management and public relations services are fairly specialized, a variety of occupations are found in this industry (table 1). Some of these occupations, such as *public relations specialists,* are specific to only one segment of the industry, whereas others, such as *bookkeeping, accounting,* and *auditing clerks*, can be found throughout the industry.

Compared with other industries, a relatively high proportion of workers are highly educated. Around 40 percent of those in management and public relations services have a bachelor's degree, compared with 18.5 of the workers throughout the entire economy. More than 25 percent have a master's degree or higher, compared with 9 percent of the workers throughout the economy. Certain jobs may have stringent entry requirements. For example, some management consulting firms prefer to hire

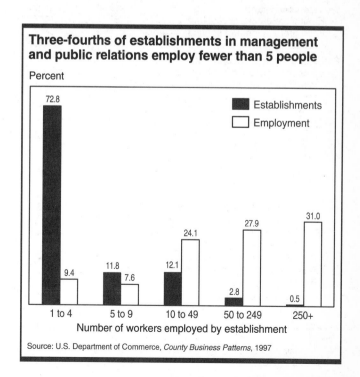

**Three-fourths of establishments in management and public relations employ fewer than 5 people**

Percent

- Establishments
- Employment

| Number of workers | Establishments | Employment |
|---|---|---|
| 1 to 4 | 72.8 | 9.4 |
| 5 to 9 | 11.8 | 7.6 |
| 10 to 49 | 12.1 | 24.1 |
| 50 to 249 | 2.8 | 27.9 |
| 250+ | 0.5 | 31.0 |

Number of workers employed by establishment

Source: U.S. Department of Commerce, *County Business Patterns*, 1997

**Table 1. Employment of wage and salary workers in management and public relations services by occupation, 2000 and projected change, 2000-10**

(Employment in thousands)

| Occupation | Employment, 2000 Number | Employment, 2000 Percent | Percent change, 2000-2010 |
|---|---|---|---|
| All occupations ........................... | 1,090 | 100.0 | 42.2 |
| **Management, business, and financial occupations** ........................... | 323 | 29.6 | 45.9 |
| Administrative services managers ....... | 11 | 1.0 | 76.0 |
| Marketing managers .............................. | 8 | 0.7 | 41.5 |
| Public relations managers ................... | 9 | 0.8 | 61.3 |
| Chief executives ................................... | 21 | 1.9 | 40.4 |
| Construction managers ........................ | 14 | 1.3 | 46.7 |
| Financial managers ............................. | 12 | 1.1 | 32.0 |
| General and operations managers ...... | 56 | 5.1 | 38.6 |
| All other managers ............................... | 11 | 1.0 | 32.0 |
| Human resources, training, and labor relations specialists ............................ | 14 | 1.3 | 35.4 |
| Management analysts .......................... | 66 | 6.0 | 44.1 |
| All other business operations specialists ............................................. | 17 | 1.6 | 46.7 |
| Accountants and auditors.................... | 16 | 1.5 | 76.0 |
| **Professional and related occupations** ........................... | 228 | 21.0 | 53.5 |
| Computer programmers ....................... | 16 | 1.4 | 19.2 |
| Computer systems analysts ................ | 10 | 0.9 | 76.0 |
| Computer software engineers ............. | 12 | 1.1 | 93.9 |
| Computer support specialists .............. | 8 | 0.7 | 120.0 |
| Engineers ............................................. | 24 | 2.2 | 40.4 |
| Drafters, engineering, and mapping technicians ....................................... | 14 | 1.3 | 35.3 |
| Environmental scientists and specialists, including health .............. | 8 | 0.7 | 46.7 |
| Market and survey researchers........... | 8 | 0.8 | 47.6 |
| Education, training, and library occupations........................................ | 9 | 0.8 | 47.8 |
| Art and design occupations ................. | 11 | 1.0 | 46.2 |
| Public relations specialists ................. | 17 | 1.6 | 61.3 |
| Registered nurses ............................... | 11 | 1.0 | 46.7 |
| Other health professionals and technicians ....................................... | 14 | 1.3 | 43.5 |
| **Service occupations** ............................... | 91 | 8.3 | 43.3 |
| Healthcare support occupations .......... | 8 | 0.8 | 47.4 |
| Food preparation and serving related occupations ........................................ | 28 | 2.5 | 28.7 |
| **Sales and related occupations** .............. | 58 | 5.4 | 36.2 |
| Sales representatives, wholesale and manufacturing, except technical and scientific products ........................... | 9 | 0.8 | 14.5 |
| All other sales and related workers ..... | 15 | 1.4 | 46.7 |
| **Office and administrative support occupations** ........................... | 287 | 26.4 | 30.4 |
| First-line supervisors/managers of office and administrative support workers ............................................. | 18 | 1.6 | 11.6 |
| Bookkeeping, accounting, and auditing clerks .................................. | 24 | 2.2 | 26.3 |
| Customer service representatives ....... | 35 | 3.2 | 38.7 |
| Receptionists and information clerks .... | 15 | 1.4 | 46.7 |
| Office clerks, general............................ | 34 | 3.1 | 46.7 |
| Executive secretaries and administrative assistants ................... | 35 | 3.3 | 32.0 |
| Secretaries, except legal, medical, and executive ...................................... | 25 | 2.3 | 17.3 |
| **Transportation and material moving occupations** ........................... | 26 | 2.4 | 40.4 |

NOTE: May not add to totals due to omission of occupations with small employment.

only workers who have a master's degree in business administration (MBA). Other positions can be attained only after many years of related experience.

In management and public relations services, workers in management and business and financial operations occupations and in office and administrative support occupations make up 56 percent of employment. These same occupations account for about 27 percent of workers across the entire economy. These workers comprise a disproportionate share of jobs in this industry because they not only manage and administer their own firms, but often manage clients' businesses or properties as well. For example, office management services and facilities support firms might need only a handful of managers, bookkeepers, and secretaries to handle their own affairs, but need many more to administer each office or facility they contract to manage.

*Chief executives* and *general and operations managers* include both the highest level managers—such as chief executive officers and vice presidents—and many middle managers with diverse duties. Top-level managers shape company policy, often with the help of other executives or a board of directors. They oversee all activities of the firm, coordinate duties of subordinate executives and managers, and often bear ultimate responsibility for a firm's performance. Mid-level managers may oversee the activities of one department or, when working for a management services firm, all the activities of one or more establishments, properties, or construction ventures. These jobs are found throughout the industry, but they are particularly concentrated in the management services and facility support services segments.

*Management analysts*, also called *management consultants*, are the highest profile employees in the management consulting industry. Their work is quite varied, depending on the nature of the project and the client's needs. In general, consultants study and analyze business-related problems, synthesizing information from many sources, and recommend solutions. Suggested solutions can range from overhauling a client's computer systems to offering early retirement incentives to middle managers, switching health plans, improving just-in-time inventory systems, hiring public relations firms, or selling troublesome parts of businesses. Because of the varied nature of these jobs, firms hire workers with diverse backgrounds, such as engineering, finance, actuarial science, chemistry, and business. Many firms require consultants to have MBA's, whereas others hire workers who have only bachelor's degrees. Many workers have experience in other industries prior to entering management consulting work.

*Construction managers* work almost exclusively for construction management firms in the industry. In construction industries, the term "construction manager" sometimes is used to refer to the jobs of constructor, construction superintendent, general construction manager, project supervisor, and any number of contractors. In the management services segment of this industry, construction managers are highly trained or experienced workers who control the entire construction process. Through precise scheduling and cost estimation techniques, these managers oversee projects to ensure that they are completed on time and at a reasonable cost. Their work requires a thorough understanding of the construction process. As a result, most construction managers have an extensive educational background—in subjects such as architecture, engineering, construction technology, law, and business administration—as well as many years of related construction experience before entering this occupation.

Other management and business and financial operations occupations include *financial managers*, who prepare financial statements and assess the financial health of firms. Often, they must have at least a bachelor's degree in accounting or finance. As one might expect, most *advertising, marketing, promotions, public relations,* and *sales managers* in the industry are employed in public relations firms, where they manage publicity campaigns and supervise *public relations specialists,* discussed below. *Administrative services managers* typically administer a firm's support services, overseeing secretaries, data entry keyers, bookkeepers, and other clerical staff. In the management services industry, they also often supervise a client's clerical and support staff. *Accountants* and *auditors* monitor firms' financial transactions and often report to financial managers.

Administrative support positions in management and public relations services resemble those in other industries. Management and facility support services firms often staff clients' businesses, so administrative support workers are needed in large numbers. Particularly numerous are *secretaries* and *administrative assistants* and *bookkeeping, accounting,* and *auditing clerks,* who record and classify financial data. The industry also employs many *supervisors* and *managers of office* and *administrative support workers,* who oversee the support staff, often reporting to administrative services managers.

One of the industry's largest professional occupations is *public relations specialists,* almost all of whom work in the public relations segment of the industry. Under the guidance of public relations managers, these workers design, implement, and analyze public relations strategies and materials. They write press releases, contact people in the media, encourage their clients to sponsor special events, prepare clients for interviews or crises, and advise them on how to achieve a desired public image. In almost all cases, workers in these jobs must have strong writing skills and a bachelor's degree; applicants with degrees in communications, journalism, English, or business and prior job experience are preferred.

Designers in this industry are mostly *graphic designers* who use a variety of print, electronic, and film media to create designs that meet clients' commercial needs. Using computer software, they develop the overall layout and design of magazines, newspapers, journals, corporate reports, and other publications. They also may produce promotional displays and marketing brochures for products and services and design distinctive company logos for products and businesses. An increasing number of graphic designers develop material to appear on Internet home pages.

The rapid spread of computers and information technology has generated a need for highly trained computer specialists to design and develop new hardware and software systems and to incorporate new technologies. *Systems analysts* design new computer systems or redesign old systems for new applications. They solve computer problems and enable computer technology to meet individual needs of an organization. For example, a systems analyst from a management consulting firm might be hired by a wholesale firm to implement an online inventory database. *Computer software engineers,* on the other hand, can be involved in the design and development of software systems for control and automation of manufacturing, business, and management processes. Other computer specialists include *computer support specialists* who provide technical assistance, support, and advice to customers and users, and *database administrators* who work with database management systems software and determine ways to organize and store data. In the

consulting segments of this industry, computer specialists such as systems analysts, computer scientists, and computer engineers sometimes are referred to simply as "consultants."

Technical workers also include *computer programmers,* who write programs and create software—often in close conjunction with systems analysts—and *engineering technicians,* who aid engineers in research and development. Like systems analysts and engineers, persons in these occupations work primarily in the business and management consulting segments of the industry.

Compared with the primary occupational groups discussed above, the industry has relatively few jobs in service occupations. These include a large number of *food preparation and serving related workers,* who prepare and serve meals in business or institutional cafeterias. These occupations are found throughout the industry, but many food preparation and serving workers are employed in facilities support services firms.

Management and public relations service firms do not produce any goods and, as a result, employ relatively few sales and production workers. Sales, production, and the remaining occupational groups make up only about 15 percent of industry employment.

## Training and Advancement

Training and advancement opportunities vary widely within management and public relations services, but most jobs in the industry are similar in three respects. First, clients usually hire management and public relations firms based on the expertise of their staffs, so proper training of employees is vital to the success of firms. Second, although a bachelor's degree or higher generally is preferred by employers, most jobs also require extensive on-the-job training or related experience. Third, advancement opportunities are best for workers with the highest levels of education.

The management and public relations services industry offers excellent opportunities for self-employment. Because capital requirements are low, highly experienced workers can start their own businesses fairly easily and cheaply; and, every year, thousands of workers in this industry go into business for themselves. Some of these workers come from established management and public relations services firms, whereas others leave industry, government, or academic jobs to start their own businesses.

Most organizations need prospective employees to possess a variety of skills. To a large extent, a degree is only one desired qualification. Workers must also possess proven analytical and problem-solving ability, excellent written and verbal communications skills, experience in a particular specialty, assertiveness and motivation, strong attention to detail, and a willingness to work long hours, if necessary.

Whereas very few universities or colleges offer formal programs of study in management consulting, many fields provide a suitable background. These include most areas of business and management, as well as computer and information sciences and engineering. Management consulting firms also provide extensive training on the job. The method and extent of training can vary, based on the type of consulting and the nature of the firm. Information systems, industrial production, and other highly technical consulting requires particularly extensive formal training, but training for other types of consulting work often is less rigorous.

Management and leadership classes and seminars are available throughout the United States; some are hosted by volunteer senior executives and management experts, representing a variety of businesses and industries. Some large firms invest a great deal of time and money in training programs, educating new hires in formal classroom settings over several weeks or even months, and some even have separate training facilities. Small firms often combine formal and on-the-job training.

Entry-level positions within the management and public relations industry involve very little responsibility at the beginning. Striving for and displaying quality work results in more responsibility. Most management consulting firms have two entry-level positions. Workers who hold bachelor's degrees usually start as research associates; those with graduate degrees usually begin work as consultants. Successful workers progress through the ranks from research associate to consultant, management consultant, senior consultant, junior partner, and after many years, to senior partner. In some firms, however, it is very difficult for research associates to progress to the next level without further education. As a result, many management consulting firms offer tuition assistantships, grants, or reimbursement plans so that workers can attain a master's in business administration or another degree.

In business consulting firms, workers usually have extensive formal education, such as a master's or doctoral degree, in a relevant field. Additionally, few start in business consulting firms without some prior experience. Often, they have worked as university or college professors or as researchers in government or private industry. New entrants normally begin as research assistants and work under experienced consultants, until they are able to carry out projects independently.

In public relations, employers prefer applicants with degrees in communications, journalism, English, or business. Some 4-year colleges and universities have begun to offer a concentration in public relations. Because there is keen competition for entry-level public relations jobs, workers are encouraged to gain experience through internships, co-op programs, or one of the formal public relations programs offered across the country. However, these programs are not available everywhere, so most public relations workers get the bulk of their training on the job. At some firms, this training consists of formal classroom education, but in most cases, workers train under the guidance of senior account executives or other experienced workers, gradually familiarizing themselves with public relations work. Entry-level workers often start as research or account assistants and may be promoted to account executive, account supervisor, vice president, and executive vice president.

Voluntary accreditation programs for public relations specialists and management consultants, respectively, are offered by the Public Relations Society of America and the Institute of Management Consultants. Both programs are recognized marks of competency in the profession and require that workers have been employed in the field for several years.

Almost all workers in management services receive on-the-job training, and the remainder usually have prior work experience in a related field. Most managerial and supervisory workers gain experience informally, overseeing a few workers or part of a project under the close supervision of a senior manager. Although it is less common, some large firms offer formal management training.

Workers who advance to high-level managerial or supervisory jobs in management services firms usually have an extensive educational background. For example, a worker with an electrical engineering degree might start work in a construction management firm as a field inspector and advance quickly. On the other hand, a worker without such a degree, but with many years of construction experience, might also hold the position of field inspector. However, the latter employee will be at a disadvantage for further advancement. Frequently, the highly technical nature of work in these firms makes it difficult for less educated workers to advance.

## Earnings

Earnings in management and public relations services typically are considerably higher than the average for the entire private sector of the economy. Nonsupervisory management and public relations workers averaged $674 a week in 2000, compared with $474 for workers throughout private industry. Earnings in the largest occupations in management and public relations services appear in table 2.

Table 2. Median hourly earnings of the largest occupations in management and public relations services, 2000

| Occupation | Management and Public Relations | All industries |
|---|---|---|
| Chief executives | $ 65.75 | $ 54.72 |
| General and operations managers | 40.68 | 29.41 |
| Financial managers | 35.32 | 32.22 |
| Construction managers | 33.00 | 28.00 |
| Management analysts | 29.47 | 26.46 |
| Public relations managers | 27.59 | 26.22 |
| Computer programmers | 27.46 | 27.69 |
| Administrative services managers | 21.36 | 22.63 |
| Public relations specialists | 21.01 | 19.03 |
| Customer service representatives | 12.43 | 11.83 |

These data do not reflect earnings for self-employed workers, who often are paid very well. Also, both managerial workers and high-level professionals can make considerably more than the industry average. According to a 2000 survey by the Association of Management Consulting Firms, the average total cash compensation (salary plus bonus/profit sharing) for research associates was $37,616; entry-level consultants, $56,285; management consultants, $69,865; senior consultants, $89,117; junior partners, $111,097; and senior partners, $191,284.

According to a 2001 survey conducted by Abbot, Langer and Associates, the median annual cash compensation for junior consultants was $40,210; consultants, $53,207; senior consultants, $74,195; principal consultants, $93,690; and senior or executive vice presidents (ownership interest), $160,000.

In addition to a straight salary, many workers receive additional compensation, such as profit-sharing, stock ownership, or performance-based bonuses. In some firms, bonuses can constitute one-third of annual pay.

Only 2.1 percent of workers in management and public relations services belong to unions or are covered by union contracts, compared with 14.9 percent of workers in all industries combined.

## Outlook

Between 2000 and 2010, wage and salary jobs in the management and public relations services industry are expected to grow by 42 percent—nearly triple the 16 percent growth projected for all industries combined, ranking it among the most rapidly growing industries. Projected job growth can primarily be attributed to the continuing complexity of business. Among other things, today's managers must deal with rapid technological innovations, such as the impact of electronic business ("e-business"). Managers also must deal with changes in government regulations, growing environmental concerns, and the continuing reduction of trade barriers resulting in an increasingly global economy. Because it has become difficult to keep abreast of these changes, corporations, institutions, and governments will increasingly need well-trained, well-informed management and public relations services professionals.

Accompanying this changing business environment will be new competitive pressures that also will help spur industry growth. Firms today must produce higher quality goods and services more cheaply, or else lose business to more efficient domestic or foreign competitors. To cut costs, firms increasingly turn to "outsourcing," which means eliminating some in-house staff—such as internal public relations specialists or office managers—and contracting with outside firms to handle these functions. Often, these outside firms are more expensive than in-house workers in the short run, but are advantageous because they can easily be dismissed, once they are no longer needed. As businesses seek to cut costs over the long term, outsourcing in areas such as information systems, strategy, public relations, and human resources planning should continue to boost employment in the management and public relations services industry.

Each segment of the industry will grow at a different rate, for a variety of reasons. The management consulting segment will continue to grow rapidly, as demand for management consulting services increase. Contributing to this growth is a rise in the demand for information technology and the expansion of e-commerce. Most organizations today have little e-business experience and rely heavily on consultants to develop e-business strategies and integrate technologies. But in this maturing market, mergers, acquisitions, and downsizing will become more common, as firms compete by attempting to offer a broader range of consulting services. The resulting consolidation will temper employment growth.

The public relations segment also should experience faster growth, due to the growing importance of business media and the corresponding role of public relations. However, employment growth in the management services and facility support services sectors is being adversely affected by competition from other establishments providing one specialized service, such as janitorial or guard services.

## Sources of Additional Information

For more information about career opportunities in management consulting, contact:

➤ ACMF—The Association of Management Consulting Firms, 3580 Lexington Ave., New York, NY 10168. Internet: **http://www.amcf.org**

For a brochure on careers in public relations, contact:

➤ Public Relations Society of America, Inc., 33 Irving Place, New York, NY 10003. Internet: **http://www.prsa.org**

For further information on career opportunities in construction management, write to:

➤ Construction Management Association of America, 7918 Jones Branch Dr., Suite 540, McLean, VA 22102. Internet: **http://www.cmaanet.org**

Additional information about careers in facility management is available from:

➤ International Facility Management Association, One East Greenway Plaza, Suite 1100, Houston, TX 77046. Internet: **http://www.ifma.org**

In addition, information on the following occupations found in the management and public relations services industry appears in the 2002-03 *Occupational Outlook Handbook*:

- Administrative services managers
- Advertising, marketing, promotions, public relations, and sales managers
- Construction managers
- Designers
- Financial managers
- Top executives
- Management analysts
- Public relations specialists

# Motion Picture Production and Distribution

**(SIC 781, 782)**

- Employment is projected to grow rapidly, with keen competition expected for the more glamorous jobs— writers, actors, producers, and directors.

- Although many films are shot on location throughout the United States and abroad, employment is centered in several major cities, particularly New York and Los Angeles.

- Many workers have formal training, but experience, professionalism, talent, and creativity are the most important factors for getting many jobs in this industry.

## Nature of the Industry

The U.S. motion picture industry produces much of the world's feature films and many of its television programs. The industry is dominated by several large studios based mostly in Hollywood. However, with the increasing popularity and availability worldwide of cable television, video recorders, digital video disks (DVDs), and the Internet, many small and medium-size independent filmmaking companies have sprung up to create films to fill the increasing demand. In addition to the production of feature films and television programs produced on film, the industry also produces made-for-television movies, music videos, and commercials.

The industry also includes companies who produce films for limited, or specialized, audiences. These include documentary films, which use film clips and interviews to chronicle actual events with real people, and educational films ranging from "do-it-yourself" projects to exercise films. In addition, the industry produces business, industrial, and government films that promote an organization's image, provide information on its activities or products, or aid in fundraising or worker training. Some of these films are short enough to release to the public through the Internet. Many of these films offer an excellent training ground for beginning filmmakers.

Making a movie can be a difficult, yet rewarding, experience. However, it is also a very risky one. Although thousands of movies are produced each year, only a small number of these account for most box office receipts. Most films do not make a full return on their investment from domestic box office revenues, so filmmakers rely on profits from other markets, such as broadcast and cable television, videocassette and DVD sales and rentals, and foreign distribution. In fact, major film companies receive a growing portion of their revenue from abroad. These cost pressures have reduced the number of film production companies. Currently, seven major studios produce most of the television and movie productions released nationally. Smaller and independent filmmakers often find it difficult to finance new productions, as large motion picture production companies prefer to support established filmmakers. However, digital technology is lowering production costs for some small-budget films, enabling more independents to succeed in getting their films released nationally.

Although studios and other production companies are responsible for financing, producing, publicizing, and distributing the film or program, the actual making of the film is often done by hundreds of small businesses and independent contractors that are hired by the studios as needed. These companies provide a wide range of services, such as equipment rental, lighting, special effects, set construction, costume design, as well as much of the creative and technical talent. The industry also contracts with a large number of workers in other industries that supply support services to the crews while filming, such as truck drivers, caterers, electricians, and make-up artists. Many of these workers, particularly in Los Angeles, depend on the motion picture industry for their livelihood.

Most motion pictures are still made using film. However, digital technology and computer-generated imaging is rapidly making inroads and impacting the industry in numerous ways. Making changes to a picture is much easier using digital techniques. Backgrounds can be inserted after the actors perform on a sound stage, or locations can be digitally modified to reflect the script. Even actors can be created digitally. Independent filmmakers will continue to benefit from this technology, as reduced costs improve their ability to compete with the major studios.

Digital technology also makes it possible to distribute movies to theaters using satellites or fiber optic cable, although there are relatively few theaters with the reception capability right now. In the future, however, more theaters will be capable of receiving films digitally and the costly process of producing and distributing bulky films will be sharply reduced.

## Working Conditions

Most individuals in this industry work in clean, comfortable surroundings. Shooting outside the studio or "on location," however, may require working in adverse weather, and unpleasant and sometimes dangerous conditions. Actors, producers, directors, cinematographers, and camera operators also need stamina to withstand the heat of studio and stage lights, long and irregular hours, and travel.

Directors and producers often work under stress as they try to meet schedules, stay within budget, and resolve personnel and production problems. Actors, producers, directors, cinematographers, and camera operators face the anxiety of rejection and intermittent employment. Writers and editors must deal with criticism and demands to restructure and rewrite their work many times until the producer and director are finally satisfied. All writers must be able to withstand such criticism and disappointment; freelance writers are under the added pressure of always looking for new jobs. In spite of these difficulties, many people find that the glamour and excitement of filmmaking more than compensate for the frequently demanding and uncertain nature of careers in motion pictures.

## Employment

In 2000, there were about 287,000 wage and salary jobs in the motion picture production and distribution industry. Most of the workers were in motion picture production and services. They involved casting, acting, directing, editing, film processing, motion picture and videotape reproduction, and equipment and wardrobe rental. Although seven major studios produce most of the motion pictures released in the United States, many small companies are used as contractors throughout the process. Most motion picture and distribution establishments employ fewer than 10 workers (chart).

Many additional individuals work in the motion picture production and distribution industry on a freelance, contract, or part-time basis, but accurate statistics on their numbers are not available. Many people in the film industry are self-employed. They sell their services to anyone who needs them, often working on productions for many different companies during the year. Competition for these jobs is intense, and many people are unable to earn a living solely from freelance work.

Employment in the production of motion pictures and other films for television is centered in Los Angeles and New York City. Studios are also located in Chicago, Orlando, Texas, and North Carolina. In addition, many films are shot on location throughout the United States and abroad.

## Occupations in the Industry

The length of the credits at the end of most feature films and television programs gives an idea of the variety of workers involved in producing and distributing films. The motion picture industry employs workers in every major occupational group. Professionals and related workers account for about 4 in 10 salaried jobs in the industry. One in four salaried workers hold jobs in transportation and material-moving occupations (table 1).

Jobs in the industry can be broadly classified according to the three phases of filmmaking: Preproduction, production, and postproduction. Preproduction is the planning phase. This includes budgeting, casting, finding the right location, set and

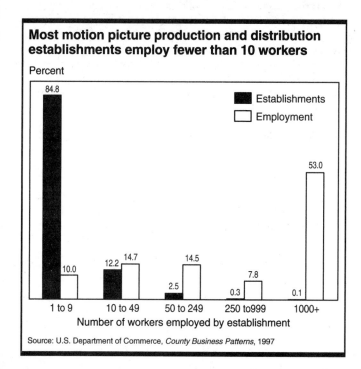

**Most motion picture production and distribution establishments employ fewer than 10 workers**

Percent

- Establishments
- Employment

| Number of workers employed by establishment | Establishments | Employment |
|---|---|---|
| 1 to 9 | 84.8 | 10.0 |
| 10 to 49 | 12.2 | 14.7 |
| 50 to 249 | 2.5 | 14.5 |
| 250 to 999 | 0.3 | 7.8 |
| 1000+ | 0.1 | 53.0 |

Source: U.S. Department of Commerce, *County Business Patterns*, 1997

**Table 1. Employment of wage and salary workers in motion picture production and distribution by occupation, 2000 and projected change, 2000-10**

(Employment in thousands)

| Occupation | Employment, 2000 Number | Employment, 2000 Percent | Percent change, 2000-2010 |
|---|---|---|---|
| **All occupations** | 287 | 100.0 | 28.7 |
| **Management, business, and financial occupations** | 18 | 6.4 | 32.8 |
| General and operations managers | 5 | 1.9 | 28.6 |
| Business operations specialists | 2 | 0.9 | 31.2 |
| Financial specialists | 2 | 0.7 | 36.3 |
| **Professional and related occupations** | 110 | 38.3 | 36.2 |
| Computer specialists | 6 | 2.0 | 63.0 |
| Multi-media artists and animators | 4 | 1.2 | 75.1 |
| Actors | 25 | 8.6 | 26.0 |
| Producers and directors | 8 | 2.7 | 38.8 |
| All other entertainers and performers, sports and related workers | 33 | 11.5 | 36.2 |
| Writers and editors | 3 | 0.9 | 34.8 |
| Audio and video equipment technicians | 7 | 2.5 | 27.5 |
| Broadcast technicians | 2 | 0.7 | 36.2 |
| Sound engineering technicians | 3 | 1.1 | 25.8 |
| Camera operators, television, video, and motion picture | 5 | 1.7 | 49.8 |
| Film and video editors | 5 | 1.8 | 36.2 |
| All other media and communication equipment workers | 3 | 1.0 | 36.2 |
| **Service occupations** | 5 | 1.7 | 26.3 |
| Security guards | 2 | 0.7 | 18.3 |
| **Sales and related occupations** | 8 | 2.7 | 19.5 |
| Sales representatives, wholesale and manufacturing, except technical and scientific products | 2 | 0.9 | 6.3 |
| **Office and administrative support occupations** | 58 | 20.3 | 26.2 |
| Customer service representatives | 4 | 1.5 | 28.8 |
| Production, planning, and expediting clerks | 24 | 8.3 | 31.2 |
| Shipping, receiving, and traffic clerks | 6 | 2.2 | 24.7 |
| Office clerks, general | 6 | 2.0 | 36.2 |
| Executive secretaries and administrative assistants | 3 | 1.0 | 22.6 |
| **Installation, maintenance, and repair occupations** | 11 | 4.0 | 24.8 |
| Maintenance and repair workers, general | 10 | 3.4 | 20.9 |
| **Production occupations** | 6 | 1.9 | 27.3 |
| Other production occupations | 3 | 1.1 | 30.0 |
| **Transportation and material moving occupations** | 70 | 24.5 | 19.7 |
| Industrial truck and tractor operators | 12 | 4.2 | 25.6 |
| Laborers and freight, stock, and material movers, hand | 12 | 4.2 | 22.6 |
| Packers and packagers, hand | 7 | 2.3 | 36.2 |
| All other material moving workers | 32 | 11.1 | 9.1 |

NOTE: May not add to totals due to omission of occupations with small employment.

costume design, set construction, and scheduling. Production is the actual making of the film. The number of people involved in the production phase can vary from a few for a documentary film to hundreds for a feature film. It is during this phase that the actual filming is done. Postproduction activities take place in the editing rooms and recording studios in which the film is shaped into its final form.

Some individuals work in all three phases. *Producers*, for example, are involved in every phase from beginning to end. These workers look for ideas that they believe can be turned into lucrative film projects or television shows. They may see many films, read hundreds of manuscripts, and maintain numerous contacts with literary agents and publishers. Producers are also responsible for all financial aspects of a film, including finding financing for its production. The producer works closely with the director on the selection of script, principal members of the cast, and filming locations, because these decisions greatly affect the cost of a film. Once financing is obtained, the producer works out a detailed budget and sees to it that the production costs stay within that budget. In a large production, the producer also works closely with *production managers* who are in charge of crews, travel, casting, and equipment. For television shows, much of this process requires especially tight deadlines.

*Directors* translate the script to film and are involved in every stage of production. They may supervise hundreds of people, from screenwriters to costume and set designers. Directors are in charge of all technical and artistic aspects of the film or television show. They conduct auditions and rehearsals and approve the location, scenery, costumes, choreography, and music. In short, they direct the entire cast and crew during shooting. *Assistant directors* help them with such details as handling extras, transportation of equipment, and arrangements for food and accommodations. Some directors assume multiple roles, such as *director-producer* or *writer-producer-director*. Successful directors must know how to hire the right people and create effective teams.

*Preproduction occupations.* Before a film or a television program moves into the production phase, it begins with an idea which *screenwriters* turn into a script. They either develop an original idea or take an existing literary work and adapt it into a screenplay or television pilot (a sample episode of a proposed television series). Screenwriters work closely with producers and directors. Sometimes they prepare a shooting script that has instructions on shots, camera angles, and lighting. They frequently make changes to reflect the directors' and producers' ideas and desires. The work, therefore, requires not only creativity, but also an ability to write and rewrite many script versions under pressure. Although the work of feature film screenwriters usually ends when the shooting begins, writing for television usually is a continuous process.

*Art directors* design the physical environment of the film or television set to create the mood called for by the script. Television art directors may design elaborate sets for use in situation comedies or commercials. They supervise many different people, including *illustrators*, *scenic designers*, *model makers*, *carpenters*, *painters*, *electricians*, *laborers*, *set decorators*, *costume designers,* and *makeup* and *hairstyling artists*. These positions can provide an entry into the motion picture industry. Many start in these jobs in live theater productions and then move back and forth between the stage, film, and television.

*Production occupations.* *Actors* entertain and communicate with the audience through their interpretation of dramatic roles. Only a small number achieve recognition in motion pictures or television. Many are cast in supporting roles or as walk-ons. Some start as background performers with no lines to deliver. Also called "extras," these are the people in the background—crowds on the street, workers in offices, or dancers at a ball. Others perform stunts, such as driving cars in chase scenes or falling from high places. Although a few actors find parts in feature films straight out of drama school, most support themselves by working for many years outside of the industry. Most acting jobs are found through an agent, who finds auditions that may lead to acting assignments.

Cinematographers, camera operators, and gaffers work together to capture the scenes in the script on film. *Cinematographers* compose the film shots to reflect the mood the director wishes to create. They do not usually operate the camera; instead, they plan and coordinate the actual filming. *Camera operators* handle all camera movements and perform the actual shooting. *Assistant camera operators* check the equipment, load the camera, operate the slate and clapsticks (now electronic), and take care of the equipment. *Commercial camera operators* specialize in shooting commercials. This experience translates easily into documentary work. *Gaffers*, or lighting technicians, set up different kinds of lighting needed for filming. They work for the *director of photography*, who plans all lighting needs. *Sound engineering technicians, film recordists*, and *boom operators* record dialogue, sounds, music, and special effects during the filming. Sound engineering technicians are the "ears" of the film. They supervise all sound generated during filming. They select microphones and the level of sound from mixers and synthesizers to assure the best sound quality. Recordists help to set up the equipment and are in charge of the individual tape recorders. Boom operators handle long booms with microphones that are moved from one area of the set to another. Because more filming is done on location and the equipment has become compact, lighter, and simpler to operate, one person often performs many of the above functions.

*Multi-media artists and animators* create the movie "magic." Through their imagination, creativity, and skill, they can create anything required by the script, from talking animals to flaming office buildings and earthquakes. Many begin as stage technicians or scenic designers. They not only need a good imagination, but also must be part carpenter, plumber, electrician, and electronics expert. These workers must be familiar with many ways of achieving a desired special effect because each job requires different skills. Computer skills have become very important in this field. Some areas of television and film production, including animation and visual effects, now rely heavily on computer technology. Although there was a time when elaborate computer animation was restricted to blockbuster movies, much of the 3-dimensional work being generated today is happening in small to mid-sized companies. Some specialists create "synthespians"—realistic digital humans—which appear mainly in science fiction productions. These digital images are often used when a stunt or scene is too dangerous for an actor.

Many individuals get their start in the industry by running errands, moving things, and helping with props. *Production assistants* and *grips* (stage hands) are often used in this way.

*Postproduction occupations.* One of the most important tasks in filmmaking and television production is editing. After the film is shot and processed, *film and video editors* study footage, select the best shots, and assemble them in the most effective way. Their goal is to create dramatic continuity and the right pace for the desired mood. Editors first organize the footage and then structure the sequence of the film by splicing and resplicing the best shots. They must have a good eye and understand the subject of the film and the director's intentions. The ability to work with digital media is also becoming increasingly important. Strong computer skills are mandatory for most jobs. However, few industry-wide standards exist, so companies often look for people with skills in the hardware/software they are currently using.

*Assistant editors* or *dubbing editors* select the sound track and special sound effects to produce the final combination of sight and sound as it appears on the screen. *Editing room assistants* help with the splicing, patching, rewinding, coding, and storing of the film. Some television networks have *film librarians*, who are responsible for organizing, filing, cataloging, and selecting footage for the film editors. There is no one way of entering the occupation of editor; however, experience as a film librarian, sound editor, or assistant editor—plus talent and perseverance—usually help.

*Sound effects editors* or *audio recording engineers* perform one of the final jobs in postproduction. They add prerecorded and live sound effects and background music by manipulating various elements of music, dialogue, and background sound to fit the picture. Their work is increasingly computer-driven as electronic equipment replaces conventional tape recording devices. The best way to gain experience in sound editing is through work in radio stations, with music groups, in music videos, or adding audio to Internet sites.

After the film or television show is finished, *marketing personnel* develop the marketing strategy for films. They estimate the demand for the film and the audience to whom it will appeal, develop an advertising plan, and decide where and when to release the film. *Advertising workers* or "unit publicists" write press releases and short biographies of actors and directors for newspapers and magazines. They may also set up interviews or television appearances for the stars or director to promote a film. *Sales representatives* sell the finished product. Many production companies hire staff to distribute, lease, and sell their films and made-for-television programs to theater owners and television networks. The best way to enter sales is to start by selling advertising time for television stations.

Large film and television studios are headed by a *chief executive officer* (CEO) who is responsible to a board of directors and stockholders. Various managers such as *financial managers* or *business managers*, as well as *accountants* and *lawyers* report to the CEO. Small film companies, and those in business and educational film production, cannot afford to have so many different people managing only one aspect of the business. As a result, they are usually headed by an *owner-producer*, who originates, develops, produces, and distributes films with just a small staff and some freelance workers. These companies offer good training opportunities to beginners because they provide exposure to many phases of film and television production.

## Training and Advancement

Formal training can be a great asset to workers in filmmaking and television production, but experience, talent, and creativity are usually the most important factors in getting a job. Many entry-level workers start out by working on documentary, business, educational, industrial, or government films, or in the music video industry. This kind of experience can lead to more advanced jobs.

Actors are usually required to have formal dramatic training or acting experience. Training can be obtained in dramatic arts schools throughout the country, although most schools are located in New York City and Los Angeles. More than 500 colleges and universities offer bachelor's or higher degrees in dramatic and theater arts. Training in singing and dance, experience in modeling, and performing in local and regional theater are especially useful. Many actors begin their career by performing in commercials and as extras. Most professional actors rely on agents or managers to find auditions for them.

There are no specific training requirements for producers and directors. Talent, experience, and business acumen are very important. An ability to deal under stress with many different kinds of people is also essential. Directors and producers come from varied backgrounds. Many start as assistant directors and producers; others gain industry experience first as actors, writers, film editors, or business managers. Formal training in directing and producing is available at some colleges and universities. Individuals interested in production management who have a bachelor's degree or 2 years of on-set experience in motion picture or television production may qualify for the Assistant Directors Training Program offered jointly by the Directors Guild of America and the Alliance of Motion Picture and Television Producers. Training is given in New York City and Los Angeles. To enroll in this highly competitive program, individuals must take a written exam and go through a series of assessments.

Although many screenwriters have college degrees, talent and creativity are even more important determinants of success in the industry. Screenwriters need to develop creative writing skills, a mastery of film language, and a basic understanding of filmmaking. Self-motivation, perseverance, and an ability to take criticism are also valuable. Feature film writers usually have many years of experience and work on a freelance basis. Many start as copywriters in advertising agencies and as writers for educational film companies, government audiovisual departments, or inhouse corporate film divisions. These jobs not only serve as a good training ground for beginners but also have greater job security than freelancing.

Cinematographers, camera operators, and sound engineers usually have either a college or technical school education, or they go through a formal training program. Computer skills are required for many editing, special effects, and cinematography positions.

In addition to colleges and technical schools, many private institutes offer training programs on various aspects of filmmaking, such as screenwriting, editing, directing, and acting. For example, the American Film Institute offers training in directing, production, cinematography, screenwriting, and production design.

The educational background of managers and top executives varies widely, depending on their responsibilities. Most managers have a bachelor's degree in liberal arts or business administration. Their majors often are related to the departments they direct. For example, a degree in accounting or finance, or in business administration with an emphasis on accounting or finance, is suitable academic preparation for financial managers.

Employers prefer individuals with an undergraduate degree in marketing, advertising, or business for top-level positions in these departments. Experience in retail and print advertising is also helpful. A high school diploma and retail or telephone sales experience are beneficial for sales jobs.

Promotion opportunities for many jobs are extremely limited because of the narrow scope of duties and skills of the occupations. Thousands of jobs are also temporary, intermittent, part time, or on a contract basis, making advancement difficult. Individual initiative is very important for advancement in these fields.

Screenwriters usually have had writing experience as freelance writers or editors and writers in other employment settings. As they build a reputation in their career, demand for their screenplays or teleplays increases, and their earnings grow. Some become directors or producers. Film and video editors often begin as editing room assistants; cinematographers usually start as assistant camera operators; and sound recordists often start as boom operators and gradually progress to sound engineer. Computer courses in digital sound and electronic mixing are often important for upward mobility.

General managers may advance to top executive positions, such as executive or administrative vice-president in their own firm, or to similar positions in a larger firm. Top-level managers may advance to chief operating officer and CEO. Financial, marketing, and other managers may be promoted to top management positions or may transfer to closely related positions in other industries. Some may start their own businesses.

## Earnings

Earnings of workers in the motion picture production and distribution industry vary, depending on education and experience, type of work, union affiliation, and duration of employment. In 2000, average weekly earnings of nonsupervisory workers in motion picture production and services were $811, compared with $474 for workers in all industries.

Based on a union contract that was negotiated in July 2001, motion picture and television actors who are members of Screen Actors Guild earn a minimum daily rate of $636, or $2,206 for a 5-day week. They also receive additional compensation for reruns. Annual earnings for many actors are low, however, because employment is very irregular. Many actors supplement their incomes from acting with other jobs outside the industry. Some well-known actors get salaries well above the minimums and, of course, earnings of the few top stars are astronomical.

Salaries for directors vary widely. Producers seldom get a set salary; instead, they get a percentage of a show's earnings or ticket sales. Earnings in selected occupations in motion picture production and distribution appear in table 2.

**Table 2. Median hourly earnings of the largest occupations in motion picture production and distribution, 2000**

| Occupation | Motion Picture production and services | All industries |
|---|---|---|
| Sound engineering technicians | $ 45.29 | $ 18.98 |
| Multi-media artists and animators | 21.80 | 19.77 |
| Audio and video equipment technicians | 18.11 | 14.57 |
| Film and video editors | 17.68 | 16.42 |
| Camera operators, television, video, and motion picture | 15.17 | 13.40 |
| Maintenance and repair workers, general | 12.80 | 13.39 |
| Production, planning, and expediting clerks | 12.40 | 14.71 |
| Customer service representatives | 11.83 | 11.83 |
| Laborers and freight, stock, and material movers, hand | 8.39 | 9.04 |
| Industrial truck and tractor operators | 8.07 | 11.74 |

Unions are very important in this industry. Virtually all film production companies and television networks sign contracts with union locals that require the employment of workers according to union contracts. Nonunion workers may be hired because of a special talent, to fill a specific need, or for a short period of time. Although union membership is not mandated, nonunion workers risk lost eligibility for future work assignments. Actors who appear in filmed entertainment—including television, commercials, and movies—belong to the Screen Actors Guild; those in broadcast television generally belong to the American Federation of Television and Radio Artists. Film and television directors belong to the Directors Guild of America. Art directors, cartoonists, editors, costumers, scenic artists, set designers, camera operators, sound technicians, projectionists, and shipping, booking, and other distribution employees belong to the International Alliance of Theatrical Stage Employees, Moving Picture Technicians, Artists and Allied Crafts (I.A.T.S.E.), or the United Scenic Artists Association.

## Outlook

The employment outlook in the motion picture production and distribution industry is very good mainly due to the explosion of programming needed to fill an increasing number of cable and satellite television channels, both in the United States and abroad. Also, more films will be needed to meet inhome demand for videos, DVDs, and films over the Internet. Responding to an increasingly fragmented audience will create many opportunities to develop films. The international market for U.S.-made films is expected to continue growing as more countries and foreign individuals acquire the ability to view our films. This will result in employment growth of 29 percent between 2000 and 2010 as compared with 16 percent for all industries. In addition, many more jobs will arise as people leave this industry, mainly for more stable employment.

There is concern in the motion picture industry, however, over the number of films that are being made abroad. In response to a number of tax breaks offered by mainly English-speaking countries, especially Canada, U.S. filmmakers have increasingly moved the production of films abroad. Lower budget films, such as made-for-television movies and commercials, have fled in large numbers to save on costs. In addition, more feature films are being made abroad, but mostly for artistic reasons. When film production leaves, it takes away the jobs of most of the noncritical supporting actors and behind-the-scenes workers who are usually hired locally. To address this issue, California has initiated some tax breaks to encourage filmmakers to stay in California. Also, the U.S. Congress has a bill before it offering tax incentives for filmmakers to stay in the United States.

Despite the loss of some film production and its impact on jobs, most occupations will still see employment growth; however, opportunities will be better in some occupations than others. Computer specialists, multimedia artists and animators, film and video editors, and others skilled in digital filming, editing and computer-generated imaging should have the best job prospects. There also will be good job opportunities for broadcast and sound engineering technicians and craftspeople, such as gaffers and set construction workers. In contrast, keen competition can be expected for the more glamorous high-paying jobs in the industry, namely writers, actors, producers, and directors, as many more people seek these jobs than are generally available. Jobs with small or independent filmmakers may provide the best job prospects, as these companies are likely to grow more quickly as the costs of production decline due to digital technology.

## Sources of Additional Information

For general information on employment as an actor, contact:

➢ Screen Actors Guild, 5757 Wilshire Blvd., Los Angeles, CA 90036-3600. Internet: **http://www.sag.org**

➢ American Federation of Television and Radio Artists—Screen Actors Guild, Suite 204, 4340 East-West Hwy., Bethesda, MD 20814. Internet: **http://www.aftra.org**

For general information about arts education and a list of accredited college-level programs, contact:

➢ National Office for Arts Accreditation in Higher Education, 11250 Roger Bacon Dr., Suite 21, Reston, VA 22091. Internet: **http://www.arts-accredit.org**

Information on many motion picture production and distribution occupations may be found in the 2002-03 *Occupational Outlook Handbook*, including the following:

- Actors, producers, and directors

- Artists and related workers

- Broadcast and sound engineering technicians and radio operators

- Television, video, and motion picture camera operators and editors

- Writers and editors

# Personnel Supply Services

(SIC 736)

## SIGNIFICANT POINTS

- Personnel supply services ranks among the fastest growing industries in the Nation and is expected to provide the most new jobs.

- Most temporary jobs in this industry only require graduation from high school, while some permanent jobs may require a bachelor's or higher degree.

- Temporary jobs provide an entry into the workforce, supplemental income, and a bridge to full-time employment for many workers.

## Nature of the Industry

Although many people associate the personnel supply services industry with temporary employment opportunities for clerical workers, the industry matches millions of people with millions of jobs, providing both temporary and permanent employment to individuals with a wide variety of education and managerial and professional work experience. Occupations in the industry range from secretary to computer systems analyst, and from general laborer to nurse. In addition to temporary jobs in these occupations, permanent positions in the industry include workers such as employment interviewers and marketing representatives who help assign and place workers in jobs.

The personnel supply services industry has two distinct segments—*employment agencies* that place permanent employees, and *help supply services*, also referred to as temporary staffing agencies, that provide employees to other organizations on a contract basis. The typical employment agency has a relatively small permanent staff, usually fewer than 10 workers (see chart), who interview jobseekers and try to match their qualifications and skills to those being sought by employers for specific job openings.

In contrast to the smaller employment agencies, half of all temporary staffing agencies employ more than 50 workers (see chart on next page). Temporary staffing services firms or agencies provide temporary employees to other businesses to support or supplement their workforce in special situations, such as employee absences, temporary skill shortages, and varying seasonal workloads. Temporary workers are employed and paid by the temporary staffing services firm but are contracted out to a client for either a prearranged fee or an agreed hourly wage. Some companies choose to use temporary workers full time on an ongoing basis, rather than employ permanent staff, who typically would receive greater salaries and benefits. As a result, the overwhelming majority of workers in the temporary staffing services segment of the industry are temporaries; relatively few are permanent staff.

Traditionally, firms that placed permanent employees usually dealt with highly skilled applicants, such as lawyers or accountants, and those placing temporary employees dealt with less skilled workers, such as administrative support occupations. However, temporary staffing services firms increasingly place workers who have a range of educational backgrounds and work experience because businesses now are turning to temporary employees to fill all types of positions—from administrative to managerial, financial, professional, and production.

## Working Conditions

The average annual workweek in the personnel supply services industry was about 32.6 hours in 2000, compared with the average of 34.5 hours across all industries. The low average work week reflects the fact that a temporary employee could work 40 or more hours a week on a contract for an extended period and then take a few weeks off from work. Most full-time temporary workers put in 35-40 hours a week, while some work longer hours. Permanent employees in employment agencies usually work a standard 40-hour week, unless seasonal fluctuations require more or fewer hours.

Workers employed as permanent staff of employment agencies or temporary staffing services firms usually work in offices and may meet numerous people daily. Temporaries work in a variety of environments and often do not stay in any one place long enough to settle into a personal workspace or establish close relationships with coworkers. Most assignments are of short duration because temporaries may be called to replace a worker who is ill or on vacation or to help with a short-term surge of

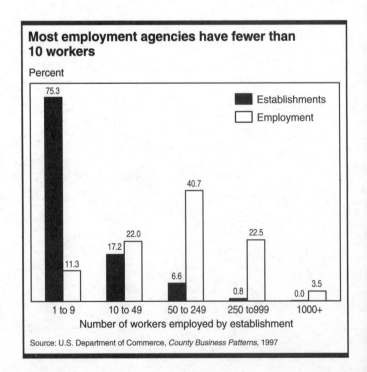

**Most employment agencies have fewer than 10 workers**

Percent

Legend: ■ Establishments □ Employment

| Number of workers employed by establishment | Establishments | Employment |
|---|---|---|
| 1 to 9 | 75.3 | 11.3 |
| 10 to 49 | 17.2 | 22.0 |
| 50 to 249 | 6.6 | 40.7 |
| 250 to 999 | 0.8 | 22.5 |
| 1000+ | 0.0 | 3.5 |

Source: U.S. Department of Commerce, *County Business Patterns*, 1997

work. However, assignments of several weeks or longer occasionally may be offered. On each assignment, temporary employees may work for a new supervisor.

Employment as a temporary is attractive to many. The opportunity for a short-term source of income while enjoying flexible schedules and opportunities to take extended leaves of absence is well-suited to students, persons juggling job and family responsibilities, those exploring various careers, and those seeking permanent positions in a chosen career. Firms try to accommodate workers' preferences for particular days or hours of work and for frequency or duration of assignments. Temporary work assignments provide an opportunity to experience a variety of work settings and employers, to sharpen skills through practice, and to learn new skills. Nevertheless, many workers in temporary assignments would prefer the stability and greater benefits associated with full-time work.

The annual injury and illness rate for the entire industry was 3.7 cases for every 100 full-time workers in 1999, lower than the rate of 6.3 for the entire private sector. Temporary workers in industrial occupations often perform work that is more strenuous and potentially more dangerous, so they may have a higher rate of injury and illness.

## Employment

The personnel supply services industry provided 3.9 million jobs in 2000, almost 3.5 million of them in help supply services firms. Although about 18,000 of the almost 63,000 establishments in the industry are employment agencies, staffing services firms employ 9 out of 10 industry workers. Employment in staffing services companies has been experiencing dramatic growth, and employment projections indicate continuing rapid growth in personnel supply services.

Employment in the personnel supply services industry is distributed throughout the United States. Workers are somewhat younger than those in other industries—nearly 50 percent of personnel supply services workers are under 35, compared with

38 percent of all workers, reflecting the large number of clerical and other entry-level positions in the industry that require little formal education.

## Occupations in the Industry

The personnel supply services industry encompasses many fields, from office and administrative support occupations to professional and production occupations (table 1). In general, occupations in the industry include the permanent staff of personnel supply services firms, and the variety of occupations supplied as temporary staff.

The permanent staff of personnel supply service agencies is responsible for the daily operation of the firm. Many of these workers are in management, business, and financial, and sales and related occupations, which combined account for only about 1 out of 10 jobs in this industry. *Managers* ensure that the agency is run effectively, and they often conduct interviews of potential clients and jobseekers. *Employment, recruitment, and placement specialists* recruit and evaluate applicants and attempt to match them with client firms. Most work in the personnel supply services industry. *Sales workers* actively pursue new client firms and recruit qualified workers. Because of fierce competition among agencies, marketing and sales work at times can be quite stressful.

The largest proportion—about 1 in 3—of all workers in this industry are in office and administrative support jobs. These positions may be either temporary or permanent. Experience in office and administrative support occupations usually is preferred for these jobs, although some persons take special training to learn skills such as bookkeeping and word processing. *Receptionists* greet visitors, field telephone calls, and perform assorted office functions. *Secretaries* perform a growing range of tasks, such as keyboarding and answering the telephone, depending on the type of firm in which they work. *Medical secretaries* make appointments and need a familiarity with common medical terms and procedures; *legal secretaries* must be familiar with the format of common legal documents. *General office clerks* file documents, type reports, and enter computer data. *File clerks* classify and store office information and records. *Data entry keyers* type information into a computer data base, either through a personal computer or directly into a mainframe computer. *Word processors and typists* enter and format drafts of documents using typewriters or computers. *Bookkeeping clerks* compute, classify, and record transaction data for financial records and reports.

Production, transportation and material moving occupations account for another 37 percent of employment in the personnel supply services industry, and the share of these workers employed as temporaries is growing. Many of these jobs seldom require education beyond high school, although related work experience may be preferred for some. Others require significant experience and on-the-job training. Highly skilled *assemblers and fabricators* may assemble and connect parts of electronic devices, while those less skilled work on production lines continually repeating the same operation. *Helpers* perform a variety of mostly unskilled tasks. *Laborers* and *freight, stock, and material movers* move goods to and from storage areas either in factories, warehouses, or other businesses. *Hand packers and packagers* wrap, package, inspect, and label materials manually, often keeping records of what has been packed and shipped.

A growing number of temporary workers also are specialized professional and service workers, which account for an-

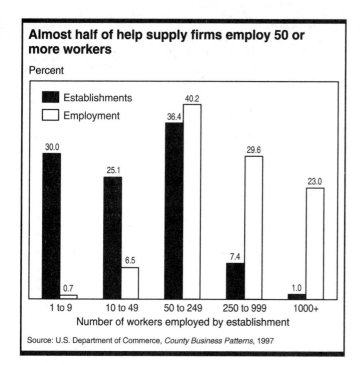

**Almost half of help supply firms employ 50 or more workers**

Percent

- ■ Establishments
- □ Employment

| Number of workers employed by establishment | Establishments | Employment |
|---|---|---|
| 1 to 9 | 30.0 | 0.7 |
| 10 to 49 | 25.1 | 6.5 |
| 50 to 249 | 36.4 | 40.2 |
| 250 to 999 | 7.4 | 29.6 |
| 1000+ | 1.0 | 23.0 |

Source: U.S. Department of Commerce, *County Business Patterns*, 1997

other 17 percent of employment. Professional and related occupations include a variety of computer specialists and health care practitioners. Most of these occupations require at least 2 to 4 years of college. *Computer programmers* write, test, and maintain the detailed instructions, called programs or software, that computers must follow to perform their functions. Other computer specialists include *computer support specialists* who provide technical assistance, support, and advice to customers and users. *Licensed practical nurses* provide basic bedside care to patients. *Registered nurses* administer medication, tend to patients, and advise patients and family members about procedures and proper care. They usually work in hospitals, but they may be assigned to private duty in patients' homes.

Service workers employed on a temporary basis also include a number of health care support occupations. *Home health aides* usually work in the home of an elderly or ill patient, allowing a patient to stay at home instead of being institutionalized. Becoming a home health aide generally does not require education beyond high school. *Nursing aides* and *orderlies* also seldom need education beyond high school, but employers do prefer previous experience. They assist nurses with patient care in hospitals and nursing homes.

The remainder of the workers in this industry includes those in farming, fishing, and forestry; installation, maintenance, and repair; and construction and extraction occupations.

## Training and Advancement

The personnel supply services industry offers opportunities in many occupations for workers with a variety of skill levels and experience. The majority of temporary jobs still only require graduation from high school or the equivalent, while some permanent jobs, such as those in management, may require a bachelor's or higher degree. In general, the training requirements of temporary workers mirror those for permanent employees in the economy as a whole. As the industry expands to include various professional and managerial occupations, therefore, a growing number of jobs will require professional or advanced degrees.

Many temporary staff services firms offer skills training to newly hired employees to make them more marketable. This training often is provided free to the temporary worker and is an economical way to acquire training in important skills such as word processing. Agency training policies vary, so persons considering temporary work should ask firms what training they offer and at what cost.

Advancement as a temporary employee usually takes the form of pay increases or greater choice of jobs. More often, temporaries transfer to full-time jobs with other employers. Turnover among temporaries within help supply firms usually is very high because few choose to work as temporaries for long; many accept offers to work full time for clients for whom they worked as temporaries. Some experienced temporaries may be offered permanent jobs with help supply firms, either as receptionists or in positions screening or training others for temporary jobs.

Permanent staff of employment agencies and temporary staff services firms typically are employment interviewers, administrative support workers, or managers. The qualifications required of employment interviewers depend partly on the occupations that the employment agency or help supply services firm specializes in placing. For example, agencies that place professionals, such as accountants or nurses, usually employ interviewers with college degrees in similar fields. Agencies specializing in placing administrative support workers, such as secretaries or word processors, are more likely to hire interviewers with less education who have experience in the occupations.

**Table 1. Employment of wage and salary workers in personnel supply services by occupation, 2000 and projected change, 2000-10**

(Employment in thousands)

| Occupation | Employment, 2000 | | Percent change, 2000-2010 |
|---|---|---|---|
| | Number | Percent | |
| **All occupations** | 3,887 | 100.0 | 49.2 |
| **Management, business, and financial occupations** | 183 | 4.7 | 54.6 |
| Employment, recruitment, and placement specialists | 57 | 1.5 | 40.4 |
| **Professional and related occupations** | 347 | 8.9 | 66.5 |
| Computer specialists | 67 | 1.7 | 95.1 |
| Registered nurses | 76 | 1.9 | 65.1 |
| Licensed practical and licensed vocational nurses | 43 | 1.1 | 46.6 |
| **Service occupations** | 329 | 8.5 | 56.0 |
| Home health aides | 47 | 1.2 | 65.1 |
| Nursing aides, orderlies, and attendants | 53 | 1.4 | 65.1 |
| Janitors and cleaners, except maids and housekeeping cleaners | 61 | 1.6 | 65.1 |
| **Sales and related occupations** | 120 | 3.1 | 48.8 |
| Telemarketers | 29 | 0.7 | 41.3 |
| **Office and administrative support occupations** | 1,305 | 33.6 | 40.5 |
| Bookkeeping, accounting, and auditing clerks | 71 | 1.8 | 42.2 |
| Customer service representatives | 103 | 2.6 | 56.2 |
| File clerks | 43 | 1.1 | 32.0 |
| Receptionists and information clerks | 92 | 2.4 | 53.9 |
| Stock clerks and order fillers | 85 | 2.2 | 65.1 |
| Data entry keyers | 121 | 3.1 | 22.7 |
| Office clerks, general | 246 | 6.3 | 37.4 |
| Executive secretaries and administrative assistants | 81 | 2.1 | 48.6 |
| Secretaries, except legal, medical, and executive | 108 | 2.8 | 32.1 |
| All other secretaries, administrative assistants, and other office support workers | 67 | 1.7 | 39.8 |
| **Construction and extraction occupations** | 122 | 3.1 | 61.6 |
| **Installation, maintenance, and repair occupations** | 55 | 1.4 | 57.1 |
| **Production occupations** | 746 | 19.2 | 47.3 |
| Team assemblers | 43 | 1.1 | 48.6 |
| All other assemblers and fabricators | 109 | 2.8 | 48.6 |
| Cutting, punching, and press machine setters, operators, and tenders, metal and plastic | 35 | 0.9 | 32.1 |
| Helpers—Production workers | 139 | 3.6 | 36.8 |
| Inspectors, testers, sorters, samplers, and weighers | 35 | 0.9 | 81.7 |
| Packaging and filling machine operators and tenders | 63 | 1.6 | 39.9 |
| **Transportation and material moving occupations** | 679 | 17.5 | 51.6 |
| Laborers and freight, stock, and material movers, hand | 335 | 8.6 | 48.6 |
| Packers and packagers, hand | 209 | 5.4 | 51.3 |

NOTE: May not add to totals due to omission of occupations with small employment.

Although permanent staff in administrative support occupations, such as receptionists, usually do not require formal education beyond high school, related work experience may be needed. Sometimes, staff experienced in administrative support occupations advance to employment interviewer positions. Employment interviewers advance to positions with higher earnings potential in which they interview persons seeking jobs with higher rates of pay. These positions often pay more because many interviewers receive a commission based on the fees paid by clients.

Most managers of employment agencies and temporary staff services firms have college degrees; an undergraduate degree in personnel management or a related field is the best preparation for these jobs. Employment, recruitment, and placement specialists often advance to managerial positions, but seldom without a bachelor's degree.

## Earnings

In 2000, earnings among nonsupervisory workers in help supply services firms were $11.07 per hour and $361 per week, lower than $13.70 an hour and $474 a week for all private industry.

Earnings vary as widely as the range of skills and formal education among workers in personnel supply services. As in other industries, managers and professionals earn more than clerks and laborers. Also, temporaries usually earn less than workers employed as permanent staff, but some experienced temporaries make as much or more than workers in similar occupations in other industries. Earnings in the largest occupations in personnel supply services appear in table 2.

**Table 2. Median hourly earnings of the largest occupations in personnel supply services, 2000**

| Occupation | Personnel supply services | All industries |
|---|---|---|
| Registered nurses | $ 22.53 | $ 21.56 |
| Employment, recruitment, and placement specialists | 16.67 | 17.54 |
| Secretaries, except legal, medical, and executive | 11.45 | 11.47 |
| Customer service representatives | 10.16 | 11.83 |
| Data entry keyers | 9.65 | 10.24 |
| Receptionists and information clerks | 9.53 | 9.63 |
| Office clerks, general | 9.38 | 10.16 |
| Laborers and freight, stock, and material movers, hand | 7.62 | 9.04 |
| Helpers—Production workers | 7.47 | 8.66 |
| Packers and packagers, hand | 7.40 | 7.53 |

Most permanent workers receive basic benefits; temporary workers usually do not receive such benefits unless they work a minimum number of hours or days per week to qualify for benefit plans. Only 3.3 percent of workers in personnel supply services are union members or are covered by union contracts, compared with 14.9 percent of workers in all industries combined.

## Outlook

Personnel supply services ranks among the fastest growing industries in the Nation and is the industry projected to provide the most new jobs. The industry is expected to gain about 1.9 million new jobs over the period. Wage and salary employment in the personnel supply services industry is expected to grow 49 percent over the 2000-10 period, more than 3 times the 16-percent growth projected for all industries combined.

Growth in demand for temporary employees has fueled the expansion of the industry and is attributable to a number of factors. As competition has grown, businesses have sought new ways to make their staffing patterns more responsive to changes in demand. To achieve this, they have increasingly hired temporary employees with specialized skills, to reduce costs and bridge areas where know-how or experience may be lacking. As governments and other organizations increasingly use temporary workers, demand is expected to continue increasing rapidly. This growth in demand, coupled with significant turnover in these positions, should create plentiful opportunities for persons who seek jobs as temporaries.

Employment agencies also are expected to continue growing, but not as fast as temporary staffing services. Growth in these agencies stems from employers' increasing willingness to allow outside agencies to perform the preliminary screening of candidates and the growing acceptance of executive recruitment services. However, online employment agencies operate without employment counselors and need fewer administrative support workers. Job postings on employer Web sites; online newspaper classified ads; and job matching sites operated by educational institutions and professional associations compete with this industry, thereby dampening employment growth.

Most new jobs will arise in the largest occupational groups in this industry—office and administrative support occupations, production, and transportation and material moving occupations. However, the continuing trend toward specialization also will spur growth among professional workers, including engineers, computer specialists, and healthcare practitioners, as well as managers, as government increasingly contracts out management functions. In addition, growth of temporary staffing firms specializing in accounting, legal, and information technology services will provide more opportunities for professional workers within those fields. Marketing and sales representative jobs in temporary staffing firms also are expected to increase along with competition among these firms for the most qualified workers and the best clients.

## Sources of Additional Information

For information concerning employment in help supply services, contact:

➤ American Staffing Association, 277 S. Washington St., Suite 200, Alexandria, VA 22314. Internet: **http://www.natss.org**

For information about employment agencies, contact:

➤ National Association of Personnel Services, 3133 Mt. Vernon Ave., Alexandria, VA 22305. Internet: **http://napsweb.org**

More information about many occupations in this industry, including the following, appears in the 2002-03 *Occupational Outlook Handbook*:

- Construction laborers
- Human resources, training, and labor relations managers and specialists
- Interviewers
- Office clerks, general
- Personal and home care aides
- Receptionists and information clerks
- Secretaries and administrative assistants

# Social Services, Except Childcare

(SIC 83, except 835)

## SIGNIFICANT POINTS

- About 7 out of 10 jobs are in professional and service occupations.

- Several occupations concentrated in social services—social and human service assistants, personal and home care aides, and home health aides—are among the fastest growing occupations in the economy.

- Average earnings are low because of the large number of part-time and low-paying service jobs.

## Nature of the Industry

Careers in social services appeal to persons with a strong desire to make life better and easier for others. Workers in this industry usually are good communicators and enjoy interacting with people. Social services workers help the homeless, housebound, and infirm cope with circumstances of daily living; counsel troubled and emotionally disturbed individuals; train or retrain the unemployed or underemployed; care for the elderly and the physically and mentally disabled; help the needy obtain financial assistance; and solicit contributions for various social services organizations. About 102,000 establishments in the private sector provided social services in 1997. Thousands of other establishments, mainly in State and local government, provided many additional social services. (For information about government social services, see the *Career Guide* statements on Federal Government, and State and local government, excluding education and hospitals.)

Social services contain four segments—individual and miscellaneous social services, residential care, job training and related services, and childcare services. (The childcare services industry, including daycare and preschool care centers, is covered in a separate *Career Guide* statement.)

*Individual and miscellaneous social services* establishments provide counseling and welfare services including refugee, disaster, and temporary-relief services. Government offices distribute welfare aid, rent supplements, and food stamps. Some agencies provide adult daycare, home-delivered meals, and home health and personal care services. Other services concentrate on children, such as big brother and sister organizations, youth centers, and adoption services. Workers in crisis centers may focus on individual, marriage, child, or family counseling. Also included are many different kinds of establishments, such as advocacy groups, antipoverty boards, community development groups, and health and welfare councils. Many miscellaneous social services organizations are concerned with community improvement and social change. They may solicit contributions, administer appropriations, and allocate funds among other agencies engaged in social welfare services.

*Residential care* facilities provide around-the-clock social and personal care to children, the elderly, and others who have limited ability to care for themselves. Workers care for residents of alcohol and drug rehabilitation centers, group homes, and halfway houses. Nursing and medical care, however, is not the main focus of establishments providing residential care, as it is in nursing or personal care facilities. (See the statement on health services, elsewhere in the *Career Guide*.)

*Job training and related services* establishments train the unemployed, underemployed, disabled, and others with job market disadvantages. Vocational specialists and counselors work with clients to overcome deficient education, job skills, or experience. Often industrial psychologists or career counselors will assess the job skills of a client and, working with both the employer and the client, decide whether the client would be better served by taking additional job training, by being placed in a different job with his or her current skills, or by having the job restructured to accommodate any skill deficiency.

## Working Conditions

Some social services establishments—such as residential care facilities—operate around the clock. Thus, evening, weekend, and holiday work is not uncommon. Some establishments may be understaffed, resulting in large caseloads for each worker. Jobs in voluntary, nonprofit agencies often are part time.

Some workers spend a substantial amount of time traveling within the local area. For example, home health and personal care aides routinely visit clients in their homes; social workers and social and human service assistants also may make home visits. In 1999, the incidence rate for occupational injury and illness in social services varied by industry sector. Compared with the rate of 6.3 per 100 full-time workers for the entire private sector, job training and related services had a higher rate of 9.2. On the other hand, individual and family services had a lower than average rate of 4.5.

## Employment

Social services provided nearly than 2.2 million nongovernment wage and salary jobs in 2000. Almost half were in individual and miscellaneous social services (table 1). About 2 percent of workers in this industry were self-employed or unpaid family workers.

In 1997, about 65 percent of social services establishments employed fewer than 10 workers; however, larger establishments accounted for most jobs (chart).

Social services workers are somewhat older than workers in other industries (table 2). About 41 percent were 45 years old or older, compared with 35 percent of all workers. Jobs in social services are concentrated in large States with heavily populated urban areas, such as New York and California.

**Table 1. Employment of nongovernment wage and salary workers in social services, except childcare, by detailed industry, 2000**

(Employment in thousands)

| Industry segemnt | Employment, 2000 Number | Employment, 2000 Percent | Percent change, 2000-2010 |
|---|---|---|---|
| Total, social services, except childcare ... | 2,191 | 100.0 | 42.2 |
| Individual and miscellaneous social services .............................. | 1,005 | 45.9 | 29.3 |
| Residential care ...................... | 806 | 36.8 | 63.5 |
| Job training and related services ........... | 380 | 17.3 | 31.7 |

## Occupations in the Industry

Almost one-third of nongovernment social service jobs are in professional and related occupations (table 3). *Social workers* counsel and assess the needs of clients, refer them to the appropriate sources of help, and monitor their progress. They may specialize in child welfare and family services, mental health, medical social work, school social work, community organization activities, or clinical social work. *Social and human service assistants* serve in a variety of social and human service delivery settings. Job titles and duties of these workers vary, but they include human service worker, case management aide, social work assistant, mental health aide, child abuse worker, community outreach worker, and gerontology aide. *Counselors* help people evaluate their interests and abilities and advise and assist them with personal and social problems.

Almost 4 out of 10 nongovernment jobs in social services are in service occupations. *Residential advisors* develop and coordinate nonmedical activities for residents of long-term care and treatment facilities, such as assisted-living housing for the elderly. The social services industry employs more than half of all residential advisors. *Personal and home care aides* help elderly, disabled, and ill persons live in their own homes instead

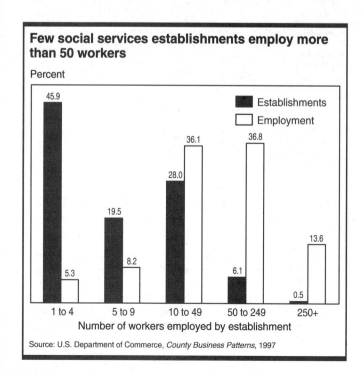

**Few social services establishments employ more than 50 workers**

Percent

Source: U.S. Department of Commerce, *County Business Patterns*, 1997

**Table 2. Percent distribution of employment in social services by age group, 2000**

| Age group | Social services | All industries |
|---|---|---|
| Total ................................................. | 100.0 | 100.0 |
| 16 to 24........................................... | 11.7 | 15.3 |
| 25 to 34........................................... | 23.4 | 22.6 |
| 35 to 44........................................... | 24.1 | 27.1 |
| 45 to 54........................................... | 23.9 | 22.0 |
| 55 to 64........................................... | 12.2 | 10.1 |
| 65 and older ................................... | 4.6 | 3.0 |

of an institution by providing routine personal care services. Although some are employed by public or private agencies, many are self-employed. Persons in *food preparation and serving related occupations* serve residents at social services institutions. *Nursing* or *home health aides* provide health-related services for ill, injured, disabled, elderly, or infirm individuals either in institutions or in their homes.

As in most industries, office and administrative support workers—secretaries and bookkeepers, for example—as well as managers account for many jobs. However, social services employ a much smaller percentage of production; installation, maintenance, and repair; and sales jobs than does the economy as a whole.

Certain occupations are more heavily concentrated in some segments of the industry than in others. Individual and miscellaneous social services, for example, employ the greatest numbers of social workers, social and human service assistants, and personal and home care aides. Job training and vocational rehabilitation services provide the most jobs for adult literacy and remedial education teachers and instructors. Nursing and psychiatric and home health aides and food preparation and serving related workers work mainly in the residential care segment of the industry.

## Training and Advancement

Some occupations in social services have very specific entrance requirements. These include most of the professional and related occupations. Those requiring specific clinical training, such as clinical social workers and clinical psychologists, also require appropriate State licensure or certification. Nevertheless, people with a limited background in social services or little education beyond high school can find a job in the industry. Nursing aids, orderlies, and attendants; home health aides; and personal and home care aides are some of these occupations. Many establishments provide on-the-job or classroom training, especially for those with limited background or training.

Many employers prefer social and human service assistants with some related work experience or college courses in human services, social work, or one of the social or behavioral sciences. Other employers prefer an associate degree or a bachelor's degree in human services or social work. A number of employers provide in-service training, such as seminars and workshops.

Entry-level jobs for social workers require a bachelor's degree in social work or in an undergraduate major such as psychology or sociology. However, most agencies require a master's degree in social work or a closely related field. Public agencies and private practice clinics that offer clinical or consultative services require an advanced degree in clinical social work; supervisory, administrative, and staff training positions usually require at least a master's degree.

**Table 3.  Employment of wage and salary workers in social services, except childcare by occupation, 2000 and projected change, 2000-10**

(Employment in thousands)

| Occupation | Employment, 2000 Number | Employment, 2000 Percent | Percent change, 2000-2010 |
|---|---|---|---|
| **All occupations** | 2,191 | 100.0 | 42.3 |
| **Management, business, and financial occupations** | 262 | 12.0 | 33.7 |
| General and operations managers | 53 | 2.4 | 33.2 |
| Social and community service managers | 37 | 1.7 | 34.5 |
| Human resources, training, and labor relations specialists | 26 | 1.2 | 23.3 |
| **Professional and related occupations** | 684 | 31.2 | 45.6 |
| Social scientists and related occupations | 16 | 0.7 | 37.4 |
| Educational, vocational, and school counselors | 21 | 1.0 | 47.2 |
| Mental health counselors | 27 | 1.3 | 26.0 |
| Rehabilitation counselors | 69 | 3.2 | 26.5 |
| Substance abuse and behavioral disorder counselors | 23 | 1.0 | 47.6 |
| Social and human service assistants | 129 | 5.9 | 76.6 |
| Child, family, and school social workers | 85 | 3.9 | 38.0 |
| Medical and public health social workers | 19 | 0.9 | 33.4 |
| Mental health and substance abuse social workers | 23 | 1.0 | 62.6 |
| Preschool teachers, except special education | 21 | 0.9 | 9.5 |
| Teacher assistants | 29 | 1.3 | 34.5 |
| Registered nurses | 30 | 1.4 | 50.4 |
| Licensed practical and licensed vocational nurses | 23 | 1.0 | 40.7 |
| **Service occupations** | 853 | 38.9 | 50.3 |
| Home health aides | 226 | 10.3 | 42.4 |
| Nursing aides, orderlies, and attendants | 62 | 2.8 | 64.9 |
| Cooks, institution and cafeteria | 29 | 1.3 | 46.8 |
| Food and beverage serving workers | 22 | 1.0 | 42.9 |
| Building cleaning workers | 61 | 2.8 | 42.6 |
| Childcare workers | 62 | 2.8 | 57.2 |
| Personal and home care aides | 225 | 10.3 | 64.2 |
| Recreation workers | 23 | 1.1 | 27.3 |
| Residential advisors | 23 | 1.0 | 30.8 |
| **Sales and related occupations** | 22 | 1.0 | 31.4 |
| **Office and administrative support occupations** | 245 | 11.2 | 21.7 |
| Bookkeeping, accounting, and auditing clerks | 28 | 1.3 | 19.6 |
| Receptionists and information clerks | 27 | 1.2 | 40.5 |
| Office clerks, general | 41 | 1.9 | 35.4 |
| Executive secretaries and administrative assistants | 38 | 1.7 | 23.1 |
| Secretaries, except legal, medical, and executive | 34 | 1.5 | 9.7 |
| **Installation, maintenance, and repair occupations** | 21 | 1.0 | 35.0 |
| **Production occupations** | 36 | 1.6 | 28.0 |
| **Transportation and material moving occupations** | 64 | 2.9 | 30.0 |
| Motor vehicle operators | 38 | 1.7 | 33.7 |

NOTE: May not add to totals due to omission of occupations with small employment.

Volunteering with a student, religious, or charitable organization is a good way for persons to test their interest in social services, and may provide an advantage when applying for jobs in this industry.

Advancement paths vary.  For example, some personal and home care aides as well as some nursing aides, orderlies, and attendants, and home health aides get additional training and become licensed practical nurses.  Formal education—usually a bachelor's or master's degree in counseling, human services, rehabilitation, social work, or a related field—almost always is necessary for social and human service assistants to advance.  Social workers with an advanced degree and the appropriate license can advance to supervisor, program manager, assistant director, or executive director of an agency or department.  They also may enter private practice and provide psychotherapeutic counseling and other services on a contract basis.  Private practice for social workers depends on the affordability of services, including the availability of funding from third parties.

## Earnings

Earnings in selected occupations in the social services, except childcare, industry in 2000 appear in table 4.  As in most industries, professionals and managers—whose salaries reflect higher education levels, broader experience, and greater responsibility—commonly earn more than other workers in social services.

**Table 4. Median hourly earnings of the largest occupations in social services, except childcare, 2000**

| Occupation | Individual and family services | Job training and related services | Residential care | Social services, not elsewhere classified | All industries |
|---|---|---|---|---|---|
| Registered nurses | $ 18.86 | $ 19.44 | $ 18.67 | $ 19.09 | $ 21.56 |
| Social and community service managers | 17.57 | 18.14 | 17.00 | 18.17 | 18.81 |
| Mental health counselors | 13.48 | 12.34 | 11.02 | 13.43 | 13.25 |
| Child, family, and school social workers | 13.06 | 12.08 | 12.88 | 12.47 | 15.13 |
| Rehabilitation counselors | 11.37 | 11.09 | 9.79 | 10.32 | 11.75 |
| Social and human service assistants | 10.27 | 9.71 | 9.56 | 10.49 | 10.74 |
| Home health aides | 7.89 | 8.32 | 8.16 | 8.10 | 8.23 |
| Nursing aides, orderlies, and attendants | 7.88 | 8.05 | 7.96 | 6.35 | 8.89 |
| Personal and home care aides | 7.75 | 7.85 | 7.97 | 7.56 | 7.50 |
| Child care workers | 7.67 | 6.61 | 8.71 | 7.30 | 7.43 |

About 12 percent of workers in the social services industry were union members or were covered by union contracts in 2000, compared with about 15 percent of workers throughout all industries.

## Outlook

Job opportunities in social services should be numerous through the year 2010. The number of nongovernment wage and salary jobs is expected to increase 42 percent, compared with only 15 percent for all industries combined. Expected growth rates for the various segments of the industry are 29 percent in individual and miscellaneous social services, 32 percent in job training and related services, and 64 percent in residential care over the 2000-10 period. In addition to employment growth, many job openings will stem from the need to replace workers who transfer to other occupations or stop working.

The expected growth is mostly due to expanding services for the elderly. Services also will grow for the mentally ill, the physically disabled, and families in crisis. In addition, older people make up a rapidly expanding segment of the population and are more likely than younger people to need social services, and businesses are implementing more employee-counseling programs. The growing emphasis on providing home care services rather than more costly nursing home or hospital care, and on earlier and better integration of the physically disabled and mentally ill into society, also will contribute to employment growth in the social services industry, as will increased demand for drug and alcohol abuse prevention programs. The expansion and creation of employment in the social services industry may rely on the amount of funding made available by the government and managed-care organizations.

Some of the fastest growing occupations in the Nation are concentrated in social services. Compared with industry growth of 42 percent, the number of nursing, psychiatric, and home health aides within social services is projected to grow 48 percent between 2000 and 2010; social and human service assistants, 77 percent; and personal and home care aides, 64 percent.

Overall employment of social workers will continue to grow, but not as rapidly as that of social and human service assistants, as the cost-containment efforts of managed-care organizations limit demand for clinical social workers.

## Sources of Additional Information

For additional information about careers in social work, contact:

➤ National Association of Social Workers, 750 First St. NE., Suite 700, Washington, DC 20002-4241. Internet: **http://www.naswdc.org**

For information on programs and careers in human services, contact:

➤ Council for Standards in Human Services Education, Northern Essex Community College, 100 Elliott Way, Haverhill, MA 01830. Internet: **http://www.cshse.com**

State employment service offices may also be able to provide information on job opportunities in social services.

Information on many occupations in social services, including the following, may be found in the 2002-03 *Occupational Outlook Handbook*:

- Counselors
- Nursing, psychiatric, and home health aides
- Personal and home care aides
- Social and human service assistants
- Social workers
- Teachers—adult literacy and remedial and self-enrichment education

# Government

# Federal Government, Excluding the Postal Service

## SIGNIFICANT POINTS

- More than half of Federal workers held managerial or professional jobs, double the rate for the workforce as a whole.

- About 4 out of 5 Federal employees work outside the Washington, DC, metropolitan area.

- Federal employment is projected to decline slightly due to budgetary constraints, the growing use of private contractors, and the transfer of some functions to State and local governments.

## Nature of the Industry

The Federal Government affects Americans in countless ways. It defends them from foreign aggression, represents their interests abroad, enforces laws, and administers many different programs and agencies. Americans are particularly aware of the Federal Government when they pay their income taxes each year, but they usually do not consider the government's role when they watch a weather forecast, purchase fresh and uncontaminated groceries, travel by highway or air, or make a deposit at their bank. Workers employed by the Federal Government play a vital role in these and many other aspects of American life. (While career opportunities in the U.S. Postal Service and the Armed Forces are not covered here, both are described in the 2002-03 edition of the *Occupational Outlook Handbook*. See the *Handbook* statements on postal service workers and job opportunities in the Armed Forces.)

Over 200 years ago, the founders of the United States gathered in Philadelphia, PA, and created a constitution for a new national government and laid the foundation for self-governance in America. The Constitution of the United States, ratified by the last of the 13 original states in 1791, created the three branches of the Federal Government and granted certain powers and responsibilities to each. The legislative, judicial, and executive branches were created with equal powers but very different responsibilities that act to keep their powers in balance.

The legislative branch is responsible for forming and amending the legal structure of the Nation. Its largest component is Congress, the primary U.S. legislative body, which is made up of the Senate and the House of Representatives. This body includes senators, representatives, their staffs, and various support workers. The legislative branch employs only about 1 percent of Federal workers, nearly all of whom work in the Washington, DC, area.

The judicial branch is responsible for interpreting the laws that the legislative branch enacts. The Supreme Court, the Nation's definitive judicial body, makes the highest rulings. Its decisions usually follow an appeal of a decision made by the one of the regional Courts of Appeal, which hear cases appealed from U.S. District Courts, the Court of Appeals for the Federal Circuit, or State Supreme Courts. U.S. District Courts are located in each State and are the first to hear most cases under Federal jurisdiction. The judicial branch employs about the same number of people as the legislative branch, but its offices and employees are dispersed throughout the country.

Of the three branches, the executive branch—through the power vested by the Constitution in the office of the President—has the widest range of responsibilities. Consequently, it employed about 97 percent of all Federal civilian employees (excluding postal workers) in 2000. The executive branch is composed of the Executive Office of the President, 14 executive cabinet departments, and nearly 90 independent agencies, each of which has clearly defined duties. The Executive Office of the President is composed of several offices and councils that aid the President in policy decisions. These include the Office of Management and Budget, which oversees the administration of the Federal budget; the National Security Council, which advises the President on matters of national defense; and the Council of Economic Advisers, which makes economic policy recommendations.

Each of the 14 executive cabinet departments administers programs that oversee an element of American life. The highest departmental official of each cabinet department, the Secretary, is a member of the President's cabinet. Each, listed by employment size, is described below (table 1).

- *Defense:* Manages the military forces that protect our country and its interests, including the Departments of the Army, Navy, Air Force, and a number of smaller agencies. The civilian workforce employed by the Department of Defense performs various support activities, such as payroll and public relations.
- *Veterans Affairs:* Administers programs to aid U.S. veterans and their families, runs the veterans' hospital system, and operates our national cemeteries.
- *Treasury:* Regulates banks and other financial institutions, administers the public debt, prints currency, collects federal income taxes, and carries out law enforcement in a wide range of areas, including counterfeiting, tax, and customs violations.
- *Justice:* Enforces Federal laws, prosecutes cases in Federal courts, and runs Federal prisons.
- *Agriculture:* Promotes U.S. agriculture domestically and internationally and sets standards governing quality, quantity, and labeling of food sold in the United States.
- *Interior:* Manages Federal lands including the national parks and forests, runs hydroelectric power systems, and promotes conservation of natural resources.
- *Transportation:* Sets national transportation policy; runs the Coast Guard (except in time of war); plans and funds the construction of highways and mass transit systems; and regulates railroad, aviation, and maritime operations.
- *Health and Human Services:* Sponsors medical research, approves use of new drugs and medical devices, runs the Public Health Service, and administers Medicare.
- *Commerce:* Forecasts the weather, charts the oceans, regulates patents and trademarks, conducts the census,

compiles statistics, and promotes U.S. economic growth by encouraging international trade.

- *Energy:* Coordinates the national use and provision of energy, oversees the production and disposal of nuclear weapons, and plans for future energy needs.
- *Labor:* Enforces laws guaranteeing fair pay, workplace safety, and equal job opportunity; administers unemployment insurance; regulates pension funds; and collects and analyzes economic data at the Bureau of Labor Statistics.
- *State:* Oversees the Nation's embassies and consulates, issues passports, monitors U.S. interests abroad, and represents the United States before international organizations.
- *Housing and Urban Development:* Funds public housing projects, enforces equal housing laws, and insures and finances mortgages.
- *Education*: Provides scholarships, student loans, and aid to schools.

**Table 1. Federal Government executive branch civilian employment, except U.S. Postal Service, September 2000**
(Employment in thousands)

|  | United States | Washington, DC area |
|---|---|---|
| Total ................................................ | 1,700 | 272 |
| **Executive departments** ........................ |  |  |
| Defense, total ........................................ | 623 | 64 |
| Army ................................................ | 207 | 19 |
| Navy ................................................ | 177 | 25 |
| Air Force .......................................... | 148 | 5 |
| Other .............................................. | 91 | 14 |
| Veterans Affairs ................................... | 216 | 7 |
| Treasury ............................................. | 142 | 23 |
| Justice ............................................... | 123 | 22 |
| Agriculture ......................................... | 103 | 11 |
| Interior ............................................. | 73 | 8 |
| Transportation .................................... | 63 | 10 |
| Health and Human Services ................. | 62 | 28 |
| Commerce ........................................... | 47 | 21 |
| Energy ............................................... | 16 | 5 |
| Labor ................................................. | 16 | 5 |
| State .................................................. | 11 | 9 |
| Housing and Urban Development ........... | 10 | 3 |
| Education ............................................ | 5 | 3 |
| **Independent agencies** ........................... |  |  |
| Social Security Administration ............... | 64 | 2 |
| National Aeronautics and Space Administration ........................ | 19 | 4 |
| Environmental Protection Agency ........... | 18 | 6 |
| General Services Administration ............. | 14 | 5 |
| Tennessee Valley Authority .................... | 13 | 0 |
| Federal Deposit Insurance Corporation ... | 7 | 3 |

Source: U.S. Office of Personnel Management

Numerous independent agencies perform tasks that fall between the jurisdictions of the executive departments or that are more efficiently executed by an autonomous agency. Some smaller, but well- known independent agencies include the Peace Corps, the Securities and Exchange Commission, and the Federal Communications Commission. Although the majority of these agencies are fairly small, employing fewer than 1,000 workers (many employ fewer than 100 workers), some are quite large. The largest independent agencies are:

- *Social Security Administration:* Operates various retirement and disability programs and Medicaid.
- *National Aeronautics and Space Administration:* Oversees aviation research and conducts exploration and research beyond the Earth's atmosphere.
- *Environmental Protection Agency:* Runs programs to control and reduce pollution of the Nation's water, air, and lands.
- *General Services Administration:* Manages and protects Federal Government property and records.
- *Tennessee Valley Authority:* Operates the hydroelectric power system in the Tennessee river valley.
- *Federal Deposit Insurance Corporation:* Maintains stability of and public confidence in the Nation's financial system, by insuring deposits and promoting sound banking practices.

## Working Conditions

Due to the wide range of Federal jobs, most of the working conditions found in the private sector also are found in the Federal Government. Most white-collar employees work in office buildings, hospitals, or laboratories, and most of the blue-collar workforce can be found in warehouses, shipyards, military bases, construction sites, national parks, and national forests. Work environments vary from comfortable and relaxed to hazardous and stressful, such as those experienced by law enforcement officers, astronauts, and air traffic controllers.

The vast majority of Federal employees work full time, often on flexible or "flexi-time" schedules that allow workers more control over their work schedules. Some agencies also offer telecommuting or "flexi-place" programs, which allow selected workers to perform some job duties at home or from regional centers.

Some Federal workers spend much of their time away from the offices in which they are based. Inspectors and compliance officers, for example, often visit businesses and worksites to ensure that laws and regulations are obeyed. Some Federal workers frequently travel long distances, spending days or weeks away from home. Auditors, for example, may spend weeks at a time in distant locations.

## Employment

In 2000, the Federal Government employed about 1.9 million civilian workers, or about 1.3 percent of the Nation's workforce. Although the Federal Government employs workers in every major occupational group, workers are not employed in the same proportions in which they are employed throughout the economy as a whole (table 2). The analytical and technical nature of many government duties translates into a much higher proportion of professional, management, business, and financial occupations in the Federal Government, compared with most industries. Conversely, the Government sells very little, so it employs relatively few sales workers.

Even though most Federal departments and agencies are based in the Washington, DC, area, fewer than 1 in 5 Federal employees worked in the vicinity of the Nation's Capital in 2000. In addition to Federal employees working throughout the United States, about 5 percent are assigned overseas, mostly in embassies or defense installations.

## Occupations in the Industry

Although the Federal Government employed workers in almost every occupation in 2000, about 78 percent of Federal workers were employed in professional and related; management, business, and financial; or office and administrative support occupations (table 3). Professional and related occupations comprise about 31 percent of Federal employment. The largest group of these workers are engineers, such as *chemical, civil, aeronautical, industrial, electrical, mechanical,* and *nuclear engineers*. These professionals are found in many departments of the executive branch, but they most commonly work in the Department of Defense, the National Aeronautics and Space Administration, and the Department of Transportation. In general, they solve problems and provide advice on technical programs, such as building highway bridges or implementing agency-wide computer systems.

Table 2. Percent distribution of wage and salary employment in the Federal Government and the total for all industries by major occupational group, 2000

| Occupational group | Federal Government | All industries |
|---|---|---|
| Total ............................................... | 100.0 | 100.0 |
| Professional and related ................................. | 30.7 | 18.6 |
| Management, business, and financial ............ | 26.7 | 9.5 |
| Office and administrative support ................... | 20.8 | 17.5 |
| Service............................................................ | 7.6 | 18.2 |
| Installation, maintenance, and repair .............. | 5.3 | 4.0 |
| Transportation and material moving ................ | 3.4 | 7.2 |
| Production ...................................................... | 2.6 | 9.5 |
| Construction and extraction ............................ | 2.2 | 4.6 |
| Sales and related ........................................... | 0.6 | 10.0 |
| Farming, fishing and forestry .......................... | 0.2 | 0.9 |

Other professional and related workers include *computer software engineers, computer scientists,* and *systems analysts,* who are employed throughout government. They write computer programs, analyze problems related to data processing, and keep computer systems running smoothly. Also in this group are health professionals, such as *registered nurses* and *physicians and surgeons,* most of whom are employed by the Department of Veterans Affairs (VA) in one of the many VA hospitals. Other professionals include life scientists, such as *biological scientists,* and *physical scientists,* such as *geologists, meteorologists,* and *physicists,* who examine the state of the earth and research physical phenomena. The Department of Agriculture employs the vast majority of life scientists, but physical scientists are distributed throughout government.

Other members of this group aid in research, analysis, or law enforcement. Often their tasks and skills are quite specialized, as with *engineering technicians,* who may work either directly with engineers or by themselves.

Management, business, and financial workers, who comprise about 27 percent of Federal employment, are primarily responsible for overseeing operations. *Legislators,* for example, are responsible for passing and amending laws. Managerial workers include a broad range of officials who, at the highest levels, may head Federal agencies or programs. Middle managers, on the other hand, usually oversee one activity or aspect of a program.

Others provide management support. *Accountants* and *auditors* prepare and analyze financial reports, review and record revenues and expenditures, and investigate operations for fraud and inefficiency. *Tax examiners, collectors, and revenue agents* determine and collect taxes. *Purchasing agents* handle Federal purchases of supplies; and *management analysts* study government operations and systems and suggest improvements.

More than 1 Federal worker in 5 is in an office and administrative support occupation. These employees aid management staff with administrative duties. Administrative support workers in the Federal Government include *secretaries, procurement clerks,* and *word processors and typists.*

Compared with the economy as a whole, workers in service occupations are relatively scarce in the Federal Government. More than half of all Federal workers in these occupations are protective service workers, such as *detectives and criminal investigators, police and sheriff's patrol officers,* and *correctional officers.* These workers protect the public from crime and oversee Federal prisons.

Federally employed workers in installation, maintenance, and repair occupations include *aircraft mechanics and service technicians* who fix and maintain all types of aircraft, and *electrical and electronic equipment mechanics, installers, and repairers* who inspect, adjust, and repair electronic equipment such as industrial controls, transmitters, antennas, radar, radio, and navigation systems.

The Federal Government employs a relatively small number of workers in transportation, production, and construction occupations, such as *air traffic controllers* and *inspectors, testers, sorters, samplers, and weighers.*

## Training and Advancement

Training and educational requirements in the Federal Government mirror those in the private sector for most major occupational groups. Many jobs in professional and related occupations, for example, require a 4-year college degree. Some, such as *engineers, physicians and surgeons,* and *biological* and *physical scientists,* require a bachelor's or higher degree in a specific field of study. However, *registered nurse* and many technician occupations may be entered with 2 years of training after high school. Also, because managers usually are promoted from professional occupations, most have at least a bachelor's degree. Office and administrative support workers in the government usually need only a high school diploma, although any further training or experience, such as a junior college degree, or at least 2 years of relevant work experience, is an asset. Most Federal jobs in other occupations require no more than a high school degree, although most departments and agencies prefer workers with vocational training or previous experience.

In general, each Federal department or agency determines its own training requirements and offers workers opportunities to improve job skills or become qualified to advance to other jobs. These may include technical or skills training, tuition assistance or reimbursement, fellowship programs, and executive leadership and management training programs, seminars, and workshops. This training may be offered on the job, by another agency, or at local colleges and universities.

Advancement in the Federal Government is commonly based on a system of occupational pay levels, or "grades." Workers enter the Federal civil service at the starting grade for an occupation and begin a "career ladder" of promotions until they reach the full-performance grade for that occupation. This system provides for a limited number of noncompetitive promotions which usually are awarded at regular intervals, assuming job performance is satisfactory. Although these promotions do not occur more than once a year, they sometimes are awarded in the form of two-grade increases. The exact pay grade

## Table 3. Employment of wage and salary workers in the Federal Government, excluding the Postal Service, by occupation, 2000 and projected change, 2000-10

(Employment in thousands)

| Occupation | Employment, 2000 Number | Employment, 2000 Percent | Percent change, 2000-2010 |
|---|---|---|---|
| **All occupations** | 1,917 | 100.0 | -7.6 |
| **Management, business, and financial occupations** | 513 | 26.7 | -5.9 |
| Engineering managers | 18 | 0.9 | -22.3 |
| Purchasing agents, except wholesale, retail, and farm products | 30 | 1.6 | -5.0 |
| Compliance officers, except agriculture, construction, health and safety, and transportation | 36 | 1.9 | -5.0 |
| Management analysts | 45 | 2.3 | 12.0 |
| All other business operations specialists | 127 | 6.6 | -5.0 |
| Accountants and auditors | 38 | 2.0 | -24.0 |
| Tax examiners, collectors, and revenue agents | 39 | 2.1 | 4.5 |
| **Professional and related occupations** | 589 | 30.7 | -3.2 |
| Computer scientists and systems analysts | 15 | 0.8 | 10.0 |
| Computer software engineers | 14 | 0.7 | -6.9 |
| Electronics engineers, except computer | 22 | 1.1 | -16.0 |
| Engineering technicians, except drafters | 23 | 1.2 | -11.7 |
| Biological scientists | 18 | 0.9 | -5.0 |
| Physical scientists | 32 | 1.6 | -4.3 |
| Lawyers | 25 | 1.3 | 14.0 |
| Physicians and surgeons | 23 | 1.2 | 4.5 |
| Registered nurses | 49 | 2.6 | 4.5 |
| **Service occupations** | 145 | 7.6 | 2.8 |
| Healthcare support occupations | 25 | 1.3 | -4.8 |
| Correctional officers and jailers | 14 | 0.7 | 13.3 |
| Detectives and criminal investigators | 22 | 1.2 | 28.3 |
| Police and sheriff's patrol officers | 16 | 0.8 | 28.3 |
| Food preparation and serving related occupations | 16 | 0.8 | -23.6 |
| **Office and administrative support occupations** | 398 | 20.8 | -18.7 |
| First-line supervisors/managers of office and administrative support workers | 24 | 1.3 | -5.0 |
| Procurement clerks | 19 | 1.0 | -25.5 |
| Word processors and typists | 20 | 1.0 | -38.2 |
| Secretaries, except legal, medical, and executive | 48 | 2.5 | -24.0 |
| **Construction and extraction occupations** | 43 | 2.2 | -10.0 |
| Construction trades and related workers | 36 | 1.9 | -10.8 |
| **Installation, maintenance, and repair occupations** | 101 | 5.3 | -10.5 |
| Electrical and electronic equipment mechanics, installers, and repairers | 19 | 1.0 | -18.5 |
| Aircraft mechanics and service technicians | 19 | 1.0 | -14.5 |
| **Production occupations** | 49 | 2.6 | -13.5 |
| Inspectors, testers, sorters, samplers, and weighers | 15 | 0.8 | -24.0 |
| **Transportation and material moving occupations** | 64 | 3.4 | -4.8 |
| Air traffic controllers | 24 | 1.2 | 4.5 |

NOTE: May not add to totals due to omission of occupations with small employment.

associated with a job's career track depend upon the occupation. Typically, workers without a high school diploma who are hired as clerks start at grade 1, and high school graduates with no additional training hired at the same job start at grade 2 or 3. Entrants with some technical training or experience who are hired as technicians may start at grade 4. Those with a bachelor's degree generally are hired in professional occupations, such as economist, with a career ladder that starts at grade 5 or 7, depending on academic achievement. Entrants with a master's degree or Ph.D. may start at grade 9. Individuals with professional degrees may be hired at the grade 11 or 12 level.

New employees usually start at the first step of a grade; however, if the position in question is difficult to fill, entrants may receive somewhat higher pay or special rates. Almost all physician and engineer positions, for example, fall into this category.

Once nonsupervisory Federal workers reach the full-performance level of the career track, they usually receive periodic step increases within their grade if they are performing their job satisfactorily. They must compete for subsequent promotions, and advancement becomes more difficult. At this point, promotions occur as vacancies arise, and they are based solely on merit. In addition to within-grade longevity increases, Federal workers are awarded bonuses for excellent job performance.

Workers who advance to managerial or supervisory positions may receive within-grade longevity increases, bonuses, and promotions to higher grades. The top managers in the Federal civil service belong to the Senior Executive Service (SES), the highest positions Federal workers can reach without being specifically nominated by the President and confirmed by the U.S. Senate. Relatively few workers attain SES positions, and competition is intense. Bonus provisions for SES positions are even more performance based than those for lower-level positions. Because it is the headquarters for most Federal agencies, the Washington, DC, metropolitan area offers the best opportunities to advance to upper-level managerial and supervisory jobs.

## Table 4. Federal Government General Schedule pay rates, 2001

| GS level | Entrance level | Step increase | Maximum level |
|---|---|---|---|
| 1 | $14,244 | $ varies | $17,819 |
| 2 | 16,015 | varies | 20,156 |
| 3 | 17,474 | 582 | 22,712 |
| 4 | 19,616 | 654 | 25,502 |
| 5 | 21,947 | 732 | 28,535 |
| 6 | 24,463 | 815 | 31,798 |
| 7 | 27,185 | 906 | 35,339 |
| 8 | 30,107 | 1,004 | 39,143 |
| 9 | 33,254 | 1,108 | 43,226 |
| 10 | 36,621 | 1,221 | 47,610 |
| 11 | 40,236 | 1,341 | 52,305 |
| 12 | 48,223 | 1,607 | 62,686 |
| 13 | 57,345 | 1,912 | 74,553 |
| 14 | 67,765 | 2,259 | 88,096 |
| 15 | 79,710 | 2,657 | 103,623 |

SOURCE: U.S. Office of Personnel Management

## Earnings

There are several pay systems governing the salary rates of Federal civilian employees. In 2000, the majority of Federal workers were paid under the General Schedule (GS). The General Schedule, shown in table 4, has 15 grades of pay for civilian white-collar and service workers, and smaller within-grade step increases that occur based on length of service and quality of performance. Workers in localities with high costs of living are paid as much as an additional 17 percent, and some hard-to-fill occupations are paid more as an incentive. In general, this schedule is amended every January to reflect changes in the cost of living.

In 2000, the average worker paid under the General Schedule earned $51,565. At $102,392, patent administrators had the highest average earnings (table 5), while some administrative support workers started at salaries less than $15,000.

Table 5.  Average annual salaries in the Federal Government in selected occupations, March 2001

| Occupation | Salary |
| --- | --- |
| All occupations | $51,565 |
| | |
| Patent administrator | 102,392 |
| Astronomer | 89,734 |
| Attorney | 86,673 |
| Financial manager | 79,840 |
| Computer scientist | 75,351 |
| Economist | 74,089 |
| Podiatrist | 73,172 |
| Chemist | 70,435 |
| Electrical engineer | 69,560 |
| Statistician | 68,901 |
| Architect | 68,872 |
| Microbiologist | 67,835 |
| Accountant | 64,767 |
| Personnel manager | 64,411 |
| Librarian | 63,651 |
| Chaplain | 63,366 |
| Ecologist | 61,936 |
| Intelligence agent | 61,424 |
| Budget Analyst | 56,706 |
| Physical therapist | 55,213 |
| Social worker | 54,129 |
| Botanist | 53,131 |
| Nurse | 51,019 |
| Engineering technician | 50,850 |
| Law clerk | 46,533 |
| Border Patrol agent | 43,917 |
| Fire protection and prevention worker | 33,915 |
| Secretary | 33,354 |
| Police officer | 32,934 |
| Medical technician | 30,183 |
| Dental assistant | 27,387 |
| Nursing assistant | 26,992 |
| Mail and file clerk | 26,038 |

SOURCE:  U.S. Office of Personnel Management

The Federal Wage System (FWS) is used to pay most Federal workers in craft, repair, operative, and laborer jobs. This schedule sets Federal wages so that they are comparable to prevailing regional wage rates for similar types of jobs. As a result, wage rates paid under the FWS can vary significantly from one locality to another.

In addition to base pay and bonuses, Federal employees may receive incentive awards. These one-time awards, ranging from $25 to $10,000, are bestowed for a significant suggestion, a special act or service, or sustained high job performance. Some workers also may receive "premium" pay, which is granted when the employee must work overtime, on holidays, on Sunday, at night, or under hazardous conditions.

Benefits are an important part of Federal employee compensation. Federal employees may choose from a number of health plans and life insurance options; premium payments for these policies are partially offset by the government. In addition,

workers hired after January 1, 1984, participate in the Federal Employees Retirement System (FERS), a three-tiered retirement plan including Social Security, a pension plan, and an optional Thrift Savings Plan. Worker participation in the Thrift Savings Plan is voluntary, but any contributions made are tax-deferred, and, up to a point, matched by the Federal Government.  In addition to other benefits, some Federal agencies provide public transit subsidies in an effort to encourage employee use of public transportation.

Federal employees receive both vacation and sick leave. They earn 13 days of vacation leave a year for the first 3 years, 20 days a year for the next 12 years, and 26 days a year after their fifteenth year of service. Workers also receive 13 days of sick leave a year, which may be accumulated indefinitely.  About 60 percent of all Federal civilian employees are represented by unions through their bargaining units, although a smaller percentage of these employees actually belong to a union.

## Outlook

Wage and salary employment in the Federal Government is projected to decline by 8 percent through the year 2010, while the salaried economy as a whole is expected to grow 16 percent. The projected reduction in Federal jobs reflects governmental cost-cutting, the growing use of private contractors, and continuing devolution—the practice of turning over the development, implementation, and management of some programs of the Federal Government to State and local governments. As a result, keen competition is expected for many Federal positions, especially during times of economic uncertainty when workers seek the stability of Federal employment.  In general, Federal employment is considered to be relatively stable because it is not affected by cyclical fluctuations in the economy, as are employment levels in many construction, manufacturing, and other private sector industries.

Because of its public nature, the factors that influence Federal Government staffing levels are unique.  The Congress and President determine the Government's payroll budget prior to each fiscal year, which runs from October 1 through September 30 of the following year.  Each Presidential administration and Congress have different public policy priorities, resulting in increasing levels of Federal employment in some programs and declines in others.  The effect of these priorities in recent years has been a decline in Department of Defense civilian employment, which equals about 40 percent of Federal civilian employment.  Although this decline is expected to level off over the next decade, the emphasis on reduced government payrolls will lead to decreases in employment in many other agencies.

Much of this decline will be carried out through attrition— simply not replacing workers who retire or leave the Federal Government for other reasons.  Layoffs, called "reductions in force," have occurred in the past, but they are uncommon and usually affect relatively few workers.  In spite of attrition and declining employment, there still will be numerous employment opportunities in many agencies due to the need to replace workers who leave the workforce, retire, or accept employment elsewhere.  Furthermore, some occupations, especially professional, managerial, and protective service occupations, will be in demand even as employment in other occupations is being reduced.

The distribution of Federal employment will continue to shift toward a higher proportion of professional and managerial workers, as employment declines will be most rapid in administrative support, installation, maintenance, and repair occupations. Employment of office and administrative support workers in the Federal Government will be adversely affected by office automation. Employment among repair, construction, and production occupations is expected to decline as many of their functions are contracted out to private companies.

## Sources of Additional Information

Information on obtaining a position with the Federal Government is available from the Office of Personnel Management (OPM) through a telephone-based system. Consult your telephone directory under U.S. Government for a local number or call (912) 757-3000; Federal Relay Service: (800) 877-8339. The first number is not tollfree, and charges may result. Information also is available from the OPM Internet site: **http://www.usajobs.opm.gov**

The duties of Federal Government workers in various occupations are similar to those of their private sector counterparts. Further information on the specific occupations discussed in this statement can be found in the 2002-03 edition of the *Occupational Outlook Handbook*.

- Accountants and auditors
- Correctional officers
- Court reporters
- Judges, magistrates, and other judicial workers
- Lawyers
- Management analysts
- Police and detectives
- Probation officers and correctional treatment specialists
- Registered nurses
- Tax examiners, collectors, and revenue agents
- Top executives
- Job opportunities in the armed forces

# State and Local Government, Excluding Education and Hospitals

## SIGNIFICANT POINTS

- An excellent economy has led to budget surpluses in many State and local governments, allowing for increased spending on programs and employment.

- State government has a larger percentage of management and professional occupations, while local government employs a higher share of service workers.

## Nature of the Industry

State and local governments provide vital services to their constituents, such as transportation, public safety, healthcare, education, utilities, and courts. Excluding education and hospitals, State and local governments employ about 7.5 million workers, placing them among the largest employers in the economy. Almost two-thirds of these employees work for local governments, such as counties, cities, special districts, and towns. (State and local government hospitals are included in the health services industry and public education is a major part of educational services, both of which appear elsewhere in the *Career Guide*.)

In addition to the 50 State governments, there are about 87,000 local governments, according to the Bureau of the Census. These include about 3,000 county governments; 19,400 municipal governments; 16,600 townships; 13,700 school districts; and 34,700 special districts. Illinois had the most local government units, with more than 6,800; Hawaii had the fewest, with 19.

In many areas of the country, citizens are served by more than one local government unit. For example, most States have *counties,* which may contain various municipalities such as cites or towns, but which also often include unincorporated rural areas. *Townships,* which do not exist in some States, may or may not contain municipalities and often consist of suburban or rural areas. Supplementing these forms of local government, *special district* government bodies are independent, limited purpose governmental units that usually perform a single function or activity. For example, a large percentage of special districts manage the use of natural resources. Some provide drainage and flood control, irrigation, and soil and water conservation services.

The Council of State Governments reports that State and local governments' responsibilities were augmented in the 1990s through "devolution," the practice through which the Federal Government turns over to State and local governments the development, implementation, and management of programs. Welfare reform typifies devolution in practice, with States receiving considerable leeway to devise programs that meet their needs as a result of the 1996 Congressional reform act that provided block grants to States. As the relationship between levels of government continues to change in the coming decade, so will the nature of services provided by State and local governments.

## Working Conditions

Working conditions vary by occupation and, in some instances, by size and location of the State or local government. For example, chief executives in very small jurisdictions may work less than 20 hours a week; in larger jurisdictions, they often work more than 40 hours per week. Chief executives in large jurisdictions work full time year round, as do most county and city managers. Most State legislators work full time only when in session, usually for a few months a year, and work part time the rest of the year. Local elected officials in some small jurisdictions work part time.

Most professional, financial operations, and office and administrative support occupations in State and local government work a standard 40-hour week in an office environment. However, workers in some of the most visible local government jobs have very different working conditions and schedules. Firefighters' hours are longer and vary more widely than those of most workers. Many professional firefighters are on duty for several days in a row, working over 50 hours a week, because some must be on duty at all times to respond to emergencies. They often eat and sleep at the fire station. Following this long shift, they are then off for several days in a row or for the entire next week. In addition to irregular hours, firefighting can involve the risk of death or injury. Some local fire districts also use the services of volunteer firefighters, who tend to work shorter, regularly scheduled shifts.

Law enforcement work also is potentially dangerous. The injury and fatality rates among law officers are higher than in many occupations, reflecting risks taken in apprehending suspected criminals and responding to various emergency situations such as traffic accidents. Most police and detectives work 40 hours a week, with paid overtime when they testify in court or work on an investigation. Because police protection must be provided around the clock, some officers work weekends, holidays, and nights. Many officers are subject to call anytime their services are needed and are expected to intervene whenever they observe a crime, even if off duty.

Most driver/operator jobs in public transit systems are stressful and fatiguing because they involve dealing with passengers, tight schedules, and heavy traffic. Busdrivers with regular routes and subway operators generally have consistent weekly work schedules. Those who do not have regular schedules may be on-call and must be prepared to report for work on short notice. To accommodate commuters, many operators work "split shifts," for example, 6 a.m. to 10 a.m. and 3 p.m. to 7 p.m., with time off in between.

A number of other State and local government jobs also require weekend or night work. Because electricity, gas, and water are produced and used continuously throughout each day, for example, split, weekend, and night shifts are common for utility workers.

## Employment

State and local governments, excluding education and hospitals, employed about 7.5 million people in 2000. Local government employed the largest number of workers, accounting for 2 out of every 3 jobs (table 1).

**Table 1. Wage and salary employment in State and local governments, excluding education and hospitals, 2000**

(Employment in thousands)

| Jurisdiction | Employment | Percent |
|---|---|---|
| State and local ................................ | 7,461 | 100.0 |
| Local .......................................... | 5,051 | 67.7 |
| State .......................................... | 2,410 | 32.3 |

## Occupations in the Industry

Service occupations comprised the largest share of employment in State and local governments, accounting for 31 percent of all jobs (table 2). Of these, *police and sheriff's patrol officers, correctional officers and jailers,* and *firefighters* were the largest occupations. Office and administrative support occupations accounted for 21 percent of employment; professional and related occupations accounted for 21 percent, and management, business, and financial occupations, 12 percent.

Local government employs a smaller proportion of management, business, financial, and professional workers than does State government. Local government, on the other hand, employs a larger share of service workers, particularly firefighters and law enforcement workers (see chart).

State and local governments employ people in occupations that are found in nearly every industry in the economy, including chief executives, managers, engineers, computer occupations, secretaries, and technicians. Certain occupations, however, are mainly or exclusively found in governments, such as legislators; tax examiners, collectors, and revenue agents; urban and regional planners; judges, magistrates, and other judicial workers; police and sheriff's patrol officers; and correctional officers and jailers.

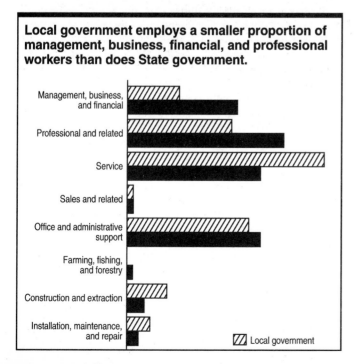

**Local government employs a smaller proportion of management, business, financial, and professional workers than does State government.**

*Chief executives, general and operations managers,* and *legislators* establish government policy and develop laws, rules, and regulations. They are elected or appointed officials who either preside over units of government or make laws. Chief executives include governors, lieutenant governors, mayors, and city managers. General and operations managers include district managers and revenue directors. Legislators include State senators and representatives, county commissioners, and city council members.

*Tax examiners, collectors, and revenue agents* determine tax liability and collect past-due taxes from individuals or businesses. *Urban and regional planners* draft plans and recommend programs for the development and use of resources such as land and water. They also propose construction of physical facilities such as schools and roads under the authority of cities, counties, and metropolitan areas. Planners devise strategies outlining the best use of community land and identify the places in which residential, commercial, recreational, and other types of development should be located.

*Judges* arbitrate, advise, and administer justice in a court of law. They oversee legal processes in courts and apply the law to resolve civil disputes and determine guilt in criminal cases. *Magistrates* resolve criminal cases not involving penitentiary sentences and civil cases involving damages below a sum specified by State law.

*Social workers* counsel and assess the needs of clients, refer them to the appropriate sources of help, and monitor their progress. *Eligibility interviewers, government programs* interview and investigate applicants and recipients to determine eligibility to receive, or continue receiving, welfare and other types of social assistance. *Social and human service assistants'* duties vary with specific job titles. These workers include social service technicians, case management aides, social work assistants, residential counselors, alcoholism or drug abuse counseling aides, child abuse workers, community outreach workers, and gerontology aides.

*Court, municipal, and license clerks* perform a variety of State and local government administrative tasks. *Court clerks* prepare dockets of cases to be called, secure information for judges, and contact witnesses, lawyers, and attorneys to obtain information for the court. *Municipal clerks* draft agendas for town or city councils, record minutes of council meetings, answer official correspondence, keep fiscal records and accounts, and prepare reports on civic needs. *License clerks* keep records and help the public obtain motor vehicle ownership titles, operators permits, and a variety of other permits and licenses.

*Firefighters* control and extinguish fires, assist with emergency medical treatment, and assist in recovery from natural disasters such as earthquakes and tornadoes. *Fire inspectors* inspect public buildings for conditions that might present a fire hazard.

*Police and sheriff's patrol officers* and *detectives and criminal investigators* have duties that range from controlling traffic to preventing and investigating crimes. They maintain order; enforce laws and ordinances; issue traffic summonses; investigate accidents; give evidence in court; serve legal documents for the court system; and apprehend, arrest, and process prisoners. State and local *correctional officers* guard inmates in jails, prisons, or juvenile detention institutions. *Bailiffs* keep order in courts.

*Busdrivers* and *subway and streetcar operators* pick up and deliver passengers at prearranged stops throughout their assigned routes. Operators may collect fares, answer questions about schedules and transfer points, and in some cases announce stops.

**Table 2. Employment of wage and salary workers in State and localgovernment, except education and health, by occupation, 2000 and projected change, 2000-10**

(Employment in thousands)

| Occupation | Employment, 2000 Number | Percent | Percent change, 2000-2010 |
|---|---|---|---|
| All occupations | 7,461 | 100.0 | 11.5 |
| **Management, business, and financial occupations** | 895 | 12.0 | 10.0 |
| Chief executives | 29 | 0.4 | 7.6 |
| General and operations managers | 77 | 1.0 | 6.1 |
| Legislators | 54 | 0.7 | 12.8 |
| Accountants and auditors | 66 | 0.9 | 12.2 |
| Tax examiners, collectors, and revenue agents | 39 | 0.5 | 12.1 |
| **Professional and related occupations** | 1,559 | 20.9 | 16.2 |
| Computer specialists | 119 | 1.6 | 38.6 |
| Drafters, engineering, and mapping technicians | 74 | 1.0 | 0.7 |
| Urban and regional planners | 24 | 0.3 | 13.0 |
| Probation officers and correctional treatment specialists | 81 | 1.1 | 23.4 |
| Social and human service assistants | 71 | 1.0 | 31.1 |
| Child, family, and school social workers | 118 | 1.6 | 18.7 |
| Judges, magistrates, and other judicial workers | 38 | 0.5 | 2.3 |
| Lawyers | 84 | 1.1 | 17.1 |
| Library, museum, training, and other education occupations | 144 | 1.9 | 12.8 |
| Registered nurses | 102 | 1.4 | 12.5 |
| **Service occupations** | 2,276 | 30.5 | 17.6 |
| Nursing aides, orderlies, and attendants | 75 | 1.0 | 12.6 |
| First-line supervisors/managers of police and detectives | 111 | 1.5 | 14.4 |
| Firefighters | 240 | 3.2 | 8.5 |
| Correctional officers and jailers | 377 | 5.1 | 31.5 |
| Detectives and criminal investigators | 70 | 0.9 | 12.6 |
| Police and sheriff's patrol officers | 579 | 7.8 | 23.3 |
| Recreation workers | 99 | 1.3 | 12.9 |
| **Office and administrative support occupations** | 1,590 | 21.3 | 1.3 |
| First-line supervisors/managers of office and administrative support workers | 104 | 1.4 | 9.5 |
| Bookkeeping, accounting, and auditing clerks | 101 | 1.4 | -3.2 |
| Court, municipal, and license clerks | 101 | 1.4 | 12.6 |
| Eligibility interviewers, government programs | 110 | 1.5 | -10.1 |
| Police, fire, and ambulance dispatchers | 78 | 1.0 | 12.9 |
| Word processors and typists | 91 | 1.2 | -27.0 |
| Office clerks, general | 302 | 4.0 | 12.4 |
| Secretaries, except legal, medical, and executive | 157 | 2.1 | -10.0 |
| **Construction and extraction occupations** | 418 | 5.6 | 7.5 |
| Highway maintenance workers | 132 | 1.8 | 3.4 |
| **Installation, maintenance, and repair occupations** | 241 | 3.2 | 7.4 |
| Maintenance and repair workers, general | 88 | 1.2 | 0.1 |
| **Production occupations** | 124 | 1.7 | 9.3 |
| Water and liquid waste treatment plant and system operators | 68 | 0.9 | 12.9 |
| **Transportation and material moving occupations** | 293 | 3.9 | 8.6 |
| Busdrivers, transit and intercity | 85 | 1.1 | 12.9 |

NOTE: May not add to totals due to omission of occupations with small employment.

## Training and Advancement

The education level and experience needed by workers in State and local government varies by occupation. Voters elect most chief executives and legislators, so local support is very important. Volunteer work and community services are valuable ways to establish vital community support. Those elected to these positions come from a variety of backgrounds, but must conform to age, residency, and citizenship regulations. Advancement opportunities for most elected public officials are limited to other offices in the jurisdictions in which they live. For example, a local council member may run for mayor or for a position in State government, and State legislators may decide to run for governor or Congress.

A master's degree in public administration is widely recommended, but not required, for city managers. They may gain experience as management analysts or assistants in government departments working with councils and mayors. After several years, they may be hired to manage a town or a small city and eventually become manager of larger cities.

For most professional jobs, a college degree is required. To obtain an entry-level urban or regional planning position, most State and local government agencies require 2 years of graduate study in urban and regional planning or the equivalent in work experience. To become a judge, particularly a State trial or appellate court judge, one usually is required to be a lawyer. About half of all State judges are appointed, and the other half are elected in partisan or nonpartisan elections. Most State and local judges serve fixed terms, ranging from 4 or 6 years for limited jurisdiction judges to 14 years for some appellate court judges.

Most applicants for firefighting jobs must have a high school education or its equivalent and pass a civil service examination. In addition, they need to pass a medical examination and tests of strength, physical stamina, coordination, and agility. Experience as a volunteer firefighter or as a firefighter in the Armed Forces is helpful, as is completion of community college courses in fire science. Recruits study firefighting techniques, fire prevention, local building codes, emergency procedures, and the proper use of rescue equipment. Firefighters may be promoted depending on written examination results and job performance.

Busdrivers must comply with Federal regulations that require drivers who operate vehicles designed to transport 16 or more passengers to obtain a commercial driver's license from the State in which they live. To qualify for a commercial driver's license, applicants must pass a written test on rules and regulations and demonstrate that they can operate a commercial vehicle safely. For subway and streetcar operator jobs, applicants with at least a high school education have the best chance. In some cities, prospective subway operators are required to work as busdrivers for a specified period. Successful applicants generally are in good health, possess good communication skills, and are able to make quick, sound judgments. Because busdrivers and subway operators deal with passengers, they need an even temperament and emotional stability. Driving in heavy, fast-moving, or stop-and-go traffic and dealing with passengers can be stressful.

Police departments in most areas require applicants to be U.S. citizens of good character, at least 20 years old, and able to meet rigorous physical and mental standards. Police departments increasingly encourage applicants to take college courses, and some require a college degree. Many community and junior colleges, as well as colleges and universities, offer programs in law enforcement or criminal justice. Officers usually attend a local or regional police academy, which includes classroom instruction in constitutional law, civil rights, and State and local law. They also receive training in patrol, accident investigation traffic control, using firearms, self-defense, first aid, and emergency management. Promotions for police officers are highly influenced by scores on a written civil service examination and subsequent performance evaluations by their superiors.

## Earnings

Earnings vary by occupation, size of the State or locality, and region of the country. As in most industries, professionals and managers earn more than other workers. Earnings in the occupations having the largest employment in State and local government appear in table 3.

**Table 3. Median hourly earnings of the largest occupations in State and local government, 2000**

| Occupation | State government | Local government | All industries |
|---|---|---|---|
| First-line supervisors/ managers of police and detectives | $ 25.94 | $ 27.42 | $ 27.50 |
| Bus drivers, transit and intercity | 23.54 | 14.68 | 12.36 |
| Police and sheriff's patrol officers | 21.35 | 19.09 | 19.13 |
| Registered nurses | 20.51 | 22.67 | 21.56 |
| Fire fighters | 16.28 | 16.71 | 16.43 |
| Child, family, and school social workers | 15.80 | 17.20 | 15.13 |
| Correctional officers and jailers | 15.32 | 14.06 | 14.99 |
| Recreation workers | 14.47 | 8.40 | 8.24 |
| Eligibility interviewers, government programs | 14.27 | 13.57 | 13.65 |
| Highway maintenance workers | 13.80 | 12.54 | 12.82 |

The International City/County Management Association (ICMA) reported the 2000 median annual salaries of selected executive and managerial occupations in local government shown in table 4.

Employer-provided benefits—including health and life insurance and retirement benefits—are more common among State and local government employees than among workers in the private sector.

## Outlook

Wage and salary employment in State and local government is projected to increase about 11 percent during the 2000-2010 period, slower than the 16 percent growth projected for all sectors of the economy combined. Employment growth will stem from the rising demand for services at the State and local levels. An increasing population and State and local assumption of responsibility for some services previously provided by the Federal Government are fueling the growth of these services. Despite the increased demand for the services of State and local governments, employment growth will be dampened by budgetary constraints due to reductions in Federal aid, especially at the county level, and resistance from citizens to tax increases.

Professional and service occupations will account for almost three-fourths of all new jobs in State and local government. Most new jobs will stem from rising demand for protective services, community and social services, health

services, and information technology. For example, rapid increases in demand for services for the elderly, the mentally impaired, and children will spur growth of social workers and social and human service assistants. Employment growth in protective service occupations will be spurred by rising demand for law enforcement and correctional officers to oversee the increasing population of convicted offenders.

**Table 4. Median annual salary for selected executive and managerial occupations in local government, 2000**

| Occupation | Salary |
|---|---|
| City manager | $75,000 |
| Engineer | 64,596 |
| Information services director | 61,657 |
| Assistant chief administrative officer | 60,427 |
| Chief administrative officer | 59,664 |
| Chief financial officer | 60,882 |
| Economic development /planning director | 58,220 |
| Fire chief | 57,000 |
| Chief law enforcement official | 55,862 |
| Human resources director | 54,440 |
| Public works director | 54,309 |
| Health officer | 52,125 |
| Human services director | 50,396 |
| Parks and recreation director | 50,086 |
| Purchasing director | 47,467 |
| Chief librarian | 42,940 |
| Clerk | 39,811 |
| Treasurer | 38,508 |
| Chief elected officials | 5,400 |

Source: International City/County Management Association (ICMA).

Slower growth is projected for management and administrative support occupations. Employment of chief executives and general managers will grow slowly through the year 2010 because the number of these positions generally remains fairly stable. Employment change occurs in rare situations, such as when a small town switches from a volunteer chief executive to a manager or paid mayor. Employment in office and administrative support occupations in State and local government is expected to increase very little and employment in many occupations is projected to decline, as the increasing use of personal computers by professionals and managers continues to reduce the need for secretaries, word processors and typists, and bookkeeping, accounting, and auditing clerks.

Employment of production and repair workers will grow slowly in response to governments' increasing tendency to contract out some services. Increased demand for transportation services should produce slow growth in employment of transportation and material-moving occupations through the year 2010.

## Sources of Additional Information

Individuals interested in working for State or local government agencies should contact the appropriate agencies. City, county, and State personnel and human resources departments, and local offices of State employment services have applications and additional information.

Other information about careers in government is available from:

➢ The Council of State Governments, P.O. Box 11910, Lexington, KY 40578-1910.
Internet: **http://www.csg.org**

- International City Management Association (ICMA), 777 North Capital NE., Suite 500, Washington, DC 20002. Internet: **http://www.icma.org**
- International Personnel Management Association, 1617 Duke Street, Alexandria, VA 22314. Internet: **http://www.ipma-hr.org**
- National Association of Counties, 440 First Street NW., Suite 800, Washington, DC 20001. Internet: **http://www.naco.org**
- National Association of State Personnel Executives, P.O. Box 11910, Lexington, KY 40578-1910. Internet: **http://www.naspe.net**
- National League of Cities, 1301 Pennsylvania Avenue, NW., Washington, DC 20004-1763. Internet: **http://www.nlc.org**

Information on many occupations commonly employed by State and local government may be found in the 2002-03 *Occupational Outlook Handbook*:

- Busdrivers
- Correctional officers
- Court reporters
- Firefighting occupations
- Judges, magistrates, and other judicial workers
- Lawyers
- Police and detectives
- Probation officers and correctional treatment specialists
- Social and human service assistants
- Social workers
- Tax examiners, collectors, and revenue agents
- Top executives
- Urban and regional planners

# Sources of State and Local
# Job Outlook Information

The *Career Guide* provides information for the Nation as a whole. State or local area information is available from:

*State Employment Security Agencies*. These agencies develop detailed information about local labor markets, such as current and projected employment by occupation and industry, characteristics of the workforce, and changes in State and local area economic activity. Listed below are the Internetaddresses of these agencies and addresses and telephone numbers of the directors of research and analysis in these agencies.

Most States have career information delivery systems (CIDS). Look for these systems in secondary schools, postsecondary institutions, libraries, job training sites, vocational rehabilitation centers, and employment service offices. The public can use the systems' computers, printed material, microfiche, and toll-free hotlines to obtain information on occupations, educational opportunities, student financial aid, apprenticeships, and military careers. Ask counselors for specific locations.

State occupational projections also are available on the Internet: **http://www.dws.state.ut.us/bls**

**Alabama**
Chief, Labor Market Information, Alabama Department of Industrial Relations, 649 Monroe St., Room 422, Montgomery, AL 36130. Phone: (334) 242-8800.
Internet: **http://www.dir.state.al.us/lmi**

**Alaska**
Chief, Research and Analysis, Alaska Department of Labor and Workforce Development, P.O. Box 25501, Juneau, AK 99802-5501. Phone: (907) 465-4500.
Internet: **http://www.labor.state.ak.us**

**Arizona**
Research Administrator, Arizona Department of Economic Security, Site Code 733A, P.O. Box 6123, Phoenix, AZ 85005. Phone: (602) 542-3871.
Internet: **http://www.de.state.az.us/links/economic/webpage/page6.html**

**Arkansas**
Robert Mantione, LMI Director, Arkansas Employment Security Department, P.O. Box 2981, Little Rock, AR 72203-2981. Phone: (501) 682-3159. Internet: **http://www.state.ar.us/esd**

**California**
Chief, Labor Market Information Division, California Employment Development Department, P.O. Box 826880, MIC 57, Sacramento, CA 94280-0001. Phone: (916) 262-2160. Internet: **http://www.calmis.cahwnet.gov**

**Colorado**
Colorado Department of Labor and Employment, Labor Market Information, 1515 Arapahoe St., Tower 2, Suite 400, Denver, CO 80202-2117. Phone: (303) 318-8850.
Internet: **http://lmi.cdle.state.co.us**

**Connecticut**
Director, Office of Research and Information, Connecticut Labor Department, 200 Folly Brook Blvd., Wethersfield, CT 06109-1114. Phone: (860) 263-6255.
Internet: **http://www.ctdol.state.ct.us/lmi/index.htm**

**Delaware**
Office of Occupational and Labor Market Information, Delaware Department of Labor, P.O. Box 9965., Wilmington, DE 19809-0965. Phone: (302) 761-8060.
Internet: **http://www.oolmi.net**

**District of Columbia**
Chief of Labor Market Information, District of Columbia Department of Employment Services, 500 C St. NW., Room 201, Washington, DC 20001. Phone: (202) 724-7213.
Internet: **http://does.dc.gov/info/labor_mkt.shtm**

**Florida**
Agency for Workforce Innovation, Labor Market Statistics, Commerce Industrial Center Building B, 367 Marpan Lane, Tallahassee, FL 32305. Phone: (850) 488-1048.
Internet: **http://www.labormarketinfo.com**

**Georgia**
Director, Labor Market Information, Georgia Department of Labor, 148 International Boulevard NE., Atlanta, GA 30303-1751. Phone: (404) 656-3177.
Internet: **http://www.dol.state.ga.us/lmi**

**Guam**
Administrator, Department of Labor, Guam Employment Services, P.O. Box 9970, Tamuning, GU 96931-9970. Phone: (671) 647-7066.
Internet: **http://gu.jobsearch.org**

**Hawaii**
Chief, Research and Statistics Office, Hawaii Department of Labor and Industrial Relations, 830 Punchbowl St., Room 304, Honolulu, HI 96813. Phone: (808) 586-8999. Internet: **http://dlir.state.hi.us**

**Idaho**
Bureau Chief, Research and Analysis, Idaho Department of Labor, 317 Main St., Boise, ID 83735-0001. Phone: (208) 332-3570 x3136.
Internet: **http://www.sde.state.id.us/cis**

**Illinois**
Economic Information and Analysis Manager, Illinois Department of Employment Security, 401 South State St., Suite 743, Chicago, IL 60605. Phone: (312) 793.-2316.
Internet:**http://www.ioicc.state.il.us/LMI/default.htm**

**Indiana**
Director, Labor Market Information, Indiana Department of Workforce Development, Indiana Government Center South, E211, 10 North Senate Ave., Indianapolis, IN 46204-2277. Phone: (317) 232-7460.
Internet: **http://www.dwd.state.in.us**

**Iowa**
Division Administrator, Research and Information Services, Iowa Workforce Development, 1000 East Grand Ave., Des Moines, IA 50319-0209. Phone: (800) JOB-IOWA.
Internet: **http://www.state.ia.us/iwd**

**Kansas**
Chief, Labor Market Information Services, Kansas Department of Human Resources, 401 SW Topeka Blvd., Topeka, KS 66603-3182. Phone: (785) 296-5058.
Internet: **http://laborstats.hr.state.ks.us**

**Kentucky**
Manager, LMI Branch, Division of Administration/Financial Management, Department of Employment Services, 275 East Main St., Suite 2-C, Frankfort, KY 40621. Phone: (800) 542-8840.
Internet: **http://www.des.state.ky.us/agencies/wforce/des/lmi/lmi.htm**

**Louisiana**
Louisiana Department of Labor, Office of Occupational Information, Research and Statistics Division, P.O. Box 94094, Baton Rouge, LA 70804-9094. Phone: (888) 302-7662.
Internet: **http://www.ldol.state.la.us/LMIQM.asp**

**Maine**
Director, Labor Market Information Services, Maine Department of Labor, 20 Union St., Augusta, ME 04330. Phone: (207) 287-2271.
Internet: **http://www.state.me.us/labor/lmis/frdef.htm**

**Maryland**
Director, Office of Labor Market Analysis and Information, Maryland Department of Labor, Licensing and Regulations, 1100 North Eutaw St., Room 601, Baltimore, MD 21201. Phone: (410) 767-2250.
Internet: **http://www.dllr.state.md.us/lmi/index.htm**

**Massachusetts**
Labor Market Information and Research Director, Massachusetts Division of Employment and Training, 19 Staniford St., 2 nd Floor, Boston, MA 02114. Phone: (617) 626-5744. Internet: **http://www.detma.org/lmi**

**Michigan**
Director, Office of Labor Market Information, Department of Career Development, Employment Service Agency, 7310 Woodward Ave., Room 520, Detroit, MI 48202. Phone: (313) 872-0990.
Internet: **http://www.michlmi.org**

**Minnesota**
Director, BLS Programs, Research and Statistical Office, Minnesota Department of Economic Security, 390 North Robert St., 5th Floor, St. Paul, MN 55104. Phone: (651) 296-4087.
Internet: **http://www.mnworkforcecenter.org/lmi/careers/index.htm**

**Mississippi**
Labor Market Information Director, Mississippi Employment Security Commission, P.O. Box 1699, Jackson, MS 39215-1699. Phone: (601) 961-7424.
Internet: **http://208.137.131.31/lmi/index.html**

**Missouri**
Department of Economic Development, Division of Workforce Development, Labor Market Information Section, P.O. Box 1087, Jefferson City, MO 65102. Phone: (573) 751-3595.
Internet: **http://www.works.state.mo.us/lmi**

**Montana**
Research and Analysis Bureau, Job Services Division, Montana Department of Labor and Industry, P.O. Box 1728, Helena, MT 59624-1728. Phone: (406) 444-2430; within Montana at (800) 633-0229; outside Montana at (800) 541-3904. Internet: **http://rad.dli.state.mt.us**

**Nebraska**
Labor Market Information Administrator, Nebraska Department of Labor, 550 South 16th St., P.O. Box 94600, Lincoln, NE 68509-4600. Phone: (402) 471-2600.
Internet: **http://www.dol.state.ne.us/nelmi.htm**

**Nevada**
Chief, DETR, Bureau of Research and Analysis, Information Development and Processing Division, 500 East Third St., Carson City, NV 89713-0001. Phone: (775) 684-0450.
Internet: **http://detr.state.nv.us/lmi/index.htm**

**New Hampshire**
Director, Economic and Labor Market Information Bureau, New Hampshire Department of Employment Security, 32 South Main St., Concord, NH 03301. Phone: (603) 228-4123.
Internet: **http://www.nhworks.state.nh.us/lmipage.htm**

**New Jersey**
Assistant Commissioner, Labor Planning and Analysis, New Jersey Department of Labor, P.O. Box 56, 5th Floor, Trenton, NJ 08625-0056. Phone: (609) 292-2643.
Internet: **http://www.state.nj.us/labor/lra**

**New Mexico**
Economic Research and Analysis Bureau, New Mexico Department of Labor, 401 Broadway Blvd. NE, P.O. Box 1928, Albuquerque, NM 87103. Phone: (505) 841-8645. Internet: **http://www3.state.nm.us/dol/dol_lmif.html**

**New York**
Director, Division of Research and Statistics, New York Department of Labor, State Office Building Campus, Room 400, Albany, NY 12240. Phone: (518) 457-6369.
Internet: **http://www.labor.state.ny.us/html/career/lmi.htm**

**North Carolina**
Director, Labor Market Information, North Carolina Employment Security Commission, P.O. Box 25903, Raleigh, NC 27611. Phone: (919) 733-2936. Internet: **http://www.esc.state.nc.us**

**North Dakota**
Program Support Area Manager, Job Service North Dakota, 1000 East Divide Ave., P.O. Box 5507, Bismarck, ND 58506-5507. Phone: (701) 328-2868.
Internet: **http://www.jobsnd.com**

**Ohio**
Director, Ohio Department of Job and Family Services, ORAA, LMI Bureau, 4300 Kimberly Parkway, 3rd Floor, Columbus, OH 43232. Phone: (614) 752-9494.
Internet: **http://lmi.state.oh.us**

**Oklahoma**
Director, Labor Market Information, Economic Research and Analysis Division, Oklahoma Employment Security Commission, P.O. Box 52003, Oklahoma City, OK 73152-2003. Phone: (405) 525-7265.
Internet: **http://www.oesc.state.ok.us/lmi/default.htm**

**Oregon**
Labor Market Information Director, Oregon Employment Department, 875 Union St. NE., Salem, OR 97311. Phone: (503) 947-1212.
Internet: **http://olmis.emp.state.or.us**

**Pennsylvania**
Director, Center for Workforce Information and Analysis, Pennsylvania Department of Labor and Industry, 7th and Forester Streets., Room 220, Labor and Industry Building, Harrisburg, PA 17120-0001. Phone: (877) 4WF-DATA. Internet: **http://www.dli.state.pa.us/workforceinfo**

**Puerto Rico**
Director, Research and Statistics Division, Puerto Rico Bureau of Employment Security, 505 Munoz Rivera Ave., 17th Floor, Hato Rey, PR 00918. Phone: (787) 754-5385.
Internet: **http://www.interempleo.org**

**Rhode Island**
Director, Labor Market Information, Rhode Island Department of Labor and Training, Building 73, 2nd Floor, 1511 Pontiac Ave., Cranston, RI 02920-4407. Phone: (401) 462-8740.
Internet: **http://www.det.state.ri.us/webdev/lmi/lmihome.html**

**South Carolina**
Director, Labor Market Information, South Carolina Employment Security Commission, 631 Hampton St., P.O. Box 995, Columbia, SC 29202. Phone: (803) 737-2660.
Internet: **http://www.sces.org/lmi/index.htm**

**South Dakota**
Director, Labor Market Center, South Dakota Department of Labor, P.O. Box 4730, Aberdeen, SD 57402-4730. Phone: (605) 626-2314.
Internet: **http://www.state.sd.us/dol/lmic/index.htm**

**Tennessee**
Director, Research and Statistics Division, Tennessee Department of Labor and Workforce Development, 500 James Robertson Pkwy., Davy Crockett Tower, 11th Floor, Nashville, TN 37245-1000. Phone: (615) 741-2284. Internet: **http://www.state.tn.us/esdiv.html**

**Texas**
Director of Labor Market Information, Texas Workforce Commission, 9001 IH-35 North, Suite 103A, Austin, TX 78753. Phone: (866) 938-4444.
Internet: **http://www.texasworkforce.org/lmi/lfs/lfshome.html**

**Utah**
Director, Labor Market Information, Utah Department of Workforce Services, 140 East 300 South, P.O. Box 45249, Salt Lake City, UT 84145-0249. Phone: (801) 526-9675.
Internet: **http://www.dws.state.ut.us**

**Vermont**
Chief, Research and Analysis, Vermont Department of Employment and Training, 5 Green Mountain Dr., P.O. Box 488, Montpelier, VT 05601-0488. Phone: (802) 828-4153.
Internet: **http://www.det.state.vt.us**

**Virgin Islands**
Chief, Bureau of Labor Statistics, Virgin Islands Department of Labor, 53A and 54A&B Kronprindsens Gade, Charlotte Amalie, St. Thomas, VI 00802. Phone: (340) 776-3700.
Internet: **http//www.vidol.org**

**Virginia**
Director, Economic Information and Services Division, Virginia Employment Commission, 703 East Main St., P.O. Box 1358, Richmond, VA 23218-1358. Phone: (804) 786-8223.
Internet: **http://www.vec.state.va.us/lbrmkt/lmi.htm**

**Washington**
Director, Labor Market and Economic Analysis, Employment Security Division, Mail Stop 6000—P.O. Box 9046, Olympia, WA 98507-9046. Phone: (800) 215-1617. Internet: **http://www.wa.gov/esd/lmea**

**West Virginia**
Director, Research, Information and Analysis, West Virginia Bureau of Employment Programs, 112 California Ave., Charleston, WV 25305-0112. Phone: (304) 558-2660.
Internet: **http://www.state.wv.us/bep/lmi/default.htm**

**Wisconsin**
Chief, LMI Data Development, Wisconsin Department of Workforce Development, 201 East Washington Ave., Room G200, Madison, WI 53702. Phone: (608) 266-2930.
Internet: **http://www.dwd.state.wi.us/lmi**

**Wyoming**
Manager, Research and Planning, Employment Resources Division, Wyoming Department of Employment, P.O. Box 2760, Casper, WY 82602-2760. Phone: (307) 473-3801.
Internet: **http://wydoe.state.wy.us**

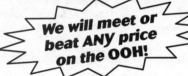